Pupil's Book

Paul Chambers Jim Marshall
Nicky Souter Rae Stark

Hodder Gibson
A MEMBER OF THE HODDER HEADLINE GROUP

Photo Acknowledgements

The publishers would like to thank the following individuals, institutions and companies for permission to reproduce copyright photographs in this book. Every effort has been made to trace and acknowledge ownership of copyright. The publishers will be glad to make suitable arrangements with any copyright holders whom it has not been possible to contact.

AKG Photo 108 (right); Ameritek USA Inc. 53; Andrew Lambert 14 (both), 32 (top right), 33 (right), 56, 64 (top), 100; Audi 79; Billie Love 110 (right); Bruce Coleman Collection 92 (top right), 108 (left), 112 (right); Bryan and Cherry Alexander Photography 72 (bottom); Corbis 24 (bottom), 32 (left), 36 (both), 39, 46, 72 (top), 74, 76 (both), 114, 116 (both), 118 (right), 120 (right); Dr Robert Rothman, Department of Biological Sciences, Rochester Institute of Technology 110 (left pair); Food Standards Agency 84 (top), 87; Hodder & Stoughton Educational 17 (top), 20, 24 (top), 29 (top), 34; Holt Studios 25, 83 (right), 86 (all), 92 (middle), 109 (top), 118 (bottom left), 120 (left pair); Life File 78, 92 (bottom right); NASA 38 (left); Nestle 32 (bottom right); Oxford Scientific Films 106, 109 (bottom); R D Battersby 29 (bottom), 65, 92 (far left); Science Photo Library 4, 7, 10, 13 (both), 17 (bottom), 26, 33 (left), 38 (right), 40, 58, 62, 64 (bottom), 82, 83 (left), 84 (left and right), 88 (both), 90 (both), 91 (both), 94 (all), 95 (both), 96, 112 (left), 113, 118 (top left); Skyscan 3, 115; Wellcome Picture Library 84 (middle).

Orders: please contact Bookpoint Ltd, 130 Milton Park, Abingdon, Oxon OX14 4SB. Telephone: (44) 01235 827720. Fax: (44) 01235 400454. Lines are open from 9.00 – 6.00, Monday to Saturday, with a 24 hour message answering service. You can also order through our website www.hodderheadline.co.uk.

British Library Cataloguing in Publication Data
A catalogue record for this title is available from the British Library

ISBN 0 340 80042 9

Published by Hodder Gibson, 2a Christie Street, Paisley, PA1 1NB.
Tel: 0141 848 1609; Fax: 0141 889 6315; Email: hoddergibson@hodder.co.uk
First Published 2003
Impression number 10 9 8 7 6 5 4 3 2
Year 2009 2008 2007 2006 2005 2004 2003

Typeset by J&L Composition, Filey, North Yorkshire

Printed in Italy for Hodder Gibson, 2a Christie Street, Paisley, PA1 1NB, Scotland, UK.

Preface

Science 5–14 has been written to match the science component of the revised Environmental Studies 5–14 National Guidelines. Pupil's Book S2 is intended to cover content from level E, where it would provide coherence continuity and progression, although the main coverage within this text is towards the targets described in level F.

The book is divided into three sections which correspond to the Knowledge and Understanding outcomes Earth and Space, Energy and Forces and Living Things and the Processes of Life.

S2 includes significant transitions from junior to middle secondary which is highlighted by option selection. Chapters 18, 38 and 58 introduce the three main subject choices – Biology, Chemistry and Physics.

As part of the 5–14 programme, pupils are encouraged to develop informed attitudes towards the environment around them. Chapters 19, 39 and 59 allow pupils to develop an understanding of the world in which they live and of current environmental issues.

Science provides a number of contexts for pupils to develop a wide range of skills. Investigating skills are focused on in Chapters 20, 40 and 60.

It is hoped that this book provides opportunities for pupils to relate science to their everyday experiences and that through this process, it stimulates interest and enjoyment in science.

Contents

Earth and Space

1 Life, the Universe and everything 2
2 Evidence for the Big Bang 4
3 Is there intelligent life elsewhere? 6
4 Searching for extra-terrestrial life on distant planets 8
5 Nuclear model of the atom 10
6 The structure of the Periodic Table 12
7 How elements combine 14
8 Elements in transition 16
9 Halogens 18
10 The water cycle 20
11 Reaction rates 22
12 Exothermic and endothermic reactions 24
13 Catalysts 26
14 Enzymes 28
15 Physical changes 30
16 Chemical changes 32
17 Equations 34
18 This is chemistry 36
19 Should we spend valuable resources on space research? 38
20 Investigating reactions 40

Energy and Forces

21 Heat radiation 42
22 Light and colour 44
23 Mixing colours of light 46
24 Seeing the sound 48
25 Magnets and their uses 50
26 Electromagnets and their uses 52
27 Current in series and parallel circuits 54
28 Electrical safety 56
29 Electronics 58
30 Electronic systems 60

31 Gravitational potential energy 62
32 Chemical potential energy 64
33 Mass and weight 66
34 How forces act 68
35 Force and motion 70
36 Force and pressure 72
37 Pressure in liquids 74
38 This is physics 76
39 Let's talk rubbish! 78
40 Investigation: Boarding school 80

Living Things and the Processes of Life

41 Microorganisms are useful! 82
42 Microorganisms can be harmful! 84
43 Food biotechnology 86
44 Medical biotechnology 88
45 DNA, chromosomes and genes 90
46 Inheritance 92
47 Adapted cells in animals 94
48 Adapted cells in plants and phytoplankton 96
49 Cellular respiration 98
50 Enzymes at work 100
51 Influencing enzymes 102
52 Ecological energetics 104
53 Darwin and his theory 106
54 Natural selection 108
55 Evolution, looking for evidence 110
56 Adaptation 112
57 Inside a modern glasshouse 114
58 This is biology 116
59 Great Scot! 118
60 Ecological investigations 120

Index 122

Life, the Universe and everything

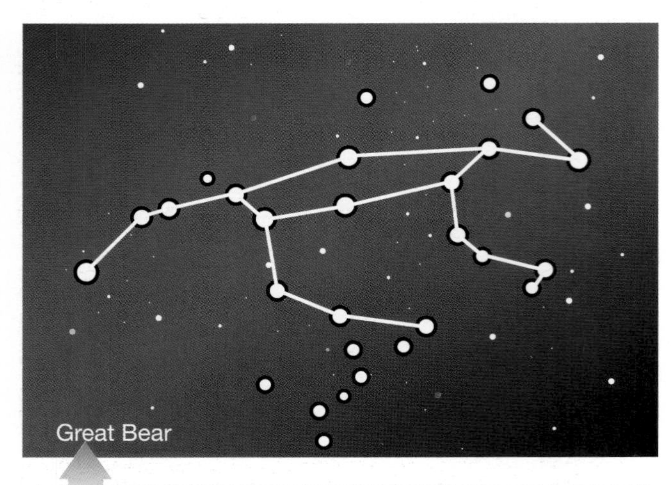

Figure 1 The Great Bear constellation

Ever since mankind has been able to think independently, people have tried to describe our place in the Universe. Astronomers from China and Asia have a long history of studying the stars and the heavens and the records of the sightings those astronomers took are still used.

Those astronomers were concerned with questions that are still of interest to scientists today.

- Where do all the stars and galaxies come from?
- Is there other intelligent life out there?
- How large is the Universe?

A number of theories have been put forward that try to explain the origin of the Universe.

These have included the 'Steady State' and 'Big Bang' theories.

The Steady State theory was first proposed in 1948 by Sir Fred Hoyle and other scientists. It claimed that the Universe was the same at all times. It suggested that any change in the Universe is balanced by the continuous creation of matter. This matter condenses into galaxies and takes the place of the galaxies that have been lost, thus maintaining the present appearance or 'steady state' of the Universe. This theory is no longer accepted by most scientists.

The Big Bang theory seems to be the more acceptable explanation of what we can observe, but the theory is *not* a proven fact. It explains a lot of what we can see but there are still some problems with it.

The Big Bang theory claims that about 14 000 000 000 years ago there was an incredible occurrence. A sort of explosion happened and all the matter in the Universe was created and fired out in all directions. Over many millions of years the matter gradually cooled and formed into stars, galaxies and planets.

This still leaves some important questions. . .

1 What was there before the Big Bang?

Not a lot really, in fact, absolutely nothing. The theory includes the idea that space and time actually began when the Big Bang took place.

2 How large is the Universe?

The size of the Universe is increasing all the time. The Universe is still expanding outwards from the original Big Bang. There is no real limit to the size of the Universe. It can expand for as long as it is able – perhaps forever!

These ideas are very difficult to imagine. The evidence for the theory comes from measurements that certain scientists (**astrophysicists**) gather. They use various telescopes and satellites to collect light and other energies from the **electromagnetic spectrum** from space.

Most scientists accept the Big Bang theory but there are still some parts of the theory that are not accepted.

Figure 2 The 'Big Bang'

Why can't scientists agree?

The difficulty is in collecting accurate information to provide the evidence we need. We are on a small planet, on a spiral arm of a galaxy called the Milky Way. We cannot travel through the Universe examining all the stars and galaxies we would like to study.

We have to design and build better and larger telescopes that peer further and further into the far reaches of the Universe to allow astrophysicists to collect this information.

Early telescopes such as that used by Galileo were **optical telescopes** and had to be used in a clear sky at night to collect information. This means that if the conditions were poor then viewing could be badly affected.

Land based telescopes such as the one shown in Figure 3 are now sited high in mountain ranges away from the background light produced by man's towns and cities and not hampered by thick cloud cover.

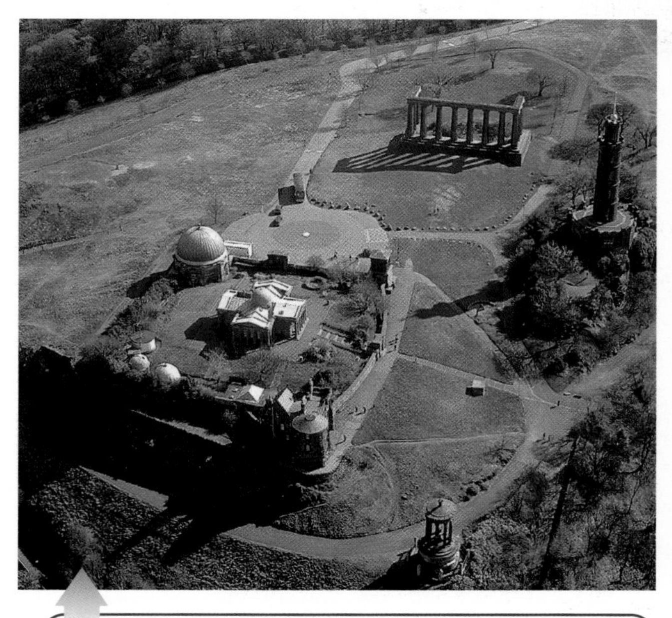

Figure 3 The Royal Observatory in Edinburgh

To further improve the quality of the information collected, NASA designed and built a telescope that was placed into orbit above the Earth's atmosphere.

Key ideas

- ★ The Universe was created by an enormous explosion about 14 billion years ago
- ★ Obtaining information from space is difficult
- ★ Astronomers collect information by using optical, ultra violet, infra red and radio telescopes
- ★ Satellites and telescopes are used to detect a range of energies from the electromagnetic spectrum

Questions

1. Describe how scientists believe the Universe was formed.
2. Why are some scientists not convinced that the Big Bang theory is correct?
3. List two questions about the Universe that are difficult to answer even with the Big Bang theory.
4. List three ways in which scientists gather information from deep space?

Wordbank

Astrophysicist – scientist who studies the stars and their formation

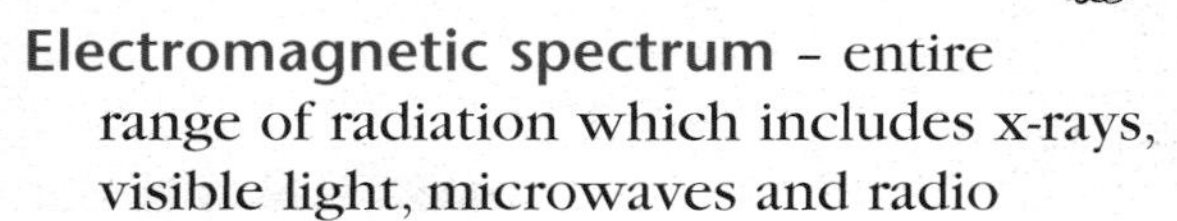

Electromagnetic spectrum – entire range of radiation which includes x-rays, visible light, microwaves and radio

Optical telescope – a telescope which detects visible light

Evidence for the Big Bang

For many years astrophysicists did not know the shape, structure and position of the various galaxies in the Universe. It was not until large scale, high quality telescopes were built that astrophysicists could make some accurate measurements of the stars and galaxies around us.

Figure 1 The Hubble space telescope – named in honour of Edwin Hubble

In 1929, Edwin Hubble, using a large optical telescope, observed many distant galaxies and examined the **spectra** of the light that came from them. The light detected from each galaxy was different from what he had expected.

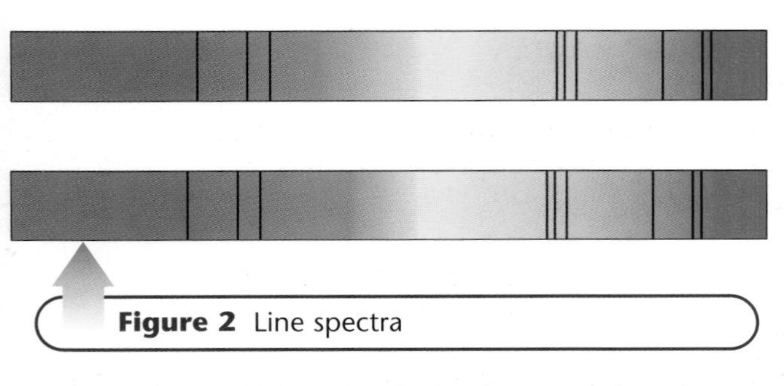

Figure 2 Line spectra

Hubble noticed that the light from each galaxy had shifted (red shift) along slightly from where it was expected. This tells us that the objects (the galaxies) are actually moving away from us. Surprisingly, he noticed that *every* galaxy he looked at was moving away from us.

What is Red Shift?

Red Shift is an effect that is similar to the everyday Doppler shift.

Doppler Shift is what makes an alarm or siren sound lower-pitched as it moves away from you. It turns out that a special version of this everyday effect applies to light as well – if an astronomical object is moving away from the Earth, its light will be shifted to longer (red) wavelengths. All distant objects we look at show this red shift. This means they all must be moving away from us.

Hubble also found that the distant galaxies were moving more quickly than the nearby galaxies.

He measured the distances and the speeds (velocities) of the galaxies and found that distance ÷ speed was roughly constant.

This is known as the **Hubble** constant **(H)** and is one of the most important terms in astronomy.

The current value for H is that $H = 65 \pm 8$ (it is very difficult to measure so all answers have to be approximate).

Why does this suggest the Universe was created by the Big Bang?

Think Hard!!

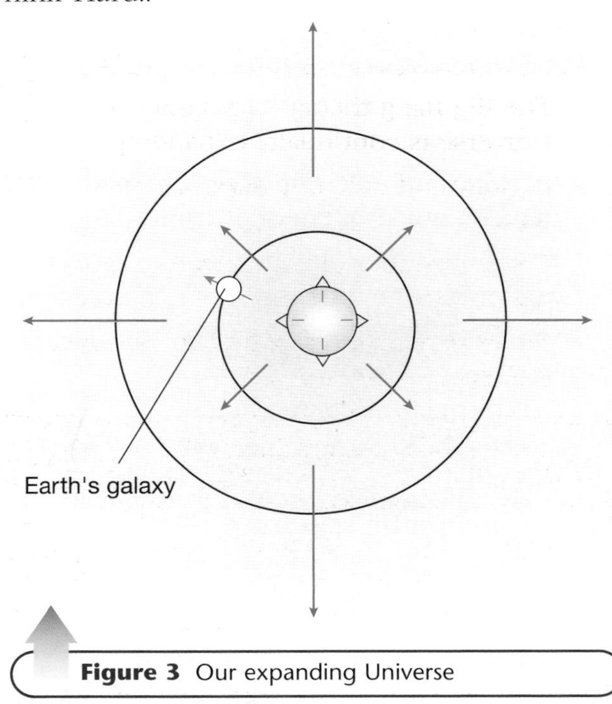

Figure 3 Our expanding Universe

We can explain why every galaxy in the Universe is moving away from us if we imagine that we occupy a position similar to the one shown in Figure 3.

The galaxies near the centre are moving outwards more slowly than Earth's galaxy.

The galaxies far away from the centre are moving outwards more quickly than Earth's galaxy.

If we look at the inner galaxies, they are moving more slowly than us, so they appear to be moving away from us.

If we look at the outer galaxies they are travelling more quickly than us, so they appear to be moving away from us.

In fact, if we look at any galaxy in any position it will be moving away from us. This ties in with the idea of a 'big bang' firing matter out in all directions. This is one piece of evidence to support the Big Bang theory.

Cosmic microwave background radiation

Astronomers who worked on the Big Bang theory predicted that there would be some background radiation (in the microwave region of the spectrum) left over from the Big Bang.

In 1965 this background radiation was discovered. It agreed very closely with the predictions and this was hailed as further convincing evidence that the Big Bang theory was correct.

You can see the effect of this yourself. When you tune your television set you can see lots of 'snow' between channels. Some of this 'snow' is caused by microwave radiation from space that was left over from the Big Bang.

Dark stuff

Some difficulties still exist with the theory and many scientists are working to clarify these difficulties. One of the problems is explaining why the Universe is still expanding. Stars and galaxies are brought together because of gravitational attraction between them. If the galaxies are all attracting each other it would seem reasonable that the galaxies should slow down. But they're not!. . .

It may be that the expansion has increased.

To explain this astrophysicists have proposed the existence of **dark matter** or dark energy.

This is a type of matter that cannot be seen by any conventional method. However if it exists in the Universe it could cause the galaxies to continue to expand despite the forces of gravity.

Confusing, isn't it!

Key ideas

- ★ The Big Bang theory states that the Universe is continually expanding
- ★ Background radiation supports this theory
- ★ The movement of the galaxies supports this theory
- ★ There may be dark matter in the Universe which we cannot detect

Wordbank

Spectra – light separated into its constituent wavelengths

Dark matter – undiscovered matter which may exist in the Universe

Questions

1. What did Edwin Hubble observe that led him to think that the Universe was expanding?
2. What additional information supported the theory?
3. Prepare a small report on the Big Bang theory. Read about it using encyclopaedias and/or CD ROMs and see if you can gather any good explanations.

Is there intelligent life elsewhere?

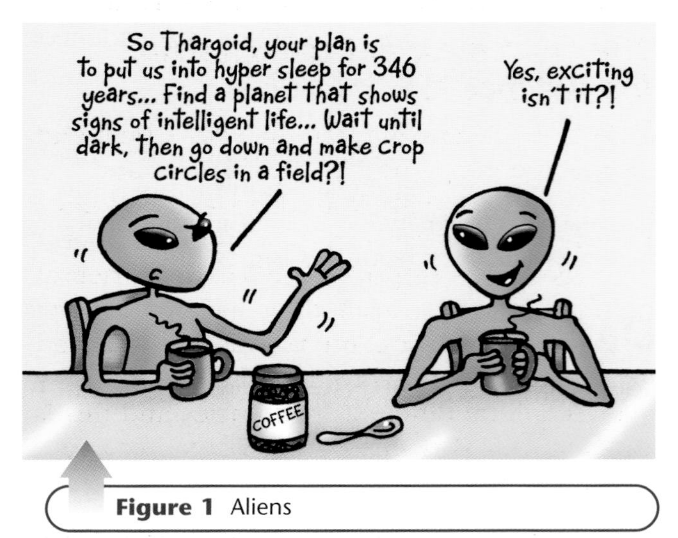

Figure 1 Aliens

Humans have always been curious about whether or not we are the only intelligent life in the Universe. If there were intelligent life on other planets, how would we communicate with it?

Early radio pioneers such as Heinrich Hertz and Guglielmo Marconi, discussed the possibility of using radio waves for interplanetary communication. In 1919, Marconi detected some unusual radio signals and tried to locate their source (causing quite a stir at the time).

Albert Einstein suggested using a light source as a means of planetary communication. However, light has a major drawback for communication over large distances. It can be blocked and dispersed by clouds and interstellar dust.

Radio waves and microwaves are not affected to the same extent by clouds and dust and would be able to travel across large distances. They also travel at the speed of light which is 300 000 km per second.

What are the chances of intelligent life?

This question is difficult to answer. Many scientists have tried to calculate the possibility of other parts of the Universe having intelligent life.

In the early 1960s an astronomer, Frank Drake, came up with a formula that gave an indication of the possibility of intelligent life.

The Drake formula includes such factors as:

1. The fraction of stars that can support planet formation.
2. The number of planets where life *may* be able to form.
3. The fraction of planets where life actually emerges.
4. The fraction of planets where *intelligent* life occurs.
5. The fraction of planets where *intelligent* life can communicate (radio etc.).
6. The length of time during which such civilisations remain detectable.

Attempts to complete the formula arrived at a figure of around 10 000. This means there could be 10 000 lifeforms that are intelligent, have radio technology, currently exist etc., spread throughout the Universe which could be contacted.

The answer is not much more than informed guesswork but it was done in an attempt to start the debate in terms of searching for intelligent life elsewhere.

The term 'intelligent life' is used in a particular context. Organisms resembling grass may exist on some other world but cannot not send out radio waves. They are not really thought of as intelligent.

Figure 2 Are these intelligent life forms?

What about dolphins or 16th century humans? They are intelligent but not able to send signals into space. There may be a huge range of alien life out there with which we may never be able to communicate.

So, if we are to detect signals from other worlds they must be able to send some form of radio signal.

How can we search for extra-terrestrial intelligence?

Mainly by detecting radio signals from space.

Figure 3 The Arecibo radio observatory

These telescopes detect radio waves from space across a wide range of frequencies. The waves are then analysed and any regular pattern is looked for, something like Morse code or regular beeps. This is a huge task! Radio waves can be broadcast over millions of different frequencies. Every frequency has to be analysed for signs of a repeated signal.

The Search for Extra-Terrestrial Intelligence (SETI)

SETI was a NASA programme which built and designed equipment that could detect and analyse radio signals from deep space. It ran for a number of years in the early 1990s but the project was stopped in 1993. Since then a number of smaller institutions have continued with some SETI programmes. SETI requires a very large amount of computing time to analyse all the different frequencies and this is expensive. A very clever way of trying to get round this was developed.

A screensaver was posted on the SETI website. People interested in SETI could download the screensaver free of charge. However, the screensaver contained a radio analysing programme and when your computer was not busy, SETI would send small bundles of signals and get your computer to look through the data for patterns. If nothing was found, your computer would then receive more for analysis and so on.

So, instead of one very large super-computer handling millions of pieces of data, there were millions of smaller computers handling small amounts of data. How intelligent!

Key ideas

- ★ It is probable that other life forms exist
- ★ In order to communicate with us alien life must be able to send radio signals
- ★ We receive and detect many radio signals from space
- ★ It is difficult to analyse all these signals
- ★ SETI led the way in attempting to locate alien life

Questions

1. Do you think there is intelligent life on other planets? Why?
2. If an alien did travel to Earth, who should it make contact with?
3. How could we try to contact other civilisations?
4. Why do so many people believe that aliens have visited this planet even though they have not made themselves visible to large communities?

Wordbank

SETI – Search for Extra-Terrestrial Intelligence

4 Searching for extra-terrestrial life on distant planets

The SETI project was designed to search for and analyse radio and microwave signals that come from deep space. Any life form that we could contact will need to exist on a planet.

Astrophysicists have been searching for planets outside our solar system for some time and have recently been successful.

Figure 1 Exoplanets

Planets that orbit other stars are known as **exoplanets** and over one hundred have been discovered to date.

How can we observe planets that are so far away?

With great difficulty!

We can see Venus, Mercury and other local planets because the light from the Sun is reflected off the surface of the planets. As they are relatively close to us, we can see the reflected light clearly. With exoplanets, the distances are so vast that we will never be able to detect the light from them. The planets are so small that the light reflected from them is extremely faint. (It is like trying to see the light from a candle being reflected off a black snooker ball at a distance of 100 miles!)

So how do we find them?

Blocking light

If a planet's orbit causes it to pass in front of a star, it blocks a little of the light from that star.

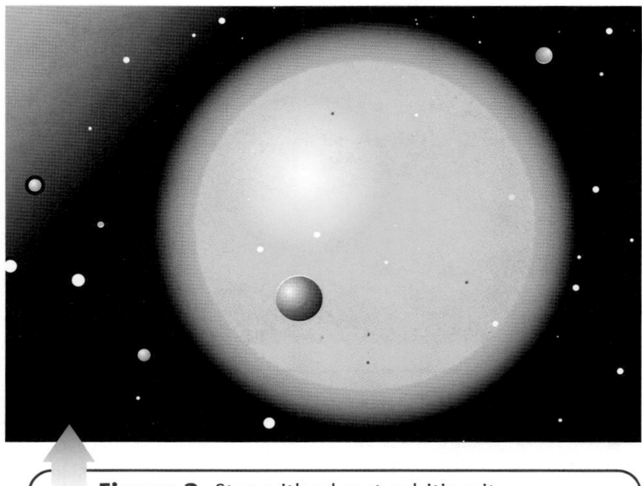

Figure 2 Star with planet orbiting it

The brightness of the star will fade slightly whenever the planet passes in front of it. For example, if the light from the star 'dims' every 30 days, we think that the star has a planet in front of it and that the planet orbits every 30 days.

Pulsing and wobbling

Certain stars emit regular 'pulses' of energy, mainly radio waves. The pulses are extremely regular. If a small planet passes near the star it causes the pulses to change slightly. Astronomers search for these pulsing stars and then examine the pulses.

If a large planet passes close to a star it can cause that star to wobble slightly. As the planet passes by, the gravitational attraction is enough to pull the star slightly. As the planet moves away the star goes back to its normal route but as it does so it wobbles slightly. Astronomers measure the orbit of stars closely and try to detect wobbles.

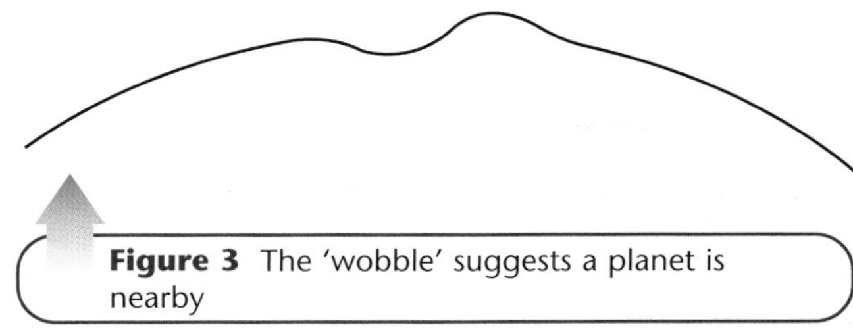

Figure 3 The 'wobble' suggests a planet is nearby

As you can gather, trying to find distant planets is very, very difficult. We can't see them so instead we look for the effect that they have on other larger, detectable objects.

Dust searching

The European Space Agency (ESA) has proposed that stars which could hold planets near to them will be surrounded by a disc of dust.

Planets are thought to have been made from clouds of gas and small, solid particles known generally as interplanetary dust. When these materials condense (come together) they form planets. Planets usually form near to the star where most of the material is found. Further away from the star the leftover dust forms a ring of small icy particles.

Our own solar system has one of these rings and it is known as the Kuiper belt. It is located beyond Pluto.

It is thought that these dust rings will only form round stars which have planets or asteroid belts. They emit a large amount of infra-red radiation and this can be detected by special telescopes. If these rings are detected then it will narrow the huge number of stars that have to be examined for exoplanets.

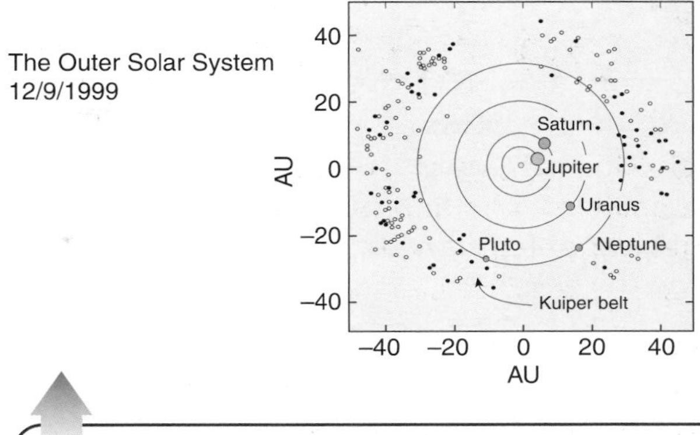

Figure 4 Location of Kuiper belt

Where next?

Some scientists have recently analysed the light that reflects off particular exoplanets. If they get enough of the light they can detect what the atmosphere may contain. One planet's atmosphere was found to contain sodium.

The overall goal is to ultimately find potentially habitable planets and probe them for signs of life.

A device known as an interferometer would help. It is a very sensitive device for analysing radiation. There are some on Earth but if we could put one in space it would detect a great deal more.

NASA has not yet committed to building a space-based interferometer, but an early model that would test the concept under a limited budget, a craft dubbed 'Star Light', could fly in 2006 if funding comes through.

Key ideas

★ Planets outside our solar system are difficult to detect

★ Planets can affect the orbit and the energy emitted from various stars and we can detect these changes caused by planets

Wordbank

Exoplanet – planet existing outside our own solar system

Questions

1 Why is it so difficult to detect planets from other systems?

2 Explain one of the ways in which we try to detect exoplanets.

3 Do you believe we should search for planets in other solar systems? Give reasons for your opinion.

Nuclear model of the atom

The word atom is derived from the Greek word *atomos* meaning indivisible. The philosopher Democritus (460–370 BC) believed that matter was composed of indivisible particles, called *atomos*.

So what are atoms really like?

We use the terms atoms, molecules, elements and compounds to help us describe how materials combine and how they react. It took scientists many hundreds of years before they could explain the structure of the atom in a way that supported the experiments scientists were doing.

Figure 1 An alchemist

Alchemists were early 'scientists' who attempted many strange experiments. Their ultimate aim was to change 'poorer' metals such as lead into gold. They were unsuccessful but in their attempts they did carry out many experiments which gave clues as to how materials react with each other.

In the late 1700s, Antoine Lavoisier managed to combine and then separate mercury and oxygen. He repeated the experiment over and over again and noticed that the amounts of mercury and oxygen used were always in the same proportion.

Experiments like this led to an Englishman, John Dalton, proposing the idea that the elements combined as individual blocks of atoms. He published his results in 1805. He proposed that these 'atoms' were the basic units of matter and that different chemicals had different atoms. This was the foundation of modern atomic theory and provided the basis upon which other theories could be refined.

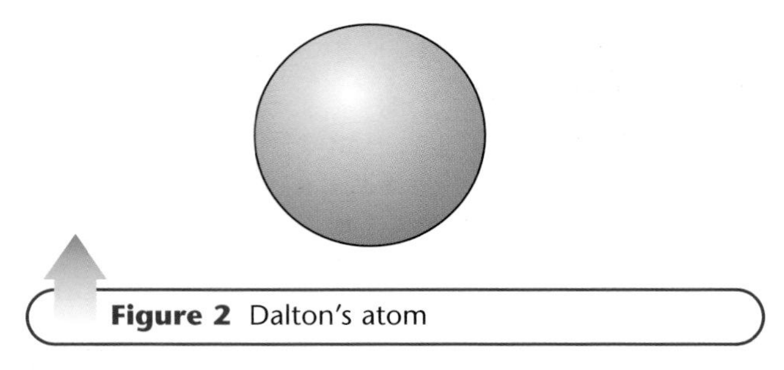

Figure 2 Dalton's atom

A closer look at the atom

By 1900 scientists were refining their theories. They now had evidence that the atom was made up of different parts. In 1897, JJ Thomson discovered a **sub-atomic** particle known as the electron. This has a negative charge.

In 1911, Ernest Rutherford showed that an atom was composed of a central core where most of the mass is found. Electrons orbit this central core.

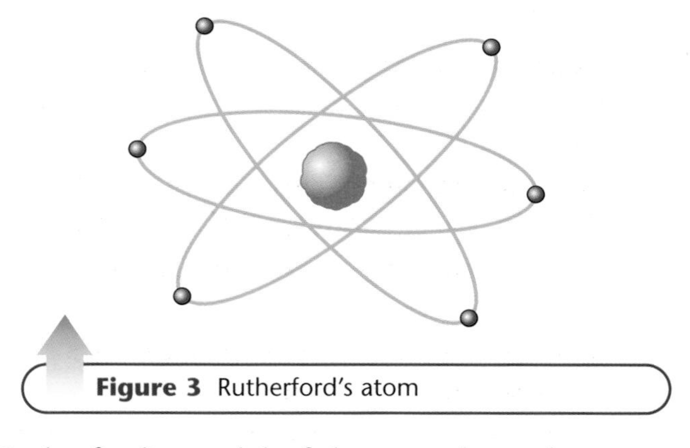

Figure 3 Rutherford's atom

Rutherford's model of the atom has a heavy, central core which has a positive charge and negatively charged electrons orbiting this core.

Neils Bohr

In papers published between 1913 and 1915 Neils Bohr took Rutherford's model of the atom and explained how the electrons were arranged around the atom.

Bohr discovered that the electrons do not orbit the atom in a random manner. He suggested that the electrons are in certain orbits or levels around the atom. They orbit at different levels and take in and give out energy when they move between levels.

James Chadwick

The neutron was first identified in 1932 by the British physicist James Chadwick. The neutron which has no charge is found along with the protons in the nucleus of the atom.

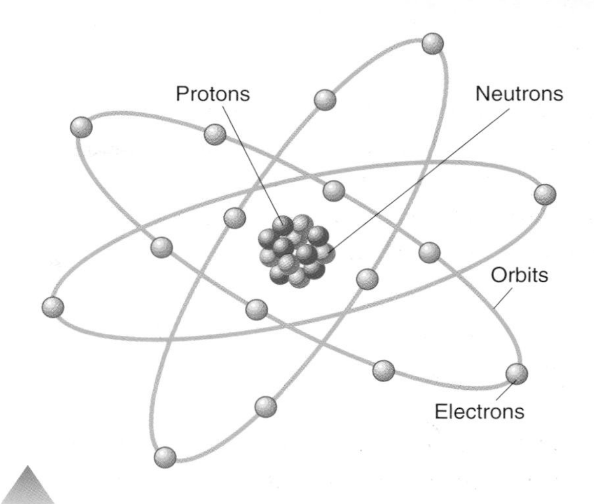

Figure 4 An atom with its nucleus of protons and neutrons and electrons orbiting

Current model of the atom

Each atom has a specific number of protons present in the nucleus. This is what determines which element it is. The number of protons present is the **atomic number** for that atom.

The number of protons and neutrons present in the nucleus is the **mass number** of that atom.

Electrons have very little mass in comparison to neutrons and protons.

Key ideas

- ★ Protons are large particles located within the nucleus and are positively charged
- ★ Neutrons are large particles located within the nucleus and carry no electrical charge
- ★ Electrons are small particles which orbit the nucleus and are negatively charged
- ★ Atomic number is the number of protons in the nucleus of an atom
- ★ Mass number is the number of protons and neutrons in an atom

Questions

1. Draw a diagram of an atom showing where the protons, neutrons and electrons are situated.
2. When was the idea that matter is composed of atoms first put forward?
3. Dalton put forward some other points as part of his general theory. List what these other points were.

Wordbank

Alchemist – an early scientist who tried to change materials into gold or valuable metal

Sub-atomic – part of an atom

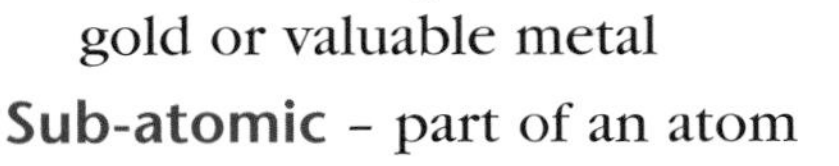

The structure of the Periodic Table

Group →

Period ↓

1	2											3	4	5	6	7	'0'
1 **H** hydrogen 1																	1 **He** helium 4
3 **Li** lithium 7	4 **Be** beryillium 9											5 **B** boron 11	6 **C** carbon 12	7 **N** nitrogen 14	8 **O** oxygen 16	9 **F** flourine 19	1 **Ne** neon 20
11 **Na** sodium 23	12 **Mg** magnesium 24											13 **Al** aluminium 27	14 **Si** silicon 28	15 **P** phosphorus 31	16 **S** sulphur 32	17 **Cl** chlorine 35.5	18 **Ar** argon 40
19 **K** potassium 39	20 **Ca** calcium 40	21 **Sc** scandium 45	22 **Ti** titanium 48	23 **V** vanadium 51	24 **Cr** chromium 52	25 **Mn** magnesuim 55	26 **Fe** iron 56	27 **Co** cobalt 59	28 **Ni** nickel 59	29 **Cu** copper 63.5	30 **Zn** zinc 65.4	31 **Ga** gallium 70	32 **Ge** germanium 73	33 **As** arsenic 75	34 **Se** selenium 79	35 **Br** bromine 80	36 **Kr** krypton 84
37 **Rb** rubidium 85	38 **Sr** strontium 88	39 **Y** yitrium 89	40 **Zr** zirconium 91	41 **Nb** niobium 93	42 **Mo** molybendium 96	43 **Tc** technetium	44 **Ru** ruthenium 101	45 **Rh** rhodium 103	46 **Pd** palladium 106	47 **Ag** silver 108	48 **Cd** cadmium 112	49 **In** indium 115	50 **Sn** tin 119	51 **Sb** antimony 122	52 **Te** tellurium 128	53 **I** iodine 127	54 **Xe** xenon 131
55 **Cs** caesium 133	56 **Ba** barrium 137	57 **La** lanthanum 139	72 **Hf** halfnium 178	73 **Ta** tantaium 181	74 **W** tungsten 184	75 **Re** rhenium 186	76 **Os** osmium 190	77 **Ir** indium 192	78 **Pt** platinum 195	79 **Au** gold 197	80 **Hg** mercury 201	81 **Ti** thallium 204	82 **Pb** lead 205	83 **Bi** bismuth	84 **Po** polonium	85 **At** aslatine	86 **Rh** radon
87 **Fr** francium 223	88 **Ra** radium 226	89 **Ac** actinium 227	104 **Rf** rutherfordium	105 **Db** dubium	106 **Sg** seaborgium	107 **Bh** bohrium	108 **Hs** hassium	109 **Mt** meitnerium	110 **Uun** ununnilium	111 **Uuu** ununnium	112 **Uub** ununnbium						
			58 **Ce** cerium 140	59 **Pr** praseodymium 141	60 **Nd** neodymium 144	61 **Pm** promethium	62 **Sm** samarium 150	63 **Eu** europium 152	64 **Gd** gadolinium 157	65 **Tb** terbium 159	66 **Dy** dysprosium 163	67 **Ho** holmium 165	68 **Er** erbium 167	69 **Tm** thulium 169	70 **Yb** ytterbium 173	71 **Lu** lutetium 175	
			90 **Th** thorium 232	91 **Pa** protactinium 231	92 **U** uranium 238	93 **Np** neptunium 2371	94 **Pu** plutonium	95 **Am** americium	96 **Cm** curium	97 **Bk** berkelium	98 **Cf** californium	99 **Es** einstein	100 **Fm** fermium	101 **Md** mendelevium	102 **No** nobelium	103 **Lr** lawrencium	

Figure 1 The Periodic Table

The Periodic Table classifies all the elements that are currently known to exist. There are over one hundred elements; some are common, such as carbon and some uncommon, such as technetium.

Each element differs from another element by the number of protons it has in its nucleus (atomic number). Oxygen has 8 protons in its nucleus, iron has 26 protons in its nucleus.

The Periodic Table is not just a simple way of listing the elements. It lists them in a particular order. They are grouped together because some elements have similar properties to others. This way of organising them was originated by a Russian chemist called Dmitri Mendeleyev in 1869.

Mendeleyev was passionate about elements and studied their characteristics closely.

He wrote the elements out on cards and then played a sorting game with them. This led to the shape of the Periodic Table.

Groups in the Periodic Table

The Periodic Table is arranged in vertical columns or groups. All the elements in a group have the same number of electrons in their outer energy level.

The column on the far left hand side is Group 1. The column on the far right hand side is Group 0.

Group 1

Elements in Group 1 have one electron in their outer energy level. The elements in Group 1 include lithium, sodium and potassium. They are all metals and are all very reactive. If you add any metals from this group to water they will react violently. Potassium will fizz about the surface of the water and burst into a lilac flame. Sodium will roll into a ball and occasionally burst into flame.

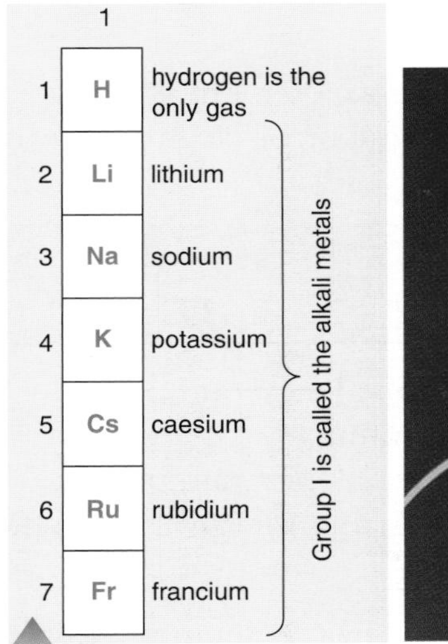

Figure 2 Group 1 metals are very reactive!

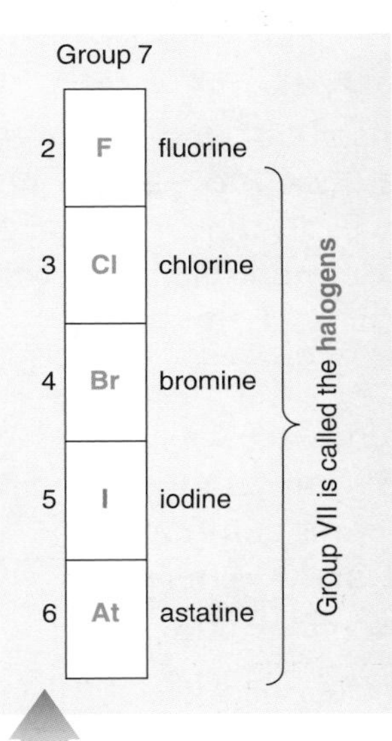

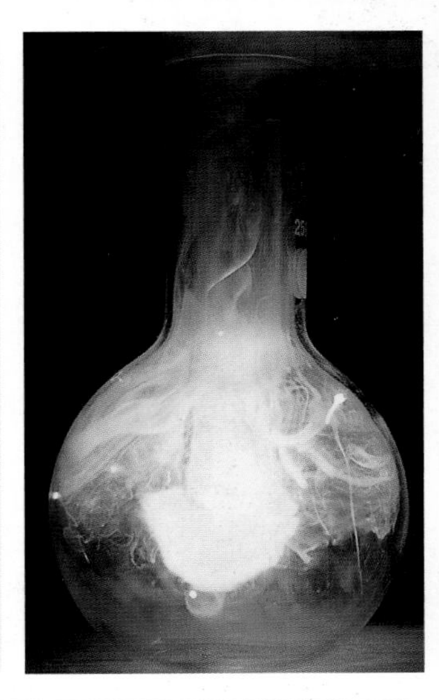

Figure 3 Group 7 elements react to form salts

This group is known as the alkali metals as they also produce an alkali when they react with water.

Group 7

Elements in Group 7 have seven electrons in their outer energy level. All the elements in Group 7 are non-metals. The first two elements, fluorine and chlorine, are gases. Bromine is a liquid, and iodine and astatine are solids.

They are all very reactive. Fluorine and chlorine are particularly reactive and can react violently with other chemicals. They are known as the **halogens** because they form chemicals such as copper chloride, which is a salt. Halogen means 'salt maker'.

Periods in the Periodic Table

The elements are also arranged in rows or periods. Elements in the same period have the same number of energy levels orbiting the atomic nucleus. The first period has one energy level for its electrons. The second period has two energy levels and so on. The energy levels are often described as **shells** which orbit the nucleus. Each shell has a maximum number of electrons which it can hold.

Key ideas

- ★ Elements are arranged in the Periodic Table according to their properties
- ★ Elements are placed into groups according to the number of electrons in their outer energy level
- ★ Elements are placed into rows according to the number of energy levels present

Wordbank

Halogens – salt forming elements found in Group 7 of the Periodic Table

Shells – energy levels of electrons which orbit an atomic nucleus

Questions

1. Silicon is used in the construction of semi-conductor materials. Which of the following could be used for the same purpose – Te, Rb, Ge, Mg or Kr?
2. What happens to the atomic number of the elements as you go across the Periodic Table?
3. What happens to the number of energy levels as you go down the periods of the Periodic Table?
4. What do elements Au, Pt and Ag have in common?
5. Suggest another element which will have 6 electrons in its outer shell.

How elements combine

The Periodic Table contains about one hundred different elements but there are more than one hundred different substances in the Universe. This is because atoms of different elements can react with others to form new chemicals known as compounds.

These compounds can then react with other elements or each other to form an ever increasing number of different compounds. The Earth is composed of many different compounds such as rocks, metals and plants.

The chemicals combine in a process called a chemical reaction.

Valency

Valency is a term used when chemical reactions are studied. The valency number of an element can be used to predict how it will combine.

In 1916, an American chemist Gilbert Lewis put forward the idea that atoms bonded together when the electrons in the outer shells interacted with each other.

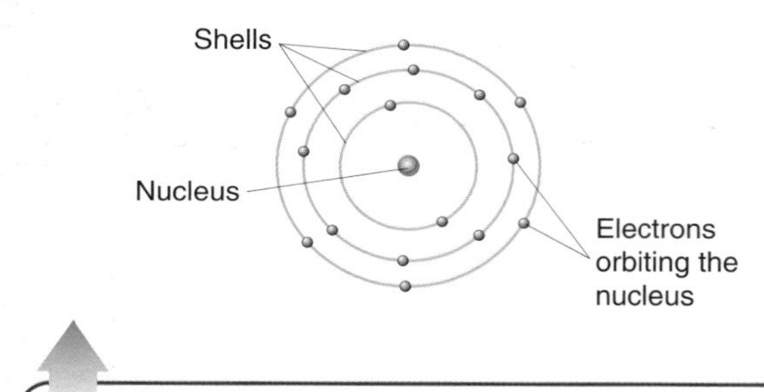

Figure 1 Electrons orbiting in a sulphur atom

The number of electrons in the outer shell is responsible for deciding how 'reactive' an element is.

Compounds generally form so that the outer shells of the reacting elements are completely filled with electrons.

Elements from Group 0 of the Periodic Table which have 8 electrons in their outer shell are very stable. Chemicals such as neon and argon have 8 electrons in their outer shells and do not need to combine with other elements as their outer shells are already completely filled with electrons.

The valency number of an element is calculated using the number of electrons in the outer shell.

Group number	1	2	3	4	5	6	7	0
Valency	1	2	3	4	3	2	1	0

- For Groups 1–4 the valency number is the same as the group number.
- For Groups 5–7 the valency number is calculated by subtracting the group number from 8.

For example if an atom has 5 electrons in its outer shell it requires 3 more electrons to become stable – the valency power is 3.

These outer electrons form the basis of how chemicals bond and there are two main types of bonding.

Ionic bonding

Let's examine sodium. It is a silver coloured metal from Group 1. This means it has one electron in its outer shell.

Chlorine is a gas from Group 7. It has seven electrons in its outer shell.

Sodium and chlorine combine easily to form sodium chloride, common salt.

Figure 2 This metal and gas react to make salt!

When sodium and chlorine react, the outer electron from the sodium atom is transferred to the outer shell of the chlorine atom.

This means that the sodium atom is now positively charged (it has lost an electron) and that the chlorine atom is now negatively charged (it has gained an electron). These charged particles are called **ions**.

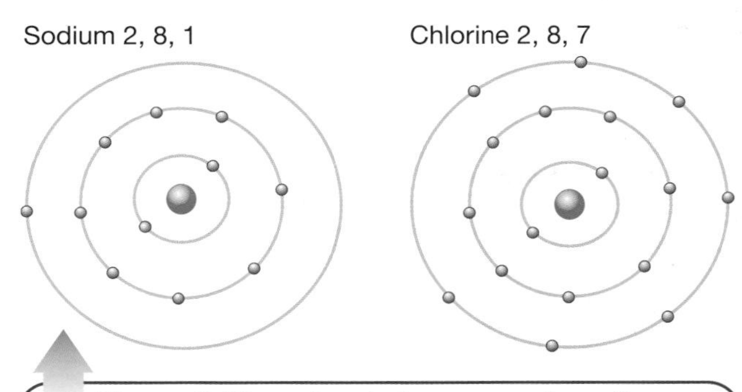

Figure 3 The outer electron moves from the sodium to the chlorine atom

An ion is formed when an atom gains or loses electrons. The positive sodium is now attracted to the negative chlorine and this forms the basis of the chemical bond. It is called an **ionic bond**. An ionic bond is an attraction between positive and negative ions.

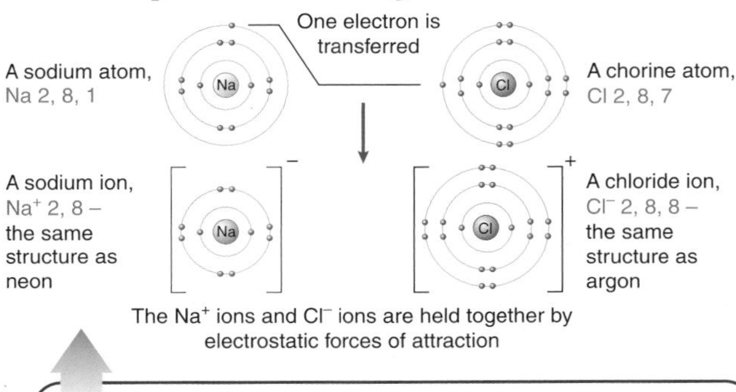

Figure 4 Ionic bonding

Covalent bonding

A second type of bonding occurs when atoms share electrons. Water is a simple covalent compound which has **covalent bonds**.

An oxygen atom has six electrons in its outer shell and a hydrogen atom has one.
If one oxygen atom joins with two hydrogen atoms and *shares* its electrons, this will give the oxygen eight electrons in its outer level. This will make water a stable compound.

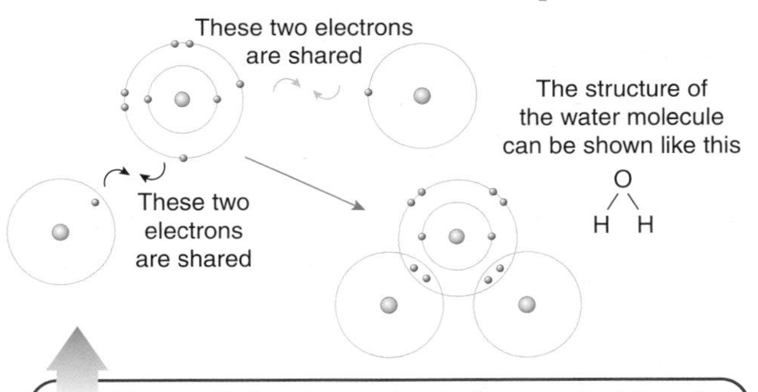

Figure 5 A water molecule has covalent bonds

In covalent bonds each atom shares the electrons between them. Neither electron belongs to any one atom. A covalent bond is a shared pair of electrons.

Key ideas

- ★ Valency of an atom is determined by the number of electrons in an atom's outer shell
- ★ Chemicals bond in a process known as a chemical reaction
- ★ Outer electrons are used in bonding
- ★ In ionic bonds electrons move from one atom to another
- ★ In covalent bonds electrons are shared between atoms

Wordbank

Valency – the chemical combining power of an element's atoms

Ionic bond – an attraction between positive ions and negative ions

Covalent bond – formed by a shared pair of electrons

Questions

1 Copy and complete this table.

Atom	Valency
Li	
Al	
Kr	
Ca	
N	
C	
Mg	

2 Explain how potassium and bromine could combine.

3 What type of bond is formed when electrons are shared?

4 Draw a diagram of a water molecule.

5 Which of the following elements could form an ionic bond with magnesium – Al, N, He or O? Explain why.

Elements in transition

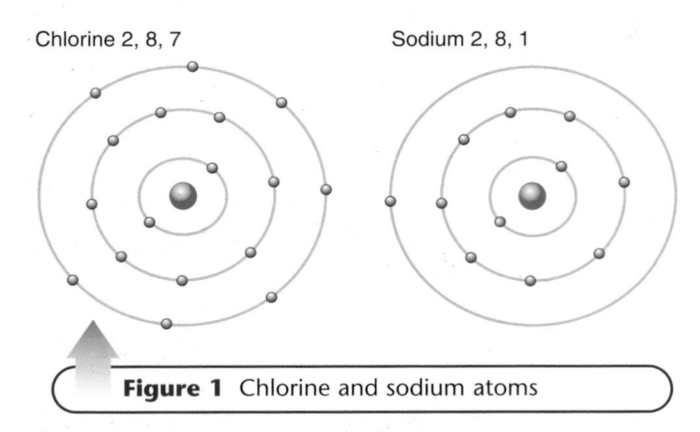

Figure 1 Chlorine and sodium atoms

The elements of the Periodic Table are arranged according to groups and periods.

Elements are arranged into groups according to the **valency** of the elements. The number of electrons in its outer shell determines the element's valency.

Elements are arranged into periods according to the number of energy levels or shells of their electrons.

When the Periodic Table was being constructed a number of elements called the transition metals did not easily fit into place.

The transition metals

The transition metals are rather more complicated in terms of the ways that the electrons are organised. These elements can be found between Groups 2 and 3 of the Periodic Table.

The properties of transition metals depend on the way that the outer electrons are organised in the outer two energy levels (shells).

Unlike other parts of the Periodic Table, similarities also exist across the periods as well as down the groups. Some of the properties of transition metals include:

- Forming **alloys** with other elements. For example, brass is an alloy of zinc and copper. A 2p coin is an alloy of copper and nickel. Stainless steel is an alloy of iron, chromium and manganese. Plumber's solder is an alloy of lead and tin.

Figure 2 The Periodic Table

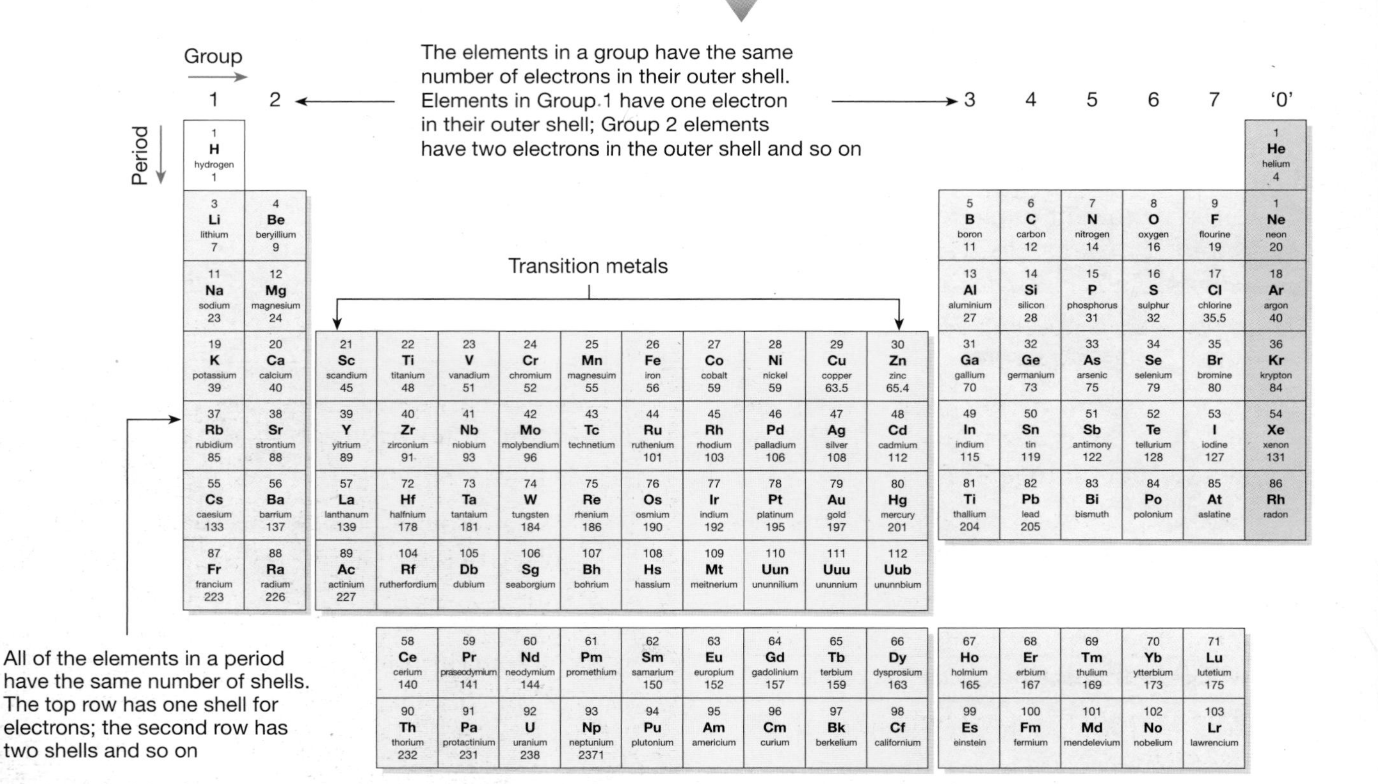

1	2											3	4	5	6	7	'0'
1 H hydrogen 1																	1 He helium 4
3 Li lithium 7	4 Be beryillium 9											5 B boron 11	6 C carbon 12	7 N nitrogen 14	8 O oxygen 16	9 F flourine 19	1 Ne neon 20
11 Na sodium 23	12 Mg magnesium 24											13 Al aluminium 27	14 Si silicon 28	15 P phosphorus 31	16 S sulphur 32	17 Cl chlorine 35.5	18 Ar argon 40
19 K potassium 39	20 Ca calcium 40	21 Sc scandium 45	22 Ti titanium 48	23 V vanadium 51	24 Cr chromium 52	25 Mn magnesuim 55	26 Fe iron 56	27 Co cobalt 59	28 Ni nickel 59	29 Cu copper 63.5	30 Zn zinc 65.4	31 Ga gallium 70	32 Ge germanium 73	33 As arsenic 75	34 Se selenium 79	35 Br bromine 80	36 Kr krypton 84
37 Rb rubidium 85	38 Sr strontium 88	39 Y yitrium 89	40 Zr zirconium 91	41 Nb niobium 93	42 Mo molybendium 96	43 Tc technetium	44 Ru ruthenium 101	45 Rh rhodium 103	46 Pd palladium 106	47 Ag silver 108	48 Cd cadmium 112	49 In indium 115	50 Sn tin 119	51 Sb antimony 122	52 Te tellurium 128	53 I iodine 127	54 Xe xenon 131
55 Cs caesium 133	56 Ba barrium 137	57 La lanthanum 139	72 Hf halfnium 178	73 Ta tantaium 181	74 W tungsten 184	75 Re rhenium 186	76 Os osmium 190	77 Ir indium 192	78 Pt platinum 195	79 Au gold 197	80 Hg mercury 201	81 Ti thallium 204	82 Pb lead 205	83 Bi bismuth	84 Po polonium	85 At aslatine	86 Rh radon
87 Fr francium 223	88 Ra radium 226	89 Ac actinium 227	104 Rf rutherfordium	105 Db dubium	106 Sg seaborgium	107 Bh bohrium	108 Hs hassium	109 Mt meitnerium	110 Uun ununnilium	111 Uuu ununnium	112 Uub ununnbium						

58 Ce cerium 140	59 Pr praseodymium 141	60 Nd neodymium 144	61 Pm promethium	62 Sm samarium 150	63 Eu europium 152	64 Gd gadolinium 157	65 Tb terbium 159	66 Dy dysprosium 163	67 Ho holmium 165	68 Er erbium 167	69 Tm thulium 169	70 Yb ytterbium 173	71 Lu lutetium 175
90 Th thorium 232	91 Pa protactinium 231	92 U uranium 238	93 Np neptunium 2371	94 Pu plutonium	95 Am americium	96 Cm curium	97 Bk berkelium	98 Cf californium	99 Es einstein	100 Fm fermium	101 Md mendelevium	102 No nobelium	103 Lr lawrencium

- They are useful as **catalysts**. Transition metals and alloys of transition metals can speed up the rate of chemical reactions e.g. platinum is used in catalytic converters in car exhausts.

Figure 3 The honeycomb structure inside this catalytic converter provides maximum surface area for chemical reactions

- Their compounds are usually coloured. Haemoglobin found in human blood contains the transition element iron.
- They have typical properties of metals such as metallic **lustre**, high conductivity of heat and electricity, **malleability** and **tensile strength**.

Figure 4 The micro-wires in silicon chips are made of gold as it is an excellent conductor of electricity

Key ideas

★ Elements are placed into periods and groups in the Periodic Table

★ Elements in a period have the same number of shells

★ Elements in a group have the same number of electrons in their outer shell

★ Transition metals have complicated arrangements of electrons

★ Similarities exist across the periods as well as down the groups within the transition elements

Wordbank

Valency – the chemical combining power of an element

Alloy – a mixture of two or more metals or a mixture of metals and non-metals, melted together

Catalyst – a substance that can change the rate of chemical reactions

Lustre – bright and shiny condition

Malleability – ability to shape or bend without breaking

Tensile strength – stretching force of a material

Questions

1 What is the approximate number of transition elements in the Periodic Table?

2 Name two transition metals and their uses.

3 In groups, prepare a display about one group of the transition elements.

4 Find out more and prepare a display about one of the following:

- the atom
- alloys
- catalysts

5 Myoglobin is an important chemical found in animal muscle. Which transition metal is associated with this compound?

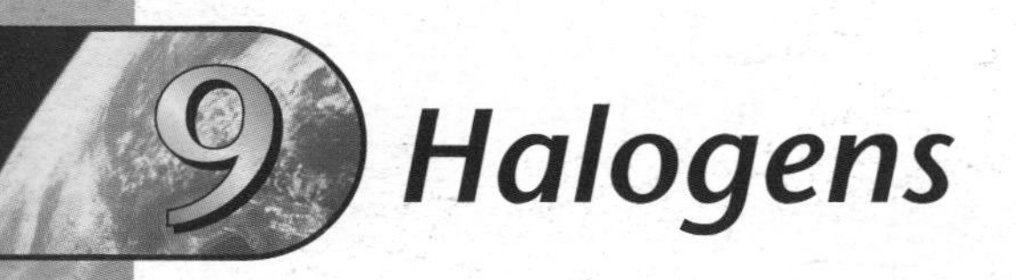

Halogens

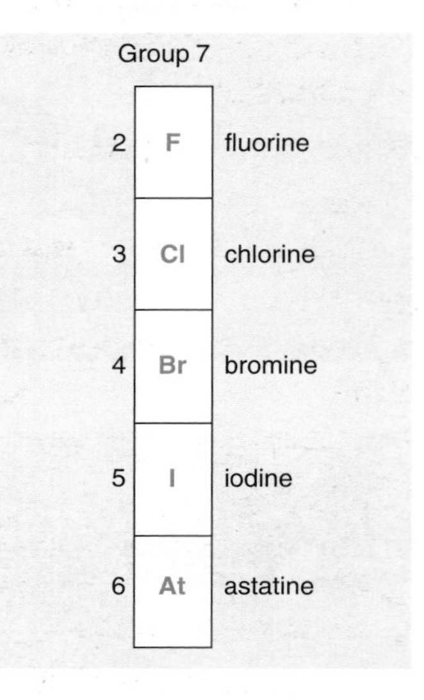

Figure 1 Group 7 elements

Group 7 of the Periodic Table contains the five elements known as **halogens**. They are the most reactive group of non-metals. In 1869, Mendeleyev organised the 63 known elements into the Periodic Table. He was able to predict the properties of elements that were still to be discovered because they were so similar.

Halogen factfile

1 The halogens as a group display very similar properties. We know now that they are all only one electron short of a complete shell.

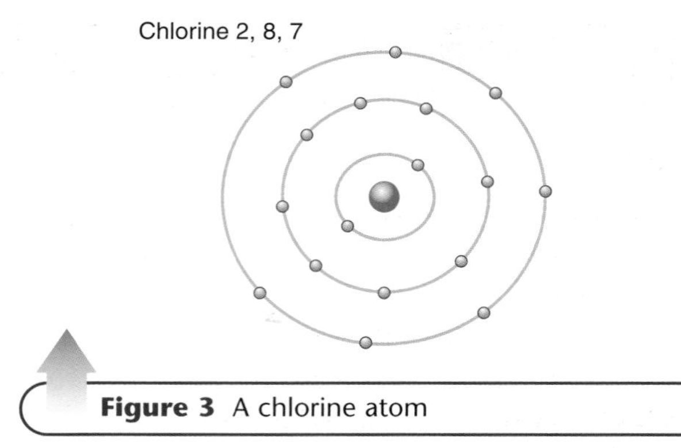

Figure 3 A chlorine atom

2 The word halogen means 'salt maker'. The halogens form salts with metals. All halogens have 7 electrons in their outer shells, requiring one more to fill it. This makes them very reactive.

3 Halogens react readily with hydrogen to produce hydrogen halides e.g. hydrogen fluoride, hydrogen chloride etc. Hydrogen halides dissolve in water to form acidic solutions such as hydrochloric acid. These acids are important economically.

4 The halogens exist as **diatomic** molecules. This is a molecule with two atoms – F_2, Cl_2, Br_2 or I_2.

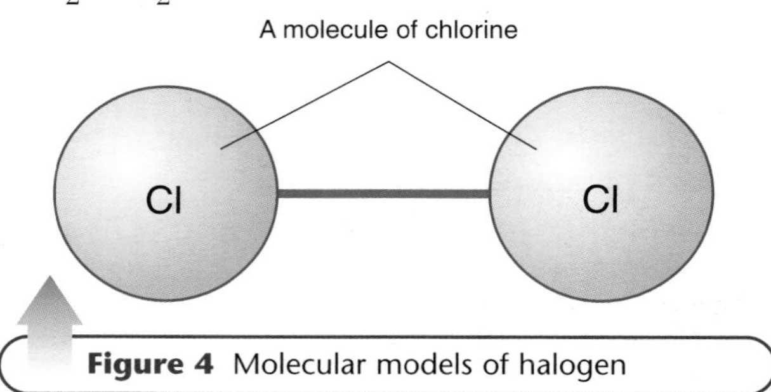

Figure 4 Molecular models of halogen

Figure 2 Mendeleyev's Periodic Table

Reihen	Gruppe I. – R^2O	Gruppe II. – RO	Gruppe III. – R^2O^3	Gruppe IV. RH^4 RO^2	Gruppe V. RH^3 R2O5	Gruppe VI. RH^2 RO^3	Gruppe VII. RH R^2O^7	Gruppe VIII. – RO^4
1	*H* = 1							
2	*Li* = 7	*Be* = 9,4	*B* = 11	*C* = 12	*N* = 14	*O* = 16	*F* = 19	
3	*Na* = 23	*Mg* = 24	*Al* = 27,3	*Si* = 28	*P* = 31	*S* = 32	*Cl* = 35,5	*Fe* = 56, *Co* = 5
4	*K* = 39	*Ca* = 40	– = 44	*Ti* = 48	*V* = 51	*Cr* = 52	*Mn* = 55	*Ni* = 59, *Cu* = 63
5	(*Cu* = 63)	*Zn* = 65	– = 68	– = 72	*As* = 75	*Se* = 78	*Br* = 80	
6	*Rb* = 85	*Sr* = 87	? *Yt* = 88	*Zr* = 90	*Nb* = 94	*Mo* = 96	– = 100	*Ru* = 104, *Rh* = 1 *Pd* = 106, *Ag* = 1
7	*Ag* = 108	*Cd* = 112	*In* = 113	*Sn* = 118	*Sb* = 122	*Te* = 125	*J* = 127	
8	*Cs* = 133	*Ba* = 137	? *Di* = 138	? *Ce* = 140	–	–	–	– – – –
9	(–)	–	–	–	–	–	–	
10	–	–	? *Er* = 178	? *La* = 180	*Ta* = 182	*W* = 184	–	*Os* = 195, *Ir* = 19 *Pt* = 198, *Au* = 1
11	(*Au* = 199)	*Hg* = 200	*Tl* = 204	*Pb* = 207	*Bi* = 208	–	–	
12	–	–	–	*Th* = 231	*H* = 1	*U* = 240	–	– – – –

5 The halogens exist at room temperature in the three states of matter:

Solid	Liquid	Gas
Iodine	Bromine	Fluorine
Astatine		Chlorine

6 Fluorine is a poisonous pale yellow gas. There are naturally occuring fluorine compounds called ores. Fluorine ores are fluorspar, calcium fluoride and cryolite. Fluorine is extracted from its ore by **electrolysis**. The gas must be collected in a non-reactive container – glass is unsuitable as fluorine will react with it! Fluorine compounds are present in toothpaste. It can be added to water supplies to help prevent tooth decay. Teflon, the slippiest substance in the world, includes fluorine.

7 Chlorine is a poisonous pale green gas. Chlorine is extracted from molten rocksalt or seawater by electrolysis. Chlorine is used for chlorinating drinking water and to make **organochlorine** compounds e.g. the insecticide DDT. Hypochlorites are used in domestic bleaches.

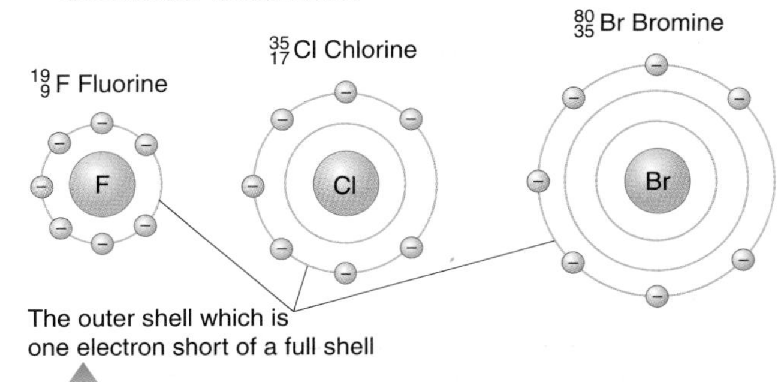

Figure 5 Fluorine, chlorine and bromine

8 Bromine is a toxic and caustic brown volatile liquid. Bromine is also extracted from seawater. Bromine salts are now used to manufacture dyes, disinfectants and photographic chemicals.

9 Iodine is a shiny black solid, which easily **sublimes** to form a violet vapour on heating. Iodine is mined as sodium iodate, which is present in small quantities in the ore Chile saltpetre. It may also be extracted from seaweed. Radioactive **isotopes** of iodine are used in medical tracer work involving the thyroid and to treat thyroid diseases. Government agencies hold supplies of potassium iodate tablets for use in the event of a nuclear accident.

Key ideas

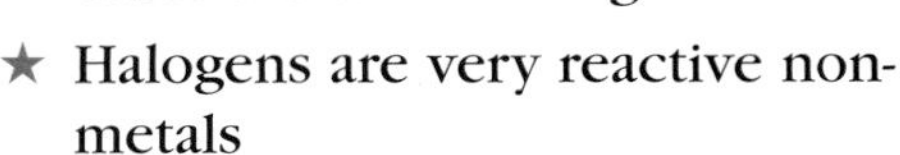

★ Group 7 elements of the Periodic Table are called halogens

★ Halogens are very reactive non-metals

★ Hydrogen halides dissolve in water to form acids

★ Halogen products are important economically

Wordbank

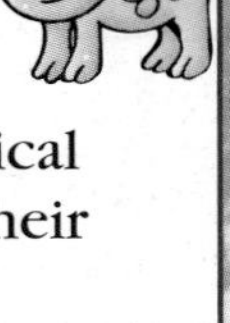

Halogens – Group 7 elements

Diatomic – any molecule which contains only two atoms

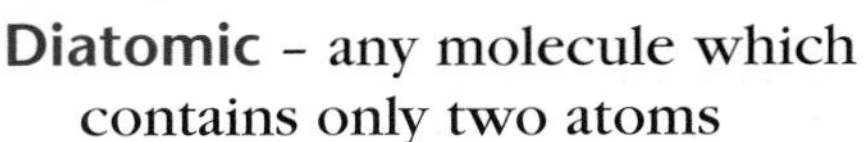

Electrolysis – process that uses electrical energy to separate elements from their compound

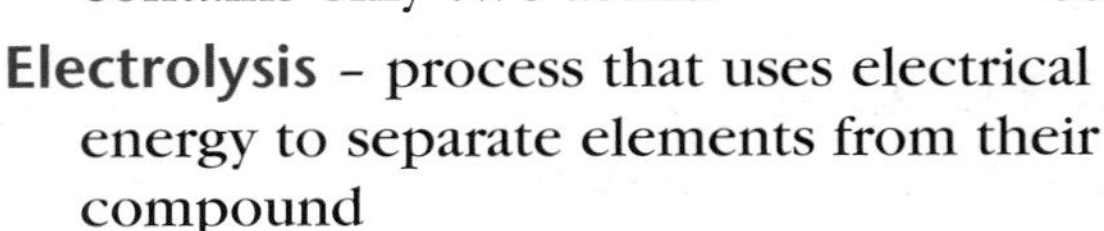

Organochlorines – compounds of carbon and chlorine

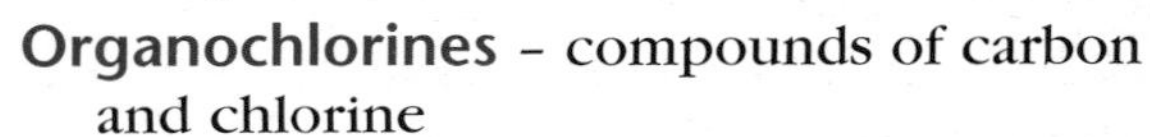

Sublimation – process where a solid turns to a gas or a gas turns to solid without becoming a liquid

Isotope – atoms of the same element which have different numbers of neutrons (they have the same atomic number but a different atomic mass)

Questions

1 Draw a diagram of each of the halogen atoms showing the electrons in the outer shell.

2 Design a container that could be used to pour liquid iodine. (Read the passage on iodine very carefully so that you can apply suitable design criteria.)

3 Name two commercial uses for fluorine, chlorine, bromine and iodine.

4 Find out some more about fluorocarbons e.g. Teflon, or organochlorine compounds e.g. DDT.

The water cycle

The water cycle involves the continuous circulation of water between the oceans, the **atmosphere**, the living things of the **biosphere** and the land of the **geosphere**. It is the presence of the enormous amount of water on Earth that distinguishes it from the other planets of our solar system and its presence is essential for life to exist.

Figure 1 Look at all the water on the surface of the Earth!

Over 1304 million cubic kilometres of water exist on Earth with 97.24% of it being the salt water of the oceans. A cubic kilometre of water contains more than a **billion** gallons.

Water source	Water volume in cubic km	Percent of total water
oceans	1268 000 000	97.24%
icecaps, glaciers	28 000 000	2.14%
ground water	8 000 000	0.61%
fresh-water lakes	120 000	0.009%
inland seas	100 000	0.008%
soil moisture	64 000	0.005%
atmosphere	12 400	0.001%
rivers	1200	0.0001%
Total water volume	**1304 000 000**	**100.00%**

Of the remaining 2.76% which is fresh water most of it, about 69%, is locked up as ice and snow mainly in the polar regions of the Earth. Around 30% is stored beneath the Earth's surface as groundwater. The remaining 1% of this 2.76% is made up from all the lakes, inland seas, moisture trapped in soil, rivers and atmospheric water.

Processes within the cycle

When the atoms of a liquid water molecule gain sufficient energy, normally from the Sun, they evaporate into the air. The process of evaporation describes the change in state from liquid to gas of the water molecules. These warmed molecules of water change from the liquid state into the gaseous state. This gas (water vapour) spreads out into the atmosphere. Evaporation can occur from plants and animals as well as from the liquid found in oceans, streams and puddles.

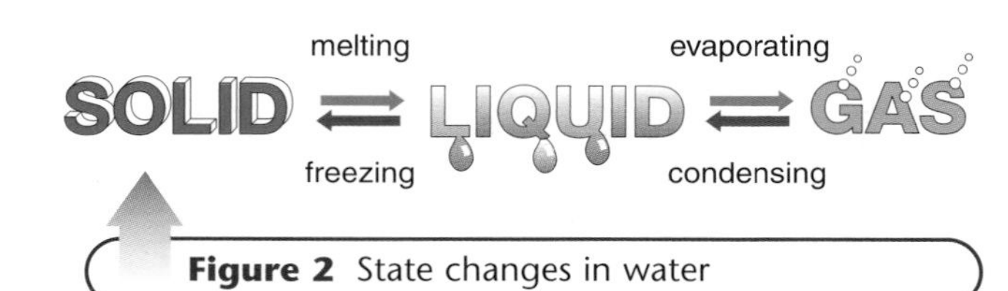

Figure 2 State changes in water

As the water vapour rises into the atmosphere it begins to cool down causing condensation of the vapour back into a liquid. The newly condensed water molecules are once again in a liquid state and they form clouds of water droplets which increase in size as they continue to cool. The condensed water molecules join together forming larger droplets of water. Eventually the water droplets **precipitate** forming raindrops, snowflakes or hailstones and fall back to Earth. Snow or hail form when the liquid water molecules lose enough energy to cause them to freeze and change state into a solid. In high altitude areas which are cold enough the snow will remain stored in the solid form. If the temperature rises, as happens when seasons change, then some of the snow melts which adds to the water which flows down the hillsides forming streams and eventually flowing into rivers.

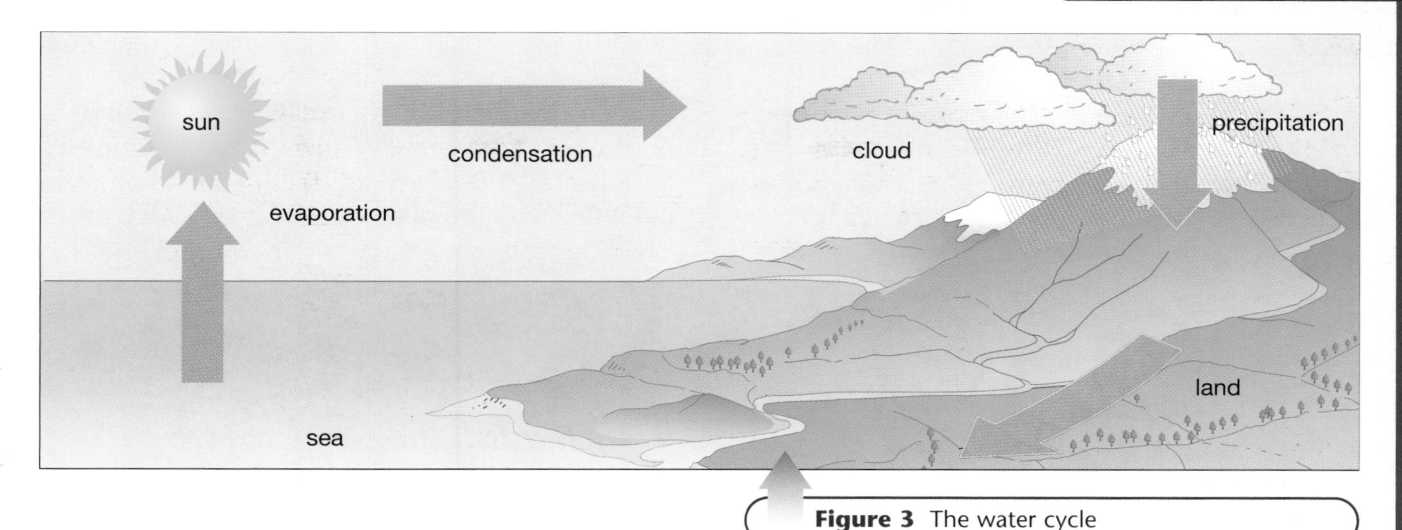

Figure 3 The water cycle

Some of the precipitation will be directly absorbed by plants and is often recycled back into the atmosphere without it reaching the ground. When the precipitation does reach the ground it normally seeps down into the soil eventually percolating down to form a store of groundwater. Indeed there is much more fresh water stored beneath the Earth's surface than there is on the surface itself.

Where the soil is already saturated with water the excess flows downhill to the nearest stream as overland flow. This water eventually forms rivers which flow into the sea.

A large percentage of the precipitation is returned to the atmosphere by evaporation from moist surfaces, puddles, ponds and lochs.

Key ideas

- ★ Water is essential to allow life to exist
- ★ Enormous quantities of water exist on Earth
- ★ Water is continually recycled in nature
- ★ The water cycle involves frequent changes of state
- ★ When rain or snow falls it is called precipitation

Wordbank

Atmosphere – the gaseous mass or envelope surrounding the Earth

Biosphere – the living organisms and their environments on Earth

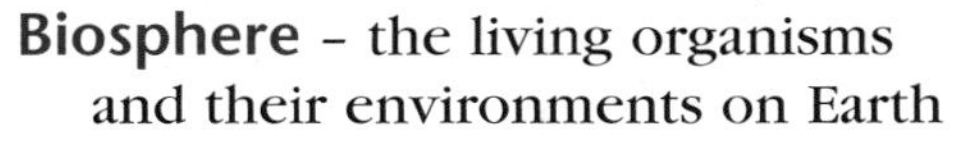

Geosphere – the soils and rocks of the Earth

Billion – 1000 000 000

Precipitation – the process of rain, hail or snow falling from the clouds

Questions

1. Where is the bulk of water stored on Earth?
2. What is the name of the process which describes water forming on the insides of windows in the classroom?
3. What is the name of the process which describes wet clothes on a washing line becoming dry?
4. What is the name of the structures in the sky where water droplets are stored?
5. Describe what happens to a water molecule as it goes through the water cycle.
6. What percentage of water found in and on the Earth is freshwater?
7. Considering the enormous volumes of water on the planet, why are some scientists concerned about the availability of useable water for the planet's population?

11 Reaction rates

A chemical reaction is a process in which one or more new substances are formed. This involves atoms of the starting materials, the **reactants**, changing to produce the new substances, the **products**.

Figure 1 Oxygen and hydrogen react to make water

Water contains the elements hydrogen and oxygen. Water is a very common compound found in vast quantities on the Earth. To make water the elements hydrogen and oxygen (the reactants), combine together to form hydrogen oxide or water (the product).

hydrogen + oxygen → water (hydrogen oxide)
reactants product

Listed in the Periodic Table there are over 100 elements currently known to man. Of these, 92 are naturally occurring. Very few elements are found in their pure state. Most are combined with one or more other elements to form a compound.

Some elements react more quickly than others. Consider the reactivity series for metals shown in the table in Figure 2. This puts metals in order of their ability to react with other elements.

A piece of calcium metal left exposed to the air will quickly lose its lustre as it reacts quickly with the oxygen in the air to form calcium oxide.

A piece of iron of equivalent size and shape will take longer to react and so loses its lustre more slowly as it forms iron oxide.

A piece of gold of equivalent size and shape will not lose its lustre as it does not react with oxygen.

Reacting particles must collide for a chemical reaction to take place. The greater the number of collisions the faster the rate of the chemical reaction. Not all collisions result in a reaction. The reactants must have a minimum energy to collide successfully.

The rate at which a reaction takes place between substances can be affected by the following:

1 Increasing the temperature

If the reactants are given more energy then the chances of the molecules colliding successfully increases and so the reaction rate will be faster.

For example, a car exhaust will rust faster than the bodywork as it is at a higher temperature.

2 Increasing the concentration of reactants

If the concentration of the reactants is increased then the chances of the reactant molecules colliding will increase resulting in a faster reaction.

In an experiment, a piece of magnesium metal in ribbon form was added to a beaker containing 50 ml of very dilute sulphuric acid. The time taken for the magnesium ribbon to dissolve was measured.

Potassium	K	**Most reactive**
Sodium	Na	↓
Calcium	Ca	
Magnesium	Mg	
Aluminium	Al	
Zinc	Zn	
Iron	Fe	
Lead	Pb	
Copper	Cu	
Mercury	Hg	
Silver	Ag	
Gold	Au	**Least reactive**

Figure 2 The reactivity series

Second and third pieces of magnesium ribbon were added to two other beakers, one containing 50 ml of dilute sulphuric acid and the other containing 50 ml of concentrated sulphuric acid. The time taken for these to dissolve was similarly measured.

The results are as shown below:

Type of acid	Time taken for Mg to dissolve
very dilute acid	4 min 20 sec
dilute acid	3 min 30 sec
concentrated acid	1 min 25 sec

As the acid concentration increases the time taken for the reaction to complete decreases, i.e. the reaction becomes faster.

3 Particle size

The smaller the particle size the faster the reaction rate. The smaller the particle size the greater the surface area and so more reacting particles come into contact resulting in more collisions and a faster reaction rate.

The previous experiment was repeated using the same mass of magnesium, but instead of using ribbon it was dropped in as granules. The following results were measured:

Type of acid	Time taken for Mg to dissolve
very dilute acid	3 min 20 sec
dilute acid	2 min 30 sec
concentrated acid	0 min 25 sec

The time taken for the magnesium granules to dissolve was less than the ribbon form in all three acids.

If magnesium powder had been used the reaction would have happened more quickly because the magnesium powder has a smaller particle size.

Key ideas

- ★ Chemical reactions involve the formation of one or more new substances
- ★ Chemical reactions can take place at different rates
- ★ The chemical reaction involves changing the reactants into the products
- ★ Increasing temperature increases rate of reaction
- ★ Increasing concentration of reactants increases rate of reaction

Wordbank

Reactants – raw materials in a chemical reaction

Products – substance produced by a chemical reaction

Reaction rate – the speed at which a chemical reaction takes place

Questions

1. Name 3 elements found in a combined state on Earth.
2. Name 3 elements found in a pure state on Earth.
3. Place the following metals in order from the most reactive to the least reactive – gold, zinc, lead, sodium, aluminium, silver, iron.
4. The following apparatus is used to produce carbon dioxide gas in the lab.

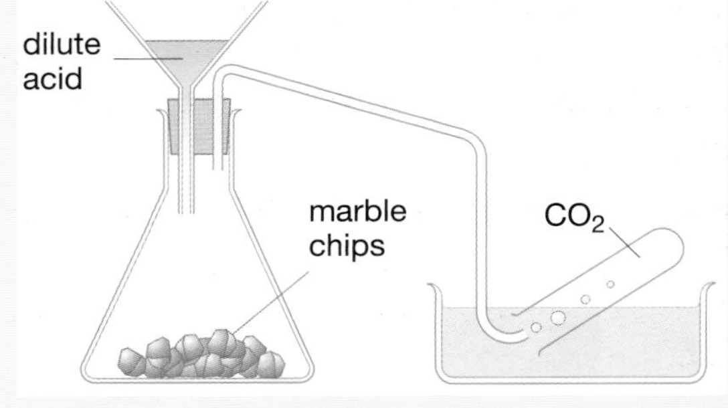

Suggest two ways you could alter the apparatus to speed up the production of gas.

5. In the experiment with the magnesium granules, what could be done to further increase the rate of reaction?

Exothermic and endothermic reactions

The term **exothermic** means to give out heat. This is a common occurrence which you witness every day, for example when a cooker ring is switched on. The ring is physically changed by the heating process and when it is switched off it will return to its original condition.

Figure 1 An exothermic event

The term **endothermic** means to absorb heat. An ice cube which melts undergoes a physical change. The ice absorbs heat in order to change into a liquid. The molecules of water have changed state but the atoms present are still the same.

In both of the above examples the chemistry of the substances has not changed.

A chemical reaction involves making a product from reactants. This involves the release or absorption of energy.

Every day you witness chemical reactions. Most of these reactions produce heat, such as when you light a match or a candle.

Figure 2 An exothermic reaction

Other chemical reactions absorb heat. The breakdown of water into hydrogen and oxygen requires the input of energy to separate the compound.

The study of energy changes in chemical reactions is called **thermochemistry**.

In thermochemistry we investigate the bonds which hold atoms together. If we break a bond then energy needs to be absorbed to cause the change. If we form a bond then energy will be released.

Exothermic reactions

A common exothermic reaction is the burning of fuels. When natural gas (which contains carbon and hydrogen) burns, several reactions occur. The carbon atoms combine with the oxygen from the air to form carbon dioxide and the hydrogen atoms combine with oxygen atoms to form water. The rearrangement of the **chemical bonds** linking the atoms releases a great deal of energy as heat and light.

natural gas + oxygen → carbon dioxide + water + HEAT

Energy is absorbed to break the bonds between the carbon and hydrogen atoms in the fuel. This is much less than the energy released when the two elements combine with oxygen. The overall reaction is exothermic because more energy is released when the new bonds are formed than is put in to break the bonds in the reactant molecules.

When an acid such as hydrochloric acid neutralises an alkali such as sodium hydroxide solution, the reaction gives out heat. The solution gets warm as the products of sodium chloride and water are formed. This is an exothermic reaction.

hydrochloric acid + sodium hydroxide → sodium chloride + water

REACTANTS → PRODUCTS

Endothermic reactions

In endothermic reactions the overall energy absorbed is greater than that released. In the production of iron from its ore, which comprises mainly iron oxide, the ore is heated to very high temperatures in the presence of carbon. The oxygen from the ore joins with the carbon to form carbon dioxide leaving the iron metal behind. This process requires an enormous amount of energy to be absorbed.

iron oxide + carbon ➔ iron + carbon dioxide + HEAT

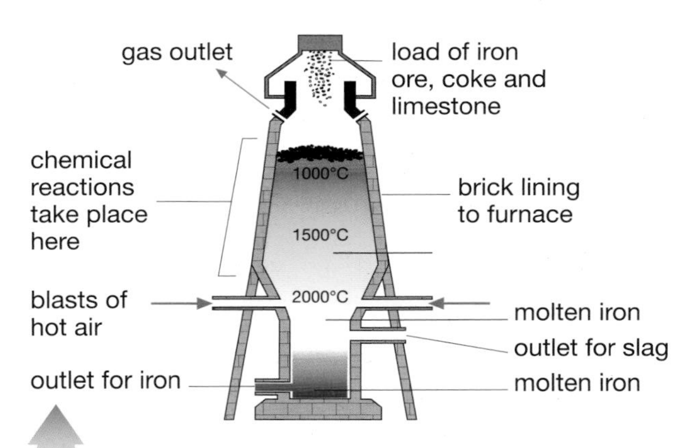

Figure 3 Heat is used in this smelter to help produce iron from its ore

Another common endothermic reaction is the reaction which takes place in leaves called photosynthesis. This is in fact a series of reactions which use the energy from sunlight to change carbon dioxide and water into glucose and oxygen.

carbon dioxide + water ➔ glucose + oxygen

Figure 4 The reactions inside these leaves are endothermic

Key ideas

- ★ Chemical reactions can be classified as exothermic or endothermic
- ★ To break a chemical bond requires energy to be absorbed
- ★ To make a chemical bond requires energy to be released
- ★ A chemical reaction is classed as exothermic or endothermic dependant upon the sum of the energy absorbed and released

Wordbank

Exothermic – a change in a substance that releases energy

Endothermic – a change in a substance that absorbs energy

Thermochemistry – the study of energy changes in chemical reactions

Chemical bond – a force linking atoms in a molecule or compound

Questions

1. Name two chemical reactions which are exothermic.
2. Name two chemical reactions which are endothermic.
3. Name a physical change which is exothermic.
4. Name a physical change which is endothermic.
5. When a bond is broken is it exothermic or endothermic?

Catalysts

A **catalyst** is a substance that alters the rate of a chemical reaction. A catalyst is often used to make a chemical reaction go faster. The catalyst is not changed by the reaction. It is not used up in the reaction and is still present when the reaction has been completed. The amount of the catalyst present at the start of the reaction is the same as at the end of the reaction. The catalyst can be used over and over again. Some common catalysts are **transition metals** from the Periodic Table.

For example, platinum is used in the manufacture of nitric acid, palladium is used in catalytic converters in cars, and nickel is used in the manufacture of margarine. Some transition metal oxides such as manganese dioxide and vanadium oxide are also commonly used as catalysts.

How does a catalyst work?

In a chemical reaction the process can be speeded up by increasing the chance of collisions between the molecules involved in the reaction. We have seen that this is possible by increasing the temperature or increasing the concentration of the reactants involved. Catalysts work by providing a convenient surface on which the reaction can occur. The catalyst allows the reaction to take place along a different pathway which requires less energy.

Hydrogen peroxide is a very toxic substance made from hydrogen and oxygen. It looks like water but has quite different properties, for example it is used as a bleach. It will slowly break down into water and oxygen but it can be dramatically speeded up by the addition of a catalyst.

Group →

Period ↓

Transition metals

1	2											3	4	5	6	7	'0'
1 H hydrogen 1																	1 He helium 4
3 Li lithium 7	4 Be beryllium 9											5 B boron 11	6 C carbon 12	7 N nitrogen 14	8 O oxygen 16	9 F flourine 19	1 Ne neon 20
11 Na sodium 23	12 Mg magnesium 24											13 Al aluminium 27	14 Si silicon 28	15 P phosphorus 31	16 S sulphur 32	17 Cl chlorine 35.5	18 Ar argon 40
19 K potassium 39	20 Ca calcium 40	21 Sc scandium 45	22 Ti titanium 48	23 V vanadium 51	24 Cr chromium 52	25 Mn magnesuim 55	26 Fe iron 56	27 Co cobalt 59	28 Ni nickel 59	29 Cu copper 63.5	30 Zn zinc 65.4	31 Ga gallium 70	32 Ge germanium 73	33 As arsenic 75	34 Se selenium 79	35 Br bromine 80	36 Kr krypton 84
37 Rb rubidium 85	38 Sr strontium 88	39 Y yitrium 89	40 Zr zirconium 91	41 Nb niobium 93	42 Mo molybendium 96	43 Tc technetium	44 Ru ruthenium 101	45 Rh rhodium 103	46 Pd palladium 106	47 Ag silver 108	48 Cd cadmium 112	49 In indium 115	50 Sn tin 119	51 Sb antimony 122	52 Te tellurium 128	53 I iodine 127	54 Xe xenon 131
55 Cs caesium 133	56 Ba barrium 137	57 La lanthanum 139	72 Hf halfnium 178	73 Ta tantaium 181	74 W tungsten 184	75 Re rhenium 186	76 Os osmium 190	77 Ir indium 192	78 Pt platinum 195	79 Au gold 197	80 Hg mercury 201	81 Ti thallium 204	82 Pb lead 205	83 Bi bismuth	84 Po polonium	85 At aslatine	86 Rh radon
87 Fr francium 223	88 Ra radium 226	89 Ac actinium 227	104 Rf rutherfordium	105 Db dubium	106 Sg seaborgium	107 Bh bohrium	108 Hs hassium	109 Mt meitnerium	110 Uun ununnilium	111 Uuu unununium	112 Uub ununbium						

58 Ce cerium 140	59 Pr praseodymium 141	60 Nd neodymium 144	61 Pm promethium	62 Sm samarium 150	63 Eu europium 152	64 Gd gadolinium 157	65 Tb terbium 159	66 Dy dysprosium 163	67 Ho holmium 165	68 Er erbium 167	69 Tm thulium 169	70 Yb ytterbium 173	71 Lu lutetium 175
90 Th thorium 232	91 Pa protactinium 231	92 U uranium 238	93 Np neptunium 2371	94 Pu plutonium	95 Am americium	96 Cm curium	97 Bk berkelium	98 Cf californium	99 Es einstein	100 Fm fermium	101 Md mendelevium	102 No nobelium	103 Lr lawrencium

Figure 1 Transition metals

An example of catalysts is found in catalytic converters fitted to car exhaust systems. The catalysts used are platinum and palladium metals coated on ceramic honeycomb housed in the muffler section of the exhaust tube.

The catalysts are responsible for speeding up the chemical reactions which change toxic gases such as unburnt fuel, carbon monoxide and nitrogen oxides into less harmful pollutants. The catalytic converter converts the hydrocarbons into carbon dioxide and water, the carbon monoxide into carbon dioxide, and the nitrogen oxides into nitrogen and oxygen. Without the presence of the catalyst the reactions could not take place fast enough.

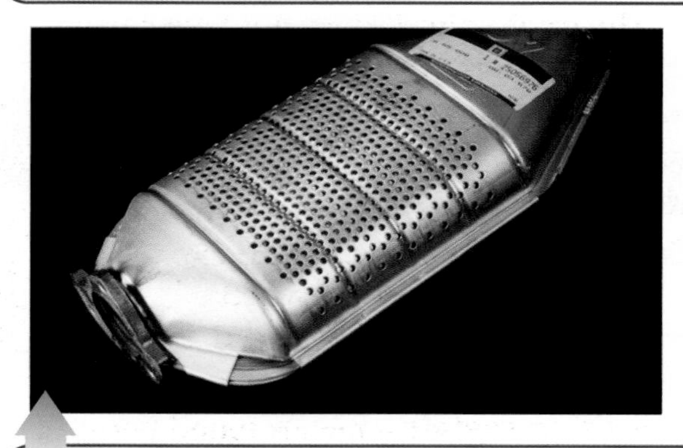

Figure 2 Catalytic converters contain the transition elements platinum and palladium

A student added 10 ml of hydrogen peroxide to each of three large test tubes with a delivery tube. All three were kept at the same temperature. A small spatula of the catalyst manganese dioxide was added to the first, a small spatula of the catalyst silica was added to the second and nothing was added to the third test tube. The volume of gas produced by each tube was found by measuring the displacement of water from a gas jar.

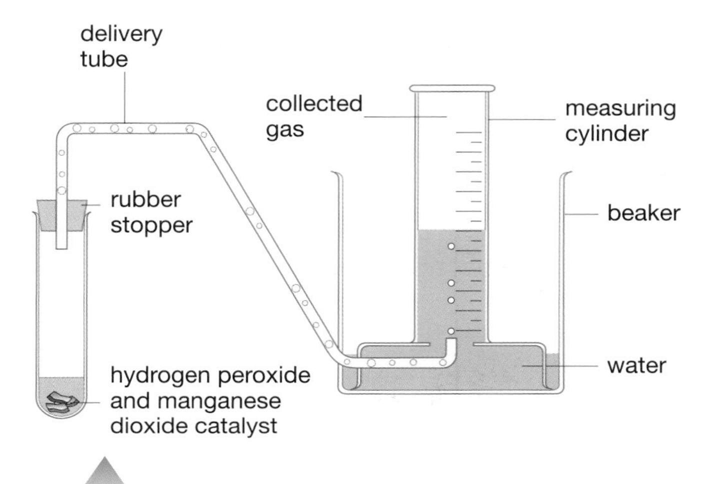

Figure 3 Production of oxygen gas

The results of the experiment are shown in the table on the right.

The results suggest that different catalysts do not have the same effect on the same chemical reaction. Indeed different catalysts have to be used for different chemical reactions. In this case manganese dioxide is a good catalyst for speeding up the breakdown of hydrogen peroxide. Silica however is not a good catalyst for this reaction. Catalysts are specific and different catalysts are used to speed up different chemical reactions.

Catalysts are used in industry to speed up chemical reactions. Not only do they allow the reaction to proceed more quickly, they allow the reaction to take place at a lower temperature thus reducing costs.

Catalysts are of major importance in today's industrial world. It has been estimated that about 20% of the United States' Gross National Product is generated through the use of catalytic processes.

Examples of industrial catalysts include compounds of titanium, aluminium or chromium which are used in the manufacture of polythene plastic from refined oil.

Test tube	Volume of gas
manganese dioxide added	250 ml
silica added	5 ml
no catalyst added	5 ml

Key ideas

- ★ A catalyst is used to make a reaction go faster
- ★ The catalyst is not changed at the end of the reaction
- ★ The catalyst itself does not take part in the reaction

Wordbank

Catalyst – a substance which alters the rate of a chemical reaction but is chemically unchanged at the end of the reaction

Transition metals – metals found between Groups 2 and 3 in the Periodic Table

Questions

1. What is a catalyst?
2. Name three catalysts.
3. Name three harmful products of a car's engine which are changed into less harmful substances by a catalytic converter.
4. Catalysts are often used in the form of granules or powder rather than as solid block. Suggest why.

14 Enzymes

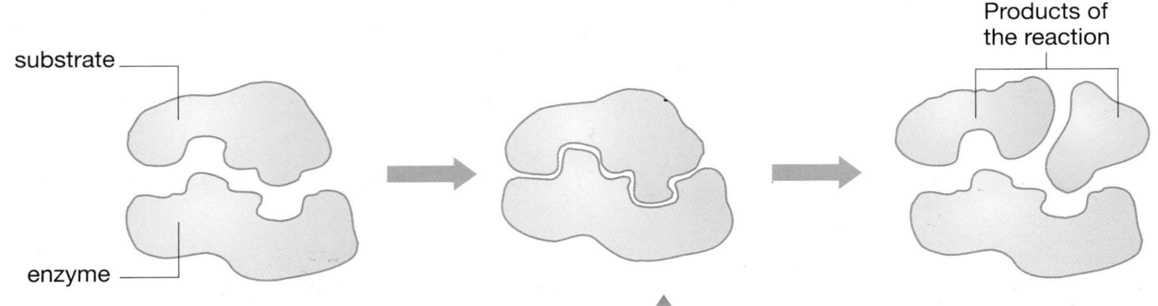

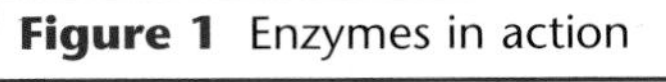

Figure 1 Enzymes in action

Catalysts are substances which alter the rate of a chemical reaction. **Enzymes** are a special type of catalyst. They are made from protein and regulate the speed of chemical reactions involved in the metabolism of living organisms. Enzyme names often end in -ase. This suffix is sometimes added to the name of the reactants with which they act. For example the enzyme that controls urea **decomposition** is called urease and the class of enzymes that affect proteins are called **proteases**. Like their chemical catalysts enzymes are designed to control a specific reaction.

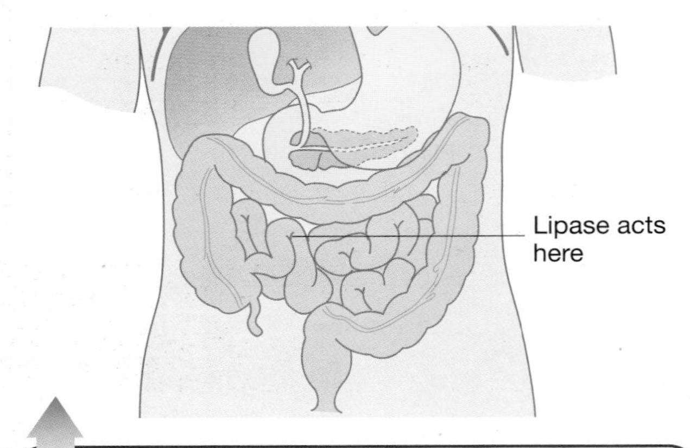

Figure 2 Lipase is a lipid-digesting enzyme at work in the human gut

Enzymes bind temporarily to one or more of the reactants. This reduces the energy needed to bring about the chemical change. This normally speeds up the reaction causing swifter delivery of the products of the reaction.

The enzyme catalase controls the breakdown of hydrogen peroxide into water and oxygen in the same way as the catalyst manganese dioxide. Each catalase molecule breaks down 40 million molecules of hydrogen peroxide per second.

The most important factor in allowing the enzyme to work efficiently is it's physical shape. In order that the enzyme can bind with the reactants the shape of the enzyme is **complimentary** to the shape of the reactants – like a key and lock.

Protein molecules such as enzymes are sensitive to temperature. High temperatures cause the protein structure to deform thus preventing it from binding with its reactant(s). Enzymes therefore work best at a particular temperature depending on which living thing they are found in. For example the lipid-digesting enzyme of the human gut called **lipase** works best at a temperature of 37°C. This is normal body temperature.

The temperature at which the enzyme works best is called its **optimum** temperature.

The following graph shows how activity increases as temperature increases up to its optimum and the rapid fall off beyond this temperature.

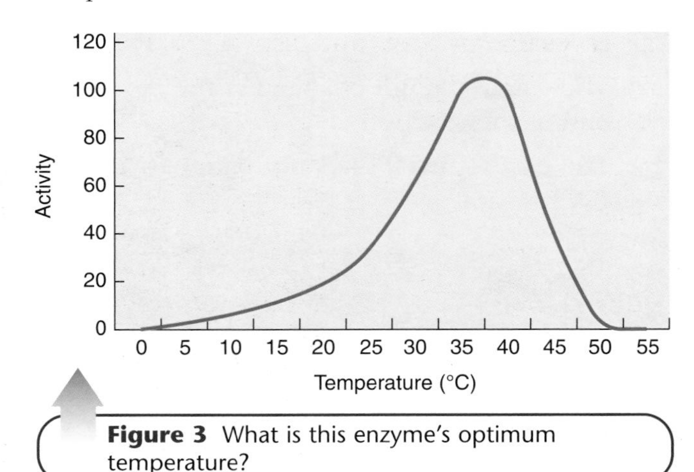

Figure 3 What is this enzyme's optimum temperature?

Other factors such as pH and inhibitor chemicals can also affect the efficiency of enzyme action.

Uses of enzymes

Enzymes are not only found in living things but are also used by humans. One of the oldest uses by humans of enzymes is in the fermentation of alcohol. Yeast is a microscopic fungus which contains the enzymes required to control the production of sugar into alcohol.

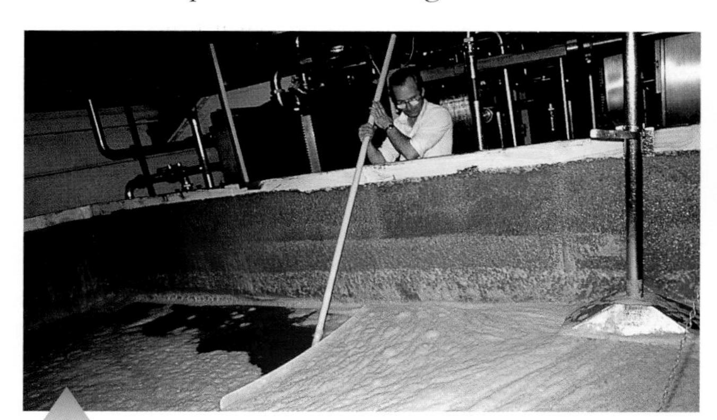

Figure 4 Yeast causes this foam in brewery tanks

Enzymes found in yeast are also used to produce the carbon dioxide in bread prior to baking.

In the textile industry, stonewashed jeans were produced by the action of pumice stones added to a washer. With the addition of cellulase, an enzyme which acts on cellulose, the stonewashing cycle time has been cut in half. This has resulted in an improvement of the finished fabric as well as reducing costs.

In biological washing powders, protease enzymes are added to improve the cleaning ability of the detergent. The protease enzyme can break down protein stains such as blood, egg etc. while the clothes are being washed at much lower temperatures than would normally be required. This saves energy costs and also means that coloured fabrics are more easily cleaned.

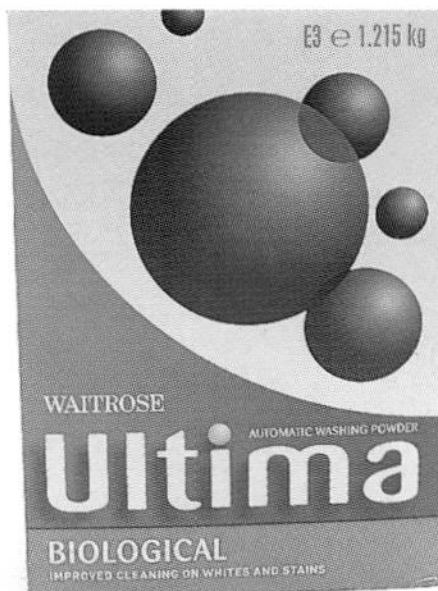

Figure 5 Biological washing powders offer improved cleaning power

Some of the latest beauty aid treatments use the action of enzymes to bring about their claimed effects. Some enzymes treatments prescribed by doctors are used to assist poor digestive processes and as a method to break up blood clots.

Key ideas

- ★ Enzymes are a special kind of catalyst
- ★ Enzymes are made from protein
- ★ Enzyme names end in -ase
- ★ Enzymes are sensitive to factors which can affect their efficiency

Wordbank

Catalyst – a substance which alters the rate of a chemical reaction but is chemically unchanged at the end of the reaction

Enzyme – a special kind of catalyst found in living things

Decomposition – breakdown of a substance

Protease – name of an enzyme which acts on proteins

Complimentary shape – a shape which is a mirror image of the other constituent

Lipase – name of an enzyme which acts on lipids

Optimum – range at which an enzyme works best

Questions

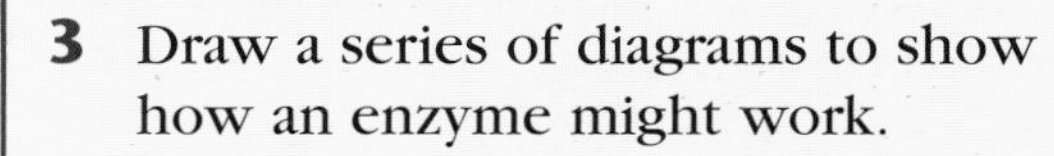

1. Name two enzymes.
2. What are enzymes made from?
3. Draw a series of diagrams to show how an enzyme might work.
4. Why is the shape of the enzyme important?
5. Name an enzyme found in the human gut.
6. Name two factors which can affect the activity of an enzyme.
7. Suggest the temperature at which biological washing powders work best.

15 Physical changes

Whenever you observe the world around you, you are really describing the current appearance of matter. Properties such as colour, shape, texture, temperature, size, smell and so on are used to describe the current appearance of a substance. These properties are subject to change according to the following rules:

- **Rule 1** The properties of matter change over time – all changes in matter involve the loss or addition of energy to the substance.
- **Rule 2** The properties of matter can change in two ways – physically and chemically. Physical changes involve changing the appearance of a substance, but not its chemical identity. Chemical changes or reactions involve changing substances into other ones.

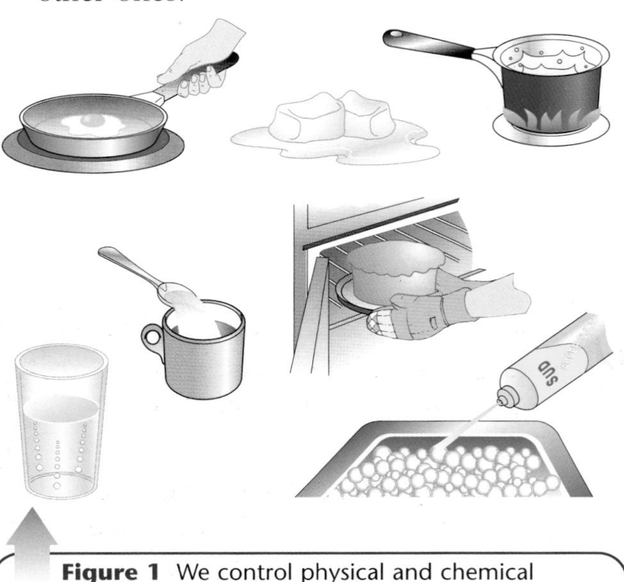

Figure 1 We control physical and chemical changes in the kitchen

Common physical changes include:

- Changes of state – when a substance changes from a solid into a liquid, or a liquid into a gas, a gas into a liquid, a liquid into a solid.
- Dissolving – when a substance dissolves in a solvent.
- Distilling – when a substance is separated from another substance by heating it, causing it to evaporate.
- Crystallisation – when a substance changes into crystals of a solid as it cools from its liquid state.

Detecting physical changes – the senses

We use our senses of seeing, hearing, smelling, tasting, and touching to describe materials. Stainless steel is shiny, while pewter is dull and non-reflective. Sour milk has an unpleasant smell while garden flowers are pleasant. Sighted people rely on seeing to describe the world – blind people learn to develop their other senses to find out the same information about the world.

We use language to describe the changes that we see – much of the language that we use depends on the way that we perceive the world. It is well known that Inuit people use many words to describe snow while we only have one. Much of the language we use relies on our sense of sight.

Detecting physical changes – making measurements

Changes can be measured in the laboratory and out of doors by using instruments. You will already have used many instruments to make measurements in science. Measurements are essential since our senses are sometimes fooled.

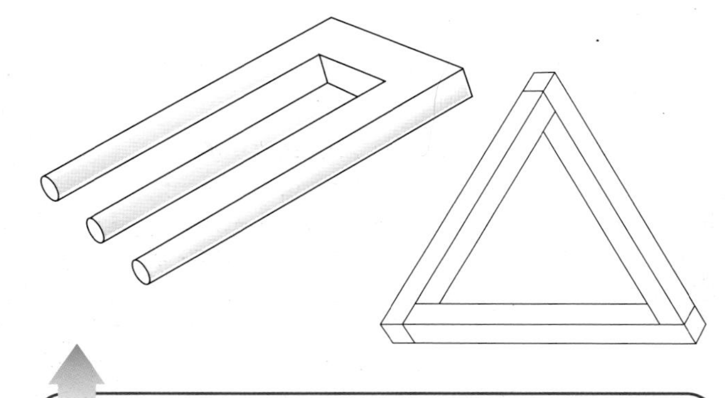

Figure 2 How many stumps are there? Which direction does the triangle point?

Physical properties change and can easily be measured without damaging the substance. Thermometers are used to measure small changes in temperature; meters are used to measure electrical voltage, current and resistance; volume is measured with several different pieces of apparatus depending on the accuracy required, for example syringes, measuring cylinders and other glassware. **Viscosity** and other properties require specialised apparatus for measuring.

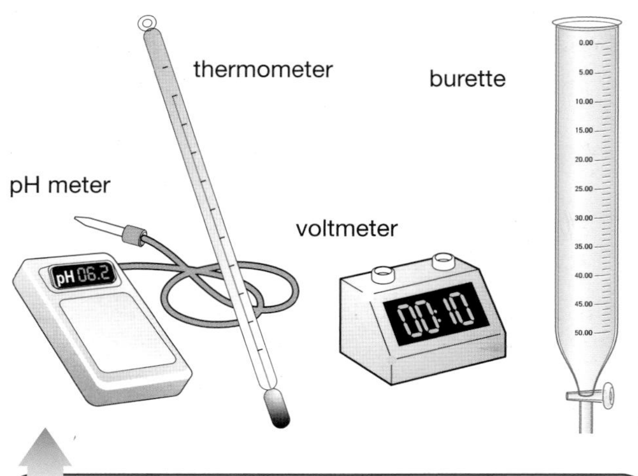

Figure 3 Different instruments measure different properties

Look at the different measuring instruments in Figure 3.

- The thermometer is used to measure temperature. The scale used is the Celsius scale (°C). It is essential that when measuring with a thermometer the bulb is in contact with what is being measured.
- The pH meter measures how acid or alkaline a substance is. Its numerical scale ranges from:

Acid ←	Neutral	→ Alkaline
1	7	14

  The probe has to be in contact with the substance being measured.
- A voltmeter is used to measure the voltage of an electrical circuit. Voltage is measured in Volts (V).
- A burette is used to measure the volume of a liquid accurately. It is measured in millilitres (ml).

Key ideas

- ★ Matter can be changed in two ways – physical changes and chemical changes
- ★ Energy is involved in all physical changes
- ★ A physical change involves changing the appearance of a substance, but not its chemical composition
- ★ We detect changes with our senses but these can be inaccurate
- ★ Instruments are used to accurately measure the physical properties of matter

Questions

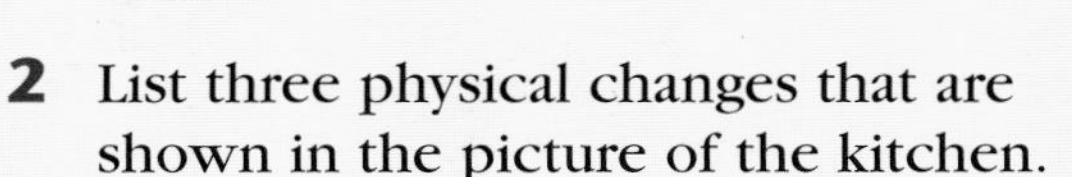

1. Make a note of how to compare physical and chemical changes in matter.
2. List three physical changes that are shown in the picture of the kitchen.
3. List three chemical changes that are shown in the picture of the kitchen.
4. Make a table showing two ways we use each of the main senses.
5. Design an experiment that could compare the viscosity of different liquids in the picture of the kitchen.

Wordbank

Viscosity – resistance of a liquid to flow, i.e. describes its thickness

Chemical changes

Chemical changes happen all around us – when we drive a car, light the gas or play football. During chemical reactions substances are changed into new ones. Chemical changes occur according to the following rules:

Figure 1 An alchemist's laboratory

Rule 1 A chemical reaction is the process by which the atoms in substances break old chemical bonds, or make new bonds with each other.

Rule 2 When chemical reactions take place energy is either released or taken in.

Rule 3 The substances that are changed are called **reactants** and the substances that are made are called **products**.

Chemical reactions happen when one substance changes into another. We can recognise that chemical changes have happened when for example the colour or temperature changes, a gas is released or a **precipitate** forms.

Evidence of chemical changes

Colour changes

Iron reacts with oxygen to produce iron oxide (rust) and the product is a different colour from the reactants.

Figure 2 What colour were these pieces of machinery before they rusted?

Heat energy changes

Heat energy is always given out or taken in during a chemical reaction.

Figure 3 This coffee is heated in the can by a chemical reaction

Production of a gas

Bubbles can be seen and heard when some chemical reactions take place.

The tablets react with water to release carbon dioxide gas. The gas could be tested by passing it through a solution of bicarbonate indicator which will change from a red to a yellow colour.

Figure 4 Effervescence caused by this headache cure reacting with water

Formation of a precipitate

When insoluble products are formed following a reaction between two liquids, they form a precipitate. This happens when lead nitrate is added to potassium iodide solution.

Figure 5 When lead nitrate and potassium iodide are mixed, a precipitate of lead iodide is formed

The solid precipitate will slowly separate from the liquid and settle at the bottom of the test tube.

Key ideas

- ★ Chemical reactions change substances
- ★ New bonds are formed between atoms as a result of chemical reactions
- ★ Energy is always taken in or released during chemical reactions
- ★ Chemical changes can be recognised in several ways

Wordbank

Reactants – substances taking part in a chemical reaction

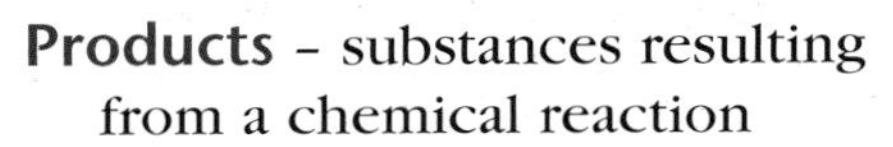

Products – substances resulting from a chemical reaction

Precipitate – a solid that separates from a solution, following a chemical reaction

Questions

1 Make a table to compare physical and chemical changes.

2 List the reactants and the products in each of the following chemical reactions:

a) burning toast
b) a car engine running
c) neutralising an acid with an alkali
d) photosynthesis

3 Copy and complete the diagram to represent the different things that can happen in chemical reactions.

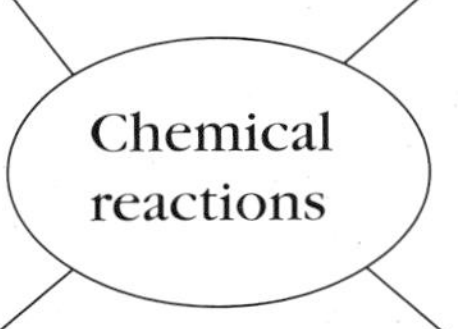

17 Equations

A chemical reaction is a process involving atoms which results in a change in their molecular composition.

A chemical reaction can be described using a **word equation** and a **chemical equation**.

Word equations only tell us what substances are involved in the reaction.

Chemical equations tell us what substances are reacting (the reactants) and what substances are being made (the products). If the equation is balanced it also tells us the number of atoms of each element present and the ratio of atoms involved.

Chemical equations use symbols to describe the elements. We can write an equation for every chemical reaction. These describe how **molecules** react.

Consider the reaction when hydrogen burns in oxygen.

Word Equation: hydrogen + oxygen → water

Chemical Equation: $2H_2 + O_2 \rightarrow 2H_20$

This has practical consequences whenever chemicals react.

Figure 1 Space shuttle launch

The large middle tank of the space shuttle actually has two smaller tanks inside it, one holding liquid oxygen and one holding liquid hydrogen. The tank containing liquid hydrogen holds twice as much as the tank containing oxygen. If the tanks were the same volume then the hydrogen would be used up when the oxygen tank was still half full.

How to read a chemical equation

1 The reactants are always shown on the left side of a chemical equation and the products are always shown on the right side.

2 The arrow in the middle separates the left from the right side and means 'produces'.

3 In equations the letters represent the chemical symbols from the Periodic Table.

4 The numbers tell how many atoms are required. If the numbers are in front of the formula then this applies to each element in that formula. If the number comes after an element within a formula then that number only applies to that element.

Balancing equations

The Law of **Conservation of Matter** states:

During an ordinary chemical change, there is no detectable increase or decrease in the quantity of matter.

This means that in a chemical equation the number of atoms of each element on the left side must equal the number of atoms on the right hand side. This is called a balanced equation.

Example 1

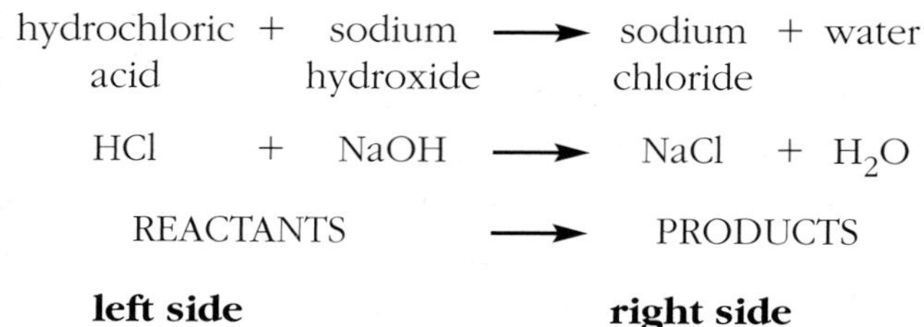

hydrochloric acid + sodium hydroxide → sodium chloride + water

$HCl + NaOH \rightarrow NaCl + H_2O$

REACTANTS → PRODUCTS

left side	**right side**
2 hydrogen atoms	2 hydrogen atoms
1 sodium atom	1 sodium atom
1 oxygen atom	1 oxygen atom

therefore left side balances the right side

Example 2

methane + oxygen ⟶ water + carbon dioxide

CH_4 + O_2 ⟶ H_2O + CO_2

REACTANTS ⟶ PRODUCTS

left side	**right side**
1 carbon atom	1 carbon atom
4 hydrogen atoms	2 hydrogen atoms
2 oxygen atoms	3 oxygen atoms

This equation is not balanced. There are different numbers of hydrogen and oxygen atoms present. To make it balance the number of molecules involved in the reaction has to be changed as follows.

methane + oxygen ⟶ water + carbon dioxide

CH_4 + $2O_2$ ⟶ $2H_2O$ + CO_2

REACTANTS ⟶ PRODUCTS

left side	**right side**
1 carbon	1 carbon
4 hydrogen	4 hydrogen
4 oxygen	4 oxygen

the left side now balances the right side

In this reaction 1 molecule of methane reacts with 2 molecules of oxygen to produce 2 molecules of water and 1 molecule of carbon dioxide.

Key ideas

★ Chemical reactions can be described using word and chemical equations

★ Reactants are shown on the left side and products on the right side

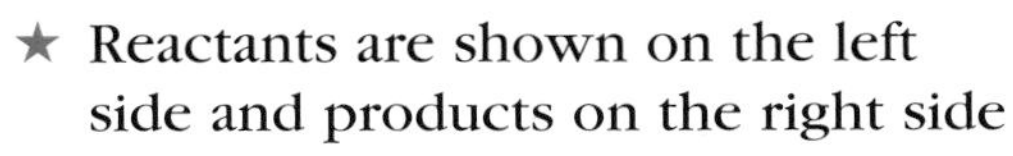

★ A balanced equation has the same number of atoms on each side of the arrow

★ The symbols from the Periodic Table are used in equations

Wordbank

Word equation – describes the substances involved in the reaction

Chemical equation – describes the elements and the ratio of those elements involved in the chemical reaction

Molecule – the smallest unit in which some atoms or groups of atoms can be present

Conservation of Matter – a law of science

Questions

1 What are the chemical symbols for the following elements – sodium, zinc, chlorine, hydrogen, gold, carbon, vanadium, and magnesium?

2 What are the chemical formulae for the following molecules?

a) 1 atom of carbon and 4 atoms of hydrogen
b) 2 atoms of hydrogen, 1 atom of sulphur and 4 atoms of oxygen
c) 1 atom of hydrogen and 1 atom of chlorine
d) 2 atoms of hydrogen and 1 atom of oxygen
e) 6 atoms of carbon, 12 atoms of hydrogen and 6 atoms of oxygen

3 How many oxygen atoms are present in each of these molecules?

a) $2NaOH$
b) $6H_2O$
c) $2KClO_3$
d) $3Ca(NO_3)_2$

4 Balance the following equations.

a) $Zn + 2\ HCl \longrightarrow ZnCl_? + H_2$
b) $2\ KClO_3 \longrightarrow 2KCl + ?O_2$
c) $S_8 + ?F_2 \longrightarrow 8SF_6$
d) $4Fe + 3O_2 \longrightarrow ?Fe_2O_3$

18 This is chemistry

There are many branches in science but the main ones are biology, chemistry and physics. All science works in the same way – it is a process of searching for the laws that govern the Universe. Scientists test their ideas with experiments. The experiments are set up in a way that allows scientists to make descriptions, explanations and predictions. **Scientific method** includes each of the following stages – making **hypotheses**, repeating experiments and generating new hypotheses.

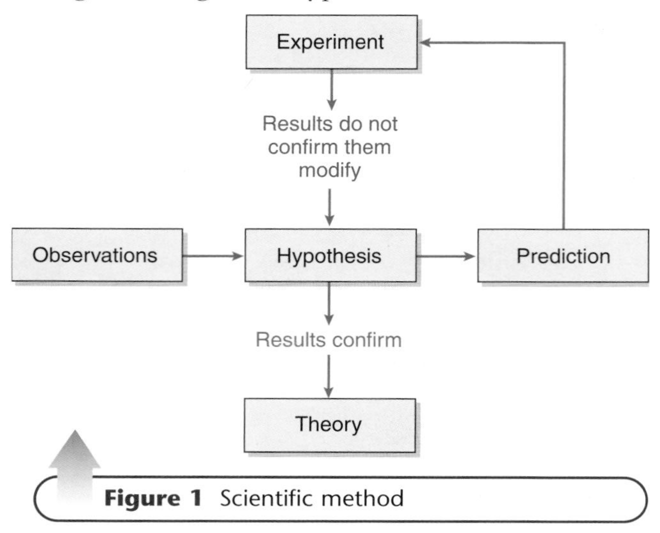

Figure 1 Scientific method

What is chemistry?

composition – the elements and compounds they are made of

properties – physical and chemical properties or conditions

Chemistry is the scientific study of the **composition**, **structure**, **properties** and **interactions** of chemicals.

interactions – the way chemicals react with other chemicals or conditions, as well as the energy changes that take place

structure – the way the atoms are put together

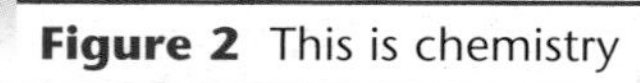

Figure 2 This is chemistry

What use is chemistry?

All the materials and substances that surround you are made from around 100 elements. Chemical reactions have taken place to heat the school, make your food and clothing, and create the inks and words in this text book. Our civilisation depends on chemistry and its products.

What do professional chemists study?

Figure 3 Professional chemists

- A **pharmacist** is commonly known as a 'chemist'. They are health professionals trained in developing and preparing drugs and other chemical medicines.
- **Analytical chemists** identify unknown materials – **forensic** chemists help solve crimes and provide evidence for use in law courts.
- **Biochemists** study the chemistry of the living world – this relates to any living thing or process. Modern biology depends on biochemistry.
- Chemistry is the study of **changing materials**. Materials involve the substances from which anything is made. Buildings, fabrics, medical equipment and appliances depend on the science of materials.
- Chemistry is the study of **materials from Earth**. Chemists study the composition and the structure of the Earth, its resources and their exploitation.
- **Inorganic** chemists study non-carbon chemistry.
- **Organic** chemists study the compounds of carbon.
- **Physical** chemists study the physical reactions of chemicals.

Famous Chemists

Robert Bunsen is considered one of the greatest chemists in the world. Bunsen discovered in 1834 the antidote that is still used today for arsenic poisoning. Although he popularised the Bunsen burner, he did not actually invent it.

Sir Harold W Kroto, a British chemist who, during research into the origins of carbon produced by stars, accidentally discovered a new family of carbon molecules known as 'fullerenes'. Unknown before 1985, fullerenes now constitute the fourth major form of carbon, along with graphite, diamond, and amorphous carbon. The discovery and synthesis of fullerenes created a new and extremely active branch of chemistry in the early 1990s.

Antoine Laurent Lavoisier, a French chemist, usually considered the founder of modern chemistry. He was largely responsible for developing the modern conception of a chemical element, and revealed the true nature of combustion.

Louis Pasteur, a French chemist and biologist who founded the science of microbiology, proved the germ theory of disease, invented the process of pasteurisation, and developed vaccines for several diseases, including rabies.

What would I study if I continued chemistry at school?

- Chemical reactions
- Speed of reactions
- Atoms and the Periodic Table
- How atoms combine
- Fuels
- Structures and reactions of Hydrocarbons
- Properties of substances
- Acids and alkalis
- Reactions of acids
- Making electricity
- Metals
- Corrosion
- Plastics and synthetic fibres
- Fertilisers
- Carbohydrates and related substances

Key ideas

★ Chemistry is a key area of modern science

★ Chemistry has many branches

★ Its approach is the same as other areas of science and involves scientific method

Questions

1 Find out more about:

a) the branches of chemistry.
b) careers in chemistry.
c) what you have already studied in chemistry.

Scientific method – a way of investigation that involves observation and making explanations (theories) to test scientific hypotheses (ideas)

Hypotheses – a scientific explanation that is to be tested by investigation

19 Should we spend valuable resources on space research?

Since developing the technology to allow people to travel through space, a number of countries have spent billions and billions of pounds exploring the Universe. As a result of this research and development many great products have been created.

At the same time millions of people have died from disease, famine, poverty and other such disasters. Could such disasters have been avoided if the resources from space research had been allocated to other causes?

Many people argue that research of all types is necessary. They believe that by attempting new or difficult things mankind can progress. Space research is only one way of attempting new or difficult investigations.

In the 1960s one of the reasons given by President Kennedy for America starting its Moon landing programme was that they were going to go there because it *was* a difficult thing to do.

NASA was the organisation given the responsibility of putting men on the moon (and bringing them back safely). NASA also have an educational mission. They have to make any information they gather available to the general public. In this way the information gathered from the research is not kept by one country and all of mankind can benefit from it.

Figure 1 NASA's mission is to understand and protect our home planet, explore the Universe and search for life, and to inspire the next generation of explorers

The technological advancements that are created by space research can be used in other fields.

- Many developments in computing and communications were driven by space research.
- The ability to place objects in precise orbits have allowed weather, remote sensing and communications satellites to give exact information on conditions all around the world.

Figure 2 A communications satellite in orbit

- Materials developed for use in the space industry can have applications in other industries. The tiles developed for the shield of the space shuttle have tremendous insulating properties.
- The development of chemicals in zero gravity may allow more effective drugs to be devised.
- Research in space may give information as to the origin of the Universe.

The case for using the resources elsewhere

Other people consider space research worthwhile to some extent but too expensive and of limited practical use. If space research had its budget cut by 75%, scientists would still be able to run a number of experiments but the resources saved could be more effectively utilised.

For example, the funds could be spent on:

- Establishing educational programmes for developing countries so that all children can be educated to a reasonable standard.
- Assisting remote communities that have difficulty in obtaining their basic needs such as food, shelter and water.

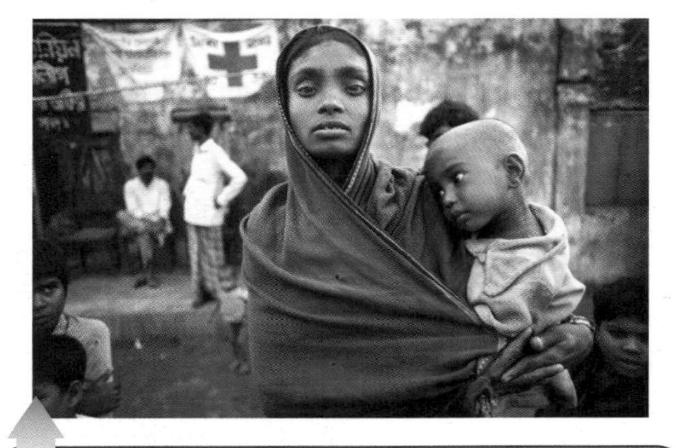

Figure 3 Organisations such as the Red Cross help provide health education and treatment to poverty stricken societies

- Establishing medical centres where basic health education and treatment can be administered to poverty stricken societies.
- Closer to home, the funds saved could be spent improving the National Health Service. Waiting times for certain procedures could be dramatically reduced if more staff were taken on.
- Council housing could be modernised and the living conditions of people in dilapidated areas improved.

Figure 4 Outdated council housing in a Scottish city

- Schools could be modernised and refurbished so our schoolchildren could be properly prepared for our technological society.

But what about the technological benefits of space research?

A portion of the saved resources would still be allocated for research. As this research would be more focussed on our current needs, technological advances would still be made. There is a good chance that similar benefits would occur in the course of other research.

A number of people believe that while space research and experiments are interesting and exciting, they are of little or no use to almost everyone in the world today.

- Who needs to know how the Universe was created?
- Would it have any effect on our lives if we did or didn't know?
- Why should we send astronauts to the Moon?
- Would it have made a difference to our lives if no one had ever been there?

These questions are difficult to answer.

Questions

1 What do you think about the resources spent on space research? Explain your decision in a small paragraph. State what your opinion is and why you hold it.

2 Imagine you are in charge of the country's finances. You have a £100 million to spend. You can spend the money on:

- Health
- Education
- Housing
- Energy
- Science

Discuss how much you would spend on each of the topics.

20 Investigating reactions

The Law of Conservation of Matter states that in a chemical reaction matter is neither created nor destroyed.

This was discovered by **Antoine Laurent Lavoisier** in around 1785.

Figure 1 Antoine Laurent Lavoisier

This means that when a chemical reaction takes place the reactants can be changed into the products but the actual atoms present are only redistributed.

A class was asked to consider this statement by investigating the chemical reaction:

magnesium + oxygen ⟶ magnesium oxide

$$2Mg + O_2 \longrightarrow 2MgO$$

The class were reminded to structure their investigation as follows:

1 What do I want to find out?

2 What equipment will I need?

3 How will I set it up?

4 What will I measure?

5 How will I make sure it is a fair test?

Two students, Lis and Helena, suggested that when magnesium metal is burned in air, oxygen atoms would combine with the magnesium atoms and would result in the product having a greater mass than the magnesium metal by itself.

Figure 2 Lis and Helena heating the magnesium ribbon

Lis and Helena took a coiled length of magnesium ribbon and placed it into a **crucible**. They placed the crucible containing the magnesium ribbon on a sensitive **electronic balance** to measure its mass. They then placed their crucible on a pipe clay triangle and heated it strongly until the magnesium burned.

After this time they reweighed the crucible and noted that the mass of the crucible and its contents had increased.

They then repeated the experiment a further two times.

Figure 3 Helena reweighing the crucible after heating

The students concluded that the crucible and its contents had gained mass because atoms of oxygen from the air had combined with the magnesium.

Helena and Lis decided to test what would happen if there was no oxygen available to the magnesium. To exclude any air from the magnesium they filled their crucible with sand and placed a lid over the top. They heated the crucible for the same length of time in the same way. They measured the mass of the crucible before and after and they found that there had been no change in mass. They also found that the magnesium had not burnt.

Figure 4 Unchanged mass of crucible with lid

These results supported their conclusion that when oxygen combines with magnesium there is an increase in mass.

Some other students were surprised that an increase in mass had been noted as they had not thought that oxygen in the air had a mass which could be detected by a balance.

They wondered if other common gases would have a measurable mass.

They considered a different reaction.

calcium carbonate → calcium oxide + carbon dioxide

$CaCO_3 \rightarrow CaO + CO_2$

Will the mass of the crucible and its contents increase or decrease? Plan their investigation for them.

Remember

- Investigations are carried out to test predictions.
- Investigations must be fair tests.
- You must measure accurately and in the same way each time.
- You must record your findings – they are the evidence for your decisions.
- Remember to be SAFE – follow all the safety rules and use safety equipment at all times. Ask your teacher if you need any help.

Wordbank

Lavoisier – famous chemist credited with discovering the Law of Conservation of Matter

Crucible – a heat resistant piece of apparatus used to heat substances strongly

Electronic balance – very sensitive and accurate chemical balance

Questions

1. Why did Helena and Lis repeat their experiment three times?
2. Why was the magnesium heated in a crucible?
3. What was the girls' hypothesis for this experiment?
4. Suggest some of the safety measures the girls would have employed during their experiment.

Further Investigations

What would happen to the mass of the magnesium if it was heated but there was no air present? Design an experiment to investigate.

How could you prove that the gas released when calcium carbonate is heated is really carbon dioxide?

21 Heat radiation

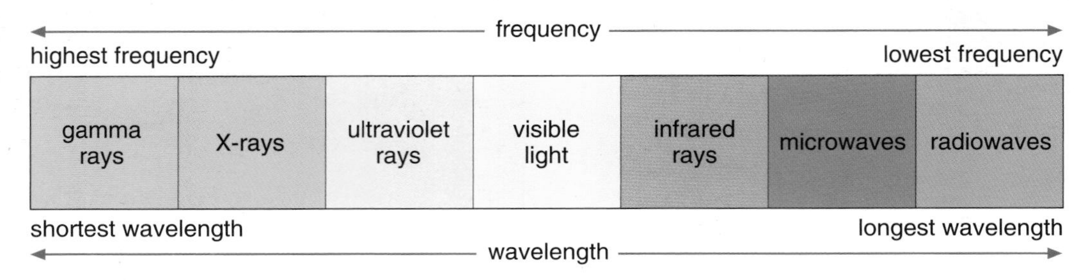

Figure 1 Electromagnetic spectrum

Heat energy can travel from a hot object to a colder object by conduction, convection and radiation. Conduction and convection require particles to be present to carry the energy.

- In conduction the energy passes from one atom to the next.
- In convection the particles of the liquid or gas circulate carrying the energy with them.
- In radiation no particles are required. The energy travels directly (radiates) from the hot object in all directions.

Heat radiation is also known as **infra red radiation**. Infra red radiation is a part of the **electromagnetic spectrum**.

Within the electromagnetic spectrum infra red radiation is close to visible light which contains all of the colours that we can see, i.e. red, orange, yellow, green, blue, indigo and violet. Ultra violet radiation lies alongside the violet end of the spectrum.

Radiated heat

Sun

(not to scale)

Earth

Figure 2 Heat radiating from the Sun to Earth

Most of the heat energy found on Earth comes from our star, the Sun. There is a **vacuum** between the Sun and Earth. The method by which heat energy travels to Earth is radiation.

The Sun has a surface temperature of around 4000°C. This is very much hotter than the surface temperature of the Earth. The heat energy will travel from the Sun to the Earth.

If you put your hand alongside a Bunsen flame it will become hotter because heat energy radiates out to your hand.

Heat energy behaves in a similar way to that of visible light. Visible light can be reflected and it can be absorbed. If you wish to reflect light then a shiny surface would work best. If you wished to absorb light then a dark dull surface would be best. This is also true for infra red radiation.

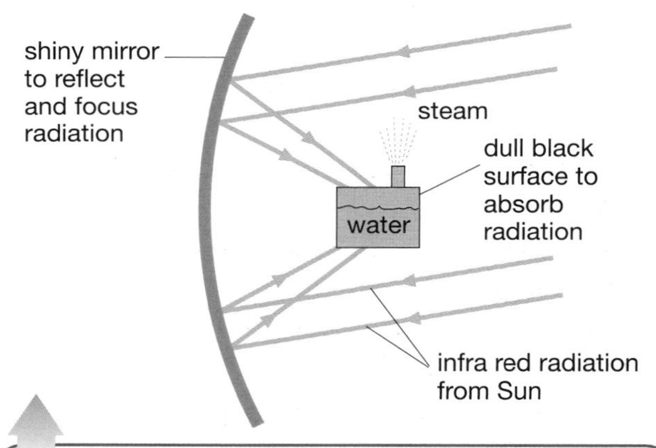

Figure 3 The infra red radiation reflects off the mirrors to the focus

A student decided to investigate the absorption of heat by differently coloured surfaces. He set up an electrical heater with two aluminium beakers placed 15 cm from the heater. One aluminium beaker was painted black and the other was left shiny. Each beaker was filled with 100 ml of water and a datalogger recorded the results.

The following results were recorded:

Time (min)	Shiny beaker temperature (°C)	Black beaker temperature (°C)
Start	20	20
1	21	22
2	22	25
3	23	28
4	24	31
5	25	34

The temperature increase of the shiny beaker was less than that of the black beaker. The shiny beaker did not absorb heat as quickly as the black beaker. The radiated energy from the heater was reflected off the shiny surface but was absorbed by the black surface.

In warm climates houses are painted white. This helps reflect heat. Solar panels are painted black to absorb heat.

In a second experiment he added 100 ml of boiling water to each beaker and recorded the temperature at the start and after 5 minutes.

His results were:

Time (min)	Shiny beaker temperature (°C)	Black beaker temperature (°C)
Start	98	98
5	89	79

Figure 4 Apparatus for measuring heat absorption

This experiment shows that the shiny beaker cooled down more slowly than the black beaker. The black beaker radiated the heat energy more quickly than the shiny beaker.

Key ideas

- ★ Heat energy travels from place to place by conduction, convection and radiation
- ★ Infra red radiation is emitted by hot objects
- ★ Infra red is a type of electromagnetic radiation
- ★ Shiny surfaces reflect heat energy better than black surfaces
- ★ Black surfaces absorb heat energy better than shiny surfaces
- ★ Black surfaces radiate heat energy better than shiny surfaces

Wordbank

Infra red radiation – form of heat energy transfer

Electromagnetic spectrum – range of radiated energies

Vacuum – empty space containing no particles of substance

Questions

1. Name the three methods by which heat energy is transferred.
2. Name four types of radiation found in the electromagnetic spectrum.
3. Where does most of the energy on Earth come from?
4. What is a vacuum?
5. What whould happen to radiated heat energy if it was directed towards a mirror?
6. The fins on heat radiators (heat sinks) in electronic circuits are often painted black. Why?

Light and colour

Artists use three primary colours: red, blue and yellow. They are known as the subtractive primary colours. These primary paint colours can be mixed to make secondary colours as follows:

red + blue = purple

red + yellow = orange

yellow + blue = green

red + blue + yellow = black

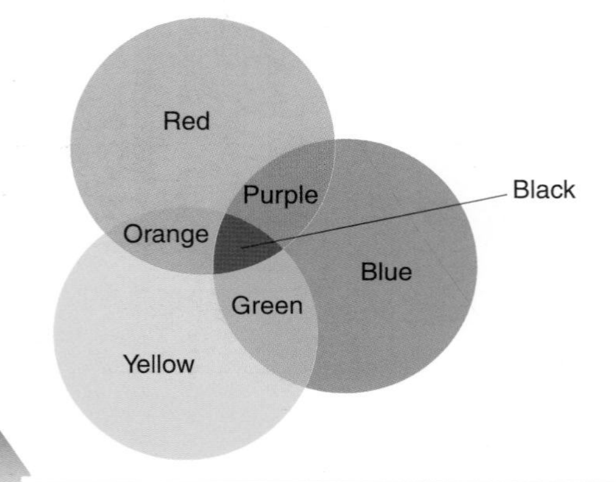

Figure 1 Colour mixing with paint

If you look at a landscape painting you can see a blue sky. The paint used appears blue because of the way light behaves. When white light strikes a surface some light is reflected and some light is absorbed. In this case the blue colour is reflected but the other colours are absorbed.

The spectrum

The visible spectrum is part of the electromagnetic spectrum and contains red, orange, yellow, green, blue, indigo and violet. The human eye cannot detect infra red or ultra violet radiation.

Figure 2 The visible spectrum lies between infra red and ultra violet radiation

Infrared

Ultra violet

All colours of the visible spectrum are distinguished from each other by having different **wavelengths**. This means that different colours have different wavelengths.

The shortest visible wavelength is violet at around 400 **nanometres** (nm). That is 400/1000 000 000 of a metre.

The longest visible wavelength is red light with a wavelength of around 700 nm. The other colours fit in between these values.

When white light is passed through a prism it separates into its different colours. These different colours can also be 'joined' to make white light.

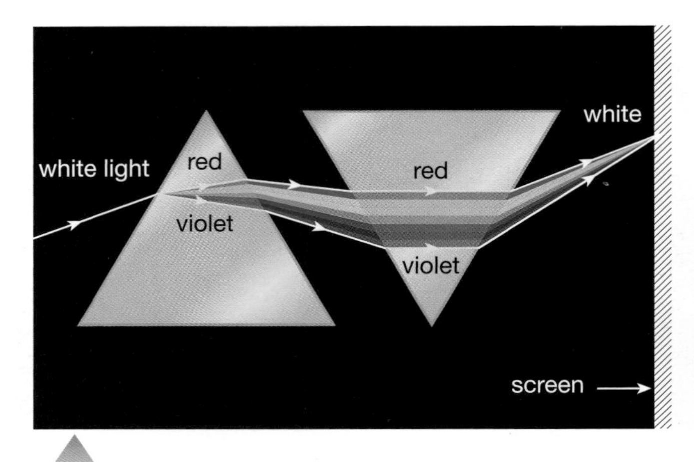

Figure 3 Prisms separating and recombining white light

Combining light

Scientists are also interested in what happens when we combine rays of light of different colours. This is different from mixing paints.

The primary colours of light are red, green and blue. These rays of light can also be combined to give different colours as follows:

red + green = yellow
red + blue = magenta
blue + green = cyan
red + green + blue = white

These are called the additive primary colours because we are making the new colours by adding different colours together.

A colour television screen contains the three additive primary colours and by combining them in different amounts it is possible to produce an image which contains the full range of colours.

The topic of colour is a complex issue. Additive and subtractive primary colours are easily confused. A small proportion of the population also have colour deficiencies in their vision and cannot see the colours other people see.

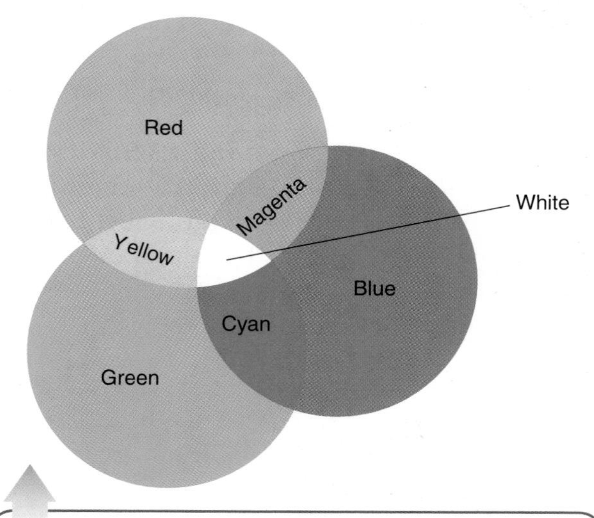

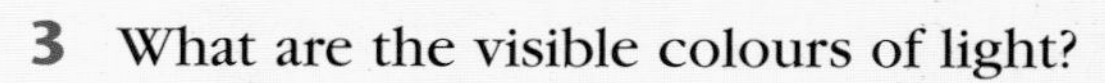
Figure 4 Colour mixing with light

Key ideas

- ★ The subtractive primary colours used in painting are red, blue and yellow
- ★ Mixing these three colours can produce all of the other secondary colours
- ★ Colours of light make up the visible part of the electromagnetic spectrum
- ★ Different colours of light have different wavelengths
- ★ Wavelengths of light can be measured in nanometres
- ★ The additive primary colours of light are red, blue and green
- ★ When mixed together they can produce all of the other secondary colours

Questions

1. What are the paint primary colours?
2. What are the secondary colours produced by the addition of the paint primary colours?
3. What are the visible colours of light?
4. What is the wavelength of blue light?
5. Name a piece of apparatus which splits light into its various colours.
6. What are the additive primary colours?
7. What three colours are used to produce the image on a television screen?

Wordbank

Wavelength – measurement of the length of a wave of light

Nanometre – a unit of measurement of wavelength

23 Mixing colours of light

The sky is blue, the grass is green. . . or is it?

The human eye has special **light sensory cells** (cones) which detect the light that enters through the pupil. The eye can detect the three additive primary colours. The number of cells stimulated determines what information is sent to the brain to be interpreted.

When we see a blue sky this means that the wavelength of light passing into the eye is blue. If the grass is green then the wavelength of light entering the eye is green.

What would happen if a coloured **filter** was placed in front of the eye?

A pure red filter works by allowing red light to pass through it but absorbing all other colours. If you hold a red filter in front of your eye and look at the grass it should be black. This is because all the green light reflected from the grass is absorbed by the red filter preventing any light from entering the eye. Any red or white objects appear red.

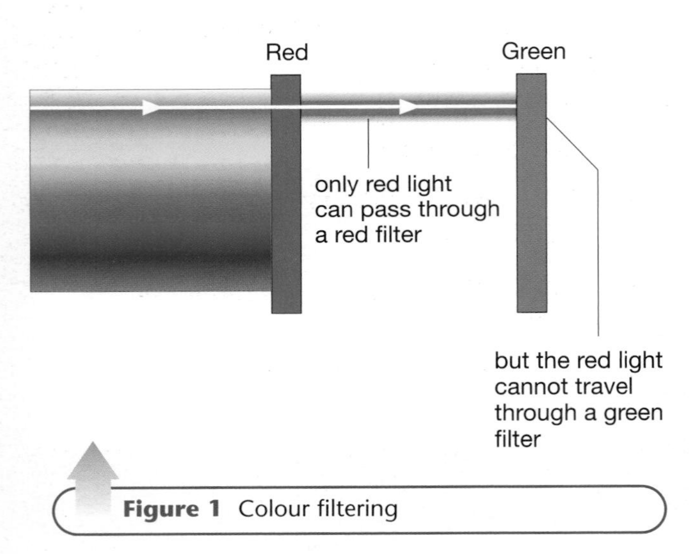

Figure 1 Colour filtering

The following tables show what light is detected using different lights and filters.

Type of light	White light	White light	White light
Type of filter	Red filter	Blue filter	Green filter
Light detected	Red	Blue	Green

Type of light	Red light	Red light	Red light
Type of filter	Red filter	Blue filter	Green filter
Light detected	Red	None	None

Type of light	Blue light	Blue light	Blue light
Type of filter	Red filter	Blue filter	Green filter
Light detected	None	Blue	None

Type of light	Green light	Green light	Green light
Type of filter	Red filter	Blue filter	Green filter
Light detected	None	None	Green

In some of the above examples no light passed through the filter.

People see colour 'normally' because we view most things in white light or sunlight. The light shines on the surface of objects and some colours are reflected.

Things look quite different if different colours of light are shone on objects. If red light is shone on a person, the 'colours' of that person's clothes would be impossible to tell.

These effects are sometimes seen in dance clubs.

Figure 2 Colours appear different under disco lights

Many animals are coloured to help them blend in with their surroundings (camouflage). The undersides of some aquatic animals are blue so that when viewed from beneath by predators they are difficult to detect. Divers at very deep sea levels come across animals with no colour because it is so dark that having a colour is of no advantage to the animal.

Stealth aircraft absorb most of the radar energy that reaches them. They reflect very little and are difficult to detect.

Colour vision and colour 'blindness'

Colour vision deficiency, or colour blindness, is the inability to distinguish certain colours.

The term 'colour blind' implies not being able to 'see' colours, whereas in fact it is really not being able to see a wide range of colours.

To people with a colour deficiency, many different colours appear to be the same. Generally, shades and lines of certain colours all appear similar.

Colour blindness affects 8% of males but only 0.5% of women.

The causes of colour blindness are mainly hereditary although eye damage can lead to a loss in colour vision.

How do our eyes detect colour?

At the back of our eyes, in the retina, there are detectors called **rods** and **cones**.

The cones are mainly responsible for colour vision and colour blind people will have a deficiency in this area.

Key ideas

- ★ The human eye detects the additive primary colours
- ★ A blue object reflects only blue light
- ★ A coloured filter absorbs other colours

Wordbank

Light sensory cell – special cells used to detect different colours of light

Filter – material which only allows certain wavelengths of light to pass through

Questions

1. What three primary colours can the human eye detect?
2. Which wavelength of light does a red jacket reflect?
3. What wavelength(s) are reflected off a black object?
4. Which colour(s) pass through a green filter?
5. Which colour(s) pass through a yellow filter?

Seeing the sound

Sound is a form of energy. One of the main ways in which we communicate is by using sound. When we talk or listen to the radio there is great variation in the sounds we can detect. Sounds can be high, low, quiet or loud.

If we speak into a microphone that has been connected to an oscilloscope we can 'see' what sound 'looks' like.

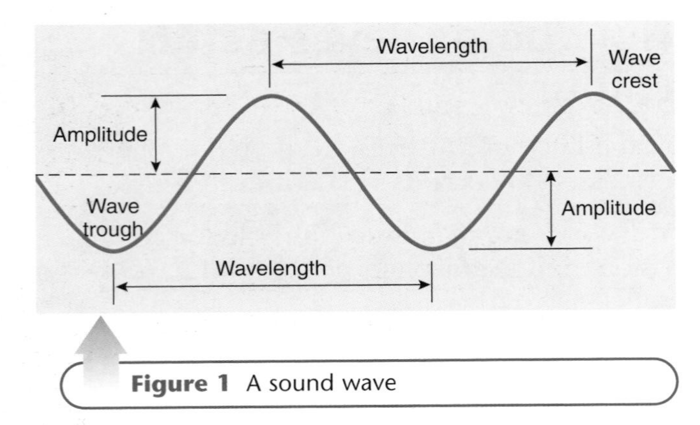

Figure 1 A sound wave

A good way of comparing sounds is to listen to them and to watch their image at the same time.

A pupil whistled into a microphone.

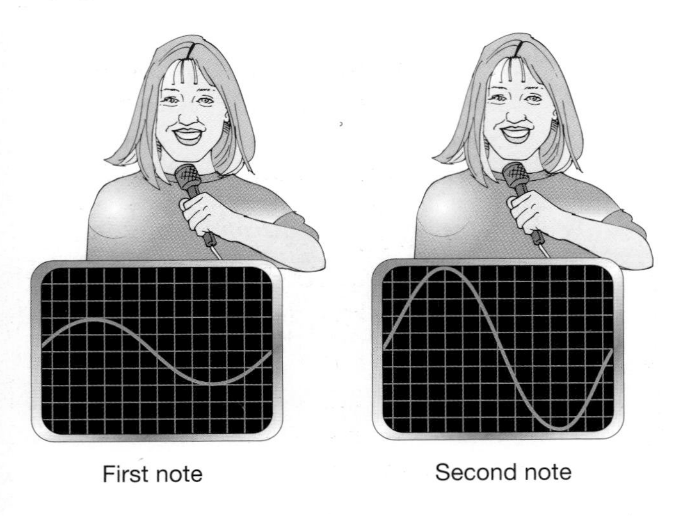

She then whistled the same note only this time louder.

She recorded in her notebook that a loud sound has a larger amplitude than a quiet sound. Loudness does not change the length of the wave.

The teacher passed the microphone to another pupil at a keyboard. The pupil played a low note followed by a higher note (the volume did not change). The notes looked like this:

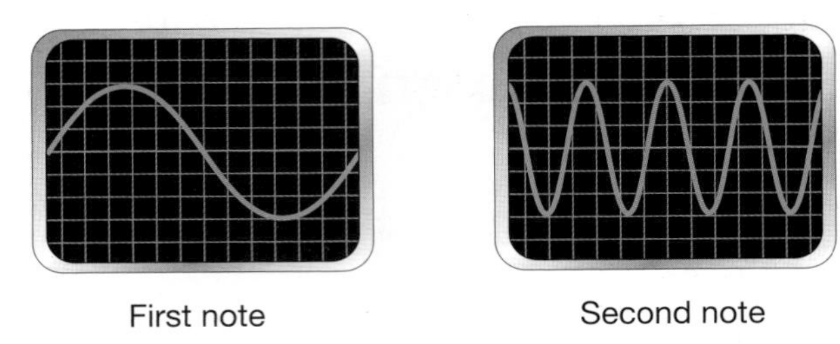

The teacher asked for an explanation.

One girl said that high pitched sounds (high notes) have a shorter wavelength than low pitched sounds. The teacher agreed and then asked about the volume.

The class said that the volume was the same (because it sounded the same).

The pupil who played the notes said that the volume was the same because the **amplitude** of both sounds was the same.

Loudness

Our ears can detect enormous variations in loudness. We can detect incredibly soft noises (whispers across the room) and withstand extremely loud noises (music systems at concerts).

Loudness is measured in decibels (dB) and this is a measure of the sound energy being emitted by an object.

Source of sound	Loudness
complete silence	0 dB
whispering	30 dB
fly buzzing	40 dB
talking normally	50 dB
nearby vacuum cleaner	70 dB
busy traffic	80 dB
nearby train	100 dB
rock concert	120 dB
nearby pneumatic drill	130 dB
nearby airplane	150 dB

Figure 2 Some sounds and their dB level – and what makes them

The decibel scale is a complicated scale and an increase of only a few dBs can mean a large increase in volume.

Sounds of over 100 decibels are very harmful and can cause temporary or possibly permanent hearing loss. A jet landing at a distance of 100 metres is about 100 decibels. Some people have been measured snoring at over 90 decibels!

High and low notes

High and low notes are best described using the term **frequency**. Frequency is the number of waves produced each second. A sound from a small bird could have a frequency of 3200 waves every second. We would describe this as a frequency of 3200 Hz.

Frequency is measured in Hertz (Hz)

The lowest sound that we can hear is about 30 Hz. The highest sound that we can hear is about 18 000 Hz.

Not everyone's hearing is the same so some people will hear higher or lower frequencies than others. The range of hearing diminishes as people get older.

Young people can hear very high notes which are completely 'silent' to older people.

Key ideas

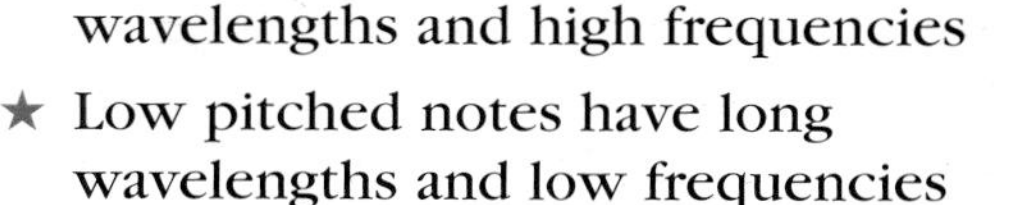

- ★ High pitched notes have short wavelengths and high frequencies
- ★ Low pitched notes have long wavelengths and low frequencies
- ★ Loudness is measured in decibels (dB)
- ★ Loud noises can cause hearing damage
- ★ Frequency is measured in hertz (Hz)

Wordbank

Frequency – number of waves in a second

Questions

1 A singer produces a note like this:

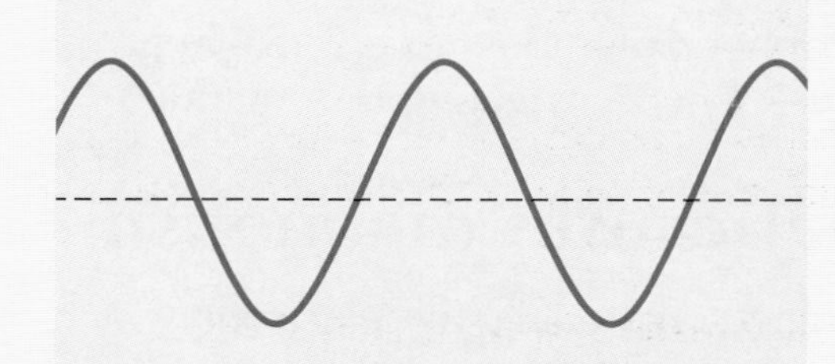

a) Draw what the sound would look like if she sang the same note but louder.

b) Draw what the sound would look like if she sang a lower note at the same volume.

c) Draw what the sound would look like if she sang a higher note but quieter.

2 List three objects that produce a low note and three musical instruments that produce a high note.

3 Prepare a small paragraph on hearing damage. Find out what occupations need ear protectors and what types of deafness there are. Are clubs and live music concerts bad for your hearing?

4 A tuning fork vibrates and produces a sound that makes 5120 waves in 20 seconds. Calculate its frequency

Magnets and their uses

Ancient Greek and early Chinese civilisations were amongst the first to observe the action of magnets. There is a legend of the Greek shepherd Magnes (~2000 BC) who was herding his sheep in an area known as Magnesia when the metal nails in his shoes became stuck on a large rock. This rock became known as magnetite. The rock could have been iron that had been struck by lightning.

People noticed that if a piece of this rock was suspended from a string it pointed in a north–south direction. These rocks were known as 'leading stones' or **lodestones**.

A compass is a magnet placed on a needle or delicate bearing.

The compass will turn and point in a north–south direction. The north pole of a magnet is the end that **points north**.

Christopher Columbus used a magnetic compass when navigating the Atlantic.

What causes magnetism?

In magnetic materials, the electrons which orbit the atom are not spinning 'normally'. It is the movement of these electrons that cause magnetism.

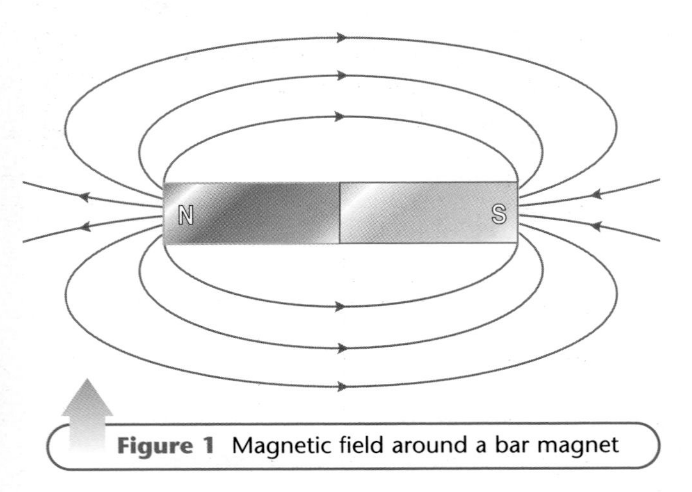

Figure 1 Magnetic field around a bar magnet

In the area around a magnet there is a magnetic field. The field for a bar magnet is shown in Figure 1. If a piece of iron is brought near to the magnetic field it will be **attracted**. If the field is strong the attraction will be strong, if the field is weak the attraction will be weak.

If we place two magnets close together their magnetic fields can affect each other.

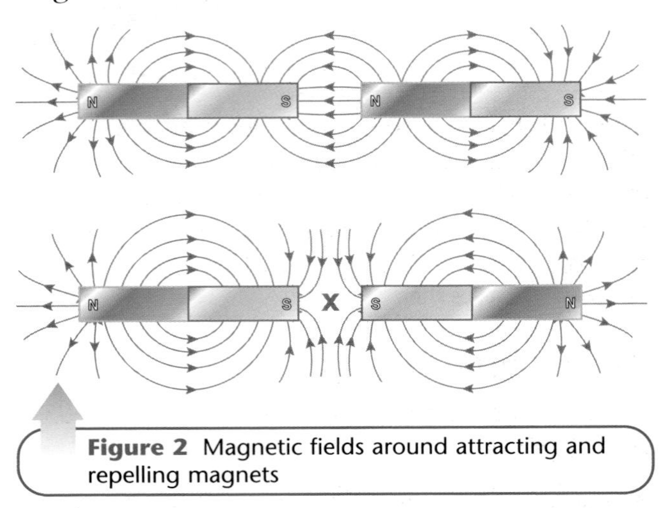

Figure 2 Magnetic fields around attracting and repelling magnets

If two north poles (or two south poles) are brought together they will **repel** each other. The force on each other pushes them away.

If a north and a south pole are brought together they will be attracted to each other.

Where can we use magnets?

Magnets are useful because they will stick to most metals or alloys containing iron. Fridge magnets are decorative and stick to doors of appliances and they can be used to spell out messages or warning signs.

There are other more practical uses of magnets which help us in everyday life.

Loudspeakers

Loudspeakers from music systems, TVs and radios contain magnets.

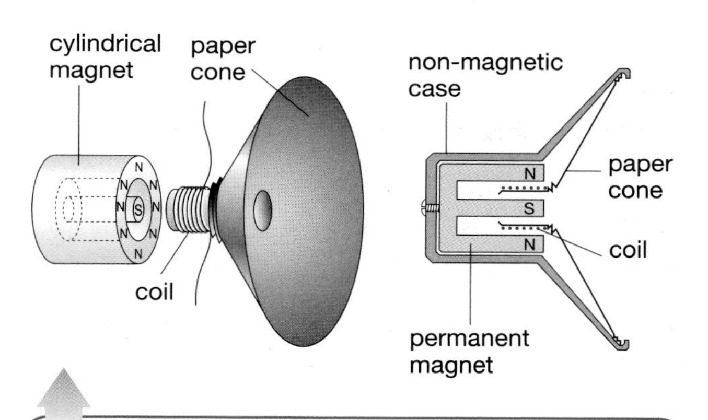

Figure 3 Inside a loudspeaker

The coil at the base of the cone becomes slightly magnetic as a current passes through the wire. The coil will then be attracted to and repelled from the magnets. This moves the speaker cone backwards and forwards to create the sound.

Alarm systems

Magnets can be used to tell when a door has been opened.

A magnet placed at the top of a door can cause two thin pieces of metal to become magnetic and attract each other. When the door is opened, the magnet is removed and the two thin pieces of metal will separate. This changes the signal in the wires and can set off an alarm.

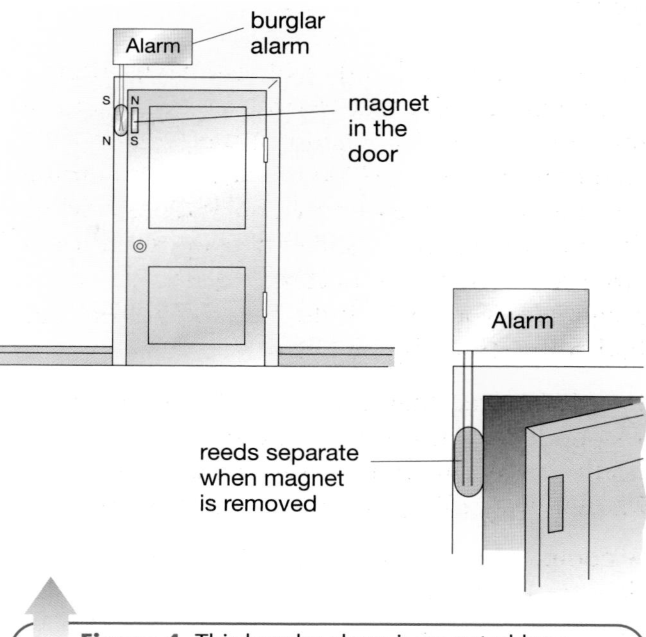

Figure 4 This burglar alarm is operated by a magnetic switch

These open wires cause a change in the signal and this could be linked to an alarm.

Electric motors

Electric motors are used widely nowadays. Electric tools, CD players and so on all have motors that turn the devices. Many motors need permanent magnets in order to provide the force that turns the device.

Key ideas

- ★ Magnets can occur naturally
- ★ Magnetism is caused by the movement of electrons
- ★ Magnets can be used in appliances such as loudspeakers and alarm systems

Wordbank

Lodestone – old name for a magnet
Attract – to pull together
Repel – to push apart

Questions

1 Copy the following diagrams and draw the magnetic field around these magnets:

a) N 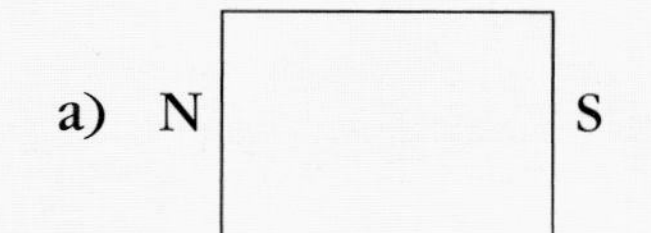 S

b) N  S N  S

2 Explain how a compass operates.

3 Why would it be foolish to place a piece of iron close to a compass?

4 Research how to make a piece of steel or iron magnetic.

Electromagnets and their uses

By the beginning of the 19th century magnetic compasses were being used in experiments dealing with electric currents.

Hans Orsted and Michael Faraday were investigating the effect of passing a current through a wire. They observed that when a current passed through a wire it changed the direction the compass was pointing to.

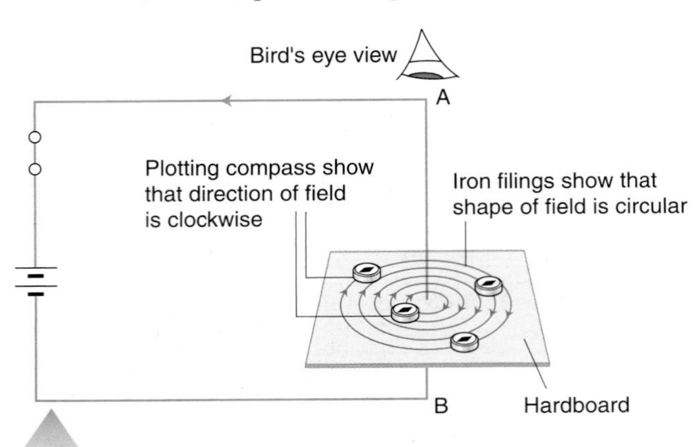

Figure 1 Magnetic field around a conducting wire

They found that by passing a current through a wire it created a magnetic field similar to that of a normal bar magnet. The magnetic field could be made stronger if the wire was coiled.

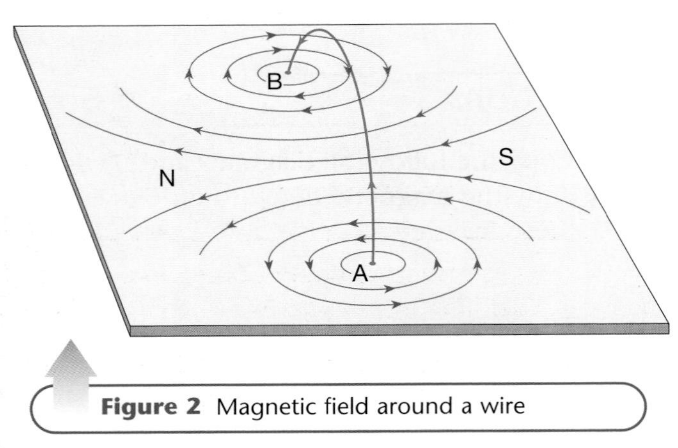

Figure 2 Magnetic field around a wire

When the current was switched off the magnetic field disappeared and the wire was no longer magnetic.

This was an interesting discovery. It meant we could create magnets when we needed them and switch them off when we didn't. We could even make the magnets stronger by having a greater current in the wire or having more coils.

These devices are known as electromagnets and have many uses.

A simple electromagnet

It is quite a simple task to make an electromagnet. You need some wire, a battery and a piece of iron.

Wrap the wire around the iron and then connect it to the battery.

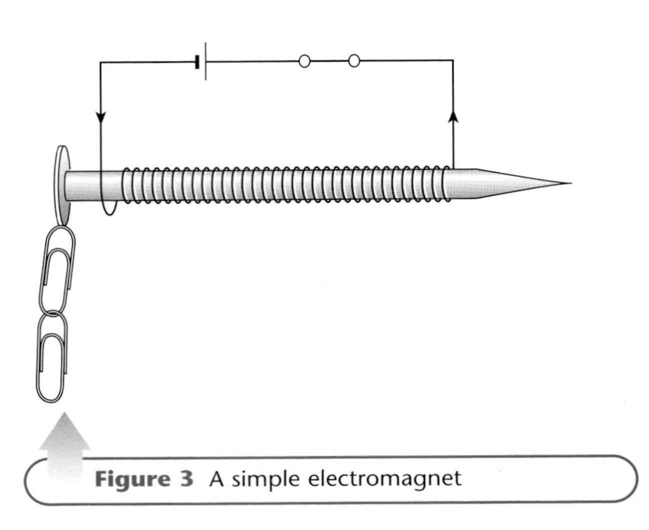

Figure 3 A simple electromagnet

An electromagnet is made when wire is wrapped around a piece of iron and a current is passed through that wire.

Uses of electromagnets

Scrapyards and metal suppliers use strong electromagnets to pick up old cars, plates of steel and so on. Electromagnets are used as they can 'attract' heavy items and lots of small pieces together.

In addition scrap metals can be separated into different groups as magnets will normally only attract iron or alloys of iron.

Medical uses

Powerful electromagnets can be used to remove small pieces of iron or steel which have become embedded in the body. Eye surgeons use **ophthalmic** electromagnets to remove small metal fragments which have entered the eye. Cutting the eye with a scalpel

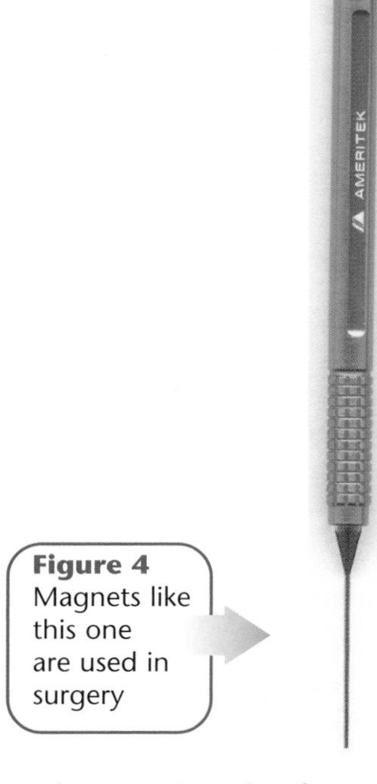

Figure 4 Magnets like this one are used in surgery

and removing the fragments with some form of grip may cause unnecessary damage to surrounding tissue.

Modern developments in magnet manufacturing have allowed the construction of very strong permanent magnets. Eye surgeons tend to use electromagnets less frequently nowadays as permanent magnets are nearly as strong, yet are smaller and more easily manipulated.

Relay switches

Some circuits that use large currents are dangerous to switch on. Switching on a light bulb or a hairdryer involves a current of only a few amps. Switching on a high power machine in a factory may involve currents of 100 A. In general it is not advisable to have a person in close contact with such a circuit.

Relay switches allow circuits to be switched on without the person having to be 'in contact' with the circuit.

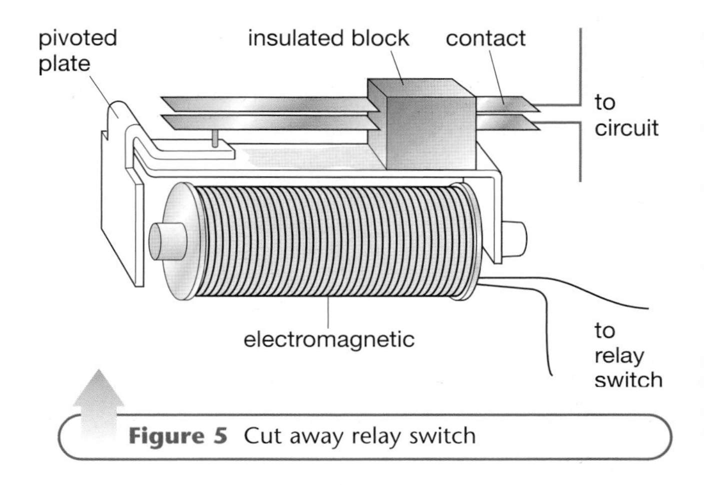

Figure 5 Cut away relay switch

Many devices have a relay switch. Starter motors for motor cars have a relay switch connected to the ignition system.

Key ideas

- ★ A current flowing in a wire can create a magnetic field around it
- ★ Wire coiled around a piece of iron can be used as an electromagnet
- ★ Electromagnets are used in many devices

Wordbank

Ophthalmic – relating to the eye

Questions

1. Draw a circuit diagram of a simple electromagnet.
2. Draw the electric field around a coil of wire with a current passing through it.
3. Why are electromagnets used to remove pieces of metals from skin?
4. Why would the switch on a computer **not** have a relay switch?
5. Find out two other uses of electromagnets.

Current in series and parallel circuits

Electrical circuits are used throughout the world to supply electrical energy to the thousands of different appliances that we use. A circuit could include a battery, some connectors and a bulb.

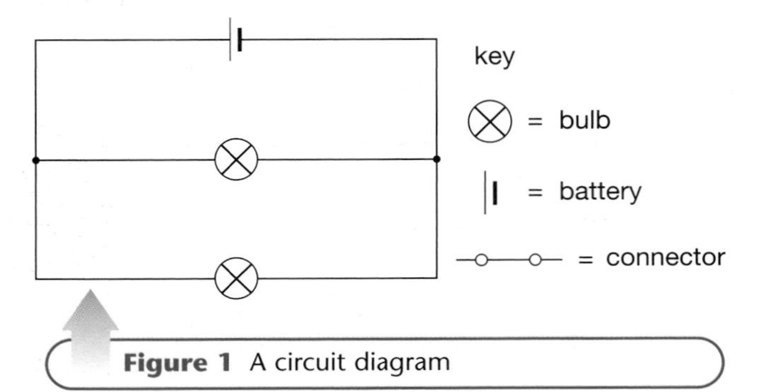

Figure 1 A circuit diagram

A pupil wanted to add another bulb to the circuit, as bright as the bulb that is already in the circuit.

The pupil had a choice. She could add another bulb to the circuit in series or add another bulb in parallel.

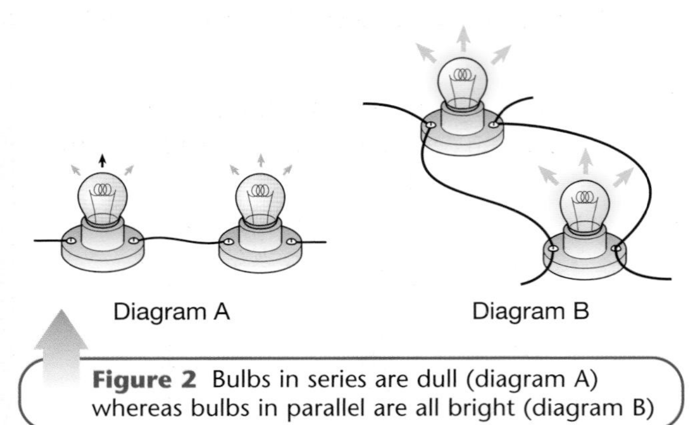

Figure 2 Bulbs in series are dull (diagram A) whereas bulbs in parallel are all bright (diagram B)

The bulbs in parallel are brighter because there is a greater current passing through them than if they were in series.

Current

In an electrical circuit, charged particles (electrons) move along the connecting wires. This movement is known as an **electrical current** and is measured in amps.

We use an ammeter to measure current and it is placed in series in the circuit.

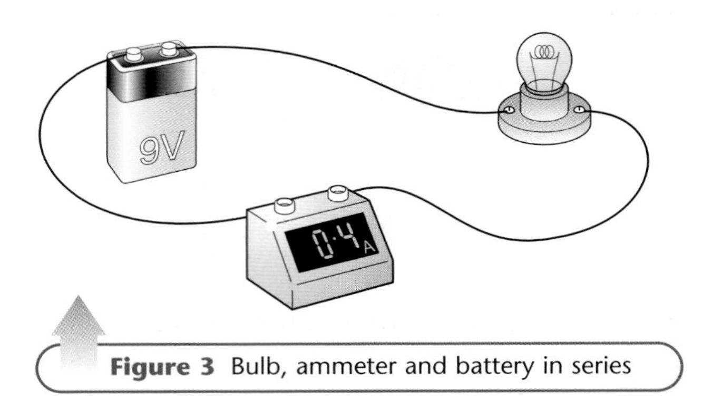

Figure 3 Bulb, ammeter and battery in series

For example, a kettle needs a current of about 5 amps to work normally, a 100W light bulb will use about 0.43 amps and a portable TV will use about 1 amp.

Current in a series circuit

A pupil was asked to measure the current in the circuit in Figure 4.

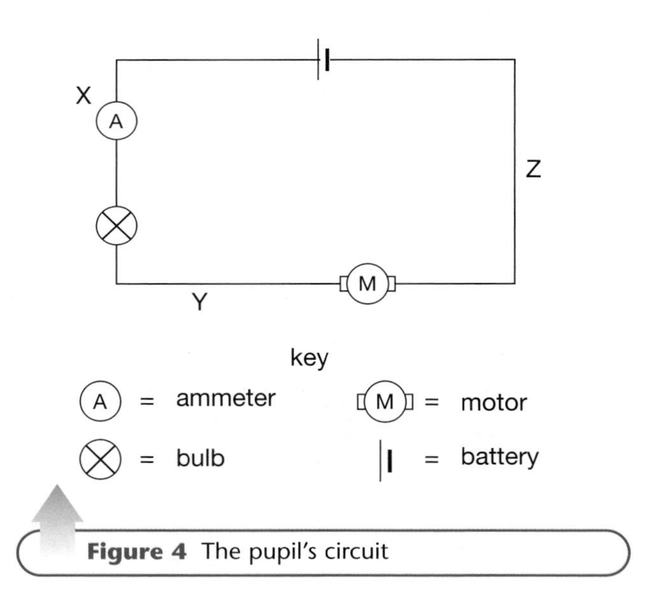

Figure 4 The pupil's circuit

He asked where in the circuit he should measure the current. His teacher said that it didn't matter where he measured it.

This puzzled him as he thought that the current at the start of the circuit would be fairly large as it has to light the bulb **and** turn the motor.

He measured the current at three points in the circuit and found the following results:

Position	Current
X	0.48 A
Y	0.48 A
Z	0.48 A

He saw that the current in a series circuit is the same at all points.

Current in a parallel circuit

The pupil was then asked to measure the current in a parallel circuit. He used the same components as the previous circuit but arranged them in a parallel circuit as shown. He measured the current in positions A, B, C and D.

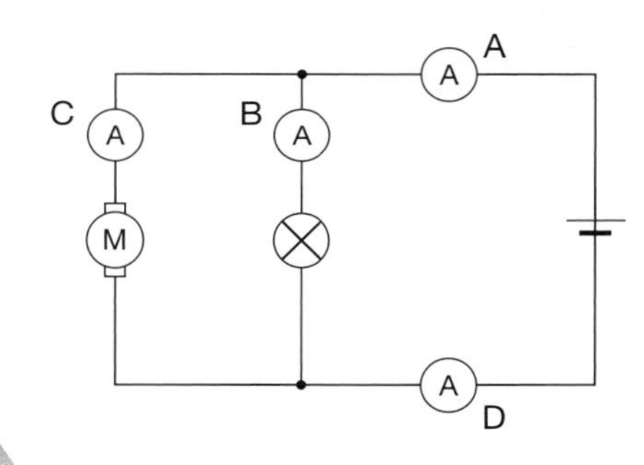

Figure 5 A simple parallel circuit

His results were as follows:

Position	Current
A	2.0 A
B	1.2 A
C	0.8 A
D	2.0 A

He noticed that the current is not the same in all parts of the circuit and that separate branches can have different currents.

A key point is that the current from the cell is 'split' when there are separate branches. When these branches 'rejoin' the current value is the same as that before the branches split.

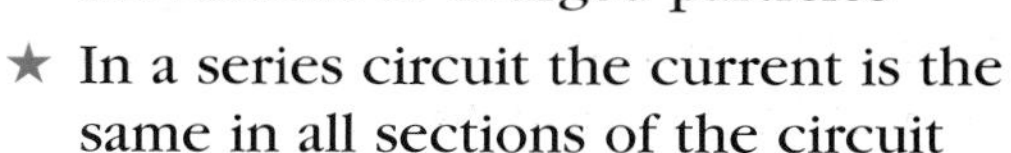

Key ideas

★ An electrical current is the movement of charged particles

★ In a series circuit the current is the same in all sections of the circuit

★ In a parallel circuit the current in separate branches can be different

Wordbank

Electrical current – a flow of charged particles

Questions

1 Draw a parallel circuit with a battery, a bulb and a motor. Indicate where you would place an ammeter to measure:

a) the current from the battery.
b) the current through the motor.

2 Explain what is meant by an electrical current.

3 Copy and complete the following diagram. Give values for the readings on all the ammeters.

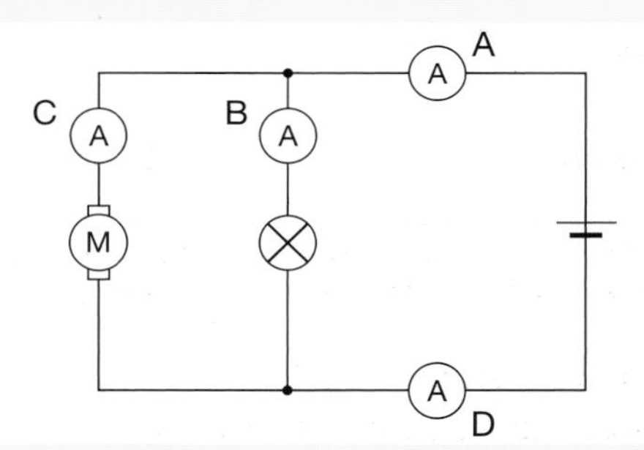

4 Copy and complete the following statement.

In a series circuit the current ....
....

In a parallel circuit the current ....
....

5 What circuit would have the larger current from the battery:

a) two bulbs connected in series?
b) two bulbs connected in parallel?

Electrical safety

Electrical circuits are used throughout the world to provide energy for the machines and appliances that we use. The main advantage of electrical energy is that it can be sent large distances quickly and efficiently and that it can be converted into many other useful types of energy.

Household electricity can however be harmful and wires and connections have to be handled safely.

Figure 1 Electrical danger symbol

In Britain we use a house wiring system that has three components. These are live, neutral and earth.

- live wire – the dangerous wire, it operates at an electrical potential of 230 volts
- neutral wire – this completes the circuit for the appliance
- earth wire – a safety device

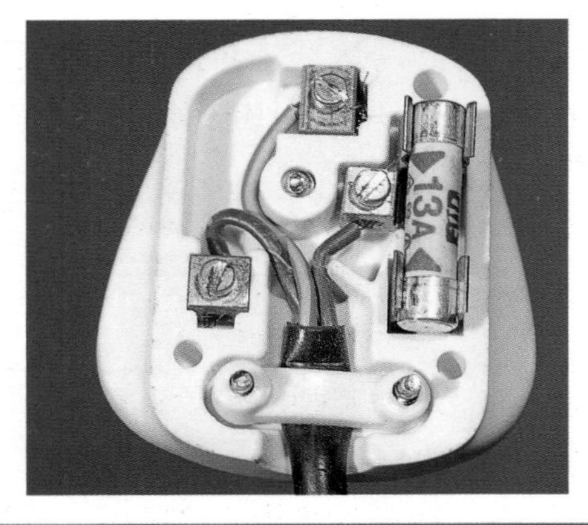

Figure 2 The live, neutral and earth wires shown in a correctly wired household plug

Many modern appliances do not have an earth wire. These appliances have a strong plastic insulation around their electrical components that make them safer to use. They are said to have 'double insulation'.

What happens if you get an electrical shock?

Figure 3 Be sure all electrical appliances are wired correctly and safely

If part of a person's body comes into contact with the live wire, or a piece of metal connected to the live wire, they can get an electrical 'shock'.

The shock occurs when their hand, for example, is at a high electrical potential and some other part of their body is at a low potential.

If you are standing on the ground your feet are at a low electrical potential.

In Figure 3 the person's hand has come into contact with a live appliance. The current travels from the high potential (the hand) to the Earth (low potential) through their body.

Effect of currents on the body

The injuries received by electrocution depend upon the size of the current and the duration of the shock. The table below gives an indication of the effect of mains electricity on the body. The current refers to the current passing through the person's body.

Current	Effect
1 mA	barely noticeable
10 mA	painful
20 mA	paralysis of muscles
90 mA	ventricular fibrillation
>100 mA	death/severe injury

The most common cause of death due to electrical shock is ventricular **fibrillation**. Fibrillation is rapid uncoordinated twitching movements of the heart that may cause a lack of circulation and therefore reduce the supply of oxygen to the brain.

Safety devices

A **fuse** or a **circuit breaker** is an important safety device that can prevent an appliance becoming live. The most serious fault that occurs in an appliance is the live wire inside the appliance breaking loose and touching the casing. At this point the casing is said to be 'live'.

Earth wires are connected to the appliance casing. They are good conductors with a low resistance. If the live wire touches the casing, there is a complete circuit from the live wire through the casing and then back to the earth wire.

Figure 5 This live wire has worked itself loose and is now touching the casing

This circuit has a low resistance. This means a high current will flow.

The high current will melt or 'blow' the fuse which cuts off the electrical supply at the plug and makes the appliance safe.

Circuit breakers operate on the same principle. A large current passing through a circuit breaker causes it to switch off. With a circuit breaker you have to switch the circuit back on. When a fuse blows you have to replace the fuse.

A major point here is that the fuse must be connected to the live wire. The energy comes into the circuit from the live. If the fuse is connected to the neutral wire it will not isolate the appliance and the danger remains.

Key ideas

★ Household wiring must be handled carefully

★ Electrical shocks can kill

★ An earth wire is a safety device

Wordbank

Fibrillation – rapid uncoordinated twitching movements that replace the normal rhythmic contraction of the heart and may cause a lack of circulation and pulse

Fuse – safety device that melts when current is too large

Circuit breaker – safety device that switches off when current is too large

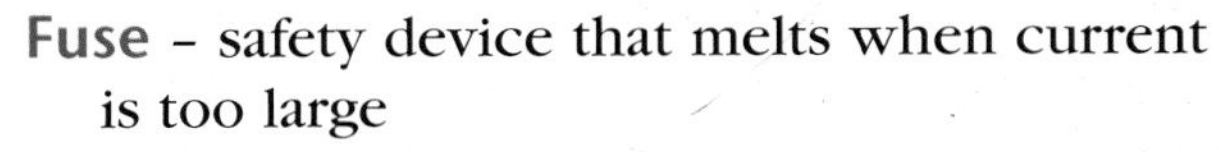

Questions

1. Name the three wires used in electrical circuits.
2. State the purpose of each wire.
3. What happens to the body if a current of 20 mA passes through it?
4. Find out the symbol for double insulation.
5. Look for appliances that may have double insulation.

29 Electronics

Electronics is a branch of science and technology which uses devices that rely upon electrons in order for them to work.

When electrons move they cause electronic components to behave in certain ways. The components can switch on or off, they can emit light and they can convert energy from one form to another.

Most devices now rely upon electronic components to control the way they operate. Computers, calculators, hi-fis, cars, mobile phones and such like all contain large amounts of electronic circuitry.

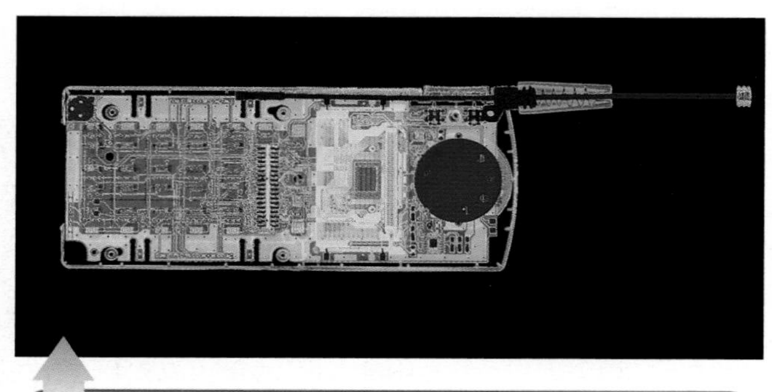

Figure 1 The inside of a mobile phone is full of circuit boards

Electronic components are now made on an extremely small scale. Some electronic circuits have components which are less than one hundredth of a millimetre long. These components are referred to as **microelectronics**.

Electronic signals – analogue and digital

Electronic devices are split into two main kinds: analogue and digital.

Analogue electronics deals with the sort of electrical signals we get from, say, someone singing into a microphone. The signal can vary continuously.

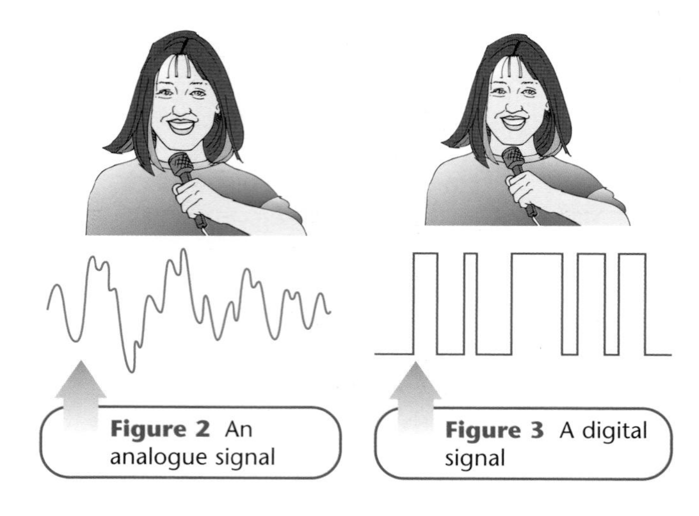

Figure 2 An analogue signal

Figure 3 A digital signal

Digital electronics deals with signals which have two stages. A digital signal could be a switch being continually pressed on or off.

Electronic devices

There are many electronic devices in production today. The simplest form of these convert one form of energy to another.

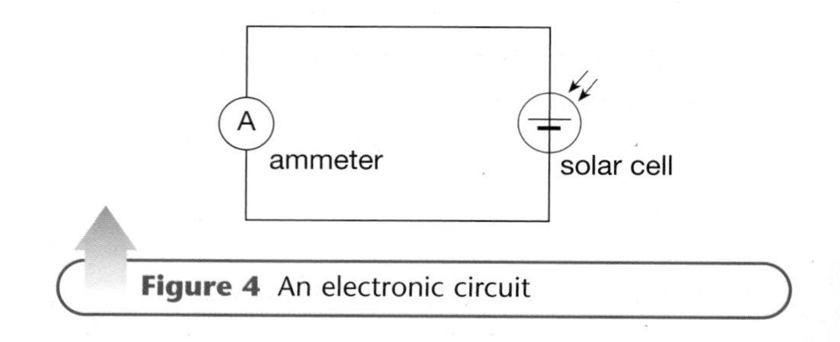

Figure 4 An electronic circuit

Solar cell

When light hits the surface of a solar cell it can cause electrons to flow round a circuit.

Solar cells may be used to power small devices such as calculators or may be used as light detectors.

Light Emitting Diodes (LEDs)

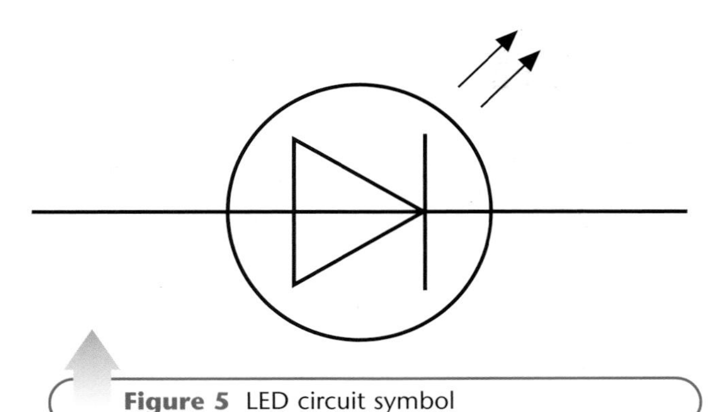

Figure 5 LED circuit symbol

Light Emitting Diodes are used widely in electronic devices. They take electrical energy and convert it into light energy. They are not like light bulbs as they do not have a filament that glows white hot. They are used widely as indicators of whether an appliance is switched on or off. The red light at the base of your television is probably an **LED**.

Initially, Light Emitting Diodes were red because that was the easiest colour to produce. Many digital alarm clocks had red numbers. Recently yellow, green and blue LEDs have become available and some high power diodes are used in street lighting and emergency torches for hillwalkers!

Key ideas

- ★ Electronic circuits are used in most modern appliances
- ★ Microelectronics circuits are extremely small
- ★ Electronic signals can be analogue or digital
- ★ Analogue signals vary continuously
- ★ Digital signals can only move between two states (on or off)

Wordbank

Microelectronics – electronic components which are extremely small

LED – Light Emitting Diode

Questions

1. List five items in your classroom that contain electronic components.
2. What does the term microelectronic refer to?
3. In an experiment to investigate what happens when light shines on a solar cell, a student set up the following experiment.

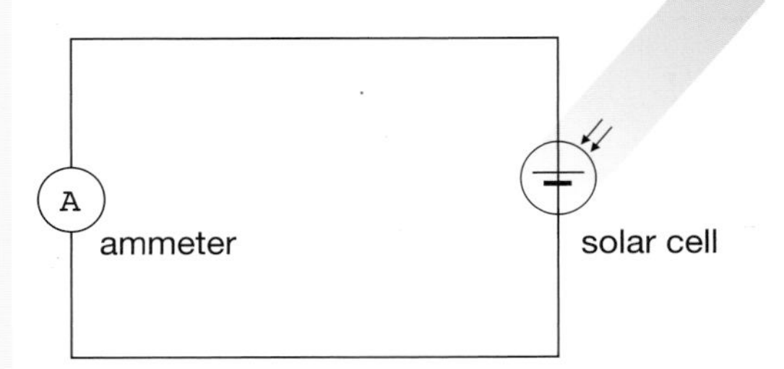

The pupil measured the brightness with a light meter and noted the current that the light caused.

Brightness	Current (mA)
0	0
25	15
60	35
80	50
100	60

a) Construct a graph of brightness against current.

b) Describe what happens to the current when the light shines on the solar cell.

c) Is the current a digital or an analogue signal?

30 Electronic systems

Electronic devices do so many operations today that it is difficult to find an appliance in everyday use that does not contain some form of electronic circuitry. When engineers and designers plan a new appliance or machine they have to decide what they want it to do and how it will operate.

Electronic circuits are described in terms of systems. It is easier to explain and describe electronic systems rather than individual components.

If you were unable to hear the music from your portable hi-fi, you could assume there is a problem with your headphones rather than that there is a problem with either the leads, connectors or loudspeaker.

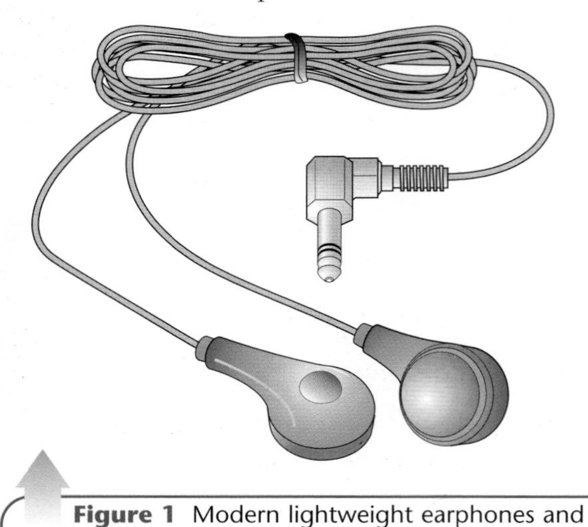

Figure 1 Modern lightweight earphones and leads

Simple systems

Input – Process – Output

It is easier to look at electronics in a 'systematic' way. That is, to think of the workings of components in smaller sections. These sections are:

Input The section that causes the system to start working.

Process The section that takes the 'information' from the input and converts or alters it.

Output The section that gives out the 'information' in a form we want.

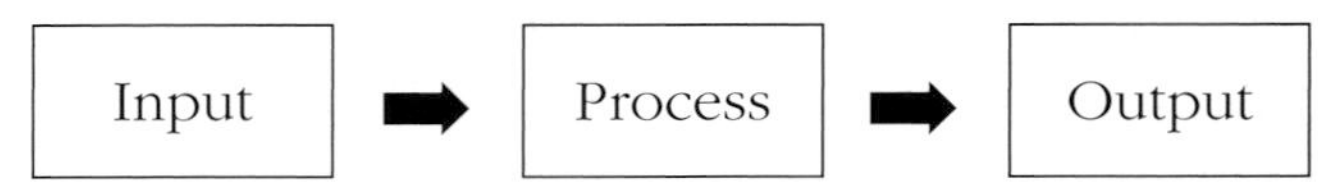

This 'system' approach helps simplify how we look at electronic devices and how they can be used to make our lives easier.

Input and output devices

Input devices

Input devices generally detect some physical quantity and convert that into electrical energy.

A microphone takes a sound signal and converts it into an electrical signal.

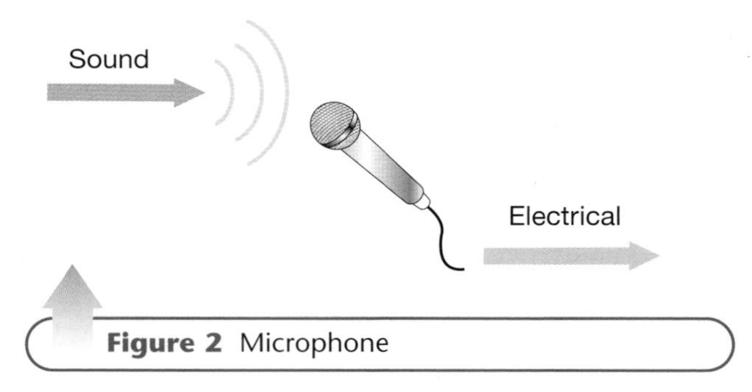

Figure 2 Microphone

A **thermocouple** is made from two different types of wires which have been welded together to form a junction. If this junction is placed somewhere hot, it converts heat energy into electrical energy.

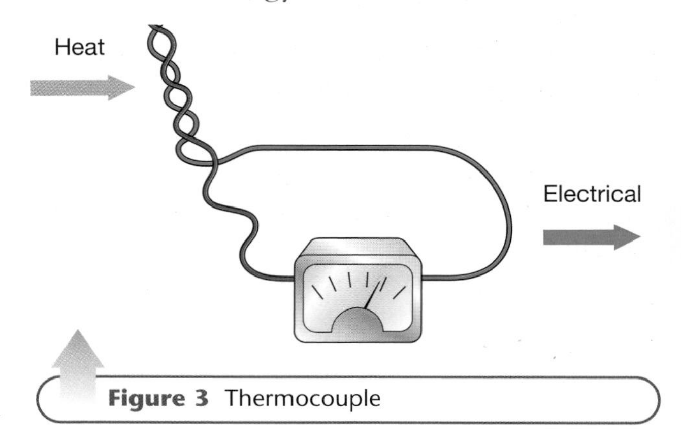

Figure 3 Thermocouple

Other input devices

- Solar cells convert light energy into electrical energy.
- Dynamos convert movement energy into electrical energy.
- Capacitors are used in time-delay switches.

Output devices

Output devices generally convert an electrical signal into some other form of energy that we want to use.

A loudspeaker takes an electrical signal and coverts it into a sound signal.

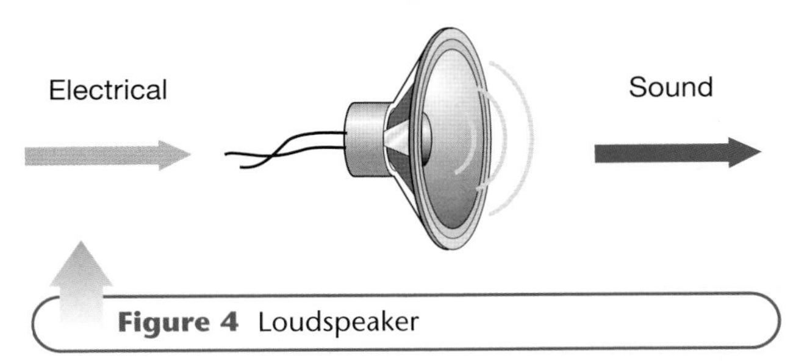

Figure 4 Loudspeaker

A light bulb takes an electrical signal and converts it into a light signal.

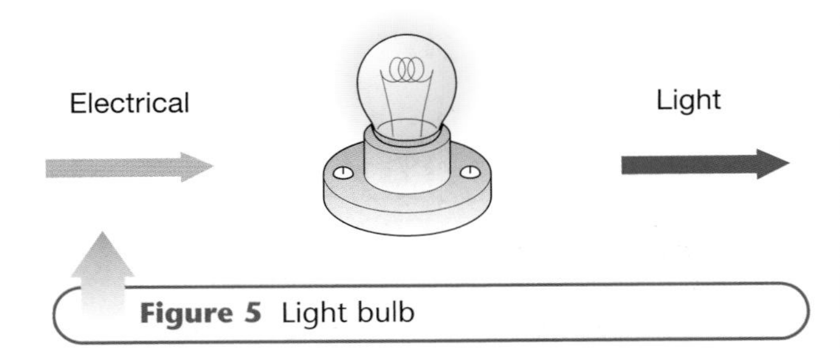

Figure 5 Light bulb

Other output devices include motors, Light Emitting Diodes and buzzers.

LEDs – Light Emitting Diodes

LEDs are similar to bulbs but emit less heat. Many streetlights are now LEDs.

In 1997, Philadelphia began replacing its traffic lights with devices containing LEDs. This reduced their power bill from $21 000 000 to $500 000.

High power LEDs will alter many bulb based operations in the near future.

Key ideas

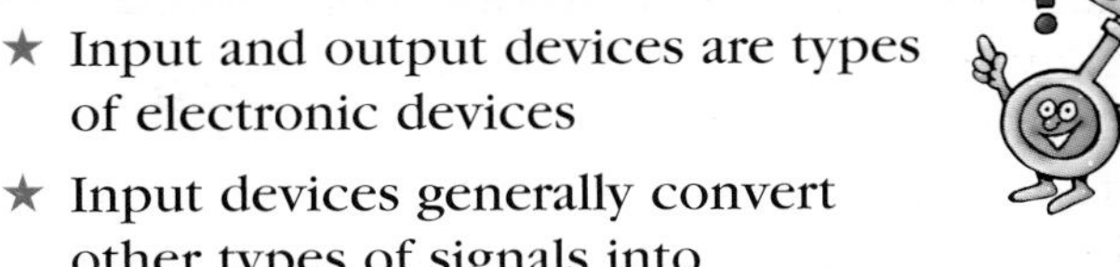

★ Input and output devices are types of electronic devices

★ Input devices generally convert other types of signals into electrical signals

★ Output devices generally convert electrical signals into other types of signals

★ The systems approach simplifies how we analyse electronic situations

Wordbank

Thermocouple – a device that converts heat energy into electrical energy

Questions

1 List five input devices.

2 List five output devices.

3 What input devices would you use in the following circuits:

a) a sound level meter?
b) a temperature control for an oven?
c) a speedometer for a bicycle?

4 What output devices would you use in the following circuits:

a) a hi-fi system?
b) a digital watch?
c) a house alarm?

Gravitational potential energy

Energy exists in many forms and can be changed from one form into another. There are a number of different ways of storing energy. For example, energy can be stored in cells (batteries), it can be stored in stretched springs and it can be stored in chemicals.

A ball held above your head has stored energy. The stored energy it has is known as **gravitational potential energy**. If that ball is released then it will fall to the ground.

It is called gravitational potential energy because we are raising the ball and this involves working against the force of gravity.

An object can be given more gravitational potential energy by raising it to a higher position.

A simple formula can be used to calculate the gravitational potential energy an object gains by being raised. The symbol for potential energy is E_p and it is measured in Joules (J).

potential energy = mass × gravitational field strength × height

This can be written as:

$$E_p = m \times g \times h$$

where m = mass of the object (in kg)

g = gravitational field strength (10 for the planet Earth)

h = height the object is raised (in metres)

So a ball of mass 2 kg raised 3 metres will have a gravitational potential energy of:

$$E_p = m \times g \times h$$
$$E_p = 2 \times 10 \times 3$$
$$2 \times 10 \times 3 = 60\text{J}$$

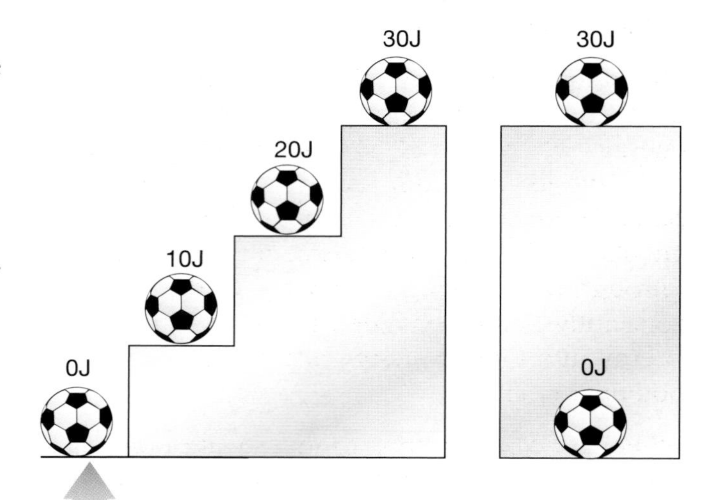

Figure 1 These balls have different values of gravitational potential energy because they are at different heights

Using a pendulum to investigate gravitational potential energy

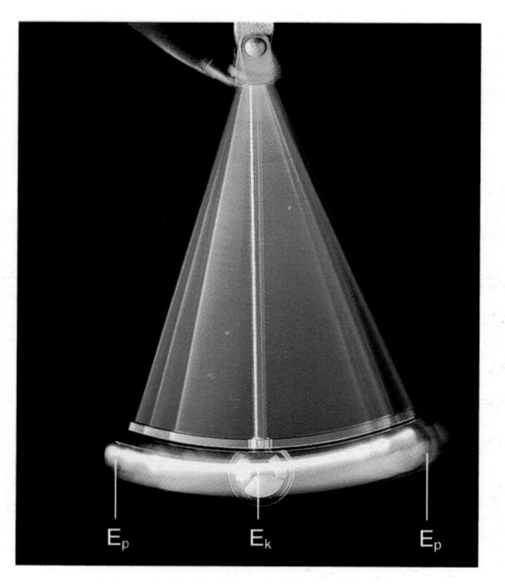

Figure 2 The amount of gravitational potential energy in this pendulum bob is constantly changing

E_k is greater at the lowest point of the swing (kinetic energy).

E_p is greater at the highest point of the swing (potential energy).

The **bob** at the end of the string will have a different value of potential energy at various points during its swing.

The height from which the bob is released will be its maximum level of gravitational potential energy. When the bob is at its lowest point it will have its minimum level of gravitational potential energy. As it swings back upwards its gravitational potential energy will increase. Throughout its swing the energy of the bob is constantly being converted from potential energy into kinetic energy and back to potential energy.

When using pendulums to investigate potential energy of an object, the factors that need to be considered are a) the mass of the bob and b) the height it was raised to. The **gravitational field strength** is constant.

Consider the results of the following experiment carried out by a group of pupils.

They set up a pendulum in the doorway of a room. They used a block of wood as the pendulum bob and measured how far another block of wood would slide when struck by the bob.

Figure 3 The pupils' pendulum hammer

The results from this experiment are shown in the following table:

Mass of bob (kg)	Release height of bob (m)	Distance travelled by wooden block (m)
1	0.1	0.1
2	0.1	0.2
5	0.3	1.5

They noted that the distance travelled was related to the potential energy gained by the bob.

Key ideas

- ★ Potential energy exists in different forms
- ★ Gravitational potential energy depends upon the mass of the object and the height it is raised to
- ★ The gravitational potential energy can be calculated using the formula $E_p = m \times g \times h$

Wordbank

Bob – object attached to the end of a string on a pendulum

Gravitational field strength – the 'pull' of gravity on an object (10 N/kg on Earth)

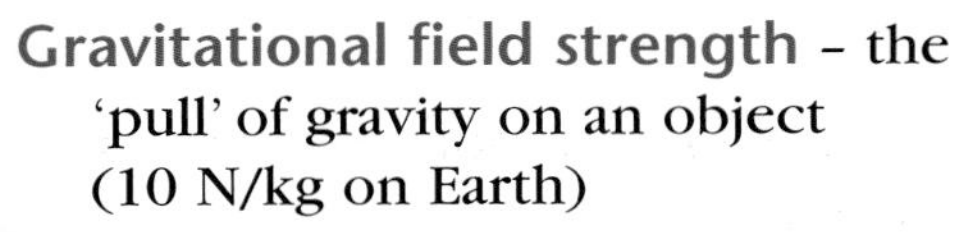

Questions

1. In what way could the potential energy of a pendulum bob be increased?
2. Write the formula used to calculate gravitational potential energy.
3. Calculate the gravitational potential energy of the following items:
   a) a brick of mass 2 kg on top of a 3 metre wall.
   b) a 55 kg man at the top of a 2 metre ladder.
   c) a 0.5 kg duster on its ledge 1.5 metres above the floor.
   d) a 2000 kg helicopter 600 metres above the school.

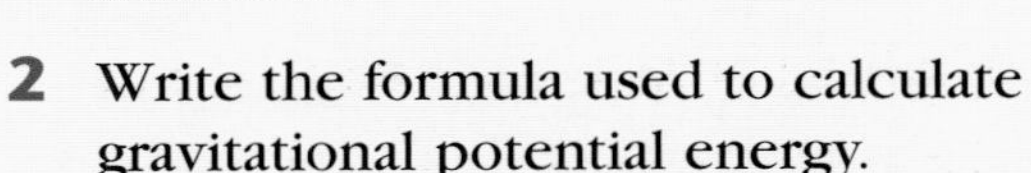

4. What are the units of measurement for gravitational potential energy?

32 Chemical potential energy

As we have already seen, energy exists in many forms and can be transformed from one form into another. Energy which is stored is known as potential energy. Chemical potential energy is stored within chemicals due to the arrangement of their atoms.

What is chemical energy?

Energy is contained within all matter. When chemical reactions take place, energy is either released or taken in. When a chemical **burns** it combines with oxygen to form a new compound.

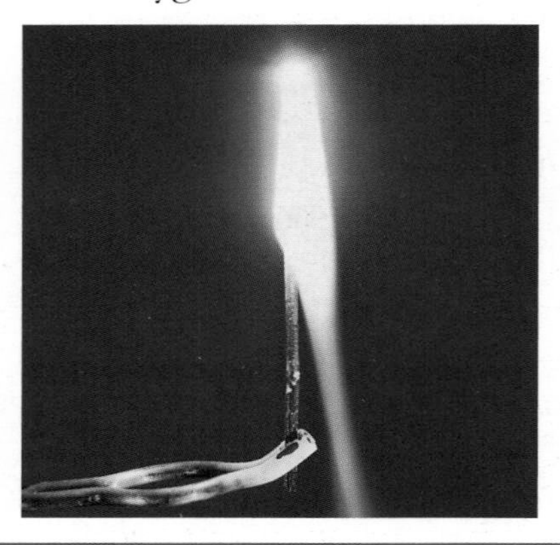

Figure 1 Burning magnesium in air

During this chemical reaction the chemical potential energy is converted into heat, light and sound energy.

The food we eat contains chemical potential energy. During respiration, cells in our bodies convert chemical energy into other forms. For example, a lot of the energy from our food is converted into heat. This heat energy is then transported around our body by the blood to maintain our body temperature at 37°C.

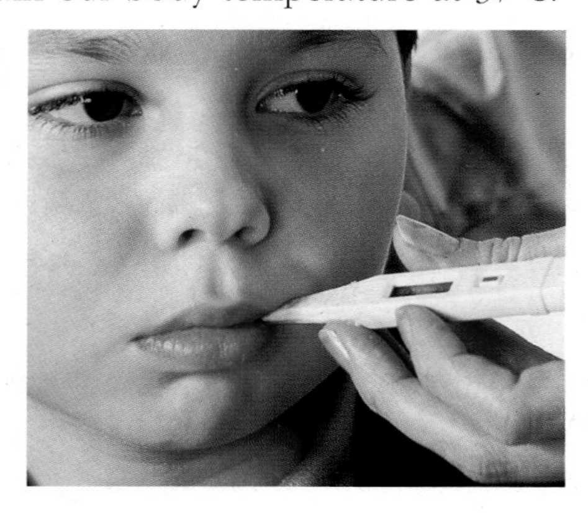

Figure 2 Using a digital thermometer to measure temperature

A piece of buttered toast contains about 315 kilojoules of energy. You could also use 315 kJ to:

- jog for 6 minutes
- cycle for 10 minutes
- walk briskly for 15 minutes
- sleep for 90 minutes
- light a 60W light bulb for 90 minutes

Energy can only be converted into another form of energy. Here are some changes in energy from one form to another.

Figure 3 Stored, light and kinetic energy

- Chemical energy in a torch battery converts to light energy when turned on.
- Food contains energy stored as chemical potential energy. Your body uses the stored energy to do work.
- If you overeat, the energy from the food is stored as chemical potential energy in fat.
- A car uses the stored chemical energy in petrol. The engine changes the chemical energy into heat and kinetic energy to power the car.

Foods

When **photosynthesis** occurs in plants, a series of chemical reactions take place. The leaf cells use light energy to combine molecules of carbon dioxide and water. They form more complex chemicals such as sugar.

A molecule of sugar contains more chemical potential energy than the molecules of carbon dioxide and water which were used to make it. This extra energy came from the light energy.

In this way green plants make all of the food that animals depend upon to stay alive. When the sugar molecule is burned inside your cells this trapped energy is released.

The basic types of food which we eat are carbohydrates, fats and proteins.

Figure 4 The carbohydrates, fats and proteins in this typical meal contain chemical potential energy

We are what we eat

The amount of energy we need to survive depends upon a number of factors: our age, size, lifestyle and so on.

Ideally, we want to take in as much energy as we 'use'. If we take in too little we will use up our stores and lose body fat. If we take in too much, the opposite occurs.

Fossil fuels

In a similar way fossil fuels (coal, oil and gas) contain a lot of chemical potential energy. They are burned to release the energy trapped within the chemicals. This energy is transformed into other types of energy which are used in our daily lives. Power stations use fossil fuels to generate electrical energy which is then used in homes and workplaces throughout the country.

Key ideas

★ Chemical potential energy is present in chemicals such as foods and fuels

★ Chemical potential energy is transformed into other forms of energy

★ Plants manufacture chemical potential energy by the process of photosynthesis

★ Fossil fuels obtained their energy originally from the Sun

Wordbank

Burning – a chemical reaction which transforms chemical potential energy into heat and light energy

Photosynthesis – series of chemical reactions which ends with the production of molecules which contain chemical potential energy

Questions

1 Describe a common chemical reaction which converts chemical potential energy into other forms of energy.

2 Name three substances which contain chemical potential energy.

3 Complete these sentences using the words *changed*, *destroyed* or *created*.

Energy can only be .... into another sort of energy. It cannot be .... nor can it be ....

4 In what form is excess food stored in the human body?

5 What is the normal temperature of the human body?

6 What is the source of chemical potential energy used by a car?

7 What compounds are changed into sugar by green plants?

8 What is the name of this process?

9 Name three fuels used in power stations to generate electricity.

33 Mass and weight

In science it is important to make accurate measurements. We measure length in metres, time in seconds and temperature in degrees Celsius.

The term **mass** is used widely in science and has a specific meaning:

Mass is the amount of matter that a substance contains and is measured in kilograms (kg) or grams (g).

Confusingly, people also measure their **weight** in kilograms. Other people who go to gyms and work out lift 'weights' which are measured in kilograms.

Figure 1 Weight training!

Mass and **weight** are not exactly the same thing however. For example, astronauts in space are weightless but they have not lost any of their mass. Their mass is still the same.

The astronauts who walked on the moon weighed only a fraction of what they did on Earth without having to go on a special diet!

Every object that contains matter has mass, but it only has weight when it is on a planet or a moon. This occurs because large objects such as planets have a gravitational field around them. Any object near to the planet will be pulled towards it. Small planets have small gravitational fields and large planets have greater gravitational fields.

Figure 2 Astronauts are weightless in space

The pull of a planet's 'gravity' on an object is its weight. Weight is measured in Newtons.

We can calculate the weight of an object by multiplying its mass (in kg) by the gravitational field strength of that planet. On Earth the field strength is 10 N/kg.

weight = mass × grav. field strength

Therefore the weight of a 25 kg object on Earth is $25 \times 10 = 250$ N.

The weight of any object on Earth can be calculated by multiplying its mass (in kg) by 10.

The terms weight and mass confuse many people, as they seem almost identical.

Figure 3 The effect of the gravitational field

Weight on other planets

We can calculate the weight of objects on other planets if we know the gravitational field strength on those planets. The field strength on the moon is 1.6 N/kg.

The weight of a 25 kg mass on the moon would be:

weight = $25 \times 1.6 = 40$ N
(compare this with 250 N on Earth)

The weight of an average person of mass 75 kg on the moon would be:

weight = $75 \times 1.6 = 120$ N
(compare this with 750 N on Earth)

The moon would be a great place to go if you only wanted to lose weight. You would weigh roughly one sixth of what you would weigh if you were back on Earth! You would still have all your fat (your mass!) but you would weigh a lot less.

If you went to a large planet such as Jupiter you would weigh over twice your normal weight.

For example, g for Jupiter = 26 N/kg so:

$$\text{weight of person} = \text{mass} \times g$$
$$= 75 \times 26$$
$$= 1950 \text{ N}$$

Imagine trying to go for a walk on Jupiter!

Key ideas

★ Mass is measured in kilograms
★ The weight of an object is how much the planet pulls it to the surface
★ Weight is calculated by multiplying mass by gravitational field strength

Wordbank

Mass – the amount of matter in an object

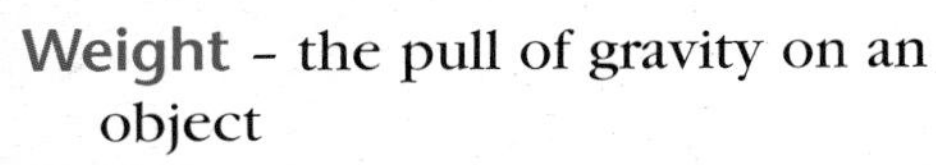

Weight – the pull of gravity on an object

Questions

1 List the units of weight and mass.

2 Why do astronauts on the moon weigh less than on Earth?

3 Copy and complete this table:

Mass (kg)	Weight on Earth (N)	Weight on Moon (N)
35		
45		
12		
7		
22		

4 An object on the moon has a weight of 640 N.

a) What is its mass?
b) What would it weigh on Earth?

5 Why would an object in deep space have no weight?

6 What would an alien from Jupiter look like if it was subject to such strong 'gravity'?

34 How forces act

There are many types of forces in the world – weight, friction, pushing and so on.

Forces can do any of three things:

- they can change the shape of an object,
- they can change the speed of an object,
- they can change the direction of an object.

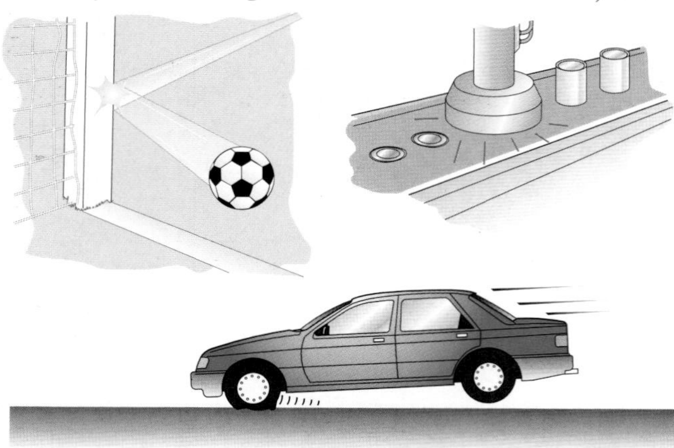

Figure 1 The effect of force on direction, shape and speed

Forces act in ways that are sometimes difficult to understand. One problem is identifying all the forces acting on an object at one particular point.

Balanced forces

Figure 2 There are lots of forces acting on these people

In the examples in Figure 2, the forces acting on the objects are said to be balanced.

- The pull of one tug of war team is balanced by the pull of the other.
- The weight of the barbell is balanced by the push of the lifter.
- The weight of the parachutist is balanced by the air friction of the parachute. (The parachutist is falling at a steady speed.)

No overall force means no change in shape, speed or direction.

In these cases the force acting in one direction is being balanced or cancelled out by an equal force acting in the opposite direction. This is the way that forces act in many circumstances.

When a child sits on a swing, the force on the chains pulling up balances the weight pulling him down. When a helicopter hovers, the force from the rotors balances the weight of the helicopter. A car at 70 mph on a motorway has the force from the tyres pushing the car balanced by the friction from the road and the air.

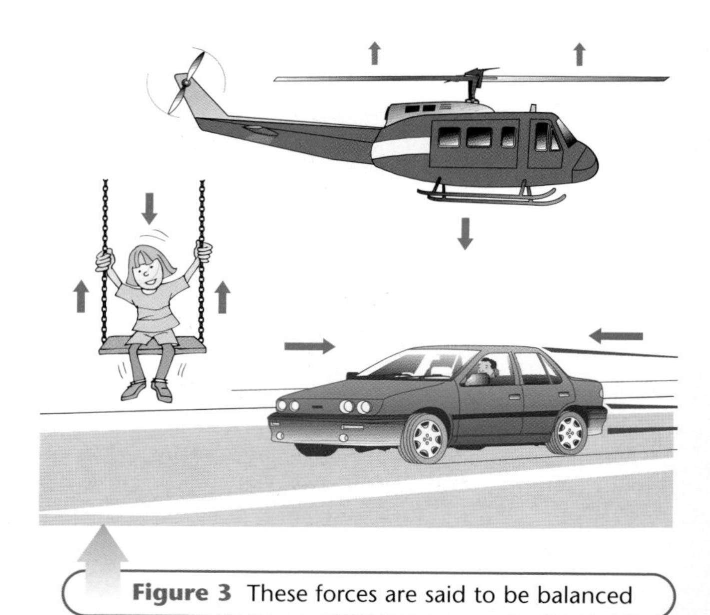

Figure 3 These forces are said to be balanced

In all of these cases the speed of the objects has not changed. It has remained constant. This occurs when the forces are balanced.

Forces in pairs

If you apply a force to an object, it does not act on its own. If you kick a ball, the ball applies a force to your foot. You may not feel it, but imagine kicking a hard ball barefoot!

When a bicycle accelerates the tyres apply a force on the road; the road also applies a force on the tyres. If this is hard to accept, consider what would happen if the bicycle tried to accelerate on slippery ice. The tyres could spin and the bike would not move.

Without grip no forces will be applied and no movement will result.

Forces act in pairs. If a force pushes an object in one direction there is a force that acts in an opposite direction.

- When a person pushes someone away, both people are pushed back.
- When a shell is fired from a cannon, the cannon is pushed back in the opposite direction from the shell. (This is referred to as recoil.)
- When a hammer hits a nail, a force is applied to the nail and an opposite force is applied to the hammer. (You would feel this force if you used your fist to hit the nail in.)

Figure 4 Forces working in pairs

In the study of physics this is referred to as **Newton's Third Law**.

If a force is applied to an object, an equal and opposite force is applied in the other direction.

Key ideas

★ When forces are balanced, speed and direction will not change

★ Forces occur in opposite pairs

Questions

1 Draw diagrams of the following situations. Mark on the directions of the forces.

a) A balloon falling slowly to the ground.
b) An elevator with some people in it (elevator not moving).
c) A boat moving at a steady speed.
d) A rugby scrum.

2 Copy and complete the following paragraph:

Forces act in .... If the forces acting on an object are .... then there will be no change in speed, ... or .... A car travelling at a steady 50 km/hr has the force from the engine .... by the friction from the air and the road.

3 Give three examples of situations where the forces are balanced. Draw a diagram and show the forces acting on the situation.

35 Force and motion

A force can make an object change its speed. If you pull or push an object it will speed up or slow down.

The term we use to describe how quickly an object speeds up (or slows down) is **acceleration**.

Sports cars and motor bikes have good acceleration. They can speed up very quickly. They have powerful engines and are quite small when compared to family cars.

The combination of an engine that can produce a large force and having a small mass means they can accelerate quickly.

To get an indication of the acceleration of vehicles, manufacturers give the time it takes for the vehicle to go from 0 to 60 mph. If a vehicle can go from 0 to 60 in a short time it has a 'quick' acceleration.

Vehicle	Time (0–60 mph)
sports car	6 seconds
saloon car	10 seconds
truck	20 seconds

How does the size of the vehicle affect its acceleration?

From the table it's obvious that large trucks cannot accelerate at the same rate as normal cars. Large trucks have very powerful engines that can exert a great force but their great size reduces their acceleration.

The acceleration of an object can be calculated by using the equation:

acceleration = force/mass

For example, a car (1200 kg) has an engine that produces a force of 3000 N.

Its acceleration is calculated using $a = F/m$

$a = 3000/1200 = 2.5$ metres/second/second

If the same engine was used to drive a van of 3000 kg the acceleration will be

$a = 3000/3000 = 1$ metres/second/second

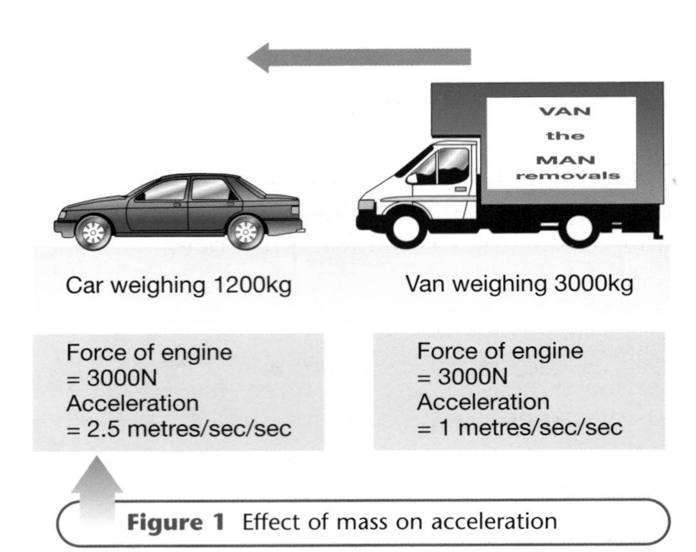

Figure 1 Effect of mass on acceleration

Why do vehicles have a top speed?

Cars, bikes, trains and aeroplanes all have a maximum speed that they cannot exceed. No matter how hard the engine is pushed there will be a maximum speed that the vehicle will reach.

This occurs because of the forces of friction and **air resistance**. You can experience these when you ride a bicycle. When you cycle you can feel the air rush against your face. If you pedal faster you will feel a greater air resistance. Cyclists try to reduce their air resistance so that they can go faster.

For motor vehicles, an engine has a maximum force that it can produce.

Let's take our example of the car mentioned earlier. Its engine can produce a force of 3000 N. As the car speeds up the air resistance increases. After a while it will reach, say, 1000 N.

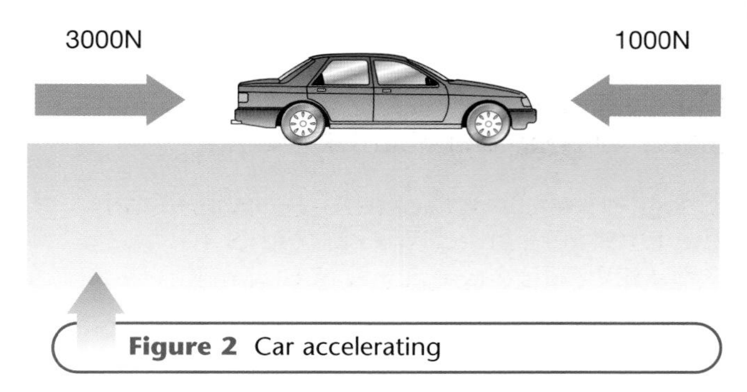

Figure 2 Car accelerating

This means the force accelerating the car is now 2000 N (3000 – 1000). Its acceleration is now less as the overall force has been reduced.

Eventually, the air resistance increases until it reaches the same size as the engine force.

At this point the force driving the car forward is balanced by the air resistance acting the other way.

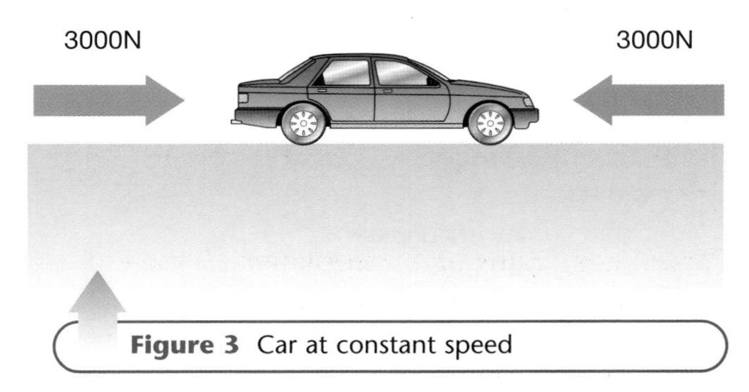

Figure 3 Car at constant speed

These forces cancel each other out and are balanced.

When forces are balanced there is no change in speed. The speed remains the same. This is the reason why cars, planes and trains etc. reach a maximum speed.

To increase the maximum speed you must either reduce your air resistance or increase the force from the engine.

Reducing Air Resistance

Cyclists use a number of methods to reduce their air resistance. Their cycles have been designed to slice through air and the cyclists adopt driving positions that reduce the air resistance (drag). They also shave off body hair and wear very smooth outfits.

Key ideas

- ★ Air resistance limits an object's speed
- ★ Air resistance increases as an object's speed increases
- ★ Acceleration depends upon the mass of the vehicle and the force produced by its engine

Wordbank

Acceleration – how quickly an object can change its speed

Air resistance – force reducing an object's movement through air

Questions

1. List five objects that can accelerate rapidly.
2. List five objects that cannot accelerate rapidly.
3. List two ways that a cyclist could reduce their air resistance.
4. A vehicle has an engine which can produce a force of 250 N. It has a mass of 150 kg. Calculate its acceleration.
5. How could large vehicles reduce their air resistance?
6. Collect data on the acceleration of family cars. Choose four cars and list their acceleration.

36 Force and pressure

Pressure is a term much used in everyday speech.

> 'pressure to do well in exams' . . . 'peer pressure' . . . 'a low pressure front moving across from the Atlantic'

Pressure has a specific meaning in science. It helps describe what happens when objects come into contact, especially when a sharp or a pointed object dents or deforms another.

Imagine a nail being hammered into a wall or a sharp knife cutting through food. In the examples, the 'pressure' on the food and wood is great. This is because the force on them is applied over a small area.

Pressure is calculated using:

pressure = force/area

For example, a person with a weight of 800 N stands in a field. The area of his feet are 0.002 m^2. The pressure he applies on the ground is:

$$\text{pressure} = \text{force/area} = 800\ \text{N}/0.002\ \text{m}^2 = 400\ 000\ \text{N/m}^2$$

The same person then stands on a garden fork which has an area of 0.0004 m^2. The pressure on the ground is now:

$$\text{pressure} = \text{force/area} = 800\ \text{N}/0.0004\ \text{m}^2 = 2\ 000\ 000\ \text{N/m}^2$$

Figure 1 Using a fork increases the pressure

Reducing pressure

Some vehicles are extremely heavy. If these vehicles were to drive over ground with normal tyres, the weight of the object concentrated over such a small area would cause them to sink into the ground.

Pressure can be reduced by making the area of the tyres very large. We can either use incredibly large tyres or lots of small tyres to spread the load.

Figure 2 Instead of tyres we can use treads or tracks to spread the load even further

Tanks are incredibly heavy and need to spread their weight as much as possible. Treads and tracks allow the pressure to be reduced to levels that allow movement.

Walking on deep snow is very difficult as the pressure from our feet is high enough to penetrate the snow. We can reduce the pressure by using snow shoes or skis.

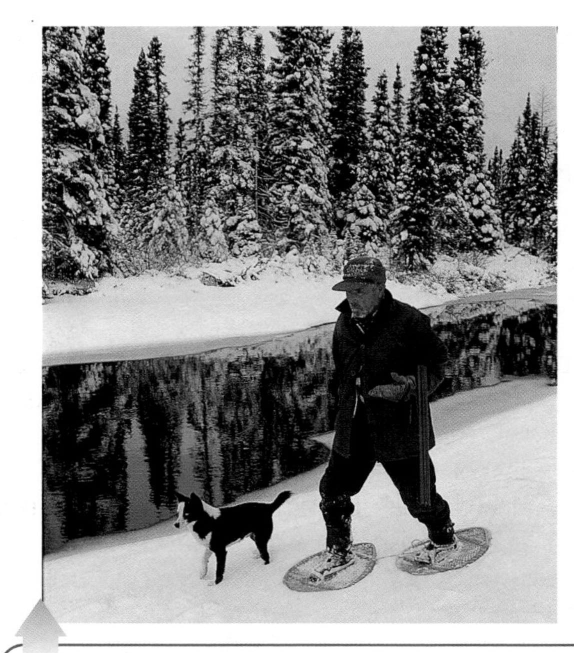

Figure 3 **Inuit** wearing snow shoes

Pressure and us

Our skin cannot take high pressure as it affects the **circulation** at that point. After a while the skin becomes painful. It can also lead to blisters and sores.

We find it comfortable to sit on soft, padded chairs which spread our weight over a fairly large area. Stools in science labs are hard and have a small surface area which makes it difficult to spread our weight evenly.

This could be why pupils continually lean forward, backwards, sideways etc. They are spreading the pressure evenly over their backsides so they do not get sores or blisters.

Figure 4 Science stools are uncomfortable

Pressure applied to an area of skin for a long time can cause minor damage. The most common skin injury is blistering.

The pressure on certain areas of skin from new or ill-fitting shoes can frequently cause blisters.

The pressure on our feet is constant if we spend long periods standing or walking.

Our feet respond to this pressure by forming corns and calluses which are tough layers of hardened skin.

Patients who are bedridden for long periods of time are monitored closely for pressure sores. If they are lying in such a way that their hip or back is pressed against the mattress for long periods of time, they can get serious bedsores.

These sores can be difficult to treat if the patient cannot get out of bed. The patient has to lie on some part of their body and this can aggravate the sore.

Key ideas

- ★ Pressure is the force of an object applied over an area
- ★ A force applied over a large area will result in a smaller pressure
- ★ A force applied over a small area will result in a larger pressure

Wordbank

Inuit – natives of northern America and Canada

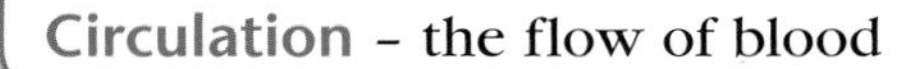

Circulation – the flow of blood

Questions

1. Calculate the pressure applied to the ground by an object of weight 800 N spread over an area of 0.05 m^2 and that same object being placed on an area of 0.0002 m^2.
2. An Inuit who weighs 750 N uses snow shoes to get around. Why is it difficult for him to walk about in normal boots?
3. Why do farm workers make one end of a fence post pointed before they hammer it into the ground?
4. Why is it uncomfortable for us to lie or lean on small stones?
5. Why do heavy lorries have a large number of tyres?
6. Why can tractors drive through ploughed fields easily?

Pressure in liquids

When a force is applied to an object it generally bends or deforms in some way. Some materials change their shape very easily.

If we trap some air in a syringe we can press the syringe down quite easily. It can be **compressed**.

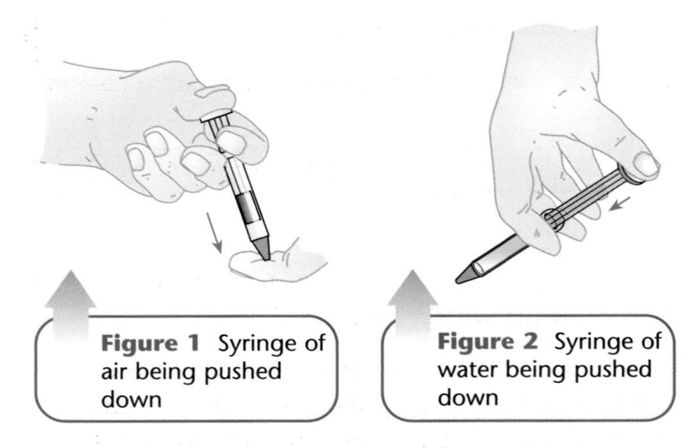

Figure 1 Syringe of air being pushed down

Figure 2 Syringe of water being pushed down

If we fill the syringe with water and press down, the plunger will not move.

Air molecules are quite widely spaced and can be squeezed together. Liquid molecules are quite closely packed and cannot be squeezed together. Divers can use cylinders of compressed air but firefighters are not able to use cylinders of compressed water.

The fact that liquids cannot be compressed has a number of uses. Many devices apply pressure to liquids and use them to transfer that pressure to other machinery. **Hydraulics** is the name given to the study of forces in liquids.

Hydraulic elevators

Originally, elevators that were used to carry people up and down buildings were lifted by cables attached to the roof of the elevator car. Many modern elevators are now raised from below by long metal pistons.

The piston is filled with a hydraulic fluid which is connected to a pump. The pump pushes the fluid at a high pressure into the piston. This fluid then pushes the piston upwards, raising the car.

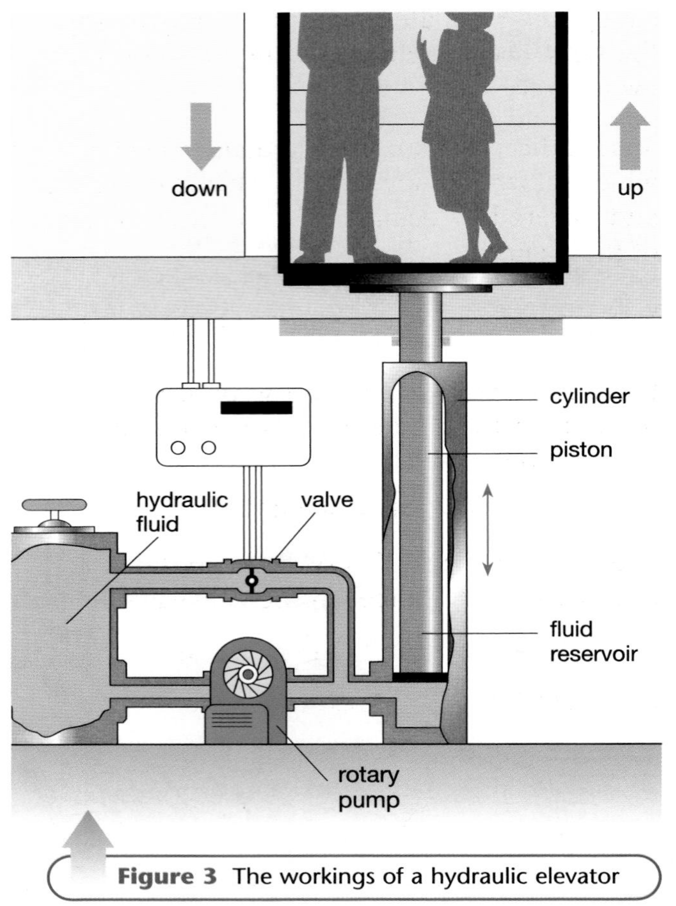

Figure 3 The workings of a hydraulic elevator

A similar machine is used to provide the forces for car crushing machines. The pistons extend and push the metal sides of the crusher together.

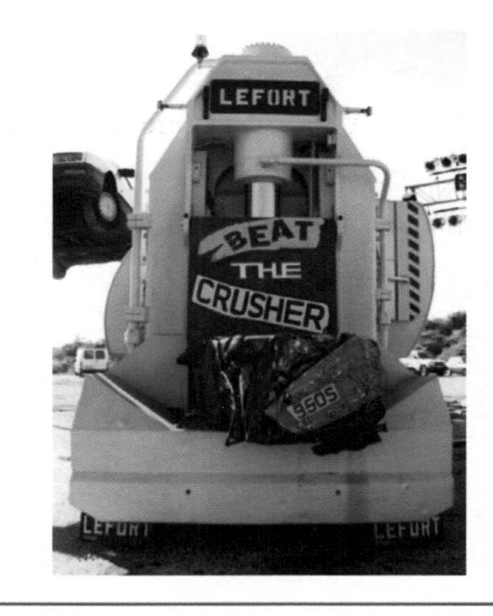

Figure 4 Car crusher

Hand operated hydraulic **jacks** are used to raise cars. It doesn't require a great deal of strength to raise a car. You need only to apply the same force again and again in order to lift even a very heavy car.

Some office chairs have a hydraulic section which allows the level of the chair to be raised and lowered by using a small lever at the side of the chair.

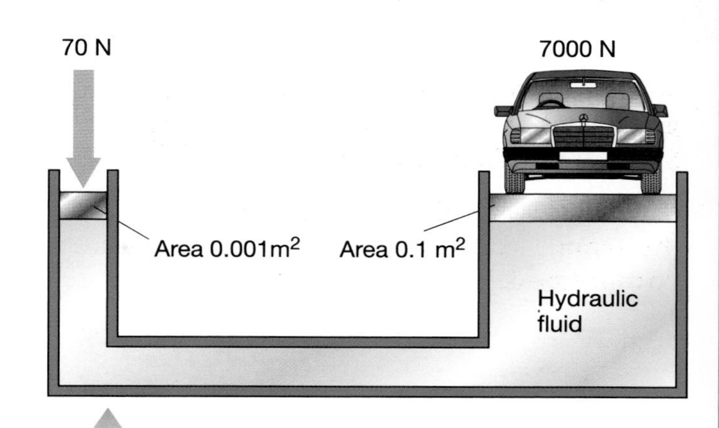

Figure 5 A hydraulic jack mechanism

How a hydraulic jack works

If we press down on a narrow piston of area 0.001 m^2 with a force of 70 N we produce a pressure of:

$P = F/A = 70/0.001 = 70\,000\ N/m^2$

The liquid transfers this pressure to the larger piston where the force can be calculated:

$F = P \times A = 70\,000\ N/m^2 \times 0.1\ m^2$

$F = 70\,000 \times 0.1 = 7000\ N$

By pushing down with a force of 70 N our jack will push up with a force of 7000 N.

Regrettably, we don't get this extra force for nothing. We have to push the small cylinder down a large distance in order for the car to be raised even a small height.

Key ideas

- ★ Liquids cannot be compressed
- ★ Hydraulic jacks can apply large forces

Wordbank

Compressed – squeezed together
Hydraulic – moving fluids
Jack – a lifting device

Questions

1. List five items that involve hydraulic devices.
2. Draw a diagram of a hydraulic car jack.
3. A mechanic used a hydraulic jack to raise a piece of machinery. He applied a force of 120 N to the small piston with a surface area of 0.001 m^2.
   a) Calculate the pressure on the piston.
   b) The large piston has an area 0.35 m^2. What force will be applied by this?
4. The brakes in a car are operated using hydraulic fluid. When you press down on the brakes, the fluid transfers the pressure to brake pads which push out and rub against the wheel. Explain why it is very important that air does not enter the hydraulic fluid. (Remember what happens to air when squeezed.)

38 This is physics

There are many branches in science but the main ones are biology, chemistry and physics. All science works in the same way by using **scientific method**.

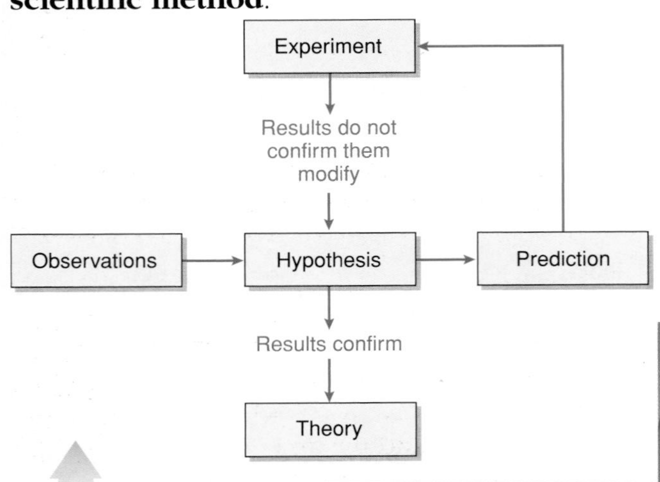

Figure 1 Scientific method

An imaginary divide exists between 'pure' and 'applied' science. Pure science involves the search for new knowledge and understanding about the Universe, and searching for scientific laws. Applied science involves devising ways in which scientific knowledge can be used to benefit mankind. The 'man on the street' debates the value of spending millions that will create nothing apart from knowledge, yet applied science often depends on the discoveries of pure science.

What is physics?

matter – a solid, liquid or gas that has mass

energy – the ability to do work in a system

Physics is the science of **matter**, **energy** and the **interactions** between them.

interactions – the way that matter and energy affect each other

Figure 2 This is physics

What use is physics?

Physicists' discoveries are often used to make things that are useful in everyday life. Famous Scots invented the telephone and the television. Many modern appliances – telephones, televisions and computers – contain miniature electronic circuits on thin slices of silicon 'chips', which were originally 'invented' by theoretical physicists. Medical diagnosis and treatment depends on many applications that were devised by physicists. Roentgen's 1895 discovery of X-rays has led to countless pictures from inside our bodies. X-rays are also used to treat cancer. The development of optical fibres is used for keyhole surgery.

What do physicists study?

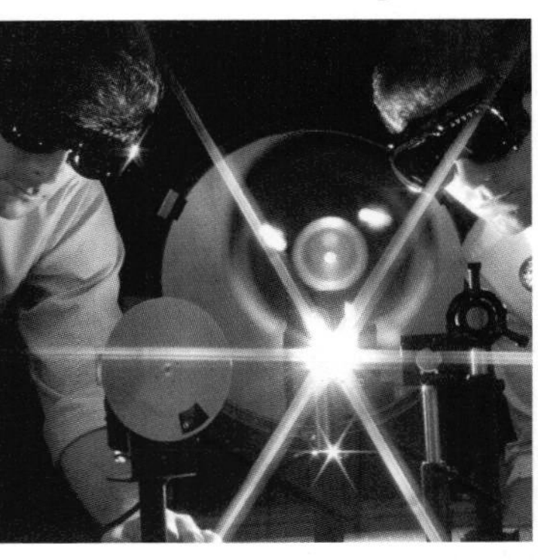

Figure 3 Professional physicists

- **Astrophysicists** study the stars, the Universe and their chemical and energetic properties.
- **Medical physicists** use and develop techniques for the treatment and diagnosis of illness.
- **Geophysicists** use their skills to make discoveries about the Earth's crust and often search for mineral reserves.
- **Engineers**, of which there are many types e.g. chemical, marine, civil, mechanical electronic and electrical. They use scientific knowledge to solve practical problems in their field.
- **Atomic and nuclear physicists** study the nature of atoms and their composition. They explore the sub-atomic particles and the energy that is involved in materials (thermodynamics).
- **Optics** involves the study of electromagnetic radiation (including light) and its interaction with matter. This area has expanded greatly with the introduction of fibre optic cables and related electronics.

What would I study if I continued physics at school?

Many schools teach topics such as:

- Telecommunications
- Using electricity
- Health physics
- Electronics
- Transport
- Energy matters
- Space physics

Famous Physicists

Albert Einstein (1879–1955) developed theories of relativity and explained the photoelectric effect.

Sir Isaac Newton (1642–1727) developed laws of mechanics and gravity. Contributed much to the fields of optics, light and heat.

James Clerk Maxwell (1831–1879), born in Edinburgh. Worked on electricity and magnetism. Developed important equations for these topics.

Richard Feynman (1918–1988), American physicist who helped understand electromagnetic interaction. Discovered the cause of the Space Shuttle 'Challenger' explosion.

Marie Curie (1867–1934), discoverer of radioactivity. Contributed greatly to the study of nuclear physics.

Sir William Thomson (1824–1907), also known as Lord Kelvin. Professor at Glasgow University from the age of 22. Developed a scientific temperature scale and was influential in many areas.

Key ideas

★ Physics is a key area of modern science

★ Physics has many branches

★ Pure and applied branches of science exist

★ Its approach is the same as other areas of science and involves scientific method

Wordbank

Scientific method – a way of investigation that involves observation, and making explanations (theories) to test scientific hypotheses (ideas)

Questions

1 Compare 'pure' and 'applied' science.

2 Find out more about:

a) the branches of physics.
b) careers in physics.
c) what you have already studied in physics.

3 Find out more about electromagnetic radiation.

Let's talk rubbish!

Rubbish is everything that we throw away or no longer use. It can be solid, liquid or gas. Scientists refer to it as waste and it can be grouped into: domestic waste (from homes); industrial and commercial waste (from factories, offices and shops); and **hazardous** waste which needs to be specially treated to prevent pollution.

Some waste is called **biodegradable** waste. This type of waste, including paper and leftover food, will break down naturally in the environment by the action of microorganisms.

Non-biodegradable waste is waste which cannot be broken down naturally.

Figure 1 Rubbish dumps full of non-biodegradable waste are an increasing concern

When dinosaurs walked the Earth there was no rubbish. Any waste that was produced by the living things was biodegradable and was recycled. Nature recycles its own waste. It is people who create rubbish. New technologies have made life easier and most of us like newer or more recent gadgets. This creates more rubbish because we discard perfectly good items and move on to the next model.

The amount of rubbish we throw away is increasing due to:

- new packaging materials used in food and electronics packaging etc.,
- greater consumption of fast and convenience foods,
- an increasing level of wealth in our society leading to a greater consumption of goods.

In Britain each household produces about 1 tonne of rubbish annually. Collectively this equates to the weight of all the people in the West of Scotland! More and more of this rubbish is non-biodegradable. It is either burnt or is buried in huge areas called landfill sites. Both of these 'solutions' pollute the environment.

Think of something you have thrown away recently. Could it have been reused? Could it have been recycled? Almost certainly, yes! However to do this needs effort from the government, councils and more importantly from ourselves.

What can be recycled?

Nearly all the rubbish in a domestic bin can be recycled.

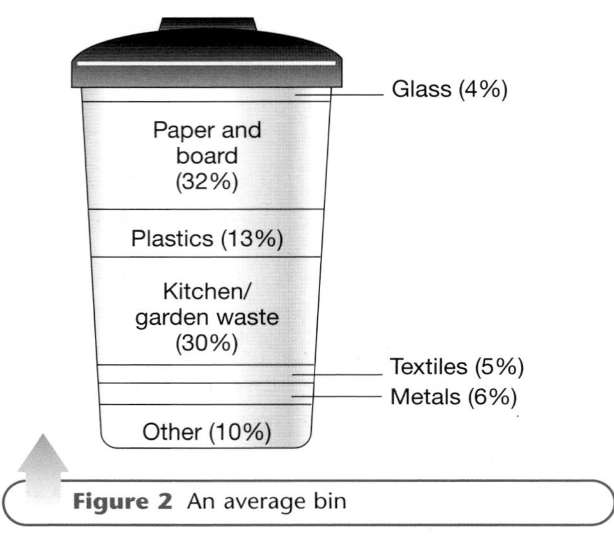

Figure 2 An average bin

You will be aware of recycling banks at the local supermarkets. These deal with bottles, paper and textiles, but what of the rubbish we create when we renew our mobile phone, computer, washing machine, fridge or car? It is estimated that there are around 90 million mobile phones lying around in homes in Britain.

Mobile phones contain many valuable materials which can be recycled and used again. They also contain very hazardous chemicals such as cadmium. If they are dumped in landfill sites then these hazardous chemicals can leak into the soil leading to toxic contamination. Many phone companies will now trade in old mobile phone handsets when a new one is purchased and will recycle the old handset.

New laws require that cars bought in and after 2006 must have an average content of 80% which can be recycled or reused.

Reduce waste

- Don't buy heavily packaged goods
- Buy loose food rather than pre-packaged
- Stop junk mail and faxes through the mailing preference service
- Cancel delivery of unwanted newspapers, donate old magazines to waiting rooms
- Use your own shopping bags or boxes. Use doorstep delivery instead of visiting the supermarket – this can use less packaging
- Grow your own vegetables – many varieties can be grown in small gardens
- Use a nappy laundry service, and save disposable ones for holidays
- Take a packed lunch to work or school in a reusable plastic container

Reuse waste

- Reuse carrier bags. Each person in the UK uses an average of 134 plastic bags per year
- Reuse scrap paper for writing notes etc.
- Reuse envelopes – stick labels over the address
- Rent or borrow items you don't use very often – e.g. party decorations and crockery. Some supermarkets hire out glasses for parties, saving on disposable cups
- Donate old computer and audio visual equipment to community groups or schools
- Buy rechargeable items
- Buy things in refillable containers e.g. washing powders
- Buy concentrated products which use less packaging
- Don't buy lots of different cleaning products for different purposes – usually the same product can be used throughout the home
- Take old clothes and books to charity shops, or have a car boot sale
- Look for long lasting (and energy efficient) appliances when buying electrical items – ensuring these are maintained will increase their lifetime
- Consider using low energy bulbs which last longer and use less energy

For more information look at:

http://www.recycle-more.co.uk/

Figure 3 This car is made from aluminium. This is more easily recyclable than steel, and is much lighter which keeps fuel consumption low

Computer **circuit boards** have contacts which are made from gold. This gold can be retrieved and reused in other circuitry if the computer is recycled.

Remember it's not enough to recycle just because we think it is good for the environment. We also have to use what we have recycled. Next time you go shopping look at the label to see if it contains recycled components.

To the left is a list of some ways to reduce rubbish.

Wordbank

Hazardous – something which can cause harm to living things

Biodegradable – material which can be recycled naturally

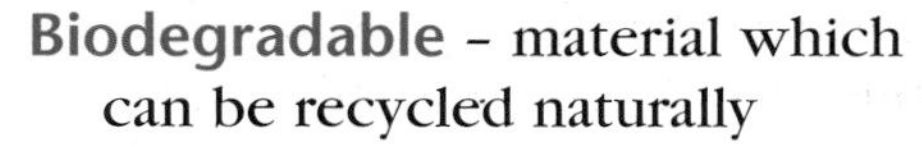

Non-biodegradable – material which cannot be recycled naturally

Circuit board – part of the electronics of modern appliances

Questions

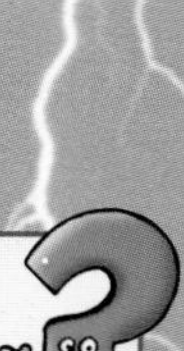

1. Why is recycling a good idea?
2. Name three things that are recycled.
3. Select a material and prepare a report on how it is recycled.
4. Select some REDUCE and REUSE suggestions for your family to employ.

40 Investigating boarding school

Trucks connect the wheels to the board allowing it to turn. Trucks can be adjusted stiff or loose by the skateboarder. **Risers** are placed between the deck and the trucks.

The deck is made from materials that must be tough and elastic. Modern boards are made from as many as seven thin layers of maple that are compressed together with glues. Once the glue has set the board is then cut and trimmed to shape. Its curved shape strengthens the board and allows skateboarders to use the nose and tail to manoeuvre the board during tricks and racing. Grip tape is placed on the surface of the board.

Figure 1 A modern skateboard

Skateboard wheels can be made of different materials such as urethane or rubber. The hardness of the materials is measured on scales that range from 0 to 100 on A, B, C and D scales. Wheels may show a hardness of 55D or 82B for example. The wheel size affects performance. They usually come in three sizes – 50, 54 or 55 mm. Wheel bearings must be durable as well as fast and smooth rolling. A scale also measures how well bearings run. The scale runs from 1 to 9. Most skateboard bearings are rated 3 or 5. Lubricants help reduce friction and enhance the performance of the skateboard. During competitions skateboarders prepare their boards to control speed and friction in order to gain as much kinetic energy as possible.

They have a lot to consider as many variables can affect their movement.

Skateboarding facts

The first ever skateboard was invented in the early 1900s.

The first skateboarding contest was held at the Pier Avenue Junior School in California in 1963. Over the next couple of years the popularity of the sport became huge.

A skateboarder was killed while skating in 1965. This led to a ban on the sport in many cities in the United States and a massive downturn in its popularity.

Advances in the technology of the deck, trucks and wheels led to safer and more manoeverable boards. In 1970, the original clay wheels were replaced with urethane wheels which had much better traction and grip.

Skateboarding is still a potentially dangerous sport. In the USA, 80 000 people a year require hospital treatement for skateboarding injuries (mainly fractures and sprains).

However, in terms of injuries, the sport remains much safer than football, rollerblading or hockey.

Despite safety concerns, the popularity of skateboarding endures because it is so much fun to do and watch.

Here are some of the amazing feats performed by skateboarders:

- The world record jump off a ramp with a skateboard is over 17 metres.
- The skateboard speed record is currently 62.55 mph.
- The highest air on a skateboard was a 5.56 m method air off a 6 m quarterpipe.
- The most mid-air skateboard rotations possible is two and a half. The '900' (as in 900° spin) is regarded as one of the hardest skateboarding tricks. So far, Tony Hawk is the first and only person to have achieved it in competition.

Questions

1. Identify 15 variables in skateboard design from the information given on these pages.
2. You are asked to investigate the factors affecting the speed of a skateboard rolling down a hill.
   Explain how you would investigate the effect that the weight of a skateboard would have on its speed at the bottom of the hill.

3. Make a list of the equipment you will need to carry out the investigation.
4. How will you set up the equipment?
5. What will you measure?
6. What will you control?
7. How will you record and present the results?
   If possible, carry out the investigation and make a report of your findings.
8. What has the investigation shown you? (Conclusion)
9. If you carried it out again, would you change anything? (Evaluation)

Remember

★ Skateboard design involves a great deal of science and technology

★ Many variables are included in everyday objects

Microorganisms are useful!

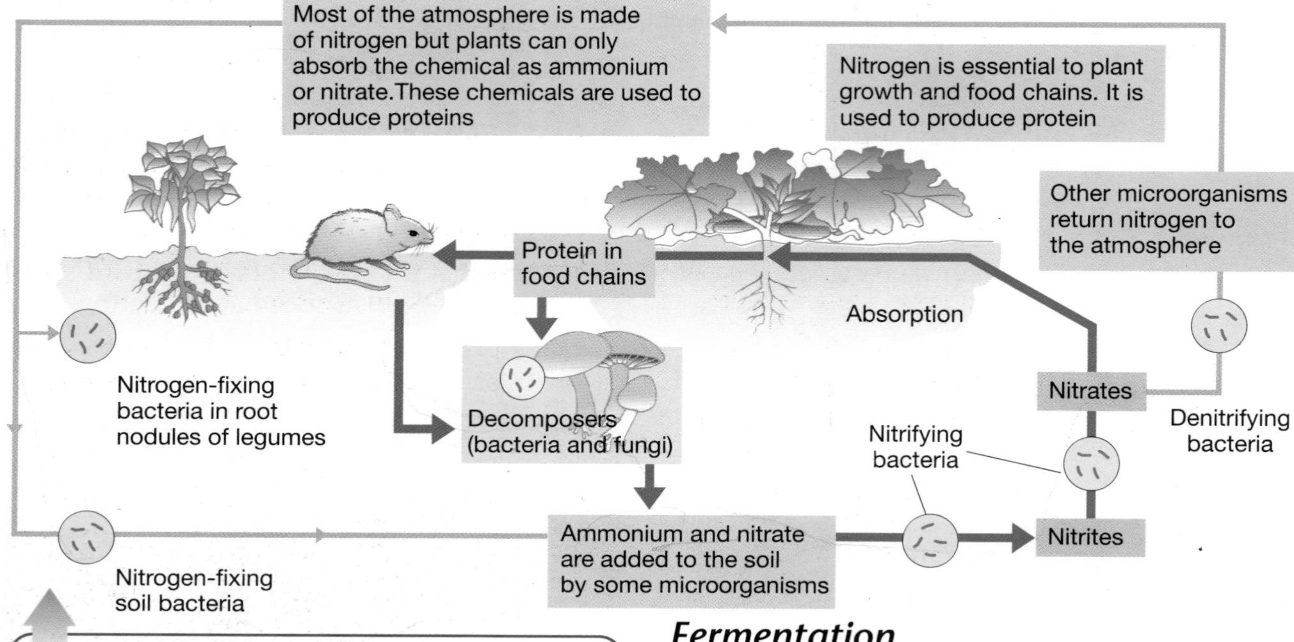

Figure 1 The nitrogen cycle

Microorganisms can exist as **bacteria**, **protists** or **fungi**. These microorganisms can have positive effects in the environment and to mankind. Microorganisms carry out essential recycling in the environment – the processes of decay and decomposition return useful materials, especially minerals, to the environment. Microorganisms are also useful in food production as well as the production of medicines.

Recycling in nature

The nitrogen cycle shows how microorganisms turn atmospheric nitrogen into chemical forms that will promote plant growth. It also shows how they return nitrogen to the atmosphere. All other minerals are recycled by natural processes.

Food production

Many foods are made by the action of microorganisms. It is possible that these were discovered accidentally when food became preserved by the action of certain microorganisms. Cheese and yoghurt are both milk products but they must be soured by specific microorganisms.

Fermentation

The process of fermentation produces wine and other alcoholic drinks. Yeast turns the sugar in fruit into ethyl alcohol. Carbon dioxide gas is also released. Several other chemicals can now be fermented by microorganisms to create new products.

Medicine

Antibiotics are drugs that fight infections. Antibiotics such as penicillin or streptomycin are made by fungi, bacteria and other organisms. These chemicals destroy other microorganisms. Antibiotics are used widely in the treatment of infectious diseases.

Vaccines – bacteria and viruses are used in the manufacture of vaccines for immunisation against infectious disease. Parts of the bacteria or weakened strains of the infection may be used to manufacture vaccines, which protect us from future diseases. A 'triple vaccine' gives protection against measles, mumps and rubella.

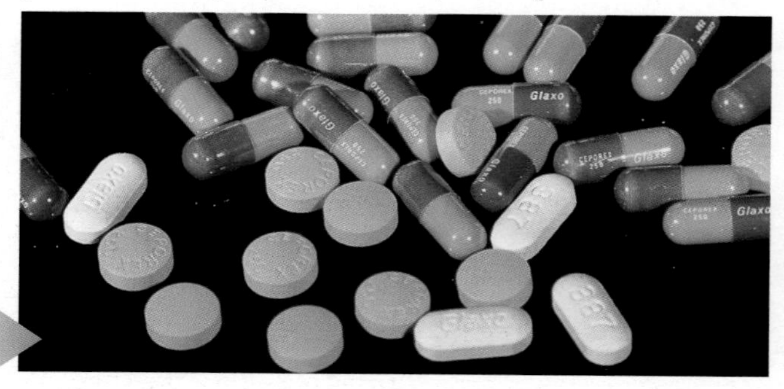

Figure 2 Oral antibiotics

Figure 3 This boy is having a tetanus booster

More than 200 years ago the English doctor Edward Jenner created the first successful vaccination, against smallpox. The last natural case of smallpox occurred in Somalia in 1977. Vaccines are now available against many diseases such as diphtheria, whooping cough, tetanus, typhoid fever and cholera. Vaccines are being developed against other **pathogens** such as **HIV**.

Antibiotics and immunisation against infectious disease are developments that have increased the life expectancy of individuals in developed countries.

Scientific research

Strain 0157 of ***E. coli*** is notorious as a food-poisoning bacterium. Other strains of *E. coli* are also grown in scientific laboratories all over the world; it is one of the best understood of all living things. Scientists have been able to conduct experiments with *E. coli* and gain a clearer understanding of living processes. Many microorganisms are studied in research laboratories, because they are easy to grow. They can also provide an alternative to using animals in research.

Modern approaches including genetic modifications of organisms (GMO) involve microorganisms.

Figure 4 A genetically modified crop ready for harvesting

Key ideas

- ★ Bacteria are useful to mankind and the environment
- ★ All nutrient cycles and therefore life depends on microbial action
- ★ Mankind makes many uses of microorganisms

Wordbank

Bacteria, protists, fungi – microorganisms

Antibiotics – drugs that fight infections

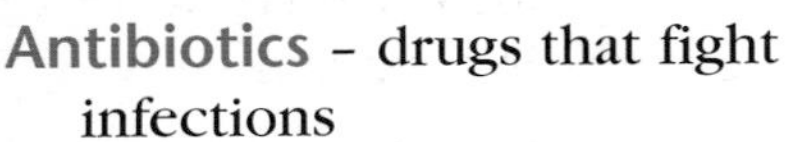

Vaccines – bacteria, viruses or their parts which protect us from future diseases

Pathogens – disease causing microorganisms

HIV – **H**uman **I**mmunodeficiency **V**irus is a virus that causes AIDS by infecting the human immune system

E. coli – a bacterium widely used in research

Questions

1 Name the three main groups of microorganism.

2 Write word equations to show three changes that bacteria carry out in the nitrogen cycle.

3 **Group activity** – prepare and present a four minute talk on one of the following:

- Microorganisms and food production
- Microorganisms and medicine production
- Microorganisms and scientific research

42 Microorganisms can be harmful!

A disease is a **pathological** condition often caused by infection with microorganisms. Diseases are identified by signs or symptoms, for example red spots in measles, stiff joints and a running nose in influenza ('flu'), and so on.

Some microorganisms are **parasites**. They can feed, grow and reproduce inside or on the surface of our bodies and cause disease. Microorganisms can infect all other living things.

Microorganisms cause many human diseases. Some release toxins, poisons that can cause fever or sickness, and others grow and multiply inside humans. A pathogen is a microorganism that causes a disease in the plant or animal it infects. Pathogens come from every group of microorganisms – bacteria, fungi and protists.

Viruses are described as perfect parasites. They use our cells to meet their needs and even use our cells to make new viruses!

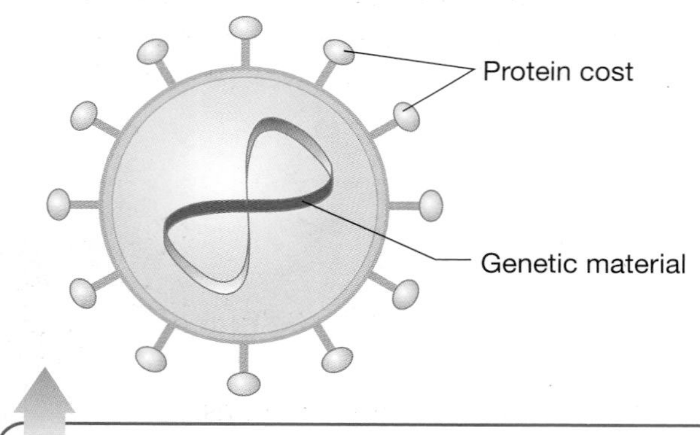

Figure 1 A virus is a parasite

Health and hygiene – prevention is better than the cure

Parasitic microorganisms can grow and multiply on or inside our bodies. We take many measures to avoid these parasites causing infection on the surface of our bodies. Washing our clothing and bodies prevents many infections. Cleaning our teeth regularly also removes the bacteria that cause dental decay and as a result those bacteria are unable to release acid that damages the enamel on the surface of our teeth.

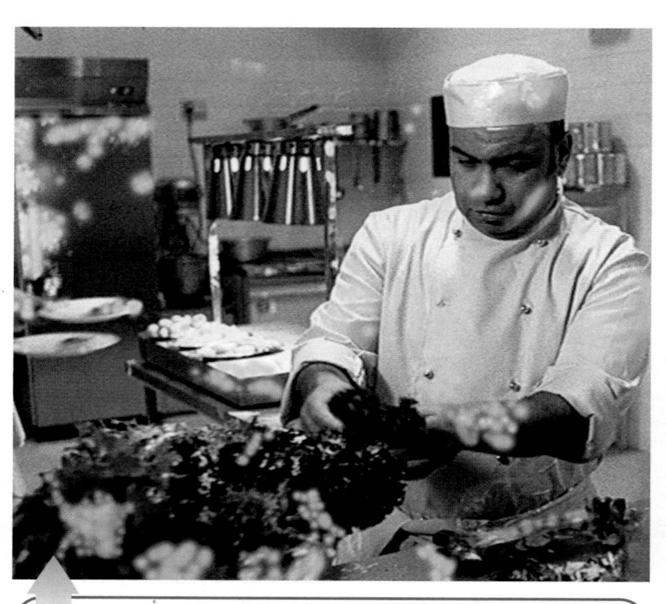

Figure 2 Food safety is everyone's responsibility

Bacterial diseases	Protist diseases	Fungal diseases
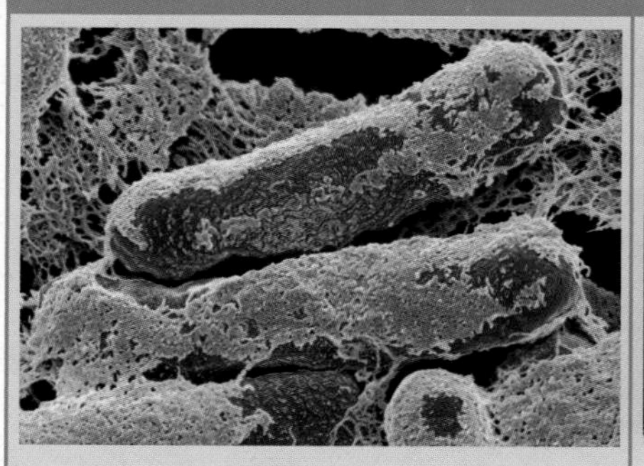	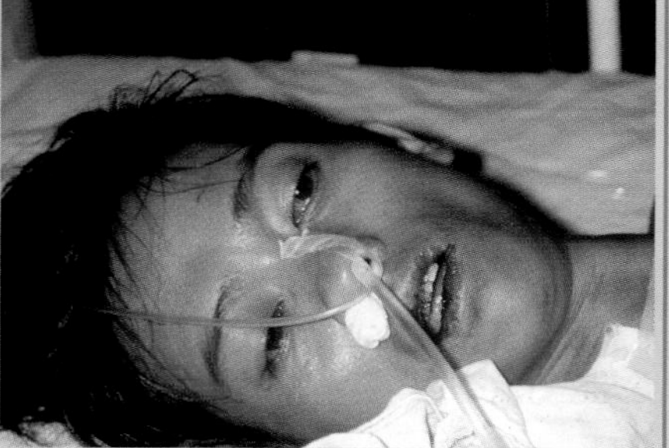	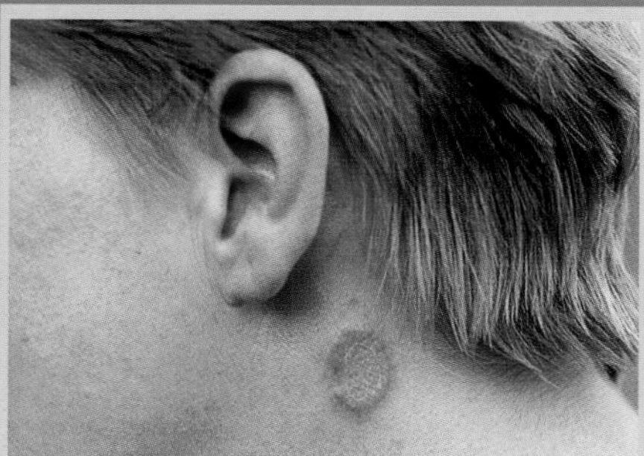
Botulism is a rare, and often fatal illness caused by a toxin released from this bacterium.	Malaria kills an African child every 30 seconds. This parasite is spread by a mosquito.	This fungal infection, ringworm, is highly contagious. Infection is often caused through contact with animals.

We could also prevent microorganisms entering our body by ensuring that food is washed and stored properly and that we are clean when we are handling food.

Wounds must always be properly cleaned so that disease-causing microorganisms may be removed and further entry should be prevented by using a sticking plaster.

The body – our defence against disease

The pathogens that cause infectious diseases are carried in food and water, through the air in coughs and sneezes, or by touching an infected person. Our bodies are so well protected against infection that it is unusual for us to become ill.

The skin is an important barrier that prevents the entry of pathogens. Mucus membranes line the mouth, nose and reproductive organs. Sticky mucus traps pathogens. The acid in our stomach also provides an additional barrier.

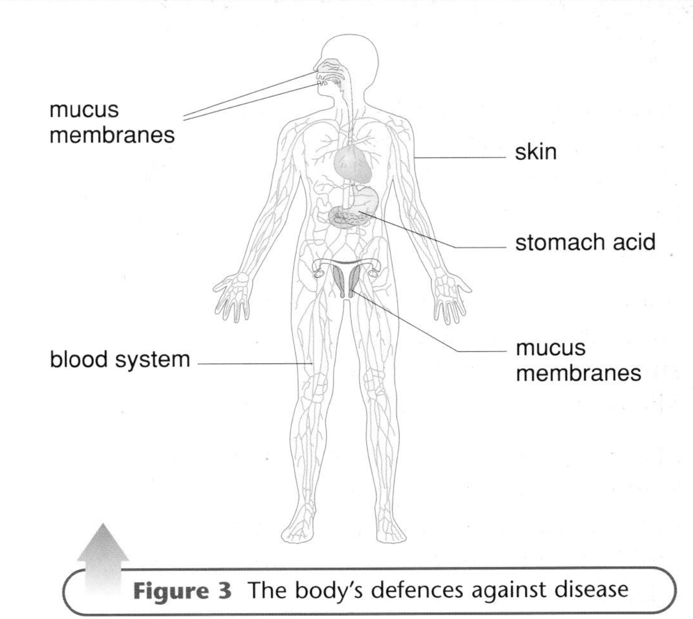

Figure 3 The body's defences against disease

When germs do get into our blood, the **immune system** recognises invading cells. **Antibodies** fight disease by 'gluing' bacteria together; white blood cells destroy them.

Fever is a high body temperature and is one symptom of infection that actually helps kill pathogens. A fever is caused by increased blood flow to the infected part of the body.

Key ideas

★ A disease is often caused by infection with microorganisms

★ Signs or symptoms identify diseases

Wordbank

Pathological – signs or symptoms that are due to disease

Parasite – an organism that grows and feeds on a different organism

Viruses – simple sub-microscopic parasites made of a core of nuclear material that is surrounded by a protein coat

Immune system – body defences that are found in the blood

Antibodies – proteins that trap foreign cells in the blood

Questions

1. List the signs or symptoms of three named infections.
2. Name two bacterial pathogens.
3. Name two protist pathogens.
4. Name two fungal pathogens.
5. Describe four ways in which we can prevent infection.
6. List four ways in which the body is protected from infection.

43 Food biotechnology

What is biotechnology?

Biotechnology is the use of living organisms, or their parts, to make a product.

Processes such as wine making or bread baking or selective breeding of plants and animals are traditional forms of biotechnology. During the second half of the 20th century, scientific discoveries on the chemical basis of inheritance (**DNA**) have allowed genetic engineering to take place. New characteristics can now be introduced to plants and animals. They are **genetically modified** (changed) by introducing genes with favourable properties from other varieties or species. This modern biotechnology is used to make foods from **GMOs** with improved flavours or nutritional properties.

Plants modified for longer shelf life

Figure 1 'Flavr-Savr' tomatoes and puree

'Flavr-Savr' tomatoes that have been genetically altered contain a gene which prevents softening. The result is that the fruit lasts longer in storage and happens to be tastier than other varieties.

Crops modified for herbicide resistance

In 1986, a herbicide-resistant soya bean was created. The advantage to the farmer is in the prevention of weeds which results in greater productivity. Environmentalists are concerned that this is increasing the use of herbicides that may build up in food chains.

Figure 2 Ripe soya crop

Yeast modified to make vegetarian cheese

Cheese production requires milk to be curdled, traditionally by an enzyme extracted from calves' stomachs. The enzyme is now produced by genetically modified yeast. The yeast has received the necessary gene to produce the enzyme.

Plants modified to produce healthy oils

Figure 3 Oilseed rape crop

Oilseed rape may be modified to improve the nutritional properties of the oil by increasing the proportions of **polyunsaturated fatty acids**. The yield of the crop is also increased.

Farmed salmon

Genetically modified salmon with increased growth rates are being developed. Environmentalists are concerned that they will escape and contaminate wild salmon populations with the altered gene.

Advantages of genetically modified foods

- Food production can be increased.
- Foods can include extra nutrients e.g. vitamins.
- Foods may carry less risk e.g. chemicals that cause cancer and heart disease, or allergens in peanuts.
- Insect and herbicide resistance improves crop yields.

Disadvantages of genetically modified foods

- Genetically modified species might contaminate wild populations.
- GMOs may introduce new food allergens e.g. peanut allergy.
- The inclusion of 'marker genes' which demonstrate resistance to antibiotics could result in resistance being passed on to humans.
- Pesticides might build up in food chains.

Regulation of GMOs

Foods are regulated in the United Kingdom by the Foods Standards Agency which protects people's health and the interests of consumers in relation to food. No evidence is available to indicate that GMOs are detrimental to food quality. Similarly, no evidence has been provided to indicate any greater antibiotic resistance.

Genetically modified foods are an issue of significant public debate.

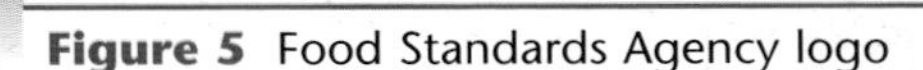

Figure 5 Food Standards Agency logo

Key ideas

★ Mankind uses and changes living things to manufacture products
★ Selective crop and animal breeding has been used traditionally
★ Modern biotechnology allows genetic modification of species
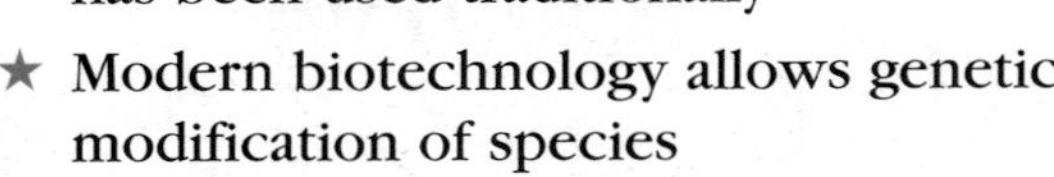
★ Several products are available
★ Advantages and disadvantages of GMOs are debated in public

Wordbank

Biotechnology – the use of living organisms, or their parts, to make a product

DNA – the chemical, contained in the cell nucleus, that contains all the genes

Genetic modification – introducing new genes into an organism to provide new characteristics

GMOs – genetically modified organisms

Polyunsaturated fatty acids – chemicals contained within oils that result in lower rates of heart disease

Questions

1. List four examples of 'traditional' biotechnology.
2. List four examples of 'modern' biotechnology that involve GMOs.
3. Prepare a note to summarise the examples of GMOs given in this chapter.

44 Medical biotechnology

Cloning technology

Much of modern biotechnology depends on **gene cloning**. Many applications are now possible – in food and medical biotechnology, waste management, agricultural and environmental uses.

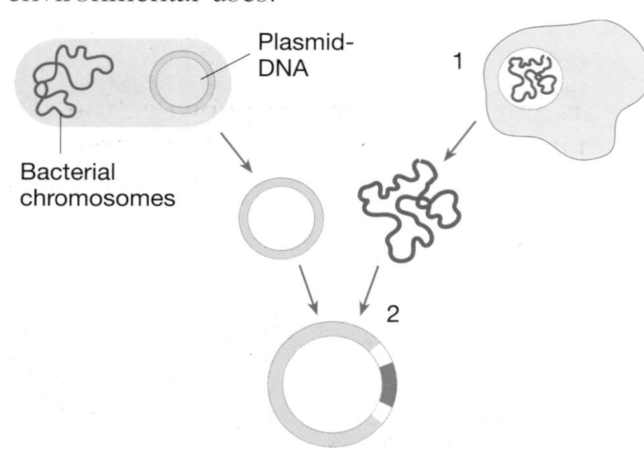

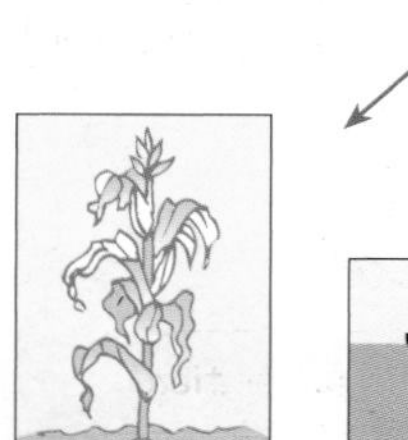

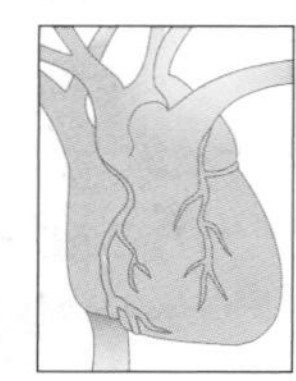

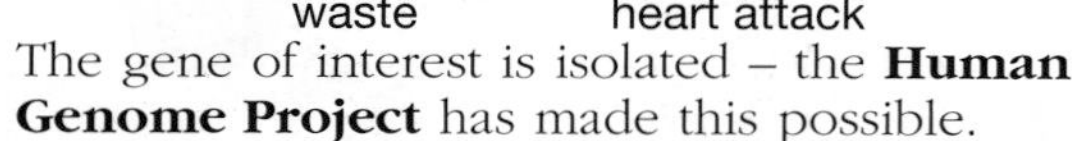

1. The gene of interest is isolated – the **Human Genome Project** has made this possible.
2. The gene is inserted into a bacterial chromosome and these multiply.
3. The copied gene can be inserted into another organism.
4. Or the protein that the gene makes is extracted and purified.

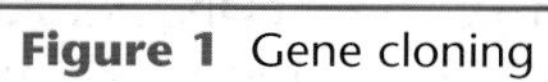

Figure 1 Gene cloning

The medical uses of biotechnology include the **diagnosis** and treatment of inherited diseases.

Diagnosis

HIV is present in the blood of infected people at extremely low levels. Advanced techniques are used to amplify the DNA in HIV to allow detection.

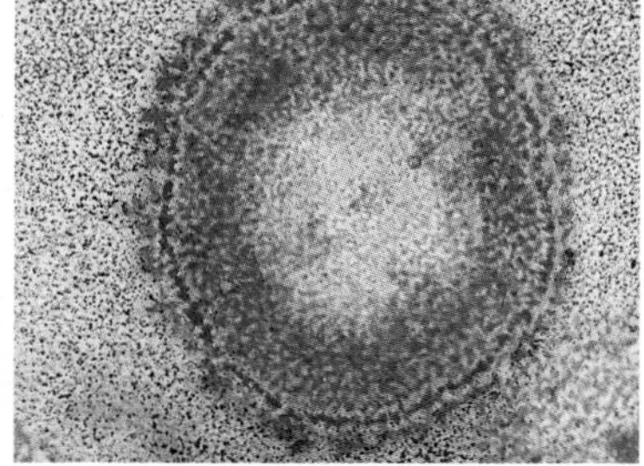

Figure 2 The HIV virus

PKU is a rare, inherited disease that affects the way that our body processes protein. All babies are screened for this at birth. PKU must be carried by both parents to be passed on. Genetic tests to detect the gene are now available.

Probes are sequences of known genes and they are used to search for a specific disease, for example cystic fibrosis.

Treatment

Gene therapy

Scientists hope to insert genes into cells affected by genetic disorders.

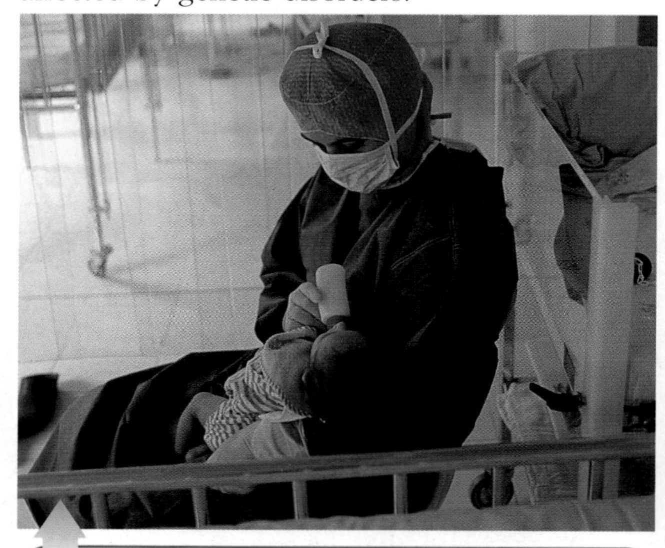

Figure 3 This baby suffers from congenital immunodeficiency and must be kept in a sterile environment. Treatments for this disorder include gene therapy. Genes may be inserted into sex cells, the embryo or bone marrow

One possibility is to genetically engineer the parents' sex cells or even to engineer the unborn embryo. The most promising method might be to insert the gene into bone marrow cells and then clone them. It is hoped that these cells will continue to grow once injected into the bone marrow and function throughout the patient's life.

Pharmaceutics – new medicines

Gene cloning in bacteria, yeast or other microorganisms can be used to produce large volumes of protein which can be used for medical purposes.

Diabetes is a disease where a hormone called insulin, made in the pancreas, is no longer produced. Diabetics have been traditionally treated with pig or beef insulin. Human insulin is made by gene cloning techniques in yeast. The insulin is identical to the natural molecule.

Heart attacks are caused by blood clots. These blood clots can be removed by a genetically engineered protein. This enzyme helps to prevent further heart attacks.

Vaccines are used to protect us from many diseases by stimulating the **immune system**. They are made from weakened pathogens or their parts. Genetic engineering approaches are being used to create new vaccines against diseases. Scientists are trying to engineer vaccines against HIV and some forms of cancer.

Ethical and moral considerations – who decides?

Genetic engineering, gene cloning and the technology that is associated with DNA manipulation has given scientists the potential to create new medicines, varieties of plants and animals as well as creating new species that could not otherwise have existed.

This is an area of significant public debate. Scientists alone cannot decide these important issues – other people and parliament must help make the decisions.

Figure 4 Biotechnology is an area of public debate

Key ideas

- ★ Biotechnology has important medical applications
- ★ New biotechnology is an important area of public debate

Questions

1. Write a note that describes the four stages of gene cloning.
2. Describe three possible approaches involving gene therapy.
3. Compare two viewpoints on the ethical and moral views on modern biotechnology.
4. Research modern biotechnology further and write a letter to your MSP expressing your conclusions.

Wordbank

Gene cloning – copying a DNA sequence by genetic engineering

Human Genome Project – an international plan to determine the complete human genome (DNA in each chromosome) sequence that was 90% accurate by 2000

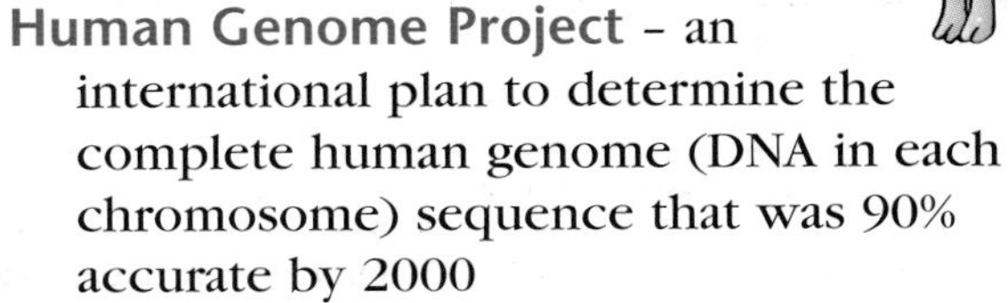

Diagnosis – recognizing a disease from its signs or symptoms

Immune system – system that protects the body from infection. It involves white cells, antibodies and the immune response

45 DNA, chromosomes and genes

Genetics is the study of inheritance. Genetic scientists are most interested in the chromosomes that are sometimes visible in the nucleus. Chromosomes are made from proteins and chemicals called nucleic acids. Chromosomes are visible during cell division and can vary in size and shape. They are normally found in pairs. Human cells have 23 pairs of chromosomes whereas a fruit fly has only 4 pairs of chromosomes.

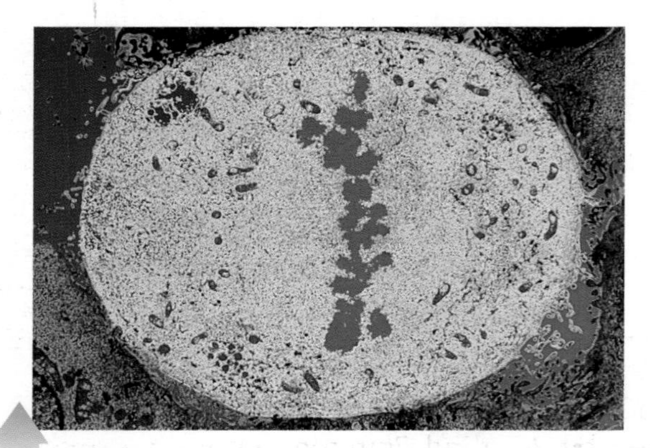

Figure 1 Human chromosomes are visible during cell division. In this photo they appear red, lined up along the centre of the cell

Specialists examine displays of the chromosomes called a **karyotype**. This is useful in searching for particular inherited abnormalities.

Here is the number of chromosomes in some other living things.

lettuce	9 pairs
tomato	12 pairs
alligator	16 pairs
potato	24 pairs
goat	30 pairs
chicken	39 pairs
king crab	104 pairs

Chromosomes and genes

Genetic information is contained in the **genes**. This controls the development of the new organism. Chromosomes contain a sequence of genes. Each gene carries the code for a protein. The proteins control the way that the body appears, for example blue eyes, or the way it works, for example to release an enzyme to digest glucose.

The genes are always found in exactly the same position along the length of a particular chromosome. This sequence allows a genetic map to be drawn.

The Human Genome Project (HGP)

This involved international cooperation to map every human gene on the 23 chromosomes. One benefit of the HGP is that treatment of inherited diseases may be possible in the future. Started in 1990 and expected to last 15 years the results of the HGP were released in 2000. The human **genome** contains around 30 000 genes.

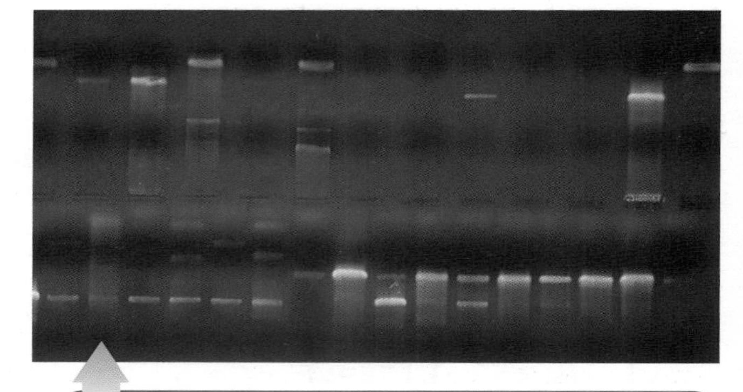

Figure 2 A DNA profile or 'genetic fingerprint'

Scientists are able to work out the sequence of **DNA** within the genes.

DNA

The discovery of the structure of DNA has led to our present understanding of how inheritance works. The structure of this complicated chemical **D**eoxyribo **N**ucleic **A**cid (DNA) was first proposed by Watson and Crick, American and English scientists working at Cambridge University in 1953. DNA is a special type of chemical molecule because its structure can be copied. It is this ability to copy itself that allows a cell to make copies of its chromosomes and then split into two new cells. Each new cell is an exact copy of the original cell. All of the cells have an identical DNA and have identical chromosomes.

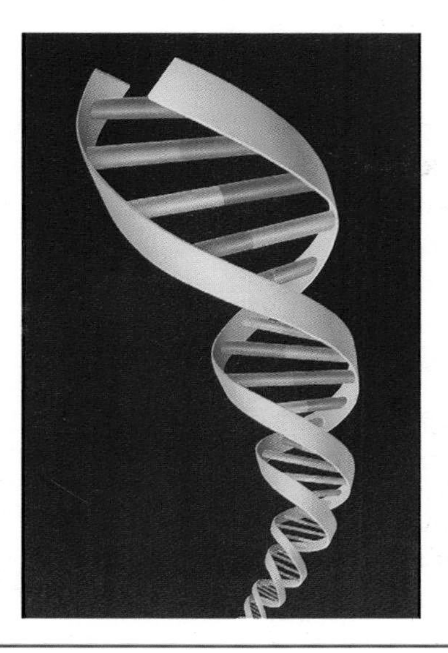

Figure 3 DNA double helix

A DNA molecule looks a little like a ladder consisting of two backbone strands linked together. The two strands twist around each other with the cross links holding the two strands in position.

James Watson, Francis Crick and Maurice Wilkins shared a Nobel Prize for Medicine in 1962 for the discovery of the structure of DNA.

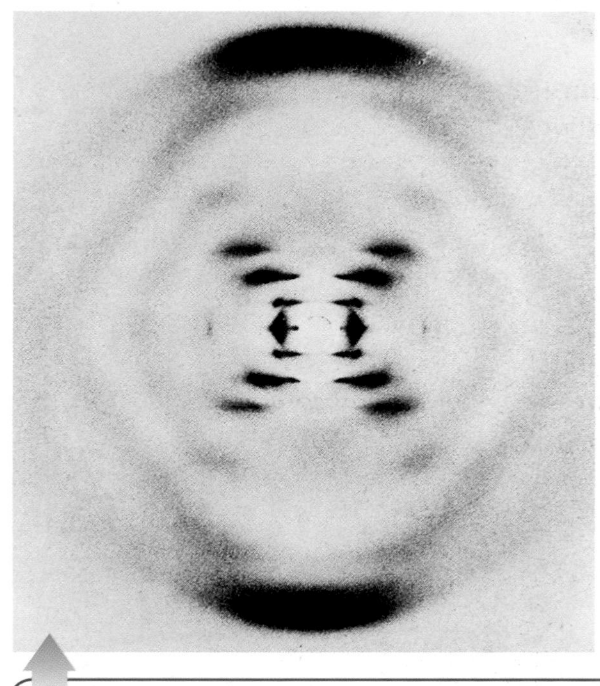

Figure 4 X-ray diffraction photograph of DNA

This photograph supplied evidence that the structure of DNA was a helix (spiral). It was taken by Rosalind Franklin, whose research was used without her knowledge or permission. Do you think that she deserved a share of the Nobel Prize?

Key ideas

- ★ Chromosomes occur in pairs
- ★ Chromosomes are composed of DNA
- ★ DNA can make copies of itself
- ★ Genes are sections of the DNA
- ★ The same genes are found at the same position on the same chromosomes of other members of the same species

Questions

1. What is genetics?
2. How many chromosomes are found in a human karyotype?
3. Who discovered the structure of DNA?

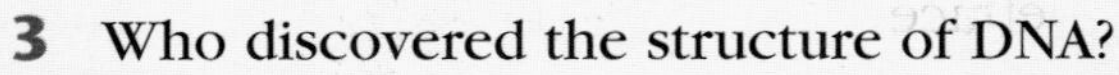

4. How long has it taken to complete the gene map for humans?
5. Find out how many genes have been identified for chromosome Number 1. (You may have to use the WWW to retrieve this information.)

Wordbank

Genetics – the study of inheritance

Karyotype – a display of an organism's chromosomes

Gene – a section of information from the chromosomes which controls a characteristic

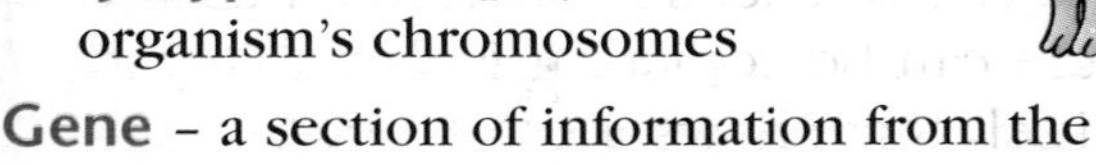

Genome – all the DNA in an organism

DNA – special type of nucleic acid

46 Inheritance

Inheritance involves passing genetic information from one generation to the next. We receive our **genes** from our parents – one set of chromosomes from each one.

Our genetic information is contained within the DNA of 46 paired chromosomes. Each chromosome pair carries information for the same characteristics – the genes. Chromosome pairs carry information from each parent for each gene.

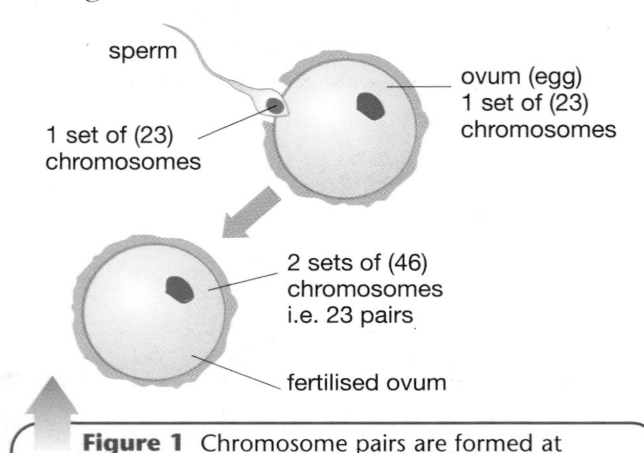

Figure 1 Chromosome pairs are formed at fertilisation

Each parent contributes a single set of chromosomes. Therefore the new organism contains two complete sets of genes, one set from each parent. These genes will determine the characteristics of each new offspring.

Sometimes characteristics can appear in different forms, for example eye colour may be blue or brown. Genes code for these different forms. In the gene for hair colour it is possible to have information for different colours of hair, and some colours are more likely to be expressed than some other colours.

Figure 2 Hair colour is inherited from your parents. Variation is possible

Hair colour is an inherited characteristic. Since each parent is brown haired we know that they carry the information for brown hair on at least one of the chromosomes that contains the gene for hair colour. Since they have a red haired child but are not red haired themselves we can **infer** three things:

- The gene for hair colour appears in different forms.
- Since the son has inherited red hair from the parents they must carry that gene.
- The form of the gene for brown hair is in some way 'stronger' than the form of the gene for red hair.

In this way much of our appearance is determined at the point of fertilisation. The gene, which is passed on from each parent, depends on chance. This is why you might have many characteristics which are the same as your brother and sister but you may have others that are different.

Selective breeding

Throughout history farmers have exploited the genetic difference of livestock and crop species to develop varieties that more fully meet consumer needs. Evidence of domesticated cattle may go back 10 000 years. **Selective breeding** in cattle has been used to increase milk yield and these herds are different from beef breeds. Other cattle breeds were bred as 'draft' animals but have been replaced by machinery in the western world.

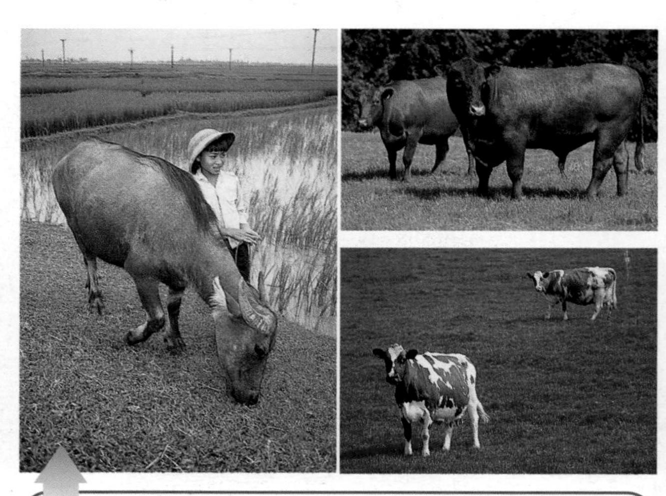

Figure 3 Cattle have been bred for draft, beef and milk purposes

Plants have also been bred to 'improve' their characteristics. Farmers have bred plants to produce a variety with desired characteristics.

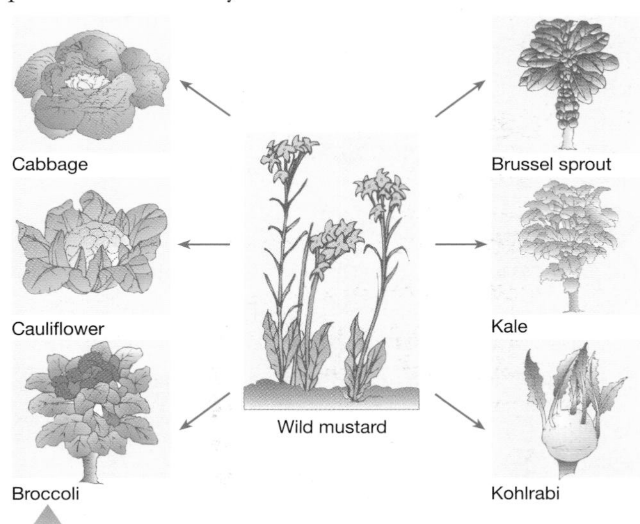

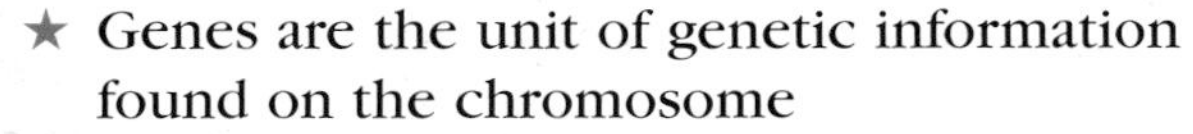

Figure 4 These plants have all been bred from a common ancestor

Genetic Engineering

Crops and livestock can now be **genetically engineered**. In its simplest form a desirable gene is transferred into another organism to provide it with the required characteristic, bringing about a change in the organism. Some plant crops such as tomatoes can have a gene inserted that brings about a longer shelf life. Some scientists have increased the size of sheep by inserting growth hormone genes into sheep embryos and this technology could also be applied to other livestock such as cattle. There are many concerns, both ethical and moral, surrounding genetic engineering.

Key ideas

- ★ The appearance of offspring depends on genetic information from both parents
- ★ Genes are the unit of genetic information found on the chromosome
- ★ The same genes are found on each chromosome pair but they can vary
- ★ Selective breeding has been used for thousands of years
- ★ Selective breeding improves varieties and breeds with particular characteristics
- ★ Genetic engineering can be used to change the information in the chromosomes of an organism

Wordbank

Inheritance – passing characteristics from one generation to the next

Gene – part of the chromosome which contains information for a characteristic of the new organism

Infer – to conclude from evidence

Selective breeding – organisms are bred with other organisms to ensure that the offspring will have specific desired characteristics

Genetic engineering – adding genes to an organism to bring about a change

Questions

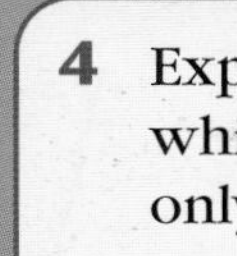

1 How many chromosomes does each human parent pass on to its offspring?

2 How many chromosomes does a newly fertilised human egg contain?

3 The form of the gene for brown hair is described by biologists as being dominant. What do you think this means?

4 Explain why a red flower fertilised with a white flower produces offspring that only have red flowers.

5 Name three animals and three plants which are the result of selective breeding by humans.

6 Suggest two advantages and two disadvantages of genetic engineering.

Adapted cells in animals

The cell is the basic unit of life. All living things are built from cells.

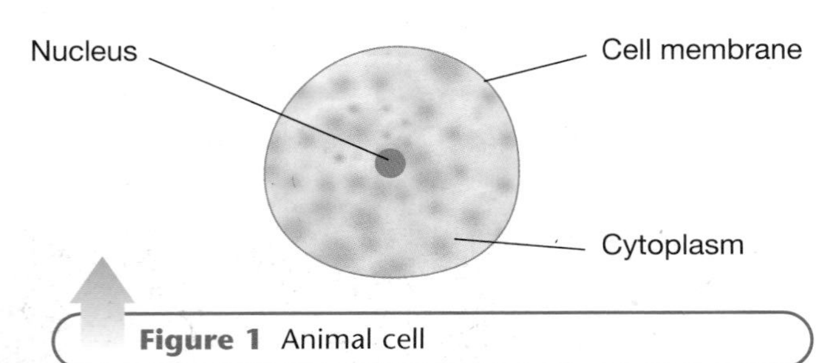

Figure 1 Animal cell

Multicellular organisms are made from many cells. These have many different jobs to do in the body and all look very different under the microscope. Similar looking cells are found in tissues. There are five main groups of tissue within the human body.

Epithelium (eppy-theel-ium) tissue

Epithelium is a special tissue which provides a lining and protective layer of cells to cover an organ surface or to line a body cavity.

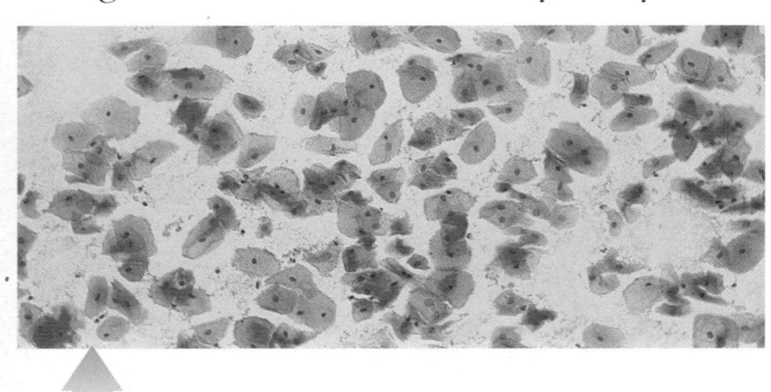

Figure 2 Epithelium tissue

The epithelium in Figure 2 is from the surface of the skin. The skin is made up of a number of layers of cells. The epithelial cells are linked with glands which secrete a variety of body fluids, for example sweat, to the surface of the body.

Connective tissue

Connective tissues support and hold parts of the body together. This group includes bone, cartilage and elastic tissues. Connective tissue in bone and cartilage help to support the body.

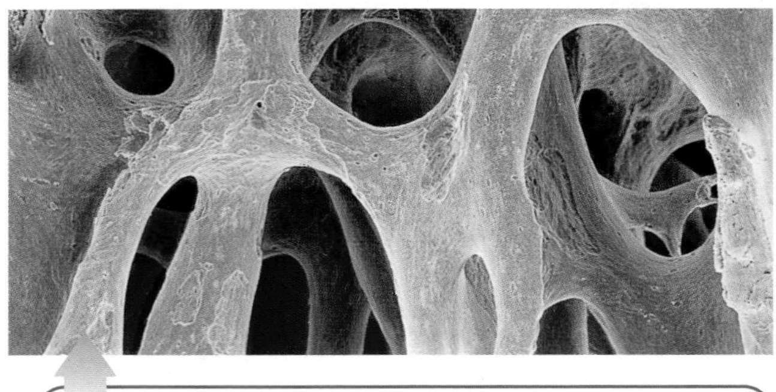

Figure 3 Bone tissue

Elastic tissue is found in tendons, ligaments and the walls of the arteries. The pulse of blood, which can be felt in arteries, is the stretching of the artery walls as the blood is pumped through.

Muscle tissue

These tissues can contract and relax to bring about movement. There are three main types of **muscle**, described in the table below.

Striated or striped muscle is mainly connected to the skeleton. This muscle is under voluntary control and quickly tires.	Smooth muscle is not under voluntary control and is found in the internal organs e.g. helping to push food through the intestines.	Cardiac muscle is not under voluntary control and makes up most of the heart. Although similar in appearance to striated muscle it does not suffer from fatigue.
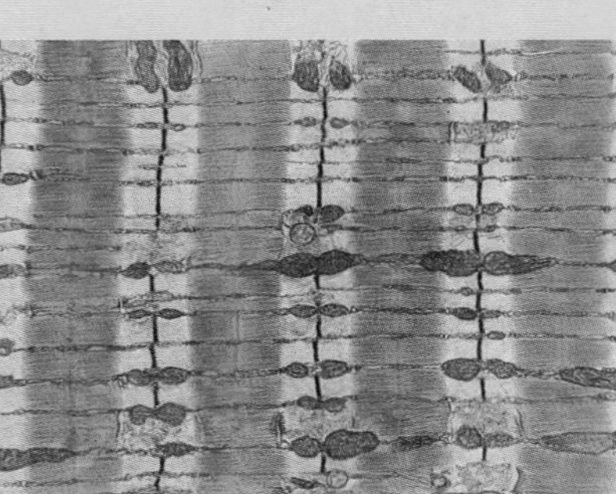	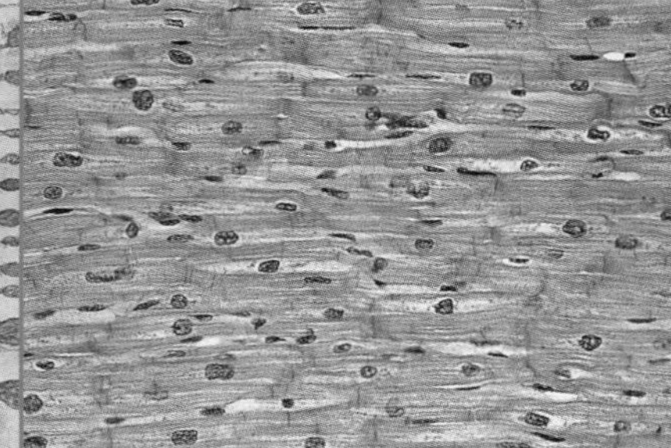	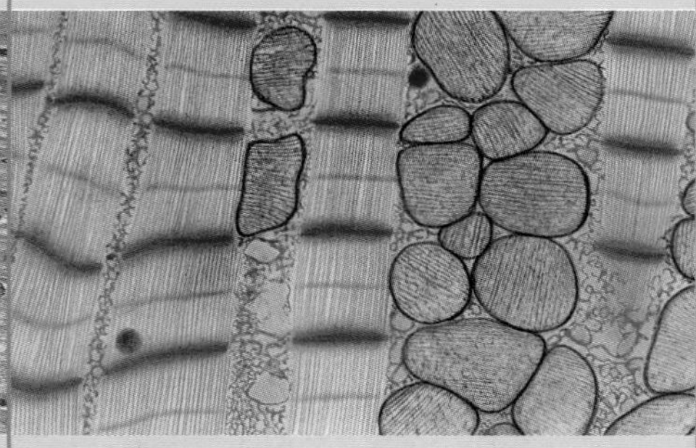
Striated muscle	Smooth muscle	Cardiac muscle

Nerve tissue

The cells connect with each other through branches called dendrites and axons. **Nerve** tissue transmits impulses to body organs such as muscles or glands.

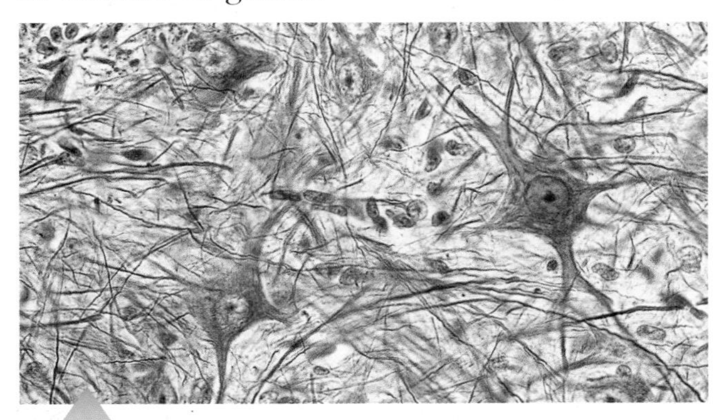

Figure 4 Nervous tissue

Fluid tissues

These include the blood and lymph, which contain specialised cells such as red blood cells and different types of white blood cells.

Red blood cells carry oxygen from the lungs to all parts of the body. They are shaped in a way that increases their ability to carry high levels of oxygen. Red blood cells are not true cells since they do not have a nucleus. White blood cells are responsible for fighting infection. They can produce special chemicals called antibodies or even eat invading bacteria.

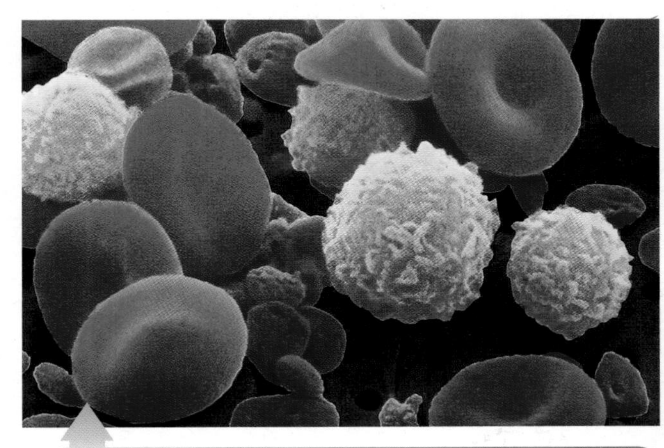

Figure 5 Blood includes several cell types

Key ideas

- ★ The cell is the basic unit of living things
- ★ Cells have different functions and appearances
- ★ Groups of cells make up tissues of which there are five main types in our bodies
- ★ These tissues make up the systems of the organism

Wordbank

Multicellular – organism composed of many cells working together

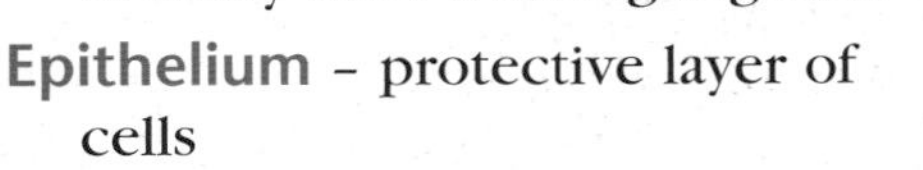

Epithelium – protective layer of cells

Connective – holds organs in place and provides support

Muscle – can bring about movement

Nerve – cells which allow communication between parts of an organism

Questions

1. What is the basic unit of all living things?
2. Name the five main groups of tissue found in the human body.
3. Make a labelled line diagram of a nerve cell.
4. In what way is the shape of red blood cells important?
5. Which type of tissue is responsible for coordination of the human body?
6. Research the characteristics of living things.

48 Adapted cells in plants and phytoplankton

Many plants exist as multicellular organisms. In multicellular plants the cells have many different appearances when viewed under the microscope. They also carry out a range of different functions.

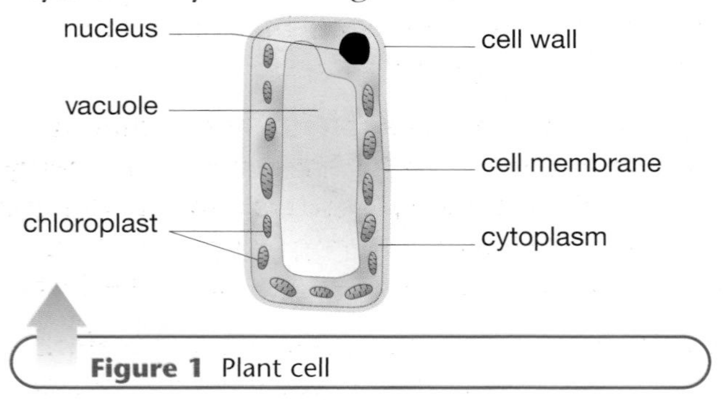

Figure 1 Plant cell

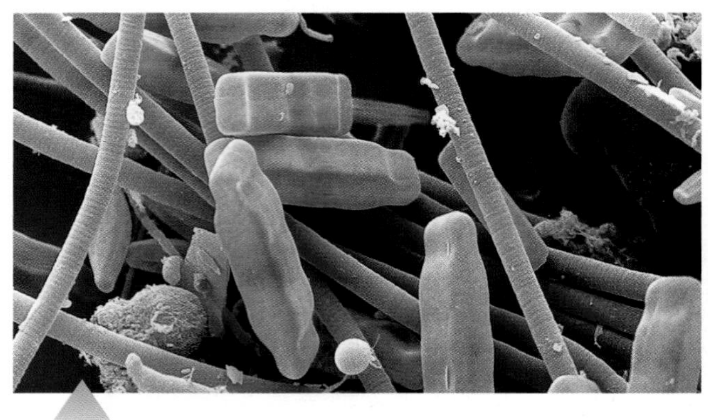

Figure 2 Variety of phytoplankton

Protista

Many protista also exist and show variety in microscopic appearance. These make up the **phytoplankton**.

The phytoplankton are important, since they carry out most photosynthesis in the world's oceans. This drives marine ecosystems as well as providing about 90% of the Earth's oxygen. Although phytoplankton appear different they must all contain the green plant pigment chlorophyll. Some phytoplankton have cell walls made from silica instead of cellulose and others are able to move.

Multicellular plants

Land plants usually include a basic structure of roots, stems and leaves. Plants cells can be specialised to perform particular functions, for example only some cells in the leaf carry out photosynthesis and only some cells in the flower are responsible for producing pollen and other reproductive cells.

Figure 3 A land plant

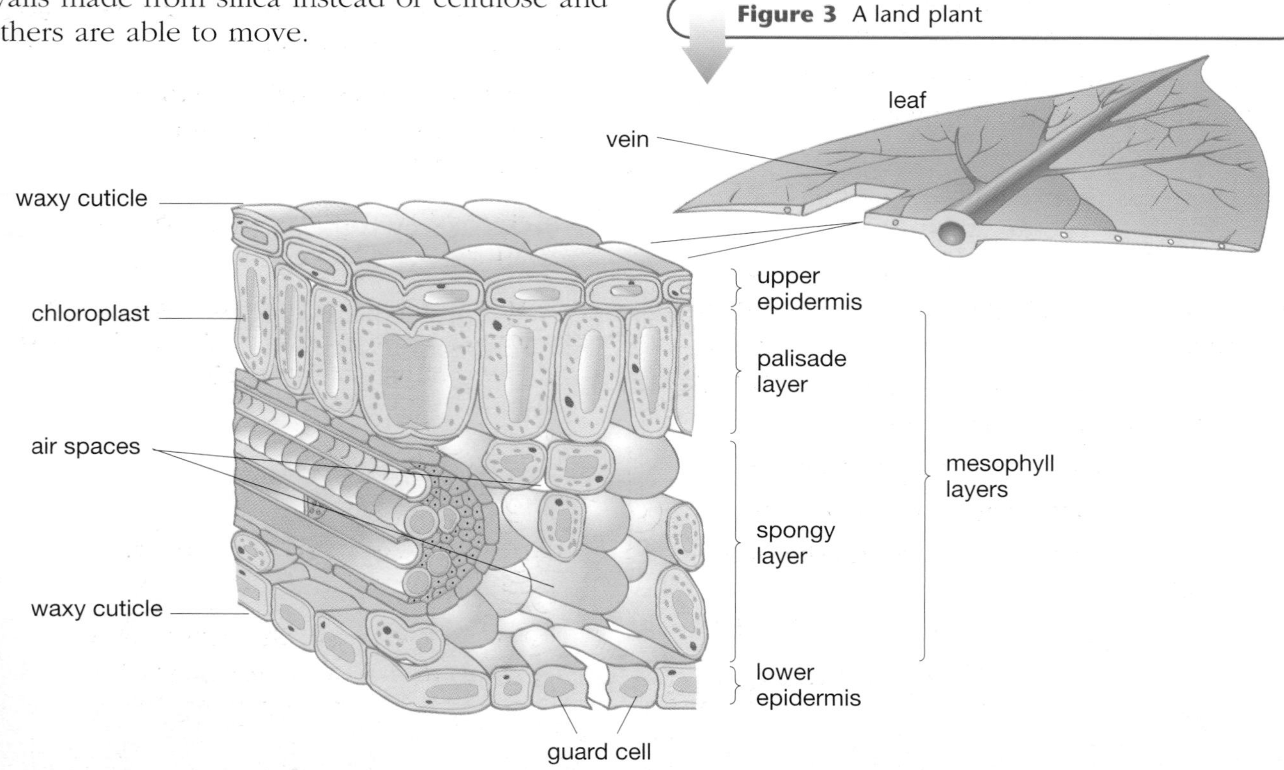

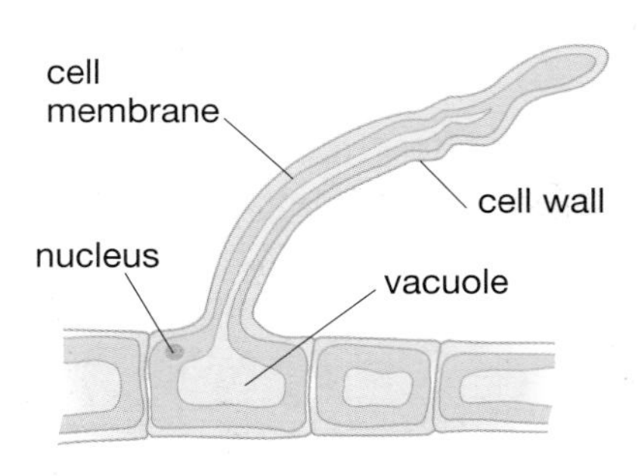

Figure 4 Many cell types are found in roots and the epidermis can appear like hairs

A cell sandwich

The leaf is really like a sandwich when you look at it through a microscope. It is designed to be thin and trap light energy – being flat with a large surface area helps this as well as allowing materials to pass quickly through the leaf.

The epidermis is coated on its outer surface with a wax layer. This waterproof cuticle ensures that water is only lost from the leaf through the pores, that are bordered with **guard cells**. These pores open and close to control the passage of oxygen and carbon dioxide in and out of the leaf. Mesophyll cells are found in the middle of the leaf and are responsible for photosynthesis.

Palisade cells are packed closely together at the top of the leaf to trap as much light energy as possible and the spongy cells trap additional energy as well as permitting oxygen, carbon dioxide and water to diffuse through the leaf.

Leaf veins include two types of cell – **xylem** cells that are really just pipes that carry water upwards from the soil, and **phloem** cells that carry sugars from the leaf and around the entire plant. Their cells have perforated ends, just like a sieve.

Key ideas

- ★ Phytoplankton is a group of unicellular protista
- ★ Multicellular plants contain root, stem, reproductive and leaf cells
- ★ Each cell type performs a different function within the organism

Wordbank

Phytoplankton – single celled protista

Root hair – specialised root cell found in multicellular plants

Xylem – specialist water transporting cells

Phloem – specialist sugar transporting cells

Guard cell – cells which surround the pores in the leaf

Questions

1 List the common factors of phytoplankton.

2 How much of the Earth's oxygen is produced by phytoplankton?

3 Explain the phrase 'drives marine ecosystems' which appeared in paragraph 3.

4 What are the four main regions of a multicellular plant?

5 Describe the appearance of each of the following plant cells by making a labelled drawing of one cell of each.

   a) root hair cell.
   b) xylem cell.
   c) phloem cell.

6 Explain the advantages to the leaf of being thin and flat.

7 What is the name of the cells which control the size of the leaf pore?

49 Cellular respiration

Cellular **respiration** is the process by which cells release energy in living things. Scientists describe one form of cellular respiration with this word equation.

glucose + oxygen ⟶ carbon dioxide + water + energy

Since it involves oxygen it is called **aerobic** respiration.

Cellular respiration takes place in animals in order to release energy from food during **digestion**. Cellular respiration also takes place in plants to release energy from stores – often in the form of starch or oil. In fact cellular respiration takes place throughout nature and in all living things whenever energy requires conversion.

Certain conditions must be met so that cells can extract the maximum quantities of energy from food. Oxygen must be present to combine with the carbon in our food. When oxygen is absent then much less energy is released. **Anaerobic** conditions reduce the efficiency of cellular respiration.

Respiration and breathing

Respiration is a chemical process that releases energy. In humans, respiration relies on the respiratory and the circulatory systems. During **breathing** muscular contractions allow air to be drawn into the lungs. Oxygen enters the bloodstream and is transported around our body in the blood for release in those tissues that need energy.

Waste products, especially carbon dioxide, must be removed from the tissues before they build up and create acid conditions. The respiratory and the circulatory systems also carry out carbon dioxide removal.

Cellular respiration takes place in the muscle cells to provide energy for movement

Digested food passes into the bloodstream from the small intestine

The carbon dioxide and water is removed in the bloodsteam

Oxygen is carried from the lungs in the circulatory system

Figure 1 Respiration releases energy

Investigating respiration in our bodies

Since we carry out respiration we can investigate it by comparing what happens to the gases in air when we breathe. The differences between **inhaled air** and **exhaled air** can be compared with the apparatus in Figure 2.

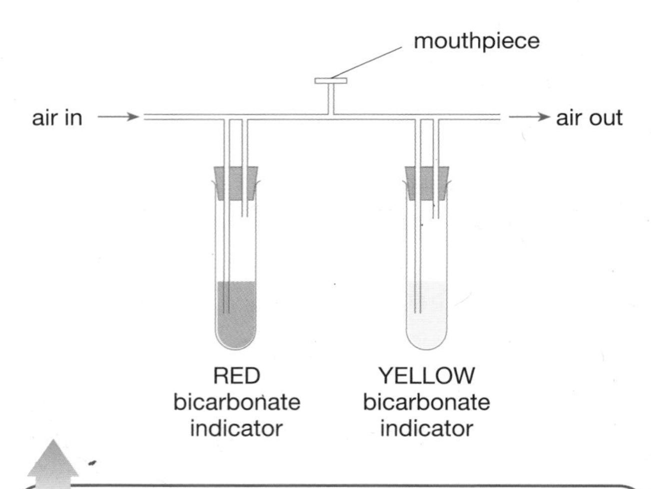

Figure 2 This apparatus compares breathed and unbreathed air. It contains a chemical which detects the presence of carbon dioxide. The red bicarbonate indicator solution turns yellow when carbon dioxide is added to it

The apparatus looked like this after a pupil had breathed in and out through the mouthpiece 10 times. Breathed and unbreathed air circulated through the apparatus and the colours changed with breathed air only. The pupil concluded that there is more carbon dioxide in exhaled air than is present in inhaled air.

In another experiment the teacher added 50 grams of **germinating** peas to a vacuum flask which contained a thermometer. The temperature was noted. After two days an increase was noted.

Pupils concluded that the food store in the peas was respired to provide the energy for growth. Some of the energy was converted to heat.

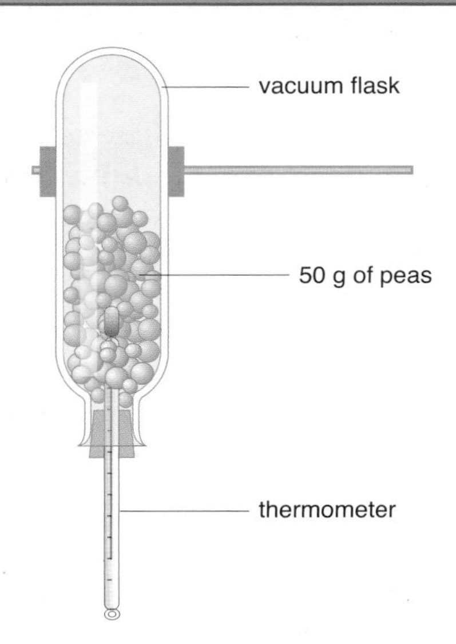

Figure 3 Germination releases energy

Key ideas

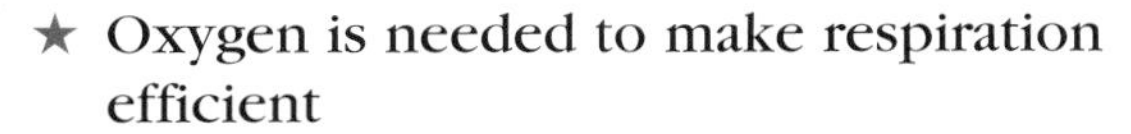

- ★ Respiration takes place in cells
- ★ Respiration releases energy from food
- ★ Oxygen is needed to make respiration efficient
- ★ Carbon dioxide and water are products of respiration
- ★ Oxygen is transported by the red blood cells from the lungs to the cells
- ★ The plasma of the blood transports glucose from the small intestine to the cells

Wordbank

Respiration – release of energy from food in cells

Aerobic – involving oxygen

Digestion – process of breaking food down into its simplest forms

Anaerobic – not involving oxygen

Breathing – process of drawing air into lungs and blowing air back out of lungs

Inhaled air – air which is drawn into the lungs

Exhaled air – air which has been in the lungs

Germinate – the first stages in growth of a seed

Questions

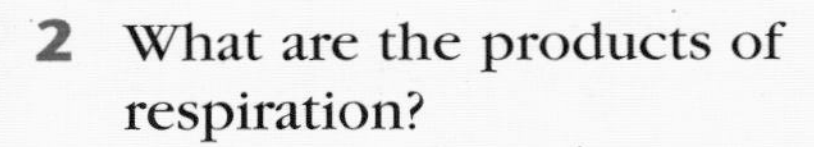

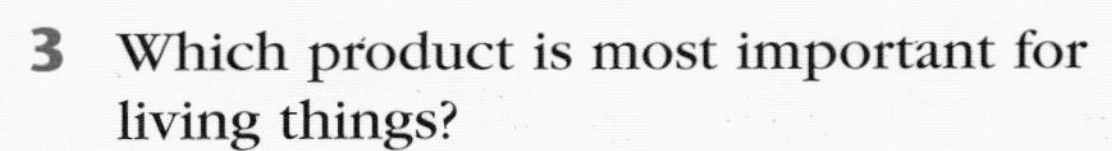

1. What are the raw materials required for respiration?
2. What are the products of respiration?
3. Which product is most important for living things?
4. Do plants carry out respiration?
5. Name the simplest form of carbohydrate food.
6. Describe the pathway of oxygen from the air in the room to an individual cell.
7. Name an indicator which detects the presence of carbon dioxide.
8. Describe the colour effect of carbon dioxide on the indicator.

50 Enzymes at work

Enzymes are chemicals that are found in all living things. Enzymes control the chemical reactions in living things. Enzymes are biological catalysts and change the rate of **biochemical** reactions. Some enzymes are important in products, for example washing powders.

Enzymes are catalysts

Catalysts are chemical substances which increase the rate of a chemical reaction. Several transition metals are catalysts. Catalysts are not changed at the end of a reaction meaning catalysts can be used again and again.

Hydrogen peroxide is a **toxic** product inside living cells. Although it normally breaks down slowly into water and oxygen a catalyst makes the reaction happen very quickly.

Figure 1 Hydrogen peroxide breaks down when catalysts are added

Enzymes are proteins

Enzymes are biological catalysts that are made from protein. Enzymes are not changed after a reaction has taken place and can be used again and again. They are however sensitive to external conditions such as temperatures and pH.

Enzymes speed up the rate of a biochemical reaction. Our liver and blood contain an enzyme that turns harmful hydrogen peroxide into water and oxygen. This enzyme, catalase, will speed up the breakdown of hydrogen peroxide into water and oxygen.

Intracellular and extracellular enzymes

Enzymes act inside (**intracellular**) or outside (**extracellular**) cells.

Intracellular enzymes control the biochemical reactions that take place during, for example, photosynthesis or respiration.

Extracellular enzymes control reactions that occur outside cells, for example in the digestive system.

A common extracellular enzyme called amylase is found in our saliva. Amylase speeds up the breakdown of starch into soluble sugars to start the process of digestion.

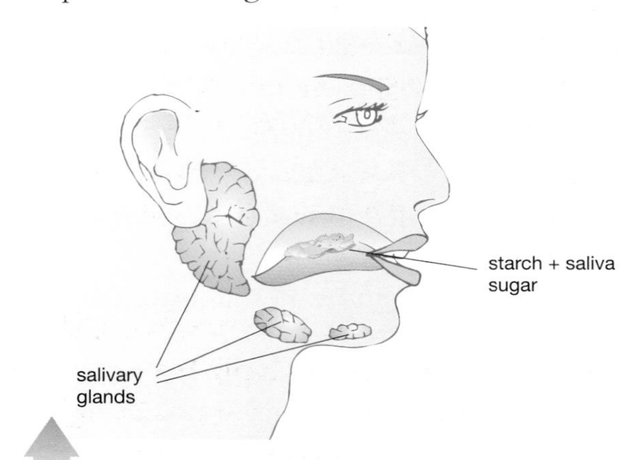

Figure 2 Food is mixed with enzymes in our mouths

Other digestive enzymes called proteases breakdown protein, and lipases breakdown lipids, fats and oils. Enzymes are easily identified by their names. They always end in -ase.

Enzymes control only one chemical reaction

Amylase has no effect on proteins and catalase will not digest starch. Each biochemical reaction is controlled by a specific enzyme. Biochemical reactions would take place very slowly without the presence of a specific enzyme. Each enzyme works by having a shape that allows the substrate, the substance to be changed, to fit into the enzyme's shape just like a key fitting into a lock. They combine for a moment, the reaction takes place and the products are released.

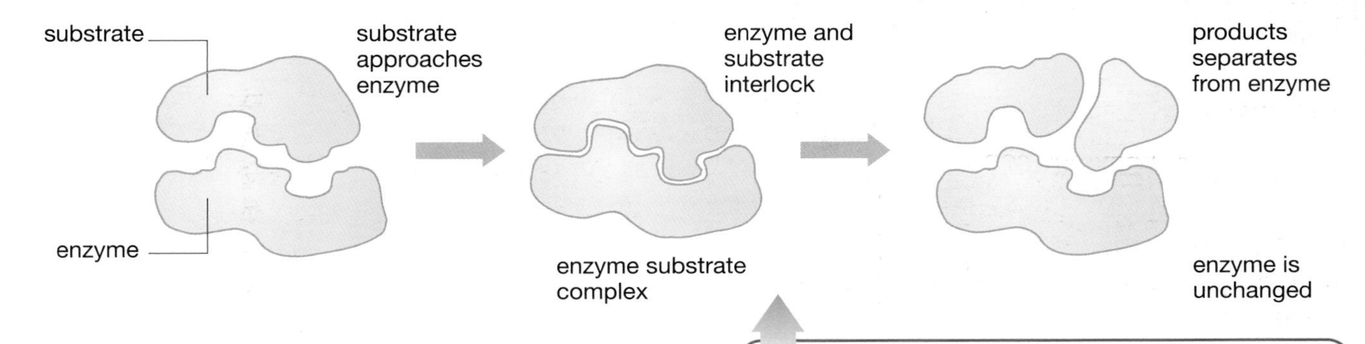

Figure 3 An enzyme controlled reaction

Industrial uses of enzymes

Chemical reactions in living things are catalysed by enzymes. Some enzymes are extracted from animal tissues for example, rennin for cheese production or plant tissues such as papain for use as a meat tenderiser. Microorganisms in industrial tanks called fermenters now make many enzymes. Genetically modified microorganisms are used to prepare the enzymes which are then purified and used in a range of processes.

Biological detergents contain enzymes that digest fat, starch, cellulose and protein stains.

The food industry uses enzymes. They clot milk to help make cheese and are also used in fruit juice production. Whisky production depends on enzymes converting starch to glucose and then into alcohol.

The clothing industry uses enzymes to prepare fabrics and to remove unwanted materials from leather.

Scientific research uses enzymes as they are specific to one substrate. The Human Genome Project and the production of new medicines all depend on enzymes.

Key ideas

- ★ Enzymes are biological catalysts
- ★ Enzymes are proteins
- ★ Intracellular and extracellular enzymes are found in our body
- ★ Enzymes control only one reaction
- ★ Their names always end in the suffix -ase
- ★ Enzymes speed up a biochemical reaction

Questions

1. Explain the role of enzymes in biochemical reactions.
2. How would you prove that the gas released by the breakdown of hydrogen peroxide is oxygen?
3. Why is it possible for an enzyme to be used again and again?
4. Using the words enzyme, substrate and product, describe which enzyme:
   a) converts starch into sugar?
   b) digests protein?
5. Construct a table to display the properties of enzymes.

Wordbank

Enzymes – proteins found in living things which catalyse biochemical reactions

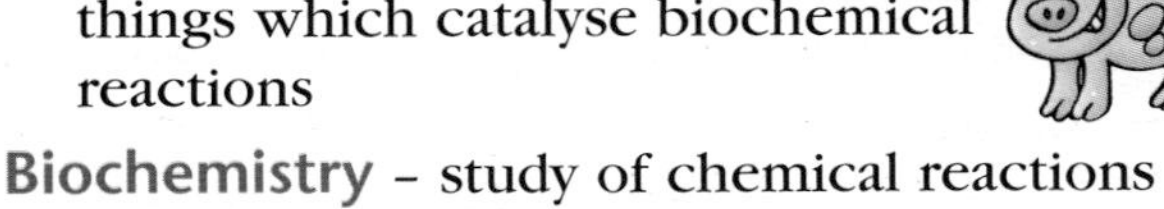

Biochemistry – study of chemical reactions that take place inside living things

Catalysts – chemical substance which changes the speed of a chemical reaction

Toxic – poisonous substance

Intracellular – within cells

Extracellular – outside cells

Influencing enzymes

Enzymes are protein catalysts that are found in all living cells. Enzymes control biochemical reactions, allowing metabolism to take place. Enzymes act on specific **substrates** according to their shape. The substrate molecule combines with the enzyme for a moment and speeds up the reaction to make a **product**. Enzymes are not used up or changed at the end of the reaction and are used time and again.

$$\text{substrate} \xrightarrow{\textit{Enzyme}} \text{product(s)}$$

e.g. $$\text{hydrogen peroxide} \xrightarrow{\textit{Catalase}} \text{water} + \text{oxygen}$$

Enzymes are sensitive to external conditions. They work best in conditions that exist in the cells or organs where they are used.

Enzymes are sensitive to temperature

Sara and Rita investigated liver catalase and varied the temperature.

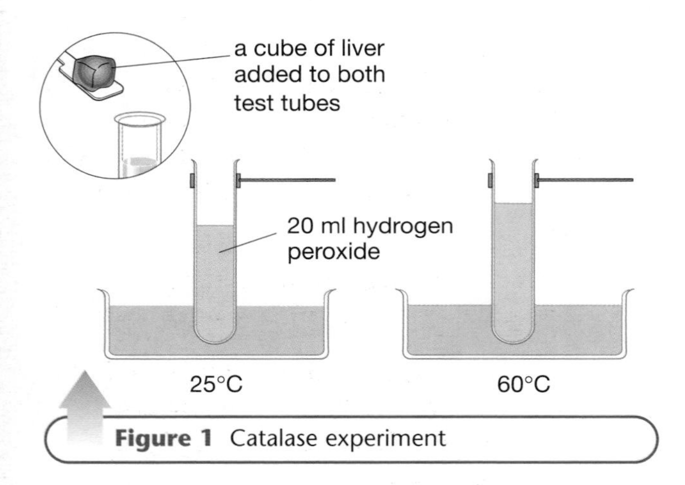

Figure 1 Catalase experiment

When the reaction took place, foam collected. The height of the foam was measured after 5 minutes.

Sara and Rita concluded that catalase was sensitive to temperature. This is because the liver catalase changed shape at 60°C and was unable to break down the hydrogen peroxide. The enzyme's shape has been permanently changed and will no longer act on the substrate. High temperatures **denature** enzymes, and all other proteins.

A further investigation by the class at varied temperatures of between 0°C and 50°C allowed the pupils to produce the following graph.

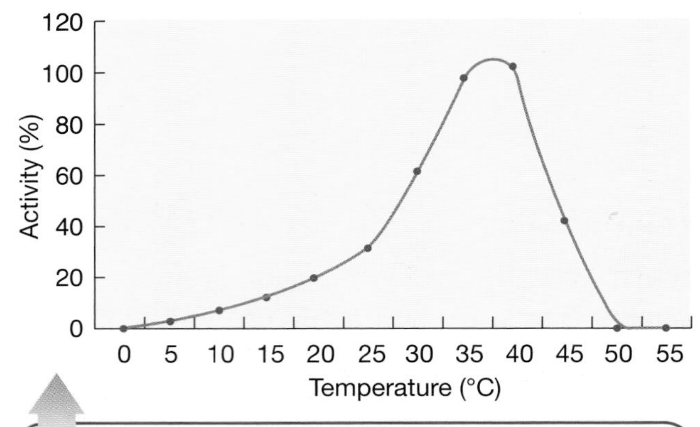

Figure 2 There is a gradual increase in activity from 0°C up to the optimum 40°C and it rapidly drops to zero beyond the optimum termperature

Explanation

As the temperature rises the rate of the reaction increases due to the extra energy available. The temperature at which that highest activity takes place is known as the **optimum** temperature.

Above this temperature the reaction rate falls. This is due to the protein structure of the enzyme being changed and eventually denatured.

This shape of graph is often found with human enzymes and they show an optimum temperature of 37°C – the same as body temperature.

Enzymes are sensitive to pH

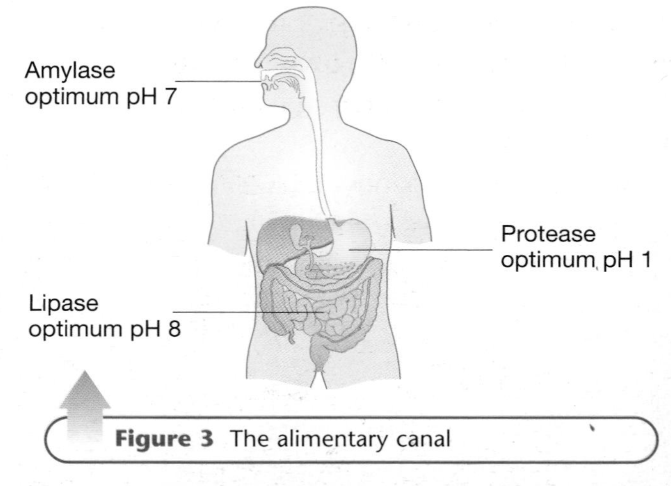

Figure 3 The alimentary canal

Investigating pH and enzymes

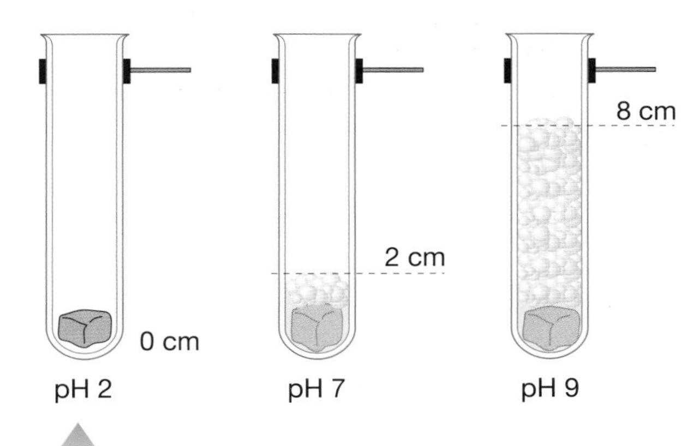

Figure 4 Investigating pH and enzymes

Catalase investigations were carried out, but this time the pH was varied. Here is what happened.

The students concluded that catalase works best in alkaline conditions. It has an optimum pH value of pH 9.

Enzymes are sensitive to temperature and pH as well as a range of other conditions that can change in cells. Several poisons work by destroying enzymes.

Key ideas

- ★ Enzymes are biological catalysts
- ★ Enzymes can be used again and again
- ★ Different enzymes work best in different conditions
- ★ Enzymes are sensitive to temperature and pH
- ★ Denatured enzymes are no longer active

Wordbank

Substrate – the substance which is changed in a chemical reaction

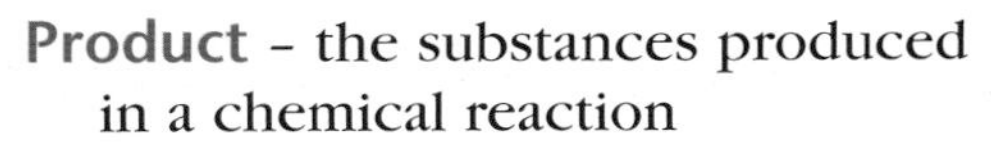

Product – the substances produced in a chemical reaction

Denatured – no longer carrying out natural activity, destroyed due to change

Optimum – condition of highest enzyme activity

Questions

1 Write a paragraph that summarises the reactions of catalase on hydrogen peroxide. Use the following terms: catalyst, enzyme, hydrogen peroxide, optimum, oxygen, product, substrate, and water.

2 At the beginning of an experiment a scientist measured that there were 20 000 molecules of enzyme present. How many molecules will be present by the end of the reaction? Explain your answer.

3 What is the optimum temperature of human enzymes? Explain your answer.

4 In the investigation into catalase and pH the students concluded that catalase has an optimum pH value of pH 9. Evaluate their conclusion.

5 Explain why denatured enzymes can no longer work.

6 Where in your body would you expect to find:

a) lipase enzyme?
b) carbohydrase enzyme?
c) protease enzyme?

Ecological energetics

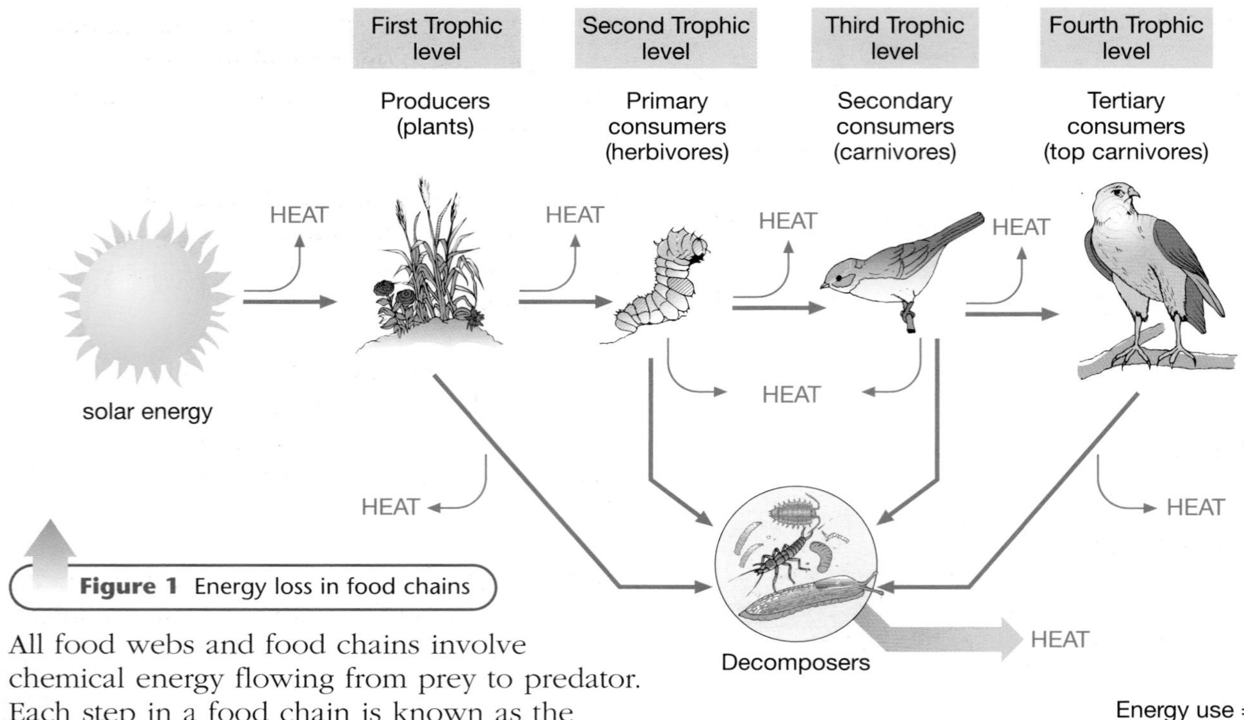

Figure 1 Energy loss in food chains

All food webs and food chains involve chemical energy flowing from prey to predator. Each step in a food chain is known as the **trophic level**. Scientists study **biomass**, the dry material at each step since water contributes no energy.

Here are some rules of food chains:

- Each trophic level in a food chain contains a certain biomass.
- Energy is lost to the environment at each stage in a food chain.
- This loss is usually as heat but some of it will be lost as undigested food.
- Only a small portion (usually no more than 10%) of food is converted into biomass.
- Much less energy is available at the next trophic level.

Scientists are able to measure the energy use and energy loss at every step in a food chain. The energy is measured in Joules. Scientists calculate the energy value of the food eaten, the energy used by the organism, as well as the energy lost as waste.

In nature the losses at each step can vary from 80% to 95%. It depends on the situation. For example Scottish farmers keep cattle inside during the cold winter months. This means that the cattle use less energy to keep warm and will use more energy for milk and meat production. Less energy will be lost to the environment from the cattle.

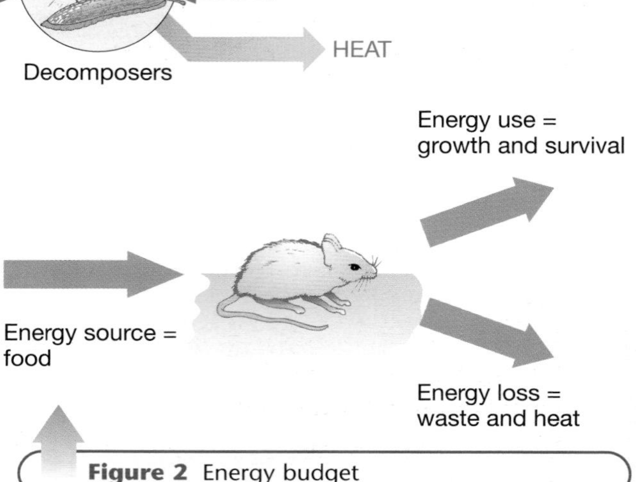

Figure 2 Energy budget

The pyramid of biomass

Since energy is lost at each step of a food chain, the biomass at each trophic level is less than the energy in the one before.

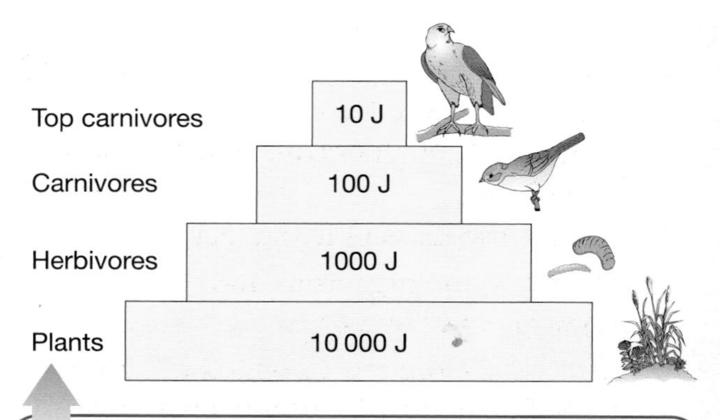

Figure 3 The pyramid of biomass shows the energy contained at each level

Productivity

Ecosystems are all different. They can be different in many physical ways as well as having different organisms living there. Some are warm and others are cold; some are wet and others are dry. The **productivity** of the ecosystems can be compared. Look at the following table for some average comparisons of different ecosystems.

Ecosystem	Average productivity ($kJ/m^2/yr$
desert	630
continental shelf	6 720
temperate grassland	10 080
agricultural land	12 600
temperate forest	26 880
tropical rain forest	36 960

The productivity of a habitat depends on its physical conditions. Productivity is an indication of the extent to which that habitat can support life. Low rainfall in a desert prevents plant growth and therefore it cannot support extensive biomass.

The oceans around the continental shelf are far more productive than the deep sea since nutrients are recycled instead of being lost to the deep ocean floor.

Fertilisers increase the productivity of agricultural land. Temperature is a major factor in productivity and is the main difference between, for example, temperate and tropical rainforest.

Scientific agriculture modifies the environment to increase productivity, for example draining wet areas or irrigating dry areas.

Key ideas

- ★ Energy flow can be calculated at each step in a food chain
- ★ Energy losses are large at each step in a food chain
- ★ The pyramid of biomass appears in every food chain
- ★ An ecosystem's productivity depends on its physical conditions

Questions

1. Explain why biomass is calculated in dry weight rather than fresh weight.
2. Make a table to show energy loss and energy gain within food chains.
3. Explain why the average productivity is measured in kilojoules per square metre per year ($kJ/m^2/yr$).
4. Explain each of the following:
   a) productivity in a desert.
   b) the differences between the productivity of agricultural land and temperate grasslands.
   c) the differences between the productivity of temperate and tropical forests.

Wordbank

Trophic level – the feeding or energy level of an organism in a food chain

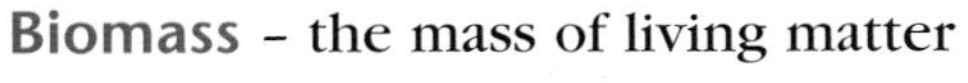

Biomass – the mass of living matter

Ecosystem – the organisms and their physical environment

Productivity – the rate at which the energy of the Sun is used by producers to make food for consumers

53 Darwin and his theory

Evolution

In 1859 Charles Darwin opened one of the greatest debates in the history of science. In his book, *On the Origin of the Species*, he asked questions about variation and how living things had changed over time. His **theory** of **natural selection** was used to explain the processes. He believed natural selection was a process that allowed only some animals and plants to survive when small climatic changes take place. When they then breed, those characteristics for survival are passed on to their offspring.

Who was Charles Darwin?

Charles Darwin was born in Shrewsbury where his father was a doctor who had married the wealthy daughter of the founder of the Wedgwood Pottery.

When he was 16 he travelled to study medicine at Edinburgh University but was horrified at the surgical practices that took place without the use of anaesthetics. In 1828 he transferred to Cambridge University to study for the ministry but became interested in, and later graduated in, zoology and geology.

Wealthy young gentlemen of that period often took the opportunity to take a 'Grand Tour' and Darwin travelled around the world on HMS Beagle from December 1831 until October 1836. During this trip Darwin was a companion to the ship's captain Fitzroy as well as being an unpaid naturalist.

Throughout the voyage Darwin was amazed at the variety of life that he found – whether it was in the South American rainforest, or the fossils on the plains of Patagonia and high in the Andes. He also found extraordinary biological diversity in the Galapagos Islands and made a large collection during this voyage.

Many scientists accept Darwin's theory of natural selection today. More **evidence** for evolution is appearing, for example with the gradual rises in air temperature due to global warming. Butterfly species are moving north as the climate gets warmer. Those butterflies have larger flight muscles and these are being passed on to their offspring, who can then fly longer and further.

Figure 2 Species are evolving

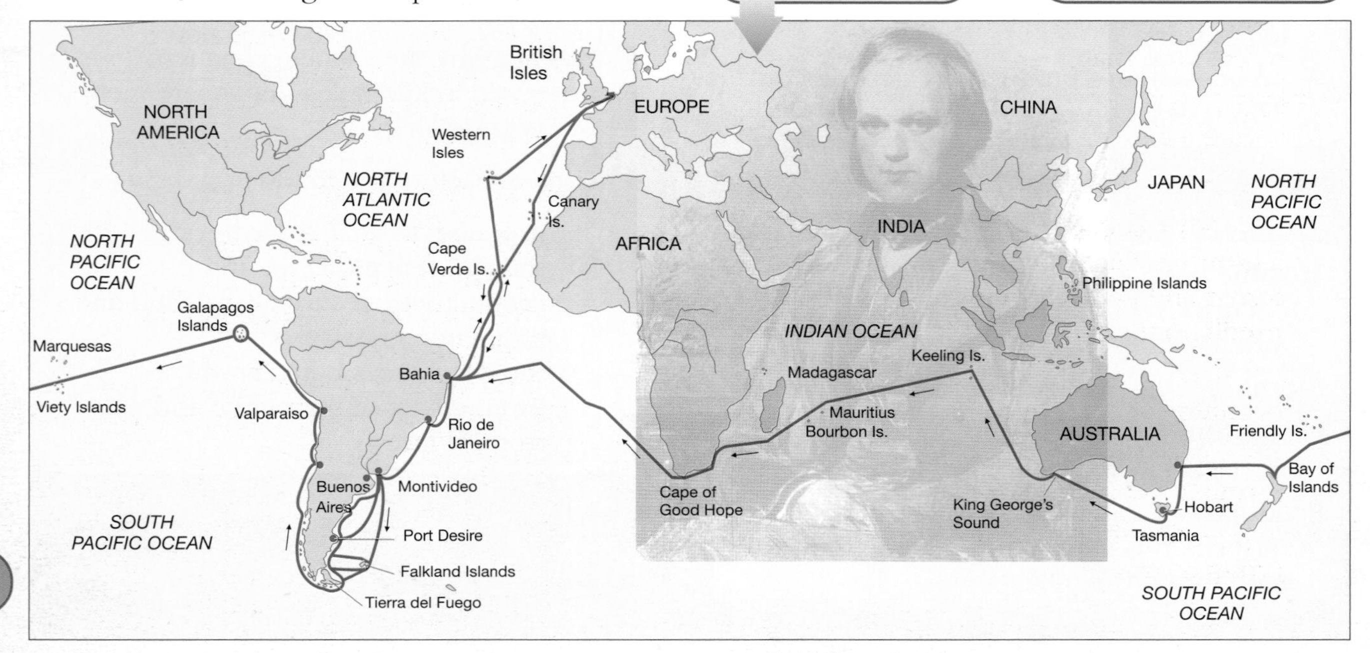

Figure 1 HMS Beagle's route

Darwin's ideas – evolution by natural selection

Charles Darwin and Alfred Wallace each developed similar ideas about evolution. They believed time and natural selection were responsible for the appearance of new species as well as the disappearance of old ones. When the dinosaurs 'ruled the Earth' for example, mammals were insignificant tree dwellers.

> *This preservation of favourable individual differences and variations, and the destruction of those which are injurious, I have called Natural Selection, or the Survival of the Fittest.*
>
> (Charles Darwin, *On the Origin of the Species*, Chapter 4)

Creation

The publication of Darwin's theory led to the **beliefs** of many faiths being challenged.

Many people believe in creation which explains how God brought the world into existence. The Old Testament describes creation as having taken place in seven days.

Across the world there are probably about 500 different creation stories to draw from – all different – but many followers of that faith believe them.

Many scientists accept Darwin's theory and are also able to believe in a particular faith. Nobody knows for sure who is correct – those who accept Charles Darwin's theories of evolution or those who believe in creation.

It is important however that all scientists accept and respect the ideas and beliefs of others.

Key ideas

- ★ Darwin explained evolution as taking place over a long period and that natural selection involved the adaptation of living things to environmental change
- ★ Darwin's theory was based largely on observations and evidence collected during a five year voyage on HMS Beagle
- ★ Evidence continues to support Darwin's theories
- ★ Some people only believe the explanation of creation that is given in the Bible

Wordbank

Theory – principles used to explain a group of facts, theories may be tested and be used to make predictions

Natural selection – the process of evolution according to Darwin's theory

Evidence – objects or data helpful in forming a conclusion

Beliefs – ideas believed or accepted by a group as true

Questions

1 What was the name of the book that contained Darwin's theory of evolution?

2 Explain the process of natural selection by placing the following statements in the correct order:

- the environment changes
- following generations survive
- organisms that do not adapt will not survive
- characteristics are passed on to successive generations
- animals and plants adapt
- organisms that adapt will survive

3 Find out more about:

- the voyage on the Beagle
- Alfred Russell Wallace
- learning about evolution in the United States
- creation *vs* evolution

54 Natural selection

Darwin's theory of **natural selection** is used to explain evolution. Natural selection includes five main ideas.

1 Natural selection happens to populations and not to individuals. Individuals pass their **genes** to their offspring. Genes pass on the design that allows the individual to survive changing conditions in the environment.

Figure 1 Natural selection involves populations

2 Natural selection takes time. The process is gradual and it takes many generations to result in the appearance of a new species. The changes that take place in the environment have tended to take hundreds or even thousands of years. Natural selection enables populations to change.

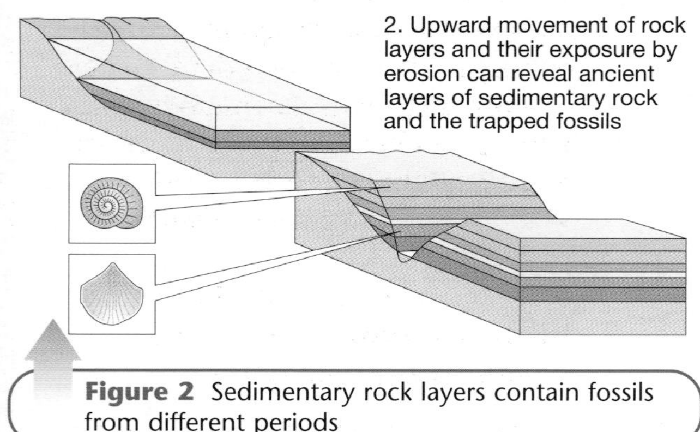

Figure 2 Sedimentary rock layers contain fossils from different periods

3 Natural selection requires success in breeding. Charles Darwin recognised that the success of an organism's reproduction and the size of the population was controlled by the resources available in the environment. Such resources include food, water and a place to live.

4 Natural selection depends on the interaction between the environment and variation within a population. Every population includes a large variety of characteristics. The environment displays seasonal change. However the environment also displays lasting change over long periods – geological time. Much of Scotland was covered with ice until quite recently – about 10 000 years ago.

The plants and animals that survived during the Ice Ages were quite different from those we find today. Favourable characteristics are passed on to the next generation when breeding takes place.

Figure 3 Characteristics of these woolly mammoths have been passed on to their modern day descendants

5 Natural selection results in the adaptation of populations of organisms to new conditions in the environment. As the environment changes only the survivors will be able to breed. They will pass their genes on to their offspring. These genes include the properties required for their survival in the altered environment. New forms of genes appear by **mutation**.

Individuals who have an advantage in their environment (e.g. defend a larger territory) are likely to leave more offspring. This increases the chance of passing on that gene to their offspring.

Figure 4 New varieties of foxgloves appear all the time – mutant white ones are now quite common in Scotland

An example of natural selection

Figure 5 Two spotted ladybirds

You might have found some unusual ladybirds – they are mainly black instead of red. These two spotted ladybirds can appear in several different forms. The most noticeable difference is that some are darker in colour. Three bits of evidence suggest that natural selection is taking place.

Observation	Explanation
Population studies have shown a decrease in the numbers of dark ladybirds in areas with low air pollution	Dark ladybirds are better camouflaged in polluted areas
Laboratory experiments have shown dark ladybirds warm up faster and have higher body temperatures and activity levels when they are heated with a light	Dark ladybirds can compete better in cold environments
Dark ladybirds tend to reproduce earlier	Dark ladybird populations may grow more rapidly

Key ideas

- ★ Natural selection is the mechanism by which evolution takes place
- ★ Natural selection acts on populations, depends on variation, and results in adaptation of populations

Wordbank

Natural selection – the process of evolution according to Darwin's theory

Genes – the unit of inheritance that determines a particular characteristic in an organism

Mutation – a change that creates a new genetic character or trait

Questions

1 Copy and complete each of the following statements by selecting the correct word or phrase:

a) Natural selection happens to *individuals/populations*.

b) Natural selection is a *gradual/sudden* process that takes place over a *short/long* time period.

c) Natural selection *depends on/does not depend on* the breeding success of individuals with favourable genes.

d) These favourable characteristics are passed on *when breeding takes place/when the environment changes*.

e) Natural selection results in *adaptation/evolution* to new environmental conditions.

2 Comment on the evidence given in the example of the two spotted ladybirds as an example of evolution taking place.

3 Find out more about:

a) Melanic moths

b) Galapagos finches

c) Ice Age mammals

Evolution, looking for evidence

Darwin's theory of natural selection suggests that species of living things have 'descended' from common ancestors. Many species have become extinct, for example dinosaurs and trilobites. Others will evolve in the future.

Darwin's finches

When Darwin visited the Galapagos Islands during his voyage on HMS Beagle he observed variation in the appearance of the 13 species of finches that are found in this island group. Although they are a similar size and colour, the main differences are in the size and shape of the beaks.

Figure 1 A vegetarian and a warbler finch, just two of the thirteen species on the Galapagos Islands

This volcanic island group appeared between 5 and 9 million years ago. According to Darwin's theory an ancestor arrived on the Islands and selection and adaptation has taken place so that the various species of finches can now be found.

Several groups of animals and plants are being studied on the Galapagos Islands. They are a 'laboratory for evolution' and there are several ways of looking for evidence of evolution.

Fossil studies

Fossils are the remains of living things that existed in a past geological age. They are usually found in rocks and only the hard parts of the organism remain such as teeth, bones, leaf skeletons, shells and insect wings. Fossils are often found in sedimentary rock.

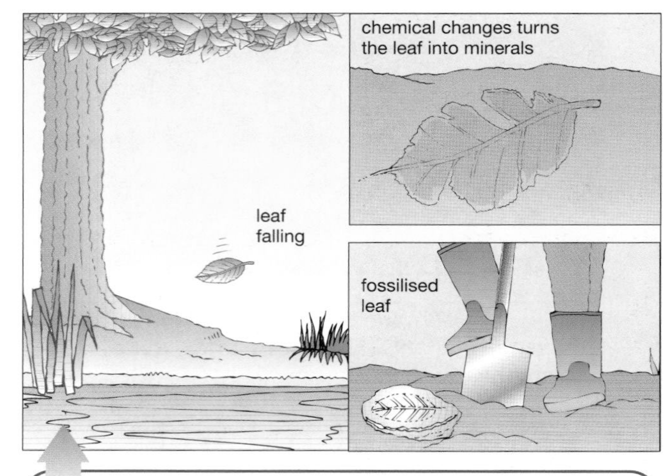

Figure 2 A leaf falls on lake side mud. The soft parts quickly decompose. The leaf skeleton is trapped by further layers of lake side mud. Chemical alterations turn the leaf into minerals

Not all fossils are rocks!

Insects may be almost perfectly preserved in amber. Woolly mammoths have been found frozen in Siberian **permafrost**. Peat is fossilised moss. The moss has been preserved by the acids that are found in wet areas. Plant remains such as pollen can be found in peat and these can give information about the climate and growing conditions in the past.

Fossil evidence is used to show the age of the remains as well as working out the relationship to the ancestors of species.

Figure 3 *Eohippus* was 20 cm high. This ancestral horse had hoofed toes, a long skull and 44 teeth. The horses' ancestor lived about 50 million years ago and lived in marshes, grazing soft leaves and plant shoots

Comparative studies

Evolutionary trends are often studied by comparing the anatomy, **embryology** or molecular biology of species that are believed to be related.

Biogeography

Biogeography is where scientists compare the natural history of different areas. The Galapagos finches are a good example of closely related species that exist in a small group of islands.

The isolated islands of St Kilda lie 65 km west of North Uist in the Outer Hebrides and some unique animals live there. On St Kilda the wrens are larger than those on the mainland. The St Kilda field mouse is now a protected species. It is heavier and a different colour from those on the mainland.

Although **marsupials** are usually associated with Australia they are also found in South America indicating that these continents were once joined to each other.

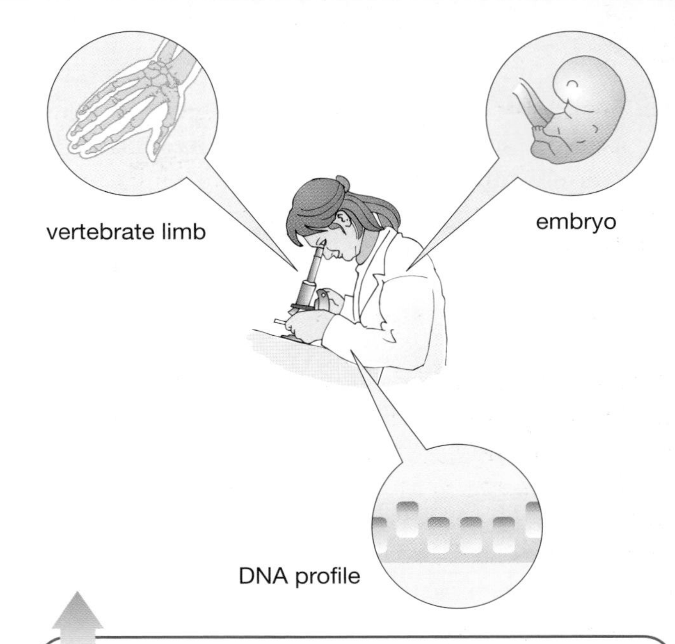

Figure 4 A human embryo is identical to a chicken or a fish at an early stage of development. The limbs of all vertebrates show 'theme and variation' on this pattern of bones. A DNA profile (genetic fingerprint) compares the chemical relationship between individuals or species. Proteins are also often compared

Key ideas

★ Darwin's theory suggests that living things are related to each other through common ancestors

★ Evidence to support the theory of evolution is found from several different areas of science

★ Evidence to support the theory of evolution is being collected from all parts of the world

Questions

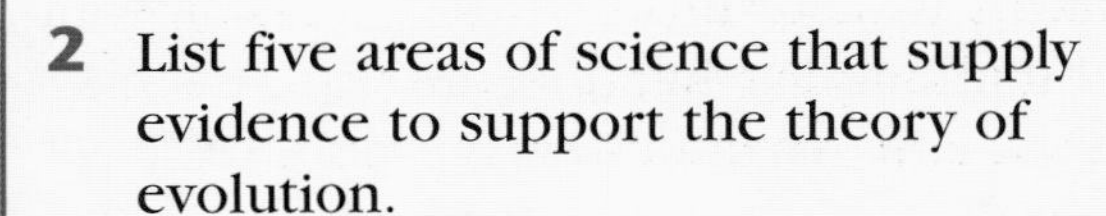

1 List three examples by which the remains of living things can be preserved.

2 List five areas of science that supply evidence to support the theory of evolution.

3 Name three parts of the world that are a 'laboratory for evolution'.

Wordbank

Permafrost – permanently frozen ground

Embryology – the study of early growth, and development of living things

Biogeography – the geographical study of the distribution of organisms

Marsupials – a group of primitive, pouch bearing mammals

56 Adaptation

Living things are **adapted** to their environment. Adaptation helps living things to survive in their environment.

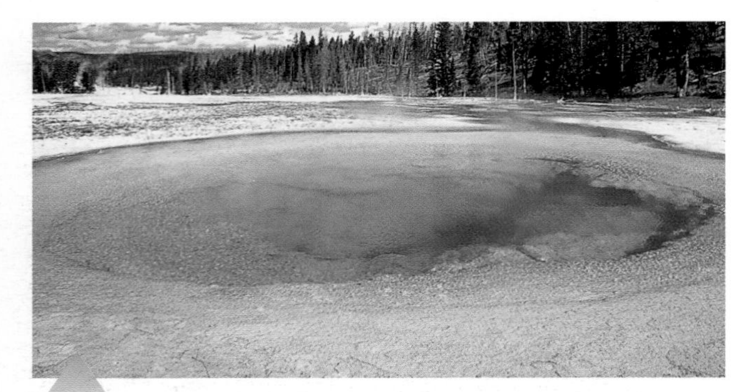

Figure 1 Some bacteria are adapted to surviving in these hot springs

Adaptations take place as the result of random genetic changes within the cells of individuals. When changes occur in the environment individuals may be able to survive better in these new conditions due to their adaptations and then pass those characteristics on to their offspring.

They **compete** better than the rest of the population. Over time there will be changes in appearance as well as the genetic makeup of a species and this eventually leads to the appearance of new ones.

Mutations change genetic traits. An organism's appearance is determined by its genes as well as its environment. Mutations are rare events and are usually harmful or have no effect, but occasionally they result in changes that can make the individual more competitive and able to survive environmental changes.

Artificial selection

Since the dawn of civilisation farmers have selected favourable characteristics in crops and livestock to increase yield, flavour and so on. Wheat is believed to have evolved in the Middle East where varieties were interbred to create the modern bread wheat. The domestic chicken (*Gallus domesticus*) was domesticated around 2000 years ago in Indochina from a red jungle fowl (*Gallus gallus*).

Genetic modification

Modern biotechnology is able to insert genes in order to accelerate traditional breeding approaches.

Adaptive behaviour

Darwin's theory depends on the ability of living things to pass on characteristics to their offspring. These include characteristics such as the colour of a ladybird's wings or the growth rate, for example, of wheat.

Animal behaviour also shows adaptation. If an animal is able to carry out a new behaviour it can gain advantages over its competitors. Many zoologists believe that they can find evidence of evolution in the study of animal behaviour. Domestic animals often show behaviour that is identical to their wild ancestors.

Figure 2 Japanese Macaque

Japanese snow monkeys (*Macaca fuscata*) have adapted to bathing in hot springs to keep warm during the winter. Large troops are fed sweet potatoes which are often coated with earth. In one troop, a young female was observed to wash the mud off in the stream and this was quickly learned by the remainder of the troop.

Animal behaviour by even the simplest animals can change their environment. Some species of ant collect food from greenflies – affecting them as well as the trees they live upon.

Figure 3 The Crens all had a common ancestor – adaptation has taken place and new species have evolved

Many animals can change their environment to match their needs, for example beavers dam up streams to create a store for their food plants to grow.

Animal communication

Animals communicate with each other in many ways such as sound, visible signals or behaviour. Most are able to detect taste and smell – house flies taste food with their feet!

Fish often detect electrical impulses. Many other animals respond to touch.

Sound is used by insects and mammals. Whale and dolphin communication has been widely studied.

Figure 3 Whales communicate with each other through a series of high frequency clicking noises

Birdsong is often used in behaviour studies. Birdsong can be different in related species, for example the song thrush repeats its song two or three times whereas its close relative the blackbird does not. It has even been shown that in some species local dialects have been recorded!

Key ideas

- ★ Living things are adapted to the environment
- ★ As the environment changes, those species that are adapted to new conditions survive
- ★ Artificial selection and genetic modification can develop new varieties of organisms
- ★ Animal behaviour shows adaptation
- ★ Animal communication shows adaptation

Wordbank

Adaptation – the process of change that takes place in living things during evolution

Competition – takes place between members of the same as well as other species

Mutation – changes in chromosomes and genes

Questions

1. Describe cat species from North America, Africa and Asia.
2. Describe the conditions where these cats live.
3. Describe adaptations to their environment.
4. Find out how each of the following is adapted to their environment:
   - camel
   - polar bear
   - cactus
   - pine tree

Inside a modern glasshouse

During the Victorian period, British explorers collected plants from around the world. As the climate can affect the distribution of living things, glasshouses were built to copy the conditions in the natural habitats of those plants.

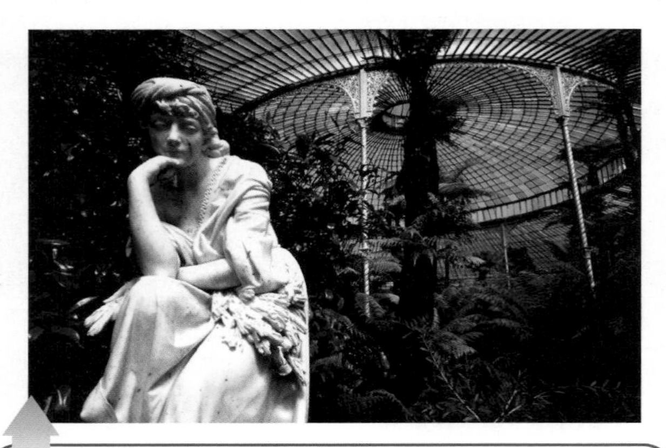

Figure 1 The Kibble palace in Glasgow's botanic gardens contains a collection of tree ferns from the tropics. This glasshouse mimics the conditions in their native environments

If collections of plants are to survive in the glasshouses, the physical or **abiotic** environment must be controlled. Gardeners now use sensors, computers and **control systems** to maintain the conditions for the best growth of the plants. Engineers can install environmental control computers. These powerful control systems each work in the same way.

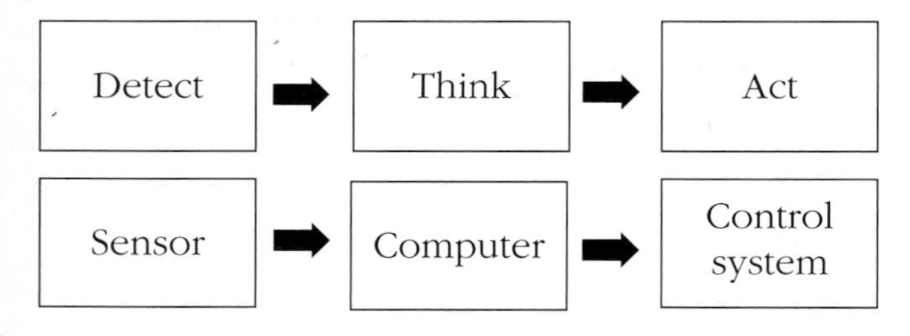

This can even include the gas inside the glasshouse – CO_2 is essential to photosynthesis. **Biotic** factors such as insect pests and disease control systems can now be included in the automatic systems. Everything affecting plant growth can be controlled by the computer except for the outside weather!

Controlled features

Sunlight

Sunlight is essential for photosynthesis and plant growth as well as supplying heat to the environment. Day length, the quality of light and the temperature can change.

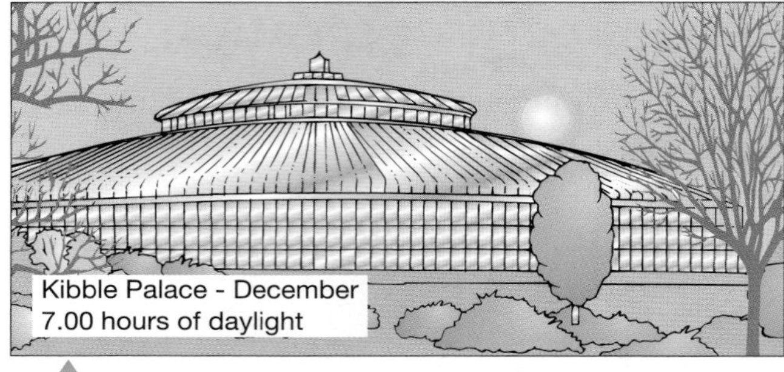

Figure 2 Daylight and temperature change through the seasons

In modern glasshouses light sensors can be used to detect the total energy or light intensity. Temperature probes contain sensitive resistors called **thermisters**. Computers can control the light levels either with artificial lights or by shading the plants. Ventilation or heating will control the temperature.

Irrigation

The quality of the soil water is also important in the modern glasshouse. The volume of water, the **nutrients** (plant foods) and the pH are all important.

Figure 3 Modern glasshouses are fully environmentally controlled. Sensors, computers and control technology can provide shade, blackout, artificial lighting, heating and cooling to imitate climatic conditions anywhere in the world. They can even control the release of bees to assist pollination!

Moisture content

Sensors can detect the soil moisture content and the computer will control automatic watering systems.

Nutrients

Nutrients, chemical salts, can also be detected electronically. These work by measuring the electrical conductivity of the solution. Nutrients, plant food, can be added by the control systems.

pH

Electronic probes can also record the pH of the soil solution. Automatic corrections can be made by the control systems.

Key ideas

- ★ Physical (abiotic) factors affect the growth of plants and consequently all food chains
- ★ Information technology and control systems can manage the abiotic environment in glasshouses

Wordbank

Abiotic – the physical or non-living part of the ecosystem

Control systems – mechanical or electronic equipment used to change a condition e.g. water or temperature

Biotic – living part of the ecosystem

Thermister – temperature sensitive resistor

Irrigation – artificially supply water

Nutrients – a chemical salt that promotes plant growth

Questions

1 List four abiotic factors.

2 Explain how a farmer can manage three abiotic factors.

3 Below is a graph which shows the change in the temperature both inside and outside a glasshouse over a 24 hour period in March. Describe, in terms of sensors, computer and control systems what has happened to maintain the temperature inside the glasshouse.

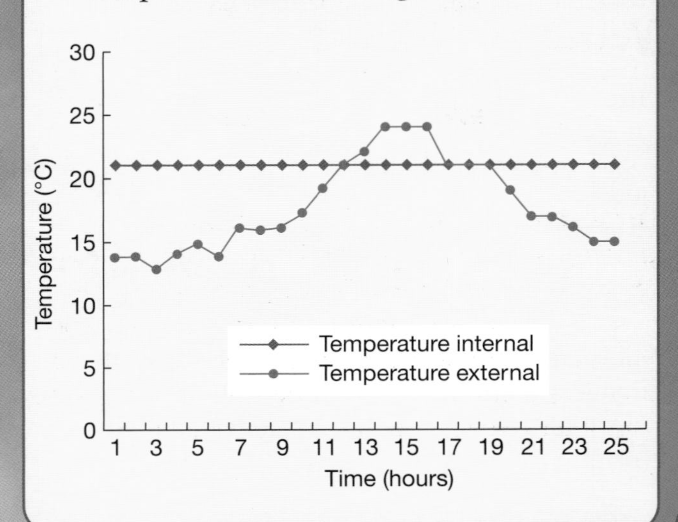

This is biology

There are many branches in science but the main ones are biology, chemistry and physics. All science works in the same way by using **scientific method**.

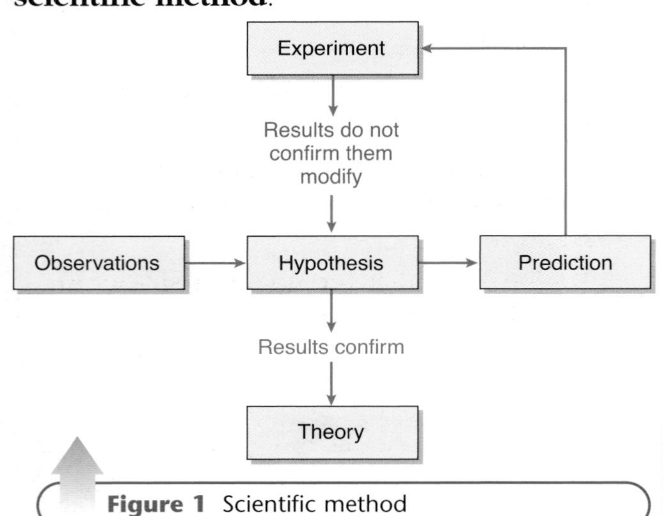

Figure 1 Scientific method

Modern scientists often work together in teams that include people from a range of scientific disciplines, for example Frances Crick who won the Nobel prize for the discovery of the structure of DNA first studied physics at university. Richard Feynman, a double Nobel prize winner in physics said:

> *. . . we humans cut nature up in different ways, and we have different courses in different departments, such compartmentalization is really artificial, and we should take our intellectual pleasures where we find them.*
>
> (The Feynman Lectures on Physics)

What is biology?

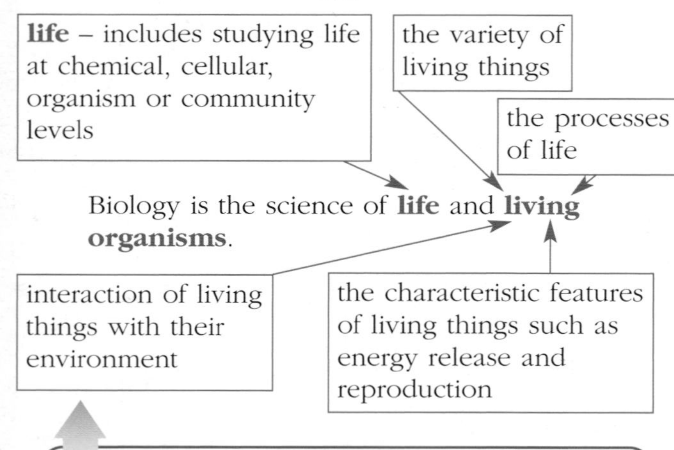

Figure 2 This is biology

What use is biology?

Living things, including ourselves, fill our world. Biological discoveries such as new drugs, medicines and treatments, improved crop varieties and environmentally friendly pesticides, are examples of the products of applied science. 'Pure' science has determined the genetic sequence of the **human genome** as well as looking at the structure of cells and classifying new species throughout the world.

What do biologists study?

Figure 3 Professional biologists

- **Environmental biologists** study environmental issues associated with ecology, agriculture, fisheries and forestry.
- **Biochemists** study chemical issues and this can also include pharmacology (drugs and their effects) and immunology (the way that bodies respond to infections).
- **Geneticists** study inheritance.
- **Psychologists** study human behaviour.
- **Botanists** (plant biologists) study the anatomy and physiology of plants.
- **Zoologists** (animal biologists) study the anatomy and physiology of animals.
- **Microbiologists** study the anatomy and physiology of microorganisms.

Famous Biologists

Richard Dawkins has popularised the 'selfish gene' theory in evolution.

Gregor Mendel (1822–1884) studied inheritance of several characteristics in pea plants, and discovered the basic laws of inheritance.

Jane Goodall has studied social behaviour in wild chimps in Tanzania for more than 40 years.

Alec Jeffries developed genetic fingerprinting in 1984, which is now routine in forensic cases and genetic research.

Rachel Carson (1907–1964) changed people's views on environmental concerns following the publication of her book *Silent Spring*.

David Attenborough is probably the best known biologist in the world. His television programmes and books have popularised zoology in particular.

What would I study if I continued biology at school?

- The Biosphere
- The world of plants
- Animal survival
- Investigating cells
- The body in action
- Inheritance
- Biotechnology

Key ideas

★ Biology is a key area of modern science

★ Biology has many branches

★ Pure and applied branches of science exist

★ Biology's aproach is the same as other areas of science and involves scientific method

★ Modern scientists often work together in multidisciplinary teams

Wordbank

Scientific method – a way of investigation that involves observation, and making explanations (theories) to test scientific hypotheses (ideas)

Questions

1 Find out more about:

a) the branches of biology.
b) careers in biology.
c) what you have already studied in biology.

David Douglas

Figure 1 Douglas firs

Britain's tallest tree is more than 64 metres high and grows near Dunkeld. The Douglas fir is a native of Western Canada and the USA. The species was named after the plant hunter David Douglas who was born in Scone, Perthshire in 1799 and died in Hawaii in 1834. While he worked at the Glasgow Botanic Gardens he was trained in plant identification and preservation by Professor William Hooker.

His adventures took him 12 000 miles on foot, horseback and canoe. He collected, preserved and identified more than 800 species which were sent to the Royal Horticultural Society. Many plants that David Douglas discovered are now garden plants, others fill our forest plantations.

Figure 2 The California poppy, *Eschscholzia californica*, was first identified by David Douglas

He died in mysterious circumstances by falling into a pit used by islanders for trapping bulls.

John Muir

John Muir was born in Dunbar two years after David Douglas died. He is famous in the United States as the first person to call for environmental action to conserve and protect wild places.

Figure 3 John Muir

John Muir emigrated as a child to the USA. Muir wrote about his travels as an explorer, naturalist and geologist, and his ideas about conservation. He influenced President Theodore Roosevelt who created the National Park System in the USA including, during Muir's lifetime, Yosemite and the Grand Canyon.

The very largest that I have yet met in the course of my explorations is a majestic old fire-scarred monument. It is thirty-five feet and eight inches in diameter inside the bark, four feet above the ground. It is burned half through, and I spent a day in clearing away the charred surface with a sharp axe and counted a little over four thousand rings. No other tree in the world, as far as I know, has looked down on so many centuries as the sequoia or opens so many impressive and suggestive views into history. These giants probably live 5000 years or more though few of even the larger trees are half as old. The age of one that was felled, for the sake of having its stump for a dancing-floor, was about 1300 years, and its diameter measured twenty-four feet inside the bark. Another that was felled in the forest was about the same size but nearly a thousand years older, though not a very old-looking tree.

(Abridged extract from John Muir, *The Yosemite*, New York: The Century Company, 1912)

Figure 4 John Muir wrote about giant redwoods he saw during a visit to Yosemite in April, 1868

Something to think about. . .

David Douglas and John Muir witnessed habitats and species that have already been changed by the activities of mankind. Habitat, genetic and species diversity – the three aspects of **biodiversity** – have all been changed by mankind. Species have been lost forever. Darwin's theory of evolution suggests that adaptation over a long time period leads to the appearance of new species – if the rate of change is too great to allow this to happen the result is a reduction of biodiversity.

Extinction is the loss of species.

Scientists are not sure how many different species live on the Earth. Estimates vary but they all agree that the number is falling at a dramatic rate due to species extinction. In the past many species became extinct due to environmental change or biological competition. A large number of species have become extinct during the past 200 years due to the actions of humans. The current rate of extinction is believed to be 1000 to 10 000 times greater than the natural rate of species extinction.

We are the only people who can make a difference. What action will you take today, tomorrow and every day for the rest of your life? Do you have what it takes to become a great Scot?

Key ideas

★ Two Scots have contributed to our understanding of biodiversity and conservation

★ Species extinction is accelerating

★ WE MUST ALL TAKE ACTION TO STOP BIODIVERSITY REDUCTION

Wordbank

Biodiversity – range of habitat, genes and species

Extinction – the loss of species

Questions

1 Prepare a website on **one** of the following:

a) David Douglas's garden plants
b) David Douglas's forest trees
c) Professor William Hooker and Kew Gardens
d) Plant hunters and the Royal Horticultural Society
e) Local environmental and conservation groups
f) Local biodiversity action plans

2 What action will you take to stop biodiversity reduction?

60 Ecological investigations

Ecology is a major area of modern science. News items often raise issues of environmental and ecological interest. Understanding ecology can influence the way that the natural environment is managed, including wildlife conservation and pollution control. It involves studying problems such as global warming and human population growth.

ecology – study of the relationships between living things and their environment

Ecological investigations often take place outdoors and take a very long time. This allows comparisons to be made. Environmental change requires investigations over long time periods. The studies examine a community in great detail. They involve identifying the plants and animals in a community as well as the non-living surroundings – the physics and chemistry of the environment.

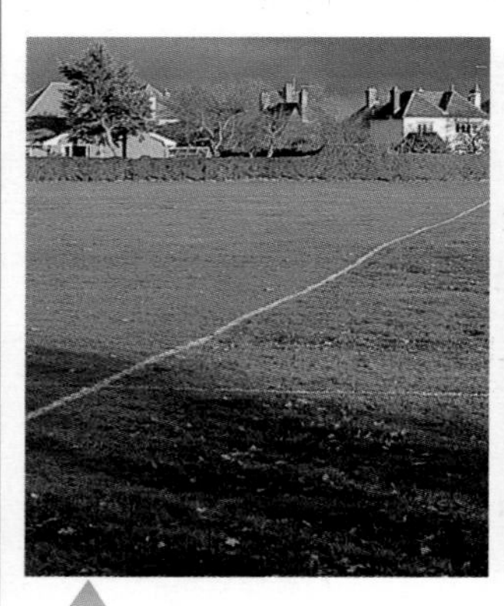

Figure 1 A casual observation on this sports pitch would describe it as grass

Figure 2 A square metre of the pitch includes several different plants. Closer examination of the lawn reveals many different plants, and the soil beneath it would reveal different animals and microorganisms as well as a complete range of chemical and physical conditions

Ecologists use several different approaches for collecting information from a community.

Sampling plant and animal life

Nets and traps are often used to collect insects and small mammals. Pitfall traps are useful for invertebrates that live on the ground. It is important that when living things are trapped that they are also returned, unharmed, to the environment.

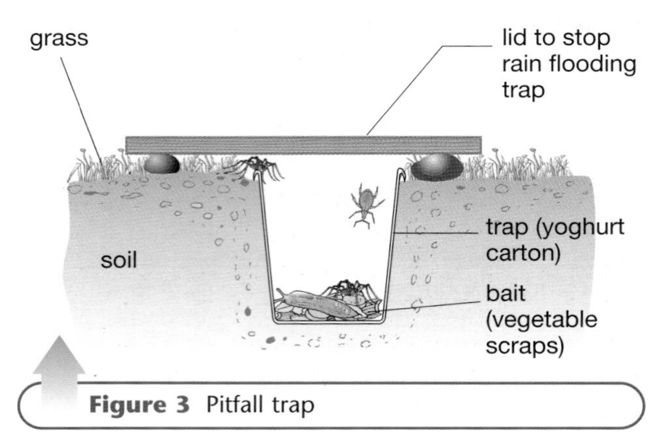

Figure 3 Pitfall trap

Direct observations

'Hides' are set up so that birds and larger mammals may be closely observed, but more often they are identified with binoculars. Video cameras are also useful.

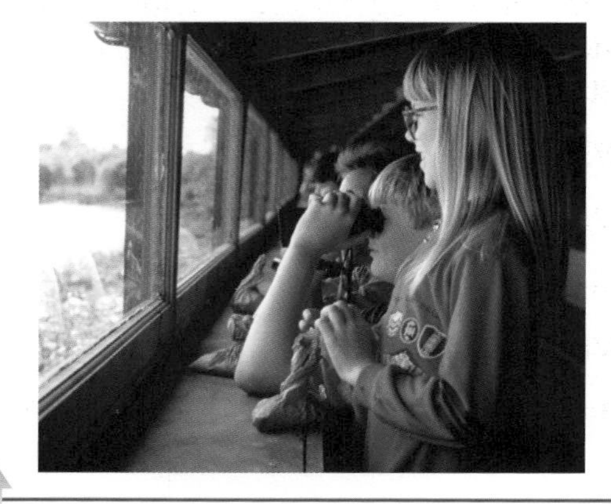

Figure 4 Enthusiasts make records of bird populations

The problems with identification is that the closer you look the more you will find!

For example, the number of different types of grass that you may find is huge – as many as 200 species are native to Britain. The best approach is to sketch or photograph the materials so that they may be used by others in the future. Preserved specimens can also be stored.

Chemical and physical analysis

The chemical and physical properties are also important in sustaining the habitat. All environmental factors – physical and chemical – will have some effect on the community.

Long term studies

In previous investigations you have identified a hypothesis and then controlled and changed variables to try to find out about the way that something worked or responded as conditions were changed. This approach is not always possible, especially in studies outdoors in the **field**.

Long term studies are required to show trends, patterns and changes in the environment. This means that careful records must be made and that these are available to other people who might study the same area in the future.

Planning an ecological investigation needs an identical approach to other scientific investigations.

1 What do I want to find out?
2 What equipment will I need?
3 How will I set it up?
4 What will I measure?
5 How will I make sure it is a fair test?

Remember

- Ecology is a major area of modern biological science
- Field investigations can contribute to scientific knowledge but may not be able to test hypotheses in the short term
- Many approaches are required in making ecological observations and they may involve all areas of science

Wordbank

Ecology – the scientific study of the interactions between living things and their environment

Field – investigations that take place out of doors, rather than in a laboratory

Questions

1 Explain why studying ecology is important.
2 Describe three ways that you could observe animals in the field.
3 Describe three ways that you could collect records of animals in the field.
4 What is the greatest problem with observing or collecting living things in the field?
5 List chemical and physical measurements that you could make in an environment.
6 Plan a class investigation in the school grounds – the records will be used by next year's class.

Index

A
abiotic factors 114, **115**
acceleration 70–1, **71**
adaptations 112–13, **113**
aerobic respiration 98, **99**
air resistance 70–1, **71**
alchemists 10, **11**
aliens 6–7
alloys 16, **17**
amylase 100
anaerobic respiration 98, **99**
analogue 58
animal behaviour 112–13
antibiotics 82, 83, **83**
antibodies 85, **85**
artificial selection 112
astrophysicist **3**
astrophysics 2
atmosphere 20, 21, **21**
atomic number 11
atoms 10–11
Attenborough, David 117

B
bacteria 82, **83**
balanced forces 68
Big Bang 2, 4–5
billion **21**
biochemistry 100, **101**
biodegradable 78, 79, **79**
biodiversity 119, **119**
biogeography 111, **111**
biology 116–17
biomass 104, **105**
biosphere 20, **21**
biotechnology 86–9, **87**
biotic factors 114, **115**
Bohr, Niels 11
breathing 98, **99**
bromine 19
Bunsen, Robert 37
burning 64, 65, **65**

C
carbon 37
carbon dioxide 98, 99
Carson, Rachel 117
catalase 102
catalysts 17, **17**, 26–7, **27**, 29, **29**, 100, 101, **101**
catalytic converters 26
cells 94–5
cellular respiration 98–9
Chadwick, James 11
chemical bonds 14–15, 24, **25**
chemical equations 34–5, **35**
chemical potential energy 64–5
chemical reactions 14, 22–7, 32–3, 40–1
chemistry 36–7
chlorine 18, 19
chromosomes 90, 92
circuit boards 79, **79**
circuit breaker 57, **57**
cloning 88, 89, **89**
colour 44–7
competition 112, **113**
complimentary shape 28, **29**
compounds 14
compression 74, 75
connective tissue 94, **95**
Conservation of Matter 34, **35**, 40
covalent bonding 15, **15**
creationism 107
crucible **41**
Curie, Marie 77
current 54–5, **55**

D
Dalton, John 10
dark matter 5, **5**
Darwin, Charles 106, 107, 110
Dawkins, Richard 116
decibels 48–9
decomposition 28, **29**
diabetes 89
diatomic, molecules 18, **19**
digestion 98, **99**
digital 58
DNA 86, **87**, 90–1, **91**
Douglas, David 118
Drake formula 6
dust 9

E
E. coli 83, **83**
ecology 104–5, 120, **121**
ecosystems 105, **105**
Einstein, Albert 77
electricity 54–7
electrolysis 19, **19**
electromagnetic spectrum 2, **3**, 42, 43, **43**, 44
electromagnets 52–3
electronic balance **41**
electronics 58–61
electrons 11
elements 12–13
embryology 111, **111**
endothermic reactions 24–5, **25**
energy 31, 62–5, 104–5
enzymes 28–9, **29**, 100–3, **101**
epithelium 94, **95**
evidence 3, 106, **107**
evolution 106–11
exoplanets 8–9, **9**
exothermic reactions 24, **25**
extinction 119, **119**
extra-terrestrials 6–7
eye 46

F
Faraday, Michael 52
fermentation 82
Feynman, Richard 77
fibrilltion 57, **57**
filters 46, 47, **47**
fluorine 19

food 64, 82, 86–7
food chains 104
food webs 104
forces 68–75
fossil fuels 65
fossils 110
frequency 49, **49**
fungi 82, **83**
fuse 57, **57**

G
Galapagos Islands 110
galaxies 4
gene therapy 88
genes 90, 91, **91**, 92, 93, **93**, 108, **109**
genetic engineering 93, **93**, 112
genetics 90–3, **91**
genome 90, **91**
geosphere 20, **21**
glasshouses 114–15
GMOs (genetically modified organisms) 86, 87, **87**
Goodall, Jane 117
gravitational field strength 63, **63**
gravitational potential energy 62–3
gravity 63
guard cells 97, **97**

H
halogens 13, **13**, 18–19, **19**
heat radiation 42–3
hertz 49
HIV (Human Immunodeficiency Virus) 83, **83**
house wiring 56
Hoyle, Sir Fred 2
Hubble constant 4
Human Genome Project 88, **89**, 90
hydraulics 74, 75, **75**
hygiene 84
hypotheses 36, **37**

I
immune system 85, **85**, 89, **89**
infra red radiation 42–3, **43**
inheritance 92–3, **93**
input 60
iodine 19
ionic bonding 14–15, **15**
isotopes 19, **19**

J
jacks 74, 75, **75**
Jeffries, Alec 117
Jenner, Edward 83

K
karyotype 90, **91**
Kroto, Sir Harold W. 37

L
Lavoisier, Antoine 10, 37, 40, **41**
leaves 96
LEDs (Light Emitting Diodes) 59, **59**
Lewis, Gilbert 14
light 8, 44–7
light sensory cell 46, **47**
lipase 28, **29**
lodestones 50, **51**
loudness 48–9
loudspeakers 61
lustre 17, **17**

M
magnetism 50–1
malleability 17, **17**
mass 66–7, **67**
mass number 11
matter 31
Maxwell, James Clerk 77
measurements 30
medical biotechnology 88–9
Mendel, Gregor 117
Mendeleyev, Dmitri 12
metals 16–17
microelectronics 58, **59**
microorganisms 82–5
microphones 60
microwave radiation 5
molecules 34, 35, **35**
motion 70–1
Muir, John 118
muscle 94, **95**
mutation 108, **109**, 112, **113**

N
nanometres 44, **45**
NASA 38
natural selection 106–9, **107**, **109**
nerves 95, **95**
neutrons 11
Newton, Sir Isaac 77
nitrogen cycle 82
non-biodegradable 78, 79, **79**
non-metals 13
nutrients 114, **115**

O
opthalmic electromagnets 52, **53**
optical telescopes 3, **3**
optimum 28, **29**, **103**
organochlorines 19, **19**
Orsted, Hans 52
oscilloscope 48
output 60, 61
oxygen 98, 99

P
parallel circuits 55
parasites 84, **85**
Pasteur, Louis 37
pathogens 83, **83**

pendulum 62
Periodic Table 12–19
phloem 97, **97**
photosynthesis 24, 64–5, **65**, 114
physical changes 30–1
physics 76–7
phytoplankton 96, **97**
PKU 88
planets 9
plants 86, 96–7
platinum 26
potassium 12
potential energy 62, 63
precipitate 32, 33, **33**
precipitation 20, 21, **21**, 32, 33
pressure 72–5
process 60
productivity 105, **105**
products 22, **23**, 32, **33**, 102, **103**
property 30
protease 28, **29**
protein 100
protista 82, **83**, 96
protons 11

R
radiation 5
radio waves 6
reactants 22, **23**, 32, **33**
reaction rates 22–3, **23**
recycling 78–9
red blood cells 95
relay switches 53
respiration 98–9, **99**
root hair cells 97, **97**
rubbish 78–9
Rutherford, Ernest 10

S
safety 56–7
scientific method 36, **37**, 76, **77**, 116, **117**
selective breeding 92–3, **93**
senses 30
series circuits 54–5
SETI (Search for Extra-Terrestrial Intellience) **7**, 7–8
shells 13, **13**
skateboards 80–1
smelting 24
sodium 12
solar cells 58
sound 48–9
space research 38–9
spectra 4, **5**
Steady State 2
Sub-atomic particles 10, **11**
sublimation 19, **19**
substrates 102, **103**
Sun 42

T
telescopes 3
temperature 30
tensile strength 17, **17**
theory 106, **107**
thermochemistry 24, **25**
thermocouple 60, **61**
Thomson, J.J. 10
Thomson, Sir William 77
transition metals 16, 26, **27**
trophic level 104, **105**

U
Universe 2

V
vaccines 82, 83, **83**
vacuum 42, 43, **43**
valency 14, **15**, 16, **17**
viruses 84, **85**
viscosity 30, **31**

W
Wallace, Alfred 107
water cycle 20–1
wavelengths 44, 45, **45**
weight 66–7, **67**
wobbles 8
word equations 34, 35, **35**

X
xylem 97, **97**

Y
yeast 29, 86

Edexcel GCSE (9-1)

Chemistry

Mark Levesley Iain Brand Nigel Saunders Sue Robilliard John Ling

ALWAYS LEARNING

PEARSON

Contents

Teaching and learning iv

SC1 States of Matter
SC2 Methods of Separating and Purifying Substances (Paper 1) 1

SC1a	States of matter	2
SC2a	Mixtures	4
SC2b	Filtration and crystallisation	6
SC2c	Paper chromatography	8
SC2d	Distillation	10
SC2d	Core practical – Investigating inks	12
SC2e	Drinking water	14
SC1–2	Preparing for your exams	16

SC3 Atomic Structure (Paper 1 and Paper 2) 17

SC3a	Structure of an atom	18
SC3b	Atomic number and mass number	20
SC3c	Isotopes	22
SC3	Preparing for your exams	24

SC4 The Periodic Table (Paper 1 and Paper 2) 25

SC4a	Elements and the periodic table	26
SC4b	Atomic number and the periodic table	28
SC4c	Electronic configurations and the periodic table	30
SC4	Preparing for your exams	32

SC5 Ionic Bonding
SC6 Covalent Bonding
SC7 Types of Substance (Paper 1 and Paper 2) 33

SC5a	Ionic bonds	34
SC5b	Ionic lattices	36
SC5c	Properties of ionic compounds	38
SC6a	Covalent bonds	40
SC7a	Molecular compounds	42
SC7b	Allotropes of carbon	44
SC7c	Properties of metals	46
SC7d	Bonding models	48
SC5–7	Preparing for your exams	50

SC8 Acids and Alkalis (Paper 1) 51

SC8a	Acids, alkalis and indicators	52
SC8b	Looking at acids	54
SC8c	Bases and salts	56
SC8c	Core practical – Preparing copper sulfate	58
SC8d	Alkalis and balancing equations	60
SC8d	Core practical – Investigating neutralisation	62
SC8e	Alkalis and neutralisation	64
SC8f	Reactions of acids with metals and carbonates	66
SC8g	Solubility	68
SC8	Preparing for your exams	70

SC9 Calculations Involving Masses (Paper 1 and Paper 2) 71

SC9a	Masses and empirical formulae	72
SC9b	Conservation of mass	74
SC9c	Moles	76
SC9	Preparing for your exams	78

SC10 Electrolytic Processes
SC11 Obtaining and Using Metals
SC12 Reversible Reactions and Equilibria
SC13 Transition Metals, Alloys and Corrosion (Paper 1) 79

SC10a	Electrolysis	80
SC10a	Core practical – Electrolysis of copper sulfate solution	82
SC10b	Products from electrolysis	84
SC11a	Reactivity	86
SC11b	Ores	88
SC11c	Oxidation and reduction	90
SC11d	Life cycle assessment and recycling	92
SC12a	Dynamic equilibrium	94
SC13a	Transition metals	96
SC13b	Corrosion	98
SC13c	Electroplating	100
SC13d	Alloying	102
SC13e	Uses of metals and their alloys	104
SC10–13	Preparing for your exams	106

SC14	**Quantitative Analysis**	
SC15	**Dynamic Equilibria, Calculations Involving Volumes of Gases**	
SC16	**Chemical Cells and Fuel Cells** (Paper 1)	107
SC14a	Yields	108
SC14b	Atom economy	110
SC14c	Concentrations	112
SC14d	Titrations and calculations	114
SC14d	Core practical – Acid–alkali titration	116
SC14e	Molar volume of gases	118
SC15a	Fertilisers and the Haber process	120
SC15b	Factors affecting equilibrium	122
SC16a	Chemical cells and fuel cells	124
SC14–16	Preparing for your exams	126

SC17	**Groups in the Periodic Table**	
SC18	**Rates of Reaction**	
SC19	**Heat Energy Changes in Chemical Reactions** (Paper 2)	127
SC17a	Group 1	128
SC17b	Group 7	130
SC17c	Halogen reactivity	132
SC17d	Group 0	134
SC18a	Rates of reaction	136
SC18b	Factors affecting reaction rates	138
SC18b	Core practical – Investigating reaction rates	140
SC18c	Catalysts and activation energy	142
SC19a	Exothermic and endothermic reactions	144
SC19b	Energy changes in reactions	146
SC17–19	Preparing for your exams	148

SC20	**Fuels**	
SC21	**Earth and Atmospheric Science** (Paper 2)	149
SC20a	Hydrocarbons in crude oil and natural gas	150
SC20b	Fractional distillation of crude oil	152
SC20c	The alkane homologous series	154
SC20d	Complete and incomplete combustion	156
SC20e	Combustible fuels and pollution	158
SC20f	Breaking down hydrocarbons	160
SC21a	The early atmosphere	162
SC21b	The changing atmosphere	164
SC21c	The atmosphere today	166
SC21d	Climate change	168
SC20–21	Preparing for your exams	170

SC22	**Hydrocarbons**	
SC23	**Alcohols and Carboxylic Acids**	
SC24	**Polymers** (Paper 2)	171
SC22a	Alkanes and alkenes	172
SC22b	Reactions of alkanes and alkenes	174
SC23a	Ethanol production	176
SC23b	Alcohols	178
SC23b	Core practical – The combustion of alcohols	180
SC23c	Carboxylic acids	182
SC24a	Addition polymerisation	184
SC24b	Polymer properties and uses	186
SC24c	Condensation polymerisation	188
SC24d	Problems with polymers	190
SC22–24	Preparing for your exams	192

SC25	**Qualitative Analysis: Tests for Ions**	
SC26	**Bulk and Surface Properties of Matter Including Nanoparticles** (Paper 2)	193
SC25a	Flame tests and photometry	194
SC25b	Tests for positive ions	196
SC25c	Tests for negative ions	198
SC25c	Core practical – Identifying ions	200
SC26a	Choosing materials	202
SC26b	Composite materials	204
SC26c	Nanoparticles	206
SC25–26	Preparing for your exams	208

Glossary	209
Index	214
The periodic table of the elements	216

Teaching and learning

The **topic reference** tells you which part of the course you are in. 'SC17c' means, 'Separate Science, Chemistry, unit 17, topic c'.

The **specification reference** allows you to cross reference against the specification criteria so you know which parts you are covering. References that end in C, e.g. C9.2C, are in Chemistry only, the rest are also in the Combined Science specification criteria.

If you see an **H** icon that means that content will be assessed on the Higher Tier paper only.

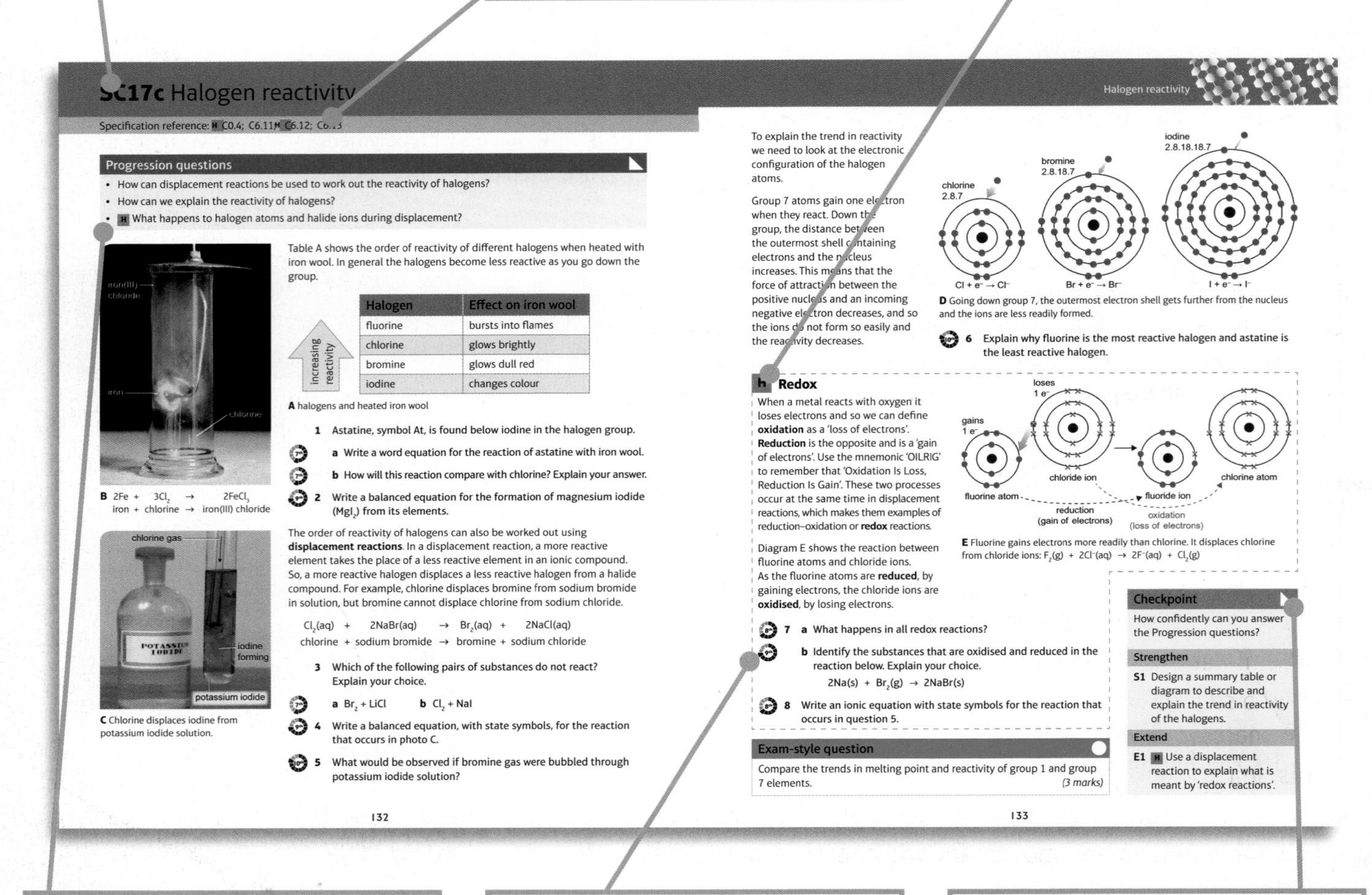

SC17c Halogen reactivity

Specification reference: H C0.4; C6.11H C6.12; C6.13

Progression questions

- How can displacement reactions be used to work out the reactivity of halogens?
- How can we explain the reactivity of halogens?
- H What happens to halogen atoms and halide ions during displacement?

Table A shows the order of reactivity of different halogens when heated with iron wool. In general the halogens become less reactive as you go down the group.

Halogen	Effect on iron wool
fluorine	bursts into flames
chlorine	glows brightly
bromine	glows dull red
iodine	changes colour

increasing reactivity

A halogens and heated iron wool

iron(III) chloride
iron
chlorine

B $2Fe + 3Cl_2 \rightarrow 2FeCl_3$
iron + chlorine → iron(III) chloride

1 Astatine, symbol At, is found below iodine in the halogen group.
a Write a word equation for the reaction of astatine with iron wool.
b How will this reaction compare with chlorine? Explain your answer.

2 Write a balanced equation for the formation of magnesium iodide (MgI_2) from its elements.

The order of reactivity of halogens can also be worked out using **displacement reactions**. In a displacement reaction, a more reactive element takes the place of a less reactive element in an ionic compound. So, a more reactive halogen displaces a less reactive halogen from a halide compound. For example, chlorine displaces bromine from sodium bromide in solution, but bromine cannot displace chlorine from sodium chloride.

$Cl_2(aq) + 2NaBr(aq) \rightarrow Br_2(aq) + 2NaCl(aq)$
chlorine + sodium bromide → bromine + sodium chloride

chlorine gas
POTASSIUM IODIDE
iodine forming
potassium iodide

C Chlorine displaces iodine from potassium iodide solution.

3 Which of the following pairs of substances do not react? Explain your choice.
a $Br_2 + LiCl$ b $Cl_2 + NaI$

4 Write a balanced equation, with state symbols, for the reaction that occurs in photo C.

5 What would be observed if bromine gas were bubbled through potassium iodide solution?

132

Halogen reactivity

To explain the trend in reactivity we need to look at the electronic configuration of the halogen atoms.

Group 7 atoms gain one electron when they react. Down the group, the distance between the outermost shell containing electrons and the nucleus increases. This means that the force of attraction between the positive nucleus and an incoming negative electron decreases, and so the ions do not form so easily and the reactivity decreases.

chlorine 2.8.7
bromine 2.8.18.7
iodine 2.8.18.18.7
$Cl + e^- \rightarrow Cl^-$
$Br + e^- \rightarrow Br^-$
$I + e^- \rightarrow I^-$

D Going down group 7, the outermost electron shell gets further from the nucleus and the ions are less readily formed.

6 Explain why fluorine is the most reactive halogen and astatine is the least reactive halogen.

H Redox

When a metal reacts with oxygen it loses electrons and so we can define **oxidation** as a 'loss of electrons'. **Reduction** is the opposite and is a 'gain of electrons'. Use the mnemonic 'OILRIG' to remember that 'Oxidation Is Loss, Reduction Is Gain'. These two processes occur at the same time in displacement reactions, which makes them examples of reduction–oxidation or **redox** reactions.

Diagram E shows the reaction between fluorine atoms and chloride ions. As the fluorine atoms are **reduced**, by gaining electrons, the chloride ions are **oxidised**, by losing electrons.

gains 1 e⁻
loses 1 e⁻
fluorine atom
chloride ion
fluoride ion
chlorine atom
reduction (gain of electrons)
oxidation (loss of electrons)

E Fluorine gains electrons more readily than chlorine. It displaces chlorine from chloride ions: $F_2(g) + 2Cl^-(aq) \rightarrow 2F^-(aq) + Cl_2(g)$

7 a What happens in all redox reactions?
b Identify the substances that are oxidised and reduced in the reaction below. Explain your choice.
$2Na(s) + Br_2(g) \rightarrow 2NaBr(s)$

8 Write an ionic equation with state symbols for the reaction that occurs in question 5.

Exam-style question

Compare the trends in melting point and reactivity of group 1 and group 7 elements. *(3 marks)*

Checkpoint

How confidently can you answer the Progression questions?

Strengthen

S1 Design a summary table or diagram to describe and explain the trend in reactivity of the halogens.

Extend

E1 H Use a displacement reaction to explain what is meant by 'redox reactions'.

133

By the end of the topic you should be able to confidently answer the **Progression questions**. Try to answer them before you start and make a note of your answers. Think about what you know already and what more you need to learn.

Each question has been given a **Pearson Step** from 1 to 12. This tells you how difficult the question is. The higher the step the more challenging the question.

When you've worked through the main student book questions, answer the **Progression questions** again and review your own progress. Decide if you need to reinforce your own learning by answering the **Strengthen question**, or apply, analyse and evaluate your learning in new contexts by tackling the **Extend question**.

Paper 1

SC1 States of Matter / SC2 Methods of Separating and Purifying Substances

Millions of tonnes of tiny bits of plastic are floating in the oceans, and they harm wildlife. Water currents cause the plastic to collect in certain areas. The biggest of these is the 'Great Pacific Garbage Patch' in the Pacific Ocean, which could be three times the area of the UK. At the age of 19, Dutch student Boyan Slat came up with the idea of using giant floating booms to direct the plastic pieces into a mechanism that would filter the plastic out of the water. The idea relies on two properties of the plastic – it floats and it is insoluble in water. Not everyone agrees that it will work, and think that the system would not survive in the oceans. In this unit you will learn about how materials can be separated from one another using their properties.

The learning journey

Previously you will have learnt at KS3:

- how particles are arranged in solids, liquids and gases and how their energy changes with changes of state
- how mixtures differ from pure substances
- how to separate some mixtures using filtration, distillation and chromatography.

In this unit you will learn:

- how to use information to predict the state of a substance
- how the arrangement, movement and energy of particles change during changes of state
- how to use melting points to tell the difference between mixtures and pure substances
- how to identify substances using melting points and chromatography
- how different methods of separation work
- how to choose a separation method based on the properties of the substances in a mixture.

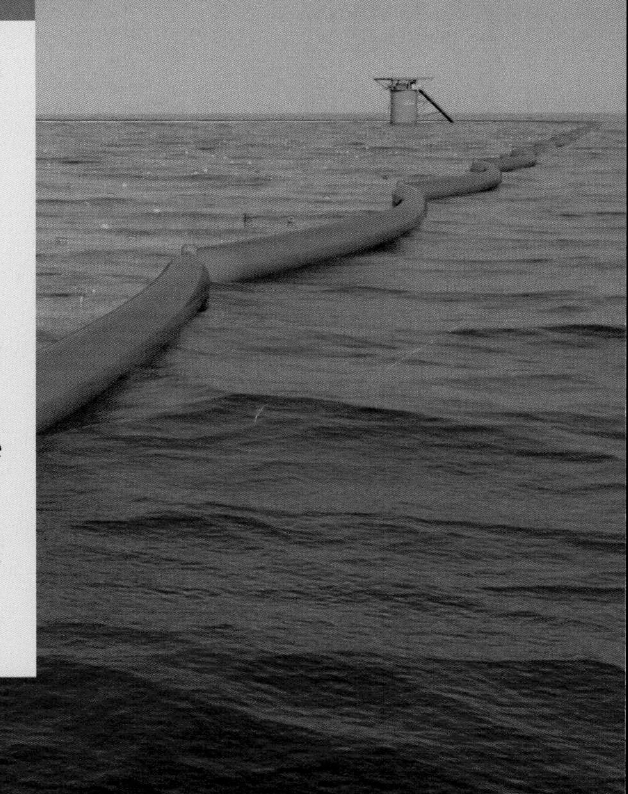

SC1a States of matter

Specification reference: C2.1; C2.2; C2.3; C2.4

Progression questions

- What are particles like in substances in the solid, liquid and gas states?
- What changes happen to particles during the different changes of state?
- How do you decide what state a substance will be in at a given temperature?

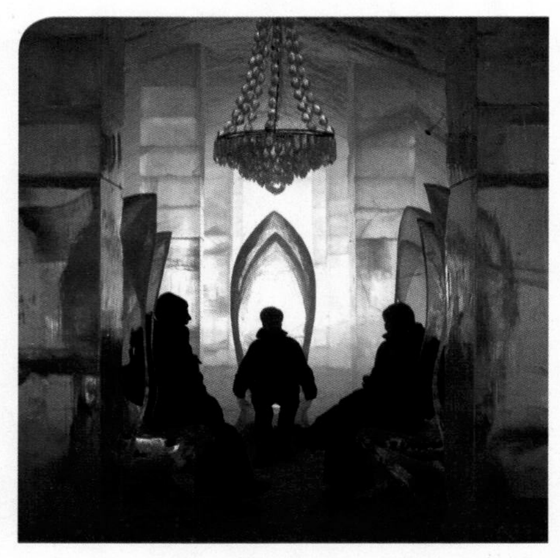

A This 'ice hotel' is made entirely from ice and snow – these are both water in the solid state.

The three **states of matter** are solid, liquid and gas. For example, water can exist in the solid state as ice, or in the familiar liquid state, or in the gas state as steam or water vapour.

The particle model

Some **particles** are large enough to see, like the dust on a computer screen. Others, like **atoms** and **molecules**, are far too small for you to see. When chemists discuss particles, they usually mean these very small particles.

The **particle model** explains state changes in a substance in terms of the arrangement, movement and energy stored in its particles.

State	Particle diagram	Arrangement of particles	Movement of particles
Gas		random far apart	fast in all directions
Liquid		random close together	move around each other
Solid		regular close together	vibrate about fixed positions

B Particles in the solid state contain the smallest amount of stored energy; particles in the gas state contain the most.

Did you know?

Science recognises 16 different types of ice, depending on the arrangement of the water molecules. A type called amorphous ice is found in space (such as on comets). A type called Ice IV is what you'll find in a kitchen freezer, here on Earth.

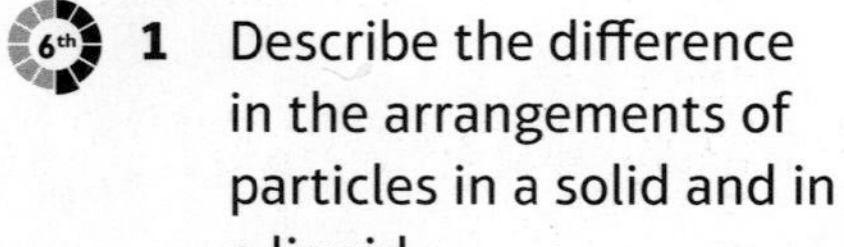

6th **1** Describe the difference in the arrangements of particles in a solid and in a liquid.

6th **2** Describe the difference in the movement of particles in a liquid and in a gas.

State changes

State changes are **physical changes**. They can be reversed, and the **chemical properties** of the substance do not change. This is because the particles themselves do not change – only their arrangement, movement and amount of stored energy.

3 State the meaning of the terms 'sublimation' and 'deposition'.

Particles are attracted to one another by weak forces of attraction. There are many of these forces in a solid. Some of these are overcome during melting. The remaining **attractive forces** between particles in a liquid are overcome during evaporation and boiling (when a substance is evaporating as fast as it can). For this to happen, energy must be transferred from the surroundings to the particles. This is why you heat ice to melt it, and why you boil water in a kettle. Diagram D shows how the temperature changes when water in the solid state is heated until it reaches the gas state.

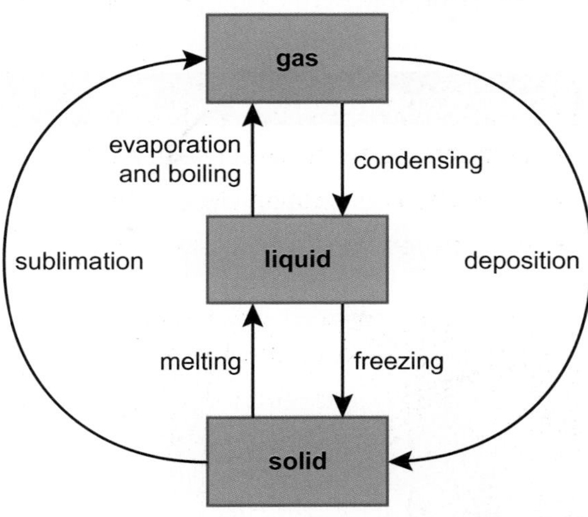

C the interconversions between the three states of matter

4 Describe how you can see from a 'heating curve' (such as diagram D) that a substance is changing state.

5 Explain what happens to the particles when a substance melts.

6 The melting point of gallium is 29.8 °C and its boiling point is 2204 °C. Predict its state at 25 °C, 100 °C and at 2205 °C.

Some attractive forces form between particles during condensing, and many attractive forces are formed during freezing. For this to happen, energy must be transferred from the particles to the surroundings. This is why water vapour turns into water droplets on a cold window, and why you put water in a freezer to make ice.

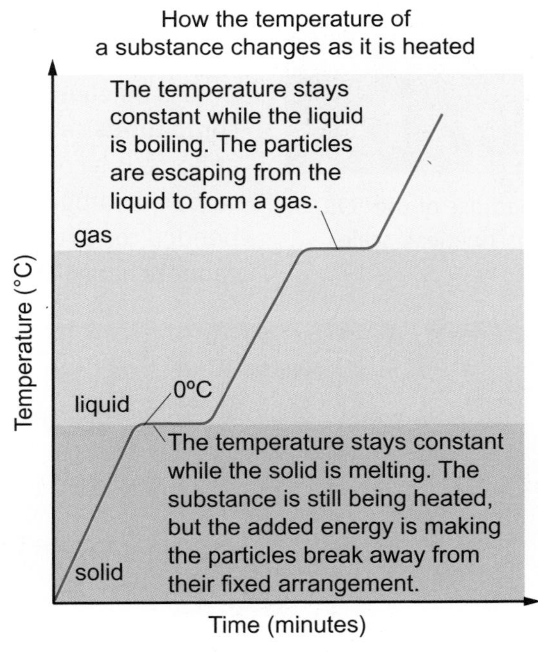

D a heating curve for water

You can predict the state of a substance if you know its temperature, and its **melting point** and **boiling point**. If the temperature is:

- below the melting point, the substance is solid
- between the melting point and boiling point, the substance is liquid
- above the boiling point, the substance is gas.

Exam-style question

Camping gas is used by campers and hikers. It is a mixture of propane and butane. Explain, in terms of the arrangement of fuel particles, why camping gas is stored in cylinders as a liquid rather than as a gas.

(2 marks)

Checkpoint

How confidently can you answer the Progression questions?

Strengthen

S1 Draw a diagram to show the states of matter. On your diagram, name each state change and describe what happens to the particles as it happens.

Extend

E1 Explain why the arrangement, movement and energy of particles change during changes of state.

SC2a Mixtures

Specification reference: C2.5; C2.6

Progression questions

- What is the difference between a pure substance and a mixture?
- What happens to its particles when a solid melts?
- How do melting points allow you to spot the differences between pure substances and mixtures?

A You can tell this gold bar is very nearly pure because of the '999.9' stamped on it. A number lower than 1000 on this 'fineness' scale means it is impure.

The composition (make-up) of a **pure** substance:

- cannot be changed
- is the same in all parts of a piece of the substance.

So, for example, pure gold contains only gold atoms.

 **1** Which type of atoms are found in a piece of pure silver?

 **2** State what is meant by the term 'impure'. Explain what the term 'impure' means.

Gold is an **element** and can be pure, but **compounds** can also be pure. The sugar we use at home is a compound called sucrose. It contains carbon, hydrogen and oxygen atoms chemically bonded together to form sucrose molecules. You cannot change the composition of pure sucrose.

Did you know?

The purest gold ever was produced in 1957 and was 999.999 on the fineness scale.

Gold purity is still often measured on the older carat scale, where 24 carat gold is pure gold.

 **3** **a** Describe what a mixture of carbon, hydrogen and oxygen might look like.

 **b** Describe how you would separate marbles from sand.

 **4** Oxygen can be removed from air by cooling. Explain why this would not be possible if air were not a mixture.

B Pure sucrose is always sucrose, no matter how finely it is ground down.

A pure substance has the same fixed composition in all its parts and so we can't separate it into other substances using physical methods (such as filtering or picking bits out).

A **mixture** contains elements and/or compounds that are not chemically joined together. You *can* use physical processes to separate mixtures into different substances.

A mixture does not have a fixed composition. For example, air is a mixture of gases. When students sit in a classroom, they use up oxygen and breathe out carbon dioxide and so the composition of the air in the room changes. We still call it 'air', but because air is a mixture its composition can change.

Melting points

When a solid melts, its particles gain enough energy to overcome the weak forces of attraction between them. They move further away from one another and the solid becomes a liquid. The temperature at which this happens is the **melting point**. This is an example of a **physical property** (how a substance responds to forces and energy).

5 What is the freezing point of pure oxygen?

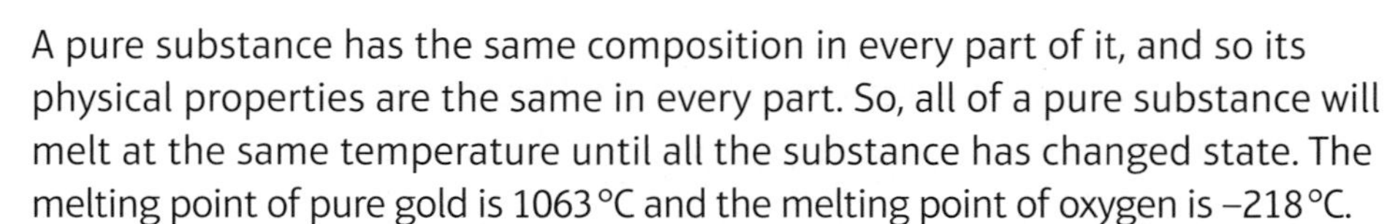

A pure substance has the same composition in every part of it, and so its physical properties are the same in every part. So, all of a pure substance will melt at the same temperature until all the substance has changed state. The melting point of pure gold is 1063 °C and the melting point of oxygen is –218 °C.

C This sweet is a mixture and so does not have a sharp melting point.

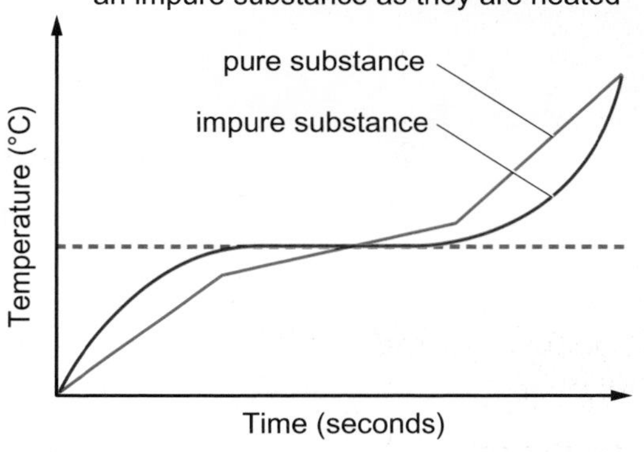

D heating curves for a pure substance and a mixture

The sweet shown in photo C has a liquid centre. The whole sweet melts over a *range* of temperatures and not all the parts melt and become liquid at the same time. This is what happens in mixtures – they do not have fixed, sharp melting points.

Substance	Melting temperatures (°C)
lead–tin alloy	183 to 258
argon	–189
carbon monoxide	–205

6 The table shows some melting temperatures.

a Identify which substances are mixtures and which are pure.

b Sketch a cooling curve for each of the three examples and explain their shapes.

Exam-style question

Explain why mixtures melt over a range of temperatures but pure substances have precise melting points. *(2 marks)*

Checkpoint

How confidently can you answer the Progression questions?

Strengthen

S1 List the ways in which pure substances are different from mixtures.

Extend

E1 A piece of gold jewellery is 750 on the fineness scale. Would you expect the jewellery to have a sharp melting temperature? Explain your answer.

SC2b Filtration and crystallisation

Specification reference: C0.6; C2.7

Progression questions

- How can filtration be used to separate mixtures?
- How can crystallisation be used to separate mixtures?
- What are the hazards and risks when separating mixtures by filtration and crystallisation?

A Some whales filter sea water with bristles (called baleen plates) to separate krill from the water.

1 a Give one example of a mixture that can be separated by filtration.

b Explain how this mixture is separated by filtration.

c Describe another type of mixture that can be separated by filtration.

Did you know?

Nearly 4 million tonnes of salt are solution mined in the UK each year.

C Salt can be produced by the evaporation of sea water.

Filters can be used to separate some mixtures. They let smaller pieces or liquids through but trap bigger pieces or **insoluble** substances.

Examples of **filtration** are to be seen all around us. Cars, vacuum cleaners and air-conditioning systems all have filters. Some whales use filters to feed. They open their mouths and take in water. When they close their mouths, they push out the water through filters. Small animals (such as krill) get stuck in the filters and are swallowed.

Crystallisation

A **solution** is a mixture made of **solutes** (dissolved substances) in a liquid called the **solvent**. Solutes can be separated from a solution by evaporating the solvent to leave the solutes behind. This is called **crystallisation**. The process forms solid crystals of various sizes. If the crystals form slowly, the particles have longer to form an ordered pattern and will make larger crystals.

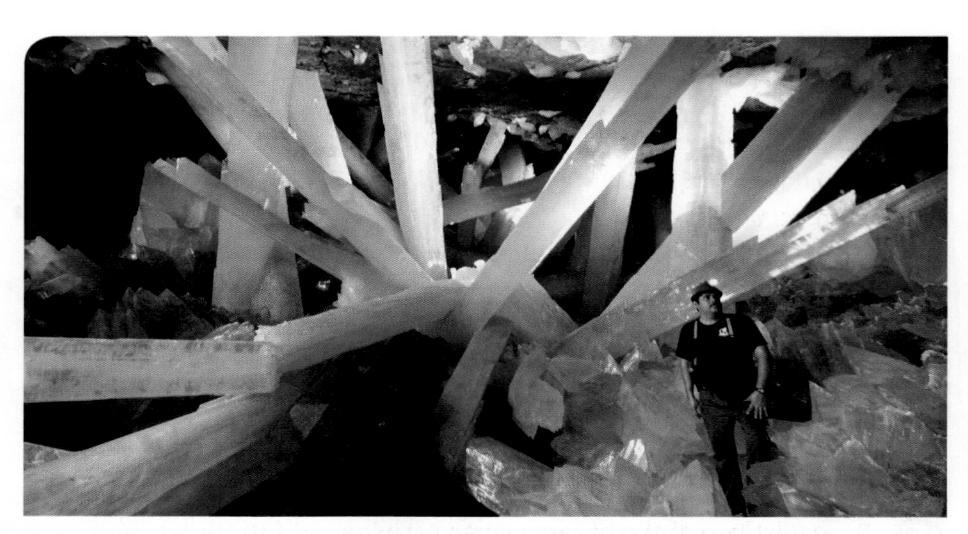

B Crystals in the Giant Crystal Cave in Mexico took over 500 000 years to form.

Table salt is produced from sea water, or is dug out of the ground or extracted using 'solution mining'. In this process water is pumped into layers of salt underground. The resulting salt solution is then heated, which evaporates the solvent and makes the solution more and more salty. Eventually it reaches a point where there is as much salt in the water as can possibly dissolve. This is a **saturated solution** and it contains the maximum amount of solute that can dissolve in that amount of solvent at that temperature. If more water evaporates and/or the solution cools, then some solute leaves the solution and salt crystals form.

Filtration and crystallisation in the lab

To filter a solution in the laboratory, a filter funnel is lined with filter paper that has fine holes in it. The solvent and solute(s) pass through the fine holes to form the **filtrate**. Bits of insoluble substances cannot fit through the holes and so leave a **residue** in the filter paper. A Bunsen burner is then used to evaporate the filtrate carefully. Care must be taken not to overheat the solution once it is saturated, because hot crystals may spit out. Further heating may also cause crystals to change chemically.

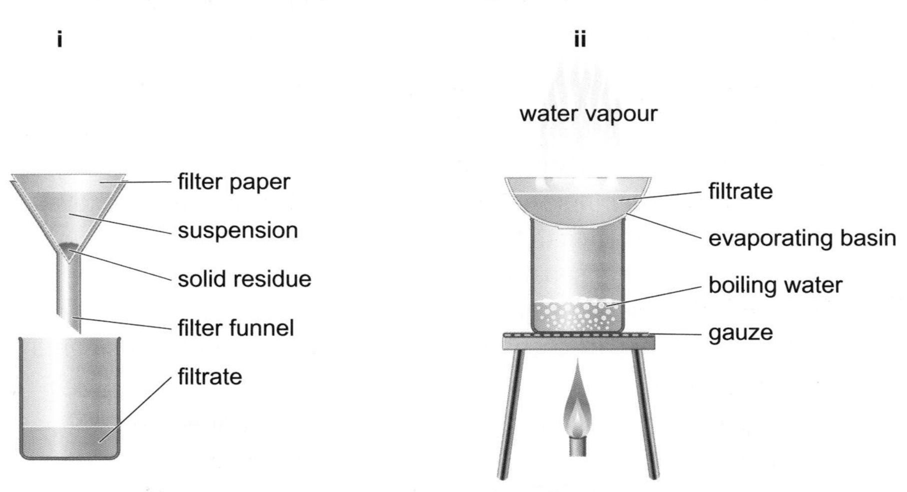

D Laboratory apparatus for (i) filtration and (ii) crystallisation.

In a **risk assessment**, the **hazards** of doing an experiment are identified. A hazard is something that could cause harm. Then ways of reducing the **risk** (chance) of a hazard causing harm are considered.

During crystallisation, the risks from spitting can be reduced by wearing eye protection, removing the Bunsen burner before the solution is completely dry and/or using steam to heat the evaporating basin gently (as above).

7 When a mixture of rock pieces, salt and water is filtered, what will be found as the:

a filtrate

b residue?

8 **a** List two of the hazards when carrying out filtration and crystallisation.

b Explain how the risks from each of your hazards can be reduced.

Exam-style question 

Explain the difference between a risk and a hazard. *(2 marks)*

2 Give the names of two mixtures that can be separated by crystallisation.

3 In the solution mining of salt, give the names of the:

a solvent

b solution

c solute.

4 When is a solution said to be 'saturated'?

5 Explain why crystals form during crystallisation.

6 Explain why the crystals in photo B are so big.

Checkpoint

How confidently can you answer the Progression questions?

Strengthen

S1 Explain how you would separate sand *and* salt from a mixture of the two.

Extend

E1 Scientists looking for new substances in plants grind up the plants with methanol. This solvent dissolves many plant compounds. However, methanol is flammable and toxic (especially if the vapour is inhaled). Large crystals can be made to help scientists work out what the compounds are made of. Explain how you would make plant-compound crystals using methanol.

SC2c Paper chromatography

Specification reference: C2.7; C2.9; C2.10

Progression questions

- How can chromatography be used to separate mixtures?
- What are the differences between mixtures and pure substances on a chromatogram?
- How do you calculate an R_f value?

A Experts restoring an old painting – they need to know what substances were mixed together to produce the paints used by the original artist.

Inks, paints and foods often contain mixtures of coloured compounds. **Chromatography** can be used to find out which coloured compounds the mixture contains. The type of chromatography used to analyse the substances in old oil paintings requires expensive machinery.

Paper chromatography is a simpler technique that works because some compounds dissolve better in a solvent than others. When a solvent moves along a strip of paper, it carries the different substances in the mixture at different speeds, so they are separated. The solvent is called the **mobile phase**. The paper contains the **stationary phase**, through which the solvent and dissolved substances move. The paper with the separated components on it is called a **chromatogram**.

1 a How many different compounds are in substance X in diagram B?

b For mixture Y, explain why the green spot is higher than the red spot.

2 Look at diagram B again. Explain why:

a the labels for substances X, Y and Z are written in pencil, not ink

b the starting positions for the different substances are above the level of solvent in the container.

3 One of the coloured compounds in diagram B has an R_f value of 0.1. Explain which compound this is likely to be.

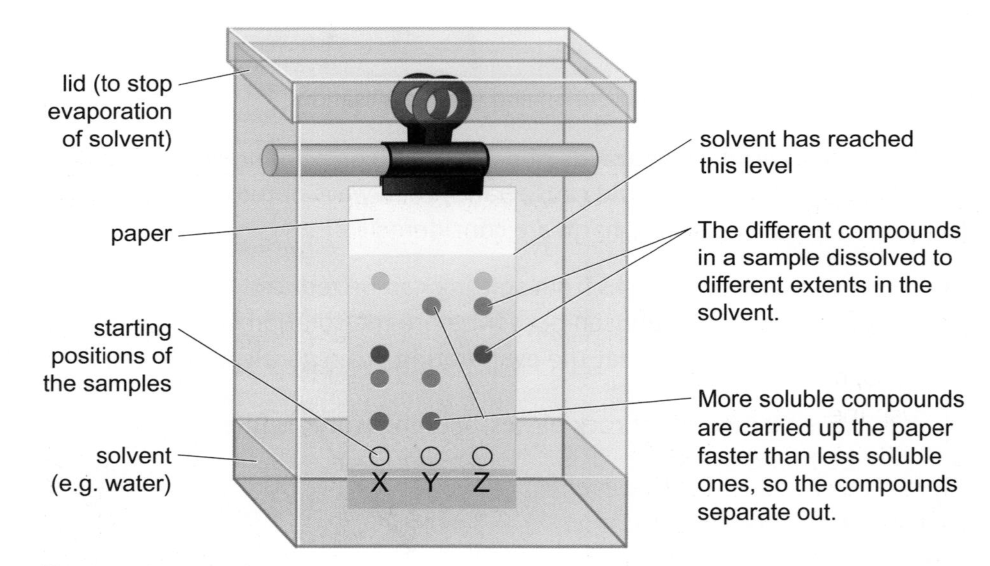

B paper chromatography

The **R_f value** is the distance the compound has risen divided by the distance the solvent has risen. Both measurements are made from the starting positions of the samples on the paper.

$$R_f = \frac{\text{distance moved by the spot}}{\text{distance moved by the solvent}}$$

The R_f value of a particular compound does not change if the chromatography conditions used remain the same.

Worked example

In diagram B, the pink spots have moved 4 cm and the solvent has moved 10 cm along the paper. Calculate the R_f value of this pink compound:

$$R_f = \frac{4}{10} = 0.4$$

A compound never rises as fast as the solvent, so R_f values are always less than 1. If you calculate an R_f value bigger than 1, you've made a mistake.

Paper chromatography can be used to:

- distinguish between pure and impure substances
- identify substances by comparing the pattern on the chromatogram with the patterns formed by known substances
- identify substances by calculating their R_f values.

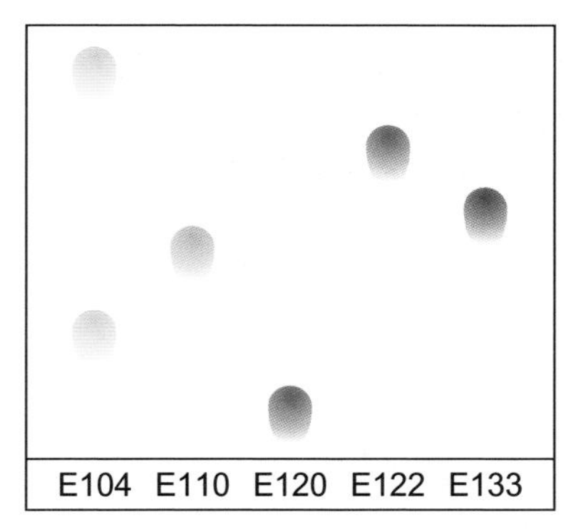

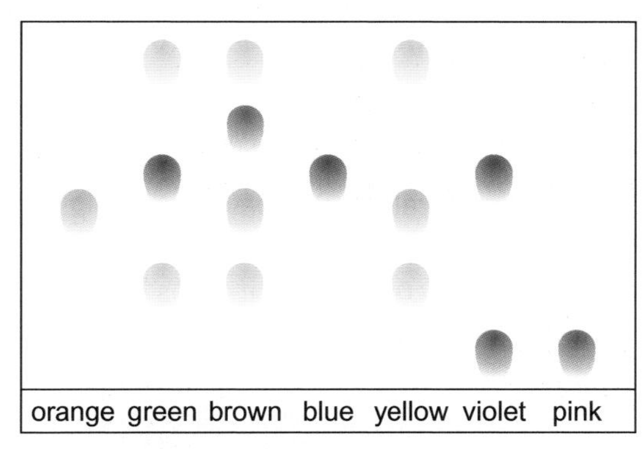

C The chromatogram on the left was done using known substances. The chromatogram on the right shows that the orange and blue sweets contain single dyes.

4 In diagram B, the yellow spots have moved 9 cm and the solvent has moved 10 cm. Calculate the R_f value of the yellow substance.

5 In diagram C, the chromatogram on the left shows some food dyes found in sweets. The chromatogram on the right shows the results for some sweets.

a Which sweets contain just one dye?

b Which dyes are in the yellow sweets?

c What is the colour of the most soluble dye?

Did you know?

In 1983, many national newspapers paid a lot of money to publish diaries allegedly written by Adolf Hitler. However, scientists used chromatography to analyse the inks in the diaries and found that they were not available during Hitler's lifetime – the diaries were fake.

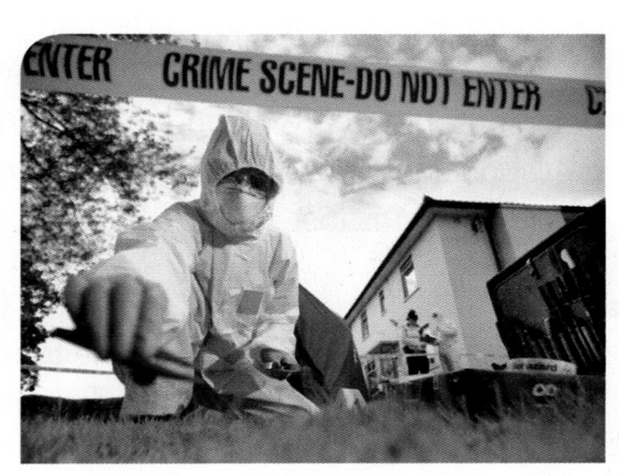

D Chromatography can be used to help identify substances at crime scenes.

Exam-style question

Two dyes have the same R_f values when tested using chromatography. Explain whether this means they are the same dye or not. *(3 marks)*

Checkpoint

How confidently can you answer the Progression questions?

Strengthen

S1 The police have taken four orange lipsticks from suspects. Explain the steps needed to find out if one of the lipsticks could have made a mark at a crime scene.

Extend

E1 A laboratory produces a list of R_f values for food colourings. Explain why R_f values are used and what other information is needed for these R_f values to be useful.

SC2d Distillation

Specification reference: C0.6; C2.7

Progression questions

- What is distillation?
- How do simple distillation and fractional distillation differ?
- How would you reduce risks when carrying out a distillation experiment?

A a steam iron

Tap water contains dissolved minerals, especially in hard water areas – tap water is a **mixture**. For some jobs it is best to use pure water (such as for chemical analysis, in car-cooling systems and older steam irons). To make water pure we need to separate it from the dissolved solids. This is done by **distillation**.

1 a What happens to the water in a steam iron when you turn the iron on?

b Explain why some irons may not work well if you use ordinary tap water.

When mineral water **evaporates**, only the water turns to a gas (vapour). The solid minerals, which have much higher boiling points, are left behind. The water vapour (steam) is pure. If the vapour is then **condensed**, it turns back to liquid water again – the liquid water will now be pure. This combination of evaporation followed by condensation is called distillation. The apparatus used is called a **still**.

Diagram B shows a simple method for distilling. Water is heated in the conical flask and the vapour travels along the delivery tube, where it condenses. This method is not very efficient because much of the vapour is lost.

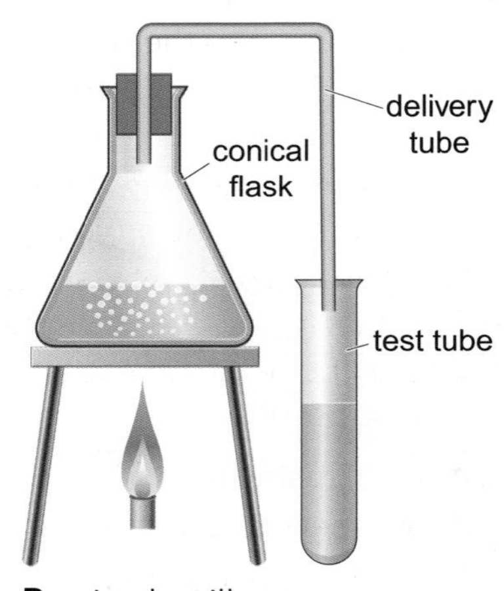

B a simple still

2 In diagram B, what is the hazard if steam escapes from the tube?

3 Suggest a way of improving a simple still so that more of the steam condenses back to water.

thermometer

anti-bumping granules (to make the liquid boil more smoothly – small bubbles of vapour form on the corners of the granules and reduce the risk of the liquid boiling over.)

cooling water out

condenser (a central tube surrounded by a jacket of cold water)

distillation flask

solution (e.g. salty water)

cooling water in

distillate (e.g. pure water)

C distillation apparatus

The type of still shown in diagram C is more efficient. The condenser keeps the tube cool, so that almost all of the vapour condenses and turns into a liquid.

4 Explain how the still in diagram C can be used to purify water.

5 Explain how:

a the condenser reduces the risk of hot vapour escaping

b the safety of the method is improved by using anti-bumping granules.

Fractional distillation

Distillation can also be used to separate two or more liquids. This works because some liquids boil more easily than others. Liquids with lower boiling points evaporate more easily than others, and will turn into a vapour first. This is called **fractional distillation**, because the original mixture will be split into several parts, or fractions. The first fraction to be collected contains the liquid with the lowest boiling point. The fractions could be pure liquids, or may still be mixtures.

Fractional distillation can be used:

- to separate the different products in crude oil
- to make alcoholic drinks such as whisky and vodka
- to separate out the gases in the air, after the air has been cooled and turned into a liquid at −200 °C.

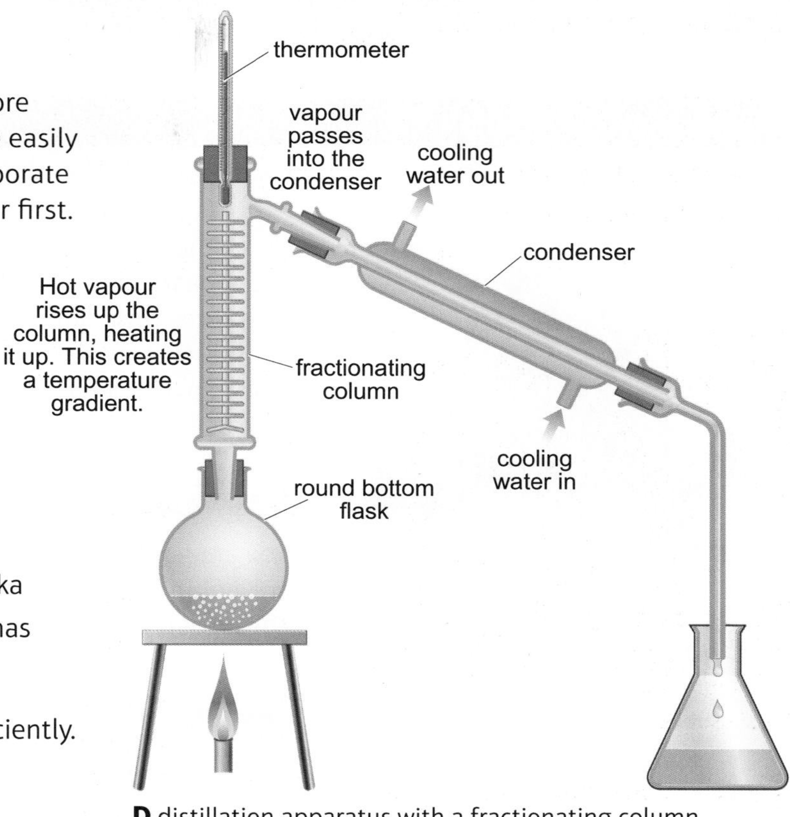

D distillation apparatus with a fractionating column

Diagram D shows how to separate liquids more efficiently. A column is fixed above the distillation flask. The hot vapour rises up the column. At first, the vapour condenses when it hits the cool glass and drips back down into the flask. As the column gradually heats up, there will be a temperature gradient – it will be hottest at the bottom and the temperature will drop as you go further up the column. The fraction with the lowest boiling point will reach the top of the column first and the vapour will then pass into the condenser. If you keep heating, fractions with higher boiling points will then rise up the column and can be collected later.

6 **Compare and contrast simple and fractional distillation.**

7 **Explain why a liquid with a lower boiling point will reach the top of a fractionating column more quickly than one with a higher boiling point.**

Did you know?

The vacuum flask that we now use to keep drinks hot was originally used to keep liquid air *cold*. It was designed by James Dewar in 1892.

Exam-style question

A student is asked to separate two liquids. Liquid A boils at 100 °C and liquid B boils at 65 °C. The student sets up a fractional distillation experiment, and after a few minutes a clear liquid is collected from the condenser. Explain which of the two liquids will be collected first. *(2 marks)*

Checkpoint

How confidently can you answer the Progression questions?

Strengthen

S1 Explain what distillation is and how the distillation apparatus (the still) works. Use a labelled diagram to make your explanation clear.

S2 Explain the safety precautions you need to take when carrying out distillation in a laboratory.

Extend

E1 Pure ethanol ('alcohol') boils at 78.5 °C. Explain how a 50:50 mixture of ethanol and water can be separated by fractional distillation.

E2 Suggest why the boiling point of the starting liquid will change with time.

SC2d Core practical – Investigating inks

Specification reference: C2.11

Aim

Investigate the composition of inks using simple distillation and paper chromatography.

A Fountain pen ink is available as a washable ink.

Ink is a mixture of coloured substances dissolved in a liquid solvent. Ink that appears to be a single colour, such as black, may contain two or more substances with different colours. Permanent inks do not run if the paper becomes wet, a useful property if you drop your homework in a puddle. Washable inks separate into their different colours if the paper gets wet, but may be removed if spilt on clothing.

Your task

You are going to use simple distillation to separate a sample of the solvent in some ink. You will also use paper chromatography to separate the coloured substances in samples of ink.

Method

Simple distillation

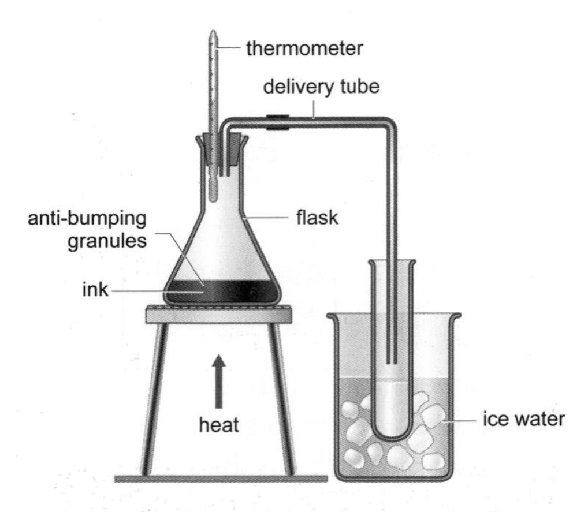

B separating ink using simple distillation

Wear eye protection.

A Set up your apparatus so that the ink is in a flask, and its vapours can be led away to be condensed. Diagram B shows some typical apparatus but yours may be different.

B Heat the flask of ink using a Bunsen burner, making sure the ink simmers gently and does not boil over into the delivery tube.

C Continue heating until you have collected a few cm^3 of distillate (distilled solvent).

D Note the maximum temperature obtained.

Paper chromatography

E Draw a pencil line on a piece of chromatography paper, about 2 cm from the bottom.

F Add a small spot of ink to the pencil line.

G Add water to a container to a depth of about 1 cm.

H Place the paper into the container. Make sure the paper is supported so that it does not slump into the water when it becomes damp. Allow the water to travel through the paper.

I Take the paper out before the water reaches the top. Immediately mark the position of the solvent front using a pencil, then leave the paper to dry.

J Measure the distance travelled by the water from the pencil line, and the distances travelled by each coloured substance.

K Calculate the R_f value for each coloured substance.

Exam-style questions

1 Explain the function of the beaker of iced water in diagram B. *(2 marks)*

2 A student carries out simple distillation on a sample of blue ink.

- **a** Predict how the appearance of the ink changes, and give a reason for your answer. *(2 marks)*
- **b** During the experiment, hot liquid solvent drips from the bulb of the thermometer. Suggest an explanation for a temperature rise from 83 °C to 100 °C as this happens. *(1 mark)*

3 Explain why simple distillation allows a pure solvent to be separated from a solution. *(3 marks)*

4 A student distils a sample of ink. Devise a simple method to show that the liquid collected is pure water. Include the expected results in your answer. *(3 marks)*

5 Propanone is a flammable solvent. A student carries out paper chromatography of ink using propanone.

- **a** Identify the mobile phase and the stationary phase in her experiment. *(2 marks)*
- **b** Explain one precaution necessary to control the risk of harm in her experiment. *(1 mark)*
- **c** Suggest an explanation for why the level of the propanone should be below the ink spot on the paper at the start. *(1 mark)*

6 Explain how paper chromatography separates coloured substances in ink. *(3 marks)*

7 A student uses paper chromatography to analyse four samples of ink (X, A, B and C). Diagram C shows his results.

- **a** Describe what the results tell you about ink sample X. *(2 marks)*
- **b** Calculate the R_f value of the substance in ink B. *(2 marks)*

8 A student uses paper chromatography to analyse the dyes present in a sample of ink. She adds a sample of the ink and four dyes (1, 2, 3 and 4) to the paper. Table D shows her results for the dyes.

- **a** Explain which dye is the most soluble in the solvent used by the student. *(2 marks)*
- **b** Explain whether each dye is a pure substance. *(2 marks)*
- **c** Suggest an explanation for why a mixture of dyes 1 and 4 may appear as a single green spot in a paper chromatogram. *(2 marks)*

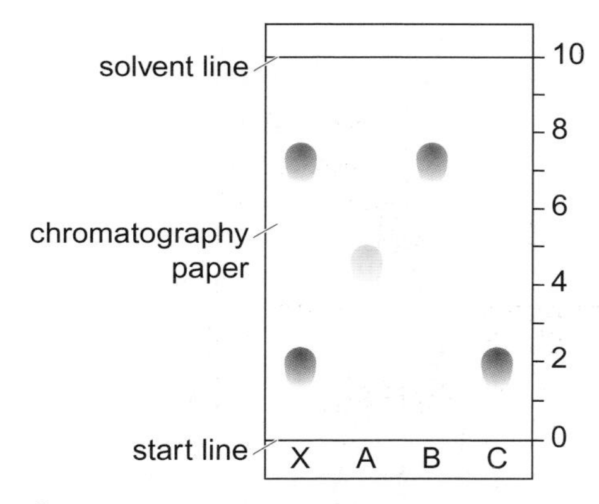

C

Dye	Spot colour	R_f
1	yellow	0.10
2	red	0.35
3	green	0.67
4	blue	0.12

D

SC2e Drinking water

Specification reference: C2.8; C2.12

Progression questions

- How would you choose which method to use to separate a mixture?
- How is drinking water produced?
- Why must water used in chemical analysis be pure?

A Personal water purifiers filter water to make it safer to drink.

1 Explain how pure water is produced using the apparatus shown in diagram B.

2 Suggest why the simple distillation of sea water may be used to provide drinking water in oil-rich coastal countries.

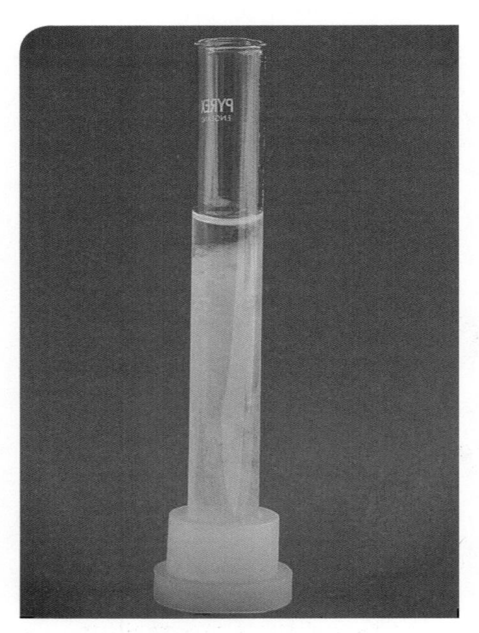

C A cloudy white precipitate forming during a chemical analysis.

About 97% of the Earth's water is in the oceans. The concentration of dissolved salts in sea water is far too high for us to drink safely. Producing pure water from sea water is called **desalination** and can be achieved using **simple distillation**.

Purifying sea water

Water is separated from dissolved salts using simple distillation. Sea water is heated so that water vapour leaves it quickly. This vapour is then cooled and condensed, forming water without the dissolved salts.

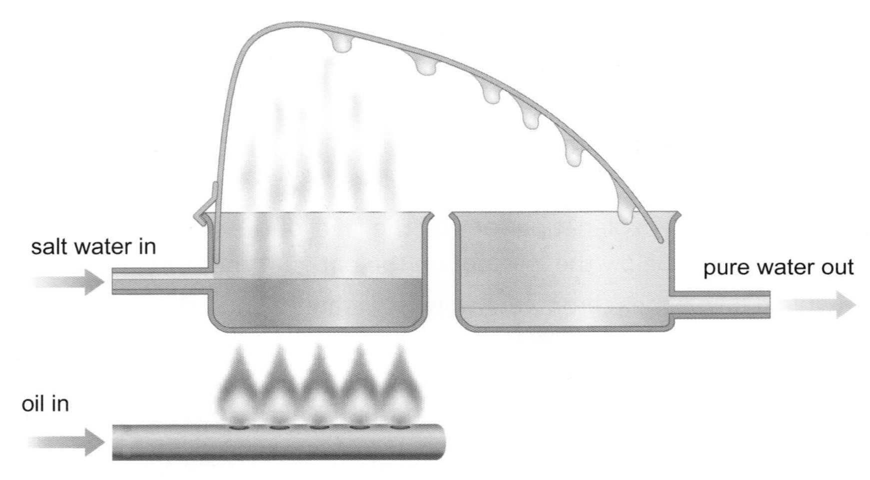

B Simple distillation of sea water using oil as a fuel.

A lot of energy must be transferred to sea water during simple distillation, so it is not usually a suitable method for producing large volumes of drinking water. It is mainly carried out on a large scale where energy resources are cheap or plentiful, and where there is an abundant supply of sea water.

Water for chemical analysis

Chemical analysis involves using chemical reactions or sensitive machines to identify and measure the substances in a sample. The water used for chemical analysis should not contain any dissolved salts, otherwise incorrect results will be obtained. Tap water contains small amounts of dissolved salts, which may react to form unexpected cloudy **precipitates**. These may hide the correct result of the analysis. Also, the machines used for analysis may detect the salts, again leading to an incorrect conclusion.

3 Explain why distilled water is more suitable than tap water for doing a chemical analysis.

Water for drinking

In the UK, the raw material for producing drinking water comes from rivers, lakes or **aquifers** (underground rocks containing groundwater). The water in these sources is often stored in reservoirs, which are artificial lakes produced by building a dam across a valley. Fresh water from these sources contains:

- objects such as leaves and twigs
- small insoluble particles such as grit and silt
- soluble substances, including salts, pesticides and fertilisers
- bacteria and other microorganisms that may be harmful to health.

Different steps are needed to deal with these impurities. They include screening using a sieve, **sedimentation** (in which small particles are allowed to settle out) and filtration using tanks containing beds of sand and gravel. Chlorine is added in a process called **chlorination**. Chlorine kills microorganisms in the treated water.

4 Explain why it may not be safe to drink water straight from a river.

Did you know?

Only about 2.5% of the Earth's water is fresh water. Of that, only 0.3% is in rivers and lakes – the rest is in icecaps, glaciers and ground water.

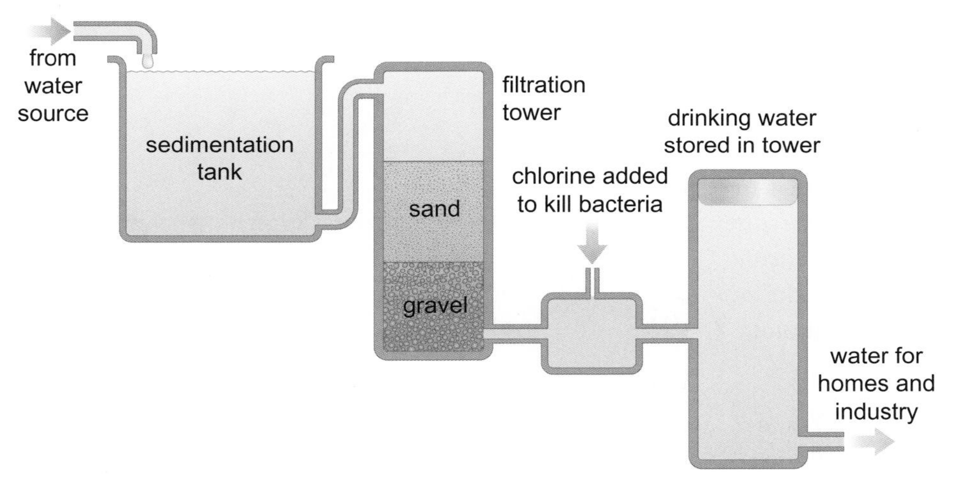

D These are the main stages in treating fresh water to make it safe to drink.

5 **a** Describe how water is treated to deal with leaves and twigs, grit and silt, and with microorganisms.

b Identify the stage missing from diagram D and draw a labelled diagram to show it.

6 Suggest why chemical reactions, rather than separation methods, are used to remove harmful substances dissolved in drinking water in the UK.

Exam-style question

Fresh water is treated to make it safe to drink. Soluble and insoluble substances are removed during this treatment, and chlorine is added to kill harmful microorganisms. State two reasons why samples of the treated water are tested regularly. *(2 marks)*

Checkpoint

How confidently can you answer the Progression questions?

Strengthen

S1 Draw flowcharts to describe two ways in which water can be made fit to drink.

Extend

E1 A bottle of water has a label saying 'Suitable for chemical analysis'. Describe how this water has been produced.

E2 Explain how you would check to see if this water really is suitable for analysis.

Methods of separating and purifying substances

A runny green mixture contains three compounds (**X**, **Y** and **Z**).

Compound	Melting point (°C)	Boiling point (°C)	State at room temperature	Notes
X	2435	4000	solid	not soluble in **Y** or **Z**
Y	−126	97.4	liquid	soluble in **Z**
Z	−114	78.4	liquid	soluble in **Y**

Plan a method to separate out **X**, **Y** and **Z**. Use the information in the table above and explain why you have suggested each step. **(6 marks)**

Student answer

Compound X is solid, and it is insoluble in the two liquids (Y and Z). This means it can be separated from them by filtration [1]. *When X is collected in the filter paper it will be wet with the two liquids, so it should be dried in a warm oven. The boiling points of the two liquids are well below the melting point of compound X, so compound X will not melt in the oven* [2].

The filtrate will be a mixture of compounds Y and Z. These can be separated using fractional distillation because their boiling points are different [3]. *When the mixture is heated, compound Z will distil off first because it has the lower boiling point* [4], *leaving compound Y behind.*

[1] This explains *why* compound X can be separated by filtration.

[2] The answer uses information from the table to explain why drying compound X will work.

[3] This makes it clear which physical property fractional distillation depends on.

[4] It is clear which liquid will be collected first, and why.

Verdict

This is a strong answer. It shows good knowledge and understanding of separation methods and uses correct scientific language.

The answer is organised logically, in the order that the practical would be carried out. Each step of the practical is linked to a scientific explanation.

Exam tip

If you are given a table of data or a graph in a question, make sure you use information from it in your answer.

Paper 1 and Paper 2

SC3 Atomic Structure

This image courtesy of Prof Richard Palmer, University of Birmingham, shows palladium atoms on a base of carbon. According to the scientists who produced it, Zhiwei Wang and David Pearmain, although they had watched with love, they had nothing to do with the spontaneous formation of the heart shape. Unfortunately this atomic valentine, being only 8 nanometres (0.000000008 metres) across, is far too small to see even with the strongest light microscope. It may, however, help to explain the nature of matter, which is central to understanding the properties of materials and the chemical reactions that form new substances. In this unit you will find out more about atoms and their structure.

The learning journey

Previously you will have learnt at KS3:

- about the particle model of matter
- how Dalton's ideas about atoms helped to explain the properties of matter
- how elements are arranged in the periodic table.

In this unit you will learn:

- how our ideas about atoms have changed
- what a relative atomic mass is
- **H** how to calculate relative atomic mass for an element.

SC3a Structure of an atom

Specification reference: C1.1; C1.2; C1.3; C1.4; C1.5

Progression questions

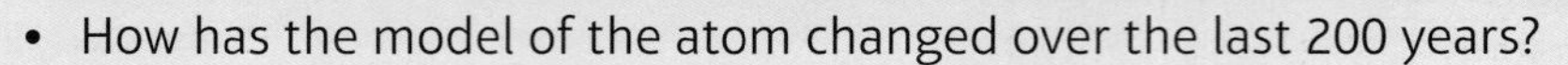

- How has the model of the atom changed over the last 200 years?
- How do the parts of atoms compare with each other?
- Why do atoms have no overall charge?

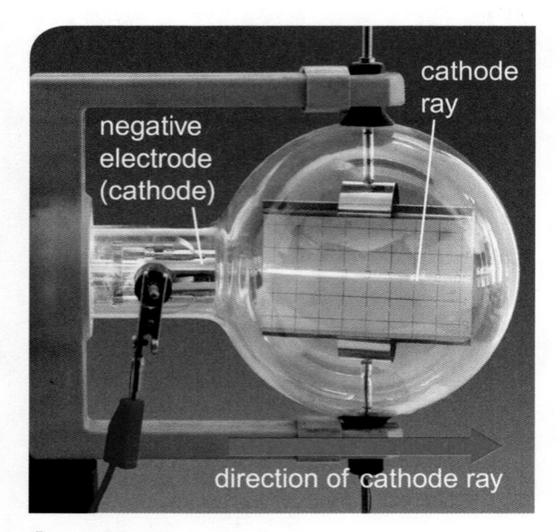

A a cathode ray tube

 **1** What are atoms?

 **2** Which of Dalton's ideas about particles is supported by the image of palladium atoms on the previous page?

In 1805 the English chemist John Dalton (1766–1844) published his atomic theory that said:

- all matter is made up of tiny particles called **atoms**
- atoms are tiny, hard spheres that cannot be broken down into smaller parts
- atoms cannot be created or destroyed
- the atoms in an **element** are all identical (but each element has its own type of atom).

Dalton's ideas helped to explain some of the properties of matter. However, experiments towards the end of the nineteenth century suggested that atoms contain even smaller particles.

When a high voltage is applied to a glass tube that has most of the air removed, glowing rays are seen. Some scientists thought that these 'cathode rays' were atoms leaving the negative electrode. In 1897, JJ Thomson (1856–1940) investigated the mass of the particles in the rays and found that they were about 1800 times lighter than the lightest atom (hydrogen). Cathode rays, therefore, did not contain atoms but **subatomic particles**, which we now call **electrons**.

The structure of atoms

Scientists have now worked out that atoms are made up of electrons together with heavier subatomic particles called **protons** and **neutrons**. All these particles have very, very small masses and electric charges. So, rather than use their actual masses and charges, it is easier to describe them by looking at their **relative masses** and **relative charges** compared to a proton. For example, if we say the mass of a proton is '1' then anything else that has the same mass is also '1'.

Did you know?

The actual mass of a proton is 0.000 000 000 000 000 000 000 001 67 g (1.67×10^{-24} g).

Subatomic particle	Relative charge	Relative mass
proton	+1 (positive)	1
electron	−1 (negative)	1/1835 (negligible)
neutron	0 (no charge)	1

B relative masses and relative charges of subatomic particles

 **3** Which subatomic particle has the lowest mass?

At the centre of all atoms is a tiny **nucleus** containing protons and neutrons. This is surrounded by fast moving electrons arranged in **electron shells** at different distances from the nucleus.

Atoms in elements always have equal numbers of protons and electrons and so have no overall charge, because the charges cancel out.

Diagram C shows two ways of modelling a beryllium atom. The three-dimensional model attempts to show how we imagine electrons to move.

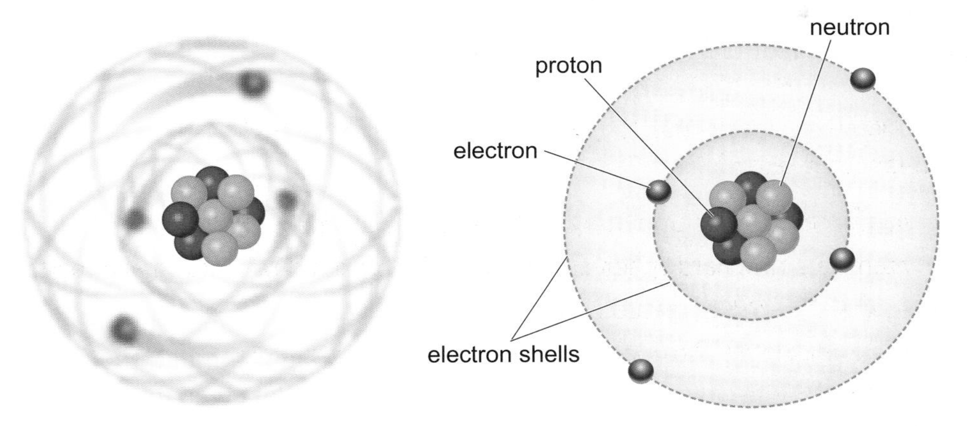

C The 'target diagram' on the right shows the arrangement of the electrons more clearly.

Models of atoms help us to understand their structure – but most models don't really give a correct impression of scale. The overall diameter of an atom can be 100 000 times the diameter of its nucleus.

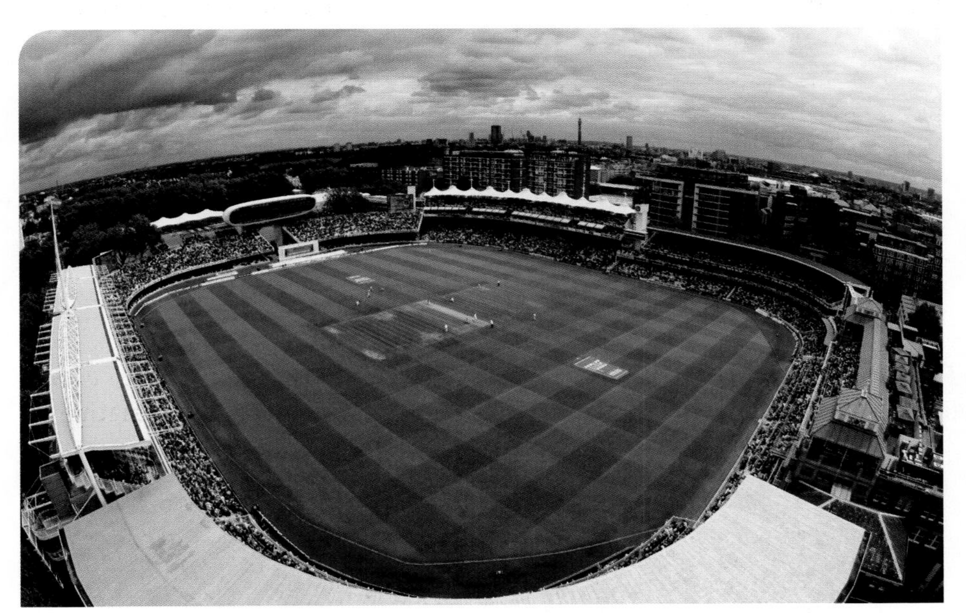

D If an atom could be made the size of the Lord's cricket ground, its nucleus would be about the size of this dot ●. Most of an atom is empty space.

4 How many protons, neutrons and electrons are in a beryllium atom?

5 A lithium atom has 3 protons, 4 neutrons and 3 electrons.

a Draw a diagram of this atom.

b Why is this atom neutral?

c How many electrons would be in an atom that has 17 protons?

Exam-style question

Compare the modern model of an atom to the atomic model proposed by John Dalton in 1805. *(2 marks)*

Checkpoint

How confidently can you answer the Progression questions?

Strengthen

S1 Draw an atom and label it to describe the arrangement and properties of its subatomic particles.

Extend

E1 Figure E (below) shows what happens when the three subatomic particles are fired through an electric field.

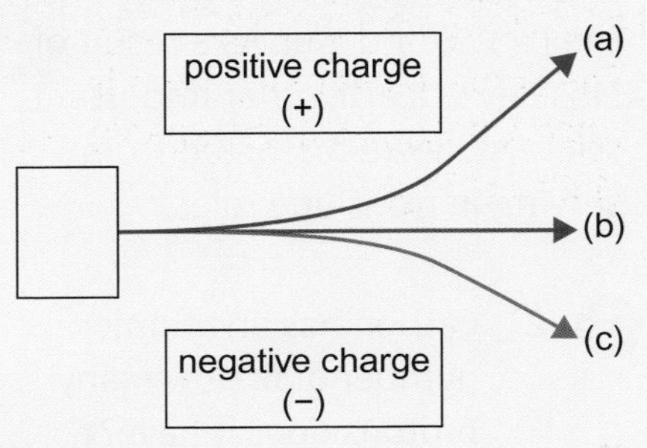

Name each particle a, b and c. Explain your answer.

SC3b Atomic number and mass number

Specification reference: C1.6; C1.7; C1.8; C1.10

Progression questions

- Why is most of the mass of an atom found in its nucleus?
- What does the atomic number tell you about an element?
- How can you calculate the numbers of protons, neutrons and electrons in atoms?

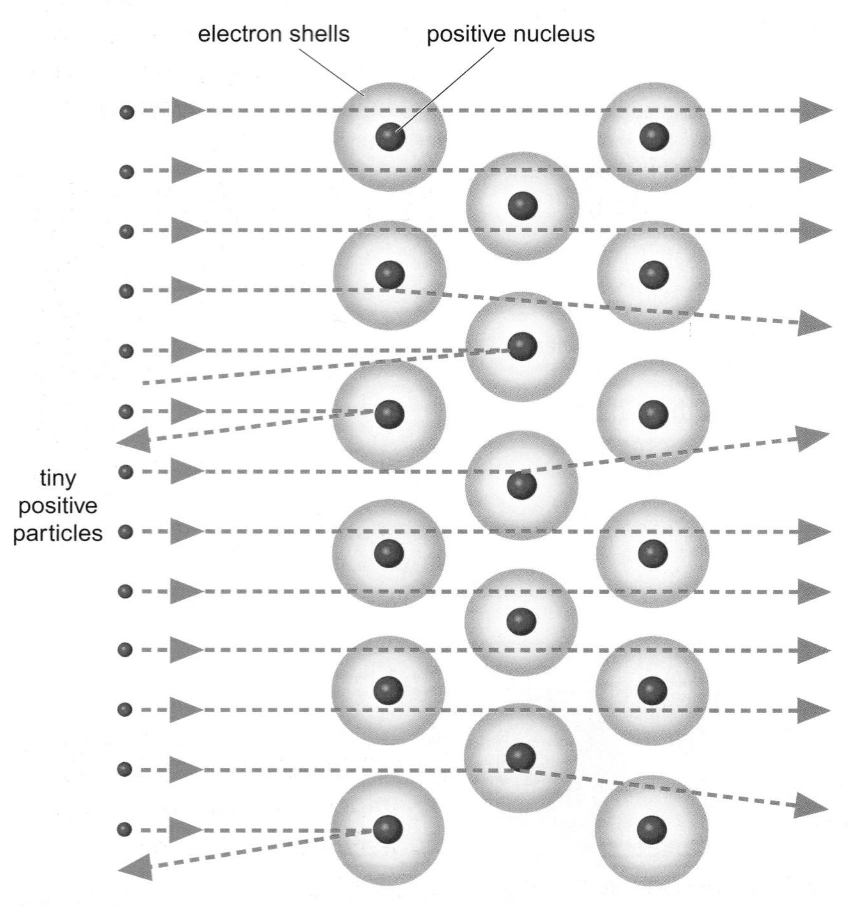

A Rutherford's scattering experiments suggested a nuclear atomic model.

The nuclear atom

In 1909, Ernest Rutherford (1871–1937) was working with others to investigate the structure of atoms. In one experiment, tiny positive particles were fired at a thin gold foil. To everyone's surprise most of the particles passed straight through the gold foil, with a few being deflected and a very small number bouncing back. Rutherford explained this by suggesting that atoms are mostly empty space, with a small positive central nucleus that contains most of the mass.

1 **a** Where is most of the mass of an atom?

b Explain how the experiment in diagram A suggests that atoms are mostly empty space.

Atomic number

The elements in the **periodic table** were originally placed in order of the masses of their atoms. However, this caused some elements to be grouped with others that had very different properties. So a few elements were swapped round to make sure that those with similar properties were grouped together, even if it meant that they were no longer in the correct order of mass.

Experiments by Henry Moseley (1887–1915) in 1913 confirmed that the rearranged order of elements in the table was actually correct. He showed that they were in order of the amount of positive charge in the nucleus. The proton was discovered about five years later. The modern periodic table places the elements in order of the number of protons in their atoms. This is the **atomic number** and it is this that defines an element – all the atoms of a particular element have the same unique atomic number.

Did you know?

Henry Moseley was killed during the First World War. As a result of Moseley's death, other important scientists were restricted from serving in front-line roles.

2 Carbon has an atomic number of 6. How many protons does it have?

3 Use a periodic table to find:

a the number of protons and electrons in atoms of:

i nitrogen **ii** potassium

b two elements whose atomic mass order does not match their atomic number order.

4 In terms of structure, what do all atoms of a certain element have in common?

Mass number

The mass of an electron is described as 'negligible' – it is so small that it can be ignored. This explains why the nucleus of any atom contains nearly all its mass. For this reason the total number of protons and neutrons in an atom is called its **mass number**.

A mass number is represented by the symbol *A* and an atomic number by the symbol *Z*. These numbers are written next to an element's symbol as shown in diagram B.

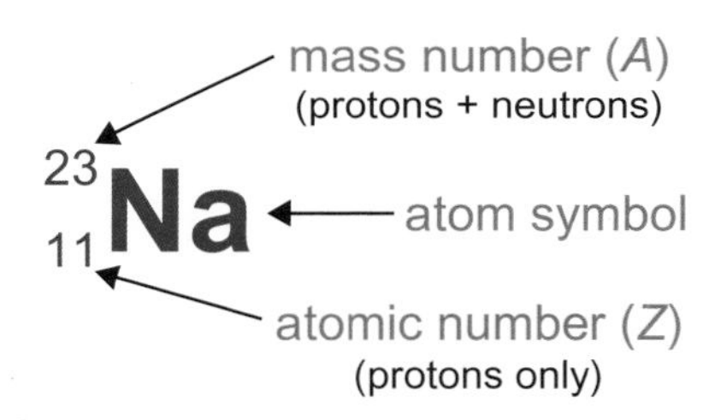

B This is how scientists write the atomic number and the mass number for a sodium atom. It shows that the atom contains 11 protons and 12 neutrons in its nucleus.

5 How many protons, neutrons and electrons are in the atom $^{27}_{13}Al$? Explain how you worked out your answer.

6 A manganese atom has 25 protons, 30 neutrons and 25 electrons. Show this information using the form shown in diagram B.

7 Look at the 'Did you know?' box on this page. Which subatomic particle does a hydrogen atom *not* have? Explain your reasoning.

Exam-style question

Complete the table below *(2 marks)*

Atom	atomic number	mass number	number of protons	number of neutrons	number of electrons
X	90	222	90	132	(i)
Y	88	(ii)	88	134	88

Did you know?

Just two elements make up most of our Universe – about 74% is hydrogen $^{1}_{1}H$ and 24% is helium $^{4}_{2}H$. These are also the two simplest atoms in the periodic table. The Sun releases energy by converting hydrogen atoms into helium atoms. Every second, over 600 million tonnes of hydrogen is converted to helium.

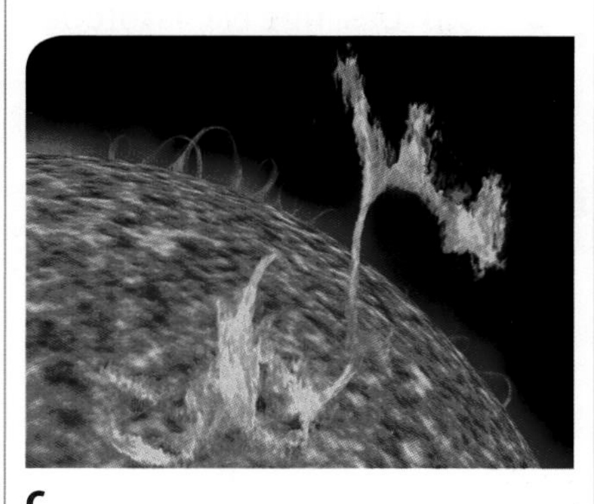

C

Checkpoint

How confidently can you answer the Progression questions?

Strengthen

S1 An atom can be represented in the form $^{65}_{29}Cu$. What does this tell you about this atom?

Extend

E1 Formulae can be written to connect the atomic number, mass number, and numbers of protons, electrons and neutrons in atoms.

For example:

atomic number = protons

Write formulae that connect the other four numbers.

SC3c Isotopes

Specification reference: C1.9; C1.10; C1.11; **H** C1.12

Progression questions

- How can you describe and identify isotopes of elements?
- Why are the relative atomic masses for some elements not whole numbers?
- **H** How do you calculate the relative atomic mass of an element?

1 **a** Write the name of each of the three lithium isotopes in diagram A.

b Describe each isotope in the format $^{A}_{Z}X$ (X is the element's symbol).

Did you know?

In 1945, at the end of the Second World War, two 'atomic bombs' were dropped on the Japanese cities of Hiroshima and Nagasaki. The bombs used nuclear fission and killed at least 129 000 people.

B

In 1932, James Chadwick (1891–1974) discovered the neutron. His discovery explains why some atoms of the same element have different masses. These atoms are known as **isotopes** – they have the same atomic number but different mass numbers. We refer to a specific isotope by adding its mass number to the element's name. The isotope on the left of diagram A is lithium-6.

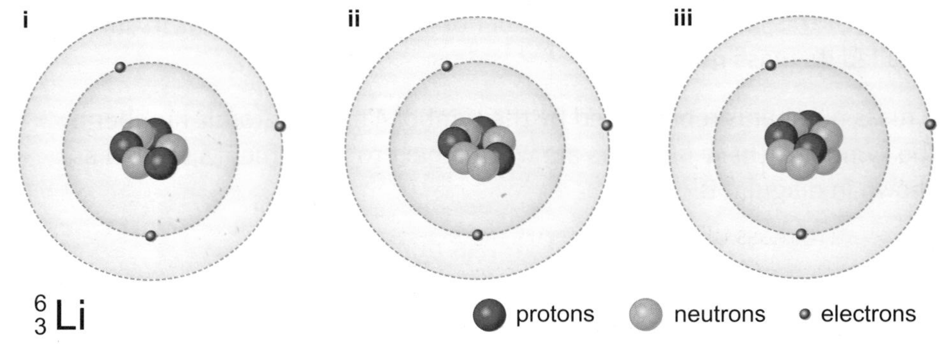

A Isotopes of the same element are chemically identical because they have the same number of protons and electrons.

Understanding neutrons led to the discovery of nuclear energy. By firing neutrons at a uranium isotope, $^{235}_{92}U$, it was discovered that a nucleus can be split (**nuclear fission**). This produces new elements and transfers large amounts of energy. Nuclear power stations use the energy from nuclear fission to produce electricity.

2 **a** State the numbers of protons and neutrons in an atom of uranium-235.

b State the number of protons, neutrons and electrons in the barium isotope formed in diagram C.

c Identify the other product. Give your answer using the format $^{A}_{Z}X$.

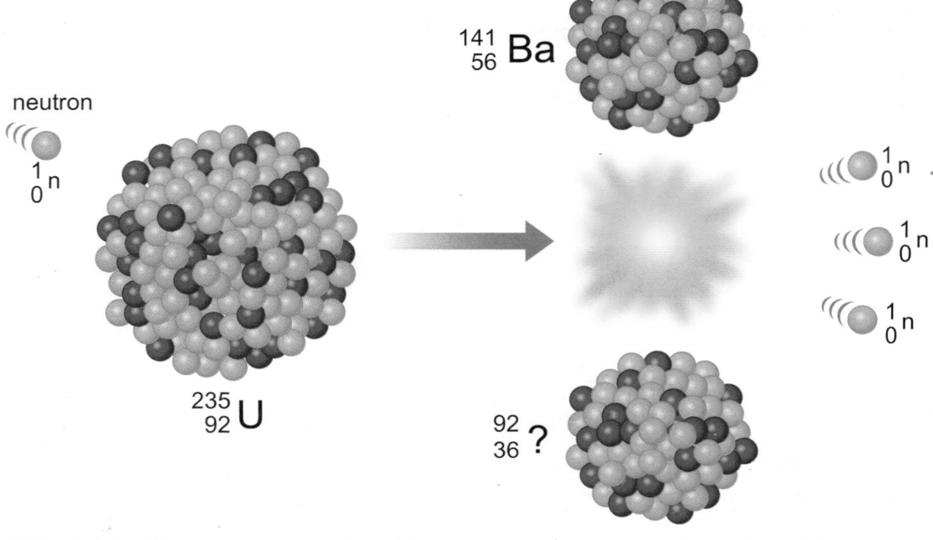

C Nuclear fission can be started by firing neutrons at atoms of uranium-235.

Relative atomic masses

The mass of an atom is incredibly small, so we measure their masses *relative to* (compared to) an atom of carbon-12. This isotope is used as a standard and given a mass of exactly 12. The masses of all other atoms are compared to this. For example, the mass of helium-4 is one-third of that of carbon-12 and so its relative mass is 4.

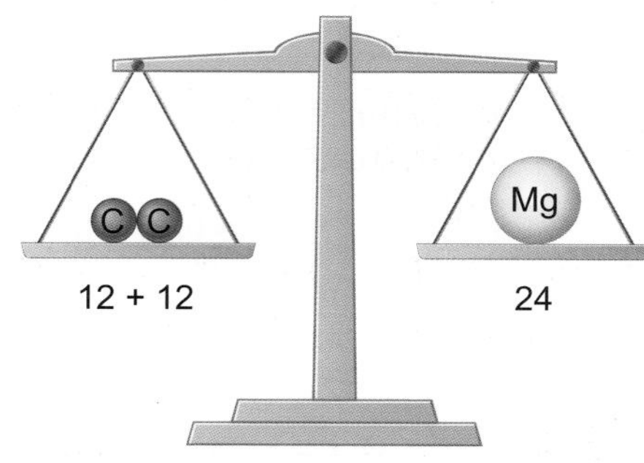

D An atom of the isotope $^{24}_{12}Mg$ has twice the mass of $^{12}_{6}C$ and so has a relative mass of 24.

3 How many $^{4}_{2}He$ atoms would be needed to balance the mass of the $^{24}_{12}Mg$ atom in diagram D?

4 Use the list of isotopes to answer the questions that follow.

$^{4}_{2}He$ $^{20}_{10}Ne$ $^{40}_{18}Ar$ $^{5}_{2}He$ $^{40}_{20}Ca$

Which two isotopes have the same:

a mass **b** chemical properties?

5 Write the mass ratios, in their simplest form, for the isotopes:

a $^{20}_{10}Ne$ and $^{40}_{18}Ar$ **b** $^{4}_{2}He$ and $^{20}_{10}Ne$

The relative mass of an isotope is its mass number. For example, chlorine has two isotopes, $^{35}_{17}Cl$ and $^{37}_{17}Cl$, and their relative masses are 35 and 37, respectively.

All elements exist as mixtures of isotopes. We use this idea to calculate an element's **relative atomic mass** (**RAM**) – the symbol is $\boldsymbol{A_r}$. A relative atomic mass is the **mean** mass of an atom of an element compared with carbon-12. It takes into account all the isotopes of the element and the amounts of each. RAMs are not whole numbers (for example the A_r of chlorine is 35.5) but most values are commonly rounded to whole numbers. The RAM of an element and its atomic number are shown on the periodic table.

6 What does the relative atomic mass of an element tell you?

7 **H** Copper has two isotopes – 69% is $^{63}_{29}Cu$ and 31% is $^{65}_{29}Cu$. Calculate the RAM of copper. Give your answer to 1 decimal place.

H

The abundances (overall proportions) of the two isotopes of chlorine are 75% of $^{35}_{17}Cl$ and 25% of $^{37}_{17}Cl$. We calculate the relative atomic mass of chlorine as follows.

If we take 100 atoms,

$$\text{the relative atomic mass} = \frac{\text{total mass of the atoms}}{\text{the number of atoms}} = \frac{(75 \times 35) + (25 \times 37)}{100}$$

$$= \frac{2625 + 925}{100} = \frac{3550}{100}$$

$$A_r = 35.5$$

Exam-style question

Neon gas has a relative atomic mass of 20.2 and is made up of two atoms: $^{20}_{10}Ne$ and $^{22}_{10}Ne$. Explain which of these isotopes is the most abundant.

(3 marks)

Checkpoint

How confidently can you answer the Progression questions?

Strengthen

S1 Describe, with examples, the similarities and differences between isotopes of the same element.

Extend

E1 **H** Describing each step, work out the relative atomic mass of magnesium – it has the composition 79% ^{24}Mg, 10% ^{25}Mg and 11% ^{26}Mg.

Isotopes

The diagram below shows the structure of two isotopes of lithium.

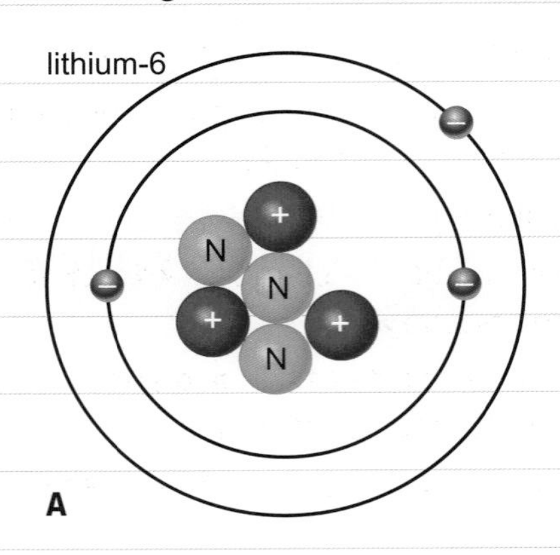

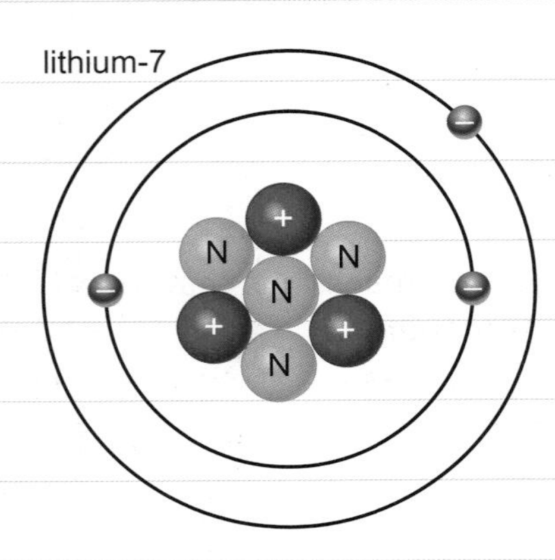

Using these lithium atoms as examples, explain the similarities and differences in the properties of different isotopes of the same element. **(6 marks)**

Student answer

Atoms that are isotopes of the same element have the same atomic numbers but different mass numbers [1]. *This means they have the same number of protons and electrons but different numbers of neutrons* [2].

Atoms that are isotopes will chemically react in the same way [3] *but be different in structure* [4].

[1] The answer gives a basic definition of isotopes.

[2] This is a good description of the similarities and differences in the number of subatomic particles, but it doesn't use the lithium isotopes to illustrate the examples.

[3] This would be better if the answer explained *why* atoms of different isotopes react in the same way.

[4] This just repeats the earlier statement about differences, without adding any further detail.

Verdict

This is an acceptable answer. It contains a basic definition of isotopes, and a description of their similarities and differences in terms of structure. The answer also notes that the isotopes will have the same chemical properties. There is some linking of scientific ideas and a basic logical structure.

This answer could be improved by referring to the examples given in the question. It would have been better if the answer had included clearer definitions of 'atomic number' and 'mass number'. The answer should also link together some more scientific ideas. For example, it could have linked reactivity with electron configuration (to explain why isotopes of the same element have the same reactivity).

Exam tip

If an exam question asks you to use examples that are given, you must include them in your answer.

Paper 1 and Paper 2

SC4 The Periodic Table

There are over 100 known elements. The modern periodic table is a chart that arranges these elements in a way that is useful to chemists. Thanks to the periodic table, chemists can make sense of patterns and trends, which lets them predict the properties of elements. This works even if only a few atoms of an element exist. The periodic table shown here includes photos of most of the elements. If an element is very rare or difficult to obtain, it shows a photo of the relevant scientist or research laboratory involved in discovering or naming the element, or a diagram representing the arrangement of its electrons.

The learning journey

Previously you will have learnt at KS3:

- about chemical symbols for elements
- that Dmitri Mendeleev designed an early periodic table
- about periods and groups in the periodic table
- about metals and non-metals, their properties and their positions in the periodic table.

In this unit you will learn:

- how Mendeleev arranged the elements known at the time in a periodic table
- how Mendeleev predicted the existence and properties of undiscovered elements
- how Henry Moseley helped to confirm Mendeleev's ideas
- how the elements are arranged in the modern periodic table
- how to use the periodic table to predict and model the arrangement of electrons in atoms.

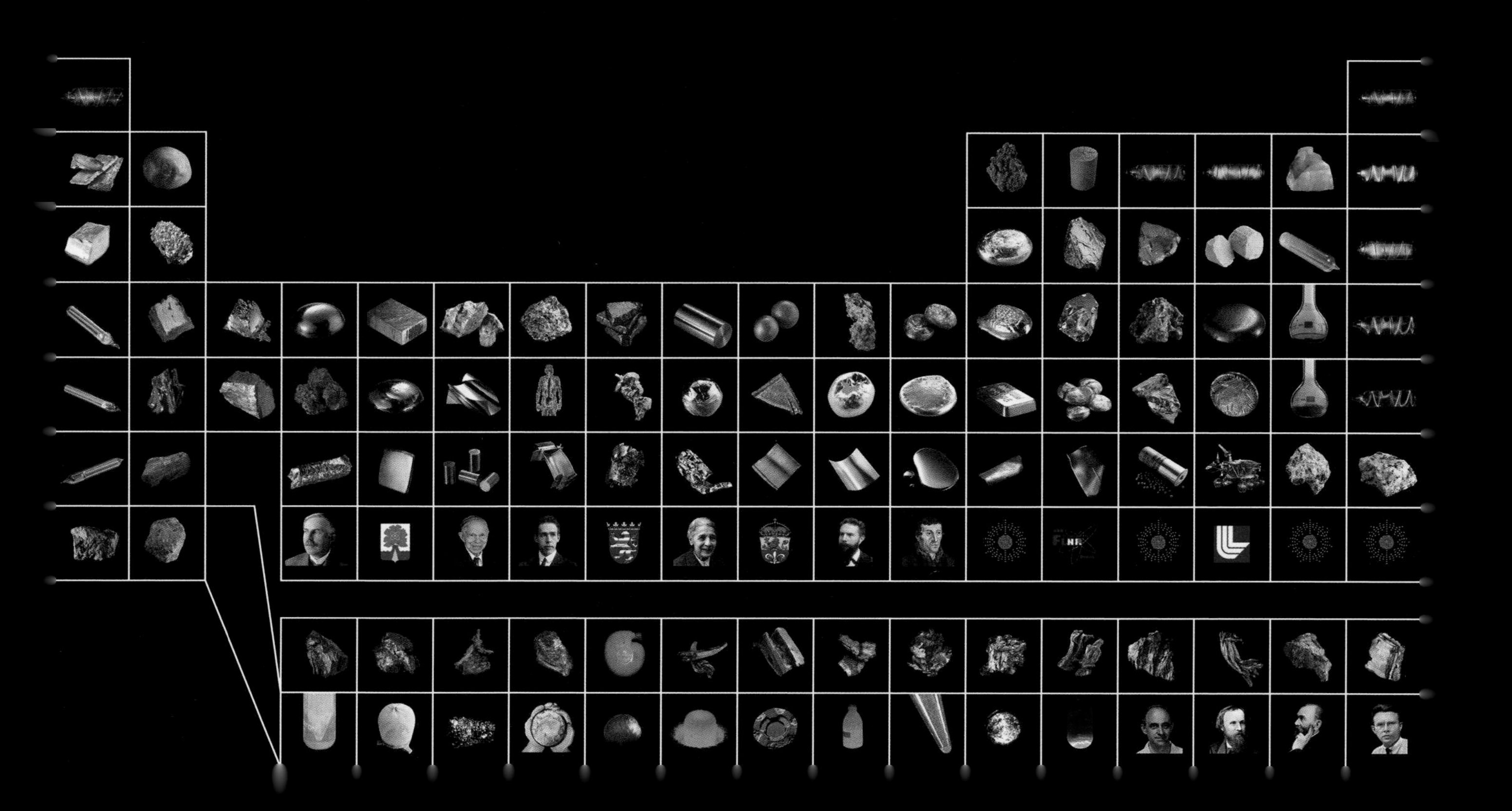

SC4a Elements and the periodic table

Specification reference: C0.1; C1.13; C1.14

Progression questions

- What are the symbols of some common elements?
- How did Mendeleev arrange elements into a periodic table?
- How did Mendeleev use his table to predict the properties of undiscovered elements?

A Towels come in all sorts of sizes, colours and patterns, just as the elements have different properties. How would you organise them?

The Russian chemist Dmitri Mendeleev (1834–1907) faced a problem early in 1869. He was busy writing the second volume of his chemistry textbook and could not decide which elements it made sense to write about next. His solution was to construct a table that led to the **periodic table** we know today.

Organising elements

Chemists had discovered 63 elements by 1869, and they were keen to organise them in a helpful way. Mendeleev arranged these elements in order of increasing **relative atomic masses** (called atomic weights then). Unlike other chemists who had tried this before, Mendeleev did not always keep to this order, and he left gaps in his table.

Mendeleev sometimes swapped the positions of elements if he thought that better suited their **chemical properties** and those of their compounds. For example, fluorine, chlorine, bromine and iodine are non-metals that do not easily react with oxygen, whereas tellurium is a metal that burns in air to form tellurium dioxide. Iodine has a lower relative atomic mass than tellurium, so Mendeleev should have placed it before tellurium according to this **physical property**. Instead, he placed iodine after tellurium so that it lined up with fluorine, chlorine and bromine (elements with similar chemical properties to iodine). Even though Mendeleev used the most accurate relative atomic masses then available, he justified this swap by stating that the value for tellurium must be incorrect.

ОПЫТЪ СИСТЕМЫ ЭЛЕМЕНТОВЪ,

ОСНОВАННОЙ НА ИХЪ АТОМНОМЪ ВѢСѢ И ХИМИЧЕСКОМЪ СХОДСТВѢ.

			Ti=50	Zr=90	?=180.
			V=51	Nb=94	Ta=182.
			Cr=52	Mo=96	W=186.
			Mn=55	Rh=104,4	Pt=197,1.
			Fe=56	Ru=104,4	Ir=198.
			Ni=Co=59	Pd=106,6	Os=199.
H=1			Cu=63,4	Ag=108	Hg=200.
	Be=9,4	Mg=24	Zn=65,2	Cd=112	
	B=11	Al=27,3	?=68	Ur=116	Au=197?
	C=12	Si=28	?=70	Sn=118	
	N=14	P=31	As=75	Sb=122	Bi=210?
	O=16	S=32	Se=79,4	Te=128?	
	F=19	Cl=35,5	Br=80	I=127	
Li=7	Na=23	K=39	Rb=85,4	Cs=133	Tl=204.
		Ca=40	Sr=87,6	Ba=137	Pb=207.
		?=45	Ce=92		
		?Er=56	La=94		
		?Yt=60	Di=95		
		?In=75,6	Th=118?		

B Mendeleev's published 1869 table. The question mark after the relative atomic mass of tellurium, Te, shows that he thought this was incorrect. He swapped the positions of iodine and tellurium so that iodine ended up in the same line as other elements with similar properties.

Mendeleev assumed that elements would continue to be discovered, so he left gaps for them. This helped him to position the existing elements so that vertical columns contained elements with increasing relative atomic mass, and horizontal rows contained elements with similar chemical properties.

1 What information about the elements did Mendeleev use to produce his first table?

2 Explain why Mendeleev swapped the positions of iodine and tellurium in his table.

Making predictions

Mendeleev continued to work on his table. By 1871, he had settled on a table in which elements with similar properties were arranged into vertical columns, just as today.

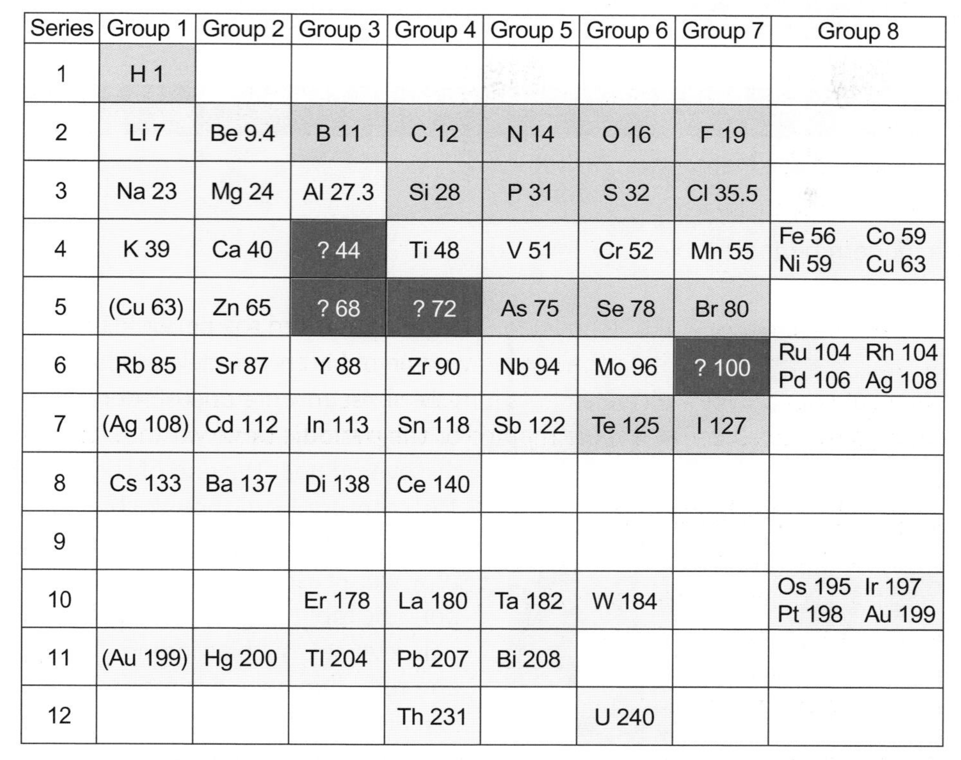

Series	Group 1	Group 2	Group 3	Group 4	Group 5	Group 6	Group 7	Group 8
1	H 1							
2	Li 7	Be 9.4	B 11	C 12	N 14	O 16	F 19	
3	Na 23	Mg 24	Al 27.3	Si 28	P 31	S 32	Cl 35.5	
4	K 39	Ca 40	? 44	Ti 48	V 51	Cr 52	Mn 55	Fe 56 Co 59 Ni 59 Cu 63
5	(Cu 63)	Zn 65	? 68	? 72	As 75	Se 78	Br 80	
6	Rb 85	Sr 87	Y 88	Zr 90	Nb 94	Mo 96	? 100	Ru 104 Rh 104 Pd 106 Ag 108
7	(Ag 108)	Cd 112	In 113	Sn 118	Sb 122	Te 125	I 127	
8	Cs 133	Ba 137	Di 138	Ce 140				
9								
10			Er 178	La 180	Ta 182	W 184		Os 195 Ir 197 Pt 198 Au 199
11	(Au 199)	Hg 200	Tl 204	Pb 207	Bi 208			
12				Th 231		U 240		

C Mendeleev's 1871 table with his relative atomic masses. The red boxes are gaps left for elements not known at the time. Di, 'didymium', was later shown to be a mixture of two elements, neodymium and praseodymium.

Mendeleev used the gaps in his table to make **predictions** about the properties of undiscovered elements, based on the properties of nearby elements. One set of predictions was for an element he called eka-aluminium. When gallium was discovered shortly afterwards in 1875, its properties closely fitted those Mendeleev had predicted for eka-aluminium.

Property	Eka-aluminium, Ea	Gallium, Ga
relative atomic mass	about 68	70
density of element (g/cm^3)	about 6.0	5.9
melting point of element (°C)	low	29.8
formula of oxide	Ea_2O_3	Ga_2O_3
density of oxide (g/cm^3)	about 5.5	5.88
reacts with acids and alkalis?	yes	yes

D Mendeleev's predicted properties of eka-aluminium and the properties of gallium. He also successfully predicted the properties of scandium (discovered in 1879), germanium (1886) and polonium (1898).

Exam-style question

Give *two* possible reasons why other scientists did not accept Mendeleev's periodic table when it was first published. *(2 marks)*

Did you know?

A 313 km diameter crater on the far side of the Moon was named in honour of Mendeleev by the Russian scientists in charge of the Luna 3 space probe. The probe, launched in 1959, was the first to photograph the far side of the Moon. Element 101 is also named after Mendeleev.

3 Mendeleev amended the relative atomic masses of some elements between 1869 and 1871. Give the symbol of one element for which its value was approximately doubled.

4 Explain how Mendeleev's 1871 table shows he was unsure where to place three elements.

5 Explain why the discovery of gallium was seen as a successful test of Mendeleev's periodic table.

Checkpoint

How confidently can you answer the Progression questions?

Strengthen

S1 What were the key features of Mendeleev's periodic table?

Extend

E1 How did Mendeleev think creatively to produce his table?

E2 What evidence supported Mendeleev's ideas?

SC4b Atomic number and the periodic table

Specification reference: C1.15; C1.16; C1.17; C1.18

Progression questions

- Why was Mendeleev right to alter the order of some elements in his table?
- What is an element's atomic number?
- How are the elements arranged in the modern periodic table?

A The modern periodic table is easily recognised. There are many fun versions including this one advertising a science park.

Development of the periodic table continued after Mendeleev's first tables. An entire group of **inert** or very unreactive elements was discovered near the end of the 19th century. Even though chemists had not predicted their existence, they were easily fitted into the periodic table as group 0. However, pair reversals such as iodine and tellurium were not properly explained, and there were still gaps. This began to change in 1913 due to a physicist called Henry Moseley.

1 Suggest why chemists in Mendeleev's time did not predict the existence of group 0 elements such as neon.

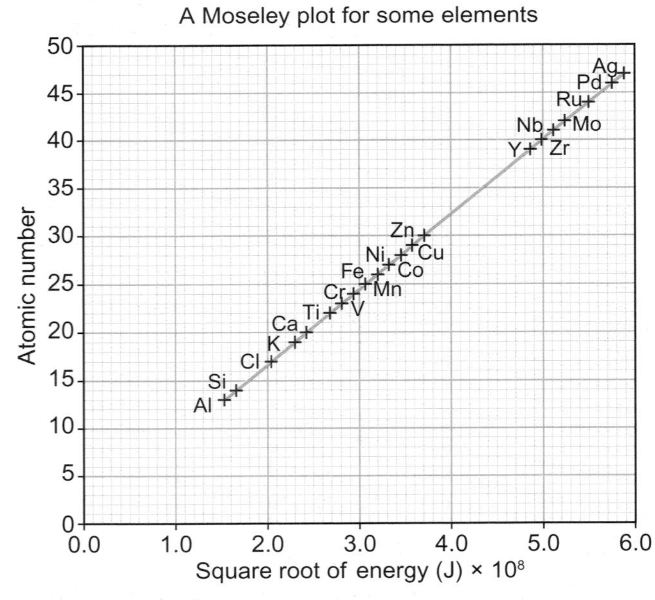

B There is a linear relationship between atomic number and the square root of the energy of emitted X-rays.

Atomic number

When scientists were beginning to accept the periodic table, an element's atomic number was just its position in the table. Moseley showed instead that it is a physical property of an element's atoms. He fired high-energy electrons at different elements, which made them give off **X-rays**. Moseley discovered that for every step increase in atomic number there was a step change in the energy of these X-rays.

Moseley realised that an atomic number was equal to the number of positive charges in the nucleus of an atom. The particle that carries this charge, the proton, was discovered a few years later. So the **atomic number** must be the number of protons in a nucleus.

2 Describe the difference between Mendeleev's atomic numbers and Moseley's modern atomic numbers.

Pair reversals

The elements in the modern periodic table are arranged in order of increasing atomic number, *Z*. When this is done:

- elements in a row or **period** are in order of increasing atomic number
- elements with similar properties are in the same column or **group**
- non-metals are on the right of the table (the other elements are metals)
- the iodine–tellurium pair reversal is explained.

Iodine exists naturally as ^{127}I but tellurium has several different isotopes. About 20% of its atoms are ^{126}Te but nearly two-thirds of its atoms are ^{128}Te or ^{130}Te, so its **relative atomic mass** is greater than that of iodine.

group 6 properties	group 6	group 7	group 7 properties
all (except oxygen) react with oxygen	oxygen, O colourless gas $A_r = 16.0$ $Z = 8$	fluorine, F pale yellow gas $A_r = 19.0$ $Z = 9$	none of them react with oxygen
none of them react with water	sulfur, S yellow solid $A_r = 32.1$ $Z = 16$	chlorine, Cl green-yellow gas $A_r = 35.5$ $Z = 17$	all react with water
	selenium, Se metallic grey solid $A_r = 79.0$ $Z = 34$	bromine, Br red-brown liquid $A_r = 79.9$ $Z = 35$	
all form compounds containing hydrogen: H_2O, H_2S, H_2Se, H_2Te	tellurium, Te silvery-white solid $A_r = 127.6$ $Z = 52$	iodine, I purple-black solid $A_r = 126.9$ $Z = 53$	all form compounds containing hydrogen: HF, HCl, HBr, HI

C These are the elements in groups 6 and 7, each with its relative atomic mass, A_r, and atomic number, *Z*.

Filling gaps

More X-ray analysis showed that just seven elements between hydrogen (*Z* = 1) and uranium (*Z* = 92) were left to be discovered. These were all discovered between 1917 and 1945. Neptunium, the first element with an atomic number above 92, was discovered in 1940. Other such 'transuranium' elements continue to be discovered, and all can be placed in the periodic table.

6 Suggest why there is a gap between calcium, Ca, and titanium, Ti, in graph B.

Exam-style question

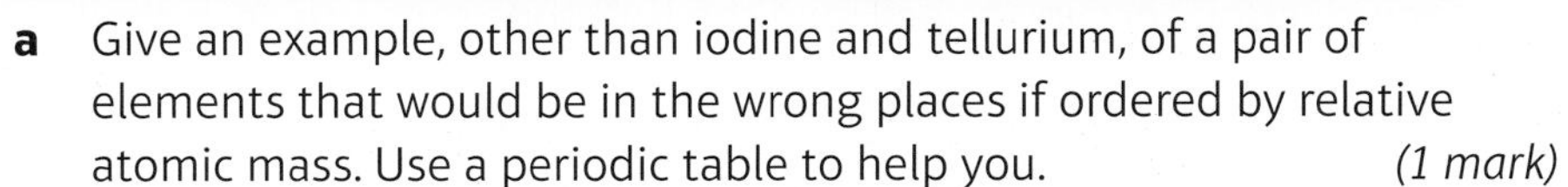

a Give an example, other than iodine and tellurium, of a pair of elements that would be in the wrong places if ordered by relative atomic mass. Use a periodic table to help you. *(1 mark)*

b Suggest why ordering by relative atomic mass would be incorrect. *(1 mark)*

Did you know?

Not all of Mendeleev's predictions were correct. For example, he predicted an element with an atomic weight of 0.4 that he called coronium. Moseley's work showed that it could not exist because it would need to contain part of a proton.

3 Give the relative atomic masses of tellurium and iodine to the nearest whole numbers.

4 Use information from diagram C to explain fully why Mendeleev was correct after all to place tellurium before iodine.

5 Use the periodic table at the back of the book to find the metals rubidium to tin, and the non-metals in groups 6 and 7. Describe the general positions of metals and non-metals.

Checkpoint

How confidently can you answer the Progression questions?

Strengthen

S1 How are the elements arranged in the modern periodic table?

Extend

E1 What are the features of the modern periodic table?

SC4c Electronic configurations and the periodic table

Specification reference: C1.18; C1.19; C.1.20

Progression questions

- What information does an electronic configuration give?
- How do you work out and show the electronic configuration of an element?
- How is the electronic configuration of an element related to its position in the periodic table?

A There are many pairs of empty seats on this bus. Where would *you* sit?

You have many choices where to sit on an empty bus but fewer choices when other people are already seated. **Electrons** fill shells in an atom, rather like filling a bus one seat at a time from the front.

Electron shells

In an atom, electrons occupy **electron shells** arranged around the nucleus. The shells can be modelled in diagrams as circles, with the electrons drawn as dots or crosses on each circle. The way in which an atom's electrons are arranged is called its **electronic configuration**. Sodium atoms each contain 11 electrons, and diagram B shows the electronic configuration for sodium.

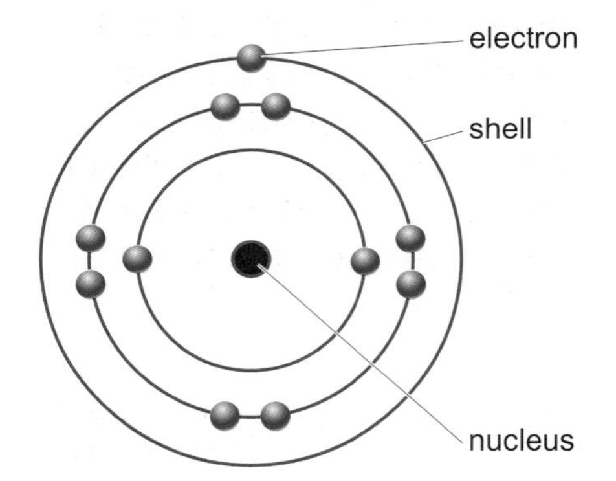

B The electronic configuration of sodium shows three occupied shells.

Each shell can contain different numbers of electrons. For the first 20 elements (hydrogen to calcium):

- the first shell can contain up to two electrons
- the second and third shells can contain up to eight electrons.

Electrons occupy the shells, starting with the innermost shell and working outwards as each one becomes full. This is why, in a sodium atom, the first shell contains two electrons, the second shell contains eight electrons and the third shell contains one electron.

1 State what is meant by the term 'electronic configuration'.

2 Explain why the electrons in a sodium atom do not all occupy one shell.

Working out configurations

Electronic configurations can also be written out rather than drawn. For example, the electronic configuration for sodium is 2.8.1 – the numbers show how many electrons occupy a shell, and the full stops separate each shell.

You can work out the electronic configuration of an element from its atomic number, *Z*. The atomic number of chlorine is 17 – each chlorine atom contains 17 protons and so also contains 17 electrons.

To fill a chlorine atom's shells:

- 2 electrons occupy the first shell (leaving 15 electrons)
- 8 electrons occupy the second shell (leaving 7 electrons)
- 7 electrons occupy the third shell.

The electronic configuration of chlorine is therefore 2.8.7 (diagram C shows this).

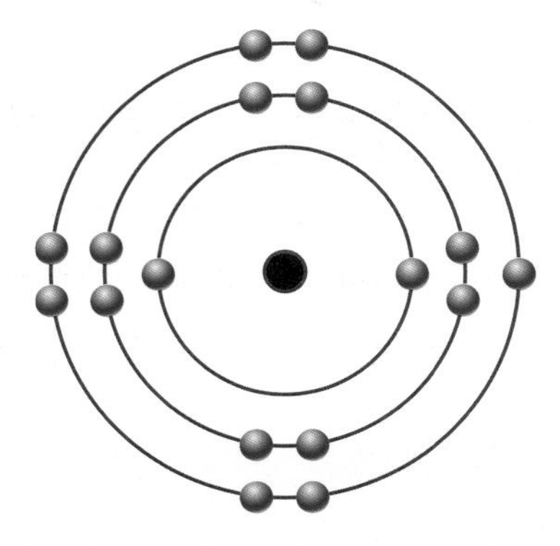

C The electronic configuration of chlorine shows three occupied shells.

 **3** Describe how you can determine the atomic number, *Z*, of an element from its electronic configuration.

4 Write the electronic configuration of phosphorus, *Z* = 15.

Connections with the periodic table

Diagram D shows the electronic configurations for the first 20 elements in the periodic table. The electronic configuration of an element is related to its position:

- the number of occupied shells is equal to the period number
- the number of electrons in the outer shell is equal to the group number (except for group 0 elements, which all have full outer shells).

1	2	3	4	5	6	7	0
H							He
Li	Be	B	C	N	O	F	Ne
Na	Mg	Al	Si	P	S	Cl	Ar
K	Ca						

D These are the electronic configurations of the first 20 elements.

 **5** What do the electronic configurations of sodium and the other elements in group 1 have in common?

 **6** Explain how you can tell from their electronic configurations that sodium and chlorine are in the same period.

Exam-style question

Explain, in terms of electrons, why magnesium and calcium are in the same group in the periodic table. *(2 marks)*

Did you know?

After calcium, the third and fourth electron shells can actually contain up to 18 electrons. For this reason the International Union of Pure and Applied Chemistry (IUPAC) now recommends the use of group numbers in the range 1 to 18. In this newer numbering system, group numbers 3 to 12 refer to the block of elements between calcium and gallium. Group numbers 13 to 17 refer to the older group numbers 3 to 7, and 18 refers to group 0.

Checkpoint

How confidently can you answer the Progression questions?

Strengthen

S1 How do you work out the electronic configuration of an element?

Extend

E1 How is the electronic configuration of an element determined, and related to its position in the periodic table?

Atomic structure and the periodic table

The table shows information about tellurium and iodine.

Element	Atomic number	Relative atomic mass, A_r
tellurium	52	127.6
iodine	53	126.9

A

Describe how Mendeleev arranged the elements known to him into a periodic table, and compare this with the arrangement in the modern periodic table.

In your answer, use information from the table above to provide examples. **(6 marks)**

Student answer

Mendeleev arranged the elements in order of relative atomic mass [1]. *He also used the properties of elements and their compounds, so he sometimes had to swap elements. For example, the A_r of iodine is 126.9, so he should have put iodine first* [2], *but he put it second. He did this so it went into the same column as similar elements* [3].

In the modern periodic table, elements are arranged in order of increasing atomic number (the number of protons in the nucleus) [4]. *This explains why Mendeleev was correct when he placed tellurium before iodine.*

[1] This shows knowledge of how Mendeleev ordered the elements, but it should say 'in order of *increasing* relative atomic mass'.

[2] The answer should be supported by comparing the A_r values for the two elements.

[3] An element in the same group, such as chlorine, could be identified using the periodic table.

[4] It is a good idea to give clear definitions like this.

Verdict

This is an acceptable answer. It shows good knowledge and understanding of the periodic table and the answer is organised in a logical way. The student has linked their knowledge of atomic structure with an understanding of Mendeleev's periodic table.

The answer could be improved by clearly quoting examples from the information given in the table. For example, in the last paragraph the answer could have included the atomic numbers for each of the elements.

Exam tip

If you are asked to use information from the question as part of your answer then make sure you include the information. It is important to make sure you *use* the information in your answer – don't just repeat what you have been given.

Paper 1 and Paper 2

SC5 Ionic Bonding / **SC6** Covalent Bonding / **SC7** Types of Substance

Using an extremely powerful 'atomic force microscope' scientists at the Berkeley Lab in California produced this amazing image showing the positions of the bonds holding the atoms of a small molecule together. Using this technique, the scientists were also able to examine the breaking and reforming of bonds during a chemical reaction. Bonds are the fundamental forces of attraction that hold our universe together. Understanding how bonds are formed and broken is essential in helping us explain even the simplest physical change or chemical reaction.

The learning journey

Previously you will have learnt at KS3:

- about the particle model of matter
- how Dalton's ideas about atoms and molecules helped to explain the properties of matter
- how elements are arranged in the periodic table.

In this unit you will learn:

- how ionic, covalent and metallic bonds are formed
- about the formation of lattice and molecular structures
- how the physical properties of a substance are linked to its bonding and structure.

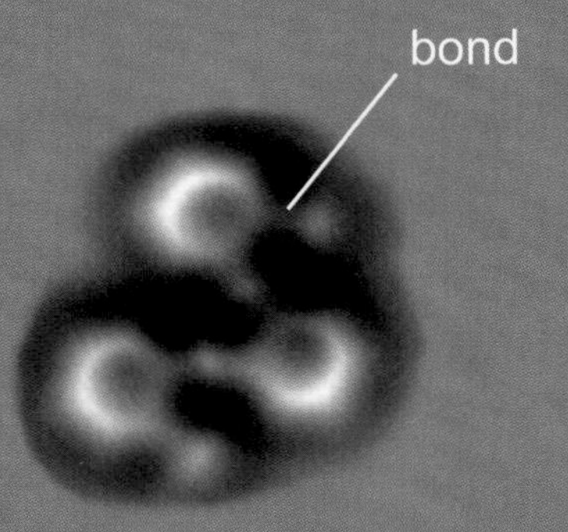

SC5a Ionic bonds

Specification reference: C0.1; C1.21;C1.22; C1.23; C1.24

Progression questions

- How are ions formed?
- How can the numbers of subatomic particles in an ion be calculated?
- What is an ionic bond?

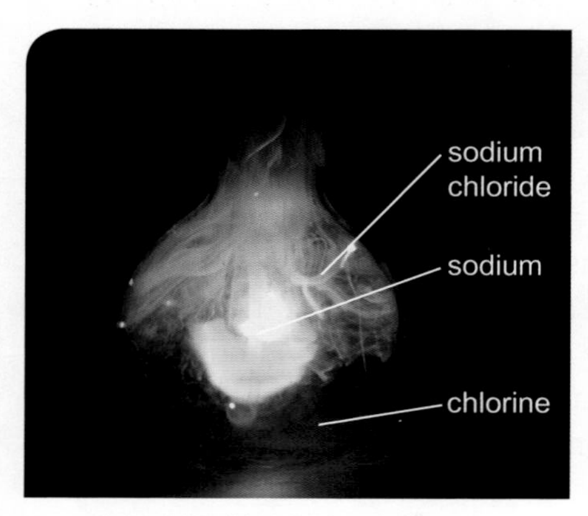

A Explosions can occur when new bonds form between sodium and chlorine atoms to form sodium chloride.

Bonds are forces of attraction that hold atoms together. When bonds form between atoms, energy is released from the atoms, making them more stable (less reactive). The most stable atoms are those of the noble gases, and scientists have found that this is because they have outer electron shells that contain as many electrons as possible – the outer shell of a noble gas atom is full.

Noble gas	Electronic configuration
He	2
Ne	2.8
Ar	2.8.8

B Atoms of all of the elements in group 0 have a stable electronic configuration (arrangement of electrons) with a complete outer shell of electrons.

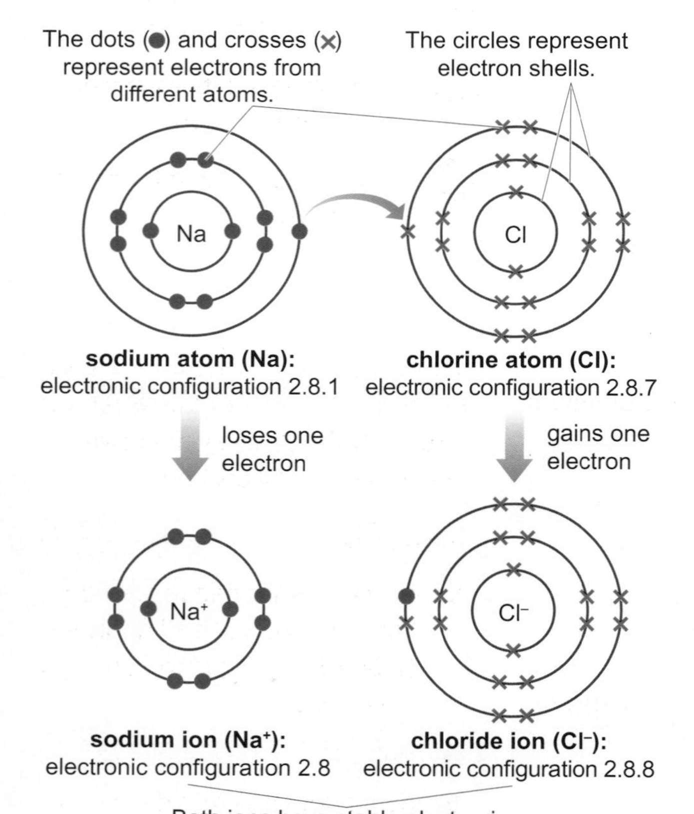

C Dot and cross diagrams can be used to show what happens when ions are formed.

Atoms are more stable if they have an outer electron shell that is full, like a noble gas. This can happen by the transfer of electrons between atoms, forming charged particles called **ions**.

Metal atoms tend to lose electrons and form positive ions, called **cations**. Cations have more protons than electrons. Non-metal atoms tend to gain electrons and form negative ions, called **anions**. Anions have more electrons than protons. The formation of sodium (Na^+) and chloride (Cl^-) ions is shown in diagram C. Note that when non-metals form negative ions the end of the name changes to –ide.

 **1 a** What are ions?

 **b** State the difference between a cation and an anion.

There are forces of attraction between all positively and negatively charged objects. These are called **electrostatic forces**. These forces hold the oppositely charged ions together, and form an **ionic bond** between them.

 **2 a** What is happening to the atoms when they form ions?

 **b** What holds the ions together in an ionic bond?

Atoms that easily form ions will have either a nearly full or a nearly empty outer electron shell. Most ionic bonds are formed between a metal and a non-metal. Table D shows the number of electrons lost or gained and the resulting ion charge of some groups of elements. The ion formed depends on the element's position in the periodic table and its number of outer electrons.

	Group 1	Group 2	Group 6	Group 7
outer electrons	1	2	6	7
electrons lost or gained	1 lost	2 lost	2 gained	1 gained
charge on ion	1+	2+	2−	1−
example	Li^+	Ca^{2+}	S^{2-}	F^-

D formation of ions by elements in groups 1, 2, 6 and 7

Diagram E shows the number of protons, neutrons and electrons in each atom and ion in the formation of the ionic bond in magnesium oxide.

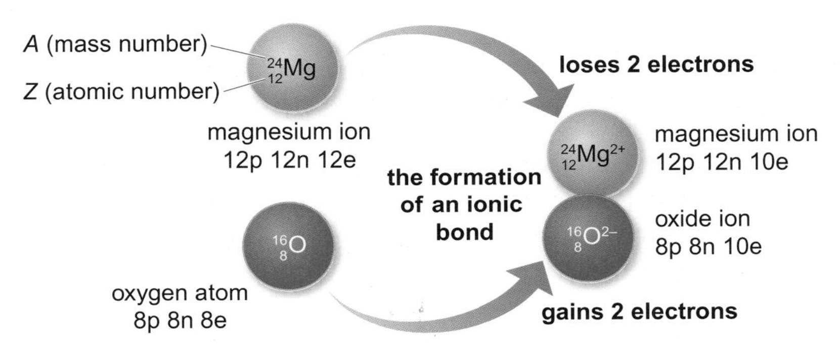

E ionic bond formation in magnesium oxide

5 An aluminium atom $^{27}_{13}Al$ loses three electrons when its ion is formed.

a How many protons, neutrons and electrons are in the aluminium ion?

b Write the symbol for the aluminium ion.

6 Draw dot and cross diagrams to show the ions in diagram E.

Exam-style question

Bromine is in group 7 of the periodic table.

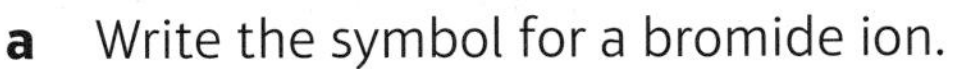

a Write the symbol for a bromide ion. *(1 mark)*

b State what the symbol tells you about the electrons in a bromide ion compared with a bromine atom. *(1 mark)*

Did you know?

The most common atom in the Universe, hydrogen, contains one proton and one electron. The hydrogen ion (H^+) is therefore just a proton. This makes it more than 100 000 times smaller than the hydrogen atom and it is the smallest particle that can take part in a chemical reaction.

3 Write the symbol for the ion formed by:

a potassium (K) in group 1

b selenium (Se) in group 6.

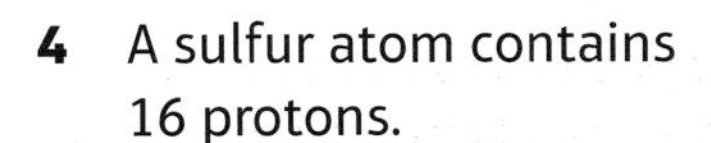

4 A sulfur atom contains 16 protons.

a How many electrons does it contain?

b Write out its electronic configuration.

c Explain why it forms S^{2-} ions.

Checkpoint

How confidently can you answer the Progression questions?

Strengthen

S1 Describe what happens when lithium (group 1) and fluorine (group 7) react to form an ionic bond.

Extend

E1 Using dot and cross diagrams, explain what happens when aluminium and oxygen form an ionic bond.

SC5b Ionic lattices

Specification reference: C0.1, C1.25, C1.26, C1.27

Progression questions

- What is an ionic lattice?
- What do the endings –ide and –ate tell you about a substance?
- How do you work out the formulae of ionic compounds?

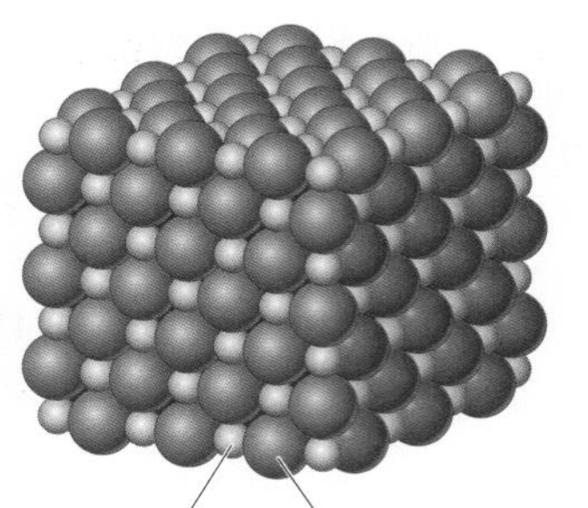

A Sodium chloride forms a cubic lattice structure.

2 Explain why the solid shown in photo B can be described as crystals.

B Sodium chloride crystals are shaped like cubes. These crystals are from a salt mine in Poland and the largest one has sides of 5 cm.

Ionic compounds, which are formed by the loss and gain of electrons, are held together by strong electrostatic forces of attraction between oppositely charged ions. These strong ionic bonds allow 'billions' of ions to be packed together in a regular repeating arrangement called a **lattice structure**. The lattice structure in sodium chloride is shown in diagram A.

1 **a** What holds ions together in an ionic bond?

b Why is the structure in diagram A described as a cubic lattice?

Ionic compounds will often form **crystals** when solid because of their regular lattice structure. Crystals are pieces of solid that have a particular regular shape, flat surfaces and sharp edges. Photo B shows crystals of sodium chloride.

Did you know?

The shapes of crystals are determined by the structure of the lattice. There are seven basic crystal or lattice structures.

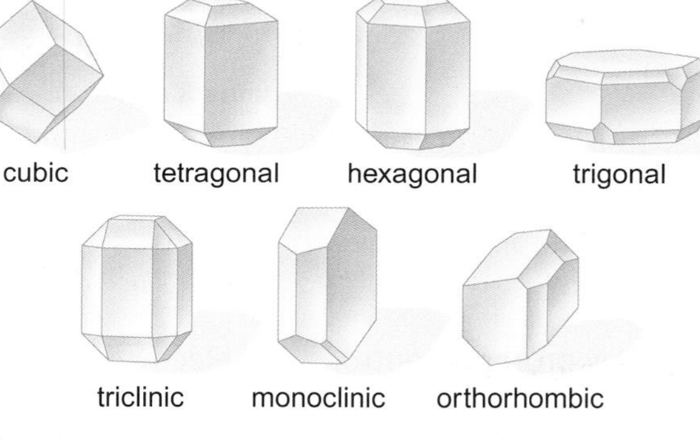

C the seven basic crystal structures

Positive ion	Ion formula	Negative ion	Ion formula
sodium	Na^+	fluoride	F^-
lithium	Li^+	chloride	Cl^-
potassium	K^+	bromide	Br^-
magnesium	Mg^{2+}	oxide	O^{2-}
calcium	Ca^{2+}	sulfide	S^{2-}
aluminium	Al^{3+}	phosphide	P^{3-}

D common ions

Working out ionic formulae

Ionic compounds are electrically neutral (they have no overall charge). So the formula of an ionic compound contains the same number of positive charges as negative charges. To work out ionic formulae we will need to use ion formulae, as shown in table D. Note that in two-element compounds the name ending of the non-metal ion is changed to –ide.

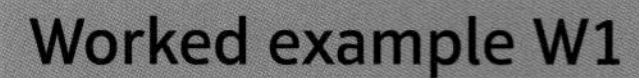

Worked example W1

Magnesium oxide contains the ions Mg^{2+} and O^{2-}.

A magnesium ion has two positive charges and an oxide ion has the same number of negative charges. One of each ion will balance the charges, and so the formula = MgO

Worked example W2

Sodium sulfide contains the ions Na^{+} and S^{2-}.

Therefore two Na^{+} ions are needed to balance the charges on the S^{2-} ion, and so the formula = Na_2S

Some ions contain more than one atom. For example, the sulfate ion, shown in diagram E, contains one sulfur atom bonded to four oxygen atoms with two added electrons. More examples of these **polyatomic ions** are shown in table F. An ion name ending '–ate' or '–ite' shows that the ion contains oxygen as well as another element.

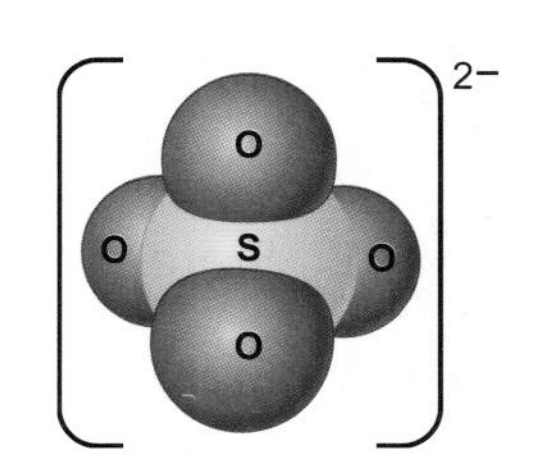

E The formula of a sulfate ion is SO_4^{2-}.

If an ionic formula contains two or more of the same polyatomic ions then the formula of the polyatomic ion must be written inside brackets.

Worked example W3

Calcium nitrate contains the ions Ca^{2+} and NO_3^{-}.

Therefore two NO_3^{-} ions are needed to balance the charges on the Ca^{2+} ion, and so the formula = $Ca(NO_3)_2$

Note that the brackets are needed around the polyatomic ion. Without brackets the formula becomes $CaNO_{32}$ and this compound is not possible.

5 Write the formulae for:

a sodium carbonate **b** ammonium sulfate.

6 Li_3PO_4 is an ionic compound.

a Suggest a name for this compound.

b Write the formulae for both of the ions.

Exam-style question

Potassium iodide and potassium iodate, which contains the ion IO_3^{-}, are both used in health supplements.

a Give the formulae for both compounds. *(1 mark)*

b Compare and contrast these two compounds. *(2 marks)*

3 Write the formulae for:

a sodium fluoride

b calcium sulfide

c magnesium bromide

d aluminium oxide.

4 The formula of iron chloride is $FeCl_3$.

a What is the charge on the iron ion?

b Explain how you worked out your answer.

Polyatomic ion name	Ion formula
ammonium	NH_4^{+}
nitrate	NO_3^{-}
hydroxide	OH^{-}
carbonate	CO_3^{2-}
sulfate	SO_4^{2-}
sulfite	SO_3^{2-}

F Polyatomic ions are groups of two or more atoms, which have become charged.

Checkpoint

How confidently can you answer the Progression questions?

Strengthen

S1 Describe with the help of a diagram the type of structure you find in ionic compounds.

Extend

E1 What does the formula $Fe_3(PO_4)_2$ tell you about the compound and its structure?

SC5c Properties of ionic compounds

Specification reference: C1.33

Progression questions

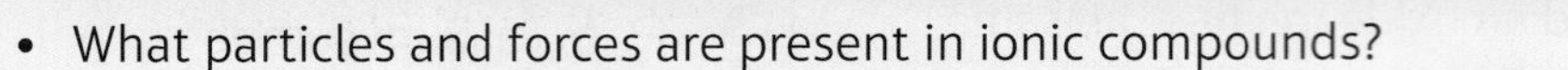

- What particles and forces are present in ionic compounds?
- Why do ionic compounds have high melting points and boiling points?
- Why do ionic compounds conduct electricity when they are liquids or dissolved in water but not when they are solids?

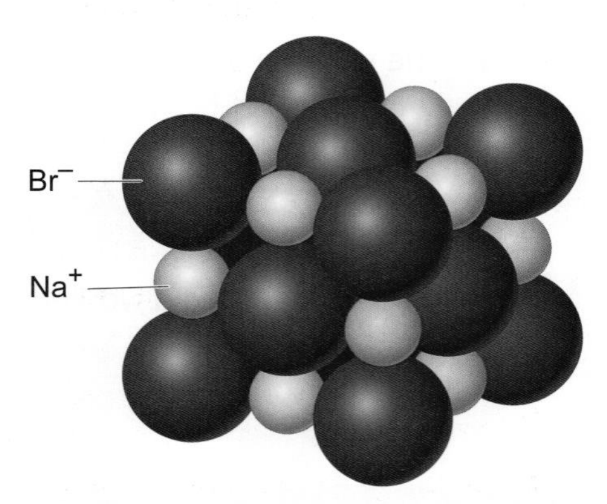

A the lattice structure of sodium bromide

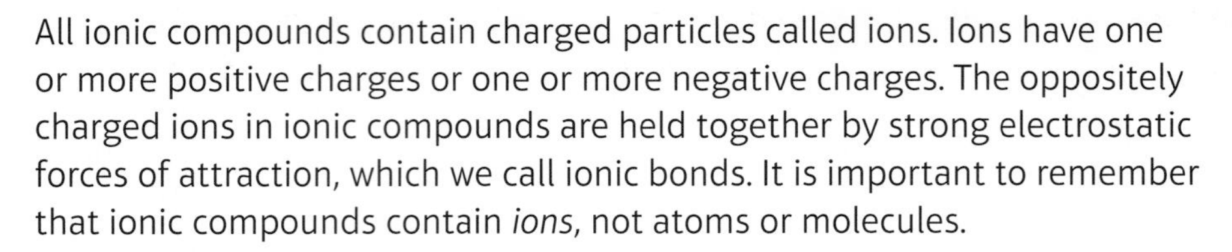

All ionic compounds contain charged particles called ions. Ions have one or more positive charges or one or more negative charges. The oppositely charged ions in ionic compounds are held together by strong electrostatic forces of attraction, which we call ionic bonds. It is important to remember that ionic compounds contain *ions*, not atoms or molecules.

In ionic compounds, huge numbers of ions are arranged in a giant structure or lattice. This has a regular pattern and so ionic compounds form crystals.

1 State the type of particles present in an ionic compound.

2 State the type of forces found in an ionic bond.

Melting points and boiling points

The electrostatic forces of attraction between oppositely charged ions are strong. A lot of energy is needed to overcome these forces in order to separate the ions and cause the substance to melt. This is why ionic compounds must be heated to high temperatures before they change state. They have high melting points and boiling points.

B molten sodium chloride

Some ions have more than one charge (such as Mg^{2+} and O^{2-}). These highly charged ions will attract other ions more strongly than ions with one charge. More energy will be needed to overcome the electrostatic forces of attraction and so the melting points will be higher.

Ionic compound	Melting point (°C)	Boiling point (°C)
sodium bromide, NaBr	747	1390
sodium chloride, NaCl	801	1413
magnesium oxide, MgO	2852	3600

C Ionic compounds have high melting points and boiling points.

3 Explain why ionic compounds have high melting points.

4 Explain why magnesium oxide has a much higher melting point than sodium chloride.

Electrical conductivity

Ionic compounds conduct electricity when they are molten or dissolved in water. They do not conduct electricity when they are in the solid state.

Two conditions must be met for a substance to conduct electricity:

- it must contain charged particles
- these particles must be free to move.

5 Samples of sodium chloride and magnesium oxide are both heated to 1080 °C. State and explain how the properties of these two compounds will or will not change at this temperature compared to room temperature.

When an ionic compound conducts electricity, it is the charged *ions* that carry the current. Ionic compounds do not conduct electricity in the solid state as the ions are not free to move from place to place. When the ionic compound is molten or in **aqueous solution**, the ions are free to move and so it does conduct electricity. Most ionic compounds are soluble in water and form an aqueous solution.

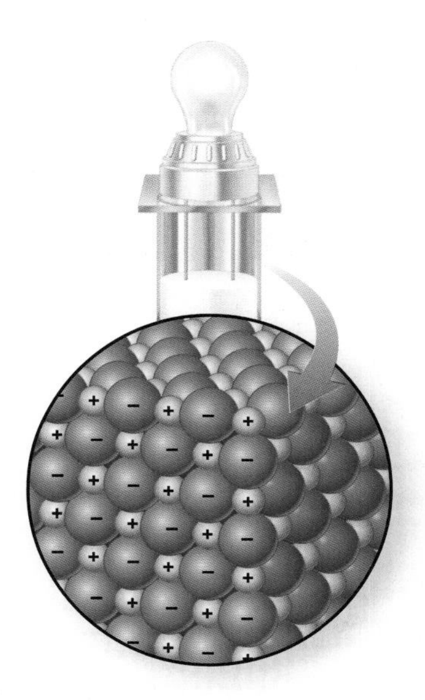

Positive and negative ions fixed in a solid do not conduct a current.

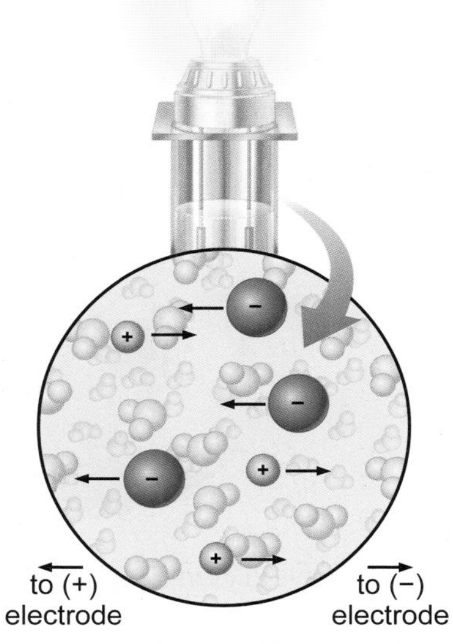

In solution, positive and negative ions move and conduct a current.

D Solid sodium chloride does not conduct electricity but aqueous sodium chloride does conduct.

The negative ions are also known as anions and they are attracted to the positive electrode, which is called the **anode**. The positive ions are also known as cations and they are attracted to the negative electrode, which is called the **cathode**.

It is important to remember that it is ions moving that enable ionic compounds to conduct electricity and that it is not *electrons* moving.

6 Explain why ionic compounds conduct electricity when they are dissolved in water.

7 Magnesium oxide is insoluble in water. State the condition needed for magnesium oxide to conduct electricity.

Exam-style question

Magnesium chloride is an ionic compound and has a high melting point. Explain why magnesium chloride has a high melting point. *(3 marks)*

Did you know?

Molten salts are used to store energy in some solar power stations. The salts are heated up by the Sun and release their thermal energy at night, allowing electricity to be generated when it is dark.

Checkpoint

How confidently can you answer the Progression questions?

Strengthen

S1 You are given a substance and asked to find out if it is an ionic compound. Describe the tests you would carry out in order to decide.

Extend

E1 Table E shows some properties of five compounds.

Compound	Melting point (°C)	Soluble in water?	Conducts when molten?
A	2072	no	yes
B	191	no	no
C	782	yes	yes
D	605	yes	yes
E	150	yes	no

E

Identify the compounds that have ionic bonding and explain your reasoning. Give reasons why the other compounds do not have ionic bonding.

SC6a Covalent bonds

Specification reference: C1.28; C1.29; C.1.30; C1.31

Progression questions

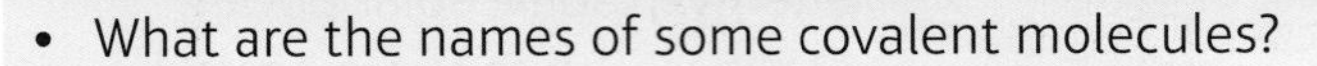

- What are the names of some covalent molecules?
- How are covalent bonds formed?
- How can dot and cross diagrams be used to explain the formation of covalent molecules?

Did you know?

A cup of tea will contain over 1 000 000 000 000 000 000 000 000 (10^{24}) water molecules. This is the same as the estimated number of stars in the Universe.

Molecular substances contain groups of atoms that are held together by strong bonds called **covalent bonds**. The number of atoms of each element bonded together in a simple **molecule** is shown by its **molecular formula.**

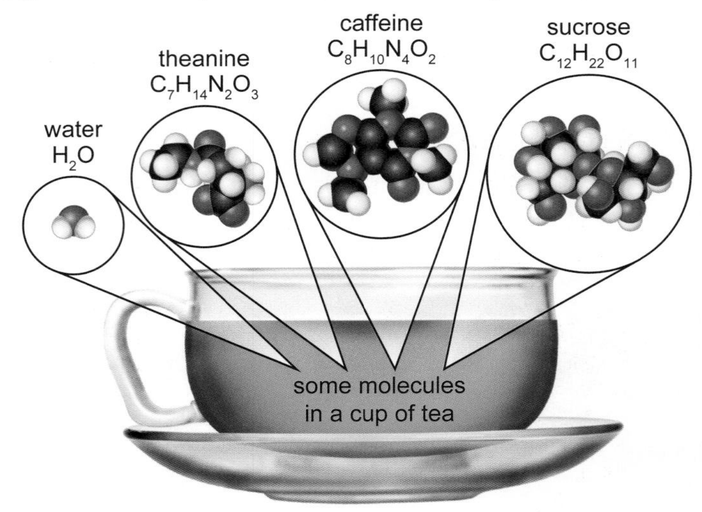

A Most of the molecules in a cup of tea are water, which has the molecular formula H_2O.

1 a What is a molecule?

b What does a molecular formula tell you about a substance?

2 Oxygen molecules consist of two oxygen atoms.

a Write the molecular formula for oxygen.

b Explain why a noble gas, such as argon, exists as single atoms and not as molecules.

Covalent bonds are usually formed between non-metal atoms and are produced by sharing pairs of electrons. By forming the bond the atoms become more stable, because they can use the shared electrons to complete their **outer electron shells**. The reason why noble gases are so stable is because they have full outer electron shells.

The **dot and cross diagrams** in diagram B show how covalent bonds are formed. Counting the shared electrons, each atom now has a complete outer shell of electrons. Sometimes atoms share more than one pair of electrons to fill their outer shells. In oxygen and carbon dioxide the atoms share two pairs of electrons, to form **double bonds**.

Dots show electrons from one atom and crosses show electrons from the other atom. This allows us to see which atoms the electrons in the bond originally came from. The electrons themselves are all identical.

single covalent bond

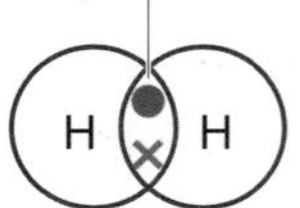

a hydrogen

H
Cl
single covalent bond

b hydrogen chloride

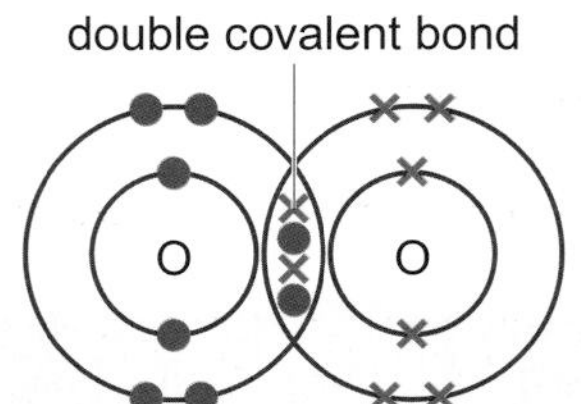

c oxygen

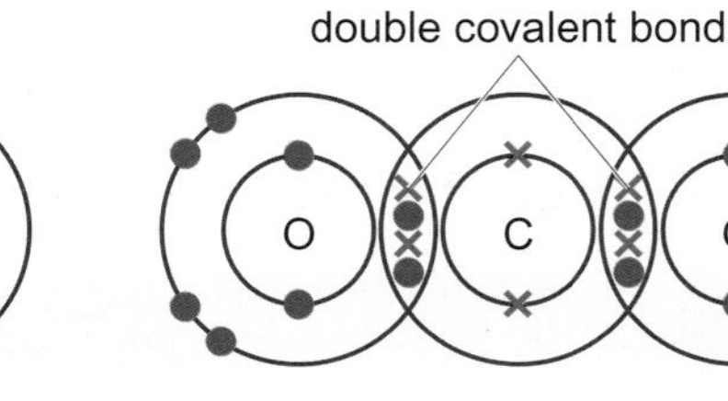

d carbon dioxide

B Dot and cross diagrams can be used to explain how covalent bonds are formed.

 **3** **a** Describe how covalent bonds are formed.

 **b** Write the molecular formulae for the substances shown in diagram B.

 **4** The electronic configuration of fluorine is 2.7. Draw a dot and cross diagram to show how fluorine molecules (F_2) are formed.

The atoms in molecules are held together by strong **electrostatic forces** of attraction between the positive nuclei and the negative electrons in the bonded atoms. There are also some forces of attraction *between* molecules but these are very weak in comparison. Atoms and molecules are extremely small, about 10^{-10} metres across, so we represent them using models, such as those shown in Diagram C.

 **5** What holds the atoms together when a covalent bond has been formed?

CH_4

molecular formula

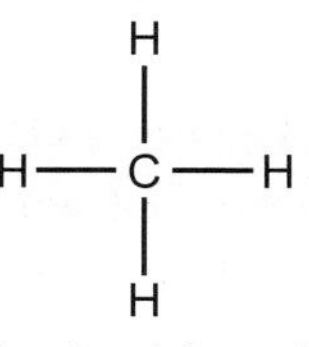

structural formula (stick bonds)

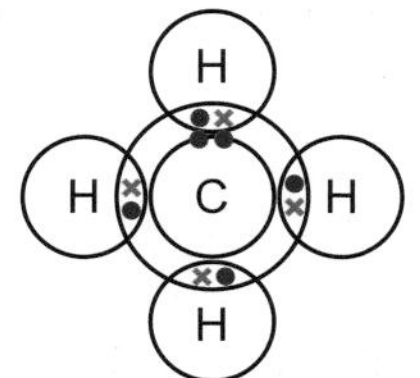

full dot and cross diagram

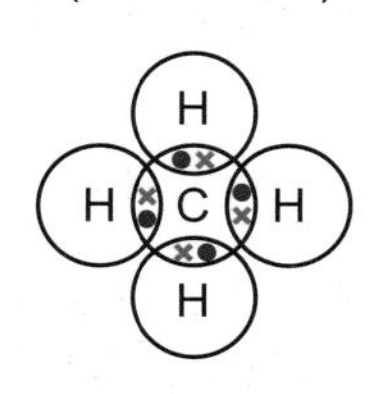

dot and cross (outer shell only)

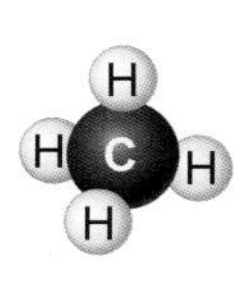

3D space filling

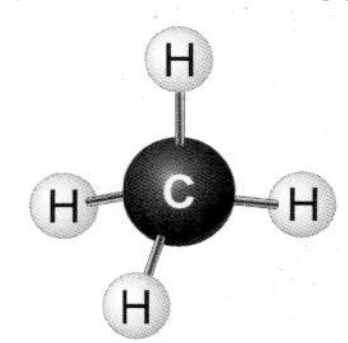

ball and stick

C different representations of methane

6 Look at diagram C.

 **a** How are bonds represented in structural formulae?

 **b** Describe the covalent bonds in methane.

 **c** Draw four different models of a water molecule, including one dot and cross diagram.

Working out molecular formulae

The numbers of covalent bonds formed by atoms of different elements are shown in table D. This is called the **valency** of the element. It is the same as the number of electrons needed to obtain a complete outer shell.

Group number	Examples	Outer electrons	Bonds formed	Valency
4	C and Si	4	4	4
5	N and P	5	3	3
6	O and S	6	2	2
7	F and Cl	7	1	1

D valencies of some elements

Diagram E shows how molecular formulae can be worked out by matching up the valencies, so that all atoms have the correct number of bonds (and so a complete outer electron shell).

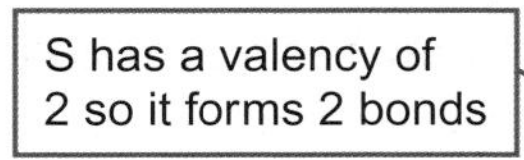

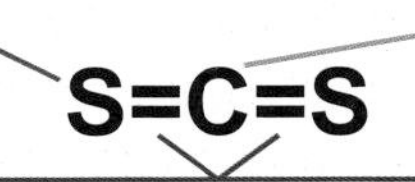

C has a valency of 4 so it forms 4 bonds

So two S atoms each form a double bond with a single C atom. As a result all atoms form the correct number of bonds.

E working out the formula of carbon sulfide

7 Work out the molecular formulae for:

 **a** oxygen fluoride **b** hydrogen sulfide **c** nitrogen chloride.

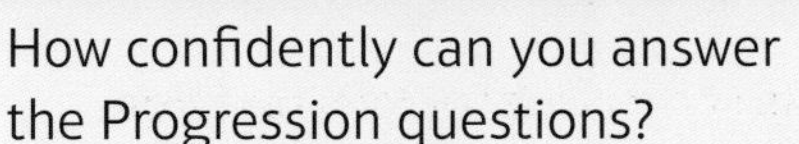

Checkpoint

How confidently can you answer the Progression questions?

Strengthen

S1 What does diagram B tell you about hydrogen chloride?

Extend

E1 Describe the bonding in a molecule of ammonia, which contains three hydrogen atoms and one nitrogen atom. Use diagrams in your answer.

Exam-style question

Describe the bonding in a molecule of water, which contains two hydrogen atoms and one oxygen atom. *(3 marks)*

SC7a Molecular compounds

Specification reference: C1.34; C1.39

Progression questions

- Why do simple molecular compounds have low boiling and melting points?
- Why are simple molecular compounds poor electrical conductors?
- What is a polymer?

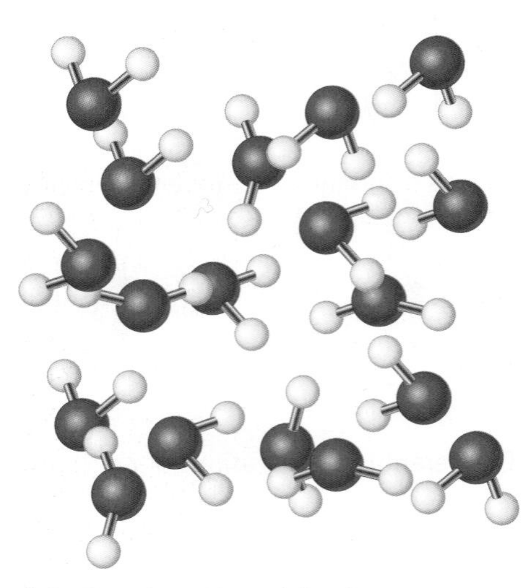

A 'ball and stick' models of H_2O molecules

All **compounds** contain atoms of more than one **element**, chemically joined together by **bonds**. The properties of a compound are influenced by its atoms and by its type of bonding.

Some compounds exist as molecules – distinct groups of atoms joined by **covalent bonds**. They have **covalent, simple molecular structures**. An example is water. One molecule of water always contains one atom of oxygen covalently bonded to two atoms of hydrogen.

1 Look at diagram A.

a What do the red and white spheres represent?

b How are bonds represented in this model?

2 Why is the ratio of oxygen to hydrogen atoms the same in every glass of water?

Melting and boiling points

The covalent bonds in a water molecule are strong forces of attraction. However, there are also weak forces of attraction *between* molecules – **intermolecular forces**. These intermolecular forces hold water molecules together and must be overcome when turning liquid water into a gas. Small, simple molecules such as water often have low melting and boiling points, because it doesn't take much energy to overcome the weak intermolecular forces.

3 Covalent bonds are strong, so why does water have a low melting point?

4 What would you expect the strength of the bonds to be like between carbon and oxygen atoms in carbon dioxide, compared to the strength of the forces between neighbouring carbon dioxide molecules?

5 **a** Methane consists of molecules (containing one carbon atom covalently bonded to four hydrogen atoms). Would you expect methane to have a high or low melting point?

b Explain your reasoning.

Did you know?

Intermolecular forces can allow water in an open container to be higher than the top of the container.

B

Conduction of electricity

An electric current is a flow of charged particles. Simple molecules have no overall charge and so cannot carry an electric current. In a covalent bond, electrons are shared between two atoms. The strong forces between the negatively charged electrons and the positively charged nuclei hold the electrons in place. The electrons cannot flow and so cannot carry a current.

6 Explain why water is a poor conductor of electricity.

Polymers

Monomers are small, simple molecules that can be joined in a chain to form a **polymer**. Carbon atoms can form up to four covalent bonds with other atoms, and so monomers are usually linked together by covalent bonds between carbon atoms. Most polymers contain a chain of carbon atoms.

Poly(ethene) (or 'polythene') is a common polymer made of ethene monomers (as shown in diagram D).

Polymer molecules can have different lengths. Longer polymers have more intermolecular forces between them. The longer chains also tend to get tangled up with one another. For these reasons, longer polymers have higher melting and boiling points than shorter ones.

7 What is a polymer?

C Poly(ethene) sheets are often used to protect things, such as plants. These are coffee beans being dried.

(i) ethene

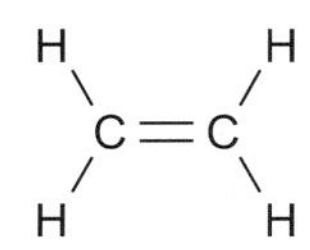

(ii) poly(ethene)

D two dimensional models of: (i) an ethene molecule (monomer) (ii) a poly(ethene) molecule

8 a What monomer is used to make poly(butene)?

b What polymer is formed by linking styrene monomers together?

9 Explain why most polymers are solids at room temperature, whereas their monomers are liquids or gases.

Exam-style question

Explain why small molecules have a lower melting point than large polymer molecules. *(3 marks)*

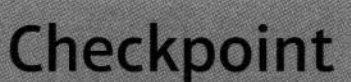

Checkpoint

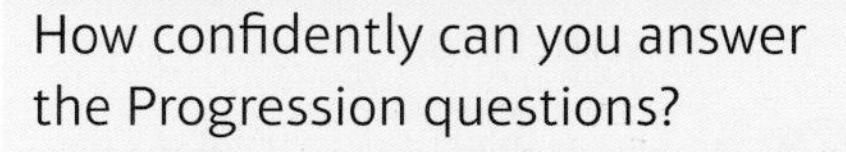

How confidently can you answer the Progression questions?

Strengthen

S1 You can ask three questions to find out if a substance consists of simple molecules or not. What questions would you ask?

Extend

E1 Propene melts at −185 °C. Explain how the melting point and electrical conduction will change if other propene molecules are added together to form a chain.

SC7b Allotropes of carbon

Specification reference: C1.35; C1.36; C1.37; C1.38

Progression questions

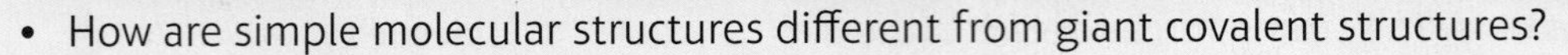

- How are simple molecular structures different from giant covalent structures?
- What are the differences in structure between the different allotropes of carbon?
- How do we explain the properties and uses of graphite, diamond and fullerenes?

Molecules are groups of atoms joined by covalent bonds. Molecules can be compounds (such as water, H_2O) or elements (such as oxygen, O_2).

The element carbon can form a number of different molecules. Different structural forms of the same element are called **allotropes**. The structure and bonding in different allotropes influences their properties and uses.

5th **1** What is an allotrope?

Fullerenes

Carbon can form simple molecules called **fullerenes**, in which each carbon atom is covalently bonded to three other carbon atoms. Fullerenes are often tubular molecules (nanotubes) or spherical. An example is buckminsterfullerene (or 'bucky ball'), which has 60 carbon atoms that form a ball with the formula C_{60}.

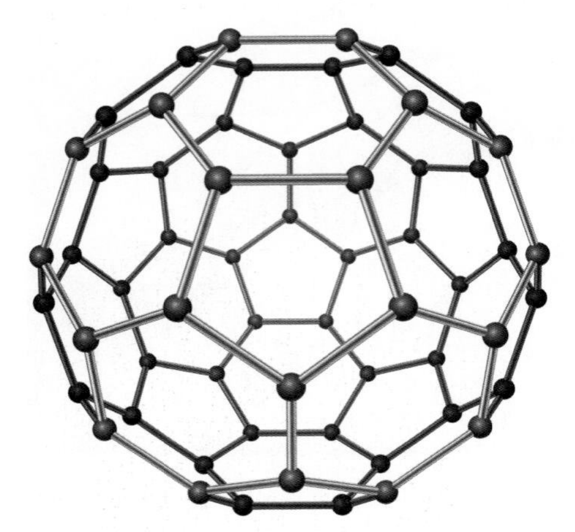

A Buckminsterfullerene is a simple molecule.

Fullerenes have weak intermolecular forces between the molecules and so have low melting points (or sublimation points). These weak forces also make them soft and slippery. However, the molecules themselves are very strong due to their covalent bonding.

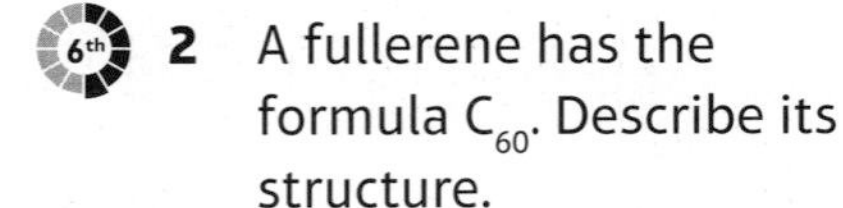

6th **2** A fullerene has the formula C_{60}. Describe its structure.

6th **3** Explain why fullerenes have low melting points.

Graphene

Graphene is similar to fullerenes but is not a simple molecule. It consists of a sheet of carbon atoms with no fixed formula. The sheet is just one atom thick, making it the lightest known material, but its covalent bonds make it extremely strong. It also allows free electrons to move across its surface and so is a good electrical conductor.

Did you know?

Buckminsterfullerene is named after an American architect called Richard Buckminster Fuller, who designed spherical buildings with a similar structure to C_{60}.

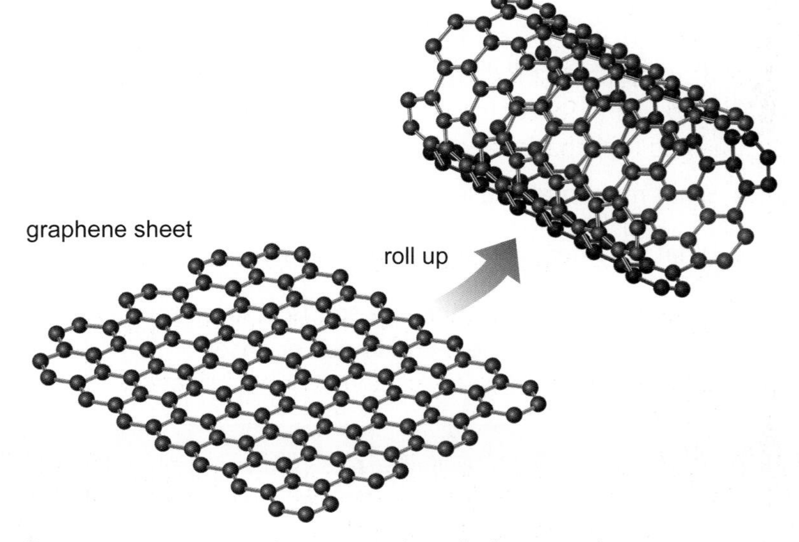

B Graphene can be a sheet or can be rolled into a tube.

6th **4** Explain why graphene is not a simple molecule.

Giant structures of carbon

Diamond and graphite are two more allotropes of carbon that are not simple molecules. They are both examples of **covalent, giant molecular structures**, which have huge three-dimensional networks of carbon atoms linked by covalent bonds.

5 How many covalent bonds will most carbon atoms form in graphite, diamond and C_{60}?

6 Describe how simple molecular structures are different from giant molecular structures.

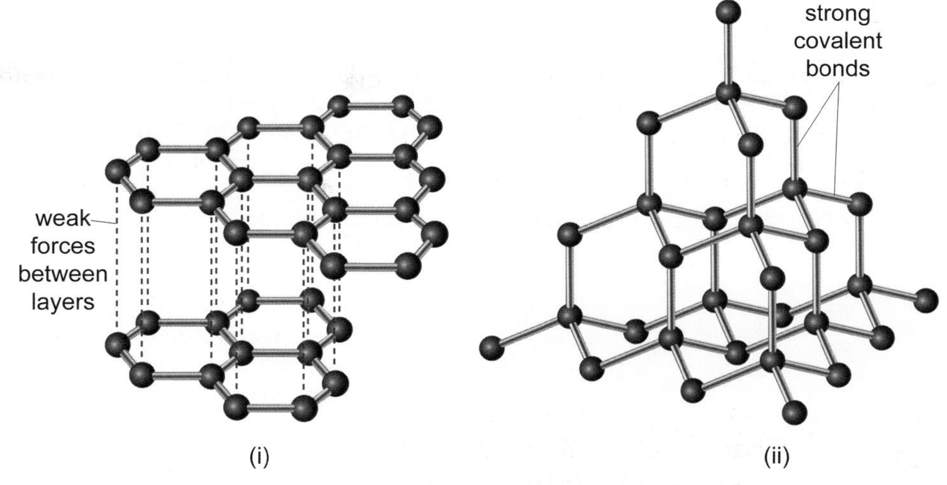

C small sections of (i) graphite and (ii) diamond to show the arrangements of atoms

Graphite and diamond both have high melting points because of the many strong covalent bonds that need to be broken to melt the solids.

However, graphite has three covalent bonds for each carbon atom, whereas diamond has four. This gives graphite a layered structure and means that not all of its electrons are held in covalent bonds. These **delocalised electrons** are free to move and can carry an electrical current. Since graphite conducts electricity well and is cheap and not very reactive, it is used as electrodes (in electrolysis).

7 Explain why graphite conducts electricity but diamond does not.

The sheets of carbon atoms in graphite are held together by weak forces of attraction (purple dashed lines in diagram C). These weak forces allow the layers to slide past each other, which makes graphite quite soft and useful as a **lubricant**.

Diamond is very hard because it has a rigid network of carbon atoms in a tetrahedral arrangement, joined by strong covalent bonds. This property makes diamond useful for tools to cut things. It is also an electrical insulator because it has no free charged particles.

8 Explain why:

a graphite is used as electrodes

b diamonds are used on cutting heads when drilling through rocks

c spherical fullerenes are used in some lubricants.

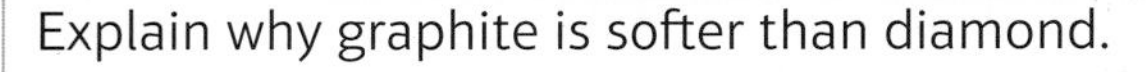

Exam-style question

Explain why graphite is softer than diamond. *(4 marks)*

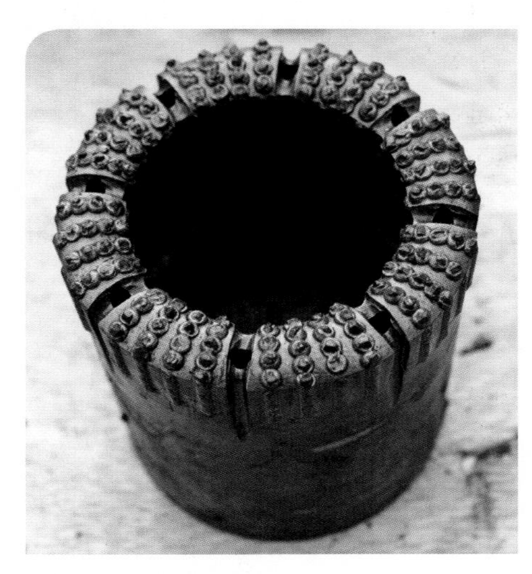

D This cutting head, used in mining, is studded with diamonds.

Checkpoint

How confidently can you answer the Progression questions?

Strengthen

S1 Describe how the structures of four allotropes of carbon cause their properties.

Extend

E1 Graphene sheets can be rolled into tubes. Predict the properties of these tubes.

SC7c Properties of metals

Specification reference: C1.40; C1.42

Progression questions

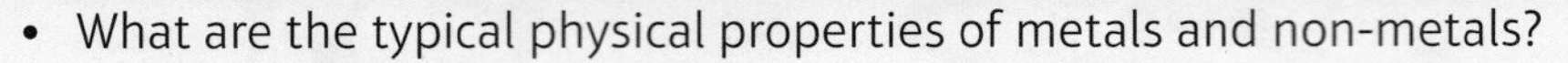

- What are the typical physical properties of metals and non-metals?
- How are the particles arranged in metals?
- How can we explain the properties of a metal in terms of its bonding and structure?

The bucket is made of iron. Metals have some common properties:
- solids with high melting points
- shiny (when polished)
- malleable
- high density
- good conductors of electricity.

Sulfur is a non-metal. Non-metals have some common properties:
- solids, liquids or gases with low melting points
- not usually shiny (when solid)
- brittle (when solid)
- low density
- poor conductors of electricity.

A Sulfur being unloaded at a port in Darwin, Australia.

Chemists classify elements into **metals** and **non-metals**, depending on their properties. Just over three-quarters of the elements are metals.

A metal or a non-metal may not have all the common properties shown in photo A.

1 Give two general properties of:

 **a** metals

 **b** non-metals.

 **2** Name a form of the non-metal carbon that is a good conductor of electricity.

Metallic structure and bonding

The atoms in a metallic element are all the same size and are packed closely together in layers to form a giant **lattice**.

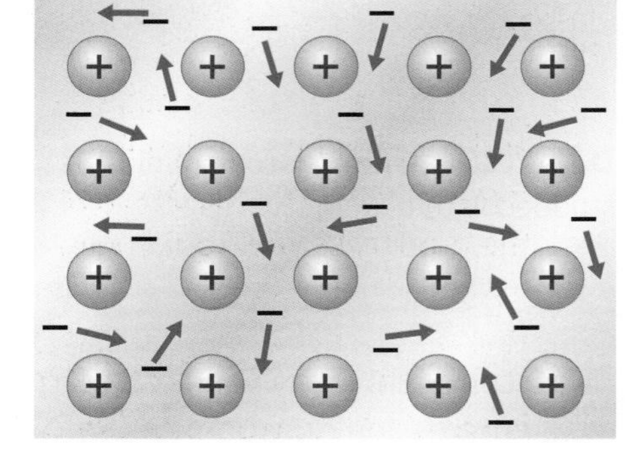

B Metals consist of stacked layers of ions in a 'sea' of delocalised ('free') electrons.

Metal atoms have one, two or three electrons in their outer shell. These outer shell electrons are lost from each atom and become free to move randomly throughout the metal. This leaves a giant lattice of positive metal ions surrounded by a 'sea' of delocalised electrons, which move randomly in all directions.

Metallic bonding is the electrostatic attraction between the positive metal ions and the negative delocalised electrons. This attraction is strong, so metals have high melting and boiling points.

 **3** **a** Describe the structure of a metal.

 **b** Describe the bonding in a metal.

 **4** Explain why most metals have high melting points.

Did you know?

Osmium is the most dense metal at room temperature (the mass of 1 cm^3 is 22.6 g). A lump of osmium the size of an average smartphone has a mass of 1.5 kg (the same as one and a half bags of sugar)!

Metals are malleable

Metals are **malleable**. This means that they can be hammered or rolled into shape without shattering. When you hit a metal, the layers of ions slide over each other. The 'sea' of electrons holds the ions together and so the metal changes shape instead of breaking.

C When hit or bent, the layers of ions in a metal can slide over each other.

 **5** Copper is used to make some saucepans. Explain why copper can be bent and shaped into a saucepan.

Metals conduct electricity

The delocalised electrons move randomly between the positive metal ions in all directions. When a potential difference (voltage) is applied between two points on a piece of metal, the electrons will flow towards the positive side. This flow of electrons transfers energy and forms an electrical current.

D Copper conducts electricity well and so is used for electrical wiring.

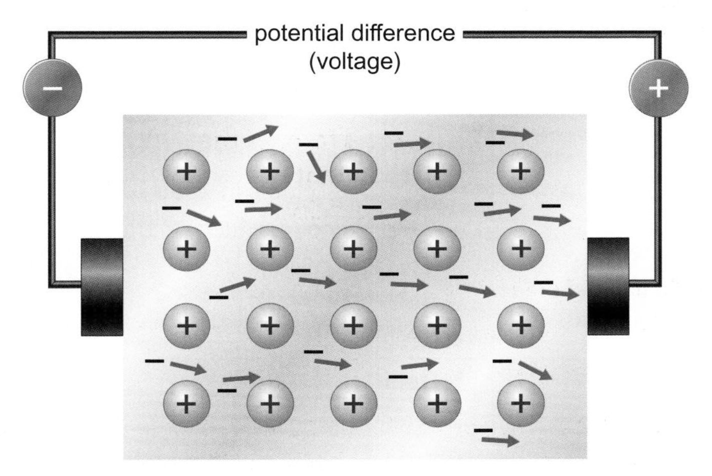

E When a voltage is applied to a piece of metal, an electrical current flows.

 **6** **Copper is used to make electrical wires. Explain why copper is a good conductor of electricity.**

Substances that conduct electricity better than others have a higher **electrical conductivity**. The electrical conductivity of the metals increases as the number of delocalised electrons increases. Each sodium ion has one positive charge, Na^+, and contributes 1 electron to the 'sea' of delocalised electrons. Each magnesium ion has two positive charges, Mg^{2+}, and contributes 2 electrons to the 'sea' of delocalised electrons, and so magnesium has a higher electrical conductivity than sodium.

 **7** **Aluminium forms Al^{3+} ions. Explain why aluminium has a higher electrical conductivity than magnesium.**

Exam-style question

Explain how metals conduct electricity. *(2 marks)*

Checkpoint

How confidently can you answer the Progression questions?

Strengthen

S1 You are given a solid substance and asked to find out if it is a metal or a non-metal. Describe the properties you would need to find out about.

Extend

E1 Elements A and B are solids at room temperature. Element A has a melting point of 98 °C, a density of 0.97 g/cm^3 and conducts electricity. Element B has a melting point of 217 °C, a density of 4.81 g/cm^3 and doesn't conduct electricity. Are these elements metals or non-metals? Explain your reasoning.

SC7d Bonding models

Specification reference: C1.32; C1.41

Progression questions

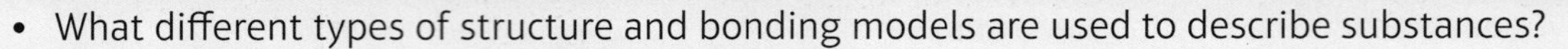

- What different types of structure and bonding models are used to describe substances?
- How do these models help explain the properties of substances?
- What are the limitations of the models that we use to show structure and bonding?

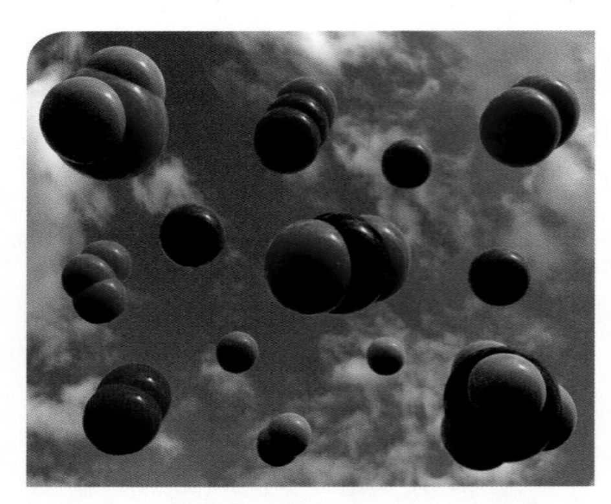

A 3D models of some gas molecules

Scientists have developed models to explain how different types of bonds and structures are formed. These models help us explain the properties of different substances. Most elements and compounds fit into one of the four main models summarised below.

Ionic

Where found: in most compounds containing metal and non-metal atoms.

Bonding: ionic bonds formed by the loss and gain of electrons to produce oppositely charged ions that attract one another.

Structure: billions of ions held together in a lattice structure.

Properties:

- high melting/boiling points
- many are soluble in water
- conduct electricity when liquid or in solution but do not when solid.

Simple molecular (covalent)

Where found: in most non-metal elements and compounds.

Bonding: covalent bonds formed when atoms share pairs of electrons.

Structure: small, distinct groups of atoms.

Properties:

- low melting/boiling points
- a few are soluble in water
- most do not conduct electricity.

Giant covalent

Where found: in a few non-metal elements and some compounds of non-metals.

Bonding: covalent bonds formed when atoms share pairs of electrons.

Structure: billions of atoms held together in a lattice structure.

Properties:

- high melting/boiling points
- insoluble in water
- most do not conduct electricity (except in carbon as graphite).

Metallic

Where found: in all metals.

Bonding: metallic bonds are the electrostatic attraction between positive metal ions and negative delocalised electrons.

Structure: billions of ions held together in a giant lattice structure of positive ions in a 'sea' of negative delocalised electrons.

Properties:

- high melting/boiling points
- insoluble in water
- conduct electricity when solid or liquid.

The models help to explain some of the properties. For example:

- Substances with high melting points have many strong bonds that need to be broken during melting. Substances with low melting points have only weak forces that need to be overcome between molecules.
- Substances that conduct electricity have charged particles that can freely move. Substances that do not conduct electricity have charged particles that cannot move or particles that are not charged.

1 Look at the substances in the box below.

potassium fluoride carbon dioxide diamond magnesium

Which substance:

a conducts electricity when solid

b is most likely to dissolve in water

c has the lowest melting point?

2 **a** Name the type of bonding and structure that usually has a low melting point.

b Explain why the melting points of these substances are usually low.

 **3** Explain why sodium metal conducts electricity when it is solid or liquid but sodium chloride conducts only when liquid.

4 A white solid with a melting point of 2614 °C does not dissolve in water.

 **a** Is the substance ionic or covalent or can you not tell? Explain your answer.

 **b** Describe a test you could do to help you answer part a.

 **5** What do sodium ions and chloride ions have in common?

Did you know?

Ideas about chemical bonds can be traced back to Roman times. The Roman poet Lucretius (*c.*95 BCE–*c.*55 BCE) imagined atoms as tiny spheres with fishhooks embedded in them. The atoms formed bonds when the fishhooks got tangled up with one another.

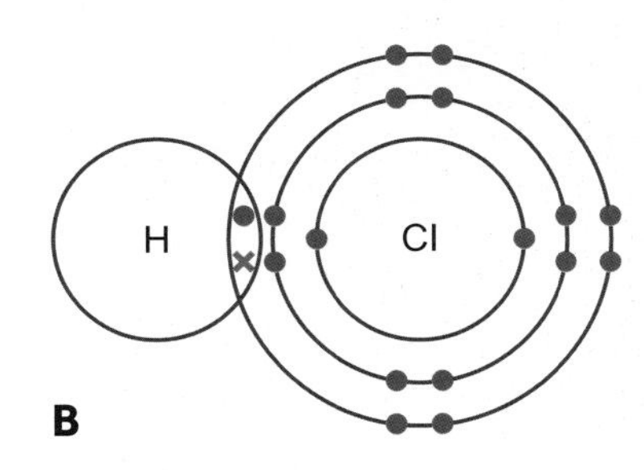

B

Problems with bonding models

The bonding models that we use to explain the properties of matter all have certain weaknesses or limitations.

- The dot and cross diagram for hydrogen chloride in diagram B shows how electrons are shared in covalent bonds. However, dot and cross diagrams do not show the structure formed and they suggest that the electrons in different atoms are different, when they are actually all the same.
- The metallic model in diagram C shows the metal ions held in a lattice and explains why it conducts electricity, but the model does not show that the ions will be vibrating all the time.

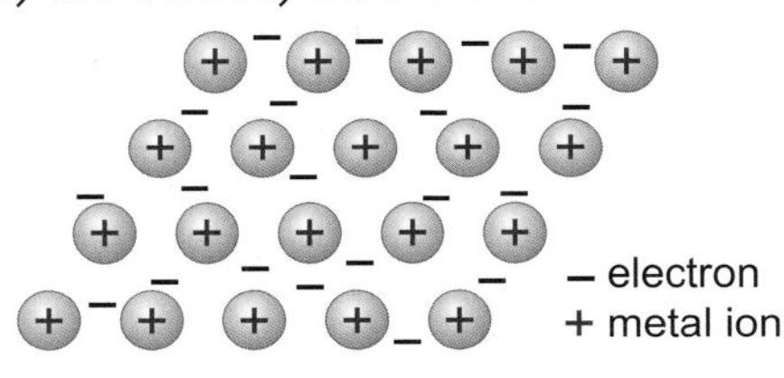

C

- 3D ball and stick models, like diagram D for diamond, show which atoms are joined together and show the shape of the structure. However, they also show the atoms too far apart and there are not really 'sticks' holding the atoms together.

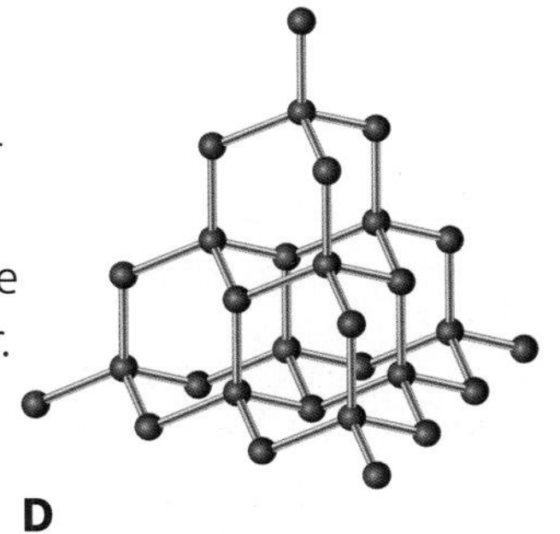
D

 **6 a** Draw a 3D structural ball and stick model of a sodium chloride lattice.

 **b** Draw a dot and cross diagram for sodium chloride.

 **c** Explain one strength and one weakness of a dot and cross diagram for sodium chloride.

 **7** Describe one strength and one weakness of the 3D models shown in photo A.

Exam-style question

Suggest an explanation why the melting point of silicon dioxide (1610 °C) is so much higher than the temperature at which solid carbon dioxide changes state (–78.5 °C), although both compounds contain covalent bonds. *(3 marks)*

Checkpoint

How confidently can you answer the Progression questions?

Strengthen

S1 Draw up a summary table describing the four 'types of bonding and structure' under the headings: 'where it occurs'; 'how bonds form'; 'type of structure'; 'properties' and 'examples'.

Extend

E1 The models below show methane.

a Draw a dot and cross diagram for methane.

b Describe one strength and one weakness of your dot and cross diagram and the two models below.

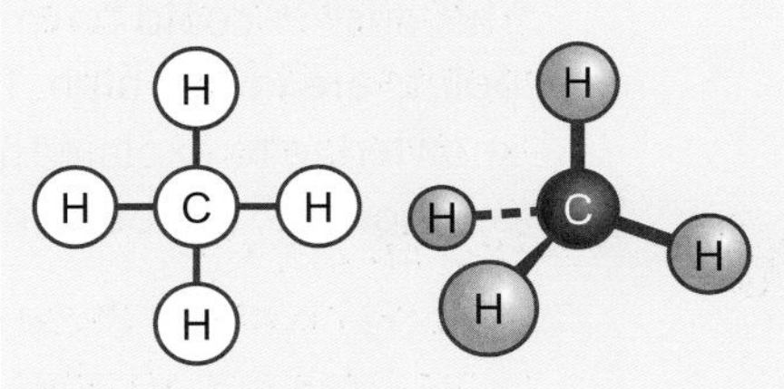

E

Bonding in compounds

Sodium chloride and hydrogen chloride are both compounds of chlorine. Sodium chloride has a boiling point of 1413 °C. Hydrogen chloride has a boiling point of –85 °C.

Explain this difference in boiling points in terms of the structure and bonding in the particles of the two compounds. **(6 marks)**

Student answer

As it is a metal and a non-metal, sodium chloride contains ionic bonds with lots of oppositely charged ions attracting each other to form a giant lattice structure [1]. *Ionic compounds contain lots of strong bonds which keep it solid* [2].

[1] This is a good description of the bonding and structure of sodium chloride.

[2] The question asked for an explanation of the high boiling point, not why it was solid.

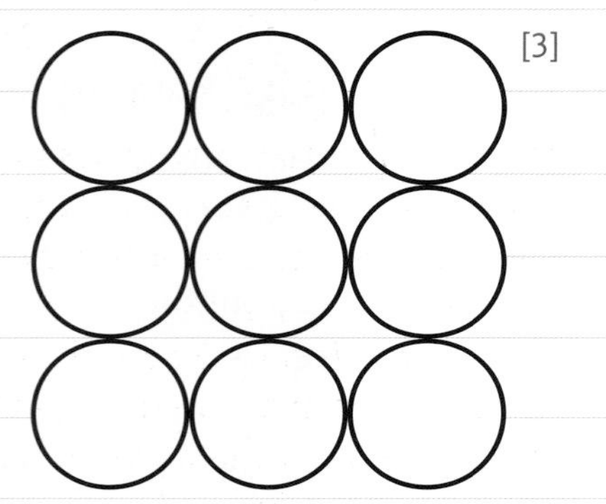

[3]

[3] The diagram will get no credit as it is not labelled or described.

Hydrogen chloride contains covalent bonds and is made up of molecules. The covalent bonds are strong bonds that hold the atoms together in the molecules. Substances which contain molecules have low boiling points [4].

[4] This part of the answer does not explain why hydrogen chloride has a low boiling point.

Verdict

This is an acceptable answer. It contains a good description of the bonding and structures of sodium chloride and hydrogen chloride. The answer has included information on both of the compounds in the question and uses correct scientific terminology.

This answer could be improved by explaining why the boiling points are low or high. The student should use scientific knowledge to explain the link between the structures of the compounds, the bonding within them and their boiling points.

Exam tip

You are more likely to get better marks in a question which requires extended writing if you plan your answer before you start. The plan can simply be a list of the keywords or phrases that you want to include. It is also useful to organise these keywords in a logical order to help structure your answer.

Paper 1

SC8 Acids and Alkalis

In the prehistoric world, lightning storms and volcanoes produced large quantities of gases that acidified our seas and lakes. Then, as now, acid rain was an environmental problem that caused extensive harm to plants and animals. We still live in a watery world, with many important chemical reactions occurring in aqueous solutions, where both the reactants and products dissolve in water. All solutions in water are either acidic, alkaline or neutral, as are many household and industrial chemicals. In this topic you will explore the nature of acidic and alkaline solutions, and investigate their most important reactions, properties and uses.

The learning journey

Previously you will have learnt at KS3:

- about solubility, solutes, solvents and solutions
- how common international hazard symbols are used
- about common acids, alkalis and neutral solutions
- about the use of indicators to test the pH of solutions
- about what happens during simple neutralisation reactions.

In this unit you will learn:

- about the ions in acids and alkalis, and how their concentrations are linked to pH
- what happens in the reactions between acids and different types of bases
- how different indicators can be used in acid–alkali titrations
- how different soluble and insoluble salts can be prepared in the laboratory.

SC8a Acids, alkalis and indicators

Specification reference: C0.5; C3.1; C3.2; C3.3; H C3.4

Progression questions

- Why are hazard symbols useful?
- What are the effects of acids and alkalis on some common indicators?
- What does the pH tell us about the ions in a solution?

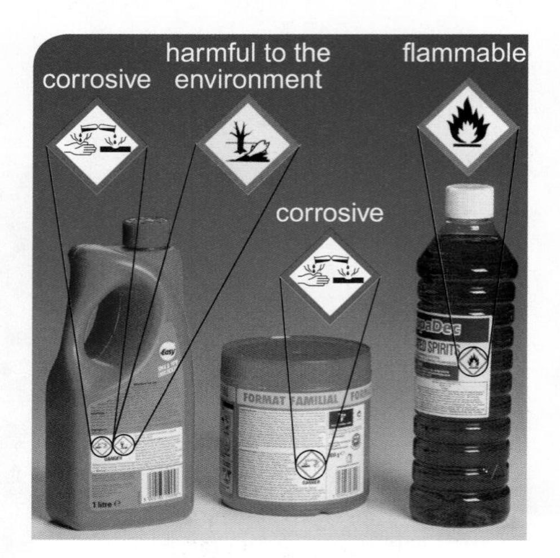

A International hazard symbols are used in all countries.

All **aqueous solutions**, including those found in many household chemicals, are either **acidic**, **alkaline** or **neutral**. Some, including those that are neutral, can cause problems. For example, some acids and alkalis can be corrosive, toxic or harmful to the environment. The hazards associated with handling particular solutions are identified by international symbols, and they indicate the precautions that need to be taken when handling them.

 **1** Name two acids and two alkalis used in the home.

 **2** **a** Suggest an advantage of having internationally agreed hazard symbols.

 **b** Suggest a safety precaution for each of the hazard symbols shown in photo A.

Indicators and pH

The **acidity** or **alkalinity** of a solution is measured on the **pH scale**. Most solutions lie between 0 and 14 on the scale. Solutions with a pH of 7 are neutral, while **acids** have a pH lower than 7 and **alkalis** have a pH greater than 7. The lower the pH, the more acidic the solution. The higher the pH, the more alkaline the solution.

The pH of a solution can be found by using **indicators** – substances that change colour depending on the pH. The **universal indicator** in photo B is made from a mixture of different indicators and produces a range of colours depending on the pH. Some other common indicators are shown in diagram C.

B Universal indicator can be used to find an approximate pH value.

 **3** Place the following pH values in order of increasing acidity. 4, 1, 7, 9, 6.

 **4** **a** What pH is the solution in photo B?

 **b** What colour would this solution turn each of the indicators in table C?

indicator	litmus	methyl orange	phenolphthalein
colour in alkaline solutions	blue	yellow	pink
colour in acidic solutions	red	red	colourless

C the colours of litmus, methyl orange and phenolphthalein

Did you know?

Plant dyes can be used as pH indicators. The juice from cherries is bright red in acid solutions but turns blue/purple in alkalis. Curry powder contains the pigment curcumin, which changes from yellow at pH 7.4 to red at pH 8.6.

Ions in acids and alkalis

An ion is an atom that has become charged by losing or gaining electrons. Losing electrons forms positive ions (e.g. Na^+, H^+). Gaining electrons forms negative ions (e.g. Cl^-, Br^-, S^{2-}).

Polyatomic ions are formed when small groups of atoms, held together by covalent bonds, lose or gain electrons. Examples include OH^-, NO_3^- and SO_4^{2-}.

Acids produce an excess of hydrogen ions (H^+) when they dissolve in water. For example, hydrochloric acid is formed when hydrogen chloride gas dissolves in water and splits into H^+ ions and Cl^- ions as shown in diagram E.

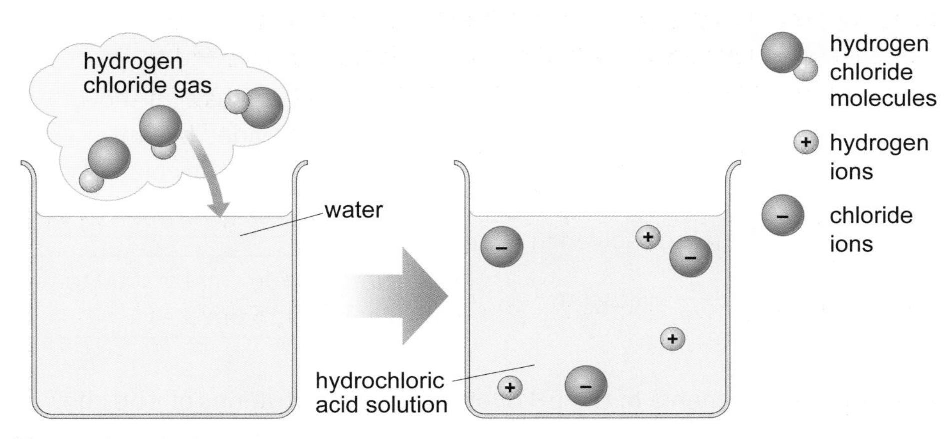

E Acids form hydrogen ions in water.

Alkalis produce excess hydroxide ions (OH^-) in water. For example, solid sodium hydroxide splits into Na^+ and OH^- ions when it dissolves.

H

The higher the number of hydrogen ions in a certain volume, the higher their **concentration**. The higher their concentration, the more acidic the solution and the lower the pH.

The higher the concentration of hydroxide ions, the more alkaline the solution and the higher the pH.

Neutral solutions, such as pure water, have a pH of 7 and contain low, equal, concentrations of hydrogen ions and hydroxide ions.

8 Describe what happens to the acidity and pH of a solution, as more hydrogen ions are added.

Exam-style question

a Explain why the pH of a hydrochloric acid increases when pure water is added. *(2 marks)*

b What would happen to the pH of salt solution (pH 7) if pure water was added? Briefly explain your answer. *(2 marks)*

Common acids	Formula
hydrochloric acid	HCl
sulfuric acid	H_2SO_4
nitric acid	HNO_3
Common alkalis	**Formula**
sodium hydroxide	$NaOH$
potassium hydroxide	KOH
calcium hydroxide	$Ca(OH)_2$

D common laboratory acids and alkalis

5 Describe what the pH scale tells us about acidity and alkalinity.

6 An acid is formed when hydrogen bromide dissolves in water.

a Suggest a possible pH for the solution and explain your choice.

b Write the symbols for the ions that form in this acidic solution.

7 What ions will each of the substances in table D produce when they dissolve in water?

Checkpoint

How confidently can you answer the Progression questions?

Strengthen

S1 Describe the differences between an acidic and an alkaline solution.

Extend

E1 Explain how the nature of a solution is changing if the pH is: **a** increasing **b** decreasing.

SC8b Looking at acids

Specification reference: H C3.5; H C3.7; H C3.8

Progression questions

- H What is the difference between dilute and concentrated solutions?
- H How do changes in the concentration of hydrogen ions affect the pH of a solution?
- H What is the difference between strong and weak acids?

H

A **concentrated** solution contains a lot of dissolved solute per unit volume, while a **dilute** solution contains only a small amount of solute.

1 25 g of sulfuric acid is dissolved in water to make 200 cm^3 of concentrated sulfuric acid solution.

a What is a concentrated solution?

b What is the concentration of this solution in $g\ dm^{-3}$?

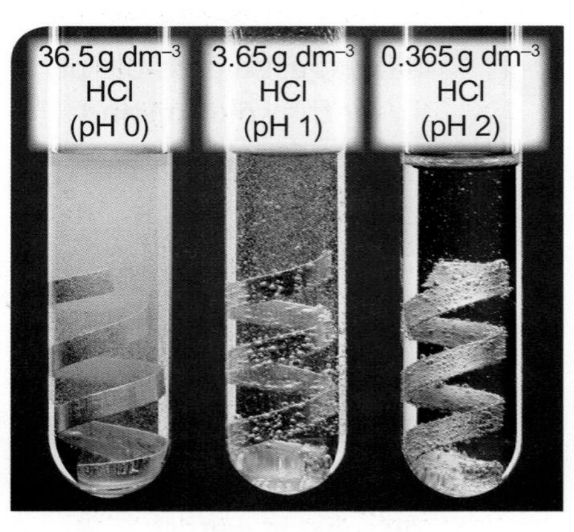

A More concentrated acids contain more hydrogen ions, so they react faster with magnesium metal.

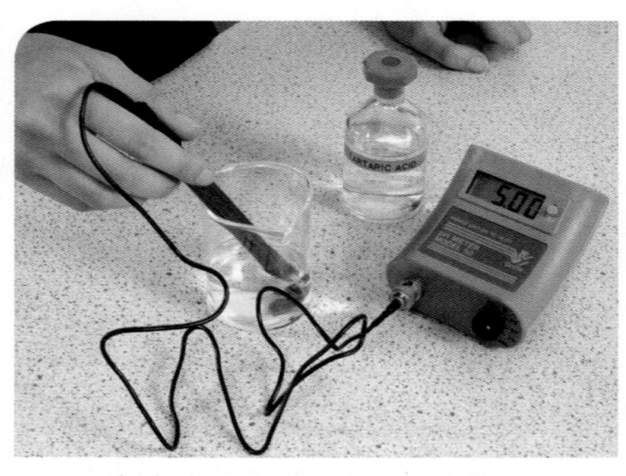

C Universal indicator only gives a rough estimate of acidity. A **pH meter** is used for accurate pH measurements.

Worked example

$$\text{Concentration} = \frac{\text{amount dissolved}}{\text{volume of solution}}$$

Units: grams per decimetre cubed, $g\ dm^{-3}$

Note: the minus sign shows that g is divided by dm^3. 1 dm^3 is the same volume as 1 litre or 1000 cm^3.

For example, if 4 g is dissolved in 50 cm^3

Note: divide cm^3 by 1000 to change into dm^3.

$$\text{Concentration} = \frac{4}{0.05} = 80\ g\ dm^{-3}$$

Accurate measurements of the pH of different concentrations of acid show that the concentration of hydrogen ions in an acid is linked to the pH. Table B shows that if the concentration of hydrogen ions is increased by a factor of 10, the pH decreases by 1. If the concentration decreases by a factor of 10, the pH increases by 1.

pH	0	1	2	3	4	5	6	7
difference in concentration of H^+ ions	× 10	× 10	× 10	× 10	× 10	× 10	× 10	

B pH and concentration

So, hydrochloric acid with a pH of 0 is 10 × 10 × 10 × 10 = 10 000 times more acidic than vinegar, with a pH of 4. This means that a solution with a pH of 0 has a concentration of H^+ ions that is 10 000 times greater than a solution with a pH of 4.

2 What does the pH of a solution measure?

3 An acid with a pH of 3 is diluted by a factor of 10. What will the new pH be?

4 The most acidic rain recorded in Britain had a pH of 2. How much more acidic is this than normal rainwater with a pH of 5?

5 What is the pH of the solution formed when 10 cm^3 of hydrochloric acid (pH 1) is made up to 1000 cm^3 with distilled water?

The pH of an acid depends on the type of acid as well as its concentration. The acids in table D with low pH values are **strong acids**. Their molecules **dissociate** (break up) completely into ions when they dissolve in water and produce high concentrations of hydrogen ions. The other acids in the table are **weak acids**. They do not dissociate completely into ions in solution. Diagram E shows the difference between a strong and a weak acid.

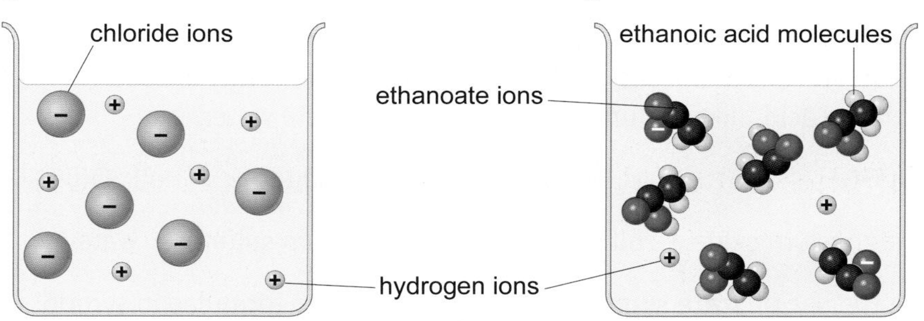

E strong and weak acids

Acids (equal concentrations)	pH
carbonic acid	3.8
nitric acid	1.0
sulfuric acid	1.2
ethanoic acid	2.9
boric acid	5.2
hydrochloric acid	1.0

D the pH of acids of the same concentration

The chemical properties of an acid depend on both the type of acid and its concentration, as shown in photo F.

6th **6** List the strong and the weak acids in table D.

7 About 1 in 60 000 butanoic acid molecules release hydrogen ions when they dissolve, while nearly all hydrogen iodide molecules do so.

6th **a** Explain which acid is a weak acid.

6th **b** Explain which acid will have the higher pH, if both are the same concentration.

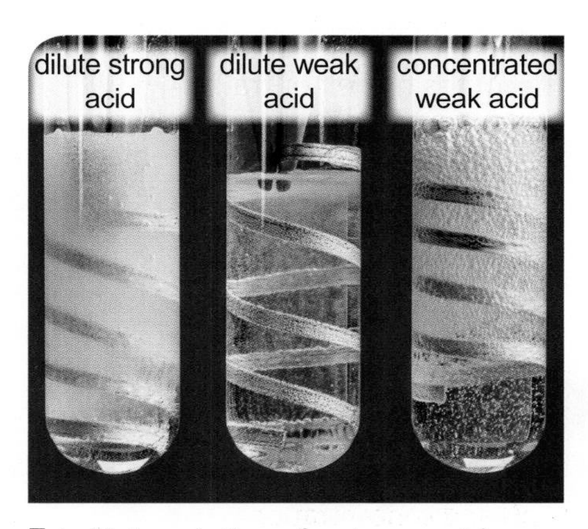

F A dilute solution of a strong acid can have a similar pH and reactivity as a concentrated solution of a weak acid. This is because they can have similar concentrations of hydrogen ions.

Exam-style question

The pH of five solutions (J–N) are described below.

J = pH 4   K = pH 12   L = pH 7   M = pH 3   N = pH 1

a Which two solutions have concentrations of hydrogen ions that differ by a factor of 10? *(1 mark)*

b State and explain which solution could be a concentrated solution of a strong acid. *(3 marks)*

Did you know?

The pH scale was developed in 1909 by Søren Sørensen (1868–1939) who was the head chemist in the Carlsberg Brewery in Copenhagen. The letters pH stand for 'power of hydrogen' where 'p' is short for the German word for power, potenz, and H is the symbol for hydrogen.

Checkpoint

How confidently can you answer the Progression questions?

Strengthen

S1 What do the following terms tell you when they are used to describe an acid solution?

a concentrated **b** dilute
c strong **d** weak

Extend

E1 Explain how a concentrated solution of a weak acid could have the same pH and similar reactions to a dilute solution of a strong acid.

SC8c Bases and salts

Specification reference: C3.9; C3.11; C3.13; C3.15

Progression questions

- Why are metal oxides bases?
- What happens during neutralisation?
- How can a soluble salt be prepared from an acid and an insoluble base?

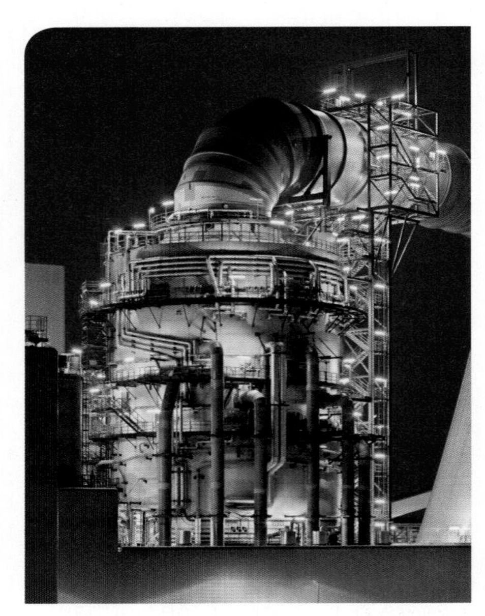

A Desulfurisation units attached to power station chimneys remove acidic sulfur-containing gases, by reacting them with the base calcium oxide.

1 What is a base?

2 Write a word equation and a symbol equation for the reaction of solid zinc oxide (ZnO) with sulfuric acid.

Bases are substances that **neutralise** acids to form a **salt** and water only. All metal oxides are bases. For example, magnesium oxide is used to neutralise acids, like sulfuric acid, in industrial waste water.

$$MgO(s) + H_2SO_4(aq) \rightarrow MgSO_4(aq) + H_2O(l)$$

magnesium oxide + sulfuric acid → magnesium sulfate + water

Note the use of **state symbols** in brackets after the formulae in symbol equations: (s) – solid; (l) – liquid; (g) – gas; (aq) – dissolved in water.

All neutralisation reactions with metal oxides occur in a similar way:

metal oxide + acid → salt + water

During neutralisation, hydrogen ions in the acid combine with oxide ions to form water. This removes the hydrogen ions and so the pH increases (becomes more neutral).

The salts are produced by replacing the hydrogen ions with metal ions, as shown in diagram B. Different acids form different salts, as shown in table C.

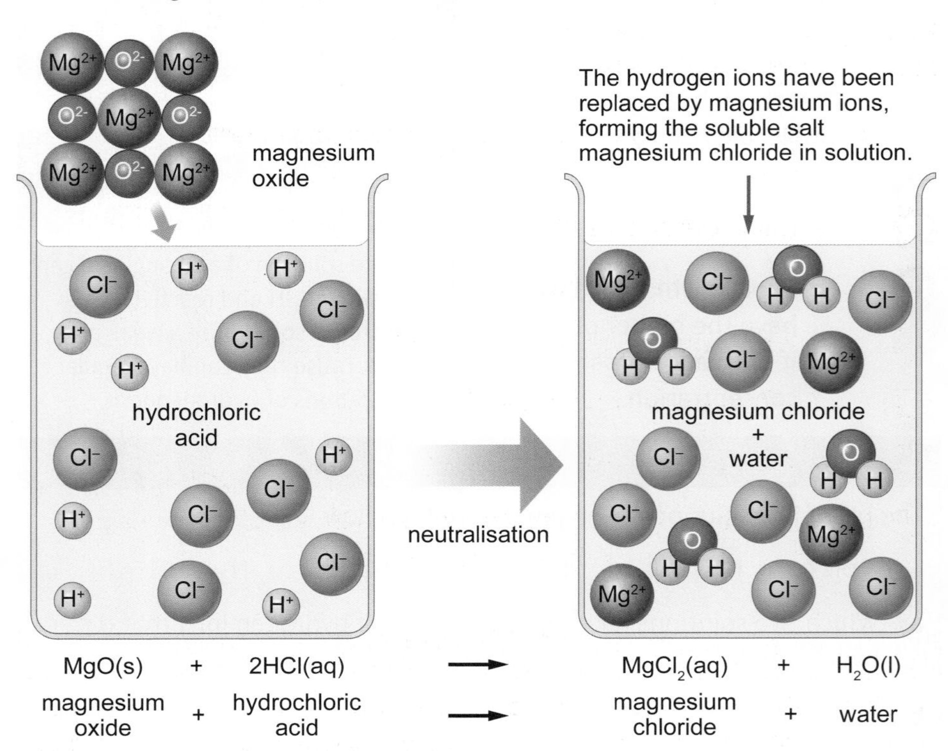

B how the salt magnesium chloride is formed

Acid	Salt formed
hydrochloric acid	chloride
sulfuric acid	sulfate
nitric acid	nitrate

C salts from acids

3 Write a word equation for the reaction between nitric acid and sodium oxide.

4 Copy and complete the symbol equation below, including the missing state symbols.

$$Li_2O(s) \; + \; ....(..) \; \rightarrow \; Li_2SO_4(aq) \; + \; ....(..)$$

Did you know?

'Limelight', meaning 'the centre of attention', originated from 19th-century stage lighting systems. These used burners to heat lumps of lime (calcium oxide), making them glow white hot.

Preparing soluble salts

The reaction between an acid and an insoluble metal oxide can be used to prepare samples of different soluble salts. For example, tin chloride can be prepared by reacting tin(II) oxide with hydrochloric acid solution. The steps involved are shown in diagram D.

An excess of the base is always added, to make sure that all the acid is used up. To make sure the prepared salt is pure, the mixture is **filtered** to remove the residue (the unreacted metal oxide) from the filtrate, leaving only the salt and water. A solid sample of the salt is then obtained by allowing the water to evaporate so that **crystallisation** of the salt occurs. Allowing the water to evaporate slowly will form larger crystals.

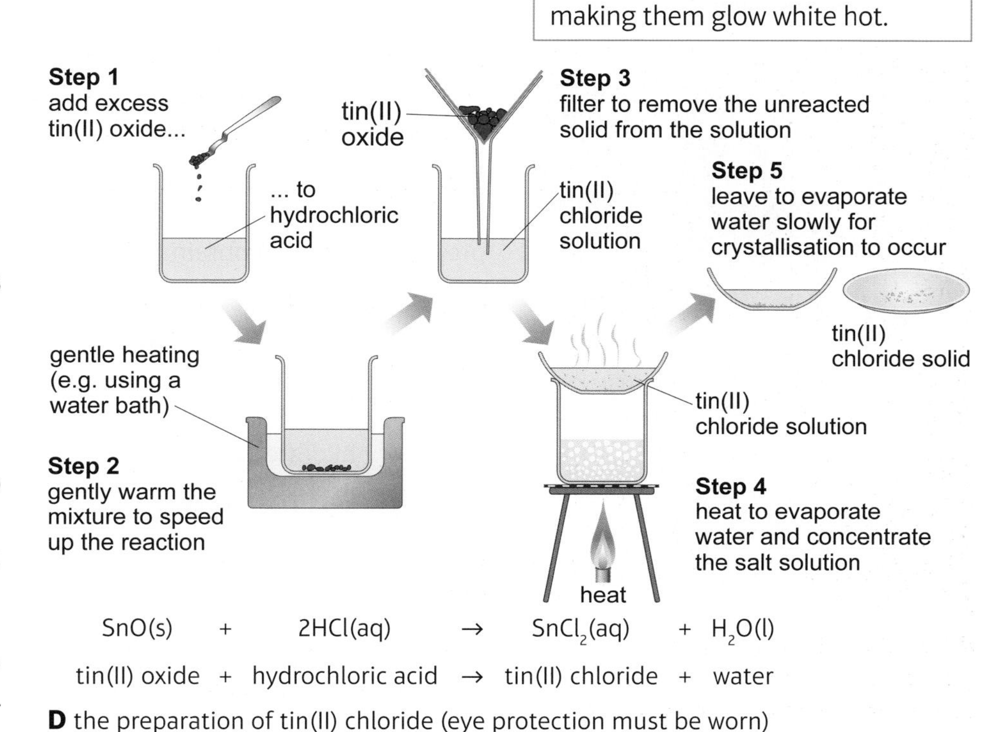

$$SnO(s) \; + \; 2HCl(aq) \; \rightarrow \; SnCl_2(aq) \; + \; H_2O(l)$$

tin(II) oxide + hydrochloric acid → tin(II) chloride + water

D the preparation of tin(II) chloride (eye protection must be worn)

5 Magnesium nitrate can be made by reacting magnesium oxide with an acid.

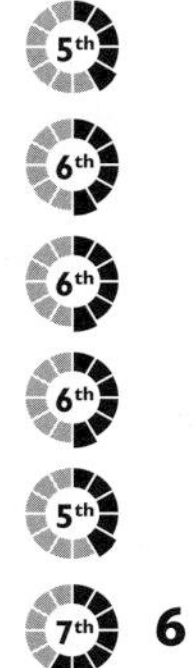

a Name the acid used.

b Why should the acid solution be warmed slightly?

c Why is the magnesium oxide added in excess?

d Why is the mixture filtered?

e Why is the salt solution heated?

6 Explain what happens to the hydrogen ions during the reaction between hydrochloric acid and tin(II) oxide.

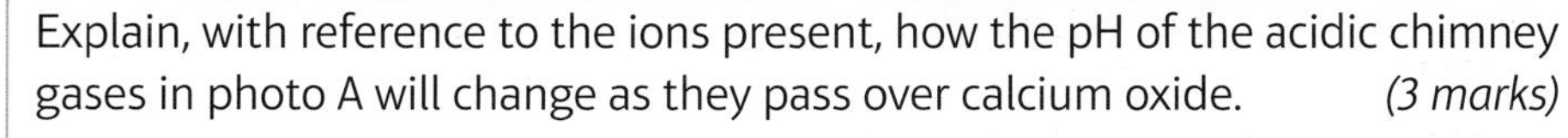

Exam-style question

Explain, with reference to the ions present, how the pH of the acidic chimney gases in photo A will change as they pass over calcium oxide. *(3 marks)*

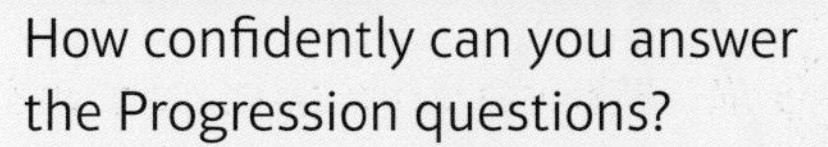

Checkpoint

How confidently can you answer the Progression questions?

Strengthen

S1 Draw a flowchart to explain the steps involved in preparing a soluble salt from an insoluble base.

Extend

E1 Aluminium nitrate, $Al(NO_3)_3$, can be made using aluminium oxide, Al_2O_3, and nitric acid, HNO_3. Describe the preparation of aluminium nitrate and explain each step of the process, including word and symbol equations.

SC8c Core practical – Preparing copper sulfate

Specification reference: C3.17

Aim

Investigate the preparation of pure, dry, hydrated copper sulfate crystals starting from copper oxide including the use of a water bath.

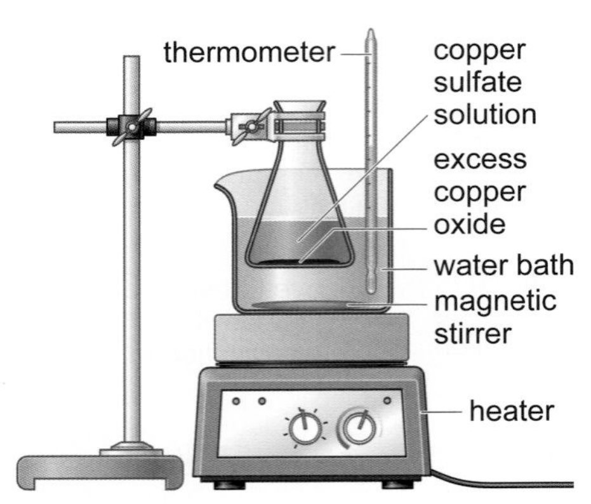

A Heating the acid makes the reaction between sulfuric acid and copper oxide faster.

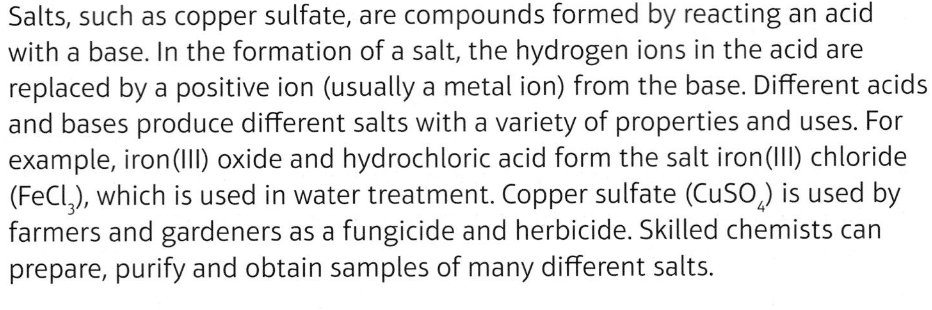

Salts, such as copper sulfate, are compounds formed by reacting an acid with a base. In the formation of a salt, the hydrogen ions in the acid are replaced by a positive ion (usually a metal ion) from the base. Different acids and bases produce different salts with a variety of properties and uses. For example, iron(III) oxide and hydrochloric acid form the salt iron(III) chloride ($FeCl_3$), which is used in water treatment. Copper sulfate ($CuSO_4$) is used by farmers and gardeners as a fungicide and herbicide. Skilled chemists can prepare, purify and obtain samples of many different salts.

Your task

Copper oxide reacts with warm sulfuric acid to produce a blue solution of the salt copper sulfate. You are going to use these reactants to prepare pure, dry hydrated copper sulfate crystals.

$$CuO(s) + H_2SO_4(aq) \rightarrow CuSO_4(aq) + H_2O(l)$$

copper oxide + sulfuric acid → copper sulfate + water

Copper oxide (the base) is insoluble in water. So when all the sulfuric acid has been used up, the excess copper oxide remains. Excess copper oxide is added to make sure that all the acid is used up. The remaining copper oxide is then separated from the copper sulfate solution by filtration. If the water is allowed to evaporate, a pure, dry sample of copper sulfate can be obtained.

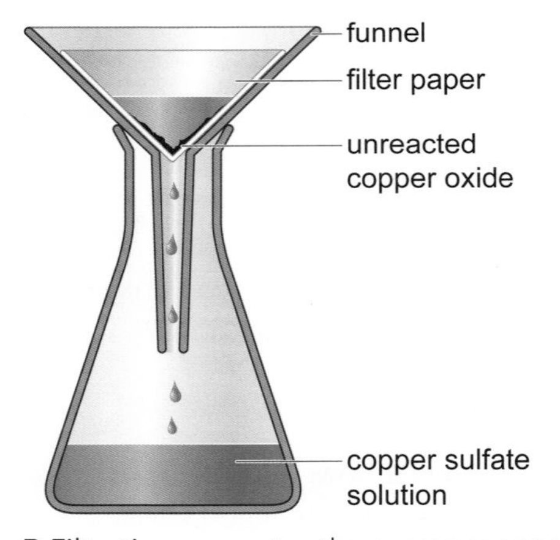

B Filtration separates the excess copper oxide (the residue) from the copper sulfate solution (the filtrate).

Method

Wear eye protection.

A Measure 20 cm^3 of dilute sulfuric acid using a measuring cylinder and pour it into a small conical flask.

B Warm the acid in a water bath set at 50 °C. Use a thermometer to measure the temperature.

C Add a little copper oxide powder to the acid and stir.

D If all the copper oxide reacts, and disappears, add a little more. Stop when the copper oxide is in excess and no longer reacts.

E Filter the mixture and transfer the filtrate to an evaporating basin.

F Heat the evaporating basin by placing it over a beaker of water heated with a Bunsen burner as shown in diagram D on the previous page. Stop heating when crystals start to form.

G Pour the solution into a watch glass and leave for a few days to allow all the water to evaporate.

Exam-style questions

1 State why copper sulfate is described as a salt. *(1 mark)*

2 State why the sulfuric acid is heated in step B. *(1 mark)*

3 In step E, explain why the copper oxide gets stuck in the filter paper while the copper sulfate goes through it. *(2 marks)*

4 Explain why a water bath is used in step B rather than heating with a Bunsen burner. *(2 marks)*

5 Explain how you know a chemical reaction has occurred in step C. *(2 marks)*

6 State how you know when all the acid has been used up. *(1 mark)*

7 Give a reason why it is important to make sure the copper oxide is in excess in step D. *(1 mark)*

8 Describe one safety precaution that should be taken during this experiment and explain why it is necessary. *(2 marks)*

9 Nickel chloride ($NiCl_2$) is a soluble salt. It can be made by reacting insoluble nickel oxide (NiO) with hydrochloric acid (HCl).

a Write a word equation for this reaction. *(1 mark)*

b Write a balanced equation with state symbols. *(2 marks)*

c Briefly describe the three main stages involved in preparing a pure, solid sample of nickel chloride. *(3 marks)*

10 Two class groups prepared some zinc chloride. One group produced lots of very small crystals while the other group produced larger crystals. Suggest an explanation for the groups producing different-sized crystals. *(2 marks)*

C Large crystals of copper sulfate form if the water evaporates slowly from a concentrated solution of copper sulfate.

SC8d Alkalis and balancing equations

Specification reference: C0.1; C0.2; C0.3; C3.10; C3.11

Progression questions

- What are alkalis?
- What happens when alkalis react with acids?
- How do we balance chemical equations?

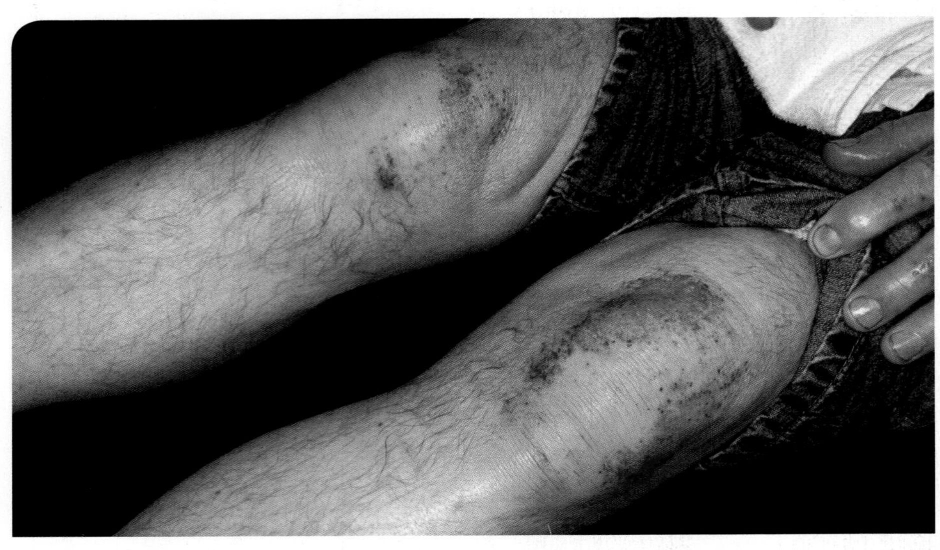

A These skin burns were caused by kneeling in wet cement, which contains an alkali called calcium hydroxide.

A base is any substance that reacts with an acid to form a salt and water only. Many bases are insoluble in water – they do not dissolve. A base that *can* dissolve in water, a *soluble* base, is called an **alkali**. Alkalis form alkaline solutions with pH values above 7.

1 Explain why all alkalis are bases, but not all bases are alkalis.

Common alkalis

Copper(II) hydroxide and most other metal hydroxides are insoluble bases.

However, these bases are soluble and therefore also alkalis:

- sodium hydroxide, NaOH, and other group 1 hydroxides
- calcium hydroxide, $Ca(OH)_2$, and other group 2 hydroxides.

Notice that the chemical formulae for these alkalis look different. In general they are MOH for group 1 hydroxides, where M stands for the metal's chemical symbol, but $M(OH)_2$ for group 2 hydroxides. This is because the ions formed by group 2 atoms have a 2+ charge, but hydroxide ions have a 1– charge. The brackets show that two OH^- ions are needed to produce a neutral compound.

Did you know?

Magnesium hydroxide is sparingly soluble. Just enough magnesium hydroxide dissolves to make an alkaline solution. It forms a cloudy white suspension in water, which is used as a medicine to neutralise excess stomach acid.

B

2 Write the formula for:

a lithium hydroxide **b** magnesium hydroxide.

Modelling reactions of alkalis with acids

Like other bases, alkalis react with acids to produce salts and water only. For example:

sodium hydroxide + hydrochloric acid → sodium chloride + water

During the neutralisation reaction, the reaction mixture becomes warmer. When an alkali is added to an acid, the pH increases and may go higher than 7 if enough alkali is added.

You can model the reaction using a **balanced equation**. In such equations, the numbers of atoms of each element must be the same on both sides of the arrow.

NaOH(aq)	+	HCl(aq)	→	NaCl(aq)	+	$H_2O(l)$
1			**Na**	1		
1			**O**			1
1		1	**H**			2
		1	**Cl**	1		

C There is one Na, one O, two H and one Cl atom on each side of this equation.

The water is formed from OH in the alkali and H in the acid.

You may need to write a number in front of one or more formulae to balance an equation. Remember that the formulae themselves cannot be changed. For example:

sodium hydroxide + sulfuric acid → sodium sulfate + water

2NaOH(aq)	+	$H_2SO_4(aq)$	→	$Na_2SO_4(aq)$	+	$2H_2O(l)$
(2 × 1) = 2			**Na**	2		
(2 × 1) = 2		4	**O**	4		(2 × 1) = 2
(2 × 1) = 2		2	**H**			(2 × 2) = 4
		1	**S**	1		

D The number 2 in front of NaOH and H_2O in the balanced equation shows that two units of these substances are needed.

Equations for the reactions of group 2 hydroxides with acids may look more complex. For example:

calcium hydroxide + nitric acid → calcium nitrate + water

$Ca(OH)_2(aq)$	+	$2HNO_3(aq)$	→	$Ca(NO_3)_2(aq)$	+	$2H_2O(l)$
1			**Ca**	1		
(1 × 2) = 2		(2 × 3) = 6	**O**	(3 × 2) = 6		(2 × 1) = 2
(1 × 2) = 2		(2 × 1) = 2	**H**			(2 × 2) = 4
		(2 × 1) = 2	**N**	(1 × 2) = 2		

E The number 2 outside the brackets for OH and NO_3 shows that there are two of these groups of atoms in the formulae for these substances.

6 Balance this equation for the reaction between potassium hydroxide solution and phosphoric acid:

$KOH(aq) + H_3PO_4(aq) \rightarrow K_3PO_4(aq) + H_2O(l)$

Exam-style question

Magnesium hydroxide solution reacts with stomach acid, which is hydrochloric acid. Magnesium chloride solution is a product. Write a balanced equation for the reaction, including state symbols. *(3 marks)*

3 Potassium hydroxide, KOH, reacts with hydrochloric acid in a similar way to sodium hydroxide. Write the balanced equation for this reaction, including state symbols.

4 Explain why the equation in diagram D is *balanced*.

5 Balance this equation for the reaction between barium hydroxide solution and sulfuric acid:

$Ba(OH)_2(aq) + H_2SO_4(aq) \rightarrow BaSO_4(s) + H_2O(l)$

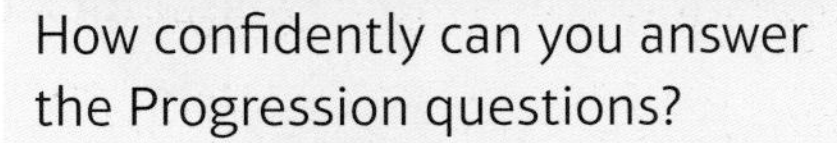

Checkpoint

How confidently can you answer the Progression questions?

Strengthen

S1 What happens when metal hydroxides react with acids?

S2 How are chemical equations balanced?

Extend

E1 Evaluate the use of balanced equations to model the reactions of metal hydroxides with acids.

SC8d Core practical – Investigating neutralisation

Specification reference: C3.6

Aim

Investigate the change in pH on adding powdered calcium hydroxide or calcium oxide to a fixed volume of dilute hydrochloric acid.

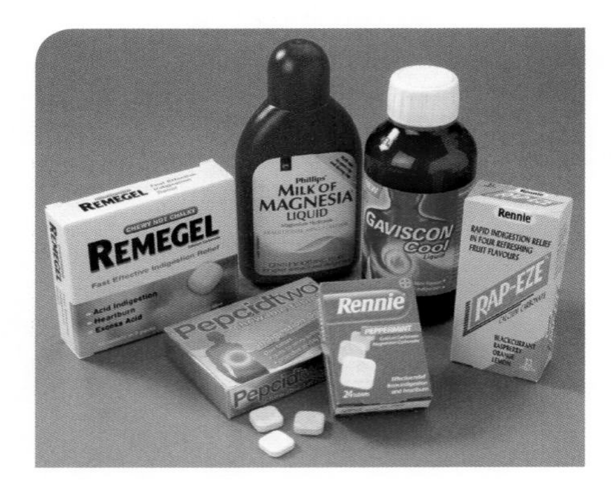

A Indigestion liquids and tablets contain different antacids.

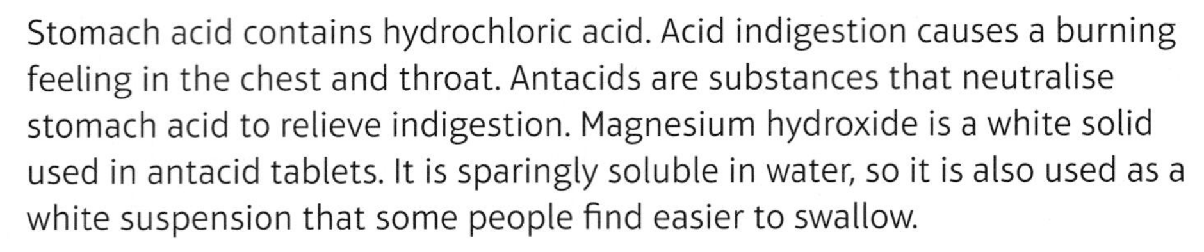

Stomach acid contains hydrochloric acid. Acid indigestion causes a burning feeling in the chest and throat. Antacids are substances that neutralise stomach acid to relieve indigestion. Magnesium hydroxide is a white solid used in antacid tablets. It is sparingly soluble in water, so it is also used as a white suspension that some people find easier to swallow.

Magnesium hydroxide neutralises hydrochloric acid:

magnesium hydroxide + hydrochloric acid → magnesium chloride + water

$$Mg(OH)_2(aq) + 2HCl(aq) \rightarrow MgCl_2(aq) + 2H_2O(l)$$

Your task

Calcium and magnesium are in group 2 of the periodic table. Calcium hydroxide has similar chemical properties to magnesium hydroxide, but it is more soluble in water. You will investigate the change in pH when you add powdered calcium hydroxide to dilute hydrochloric acid. You will add small portions of powder to the acid and record the pH of the mixture after each addition.

Method

Wear eye protection.

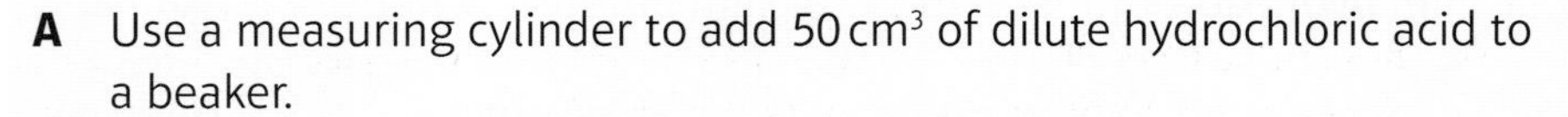

A Use a measuring cylinder to add 50 cm^3 of dilute hydrochloric acid to a beaker.

B Estimate and record the pH of the contents of the beaker.
- Put a piece of universal indicator paper onto a white tile.
- Dip the end of a glass rod into the liquid, then tap it onto the universal indicator paper.
- Wait 30 seconds, then match the colour to the appropriate pH on a pH colour chart.
- Rinse the glass rod with water.

C Measure out 0.3 g of calcium hydroxide powder onto a piece of paper or a 'weighing boat'.

D Add the calcium hydroxide powder to the beaker and stir. Then estimate and record the pH of the mixture.

E Repeat steps B and C seven times so that you add a total of 2.4 g of calcium hydroxide powder to the acid.

F Plot a graph with pH on the vertical axis and mass of calcium hydroxide on the horizontal axis.

B A pH meter may also be used to measure pH.

Exam-style questions

1 **a** Name the soluble salt formed when hydrochloric acid reacts with calcium hydroxide. *(1 mark)*

b Write the balanced equation, including state symbols, for the reaction between calcium hydroxide powder and dilute hydrochloric acid. *(3 marks)*

2 Diagrams C and D show part of the labels found on two laboratory containers.

a Give *two* reasons why hazard symbols are used on chemical containers. *(2 marks)*

b Explain why it may be more hazardous to handle calcium oxide than calcium hydroxide. *(3 marks)*

3 Give *two* reasons that explain why eye protection must be worn when using dilute hydrochloric acid. *(2 marks)*

4 A student investigates the change in pH when calcium hydroxide powder is added to 100 cm^3 of dilute hydrochloric acid.

a State *two* control variables in his experiment. *(2 marks)*

b State the independent variable in his experiment. *(1 mark)*

c Describe how the student could modify his experiment to investigate temperature changes instead of pH changes. *(1 mark)*

5 A student wants to find the mass of calcium oxide powder that produces a neutral solution when added to 75 cm^3 of dilute hydrochloric acid. She adds 0.5 g portions of the powder to the acid, and measures the pH each time with a pH meter. Table E shows her results.

a Predict the mass of calcium oxide that produces a neutral solution. *(1 mark)*

b State and explain how the student could improve her experiment to obtain a more accurate result. *(3 marks)*

6 The pH of a solution may be determined using universal indicator paper or using a pH meter.

a State why a pH meter must be calibrated using a solution with a known pH value. *(1 mark)*

b Explain whether indicator paper or a pH meter has the higher resolution. *(2 marks)*

calcium oxide
CaO
M_r = 56.0774

C

calcium hydroxide
$Ca(OH)_2$
M_r = 74.093

D

Mass of calcium oxide added (g)	pH of reaction mixture
0.0	0.3
0.5	0.6
1.0	2.8
1.5	12.3
2.0	12.5

E

SC8e Alkalis and neutralisation

Specification reference: C3.11; C3.14; C3.16; C3.18

Progression questions 

- What happens to the ions from acids and alkalis during neutralisation?
- What is titration?
- How do we make a soluble salt using titration?

A Potassium sulfate, manufactured using sulfuric acid and a soluble reactant, is a soluble salt used in fertilisers.

Soluble bases or alkalis react with acids to form a salt and water only. The type of reaction involved is neutralisation.

Did you know?

The Russian government imposed a high tax on table salt, sodium chloride, in the 17th century. This led to a 'salt riot' in Moscow in 1648.

Ions and neutralisation

Hydrochloric acid and other acids are a source of hydrogen ions, $H^+(aq)$, in solution:

$$HCl(aq) \rightarrow H^+(aq) + Cl^-(aq)$$

Sodium hydroxide and other alkalis are a source of hydroxide ions, $OH^-(aq)$, in solution:

$$NaOH(aq) \rightarrow Na^+(aq) + OH^-(aq)$$

In a neutralisation reaction, hydrogen ions from the acid react with hydroxide ions from the alkali. Water, a simple molecular substance containing covalent bonds, is formed in the reaction:

$$H^+(aq) + OH^-(aq) \rightarrow H_2O(l)$$

The other ions from the acid and alkali stay in the solution as ions of the dissolved salt. For example, $Na^+(aq)$ ions from sodium hydroxide and $Cl^-(aq)$ ions from hydrochloric acid remain after neutralisation. These ions combine to form solid sodium chloride, $NaCl(s)$, when the water evaporates.

1 Explain how water is formed in neutralisation reactions.

2 Explain, in terms of ions, how potassium hydroxide solution reacts with sulfuric acid to form water and potassium sulfate.

Soluble salts from alkalis

You can obtain a dry soluble salt from its solution by crystallisation. It is important to have a neutral solution before evaporating the water, otherwise you will contaminate the salt with an excess of one reactant.

 **3** Other than the hazards caused by hot liquids and solids, suggest a hazard caused by crystallising a salt from a solution that contains excess acid or alkali.

To obtain a neutral solution you need to mix an acid and an alkali in the correct proportions so that you end up with a solution that contains only water and the desired salt. You can do this using **titration**.

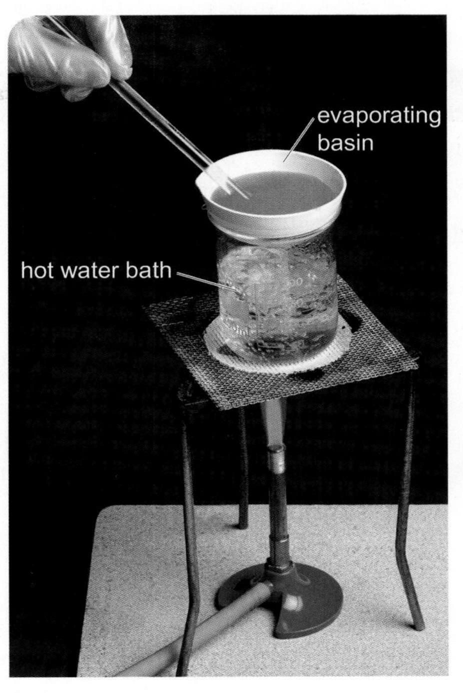

B producing a dry salt by crystallisation using a hot water bath

Titration

In a titration, acid is added from a **burette** to a fixed volume of alkali in a conical flask. The burette is a tall piece of glassware with 0.1 cm^3 graduations. You control the flow using a tap at the bottom. It is possible to add just one drop at a time.

You could use a measuring cylinder to measure out the alkali, but a **pipette** provides more accurate and repeatable measurements. A few drops of indicator are added to the alkali so you can follow the reaction. The **end-point** is when the indicator changes colour. Single indicators such as methyl orange or phenolphthalein are used because their obvious colour changes give you a sharp end-point.

To make a pure, dry salt:

- carry out a titration
- note the exact volume of acid needed to neutralise the alkali
- use the burette to add the correct volume of acid *without* the indicator
- evaporate the water from the solution formed.

 **4** In a titration, name the most suitable apparatus to add alkali to the flask, and to add acid to the alkali.

Exam-style question 

a Give a reason why universal indicator is not a good choice of indicator to use in a titration. *(1 mark)*

b Suggest a suitable indicator to use instead. *(1 mark)*

C This apparatus is used to carry out a titration. A white tile underneath the conical flask makes the end-point easier to see.

Checkpoint

How confidently can you answer the Progression questions?

Strengthen

S1 Describe how titration is used to prepare soluble salts.

Extend

E1 Evaluate the preparation of sodium and potassium salts using titration rather than by the reactions of the metals with acids.

SC8f Reactions of acids with metals and carbonates

Specification reference: H C0.4; C3.11; C3.12

Progression questions

- What happens when an acid reacts with a metal?
- What happens when an acid reacts with a metal carbonate?
- What are the tests for hydrogen and carbon dioxide?

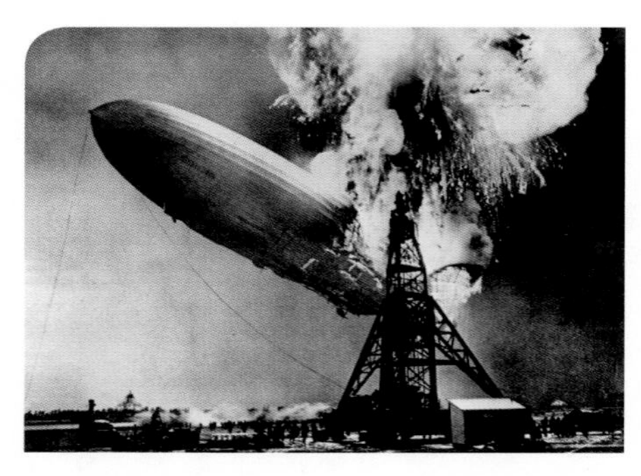

A Hydrogen gas is less dense than air and so was used to fill early air ships. Unfortunately it is also very flammable.

B Hydrogen gas is colourless and odourless. When hydrogen is mixed with air, it is highly flammable. To test for hydrogen, place a lighted splint in a hydrogen and air mixture. A squeaky pop is heard.

2 Zinc reacts with dilute hydrochloric acid. Write:

a the word equation

b the balanced equation

H **c** the half equation to show what happens to the zinc atoms.

Acids and metals

Some metals, such as copper and silver, do not react with dilute acids. Metals such as potassium and sodium react explosively with dilute acids. Metals in the middle of the **reactivity series**, such as magnesium and zinc, react steadily with dilute acids. **Effervescence** is seen as hydrogen gas bubbles are produced. The reaction also produces a salt, giving the general reaction:

metal + acid → salt + hydrogen

Magnesium reacts with sulfuric acid to form magnesium sulfate, and with hydrochloric acid to form magnesium chloride. The first name of the salt comes from the metal and the second name comes from the acid.

$$Mg(s) + H_2SO_4(aq) \rightarrow MgSO_4(aq) + H_2(g)$$

$$Mg(s) + 2HCl(aq) \rightarrow MgCl_2(aq) + H_2(g)$$

1 **Explain why gold sulfate is not formed when gold is added to dilute sulfuric acid.**

H

All acids form hydrogen ions, H^+, in aqueous solution. The metal atoms react with the hydrogen ions to form metal ions and hydrogen molecules. This can be summarised in an **ionic equation**, in which we only show the ions that change in the reaction. For example:

$$Mg(s) + 2H^+(aq) \rightarrow Mg^{2+}(aq) + H_2(g)$$

The other ions from the acid (e.g. sulfate, chloride) do not change during the reaction. They are known as **spectator ions**.

The hydrogen ions gain electrons to form hydrogen molecules. We can show what happens to electrons in a **half equation**:

$$2H^+(aq) + 2e \rightarrow H_2(g)$$

e represents an electron. It is not necessary to include the negative charge.

The magnesium atoms lose electrons:

$$Mg(s) \rightarrow Mg^{2+}(aq) + 2e$$

A loss of electrons is an **oxidation** reaction. A gain of electrons is a **reduction** reaction. You can remember this using the mnemonic OILRIG. (Oxidation Is Loss, Reduction Is Gain).

Acids and carbonates

Acids react with metal carbonates to form a salt, water and carbon dioxide. Bubbles of carbon dioxide are produced and the solid metal carbonate disappears if there is enough acid to react with it.

metal carbonate + acid → salt + water + carbon dioxide

Copper carbonate reacts with sulfuric acid to form copper sulfate, with hydrochloric acid to form copper chloride, and with nitric acid to form copper nitrate.

$$CuCO_3(s) + H_2SO_4(aq) \rightarrow CuSO_4(aq) + H_2O(l) + CO_2(g)$$

$$CuCO_3(s) + 2HCl(aq) \rightarrow CuCl_2(aq) + H_2O(l) + CO_2(g)$$

$$CuCO_3(s) + 2HNO_3(aq) \rightarrow Cu(NO_3)_2(aq) + H_2O(l) + CO_2(g)$$

During these reactions, the hydrogen ions from the acids react with the carbonate ions to form water and carbon dioxide molecules.

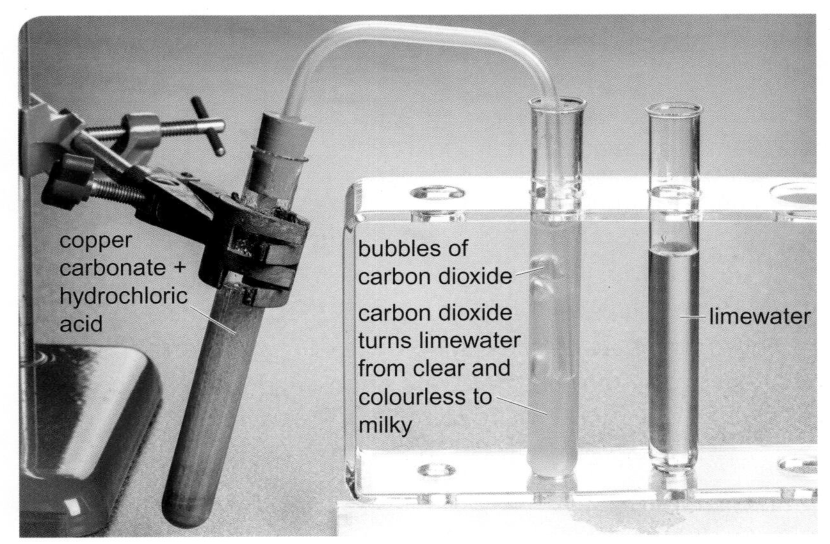

C Carbon dioxide is another colourless and odourless gas. To test for carbon dioxide, bubble the gas through limewater (calcium hydroxide solution). The limewater turns milky if carbon dioxide is present.

H

The sulfate, chloride and nitrate ions are spectator ions. The ionic equation is:

$$2H^+(aq) + CO_3^{2-}(s) \rightarrow H_2O(l) + CO_2(g)$$

6 Write the ionic equation for the reaction between magnesium carbonate and hydrochloric acid.

Exam-style question

Describe a test to show that a gas is hydrogen. *(2 marks)*

Did you know?

Carbon dioxide is denser than air and does not support burning. This makes it useful in fire extinguishers.

3 Give the formula of the salt formed when solid calcium carbonate, $CaCO_3$, reacts with dilute hydrochloric acid.

4 Explain the difference between the state symbols (aq) and (l).

5 Write the balanced equation for the reaction between zinc carbonate, $ZnCO_3$, and nitric acid, HNO_3.

Checkpoint

How confidently can you answer the Progression questions?

Strengthen

S1 Describe a reaction to make:

a hydrogen

b carbon dioxide.

Include an equation for each reaction and a description of how to test for each gas.

Extend

E1 **H** Dilute hydrochloric acid is added to zinc powder. Write word, balanced and ionic equations for the reaction that occurs. Include state symbols.

SC8g Solubility

Specification reference: H C0.4; C3.19; C3.20; C3.21

Progression questions

- What are the rules for solubility of common substances in water?
- How do you prepare a sample of a pure, dry insoluble salt?
- How do you predict whether a precipitate will be formed in a reaction?

A A red precipitate of silver chromate forms when sodium chromate solution is added to silver nitrate solution.

1 Which of the following substances are soluble in water and which are insoluble? Sodium chloride, lead nitrate, calcium sulfate, potassium hydroxide, silver chloride, calcium carbonate, ammonium carbonate.

2 Write a solubility rule for lead compounds.

Did you know?

The reaction between sodium chromate and silver nitrate is used to stain nerve cells for viewing under a microscope.

A **precipitation** reaction is one in which soluble substances in solutions cause an insoluble **precipitate** to form. Photo A shows an example. Table B shows some general rules that can be used to predict whether precipitates will form.

Soluble in water	Insoluble in water
all common sodium, potassium and ammonium salts	
all nitrates	
most chlorides	silver, lead chlorides
most sulfates	lead, barium, calcium sulfates
sodium, potassium and ammonium carbonates	most carbonates
sodium, potassium and ammonium hydroxides	most hydroxides

B some solubility rules

Solutions of lead nitrate and sodium chloride react to form soluble sodium nitrate and a white precipitate of lead chloride. The state symbols in the balanced equation show which substances are soluble and which are insoluble.

lead nitrate + sodium chloride → lead chloride + sodium nitrate

$$Pb(NO_3)_2(aq) + 2NaCl(aq) \rightarrow PbCl_2(s) + 2NaNO_3(aq)$$

The test for carbon dioxide using limewater (see CC8f) is also a precipitation reaction, in which insoluble calcium carbonate is formed:

calcium hydroxide (limewater) + carbon dioxide → calcium carbonate + water

$$Ca(OH)_2(aq) + CO_2(g) \rightarrow CaCO_3(s) + H_2O(l).$$

H

Ionic equations are also used to show the formation of precipitates. The formulae of the ions that react together to form the precipitate are shown on the left, and the formula of the precipitate is shown on the right. The ionic equation for the formation of lead chloride is:

$$Pb^{2+}(aq) + 2Cl^-(aq) \rightarrow PbCl_2(s)$$

The sodium and nitrate ions do not change, so they are spectator ions.

All salts are ionic. When two solutions containing soluble salts react together, the ions from the salts swap. For example:

copper sulfate + potassium carbonate → copper carbonate + potassium sulfate

We can predict whether a precipitate will form by checking the solubilities of the products. If both products are soluble, no precipitate will form.

In the word equation above, potassium sulfate does not form a precipitate because all potassium salts are soluble. However, copper carbonate is not in the list of soluble carbonates, so it should form as a precipitate:

$$CuSO_4(aq) + K_2CO_3(aq) \rightarrow CuCO_3(s) + K_2SO_4(aq)$$

The ionic equation is: $Cu^{2+}(aq) + CO_3^{2-}(aq) \rightarrow CuCO_3(s)$

Preparation of insoluble salts

A pure, dry sample of an insoluble salt can be prepared from two soluble salts in this way:

- Wear eye protection.
- Mix the two solutions in a beaker, then filter the mixture.
- Rinse the beaker with a little distilled water and pour this through the funnel.
- Pour a little distilled water over the precipitate in the funnel.
- Carefully remove the filter paper containing the precipitate and dry it in a warm oven.

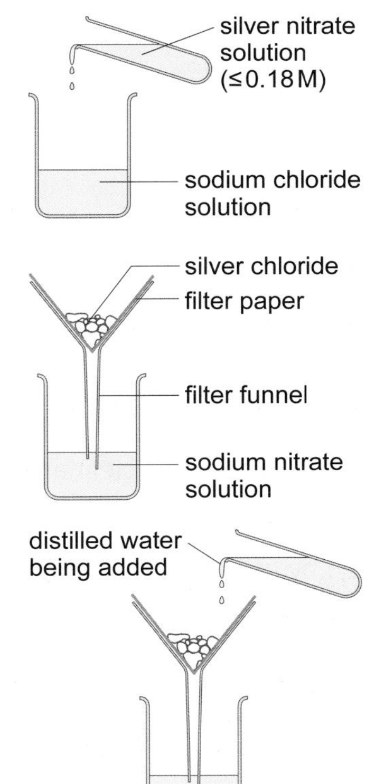

C preparing an insoluble salt

5 Explain:

a why the beaker is rinsed with a little distilled water and the washings are poured through the funnel

b why distilled water is poured over the precipitate in the funnel.

6 Suggest two other ways of drying the precipitate.

Exam-style question

Zinc carbonate is an insoluble salt. Describe how you would use solutions of potassium carbonate and zinc chloride to produce a pure, dry sample of zinc carbonate. *(4 marks)*

3 Magnesium sulfate solution reacts with barium chloride solution.

a Predict the name of the precipitate, if any.

b Write the balanced equation. Include state symbols.

H **c** Write the ionic equation for this reaction. Include state symbols.

4 Sodium chloride solution is added to copper nitrate solution.

a Predict the name of the precipitate, if any.

b Justify your answer.

Checkpoint

How confidently can you answer the Progression questions?

Strengthen

S1 Describe how to prepare a pure, dry sample of lead sulfate from two named solutions. Write a balanced equation for the reaction. Include state symbols.

Extend

E1 H The following aqueous solutions are available: sodium carbonate, copper sulfate, barium chloride. Any two of the solutions can be mixed together at a time. Predict which combinations of these solutions will produce a precipitate and name the precipitate. Write an ionic equation, including state symbols, for each reaction.

Magnesium sulfate

Soluble salts can be made by reacting an acid with an insoluble metal compound.

Plan an experiment to prepare pure, dry crystals of magnesium sulfate, $MgSO_4$, from a magnesium compound and a suitable acid. Start by choosing suitable reactants to use; you may wish to write a balanced equation to help you with your plan. **(6 marks)**

Student answer

$Mg + H_2SO_4 \rightarrow MgSO_4 + 2H$ [1]

I will make magnesium sulfate from magnesium ribbon and sulfuric acid [2].

Place 25 cm^3 of the acid in a beaker. Add magnesium ribbon a piece at a time until the bubbles of hydrogen stop. Filter the mixture and collect the solution in an evaporating basin [3]. *Heat the basin until all the water has evaporated, leaving pure, dry crystals of magnesium sulfate* [4].

[1] The balanced equation is incorrect. Hydrogen gas exists as H_2 molecules not separate hydrogen atoms.

[2] Sulfuric acid is correct, but the question asks for a magnesium compound (such as magnesium oxide). Magnesium is an element.

[3] The answer could also have explained that you need to filter the mixture to remove any excess magnesium.

[4] The last step is incorrect. If you evaporate all of the water, you will be left with a dry powder.

Verdict

This is an acceptable answer. It contains some correct chemistry, and the steps of the practical are written in a clear and logical order.

The answer could be improved by using a magnesium compound as mentioned in the question. The answer would also be better if it had a correct balanced equation, and described a suitable method for allowing crystals to form from the solution.

Exam tip

Make sure you revise the Core Practicals. The method asked for here is very similar to the preparation of copper sulfate which is a Core Practical.

Paper 1 and Paper 2

SC9 Calculations Involving Masses

In most chemical reactions it is important to mix the reactants in the correct amounts to form the maximum amount of product and to avoid waste. Iron is produced from iron ore in a blast furnace. Every tonne of iron ore needs to be mixed with 850 kg of limestone and 50 kg of coal. This should produce 350 kg of iron and 910 kg of a substance called 'slag' that can be used in concrete and for insulation. In this unit you will be learning how to calculate these amounts.

The learning journey

Previously you will have learnt at KS3:

- how to represent elements and compounds using symbols
- how mass is conserved during changes of state and chemical reactions
- how to show chemical reactions using equations.

In this unit you will learn:

- how to use relative atomic masses to calculate relative formula masses of elements and compounds
- how to work out empirical and molecular formulae of compounds
- how to calculate the mass of reactants or products in a reaction
- how to calculate the concentration of a solution
- **H** about the Avogadro constant and the quantity 1 mol of a substance
- **H** how to calculate the numbers of particles in a substance.

SC9a Masses and empirical formulae

Specification reference: C1.43; C1.44; C1.45; C1.46

Progression questions

- How do you calculate the relative formula mass of a compound?
- What is the difference between an empirical formula and a molecular formula?
- How do you determine the empirical formula of a compound?

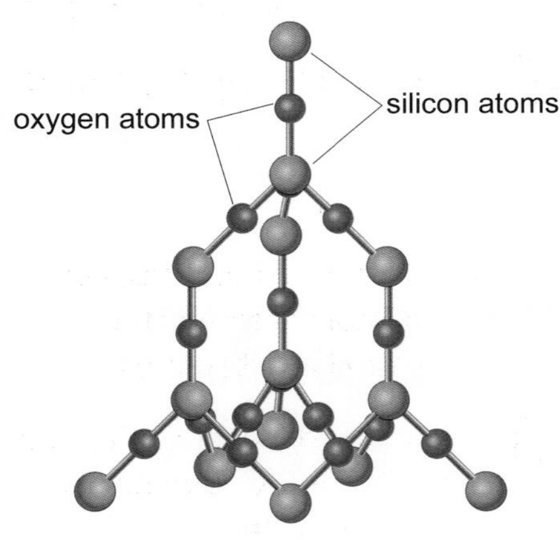

A Silicon dioxide is a giant, covalent lattice structure (of billions of atoms). Its empirical formula is SiO_2 (the ratio of silicon atoms to oxygen atom is 1:2).

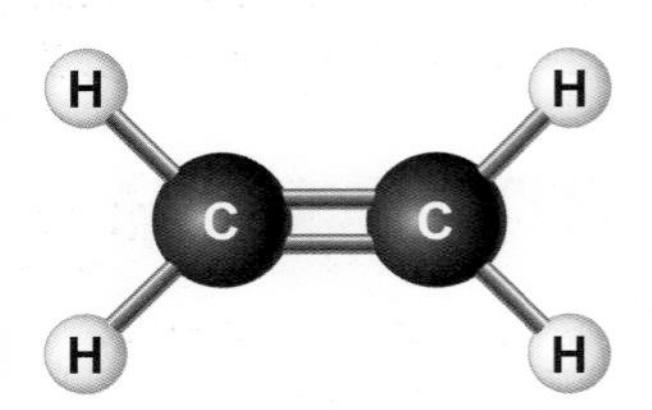

B Ethene has the molecular formula C_2H_4. CH_2 is its empirical formula.

Did you know?

The Galaxy Opal is the largest polished opal in the world. Opals consist mainly of silicon dioxide.

C

All substances have an **empirical formula**. This is the simplest whole number *ratio* of atoms or ions of each element in a substance.

Substances that are made of simple molecules also have a **molecular formula**. This represents the *actual* number of atoms of each element in one molecule.

Ethene has the molecular formula C_2H_4 but the empirical formula CH_2. Sometimes the empirical formula is the same as the molecular formula. For example, the formula for a molecule of water is H_2O and this cannot be simplified any further.

The 'formula' of a compound is its molecular formula if it is a simple molecule, or the empirical formula if it has a giant lattice structure.

1 Deduce the empirical formula of:

a C_2H_6 **b** N_2H_4 **c** C_3H_8 **d** C_6H_6 **e** $C_2H_4O_2$.

Relative formula mass

The **relative formula mass** (M_r), of a substance is the sum of the relative atomic masses (A_r) of all the atoms or ions in its formula. Relative atomic masses are given in the periodic table.

Worked examples W1

Calculate the M_r of carbon dioxide (CO_2).

$= A_r(C) + (2 \times A_r(O))$
$= 12 + (2 \times 16)$

So, M_r of $CO_2 = 44$

Calcium nitrate has a giant lattice structure. Its formula is $Ca(NO_3)_2$ (for each calcium ion there are two nitrate ions). Calculate the M_r of calcium nitrate.

$= A_r(Ca) + 2(A_r(N) + (3 \times A_r(O)))$
$= 40 + 2(14 + (3 \times 16))$

So, M_r of $Ca(NO_3)_2 = 164$

2 Calculate the relative formula masses of:

a N_2 **b** NaCl **c** NH_3 **d** H_2SO_4 **e** $(NH_4)_2SO_4$.

Finding an empirical formula

The empirical formula of a compound can be calculated from the masses of the elements used to make it. Table D shows how this is done if 10.0 g of calcium reacts with 17.8 g of chlorine.

Symbol for element	Ca	Cl
Mass (g)	10.0	17.8
Relative atomic mass, A_r	40	35.5
Divide the mass of each element by its relative atomic mass	$\frac{10.0}{40} = 0.25$	$\frac{17.8}{35.5} = 0.5$
Divide the answers by the smallest number to find the simplest ratio	$\frac{0.25}{0.25} = 1$	$\frac{0.5}{0.25} = 2$
Empirical formula	$CaCl_2$	

D To calculate an empirical formula, each element needs its own column of working.

A *molecular* formula is determined from its empirical formula and its M_r.

Worked example W2

The empirical formula for glucose is CH_2O and its relative formula mass is 180. Determine the molecular formula for glucose.

- Find empirical formula mass $A_r(C) + (2\times A_r(H)) + A_r(O)$
  $= 12 + (2 \times 1) + 16 = 30$
- Divide M_r by empirical formula mass $\frac{180}{30} = 6$

The molecular formula is six times the empirical formula, so the molecular formula is $C_6H_{12}O_6$.

Magnesium oxide can be made by heating magnesium ribbon in a limited oxygen supply, using the apparatus in diagram E. If the reactant and product are 'weighed', the empirical formula for magnesium oxide can be calculated.

5 Magnesium ribbon with a mass of 0.576 g was heated in a crucible. It produced 0.960 g of magnesium oxide. Calculate the empirical formula of magnesium oxide.

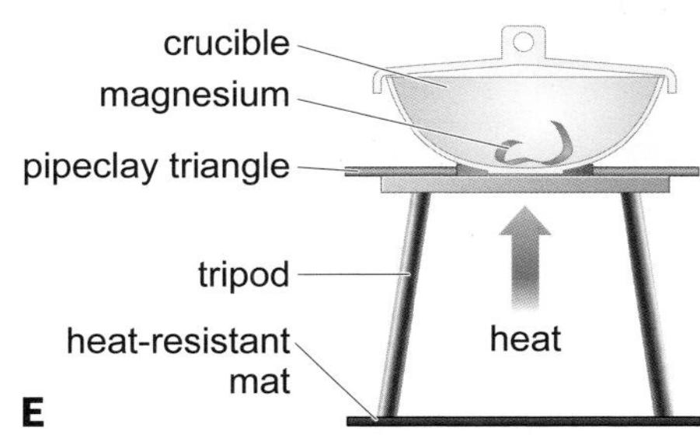

E

Exam-style question

5.6 g of iron react with 24.0 g of bromine to form iron bromide. Calculate the empirical formula of the iron bromide. (Relative atomic masses are given in the periodic table at the back of the book.) *(3 marks)*

3 Calculate the empirical formula of each of the following substances.

a lithium oxide (1.4 g Li, 1.6 g O)

b magnesium carbonate (1.2 g Mg, 0.6 g C, 2.4 g O)

c butane (1.44 g C, 0.3 g H)

4 Determine the molecular formula of each of the following substances.

a hydrogen peroxide, with empirical formula HO and M_r 34

b hexene, with empirical formula CH_2 and M_r 84

c pentane, with empirical formula C_5H_{12} and M_r 72

Checkpoint

How confidently can you answer the Progression questions?

Strengthen

S1 You are given some copper powder and a crucible. Describe an experiment to determine the empirical formula of copper oxide and explain how you would use the results to calculate the formula.

Extend

E1 A simple molecular compound contains 2.00 g of carbon, 0.33 g of hydrogen and 2.67 g of oxygen and has a relative formula mass of 60. Calculate the empirical and molecular formulae of this compound.

SC9b Conservation of mass

Specification reference: C1.47; C1.48; C1.49

Progression questions

- How do you calculate the concentration of a solution?
- How does the law of conservation of mass explain why magnesium increases in mass when it is burned?
- How do you calculate the masses of reactants and products in a reaction?

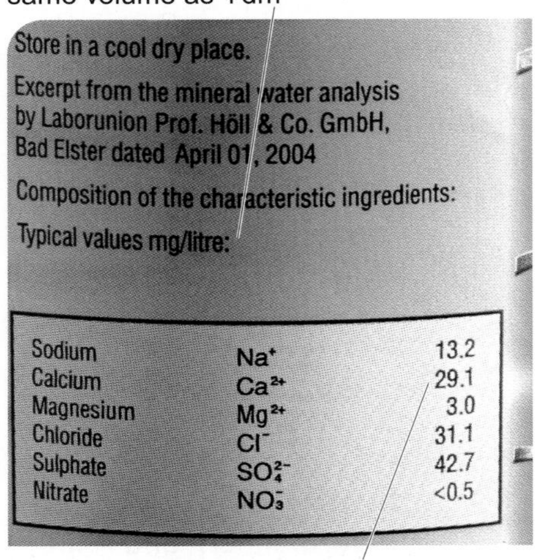

A Mineral water contains dissolved ions.

Concentrations of solutions

When a **solute** is dissolved in a **solvent** to make a **solution**, the mass of the solution is equal to the mass of the solvent *and* the mass of the solute. The overall mass of the substances does not change. This is the **law of conservation of mass**.

The amount of solute dissolved in a stated volume of a solution is its **concentration**. The units of concentration are usually 'grams per cubic decimetre', written as g dm^{-3}. 1 dm^3 is the same volume as 1 litre or 1000 cm^3.

You can calculate the concentration of a solution in g dm^{-3} using this equation:

$$\text{concentration} = \frac{\text{mass of solute in g}}{\text{volume of solution in dm}^3}$$

If the volume of the solution is given in cm^3, convert it to dm^3 by dividing by 1000.

1 Calculate the concentration, in g dm^{-3}, of the solute in these solutions.

a 20 g of sodium chloride in 2 dm^3 of solution

b 0.574 g of sodium hydroxide in 250 cm^3 of solution

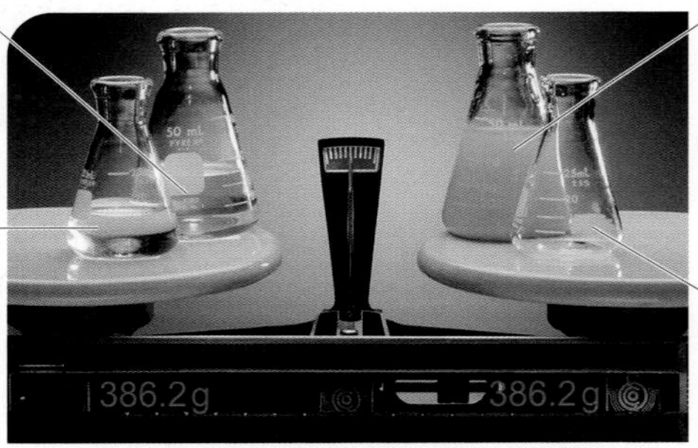

B The total mass of the reactants always equals the total mass of products.

Did you know?

Lead iodide was used as a yellow pigment in some 19th-century paintings, but it is not very stable so some of these paintings are changing colour.

$$CuCO_3(s) \rightarrow CuO(s) + CO_2(g)$$

C balanced equation for heating copper carbonate in air

Conservation of mass in reactions

Lead nitrate solution reacts with potassium iodide solution to form a yellow **precipitate** of lead iodide and a colourless solution of potassium nitrate. This is an example of a **closed system** as no new substances are added or removed.

$$Pb(NO_3)_2(aq) + 2KI(aq) \rightarrow PbI_2(s) + 2KNO_3(aq)$$

The balanced equation shows that the number of atoms does not change, and so the mass cannot change. This is another example of the law of conservation of mass.

In the reaction shown in balanced equation C, the mass of the copper oxide left is less than the mass of copper carbonate at the start. Carbon dioxide gas escapes and so the mass appears to decrease. This is a **non-enclosed system** as the gas can escape.

Some solids appear to gain in mass when they are heated in a non-enclosed system. In the reaction shown in balanced equation D, the apparent gain is due to copper reacting with oxygen from the air. However, in all systems, the mass of the products is always the same as the mass of the reactants.

$$2Cu(s) + O_2(g) \rightarrow 2CuO(s)$$

D balanced equation for heating copper in air

Calculating the masses of reactants or products

You can use relative masses and the balanced equation for a reaction to calculate the mass of a reactant or a product.

Worked example

Calculate the mass of chlorine needed to make 53.4 g of aluminium chloride.

Write the balanced equation	$2Al + \mathbf{3}Cl_2 \rightarrow \mathbf{2}AlCl_3$
Calculate relative formula masses of the substances needed	$M_r\ Cl_2 = 2 \times 35.5 = 71$ $M_r\ AlCl_3 = 27 + (3 \times 35.5) = 133.5$

Calculate ratio of masses (multiply M_r values by the balancing numbers shown in the equation).

$\mathbf{3}Cl_2$ makes $\mathbf{2}AlCl_3$

so $\mathbf{3} \times 71 = \underline{213}$ g Cl_2 makes $\mathbf{2} \times 133.5 = \underline{267}$ g $AlCl_3$

Work out the mass for 1 g of reactant or product. (Here we want 1 g of the product because that's the mass we know already.)

÷ 267 $\frac{213}{267}$ g Cl_2 makes $\frac{267}{267}$ g $AlCl_3$ ÷ 267

0.798 g Cl_2 makes 1 g $AlCl_3$

× 53.4 × 53.4

Scale up or down (*from* 1 g *to* the mass you are given)	42.6 g Cl_2 makes 53.4 g $AlCl_3$

2 12.4 g of copper carbonate was heated and formed 8.0 g of copper oxide. Calculate the mass of carbon dioxide produced.

3 1.27 g of copper was heated in air and formed 1.59 g of copper oxide. Calculate the mass of oxygen that reacted with the copper.

4 Calculate the mass of hydrogen produced when 72 g of magnesium reacts with sulfuric acid.

$$Mg + H_2SO_4 \rightarrow MgSO_4 + H_2$$

5 Calculate the mass of water produced when 500 g of methane burns.

$$CH_4 + 2O_2 \rightarrow CO_2 + 2H_2O$$

6 Calculate the mass of sodium hydroxide needed to produce 42.6 kg of sodium sulfate.

$$2NaOH + H_2SO_4 \rightarrow Na_2SO_4 + 2H_2O$$

Exam-style question

Calculate the maximum mass of magnesium oxide that could be formed by reacting 1.56 g of magnesium with excess oxygen. *(3 marks)*

$$2Mg + O_2 \rightarrow 2MgO$$

Checkpoint

How confidently can you answer the Progression questions?

Strengthen

S1 Make notes so that you can explain to a friend who missed the lesson:

a how to calculate the mass of sodium chloride formed when 5.3 g of sodium carbonate reacts with excess dilute hydrochloric acid
$Na_2CO_3 + 2HCl \rightarrow 2NaCl + H_2O + CO_2$

b why there is a loss in mass during the reaction.

Extend

E1 Calculate the loss in mass when 2.96 g of magnesium nitrate decomposes.
$2Mg(NO_3)_2(s) \rightarrow 2MgO(s) + 4NO_2(g) + O_2(g)$

SC9c Moles

Specification reference: H C1.50; H C1.51; H C1.52; H C1.53

Progression questions 

- H How do you calculate the number of moles and number of particles of a substance?
- H What controls the mass of product formed in a reaction?
- H How do you work out a balanced equation from the masses of reactants and/or products?

H

A Clockwise from top left: one mole (1 mol) each of iron(III) chloride, copper sulfate, potassium iodide, cobalt nitrate, potassium manganate(VII) and sodium chloride.

In everyday life we use special words to mean the amount of an item. A pair is two of that item and a dozen is 12 of them. In chemistry, a mole is 602 204 500 000 000 000 000 000 particles! This number is usually written in standard form as 6.02×10^{23} and is known as the **Avogadro constant.**

The SI unit symbol for 'mole' is **mol**. 1 mol of a substance contains the Avogadro constant number of particles. These can be atoms, molecules or ions and so you need to specify the type of particles.

The mass of one mole of a substance is the relative atomic mass (A_r) or relative formula mass (M_r) in grams. The relative atomic mass of magnesium is 24, so 1 mol of magnesium has a mass of 24 g and contains 6.02×10^{23} atoms.

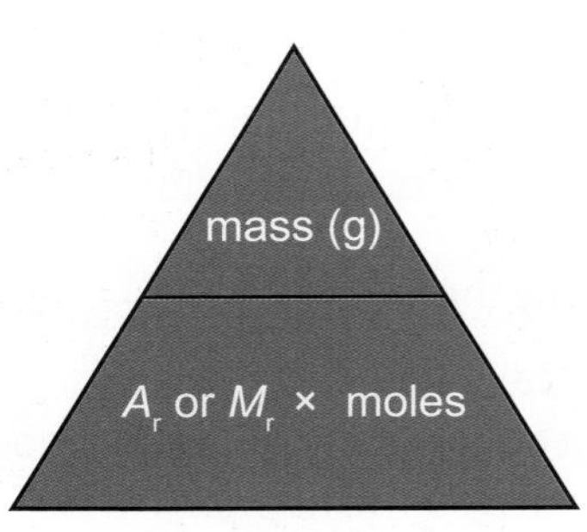

B To rearrange the equation with this triangle, cover up the quantity you want to calculate and what you can see gives you the calculation to use.

You can calculate the number of moles of any substance using this equation:

$$\text{number of moles of substance} = \frac{\text{mass of substance (g)}}{A_r \text{ or } M_r}$$

1 Give the mass of the Avogadro constant number of:

a carbon atoms **b** sodium atoms.

2 Calculate the mass of:

a 2 mol of nitrogen molecules, N_2

b 0.1 mol of sulfur dioxide molecules, SO_2.

3 Calculate the number of moles of:

a CO_2 molecules in 88 g of carbon dioxide

b CH_4 molecules in 3.2 g of methane.

Reactions

A balanced equation shows the ratios of the substances in moles.

$$2Mg + O_2 \rightarrow 2MgO$$

This equation shows that 2 mol of magnesium reacts with 1 mol of oxygen to form 2 mol of magnesium oxide. In an experiment, we usually burn magnesium in excess oxygen to make sure that all the magnesium reacts.

In a chemical reaction, one of the reactants is often added in excess and is not completely used up in the reaction. The amount of product formed is determined by the amount of reactant that is *not* in excess (and so is used up completely in the reaction). This is called the **limiting reactant**.

H

Worked example W1

1.50 g of ammonium chloride and 4.00 g of calcium hydroxide are heated together to form ammonia.

$2NH_4Cl + Ca(OH)_2 \rightarrow 2NH_3 + CaCl_2 + 2H_2O$

a Which is the limiting reactant?

b Calculate the mass of ammonia formed.

a The equation shows that 2 mol of NH_4Cl reacts with 1 mol of $Ca(OH)_2$

number of moles of $Ca(OH)_2$ = 4.00 g/(40 + 2(16 + 1)) = 0.0541 mol

We need: 2 × 0.0541 = 0.108 mol NH_4Cl to react with 0.0541 mol of $Ca(OH)_2$.

We have: 1.50 g/(14 + (4 × 1) + 35.5) = 0.0280 mol

We have less than the 0.0541 mol of NH_4Cl needed; NH_4Cl = limiting reactant.

b The equation shows that the number of moles of NH_3 made equals the number of moles of NH_4Cl used.

So, 0.0280 mol of NH_4Cl forms 0.0280 mol of NH_3

mass of NH_3 formed = mol × M_r = 0.0280 × (14 + (3 × 1)) = 0.476 g

If you know the mass of each substance in a reaction, you can calculate the number of moles of each and deduce the balanced equation. The ratio of the moles of each substance is the **stoichiometry** of the reaction.

Worked example W2

10.8 g of aluminium reacted with 42.6 g of chlorine, Cl_2, to produce aluminium chloride, $AlCl_3$. Deduce the balanced equation for the reaction.

	Al	Cl_2
Calculate the number of moles (= mass/A_r or M_r)	$\frac{10.8}{27} = 0.4$	$\frac{42.6}{2 \times 35.5} = 0.6$
Divide by the smaller	$\frac{0.4}{0.4} = 1$	$\frac{0.6}{0.4} = 1.5$
Simplest whole number ratio	1 × 2 = 2	1.5 × 2 = 3

So 2 mol of Al react with 3 mol of Cl_2. The equation is completed by adding the formula of the product and balancing in the normal way.

$2Al + 3Cl_2 \rightarrow 2AlCl_3$

Exam-style question

Calculate the number of molecules in 90 g of water, H_2O. *(2 marks)*

4 Calculate the number of molecules in:

9th **a** 16 g of oxygen molecules, O_2

9th **b** 34 g of ammonia molecules, NH_3.

10th **5** Calculate the maximum mass of magnesium oxide that can be made from 2.4 g of magnesium and 2.4 g of oxygen.

$2Mg + O_2 \rightarrow 2MgO$

9th **6** 15 g of hydrogen gas reacts exactly with 70 g of nitrogen gas to produce ammonia, NH_3. Deduce the balanced equation for the reaction.

Checkpoint

How confidently can you answer the Progression questions?

Strengthen

S1 5.00 g of iron and 5.00 g of sulfur are heated together to form iron(II) sulfide.

$Fe + S \rightarrow FeS$

a Calculate the number of moles of each reactant and state which one is the limiting reactant.

b Calculate the mass of iron(II) sulfide formed. Give your answer to 3 significant figures.

Extend

E1 Explain which of these contains the greatest number of particles.

4 g of hydrogen molecules, 16 g of oxygen molecules, 18 g of water molecules, 22 g of carbon dioxide molecules.

Empirical formula

A student carried out an experiment to determine the empirical formula of magnesium oxide using the apparatus shown.

Describe how you would use this apparatus and the results to show that the empirical formula of magnesium oxide is MgO.

(6 marks)

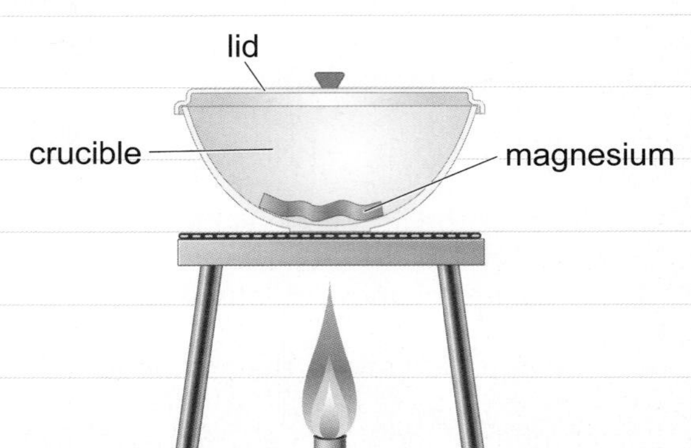

Student answer

Weigh an empty crucible, then add a piece of magnesium ribbon and weigh it again. Set up the apparatus as shown. Heat the crucible with a strong flame and lift the lid occasionally [1]. *Stop heating when all the magnesium has reacted. Let the crucible cool and reweigh it* [2].

Find the mass of magnesium used and the mass of oxygen that combined with it [3]. *Divide the masses of magnesium and oxygen by their relative atomic masses. Then, divide these answers by the smaller of the numbers to find the simplest ratio. If the simplest ratio is 1:1, the empirical formula is MgO* [4].

[1] It would be a good idea to explain why this is necessary.

[2] Overall, this is a good account of the experiment and the measurements that are needed.

[3] The correct masses are mentioned, but not how these masses are actually calculated.

[4] The explanation of the calculation is sufficient and the relationship between the simplest ratio and the empirical formula is given.

Verdict

This is a strong answer. The description of the experiment and the method of calculation are correct. The answer is written in a logical order with the description of the experiment first, and then a clear and well-ordered description of the calculations.

Exam tip

The examiner is looking for a 'well-developed, sustained line of scientific reasoning which is clear and logically structured'. When describing a process, make sure that you write down the steps in a logical order – in this case, the order that the experiment and the calculations would be carried out.

Paper 1

SC10 Electrolytic Processes / SC11 Obtaining and Using Metals / SC12 Reversible Reactions and Equilibria / SC13 Transition Metals, Alloys and Corrosion

Many metals are used for buildings, including copper, aluminium and iron, together with alloys of those metals and others. In this unit you will learn more about metals.

The learning journey

Previously you will have learnt at KS3:

- about oxidation and displacement reactions
- about the reactivity series.

You will also have learnt in *SC4 The Periodic Table*, *SC5 Ionic Bonding* and *SC8 Acids and Alkalis*:

- about anions and cations in ionic compounds
- to write balanced equations with state symbols
- how elements are arranged in the periodic table.

In this unit you will learn:

- more about reactivity, oxidation and reduction
- about how metals can be extracted
- about the advantages of recycling metals
- about the life cycle assessment of products
- to explain what happens during electrolysis and electroplating
- about equilibria in chemical reactions
- about the Haber process
- **H** how to write half equations
- about the properties of transition metals
- properties and uses of metals and their alloys.

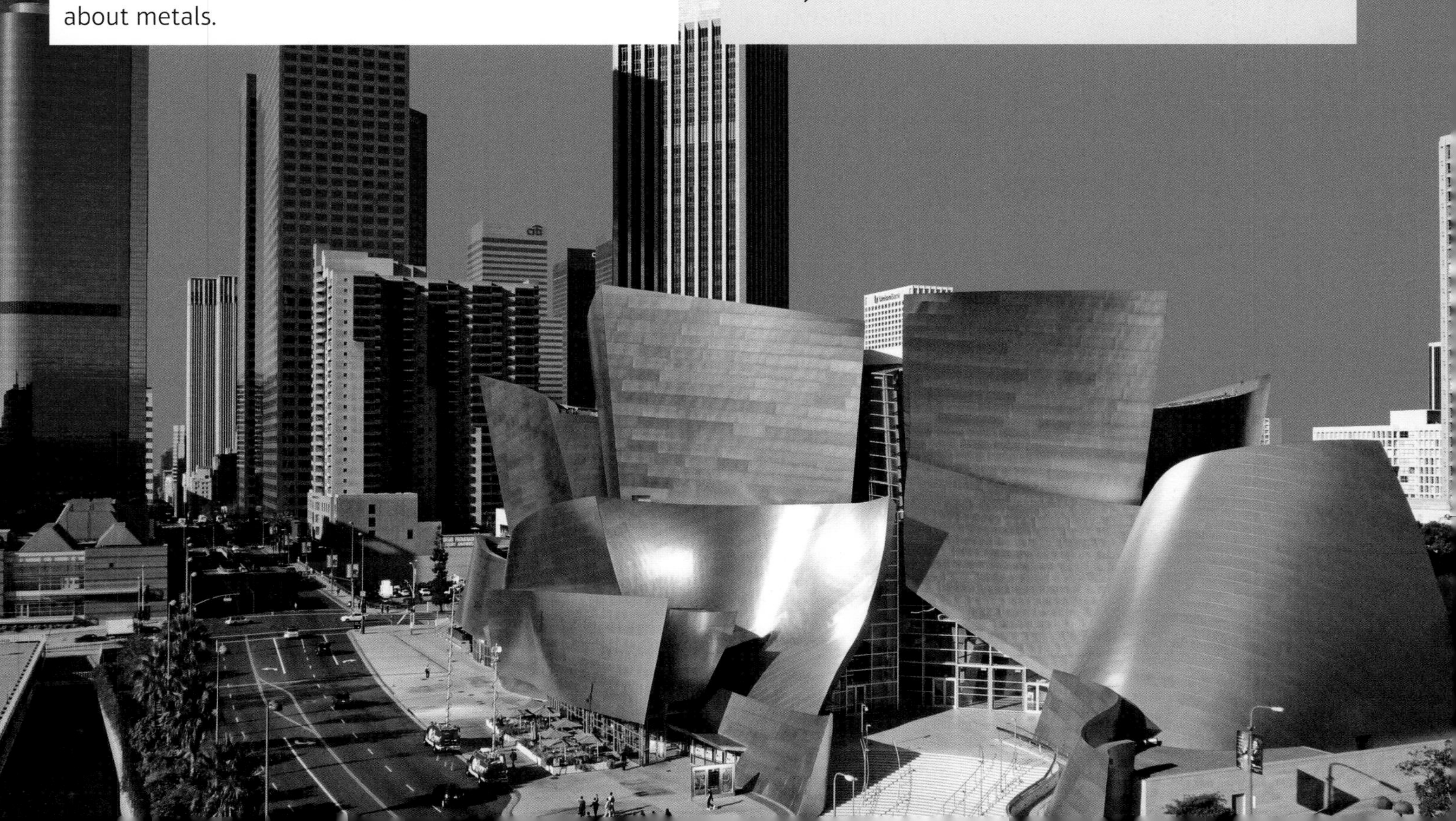

SC10a Electrolysis

Specification reference: C3.22; C3.23; C3.24; H C3.27; H C3.28; H C3.29

Progression questions

- What is an electrolyte?
- What happens to the ions during electrolysis?
- H How do you explain and represent the reactions taking place at the electrodes in electrolysis?

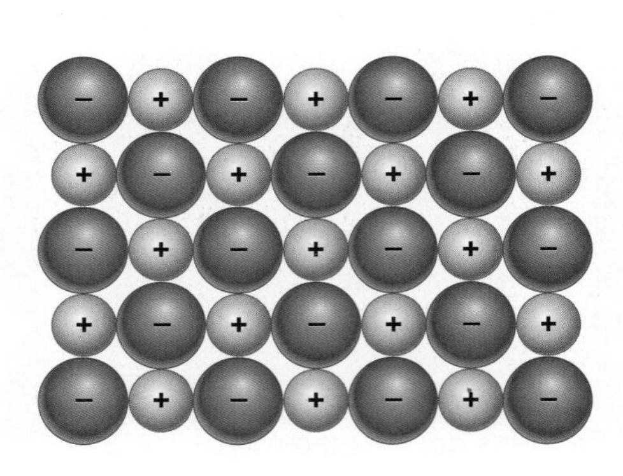

A (a) The ions cannot move in the lattice structure of solid sodium chloride.

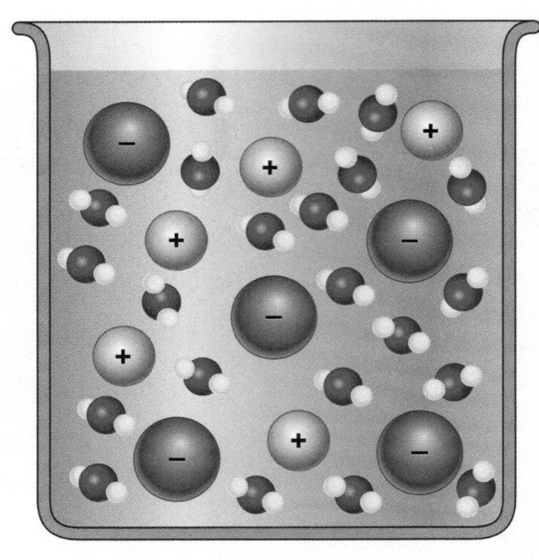

(b) The ions can move when sodium chloride is dissolved in water.

In 1800, Alessandro Volta invented the electric battery. English scientists William Nicholson and Anthony Carlisle soon discovered that electricity broke down acidified water into hydrogen and oxygen. This process is called **electrolysis** and today we use it to break down many substances.

When an ionic solid is melted or dissolved in water, its ionic bonds break. This allows the ions to move. An ionic substance with freely moving ions is called an **electrolyte** and can conduct electricity.

1 Give the meaning of the following terms.

 **a** electrolysis

 **b** electrode

Electrolysis uses energy transferred by electricity to decompose electrolytes. Two **electrodes** are connected to a direct current (d.c.) electricity supply and placed into the electrolyte. The two types of ions carry opposite charges and so migrate (move) towards the electrode with the opposite charge.

- **Cations** are positive ions and are attracted to the negative **cathode**.
- **Anions** are negative ions and are attracted to the positive **anode**.

This can be shown by placing a purple potassium manganate(VII) crystal on a piece of damp filter paper attached to a microscope slide and connected to a d.c. electricity supply. The purple colour spreads towards the anode.

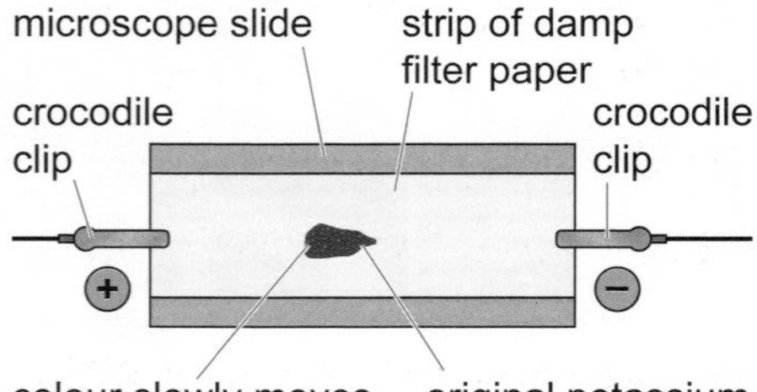

B Manganate(VII) ions are purple. Potassium ions are colourless.

 **2** Give a reason why ionic solids cannot be electrolysed.

 **3** State the type of charge on a manganate(VII) ion, giving a reason for your answer.

4 Look at these the formulae: Na^{+}, Cl^{-}, H_2O, OH^{-}, CO_2, SO_4^{2-}, Mg^{2+}

 **a** Identify the anions.

 **b** List the ions that will be attracted to the cathode during electrolysis.

H Reactions at the electrodes

At the anode, negative ions lose electrons (**oxidation**). At the cathode, electrons are transferred from the electrode to the positive ions (**reduction**).

Oxidation Is the **L**oss of electrons.

Reduction Is the **G**ain of electrons.

You can remember these by: OIL RIG.

This transfer of electrons changes charged ions into atoms or molecules, resulting in chemical changes at the electrodes. For example, in the electrolysis of molten zinc chloride, Zn^{2+} ions are attracted to the cathode, where they gain electrons and become zinc atoms. At the same time Cl^- ions migrate to the anode, where they lose electrons and become chlorine molecules.

These changes are represented by **half equations**, which show the change at each electrode.

Cathode reaction: $Zn^{2+} + 2e \rightarrow Zn$ reduction

Anode reaction: $2Cl^- \rightarrow Cl_2 + 2e$ oxidation

ReduCtion takes place at the **C**athode.

OxidAtion takes place at the **A**node.

Note that two Cl^- ions are needed to form one chlorine molecule.

5 The half equation for the reaction at the cathode during the electrolysis of molten lead bromide is:

$Pb^{2+} + 2e \rightarrow Pb$

a Explain whether this half equation shows oxidation or reduction.

b Write the half equation for the reaction of bromide ions, Br^-, at the anode.

6 The following reaction takes place at an electrode:

$Cu \rightarrow Cu^{2+} + 2e$.

Identify the electrode at which the reaction occurs, giving a reason for your answer.

Exam-style question

Solid lithium chloride cannot be electrolysed, but molten lithium chloride can be electrolysed. Explain these observations. *(2 marks)*

Did you know?

Metallic objects can be gold-plated using electrolysis. The anode is a strip of gold, the cathode is the object to be plated and the electrolyte contains gold ions.

C a gold-plated car

Checkpoint

How confidently can you answer the Progression questions?

Strengthen

S1 Give the meaning of each of the terms: electrolyte, anode, cathode, anion, cation.

S2 For each of the following ions, state which electrode it will move towards, during electrolysis: Mg^{2+}, OH^-. Give a reason for your answers.

Extend

E1 H Molten potassium bromide is electrolysed to form potassium and bromine. Write the half equations for the reactions at the electrodes, classify them as oxidation or reduction and state at which electrode they occur.

SC10a Core practical – Electrolysis of copper sulfate solution

Specification reference: C3.31

Aim

Investigate the electrolysis of copper sulfate solution with inert electrodes and copper electrodes.

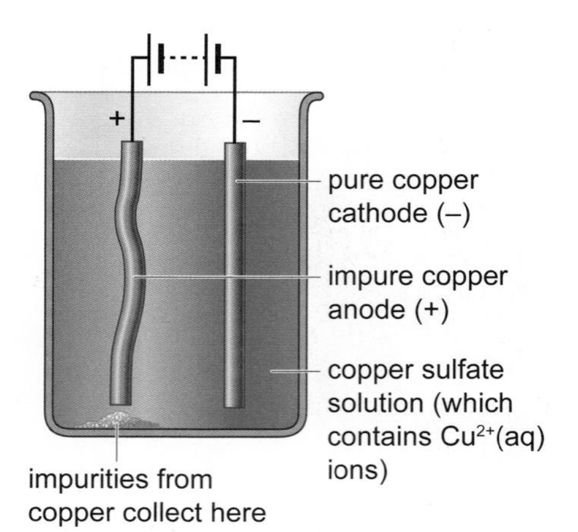

A In the purification of copper, the copper to be purified is used as the anode and some very pure copper is used as the cathode.

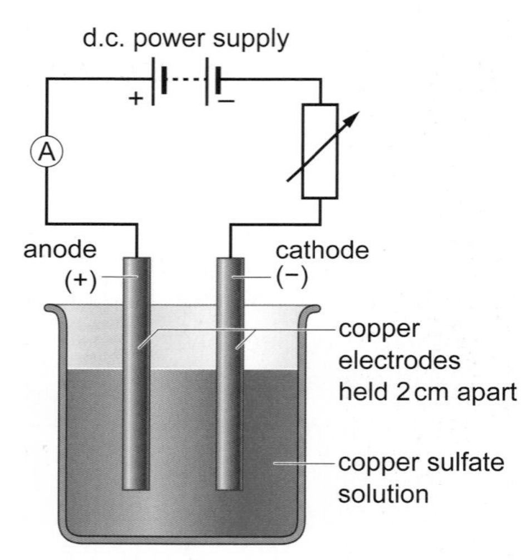

B Purifying copper by electrolysis. The copper to be purified is used as the anode and some very pure copper is used as the cathode.

The copper needed for electrical wires must be very pure and this is achieved using the electrolysis of copper sulfate solution, as shown in figure A.

During electrolysis, the copper atoms in the anode lose two electrons each to become copper ions. These ions dissolve in the solution and migrate to the cathode, where they are deposited as pure copper. So, the impure copper anode loses mass and the pure copper cathode gains mass. Impurities from the anode do not form ions and collect below the anode as a 'sludge'. The anode sludge is collected because it may contain valuable metallic elements.

H

The half equation for the anode reaction is:

$$Cu(s) \rightarrow Cu^{2+}(aq) + 2e^-$$

The half equation for the cathode reaction is:

$$Cu^{2+}(aq) + 2e^- \rightarrow Cu(s)$$

Your task

You will set up an electrolysis cell to investigate the effect of changing the current on the mass of the copper electrodes used in the electrolysis of copper sulfate solution. You will also investigate the products formed during the electrolysis of copper sulfate solution using inert (graphite) electrodes.

Method

Using copper electrodes

Wear eye protection.

A Select two clean pieces of copper foil. Label one 'anode' and the other 'cathode'. Measure and record the masses of the two electrodes.

B Set up an electrolysis circuit as shown in diagram B.

C Turn on the power and adjust the variable resistor to give a current of about 0.2 A. Record the current and adjust the variable resistor to keep it constant. Leave the power on for 20 minutes.

D Turn off the power and remove the electrodes from the beaker. Gently wash the electrodes with distilled water then dip them into propanone. Lift the electrodes out and gently shake off the propanone. Allow the remainder of the propanone to evaporate.

E Measure and record the masses of the dry electrodes.

F Repeat the experiment using currents of 0.3 A, 0.4 A and 0.5 A.

Using graphite electrodes

G Set up the circuit as shown in diagram C.

H Turn on the power and observe what happens at each electrode.

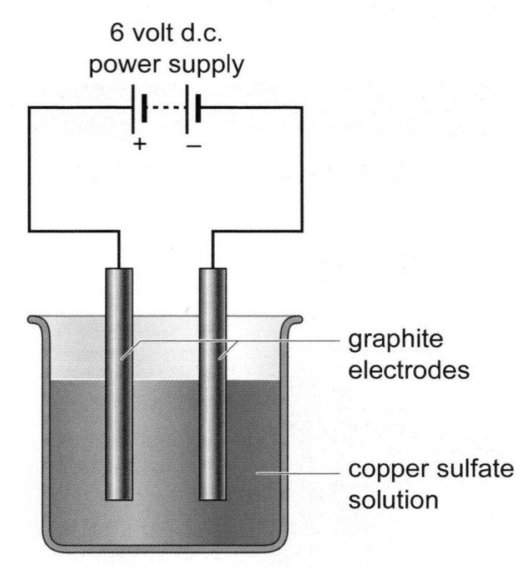

C electrolysis circuit for using graphite electrodes

Exam-style questions

1 Explain why a different product is formed at the anode when copper sulfate solution is electrolysed using graphite electrodes rather than copper electrodes. *(4 marks)*

2 Look at the method for electrolysis using copper electrodes.

- **a** State and explain *one* safety precaution *(1 mark)*
- **b** State why it is important to use clean copper electrodes. *(1 mark)*
- **c** Give a reason why a variable resistor is used in the electrolysis circuit. *(1 mark)*
- **d** Suggest a reason why the electrodes are washed at the end of the electrolysis. *(1 mark)*
- **e** Suggest a reason why propanone is used after washing the electrodes with distilled water. *(1 mark)*

3 The results of an investigation of the electrolysis of copper sulfate solution using copper electrodes are given in table D.

- **a** Calculate the changes in mass of the electrodes. *(2 marks)*
- **b** Plot a suitable graph to look for a correlation between the change in mass of each electrode and the current. *(4 marks)*
- **c** Describe the pattern in the change in mass at each electrode. *(2 marks)*
- **d** Explain the changes in mass of each electrode. *(4 marks)*
- **e** Explain the effect of increasing the current on these changes in mass. *(2 marks)*
- **f** Predict the change in mass at the anode when the current is 0.35 A. *(1 mark)*
- **g** Suggest a reason why the change in mass at the cathode is not the same as the change in mass at the anode when the same current is used. *(1 mark)*
- **h** Describe how you could improve the experiment to obtain more accurate results at the cathode. *(1 mark)*

Current (A)	0.2	0.3	0.4	0.5
Mass of anode at start (g)	2.77	2.68	2.53	2.36
Mass of anode at end (g)	2.69	2.55	2.36	2.15
Mass of cathode at start (g)	2.51	2.55	2.62	2.70
Mass of cathode at end (g)	2.58	2.66	2.76	2.87

D results of an electrolysis investigation

SC10b Products from electrolysis

Specification reference: C3.25; C3.26; C3.30

Progression questions

- How do you predict the products formed in the electrolysis of molten zinc chloride?
- How do you explain the products formed in the electrolysis of sodium chloride solution?
- How is copper purified using electrolysis?

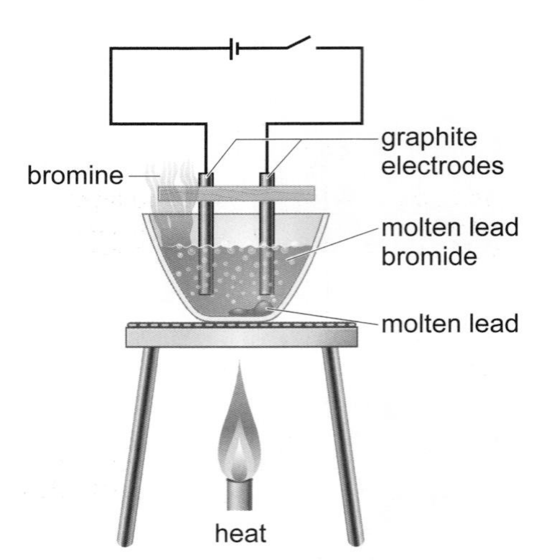

A Orange bromine gas is seen around the anode and a pool of grey liquid lead is seen under the cathode. This experiment must be carried out in a fume cupboard as bromine gas is toxic.

The electrolysis of molten or dissolved ionic salts is carried out using **inert** (unreactive) electrodes (usually graphite or platinum). When a molten salt is electrolysed, ions are **discharged** as atoms or molecules at the electrodes. When molten lead bromide is electrolysed, bromine is produced at the anode and lead is produced at the cathode.

H

Cathode reaction: $Pb^{2+}(l) + 2e \rightarrow Pb(l)$

Anode reaction: $2Br^{-}(l) \rightarrow Br_2(g) + 2e$

You can predict the electrolysis products of any molten salt. The salt will always decompose into its elements. The metal is produced at the cathode and the non-metal is produced at the anode.

8th **1** **Predict the products formed at the anode and cathode during the electrolysis of molten sodium chloride.**

9th **2** **H Explain which of the half equations in the electrolysis of molten lead bromide shows oxidation and which shows reduction.**

Electrolysis of salt solutions

Water ionises to a very small extent, so in an aqueous solution of a salt there are some hydrogen ions (H^+) and hydroxide ions (OH^-), as well as the ions of the dissolved solid. Tables B and C show the electrolysis of two salt solutions, copper chloride solution and sodium chloride solution.

Ions	$Cu^{2+}(aq)$ and $Cl^-(aq)$ (from salt), $H^+(aq)$ and $OH^-(aq)$ (from water)	
cathode	$Cu^{2+}(aq)$ and $H^+(aq)$ ions are attracted. Copper ions are discharged more readily than hydrogen ions, so copper is formed as a brown solid.	H $Cu^{2+}(aq) + 2e \rightarrow Cu(s)$ (reduction)
anode	$Cl^-(aq)$ and $OH^-(aq)$ ions are attracted. Chloride ions are discharged more readily than hydroxide ions, so chlorine is formed as a pale green gas.	H $2Cl^-(aq) \rightarrow Cl_2(g) + 2e$ (oxidation)
Overall	The copper chloride decomposes but the water does not change. $CuCl_2(aq) \rightarrow Cu(s) + Cl_2(g)$	

B copper chloride solution electrolysis

3 Describe what happens to the colour of the solution when copper chloride is electrolysed.

Ions	Na^+(aq) and Cl^-(aq) (from salt), H^+(aq) and OH^-(aq) (from water)	
cathode	Na^+(aq) and H^+(aq) ions are attracted. Hydrogen ions are discharged more readily than sodium ions, so hydrogen gas is formed.	H $2H^+(aq) + 2e \rightarrow H_2(g)$ (reduction)
anode	Cl^-(aq) and OH^-(aq) ions are attracted. Chloride ions are discharged more readily than hydroxide ions, so chlorine is formed as a pale green gas.	H $2Cl^-(aq) \rightarrow Cl_2(g) + 2e$ (oxidation)
Overall	The sodium chloride decomposes to form hydrogen and chlorine. The sodium and hydroxide ions remain in the solution. $2NaCl(aq) + 2H_2O(l) \rightarrow H_2(g) + Cl_2(g) + 2NaOH(aq)$	

C sodium chloride solution electrolysis

In the electrolysis of sodium sulfate solution, sodium ions (Na^+) and hydrogen ions (H^+) collect at the cathode, where hydrogen gas forms. At the anode, hydroxide ions (OH^-) are discharged more readily than sulfate ions (SO_4^{2-}), so oxygen gas is formed (along with water). Overall, water decomposes to form hydrogen and oxygen. The Na^+ and SO_4^{2-} ions stay in solution.

Water decomposes to form hydrogen and oxygen during the electrolysis of water acidified with dilute sulfuric acid (which contains H^+(aq) and SO_4^{2-}(aq)).

5 Use table C as a template to show the details of what happens in the electrolysis of:

8th **a** sodium sulfate **b** acidified water.

8th **6** Explain why the electrolysis of acidified water produces twice as much hydrogen as oxygen.

Copper can be purified by the electrolysis of copper sulfate solution using copper electrodes. The copper atoms in the anode lose electrons to become copper ions. These dissolve in the solution and migrate to the cathode, where they are deposited as pure copper. Impurities from the anode do not form ions and collect below the anode as a 'sludge'.

7 H Write the half equations for the reactions at the electrodes when copper sulfate is electrolysed using copper electrodes and classify them as oxidation or reduction.

Exam-style question

The electrolysis of sodium chloride solution does not produce metallic sodium. State how you would change the electrolyte to obtain metallic sodium. *(1 mark)*

4 When sodium chloride solution is electrolysed, state why hydrogen is produced instead of sodium.

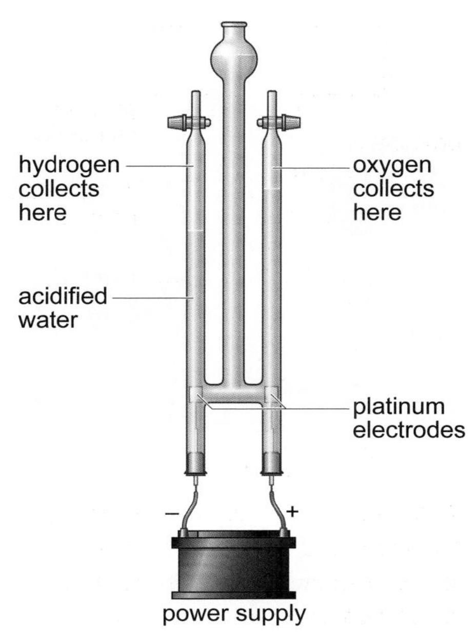

D Water is electrolysed in a Hofmann voltameter to collect the gases produced.

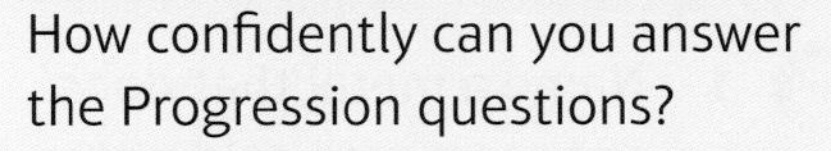

Checkpoint

How confidently can you answer the Progression questions?

Strengthen

S1 Explain the formation of the products during the electrolysis of molten zinc chloride.

S2 Predict the product formed at each electrode during the electrolysis of molten magnesium bromide. Justify your answers.

Extend

E1 Explain why the electrolysis of sodium chloride solution produces hydrogen and chlorine at the electrodes.

SC11a Reactivity

Specification reference: C4.1; H C4.2; C4.3

Progression questions

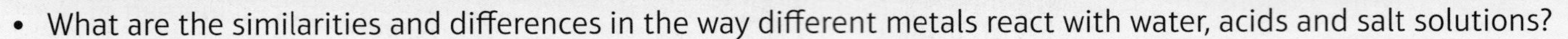

- What are the similarities and differences in the way different metals react with water, acids and salt solutions?
- What happens to metal atoms when they react with water and acids?
- H How do you explain displacement reactions as redox reactions?

A Caesium is more reactive than potassium, and so is placed above potassium in the reactivity series.

Did you know?

Caesium forms cations so easily that scientists think it could be used as a propellant in 'ion engines' for spacecraft.

1 Name a metal that does not react with cold water or dilute acid.

2 Write the word equation for the reaction of calcium with water.

3 Write the balanced equation for the reaction of magnesium with dilute hydrochloric acid. Include state symbols.

The **reactivity series** is a list of metals in order of reactivity, with the most reactive at the top.

Metal	Reaction with water	Reaction with dilute acid	Tendency of metal atoms to form cations
potassium	react with cold water to form hydrogen and a metal hydroxide	react violently	increasing ability of metal atoms to form positive ions (arrow pointing up)
sodium			
calcium		react to form hydrogen and a salt solution	
magnesium	react very slowly, if at all, with cold water but react with steam to form hydrogen and a metal oxide		
aluminium			
zinc			
iron			
copper	do not react with cold water or steam	do not react	
silver			
gold			

B the reactivity series for some metals

The metals that react with cold water form hydrogen and a metal hydroxide solution. For example:

$$2K(s) + 2H_2O(l) \rightarrow 2KOH(aq) + H_2(g)$$

The metals that react with steam form hydrogen and a solid metal oxide.

$$2Mg(s) + H_2O(g) \rightarrow 2MgO(s) + H_2(g)$$

The metals that react with dilute acids form hydrogen and a salt solution. Bubbles of gas will be seen. The more bubbles formed, the more reactive the metal.

$$Zn(s) + H_2SO_4(aq) \rightarrow ZnSO_4(aq) + H_2(g)$$

In all of these reactions, the metal atoms lose electrons to form positive ions (**cations**). The more easily a metal's atoms lose electrons, the higher the metal is in the reactivity series.

Displacement reactions

We can use the reactivity series to predict whether reactions will take place. Each metal will react with compounds of the metals below it in the series.

When zinc is dipped into copper sulfate solution, a copper coating forms on the surface of the zinc. Some of the zinc takes the place of the copper and forms zinc sulfate solution.

$$Zn(s) + CuSO_4(aq) \rightarrow Cu(s) + ZnSO_4(aq)$$

This is a **displacement reaction**. The zinc has displaced the copper.

Displacement reactions only work one way. Copper cannot displace zinc from its compounds because copper is less reactive.

4 Use the reactivity series to predict whether a displacement reaction will take place in the reaction below. Either complete the equation or write 'no reaction'.

magnesium + copper sulfate →

H

Displacement reactions are also redox reactions. The reaction between zinc and copper sulfate can be written as an ionic equation:

$$Zn + Cu^{2+} \rightarrow Cu + Zn^{2+}$$

The sulfate ions have been left out as they do not change and are called **spectator ions**. The zinc atoms lose electrons to form zinc ions. This can be shown in a **half equation**. 2e represents the two electrons.

$Zn \rightarrow Zn^{2+} + 2e$ This is **oxidation** – the loss of electrons.

The copper ions gain electrons to form copper atoms:

$Cu^{2+} + 2e \rightarrow Cu$ This is **reduction** – the gain of electrons.

A reaction in which one substance is oxidised and another is reduced is called a **redox reaction**.

6 Explain which substances are oxidised and reduced when:

$$Mg + Zn^{2+} \rightarrow Zn + Mg^{2+}$$

Exam-style question

Three metals are labelled **X**, **Y** and **Z**. Metal **X** displaces **Z** from **Z** sulfate solution. Metal **X** does not displace **Y** from **Y** sulfate solution.

State the order of reactivity of the three metals, giving a reason for your answer. *(3 marks)*

C Blue copper sulfate solution changes to colourless zinc sulfate solution as zinc displaces copper.

5 Write the balanced equation for the reaction between magnesium and zinc chloride.

Checkpoint

How confidently can you answer the Progression questions?

Strengthen

S1 Describe the reactions you could carry out to find the order of reactivity for magnesium, tin, chromium and copper. You may use the metals and the metal nitrate solutions.

Extend

E1 **H** Magnesium reacts with dilute sulfuric acid and zinc nitrate solution, as shown:

$$Mg + H_2SO_4 \rightarrow MgSO_4 + H_2$$

$$Mg + Zn(NO_3)_2 \rightarrow Mg(NO_3)_2 + Zn$$

a Write ionic equations for these reactions.

b Explain, in terms of electrons, why these are redox reactions.

SC11b Ores

Specification reference: C4.4; C4.7; **H** C4.8

Progression questions

- Which metals are found uncombined in the Earth's crust?
- How is the method of extraction of a metal related to its position in the reactivity series?
- **H** How are biological methods used to extract some metals?

A Gold occurs uncombined in the Earth's crust.

Very unreactive metals, such as gold and platinum, are found naturally in their **native state** (as uncombined elements). More reactive metals have reacted with other elements to form compounds in rocks. The process of obtaining a metal from these compounds is **extraction**.

An **ore** is a rock that contains enough of a compound to extract a metal for profit. Haematite is an ore containing iron oxide. Iron is extracted by heating the iron oxide with carbon. Carbon is more reactive than iron so it displaces it.

iron oxide + carbon → iron + carbon dioxide

This method is used for compounds of metals below carbon in the reactivity series shown in table B.

Malachite is an ore containing copper carbonate. Malachite is heated to convert it to copper oxide, which is then heated with carbon to produce copper.

Metals higher than carbon must be extracted using a more powerful method called **electrolysis**. This involves passing electricity through a molten ionic compound to decompose it into its elements. Aluminium is produced by electrolysis of aluminium oxide, found in an ore called bauxite:

aluminium oxide → aluminium + oxygen

1 Write word equations for the two reactions needed to produce copper.

2 State why copper can be produced by heating copper oxide with carbon.

increasing reactivity ↑

Metal	Method of extraction
potassium	electrolysis of a molten compound
sodium	
calcium	
magnesium	
aluminium	
(carbon)	
zinc	heat an ore with carbon
iron	
copper	
silver	found as the uncombined element
gold	

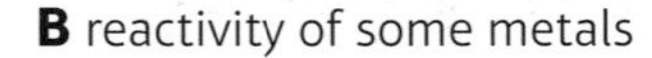

B reactivity of some metals

A lot of energy is needed to keep metal oxides molten for electrolysis, making it extremely expensive. Electrolysis is only used to extract very reactive metals that cannot be obtained by heating their oxides with carbon.

3 Name two metals that can only be extracted from their ores by electrolysis.

4 Zinc can be extracted from zinc oxide, ZnO, by heating with carbon.

a Write the balanced equation for this reaction.

b Explain why electrolysis is not used in the large-scale extraction of zinc.

H Biological methods of metal extraction

Copper is traditionally extracted by heating copper sulfide (producing copper and sulfur dioxide). However, copper ores are running out and so we need to extract copper from ores containing much smaller amounts of copper compounds.

Bioleaching uses bacteria grown on a low grade ore. The bacteria produce a solution containing copper ions, called a **leachate**. Copper is extracted from the leachate by displacement using scrap iron, then purified by electrolysis. This method can also be used for metals such as nickel, cobalt and zinc.

Phytoextraction involves growing plants that absorb metal compounds. The plants are burnt to form ash, from which the metal is extracted.

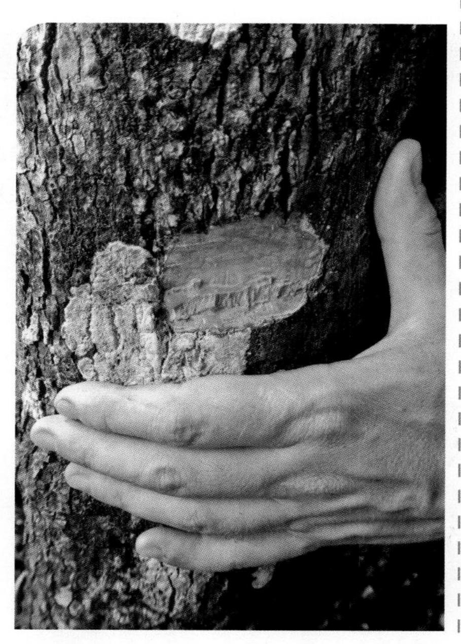

C The tree used for phytoextraction contains a nickel-rich sap, which makes it green.

Process	Advantages	Disadvantages
both bioleaching and phytoextraction	no harmful gases (e.g. sulfur dioxide) are produced causes less damage to the landscape than mining conserves supplies of higher grade ores	very slow
bioleaching	does not require high temperatures	toxic substances and sulfuric acid can be produced by the process, and damage the environment
phytoextraction	can extract metals from contaminated soils	more expensive than mining some ores growing plants is dependent on weather conditions

D some advantages and disadvantages of bioleaching and phytoextraction

5 Suggest why bioleaching and phytoextraction are very slow.

6 Copper ions, Cu^{2+}, are produced in solution during bioleaching. Write an ionic equation for the displacement reaction between these copper ions and iron. Include state symbols.

Did you know?

When aluminium was first extracted by electrolysis in the late 19th century it was more expensive than gold.

Exam-style question

Sodium is more reactive than aluminium. Describe a method to extract sodium from sodium chloride. Give a reason for your answer. *(3 marks)*

Checkpoint

How confidently can you answer the Progression questions?

Strengthen

S1 Explain why iron is extracted from iron oxide using a different method to the one used to extract aluminium from aluminium oxide.

Extend

E1 H Compare and contrast biological and non-biological methods of metal extraction.

SC11c Oxidation and reduction

Specification reference: H C4.2; C4.5; C4.6; C4.9

Progression questions

- How do you explain oxidation and reduction in terms of oxygen?
- What types of reaction happen to ores when metals are extracted?
- How is the position of a metal in the reactivity series related to its resistance to corrosion?

A Iron oxide is reduced to iron in a blast furnace.

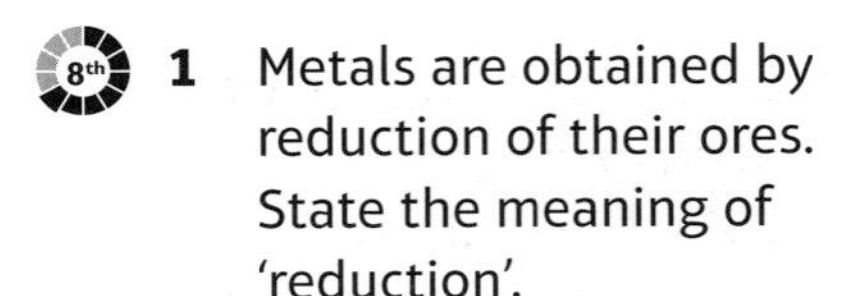

8th **1** Metals are obtained by reduction of their ores. State the meaning of 'reduction'.

9th **2** Zinc oxide reacts with carbon to form zinc and carbon dioxide in a redox reaction. Explain which substance has been oxidised and which has been reduced.

3 H Molten sodium chloride contains Na^+ and Cl^- ions. It is electrolysed to form sodium and chlorine.

8th **a** Write the half-equations for the reactions at the anode and the cathode.

10th **b** Explain whether the reaction at each electrode is oxidation or reduction.

Many metals are extracted from metal oxide ores. In order to obtain the metal from its oxide, the oxygen must be removed. When oxygen is removed from a compound, the compound is said to be 'reduced'.

Metal extraction is reduction

Oxidation is the gain of oxygen by a substance. Reduction is the loss of oxygen from a substance. Oxidation and reduction always occur together. If one substance is oxidised, another will be reduced. Reactions in which oxidation and reduction occur are called redox reactions.

Iron is obtained by removing the oxygen from iron oxide by heating with carbon. The iron oxide is reduced to iron. Carbon is oxidised to carbon dioxide.

iron oxide + carbon → iron + carbon dioxide

Aluminium is obtained by removing oxygen from aluminium oxide by electrolysis.

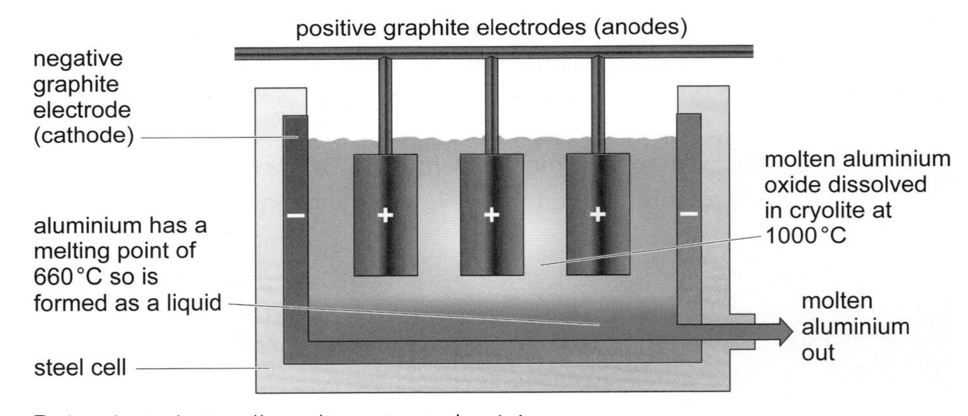

B the electrolysis cell used to extract aluminium

During electrolysis, aluminium ions (Al^{3+}) are attracted to the cathode, where they gain electrons to form aluminium. The oxide ions, O^{2-}, are attracted to the anodes, where they lose electrons to form oxygen. At the high temperature in the electrolysis cell, the oxygen reacts with the graphite (carbon) anodes to form carbon dioxide.

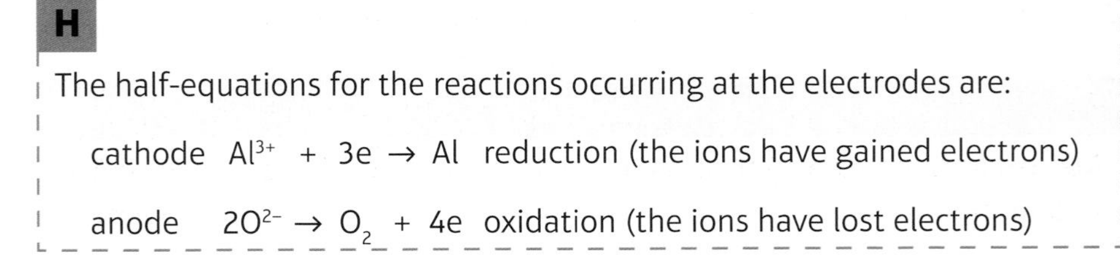

H

The half-equations for the reactions occurring at the electrodes are:

cathode $Al^{3+} + 3e \rightarrow Al$ reduction (the ions have gained electrons)

anode $2O^{2-} \rightarrow O_2 + 4e$ oxidation (the ions have lost electrons)

Corrosion

Corrosion happens when a metal reacts with oxygen, making the metal weaker over time. The metal gains oxygen so is oxidised. The corrosion of iron requires water as well as oxygen and is called **rusting**.

The more reactive a metal is, the more rapidly it corrodes. Gold does not corrode at all, which is one of the reasons it is used in jewellery.

C The Grouville Hoard was found in a field in Jersey in 2012. It contains about 70 000 coins and pieces of gold jewellery, which are 2000 years old. The gold has not corroded.

Some metals, such as aluminium, are quite reactive and would be expected to corrode quickly. However, they do not corrode because their surfaces form a protective oxide layer (a **tarnish**), which prevents further reaction.

D The iron in the Angel of the North has reacted with oxygen and water.

Exam-style question

Iron oxide is reduced by heating it with carbon. Explain what is oxidised in this process. *(2 marks)*

Did you know?

The iron originally on Mars has rusted over billions of years, making the planet red. On the Moon, however, the dark areas on its surface are made of an iron-rich rock. The iron in these rocks has not rusted.

4 Look at the Did you know? box. Explain what the different colours in the iron-rich rocks on Mars and the Moon tell us about their atmospheres.

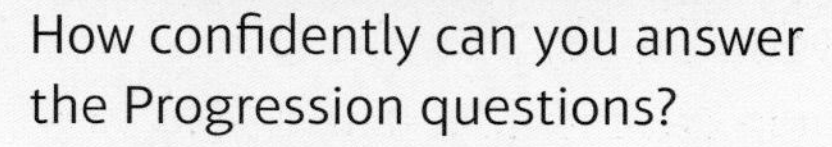

Checkpoint

How confidently can you answer the Progression questions?

Strengthen

S1 Copper oxide reacts with hydrogen:
$CuO + H_2 \rightarrow Cu + H_2O$
State, with a reason, which substance has been:
a oxidised **b** reduced.

S2 Three metals were left outside for 1 month. Metal A did not corrode at all; metal B corroded a lot; metal C corroded a little. Put the metals in order of increasing reactivity and explain your reasoning.

Extend

E1 **H** The half-equation for the reaction taking place at one of the electrodes during the electrolysis of molten magnesium chloride is:
$Mg^{2+} + 2e \rightarrow Mg$. Explain: **a** at which electrode this reaction occurs **b** whether this is oxidation, reduction or neither.

SC11d Life cycle assessment and recycling

Specification reference: C4.10; C4.11; C4.12

Progression questions

- What are the advantages of recycling a metal?
- When might recycling a material not be worthwhile?
- What are the factors to consider in a life cycle assessment of a product?

A Artists have recycled the waste washed up on the coast of Kenya into sculptures.

Every UK household is estimated to produce 1 tonne of waste each year. About 45% of this waste is recycled but there is an EU target for **recycling** to reach 70% by 2030.

An estimated 2 million tonnes of waste electrical and electronic equipment (WEEE), such as phones, TVs and toasters, are thrown away in the UK each year. These items contain a lot of precious metals worth about £1 billion, including about £36 000 000 worth of aluminium.

B The WEEE man is made from over 3 tonnes of electrical and electronic equipment that the average person in the UK throws away in a lifetime.

 **1** Describe what is meant by 'recycling metals'.

 **2** Make a table to summarise the advantages and disadvantages of recycling metals compared to extracting more of the metals from ores.

Recycling metals

Many metals can be recycled by melting them down and making them into something new. Some of the main advantages of recycling are as follows:

- Natural reserves of metal ores will last longer.
- The need to mine ores is reduced. Mining can damage the landscape as well as create noise and dust pollution.
- Less pollution may be produced. For example, sulfur dioxide is formed when some metals are extracted from metal sulfide ores.
- Many metals need less energy to recycle them than to extract new metal from the ore.
- Less waste metal ends up in landfill sites.

However, there are some disadvantages of recycling – including the costs and the energy used in collecting, transporting and sorting metals to be recycled. Sometimes it can be more expensive, and require more energy, to recycle than to extract new metal.

Life cycle assessment

A life cycle assessment (LCA) can be carried out to work out the environmental impact of a product. An example is shown in diagram C.

The LCA also helps people to decide whether it is worthwhile to manufacture and recycle a product. LCAs can be used to compare the effect of using different materials for the same product, for example making a bottle from glass or plastic.

Some data that could be used as part of an LCA for the manufacture of a sample of 1 kg of aluminium is shown in the table below.

Data on the manufacture of aluminium

- 5.5 kg of bauxite produces 1.9 kg of aluminium oxide, which produces 1.0 kg of aluminium during electrolysis
- 0.3 kg of carbon is burnt from the anodes
- 285 000 kJ of energy is needed to produce 1 kg of aluminium from bauxite
- 14 000 kJ of energy is needed to produce 1 kg of aluminium from recycled aluminium

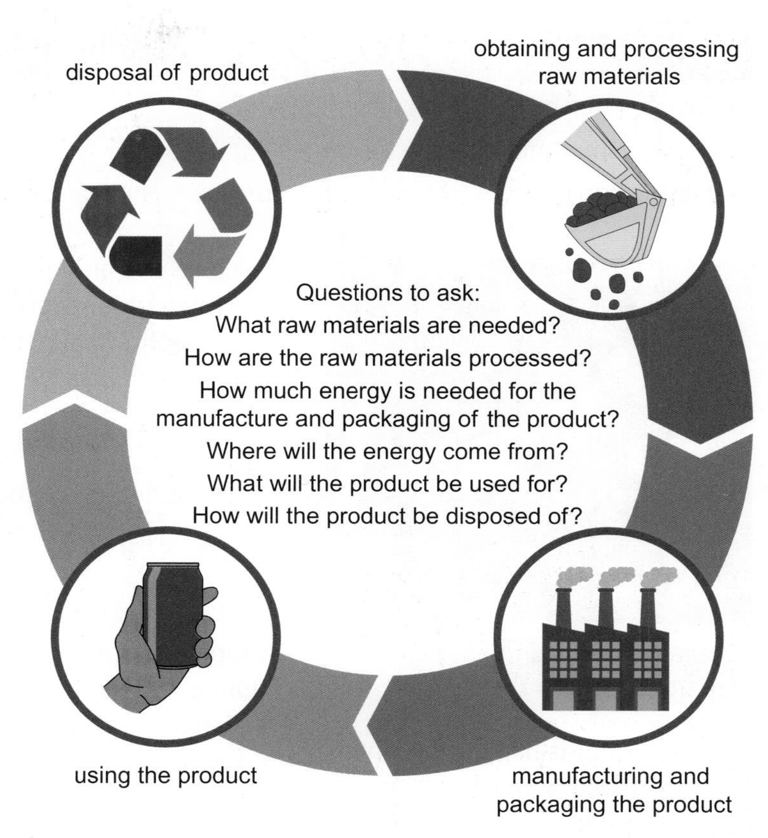

C stages in an LCA

Did you know?

The Colossus of Rhodes, one of the Seven Wonders of the Ancient World, was completed in 280 BCE using bronze from abandoned weapons. It was destroyed by an earthquake in 226 BCE. About 800 years later, the metal was recycled again.

D the Colossus of Rhodes

3 State the four stages that are considered in a life cycle assessment of a product.

4 Give two reasons why a life cycle assessment should be carried out before deciding whether to make a new product.

Exam-style question

Describe two advantages of recycling copper, rather than obtaining it from its ores. *(2 marks)*

Checkpoint

How confidently can you answer the Progression questions?

Strengthen

S1 **a** Outline how a broken aluminium saucepan is recycled to make an aluminium drinks can. **b** State the advantages and disadvantages of recycling aluminium.

Extend

E1 Discuss the life cycle assessment of aluminium, using the data shown in the data table and the extraction of aluminium in the previous topic. Include a description of other factors that need to be considered as part of the LCA.

SC12a Dynamic equilibrium

Specification reference: C4.13; C4.14; C4.15; C4.16; H C4.17

Progression questions

- What is meant by dynamic equilibrium?
- How is ammonia manufactured?
- H How do changes in temperature, pressure and concentration affect the equilibrium position?

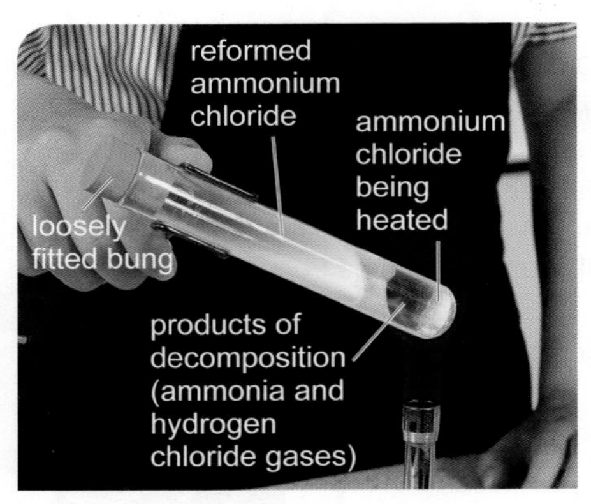

A Heating ammonium chloride is a reversible reaction.

1 What is happening when a reaction reaches 'dynamic equilibrium'?

In some chemical reactions the products react to reform the reactants. These are **reversible reactions**. In the equations for reversible reactions (such as the one shown in photo A), a double arrow '⇌' is used to show that both forward and backward reactions occur at the same time.

forward reaction →

ammonium chloride ⇌ ammonia + hydrogen

$NH_4Cl(s) \rightleftharpoons NH_3(g) + HCl(g)$

← backward reaction

Graph B shows how the percentages of the reactants and products change during the reaction. At a certain point, the forward and backward reactions are still occurring but the percentages of the reactants and products are no longer changing. This is called a **dynamic equilibrium** because the reactions are still occurring (dynamic) but the substances remain in balance (equilibrium).

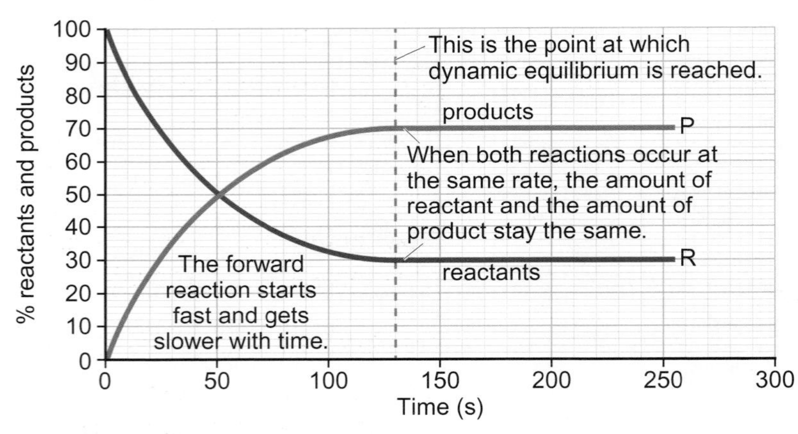

B In a reversible reaction, the backward reaction gets faster with time, and the forward reaction gets slower with time. When they are occurring at the same rate, dynamic equilibrium has been reached.

Although all reactions are reversible, dynamic equilibrium only occurs in **closed systems**, where there is no loss of reactants or products. In an **open system**, gases could escape and so equilibrium would not be achieved.

2 When calcium carbonate is heated in an open test tube it decomposes to form calcium oxide and carbon dioxide.

a Write a word equation to represent this change as a reversible reaction.

b Explain why equilibrium will not be achieved in this case.

$N_2(g) + 3H_2(g) \rightleftharpoons 2NH_3(g)$

nitrogen   hydrogen   ammonia

The manufacture of ammonia by the Haber process involves a reversible reaction between nitrogen (from the air) and hydrogen (from natural gas) that can reach a dynamic equilibrium. The 'equilibrium position' (the percentages of the products and reactants at equilibrium) is changed by the reaction conditions. In the Haber process, and all similar industrial reactions, the reaction conditions are chosen to favour the forward reaction and make a large amount of product as cheaply as possible. In the Haber process, these conditions are a temperature of 450 °C, a pressure of 200 atmospheres and the use of an iron catalyst.

3 What happens to the amount of ammonia after equilibrium is reached in the Haber process?

The equilibrium position can be altered by changes in temperature, pressure and concentration. In general, the equilibrium position shifts to reduce the effects of any changes to the system, as described in table C.

Change by ...	Equilibrium position shifts ...
increasing temperature	in the **endothermic** direction (transferring energy from the surroundings, cooling them down)
decreasing temperature	in the **exothermic** direction (transferring energy to the surroundings, heating them up)
increasing gas pressure	in the direction that forms fewer gas molecules (as this reduces pressure)
decreasing gas pressure	in the direction that forms more gas molecules (as this increases pressure)
increasing a concentration	in the direction that uses up the substance that has been added
decreasing a concentration	in the direction that forms more of the substance that has been removed

C

Photo D shows how the equilibrium position of a mixture of nitrogen dioxide and dinitrogen tetroxide depends on temperature.

$2NO_2(g) \rightleftharpoons N_2O_4(g)$ (forward reaction is exothermic)

nitrogen dioxide (brown) ⇌ dinitrogen tetroxide (colourless)

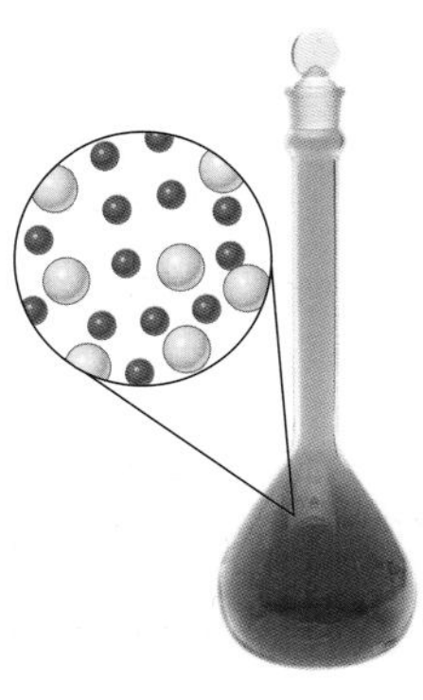

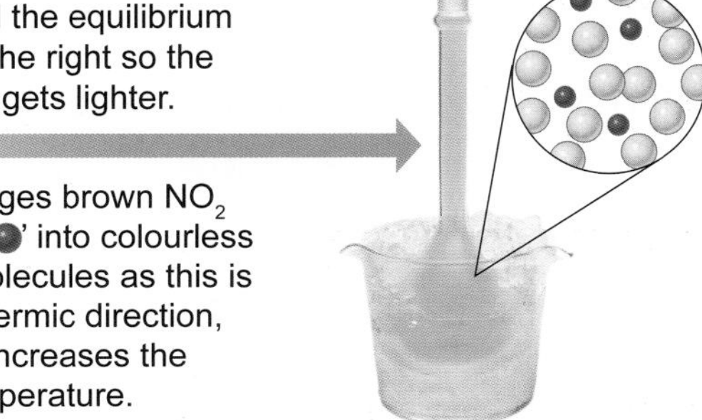

D As the temperature is decreased the equilibrium shifts in the exothermic direction.

4 Explain why the equilibrium position in industrial reactions is often controlled.

5 Describe the difference between exothermic and endothermic reactions.

6 The formation of methanol from carbon monoxide and hydrogen is a reversible reaction that is exothermic in the forward direction.

$$CO(g) + 2H_2(g) \rightleftharpoons CH_3OH(g)$$

Explain the effect on the position of equilibrium of increasing:

a temperature

b pressure

c carbon monoxide concentration.

Exam-style question

a Describe what happens in a reversible reaction. *(1 mark)*

b H Look at the equilibrium between NO_2 and N_2O_4 in diagram D. Explain why the colour changes when the pressure is increased. *(3 marks)*

Checkpoint

How confidently can you answer the Progression questions?

Strengthen

S1 Use equations to explain the formation of ammonia in a reversible reaction that reaches a dynamic equilibrium.

Extend

E1 Explain how a dynamic equilibrium is reached in the formation of ammonia.

E2 H The formation of ammonia is exothermic. Describe three ways to increase the amount of ammonia at equilibrium.

SC13a Transition metals

Specification reference: C5.1C

Progression questions

- Where are the transition metals found in the periodic table?
- What are the typical properties of transition metals?
- What properties of iron make it a typical transition metal?

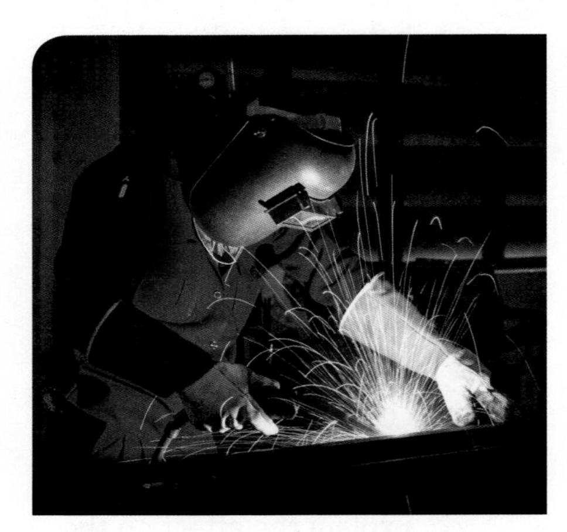

A Tungsten inert gas (TIG) welding joins pieces of steel together. The welding torch uses tungsten electrodes. The very high melting point of tungsten, 3422 °C, prevents these from melting.

1 Describe the position of the transition metals in the periodic table.

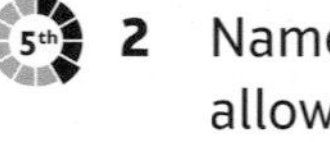

2 Name the property that allows steel car parts to be pressed into shape.

3 Bronze is a mixture of copper and tin. Suggest a reason that explains why some ancient Roman mirrors were made from polished bronze.

Tungsten and iron, like most other metals, are **transition metals**. These elements are placed in the central block of the periodic table, between groups 2 and 3. The transition metals include most of the metals used for construction, vehicles, electrical wiring, jewellery and other everyday uses.

1	2											3	4	5	6	7	0
			Ti	V	Cr	Mn	Fe	Co	Ni	Cu	Zn						
								Rh	Pd	Ag							
					W			Ir	Pt	Au	Hg						

B the transition metals, with some common examples identified

Physical properties

The transition metals have the typical properties of metals. In general, transition metals are:

- **malleable** (they can be hammered or rolled into shape without shattering)
- **ductile** (they can be stretched out to make thin wires)
- good conductors of electricity
- shiny when polished.

Iron is malleable and strong. It is used to make buildings, bridges, ships and cars. Copper is used for electrical wiring because it is ductile and a good conductor of electricity. Household mirrors consist of a sheet of glass coated with aluminium. Silver is even more shiny than aluminium, so it provides the reflective coating for the mirrors in infrared telescopes.

Compared to aluminium and the metals in groups 1 and 2, transition metals typically have:

- high melting points
- high densities.

Metal	Density (g/cm^3)	Melting point (°C)
sodium	0.968	98
magnesium	1.74	650
aluminium	2.70	660
iron	7.87	1538
copper	8.96	1085
silver	10.5	962
tungsten	19.2	3422

C Sodium (group 1), magnesium (group 2) and aluminium (group 3) have lower densities and melting points than typical transition metals such as iron.

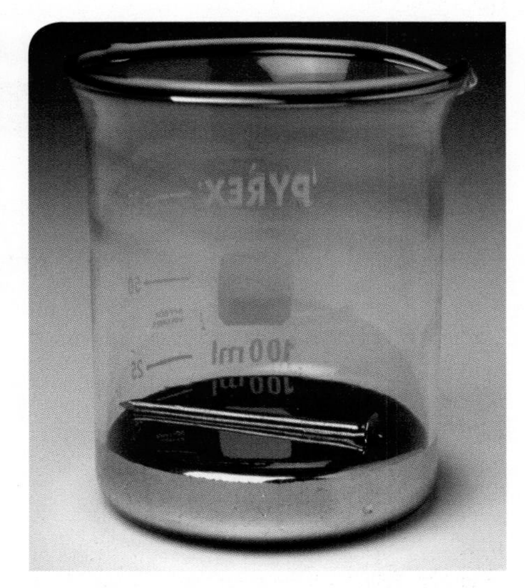

D Mercury melts at −39 °C and boils at 356 °C. A steel nail can float on it because of the high density of mercury, 13.53 g/cm^3.

Remember that these are typical properties, and there are exceptions. For example, mercury is a transition metal with a high density, but it is liquid at room temperature.

4 Explain why mercury is liquid, rather than solid or gas, at room temperature.

Chemical properties

Aluminium, and the metals in groups 1 and 2, form white or colourless compounds. However, transition metal compounds are usually coloured. For example iron(III) oxide, Fe_2O_3, is red-brown. Tungsten oxide, WO_3, is yellow. Different transition metal hydroxides are different colours. This property is used to identify the transition metal ion present in a substance (see *SC25b Tests for positive ions*). Iron(II) hydroxide, $Fe(OH)_2$, is pale green but iron(III) hydroxide, $Fe(OH)_3$, is orange-brown.

E Pure beryl is a colourless mineral. Iron impurities turn it into aquamarine, a blue gemstone.

5 Rubies are red gemstones that are mostly aluminium oxide. Suggest a reason that explains why rubies are coloured.

Transition metals and their compounds typically show catalytic activity. **Catalysts** increase the rate of a reaction without being changed either chemically or in mass at the end of the reaction. Iron is the catalyst used to manufacture ammonia by the Haber process. Iron(III) chloride, $FeCl_3$, is a catalyst used during the manufacture of poly(chloroethene) or PVC.

6 Catalytic converters in vehicles convert harmful exhaust gases into less harmful ones. Suggest a reason that explains why these devices contain platinum, Pt, and rhodium, Rh.

Exam-style question

Potassium, K, is a group 1 metal and titanium, Ti, is a transition metal. Predict *one* difference in their physical properties and *one* difference in their chemical properties. *(2 marks)*

Checkpoint

How confidently can you answer the Progression questions?

Strengthen

S1 Why is iron considered to be a typical transition metal?

Extend

E1 Compare the typical properties of transition metals with those of other metals, such as sodium and aluminium.

SC13b Corrosion

Specification reference: C5.2C; C5.3C

Progression questions

- Why do metals corrode?
- How can the surface of iron be protected from rusting?
- How does sacrificial protection prevent rusting?

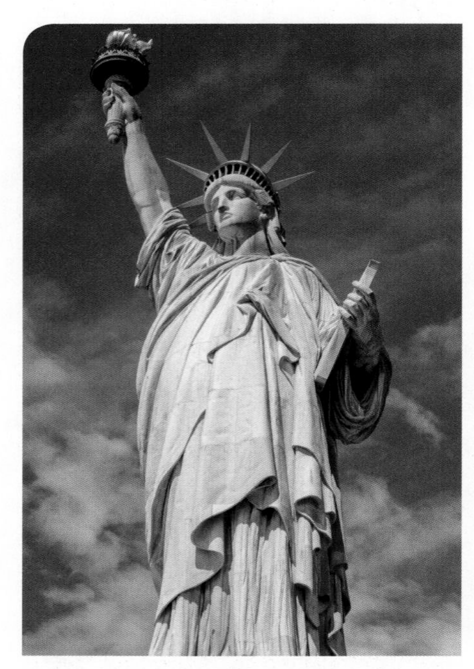

A The Statue of Liberty consists of 27 tonnes of copper sheeting over a steel frame. Its green colour is due to a natural layer of copper salts that forms when copper tarnishes.

1 **Explain why magnesium ribbon appears dull grey, but becomes silvery when rubbed with sandpaper.**

2 **Write a balanced equation for the reaction of aluminium with oxygen, forming aluminium oxide, Al_2O_3.**

When metals react with oxygen in the air, they **oxidise** to form metal oxides. Very reactive metals, such as sodium, oxidise rapidly when they are freshly cut:

sodium + oxygen → sodium oxide

$$4Na(s) + O_2(g) \rightarrow 2Na_2O(s)$$

B White sodium oxide forms quickly on shiny, freshly cut sodium.

Less reactive metals, such as silver, oxidise slowly. Gold and other very unreactive metals may not react with oxygen at all.

Metals may form a thin layer of **tarnish** when they oxidise. This layer stops oxygen reaching the metal, preventing further oxidation. The green layer of 'verdigris' on the Statue of Liberty protects the copper underneath. In a similar way, aluminium is a reactive metal protected by a natural layer of its oxide. This layer is thin enough to see the aluminium underneath.

H

Metals oxidise when they lose electrons. This happens when metals react with oxygen. It may also happen when metals react with other substances found in air. For example, silver reacts with hydrogen sulfide to form a black layer of silver sulfide:

silver + hydrogen sulfide → silver sulfide + hydrogen

$$2Ag(s) + H_2S(g) \rightarrow Ag_2S(s) + H_2(g)$$

3 **Write a half equation to model how silver oxidises to silver ions, Ag^+.**

Rusting

Corrosion happens when a metal continues to oxidise and so the metal becomes weaker over time. **Rusting** is the corrosion of iron or steel (which is mostly iron). Iron rusts when it reacts with oxygen *and* water:

iron + oxygen + water → hydrated iron(III) oxide

Hydrated iron(III) oxide is the orange-brown substance seen on rusty objects. Rust flakes off rusty iron, which exposes more metal to air and water and so the iron continues to corrode and weaken.

4 Compare and contrast tarnishing with corrosion.

5 Explain why rusting is an oxidation reaction.

Rusting can be prevented if air is kept away. This can be achieved by storing the metal in an unreactive atmosphere of nitrogen or argon. Rusting can also be prevented if water is kept away, for example using a **desiccant** powder that absorbs water vapour. Other methods of rust prevention keep both air and water away, including painting, coating with plastic, oiling and greasing.

6 Explain why a bicycle chain is oiled rather than painted.

Sacrificial protection

Sacrificial protection is a method of rust prevention that does not rely on keeping air or water away. Instead, a piece of magnesium or zinc is attached to the iron or steel object. Magnesium and zinc oxidise more easily than iron, so oxygen reacts with them rather than with the iron or steel object. This protection continues until the sacrificial metal corrodes away.

H

The more reactive a metal is, the more easily it loses electrons. Zinc and magnesium lose electrons more easily than iron does, so they are more easily oxidised.

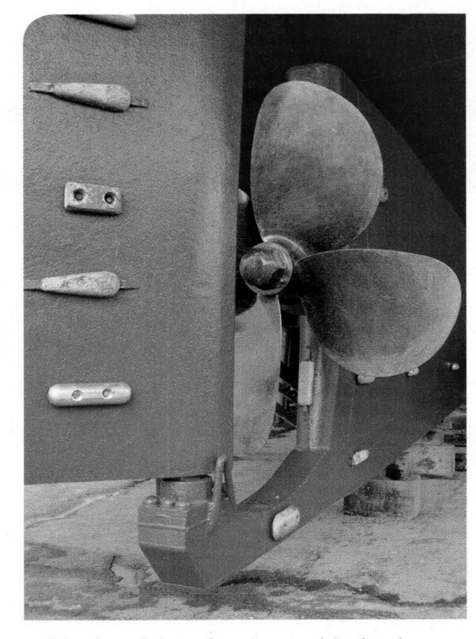

D blocks of sacrificial metal bolted onto a ship's hull

Exam-style question

Evaluate the suitability of sodium for the sacrificial protection of an offshore oil rig. *(3 marks)*

Did you know?

The Iron Pillar of Delhi is a 6 tonne iron pillar, over 1600 years old and almost free of rust. It contains a relatively high amount of phosphorus. This forms a natural layer of iron hydrogen phosphate, which prevents air and water reaching the iron below.

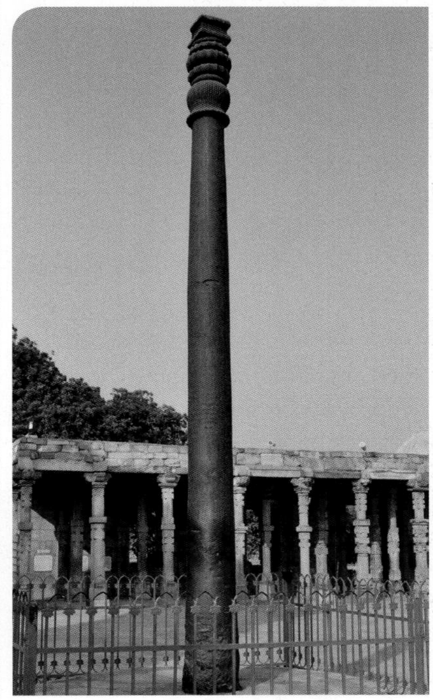

C the Iron Pillar of Delhi

7 Explain why zinc blocks are attached to a ship's hull beneath its waterline.

Checkpoint

How confidently can you answer the Progression questions?

Strengthen

S1 How do different methods of rust prevention work?

Extend

E1 How could you investigate the effect of dissolved salt on the rate of rusting?

SC13c Electroplating

Specification reference: C5.4C

Progression questions

- What is electroplating?
- Why are metals electroplated?
- How is electroplating done?

A Taps are plated with shiny chromium to improve their appearance and resistance to corrosion.

B High-end electrical connectors are plated with gold to improve their corrosion resistance.

Did you know?

Replica ancient gold and silver coins are produced by electrotyping. The two sides of a real coin are pressed into lead to make a mould. The two moulds are electroplated with gold or silver. The electroplated metal halves are removed from the moulds, then filled and glued together to make the replica coin.

Electroplating coats the surface of one metal with a thin layer of another metal. Silver and gold are attractive transition metals but they are expensive. Silver or gold can be electroplated onto cheaper 'base metals' such as copper or nickel. This produces attractive jewellery that is cheaper than solid silver or gold.

Electroplating may also be used to improve a metal object's ability to resist corrosion. Chromium is a transition metal that resists corrosion. Objects such as vehicle parts and boat parts made from steel may be 'chrome plated' using electroplating. The thin layer of chromium stops air and water reaching the steel below, preventing the object rusting.

1 Suggest two reasons that explain why a drum kit may be chrome plated.

Silver and copper are the best electrical conductors, but both tarnish in air. A layer of tarnish may form when cables and equipment are disconnected. Expensive hi-fi cables and electronic equipment may use gold-plated connectors. Gold is the third-best electrical conductor. It does not tarnish but it is much more expensive than silver or copper.

2 Cables can be made from copper.

a Describe a disadvantage of using copper cables in electronic equipment.

b Give a reason that explains why gold-plated connectors are sometimes used in expensive hi-fi equipment.

c Describe a disadvantage of using gold-plated connectors in this type of equipment.

Carrying out electroplating

To electroplate a metal object, you need:

- an **anode** (positively-charged electrode), made from the plating metal
- an **electrolyte**, which is a solution containing ions of the plating metal
- a **cathode** (negatively-charged electrode), which is the metal object itself.

3 Describe three substances you need to electroplate a steel exhaust pipe with chromium.

Diagram C shows how you could electroplate a copper ring with silver. A direct current (d.c.) flows through the electrodes and the electrolyte. Silver ions in the electrolyte move to the negatively-charged copper ring. They gain electrons and are deposited as silver atoms. At the silver anode, silver atoms lose electrons to become silver ions, which go into the electrolyte. The longer the current flows, the thicker the silver layer on the ring becomes.

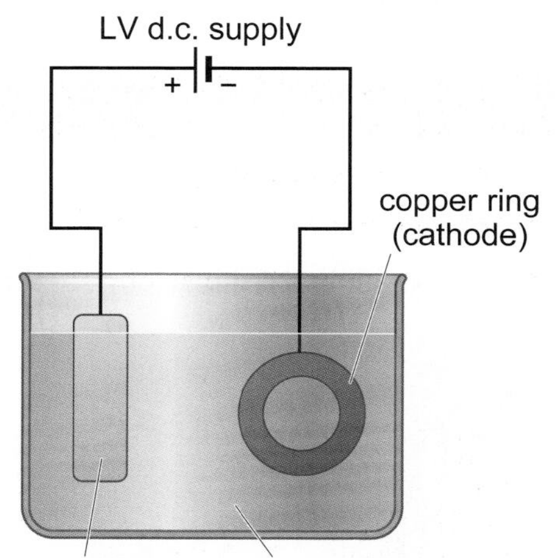

C electroplating silver onto a copper ring

These half equations model the changes that happen when copper is electroplated with silver:

at the silver anode: $Ag(s) \rightarrow Ag^{+}(aq) + e^{-}$

at the copper cathode: $Ag^{+}(aq) + e^{-} \rightarrow Ag(s)$

4 Explain whether reduction or oxidation happens at the anode.

5 Metal bicycle parts may be electroplated with nickel to improve their appearance. Nickel chloride solution, $NiCl_2(aq)$, or nickel sulfate solution, $NiSO_4(aq)$, may be used as the electrolyte. Write half equations to model the changes that happen at each electrode.

Galvanising and tin plating

Iron and steel objects can be protected from rusting by coating them with zinc. This is called **galvanising**. The thin layer of zinc improves corrosion resistance by stopping the water reaching the iron or steel, and by acting as a sacrificial metal. This sacrificial protection can continue even if the zinc layer is damaged.

Galvanising can be carried out using electroplating, or by dipping the object in molten zinc.

Food cans are made from steel. Their inner surface is protected from rusting by electroplating with tin. Tin does not react with air or water at room temperature. The tin layer stops air and water reaching the steel. However, if the tin layer is damaged, the steel can will rust faster. This is because iron is more reactive than tin, so it acts as a sacrificial metal to protect the tin.

D the surface of galvanised steel

6 a Suggest reasons that explain why galvanising a steel farm gate is desirable.

b Describe how you would use electroplating to galvanise the gate.

Exam-style question

Suggest *two* reasons that explain why a gold medal may consist of silver electroplated with gold. *(2 marks)*

Checkpoint

How confidently can you answer the Progression questions?

Strengthen

S1 Why are some metal objects electroplated with another metal?

Extend

E1 Evaluate the use of electroplating for jewellery and for metal bathroom fittings.

SC13d Alloying

Specification reference: C5.5C; C5.6C

Progression questions

- What is an alloy?
- Why is iron mixed with other metals to make alloy steels?
- Why are alloys often stronger than pure metals?

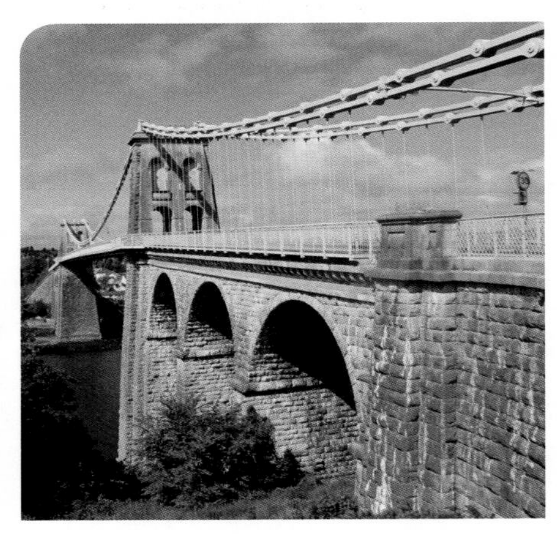

A The Menai Bridge was completed in 1826. Its original wrought iron suspension chains were replaced by steel chains in the 1930s to increase the bridge's weight limit.

1 Explain why wrought iron is an alloy.

2 Write a balanced equation for the reaction between chromium and oxygen.

3 Suggest a reason that explains why stainless steel is used for surgical instruments.

Did you know?

Alloys of iron, aluminium, carbon and manganese are lightweight but brittle. In 2015, Korean scientists discovered that adding some nickel produces an alloy as strong and lightweight as titanium, but costing ten times less.

An **alloy** is a mixture of a metal element with one or more other elements, usually metals. For example, iron straight from the blast furnace is not pure iron. It is an alloy of iron with about 4% carbon, and smaller proportions of phosphorus and other elements. Wrought iron is produced by lowering the carbon content to less than 0.08%.

Alloy steels

Alloy steels are made by deliberately adding other elements to iron. It is possible to create a huge range of alloy steels with different properties by varying their composition.

Stainless steels resist rusting, unlike other alloy steels and iron. Stainless steels contain chromium, which reacts with oxygen in the air. A layer of chromium oxide, Cr_2O_3, forms. This is thick enough to stop air and water reaching the metal below, but thin enough to be transparent. If the metal is scratched, more chromium reacts to replace the layer.

B Stainless steel is useful for domestic and professional kitchens.

Some alloy steels are very strong and tough. 'Tool steels' contain tungsten and molybdenum, and are used to make drill bits. In general, the greater the carbon content of steel, the stronger and harder it is. Mild steel has a low carbon content. However, it also contains elements such as manganese to increase its strength while maintaining its malleability. Mild steel is often used as a building material and for car body panels. Stronger steels can be more difficult to press into shape, but car manufacturers use them to produce strong but relatively lightweight car bodies.

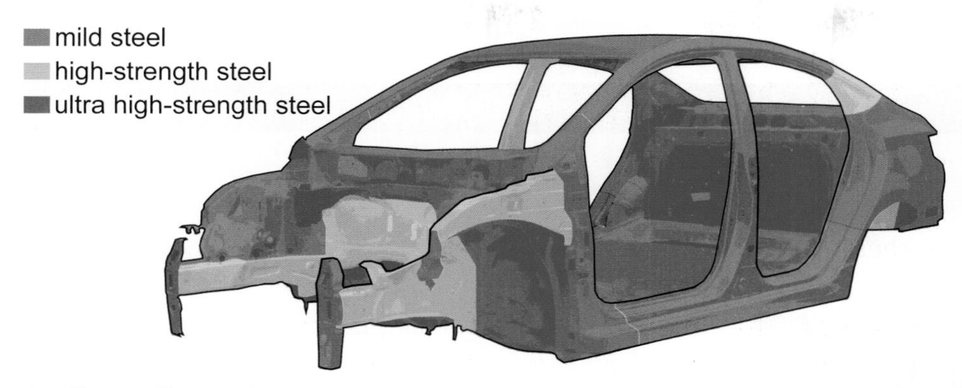

C Different alloy steels are used to make a car body.

 **4** A car body made from mild steel alone would be heavier than one that also contains high-strength steel and ultra high-strength steel (see diagram C). Give a reason that explains this.

Alloys and strength

Alloys are often stronger than the pure metals they contain. For example, pure iron is too soft for everyday use, but wrought iron is stronger even though it contains only a small amount of other elements. Alloy steels are even stronger than wrought iron.

In a solid, pure metal the atoms are all the same size and are arranged regularly in layers. These layers move past each other if enough force is applied. This is why metals are malleable and ductile. In an alloy, the atoms of other elements present may be different sizes. They distort the regular structure, making it more difficult for the layers to slide past each other. This is why alloys are often stronger than pure metals, even though they are usually still malleable and ductile.

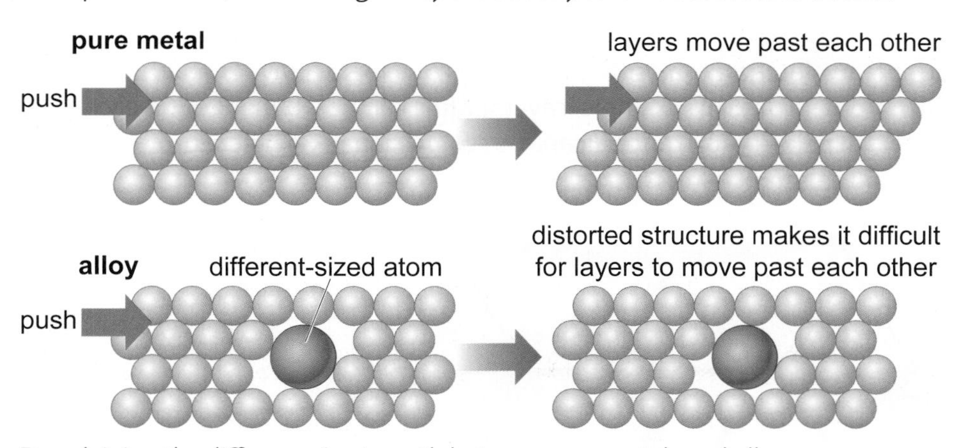

D explaining the difference in strength between pure metals and alloys

Diagram D shows a simple particle model to explain the difference in strength between a pure metal and an alloy. This is a two-dimensional model, but remember that metals have a three-dimensional structure.

 **6** Explain why car parts are made from alloy steels, rather than from pure iron or wrought iron.

Exam-style question

Jewellery gold is often an alloy of gold and copper. Explain how the presence of copper atoms can produce an alloy stronger than pure gold. *(3 marks)*

 **5** Explain, in terms of their structure, why alloys are stronger in *all* directions than the pure metals they contain.

Checkpoint

How confidently can you answer the Progression questions?

Strengthen

S1 Explain, with examples, why metals are often used as alloys rather than as pure metals.

Extend

E1 Evaluate the statement 'alloys are stronger than the individual metals they contain'.

SC13e Uses of metals and their alloys

Specification reference: C5.7C

Progression questions

- What are some common uses for aluminium, copper and gold?
- What are some common alloys containing aluminium or copper?
- Why are different metals or their alloys chosen for different uses?

A Magnalium is the name given to a range of alloys of magnesium and aluminium. When it has a high magnesium content, magnalium is brittle and flammable, making it suitable for use in signal flares and sparklers.

The uses of a metal or alloy depend upon its properties. These properties include:

- chemical properties, such as resistance to corrosion
- physical properties, such as density and ability to conduct electricity.

For example, gold and copper resist corrosion. They are also malleable, ductile and very good conductors of electricity. Both metals could be used for electrical wiring, but cost may also be an important factor. Gold is thousands of times more expensive than copper. So copper is chosen for most electrical wiring, while gold is used in tiny amounts to connect microprocessors and memory chips.

B This restorer is applying pieces of very thin gold, called gold leaf, to an antique ornament.

Aluminium resists corrosion, but it does not conduct electricity as well as copper. However, it is stronger, cheaper and less dense, so it is used for overhead electrical cables. The properties of a metal may also depend upon the intended use. For example, several wires can be wound around each other to make a cable. Such a cable is stronger than one made from a single wire of the same diameter.

C Aluminium is used in overhead electrical cables, such as these being fitted to the National Grid's new T-pylons.

1 Suggest reasons that explain why copper is used to make plumbing parts such as water pipes.

2 Suggest reasons that explain why very thin gold leaf is used to decorate the surfaces of statues and picture frames.

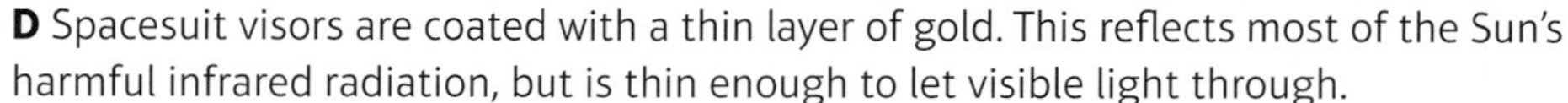

D Spacesuit visors are coated with a thin layer of gold. This reflects most of the Sun's harmful infrared radiation, but is thin enough to let visible light through.

Alloys may have more useful properties than the metals they contain. For example, brass is an alloy of copper and zinc. Copper and brass both resist corrosion. Copper is a better conductor of electricity than brass, but brass is stronger. This makes brass more suitable than copper for making electrical plug pins.

Magnalium containing 95% aluminium and 5% magnesium is an engineering alloy used for aircraft parts and scientific instruments. Table E shows some properties of the two pure metals and the alloy. Magnalium is less dense and almost four times stronger than aluminium alone. Although it is denser than magnesium, magnalium is twice as strong and has better resistance to corrosion. These properties allow the manufacture of strong but lightweight metal parts.

Metal	Density (g/cm^3)	Relative strength
aluminium	2.70	1.0
magnesium	1.74	1.9
magnalium	2.50	3.8

E properties of aluminium, magnesium and 95% Al / 5% Mg magnalium

6 Explain, using information from table E, why engineering magnalium is more suitable for aircraft parts than aluminium or magnesium alone.

Exam-style question

Jewellery gold is often an alloy of gold and copper. Other than increasing the strength of the jewellery, give *two* reasons why copper is chosen to mix with gold. *(2 marks)*

3 Suggest reasons that explain why some overhead electricity cables consist of steel wires with aluminium wires wound around them.

4 Evaluate the choice of metal, copper or aluminium, in household electricity cables and overhead electricity cables.

Did you know?

Gold is incredibly malleable and ductile. Just 1 g of gold can be hammered into a 60 cm diameter circle only 0.18 µm thick, or made into a wire nearly 3 km long.

5 Explain why brass is suitable for making coins and musical instruments.

Checkpoint

How confidently can you answer the Progression questions?

Strengthen

S1 Why are different objects made from different metals?

Extend

E1 Describe to what extent alloys are a better choice for a given purpose than a pure metal.

Electrolysis

Lead bromide contains Pb^{2+} and Br^- ions and has the formula $PbBr_2$. The diagram shows the electrolysis of lead bromide. Explain what is happening at each electrode at the start of the experiment and as the electrolyte melts. (6 marks)

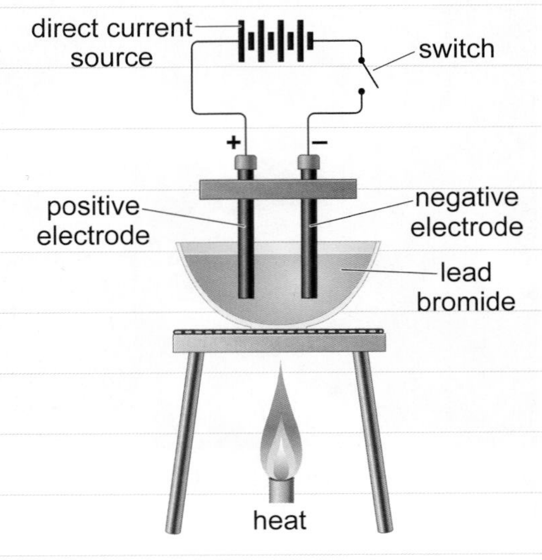

Student answer

Lead bromide contains Pb^{2+} ions and Br^- ions and has the formula $PbBr_2$ [1]*. It is a compound and has ions, so it can be used for electrolysis* [2]*. During electrolysis, the ions move towards the oppositely-charged electrodes* [3]*. The products at each electrode are lead and bromine* [4]*. Heat is needed to melt the lead bromide so that the ions can move and conduct electricity. When the lead bromide is a solid, the ions can't move, so there is no flow of electricity.*

[1] There are no marks for simply repeating information from the question.

[2] This is correct, but it is not relevant to the question which asks students to explain what is happening at the electrodes.

[3] The answer would be better if it explained what was happening at each electrode.

[4] These are the correct products, but the answer should state which product is formed at each electrode.

Verdict

This is an acceptable answer. It contains some correct chemistry, but is missing some information. There is a good explanation of why heat is needed for electrolysis, and the products of the electrolysis are given.

The answer could be improved by explaining which ions move towards which electrode and what happens at those electrodes. For example, it could explain that the positively-charged cations (Pb^{2+}) move towards the negatively-charged electrode (cathode), and once there, they gain two electrons to become lead. It would also have been more logical to have the last two sentences earlier in the explanation, starting with what happens in the circuit at the start of the experiment (when the lead bromide is still solid). There is also information that is copied from the question and some parts of the answer are not relevant.

Exam tip

Do not just repeat information from the question, and make sure that anything you write is relevant to the question that has been asked.

Paper 1

SC14 Quantitative Analysis / SC15 Dynamic Equilibria, Calculations Involving Volumes of Gases / SC16 Chemical Cells and Fuel Cells

The photo shows an ethanol production facility, where sugars are fermented into ethanol in fermentation tanks. The ethanol is then purified for use as transportation fuel. There are other methods of making ethanol, and scientists have to consider many factors before deciding on the best method to produce it, including availability and cost of raw materials, energy requirements, rate of reaction, percentage yield, and atom economy of the reaction.

The learning journey

Previously you will have learnt in *SC9 Calculations Involving Masses*:

- about the law of conservation of mass
- to calculate the maximum mass of a product formed from the mass of a reactant
- to calculate the concentration of a solution in g dm^{-3}
- **H** to calculate the number of moles of a substance in a given mass of it and vice versa.

In this unit you will learn:

- reasons why the actual yield of a reaction is less than the theoretical yield
- to calculate the percentage yield of a reaction
- what is meant by the atom economy of a reaction and how to calculate it
- how to carry out an acid–alkali titration
- **H** how to calculate an unknown concentration or volume of a solution using titration
- **H** about the factors that are considered when selecting a manufacturing method
- **H** how to interconvert between g dm^{-3} and mol dm^{-3}.

SC14a Yields

Specification reference: C5.11C; C5.12C

Progression questions

- What is meant by the terms theoretical yield and actual yield of a reaction?
- How do you calculate the percentage yield of a reaction?
- What are some reasons for the actual yield being less than the theoretical yield?

A Hydrogen is a potential fuel of the future but is very expensive to produce. Scientists have been working on using sunlight to split water into oxygen and hydrogen. A big advance was made in 2015 when scientists increased the **yield** of hydrogen by an order of magnitude (10 times) by using a substance called gallium phosphide.

If you split 36 g of water into oxygen and hydrogen, you should get 4 g of hydrogen. 4 g is the **theoretical yield** of hydrogen as it is the maximum mass of product that can be formed from the reactant. The theoretical yield is calculated from the balanced equation. In practice, you often do not get this much. The amount of product obtained when you carry out an experiment is known as the **actual yield**.

Worked example W1

Calculate the theoretical yield of hydrogen from 36 g of water.

	$2H_2O$	$\rightarrow$	$2H_2$	$+ O_2$
Calculate relative formula masses and multiply by the balancing number	$2 \times (1 + 1 + 16) = 36$		$2 \times (1 + 1) = 4$	
Add the unit symbols	36 g		4 g	

So the theoretical yield of hydrogen is 4 g.

The **percentage yield** compares the actual yield and the theoretical yield:

$$\text{percentage yield} = \frac{\text{actual yield}}{\text{theoretical yield}} \times 100$$

Worked example W2

In the reaction above, the actual yield was 3.3 g of hydrogen. Calculate the percentage yield.

$$\text{percentage yield} = \frac{3.3}{4} \times 100 = 82.5\%$$

1 Calculate the percentage yield for a reaction where the actual yield is 3.2 g and the theoretical yield is 4.0 g.

Did you know?

Scientists are trying to produce biodiesel by extracting oil from algae. The process is not very efficient at the moment, with only about 15% of the substances supplied to the algae being converted into useful oils.

2 When limestone is heated, the calcium carbonate decomposes to form calcium oxide:

$CaCO_3 \rightarrow CaO + CO_2$

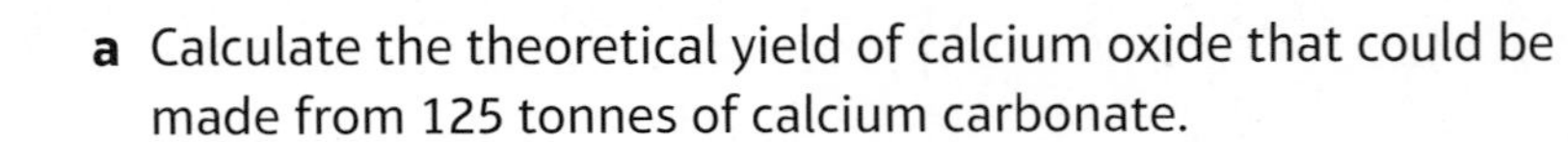

a Calculate the theoretical yield of calcium oxide that could be made from 125 tonnes of calcium carbonate.

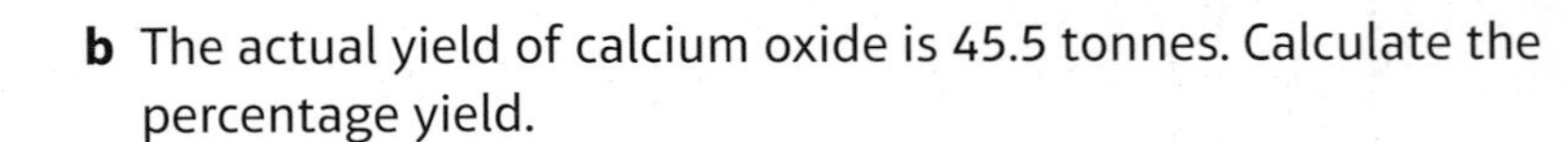

b The actual yield of calcium oxide is 45.5 tonnes. Calculate the percentage yield.

Why is the yield less than expected?

When manufacturing substances, the theoretical yield is calculated assuming that all the reactants are turned into products, and that the products are successfully separated from the reaction mixture. There are three main reasons why reactions do not give 100% yields:

- the reaction may be incomplete so not all of the reactants are used up – possibly because the reaction has not been left for long enough, or the reaction may reach equilibrium
- some of the product is lost – for example, when a liquid is transferred from one container to another, some of it will be left behind on the walls of the first container
- there may be other unwanted **side reactions** taking place – for example, some of the reactants may react to make a different product. These side reactions compete with the main reaction.

The higher the percentage yield of a reaction, the more useful the reaction is. A high yield means that fewer raw materials are used to make the same amount of product, so there is less waste and more profit can be made.

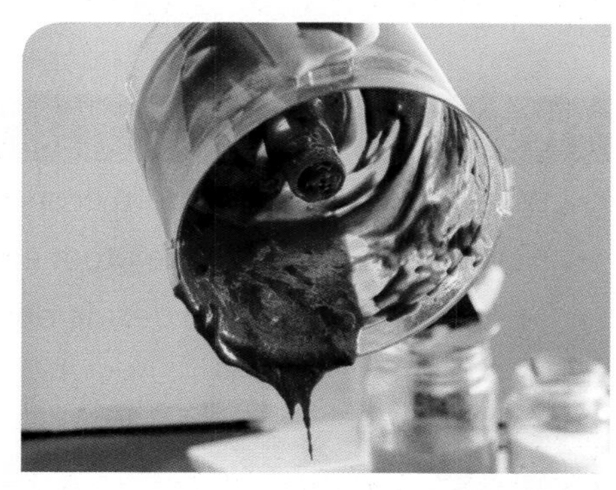

B When you bake a cake, some of the ingredients may get left behind on the scales, in the mixing bowl or in the cake tin. In a chemical reaction, some of the reactants and products may get left behind on the apparatus.

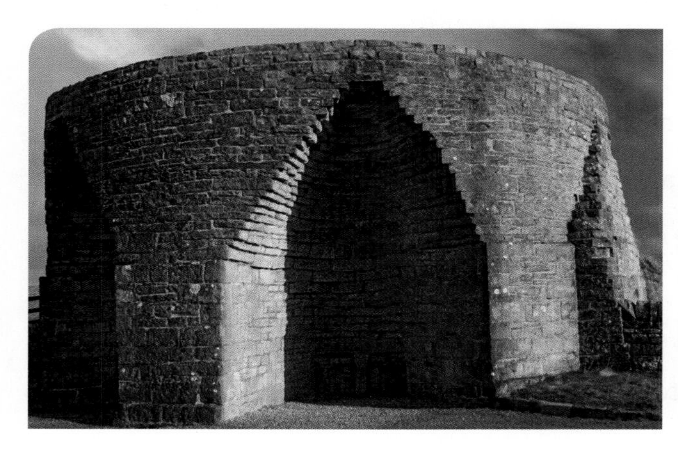

C Calcium oxide is produced by heating limestone in a lime kiln. Modern lime kilns achieve a much greater percentage yield than old kilns, such as this Roman kiln.

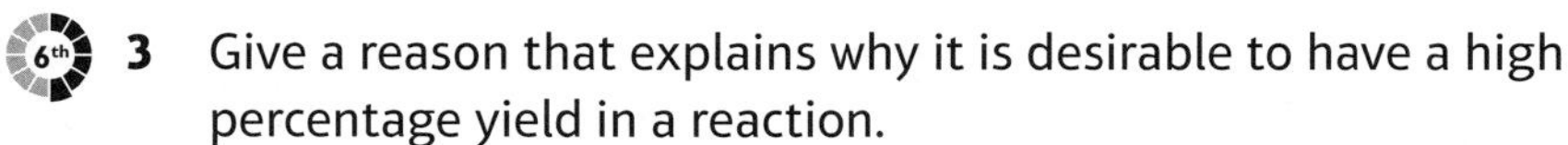

3 Give a reason that explains why it is desirable to have a high percentage yield in a reaction.

4 One of the steps in the production of sulfuric acid is:

$$2SO_2 + O_2 \rightarrow 2SO_3$$

a Calculate the theoretical yield of sulfur trioxide that could be obtained from 256 tonnes of sulfur dioxide.

b The actual yield of sulfur trioxide is 202 tonnes. Calculate the percentage yield.

Exam-style question

In an experiment to make potassium chloride, the yield is 2.5 g. The theoretical yield of potassium chloride for this experiment is 4.0 g. Calculate the percentage yield of potassium chloride. *(2 marks)*

Checkpoint

How confidently can you answer the Progression questions?

Strengthen

S1 Carbon dioxide is formed when calcium carbonate reacts with hydrochloric acid. The theoretical yield for this reaction is 44 g. Calculate the percentage yield of carbon dioxide formed when the actual yield is 32 g.

S2 Describe three reasons why the actual yield is less than the theoretical yield in a reaction.

Extend

E1 Iron is extracted from iron oxide by reducing it with carbon monoxide:

$$Fe_2O_3 + 3CO \rightarrow 2Fe + 3CO_2$$

a Calculate the theoretical yield of iron that could be obtained from 320 tonnes of iron oxide.

b The actual yield of iron is 89.6 tonnes. Calculate the percentage yield.

SC14b Atom economy

Specification reference: C5.13C; C5.14C; **H** C5.15C

Progression questions

- What is meant by the atom economy of a reaction?
- How do you calculate the atom economy of a reaction?
- **H** How is data used to decide on the best way to manufacture a product?

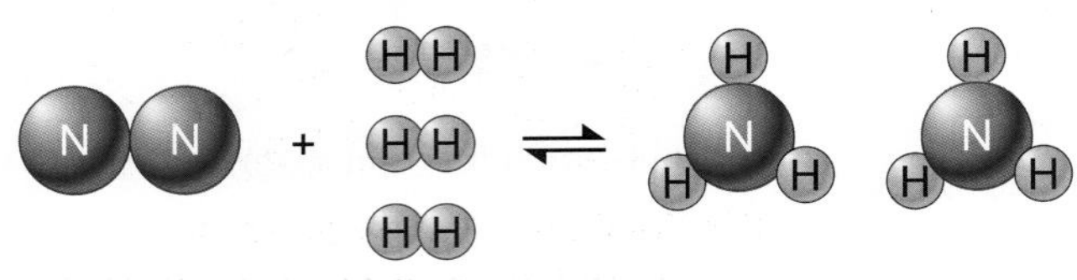

A The atom economy for making ammonia is 100%.

Atom economy is a method of showing how efficiently a particular reaction makes use of the atoms in the reactants. Many reactions form more than one product and not all of the products are useful. The atom economy shows the percentage, by mass, of useful products.

$$\text{atom economy} = \frac{\text{relative formula mass } (M_r) \text{ of the useful product}}{\text{sum of relative formula masses of all the reactants}} \times 100\%$$

Did you know?

Ibuprofen was originally made in a six-step process with an atom economy of 40%. It is now made in a three-step process with an atom economy of 77%.

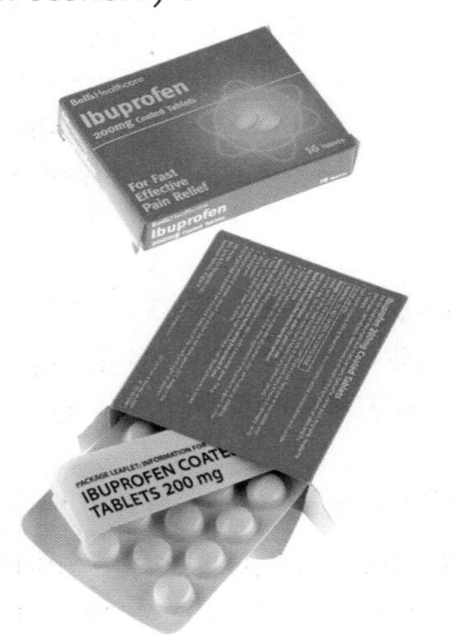

B Ibuprofen is a painkiller.

There are two ways of making ethanol, C_2H_5OH. In one method ethene, C_2H_4, is reacted with steam. All of the atoms in the reactants are present in the product, so the atom economy is 100%.

$$C_2H_4 + H_2O \rightarrow C_2H_5OH$$

1 State what is meant by the atom economy of a reaction.

2 Show that the atom economy for making ethanol from ethene is 100%.

3 The following equation shows the reaction between hydrogen and oxygen.

$$2H_2 + O_2 \rightarrow 2H_2O$$

What is the atom economy for making water in this way?

Ethanol is also produced by the fermentation of sugars, such as glucose. The atom economy of this method is much lower than making ethanol from ethene because carbon dioxide is formed as a **by-product**.

$$C_6H_{12}O_6 \rightarrow 2C_2H_5OH + 2CO_2$$

$(M_r = 180)$ $(M_r = 46)$

$$\text{atom economy for making ethanol} = \frac{2 \times 46}{180} \times 100 = 51.1\%$$

M_r of ethanol is multiplied by 2 because the equation shows that one molecule of glucose produces two molecules of ethanol.

4 Calculate the atom economy for making iron in this reaction:

$$Fe_2O_3 + 3CO \rightarrow 2Fe + 3CO_2$$

5 Zinc sulfate, $ZnSO_4$, can be made by reacting zinc carbonate with sulfuric acid:

$$ZnCO_3 + H_2SO_4 \rightarrow ZnSO_4 + H_2O + CO_2$$

Calculate the atom economy for making zinc sulfate in this way.

H Reaction pathways

Chemists often have a choice of reaction pathway to produce a substance on a large scale.

A percentage yield calculation gives no indication of the amount of waste products. A reaction can have a high percentage yield but a low atom economy, meaning that waste by-products are formed. It is better to reduce the amount of waste produced than to have to treat it later.

One way to improve the atom economy of a reaction is to find uses for the by-products of the reaction.

Chemists must consider other factors when deciding on a reaction pathway, including energy consumption, rate of reaction, raw materials and the conditions needed to produce a high yield if the reaction reaches equilibrium.

	Fermentation	Reaction of ethene with steam
raw materials	carbohydrates (e.g. from sugar cane, sugar beet, maize) – these are renewable	ethene obtained from crude oil – this is non-renewable
temperature	30–40 °C	300 °C
pressure	atmospheric pressure	high pressure (60–70 atm)
catalyst	enzymes in yeast	concentrated phosphoric acid
rate of reaction	slow	fast
purity	impure – must be fractionally distilled	pure

D comparison of two ways of making ethanol

7 a Compare the two methods of making ethanol in terms of raw materials, atom economy, energy consumption and the quality of ethanol produced.

b Brazil produces a lot of ethanol from sugar cane. Give three reasons that explain why Brazil produces ethanol from sugar cane instead of from ethene.

C In Edinburgh, Professor Martin Tangey and his team of scientists have developed a way of turning the waste products from whisky-making into butanol, for use as a biofuel.

6 Explain, in terms of waste products, whether it is better for a reaction to have a high percentage yield and a low atom economy or a low percentage yield and a high atom economy.

Exam-style question

Calculate the atom economy for making ammonia from ammonium sulfate in the following reaction:

$(NH_4)_2SO_4 + 2NaOH \rightarrow 2NH_3 + Na_2SO_4 + 2H_2O$ *(3 marks)*

Checkpoint

How confidently can you answer the Progression questions?

Strengthen

S1 Calculate the atom economy for producing hydrogen in the following reactions:

a $CO + H_2O \rightarrow CO_2 + H_2$

b $CH_4 + 2H_2O \rightarrow CO_2 + 4H_2$

Extend

E1 **H** Explain how atom economy, percentage yield and the usefulness of waste products will affect the choice of reaction pathway for manufacturing a particular product.

SC14c Concentrations

Specification reference: H C5.8C

Progression questions

- H How do you calculate the concentration of a solution in g dm^{-3}?
- H How do you calculate the concentration of a solution in mol dm^{-3}?
- H How do you convert a concentration in g dm^{-3} into mol dm^{-3} and vice versa?

A A volumetric flask is used for making an accurate solution.

A solution with an accurate concentration is made up in a **volumetric flask**. These flasks are **calibrated** to measure one volume of solution accurately, for example, 100.0 cm^3, 250.0 cm^3 or 1.00 dm^3. To make a solution, the solute is dissolved in distilled water and then made up to the graduation mark before stoppering and then shaking the flask.

It is important to measure the volume from the bottom of the meniscus and to look at it with your eyes on the same level as the graduation mark to get an accurate measurement and avoid a random error.

The concentration of a solution is the amount of solute dissolved in a stated volume of solution. The units of concentration are usually written as g dm^{-3}. 1 dm^3 is the same volume as 1 litre or 1000 cm^3.

B Fill the flask so the bottom of the meniscus is on the graduation mark.

You can calculate the concentration of a solution in g dm^{-3} using this equation:

$$\text{concentration in g dm}^{-3} = \frac{\text{mass of solute in g}}{\text{volume of solution in dm}^3}$$

If the volume of the solution is given in cm^3, convert it to dm^3 by dividing by 1000. You can use an equation triangle to help re-arrange this equation.

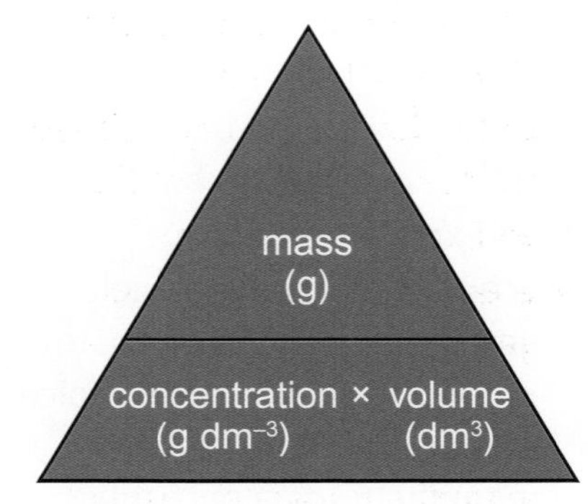

C equation triangle for working out concentration

1 Calculate the concentration, in g dm^{-3}, of the solute in these solutions:

a 15 g of sodium chloride in 3.0 dm^3 of solution

b 0.25 g of sodium hydroxide in 100 cm^3 of solution.

2 Calculate the mass of magnesium sulfate in 50 cm^3 of a solution of concentration 10 g dm^{-3}.

3 Calculate the volume of solution, in cm^3, containing 0.5 g of zinc nitrate that will have a concentration of 2.5 g dm^{-3}.

H Concentrations in mol dm^{-3}

The concentration of a solution is often given as the number of moles of solute dissolved in 1 dm^3 of solution. The unit is written as mol dm^{-3}.

You can calculate the concentration of a solution in mol dm^{-3} using this equation:

$$\text{concentration in mol dm}^{-3} = \frac{\text{number of moles of solute}}{\text{volume of solution in dm}^3}$$

4 Calculate the concentration, in mol dm^{-3}, of the solute in these solutions:

6th **a** 1.0 mol of potassium chloride in 4.0 dm^3 of solution

7th **b** 0.15 mol of copper sulfate in 250 cm^3 of solution.

7th **5** Calculate the number of moles of sodium sulfate in 100 cm^3 of a solution of concentration 0.25 mol dm^{-3}.

7th **6** Calculate the volume of solution, in cm^3, containing 0.02 mol of potassium hydroxide that will have a concentration of 0.5 mol dm^{-3}.

The two types of concentrations are related by the equation:

$$\text{concentration in mol dm}^{-3} = \frac{\text{concentration in g dm}^{-3}}{\text{relative formula mass of solute}}$$

7 Calculate the concentration, in mol dm^{-3}, of these solutions:

8th **a** sulfuric acid, H_2SO_4, of concentration 98 g dm^{-3}

8th **b** hydrochloric acid, HCl, of concentration 1.825 g dm^{-3}.

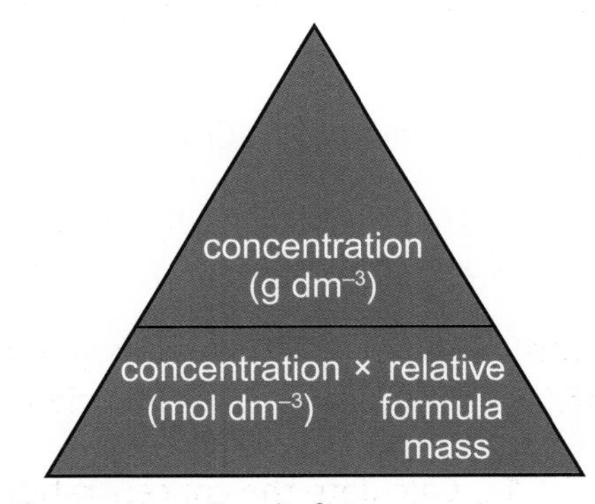

E equation triangle for converting concentrations

8 Calculate the concentration, in g dm^{-3}, of these solutions:

9th **a** sodium hydroxide, NaOH, of concentration 0.5 mol dm^{-3}

9th **b** sodium chloride, NaCl, of concentration 0.125 mol dm^{-3}.

Exam-style question

Calculate the concentration, in g dm^{-3}, of a solution of nitric acid, HNO_3, with a concentration of 0.4 mol dm^{-3}. *(2 marks)*

Did you know?

Some chemists celebrate 'Mole Day' between 6.02 am and 6.02 pm on 23 October each year.

D

Checkpoint

How confidently can you answer the Progression questions?

Strengthen

S1 A solution of sodium hydroxide, NaOH, has a concentration of 32 g dm^{-3}. Calculate the concentration of the solution in mol dm^{-3}.

S2 A solution of sodium carbonate, Na_2CO_3, has a concentration of 0.1 mol dm^{-3}. Calculate the concentration of the solution in g dm^{-3}.

Extend

E1 A student needs to make up a solution of potassium carbonate, K_2CO_3, of concentration 0.05 mol dm^{-3}. Calculate the mass of potassium carbonate needed to make up 250 cm^3 of this solution.

E2 A solution of hydrochloric acid has a concentration of 0.1 mol dm^{-3}. Calculate the number of moles of HCl in a 25.0 cm^3 portion of this solution.

SC14d Titrations and calculations

Specification reference: C5.9C; H C5.10C

Progression questions

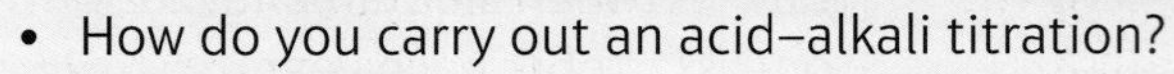

- How do you carry out an acid–alkali titration?
- H How do you calculate the number of moles of solute in a given volume of solution?
- H How do you calculate the concentration of a solution using the results of an acid–alkali titration?

1 25.0 cm^3 of sodium hydroxide solution was placed in a conical flask with a few drops of methyl orange. It was titrated with hydrochloric acid. State the indicator colour change at the end-point.

Acid–alkali titrations are used to find the exact volume of an acid that neutralises a specified volume of an alkali or vice versa. Acids and alkalis are colourless so we use indicators. The apparatus is shown in *SC14d Core practical.*

H

The concentration of one of the solutions in a titration can be calculated if the concentration of the other solution is known.

$$\text{concentration in mol dm}^{-3} = \frac{\text{number of moles of solute}}{\text{volume of solution in dm}^3}$$

The **mole ratio** is the ratio in moles of the substances in a balanced equation.

Did you know?

Titrations have many uses including: testing water samples, and analysing foodstuffs and drugs.

2 Sulfuric acid, H_2SO_4, reacts with a solution of potassium hydroxide, KOH. Write the balanced equation for this reaction.

3 25.0 cm^3 of potassium hydroxide solution was neutralised by 35.0 cm^3 of 0.750 mol dm^{-3} dilute hydrochloric acid. Calculate the concentration, in mol dm^{-3}, of the potassium hydroxide solution used.

$$HCl + KOH \rightarrow KCl + H_2O$$

Worked example W1

25.0 cm^3 of sodium hydroxide solution was titrated against 0.100 mol dm^{-3} hydrochloric acid. An average of 20.0 cm^3 of the acid neutralised the alkali. Calculate the concentration of the sodium hydroxide solution.

$HCl + NaOH \rightarrow NaCl + H_2O$ mole ratio HCl : NaOH = 1 : 1

Step 1: calculate the number of moles of the solution of known volume and concentration.

number of moles of HCl = concentration of HCl (mol dm^{-3}) × volume used (dm^3)

$$= 0.100 \times \frac{20.0}{1000} = 0.00200 \text{ mol}$$

Step 2: use the balanced equation to work out the number of moles of alkali that reacted.

1 mol of HCl reacts with 1 mol of NaOH, so 0.00200 mol of HCl reacts with 0.00200 mol of NaOH.

Step 3: calculate the concentration of the sodium hydroxide solution.

$$\text{concentration of NaOH in mol dm}^{-3} = \frac{\text{number of moles of NaOH}}{\text{volume of NaOH solution in dm}^3}$$

$$\text{volume of NaOH solution} = \frac{25.0}{1000} = 0.0250 \text{ dm}^3$$

$$\text{concentration of NaOH} = \frac{0.00200}{0.0250} = 0.0800 \text{ mol dm}^{-3}$$

H

These types of calculations can also be used to calculate the volume of one solution that will react with a given volume of another. You need to know the concentrations of both solutions and the balanced equation.

Worked example W2

25.0 cm³ of 0.200 mol dm⁻³ sodium hydroxide solution was neutralised by 0.150 mol dm⁻³ sulfuric acid. Calculate the volume of sulfuric acid needed for the neutralisation.

$2NaOH + H_2SO_4 \rightarrow Na_2SO_4 + 2H_2O$ mole ratio $NaOH : H_2SO_4 = 2 : 1$

Step 1: calculate the number of moles of the solution of known volume and concentration.

$$\text{number of moles of NaOH} = \underset{(\text{mol dm}^{-3})}{\text{concentration of NaOH}} \times \underset{(\text{dm}^3)}{\text{volume used}}$$

$$= 0.200 \times \frac{25.0}{1000} = 0.00500\ \text{mol}$$

Step 2: use the balanced equation and mole ratio to work out the number of moles of acid that reacted.

2 mol of NaOH reacts with 1 mol of H_2SO_4,

so 0.00500 mol of NaOH reacts with $\frac{0.00500}{2} = 0.00250$ mol of H_2SO_4

Step 3: calculate the volume of sulfuric acid needed.

$$\text{volume in dm}^3 = \frac{\text{number of moles of acid}}{\text{concentration in mol dm}^{-3}}$$

$$= \frac{0.00250}{0.150} = 0.0167\ \text{dm}^3 \text{ or } 16.7\ \text{cm}^3$$

Round the final answer to the same number of significant figures as used in the question.

4 10.0 cm³ of 0.140 mol dm⁻³ sodium hydroxide solution was neutralised by 12.3 cm³ of nitric acid. Calculate the concentration, in mol dm⁻³, of the nitric acid.

$HNO_3 + NaOH \rightarrow NaNO_3 + H_2O$

5 25.0 cm³ of 0.275 mol dm⁻³ potassium hydroxide solution was neutralised by 0.166 mol dm⁻³ nitric acid. Calculate the volume of nitric acid, in cm³, needed to neutralise the potassium hydroxide solution.

$HNO_3 + KOH \rightarrow KNO_3 + H_2O$

6 10.0 cm³ of 0.095 mol dm⁻³ sodium carbonate solution was neutralised by 0.15 mol dm⁻³ hydrochloric acid. Calculate the volume of hydrochloric acid, in cm³, needed.

$Na_2CO_3 + 2HCl \rightarrow 2NaCl + H_2O + CO_2$

Exam-style question

25.0 cm³ of potassium hydroxide solution reacted with 23.3 cm³ of 0.100 mol dm⁻³ hydrochloric acid. Calculate the concentration of this potassium hydroxide solution in mol dm⁻³.

$HCl + KOH \rightarrow KCl + H_2O$ *(3 marks)*

Checkpoint

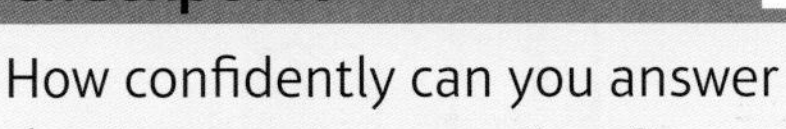

How confidently can you answer the Progression questions?

Strengthen

S1 Describe how to carry out a titration to find the exact volume of hydrochloric acid needed to neutralise 25.0 cm³ of a sodium hydroxide solution.

Extend

E1 **H** 25.0 cm³ of sodium carbonate solution was neutralised by 22.6 cm³ of 0.100 mol dm⁻³ hydrochloric acid. Calculate the concentration of the sodium carbonate solution in g dm⁻³.

$Na_2CO_3 + 2HCl \rightarrow 2NaCl + H_2O + CO_2$

SC14d Core practical – Acid–alkali titration

Specification reference: C5.9C

Aim 

Carry out an accurate acid–alkali titration, using a burette, a pipette and a suitable indicator. 

A a titration experiment

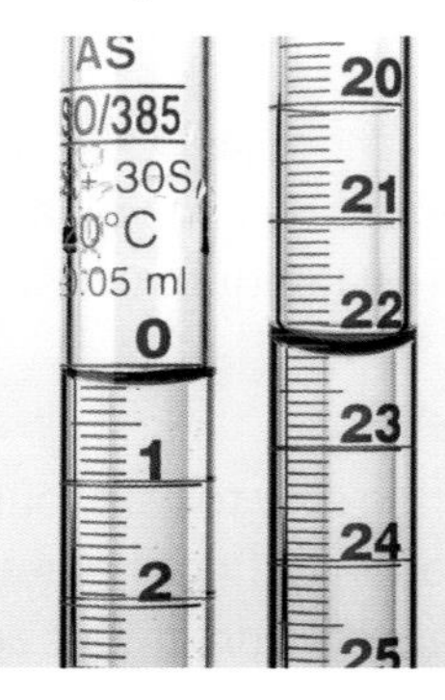

B The initial volume of solution in the burette is 0.20 cm^3 and the final burette reading is 22.20 cm^3.

C Methyl orange indicator is yellow in alkalis, peachy-orange in neutral solutions and pink in acids.

Titrations are used to find the exact volume of one solution that reacts with a fixed volume of another solution. The fixed volume of solution, often 25.0 cm^3, is measured in a pipette and the other solution is contained in a burette as these pieces of apparatus give accurate measurements. A burette has a fine scale, which gives it a good resolution. It can be read to the nearest half division, that is to ± 0.05 cm^3. Remember that the measuring instruments are calibrated for readings taken from the *bottom* of the meniscus.

The result of an acid–alkali titration can be used to prepare a soluble salt or to calculate the concentration of a solution.

Your task 

You will carry out a titration to find the exact volume of hydrochloric acid needed to neutralise 25.0 cm^3 of a solution of sodium hydroxide.

Method  

Wear eye protection. Avoid skin contact with the liquids.

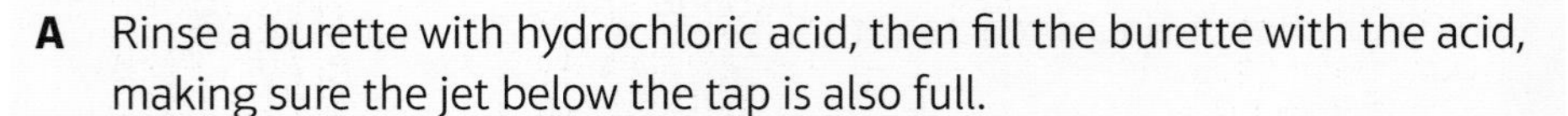

A Rinse a burette with hydrochloric acid, then fill the burette with the acid, making sure the jet below the tap is also full.

B Record the initial volume of acid in the burette.

C Rinse a pipette with sodium hydroxide solution, then fill the pipette to the 25.0 cm^3 mark and empty the solution into a conical flask.

D Add a few drops of methyl orange indicator to the flask and place the flask on a white tile under the burette.

E Add the acid to the sodium hydroxide solution while swirling the flask.

F When the indicator starts to change colour, rinse the tip of the burette and the sides of the flask with a small amount of distilled water from a wash bottle to ensure that all the acid is in the mixture, then add the acid drop by drop until the end-point is reached.

G Record the final volume of acid in the burette.

H Repeat the experiment, apart from the initial rinsing of the burette and pipette, until concordant results are obtained.

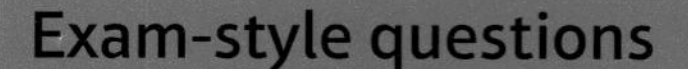

Exam-style questions

1 State a safety precaution to take in this practical and the reason for it. *(1 mark)*

2 Give a reason why the burette and pipette should be rinsed before they are filled. *(1 mark)*

3 State what you should do after filling the burette with acid and before taking the initial reading. *(1 mark)*

4 Give a reason for standing the conical flask on a white tile. *(1 mark)*

5 Suggest a reason why universal indicator is not suitable for a titration. *(1 mark)*

6 State what is meant by the 'end-point' of the titration. *(1 mark)*

7 State the colour change that would be seen at the end-point in this titration using methyl orange indicator. *(2 marks)*

8 State what is meant by 'concordant results'. *(1 mark)*

9 25.0 cm^3 of sodium hydroxide solution was titrated with dilute hydrochloric acid:

$HCl + NaOH \rightarrow NaCl + H_2O$

The following results were obtained.

	Titration 1	Titration 2	Titration 3
final burette reading (cm^3)	26.00	26.30	27.20
initial burette reading (cm^3)	0.00	1.20	1.90
volume of acid used (cm^3)	26.00	25.10	

a Calculate the volume of acid used in titration 3. *(1 mark)*

b Calculate the volume of acid that should be used to react with 25.0 cm^3 of the sodium hydroxide solution to produce the salt sodium chloride. Give a reason for your answer. *(2 marks)*

c Describe how you would use the volume calculated in **b** to obtain pure, dry crystals of sodium chloride. *(3 marks)*

d **H** The sodium hydroxide solution had a concentration of 0.100 mol dm^{-3}. Calculate the concentration, in mol dm^{-3}, of the hydrochloric acid used in this experiment. *(3 marks)*

10 **H** Give a reason for using a burette, rather than a measuring cylinder, for measuring the volume of hydrochloric acid.

11 **H** A student carried out a titration experiment following the method given, but measured the volumes of the solutions in the burette and the pipette from the top of the meniscus instead of the bottom. Explain how this error will affect the volumes measured, if at all. *(3 marks)*

SC14e Molar volume of gases

Specification reference: H C5.16C; H C5.17C; H C5.18C

Progression questions

- H What is Avogadro's law?
- H What is the molar volume of a gas?
- H How do you calculate the volume of a gas, and the mass of a solid, involved in a chemical reaction?

H

A In 1914, one way to manufacture hydrogen was the reaction between silicon and hot, concentrated sodium hydroxide solution.

Avogadro's law

The volume occupied by a sample of a gas depends on the temperature, pressure and number of particles of gas. The volume of a gas does *not* depend on its relative formula mass, M_r. Remember that the mean distance between gas particles is very large compared to the size of the particles.

Avogadro's law states that, if the temperature and pressure are the same, equal volumes of different gases contain an equal number of molecules. This lets you calculate the volumes of gases involved in a reaction. For example, nitrogen and hydrogen react together to form ammonia:

$$N_2(g) + 3H_2(g) \rightarrow 2NH_3(g)$$

The ratio of nitrogen to ammonia is 1:2. So 100 cm³ of nitrogen will produce 200 cm³ of ammonia, at the same temperature and pressure, if it reacts completely with hydrogen.

1 State two assumptions needed when using Avogadro's law in calculations.

2 Calculate the volume of hydrogen that will react completely with 100 cm³ of nitrogen.

Molar gas volume

The **molar gas volume** is the volume occupied by one mole of molecules of any gas. It is 24 dm³ or 24 000 cm³ at room temperature and pressure (rtp):

volume of gas = amount of gas (mol) × molar volume

For example, 0.5 mol of carbon dioxide occupies 0.5 × 24 = 12 dm³ at rtp.

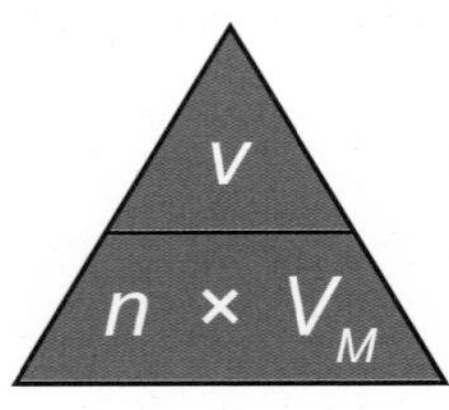

B n = amount in mol, v = volume of gas, V_m = molar volume

3 Calculate the volume, in cm³, occupied by 0.1 mol of oxygen at rtp.

If you know the volume of a gas at rtp, you can calculate its amount:

$$\text{amount of gas (mol)} = \frac{\text{volume of gas}}{\text{molar volume}}$$

For example, 96 cm³ of hydrogen contains $\frac{96}{24\,000} = 4.0 \times 10^{-3}$ mol of hydrogen molecules.

You can use calculations like these to calculate the masses of solids and volumes of gases in chemical reactions.

4 Calculate the amount of chlorine molecules, in mol, in 16 dm³ of chlorine. Give your answer to 2 significant figures.

H

Worked examples

1 Sodium reacts with chlorine to form sodium chloride:

$2Na(s) + Cl_2(g) \rightarrow 2NaCl(s)$

a Calculate the minimum volume at rtp, in dm^3, of chlorine needed to react completely with 0.92 g of sodium.

amount of sodium $= \frac{0.92}{23} = 0.040$ mol

From the balanced equation, 2 mol of Na reacts with 1 mol of Cl_2

So 0.040 mol of Na reacts with $\frac{0.040}{2} = 0.020$ mol of Cl_2

volume of $Cl_2 = 0.020 \times 24 = 0.48\ dm^3$

b Calculate the maximum mass of sodium chloride that can be made from 960 cm^3 of chlorine at rtp and an excess of sodium.

amount of chlorine $= \frac{960}{24\,000} = 0.040$ mol

From the balanced equation, 1 mol of Cl_2 produces 2 mol of NaCl

So 0.040 mol of Cl_2 produces $2 \times 0.040 = 0.080$ mol of NaCl

mass of NaCl $= 0.080 \times 58.5 = 4.68$ g (4.7 g to 2 significant figures)

2 Copper carbonate decomposes when heated:

$CuCO_3(s) \rightarrow CuO(s) + CO_2(g)$

Calculate the minimum mass of copper carbonate needed to produce 1.44 dm^3 of carbon dioxide at rtp.

amount of carbon dioxide $= \frac{1.44}{24} = 0.060$ mol

From the balanced equation, 1 mol of CO_2 is made from 1 mol of $CuCO_3$

So 0.060 mol of CO_2 needs $1 \times 0.060 = 0.060$ mol of $CuCO_3$

mass of $CuCO_3 = 0.060 \times 123.5 = 7.41$ g (7.4 g to 2 significant figures)

Exam-style question

Silicon reacts with hot, concentrated sodium hydroxide solution to produce sodium silicate and hydrogen:

$Si(s) + 4NaOH(aq) \rightarrow Na_4SiO_4(s) + 2H_2(g)$

Calculate the minimum mass of silicon needed to produce 1000 dm^3 of hydrogen at rtp. *(2 marks)*

C Hot sodium burns in chlorine with a yellow flame, producing sodium chloride.

5 Sodium reacts with water to produce sodium hydroxide and hydrogen:

$2Na(s) + 2H_2O(l) \rightarrow 2NaOH(aq) + H_2(g)$

a Calculate the maximum volume at rtp, in dm^3, of hydrogen that can be produced from 4.6 g of sodium.

b Calculate the minimum mass of water needed to produce 0.36 dm^3 of hydrogen at rtp.

Checkpoint

How confidently can you answer the Progression questions?

Strengthen

S1 How do you calculate the volumes of gases involved in chemical reactions?

Extend

E1 Flying in the 1930s, the *Hindenburg* was the largest ever airship. Calculate the mass of zinc that would be needed, when reacted with excess sulfuric acid, to produce the 200 000 m^3 of hydrogen it contained.

SC15a Fertilisers and the Haber process

Specification reference: C5.19C; C5.22C; C5.23C; C5.24C

Progression questions

- What are fertilisers?
- What are the similarities and differences between making a fertiliser in a laboratory and in a factory?
- How is the Haber process used in the manufacture of ammonium nitrate?

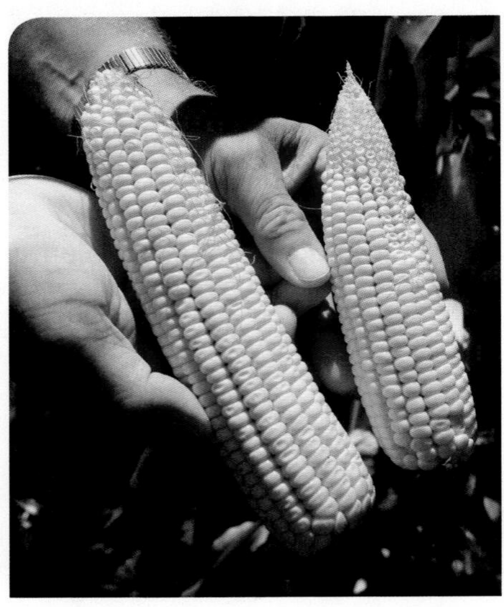

A The corn cob on the left has been grown using a nitrogen-rich fertiliser, while the one on the right has not.

Did you know?

The annual world production of ammonia by the Haber process is around 175 million tonnes (about 24 kg per person per year). About 85% of this is used to make nitrogenous fertilisers.

2 State and explain the type of reaction involved in making:

a ammonium nitrate

b nitric acid.

Plants absorb water and mineral ions through their root hair cells. This gradually reduces the concentration of mineral ions in the soil. Plants may then not grow properly and may suffer from deficiency diseases, such as stunted shoots and discoloured leaves.

Fertilisers replace the mineral ions needed by plants and so promote plant growth. Nitrogen, phosphorus and potassium (N, P and K) are important elements, but fertilisers must provide them as soluble compounds because root hair cells only absorb mineral ions that are dissolved in water.

1 Explain why potassium nitrate, KNO_3, and ammonium phosphate, $(NH_4)_3PO_4$, are suitable compounds to use in fertilisers.

Ammonium nitrate

Nitrogenous fertilisers are a source of soluble nitrogen compounds. Ammonium nitrate is one such nitrogen-rich fertiliser. Ammonium nitrate is a salt manufactured by reacting ammonia solution with dilute nitric acid:

ammonia + nitric acid → ammonium nitrate

$$NH_3(aq) + HNO_3(aq) \rightarrow NH_4NO_3(aq)$$

Ammonia is manufactured by the Haber process, in which nitrogen and hydrogen react together in a **reversible reaction** (see *SC12a Dynamic equilibrium*).

Nitric acid is manufactured from ammonia in stages. Overall, the reaction may be represented as:

ammonia + oxygen → nitric acid + water

$$NH_3(g) + 2O_2(g) \rightarrow HNO_3(aq) + H_2O(l)$$

Ammonium sulfate

Ammonium sulfate is also a nitrogenous fertiliser. It is made in the laboratory by reacting ammonia solution with dilute sulfuric acid:

ammonia + sulfuric acid → ammonium sulfate

$$2NH_3(aq) + H_2SO_4(aq) \rightarrow (NH_4)_2SO_4(aq)$$

Preparing ammonium sulfate in the laboratory is very different from its industrial production. Table B shows some differences.

	Laboratory preparation	Industrial production
scale of production	small scale	large scale
starting materials	ammonia solution and dilute sulfuric acid	raw materials for making ammonia and sulfuric acid
stages	titration (see *SC8 Acids and Alkalis*), then crystallisation	several stages
type of process	batch	continuous

B some features of making ammonium sulfate in the laboratory or industrially

For the laboratory preparation of ammonium sulfate, ammonia solution and dilute sulfuric acid are bought from chemical manufacturers. For industrial production, these substances are often made on-site from their raw materials (see diagram C).

C flow chart for the industrial production of ammonium sulfate

3 Use diagram C to name the raw materials needed to make sulfuric acid and ammonia in industry.

4 One of the stages in the manufacture of sulfuric acid is a reversible reaction. Sulfur dioxide, SO_2, reacts with oxygen from the air to produce sulfur trioxide, SO_3. Write a balanced equation, including state symbols, for this reaction.

The laboratory preparation of ammonium sulfate is a **batch process**. A small amount is made, the apparatus is cleaned, and then another small amount is made. Industrial preparation is a **continuous process**, in which reactants are constantly fed into the reactors and products are removed. The process is stopped only rarely to maintain and clean the equipment. Batch processes are difficult to automate. However, continuous processes are usually automated, so they need fewer people to make a given amount of product.

5 The rate at which each reactant is fed into the reactor in a continuous process must be carefully controlled. Suggest reasons that explain this.

6 Describe two advantages of a continuous process compared to a batch process.

Exam-style question

Suggest reasons that explain why farmers may apply 'NPK' fertilisers to their fields. *(2 marks)*

Checkpoint

How confidently can you answer the Progression questions?

Strengthen

S1 How are nitrogenous fertilisers made in the laboratory?

S2 How are nitrogenous fertilisers made on an industrial scale?

Extend

E1 Compare the advantages and disadvantages of ammonia and ammonium sulfate as nitrogenous fertilisers.

SC15b Factors affecting equilibrium

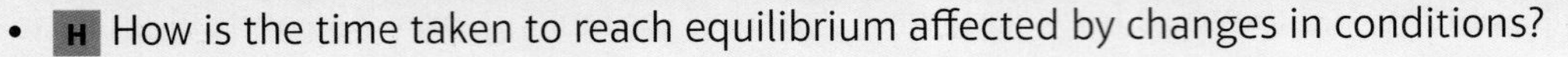
Specification reference: H C5.15C; H C5.20C; H C5.21C

Progression questions

- H How is the time taken to reach equilibrium affected by changes in conditions?
- H How are conditions chosen for industrial chemical reactions?
- H How are reaction pathways chosen for industrial processes?

H

A Nitric acid is made using nitrogen monoxide, produced from nitrogen and oxygen in an endothermic reaction. Nitrogen monoxide is made during thunderstorms because lightning causes the very high temperatures needed to move the equilibrium position in the direction of the endothermic reaction.

1 Compare the effect of catalysts on equilibria with the effects of changing temperature, pressure or concentration.

2 Why might an industrial reaction *not* be allowed to reach equilibrium?

Reversible reactions may reach equilibrium (see *SC12a Dynamic equilibrium*). This only happens when they are in a **closed system**, such as a stoppered flask, in which no substances can enter or leave.

In a **dynamic equilibrium**:

- the forward and backward reactions still happen, and at the same rate
- the concentrations of all reacting substances do not change.

The position of a dynamic equilibrium, and how quickly equilibrium is reached, are affected by changes in conditions (see table B).

Change in conditions	Position of equilibrium	Time taken to reach equilibrium
temperature increased	moves in the direction of the endothermic reaction	decreases
pressure increased in a reaction involving gases	moves towards the side of the balanced equation with the fewer molecules of reacting gas	decreases
concentration of a reacting substance increased	moves away from the reacting substance in the balanced equation	decreases
catalyst added	no change	decreases

B effects of reaction conditions on dynamic equilibria

Equilibria and industrial processes

Chemical manufacturers must make a profit. They choose reaction conditions to produce an acceptable product **yield** in an acceptable time. This may mean that reactions are not allowed to reach equilibrium – it is not profitable to achieve equilibrium if it takes years. In addition, choosing conditions that give a high rate of reaction is not worthwhile if they are too expensive.

In the Haber process, nitrogen and hydrogen react together to produce ammonia:

$$N_2(g) + 3H_2(g) \rightleftharpoons 2NH_3(g)$$

There are fewer molecules of reacting gas on the right-hand side of the equation. As the pressure is increased, the position of equilibrium moves to the right.

H

High pressures increase the equilibrium yield of ammonia *and* increase the rate of reaction. The pressure chosen, 200 atmospheres, is a compromise because very high pressures are too expensive to maintain.

The forward reaction is exothermic, so the backward reaction is endothermic. As the temperature is increased, the position of equilibrium moves to the left (in the direction of the endothermic reaction). Low temperatures increase the equilibrium yield of ammonia but reduce the rate of reaction. The temperature chosen, 450 °C, is a compromise that gives an acceptable yield of ammonia in an acceptable time.

An iron catalyst is used because, although it does not change the position of equilibrium, it *does* increase the rate of reaction.

3 Explain why the Haber process does not use very high pressures or low temperatures.

Choosing reaction pathways

There is usually more than one way to make a product. A particular **reaction pathway** is chosen by taking into account factors such as:

- availability and cost of raw materials and energy supplies
- the rate of reaction and the equilibrium position
- atom economy, yield and usefulness of **by-products** (see *SC14b Atom economy*).

In the past, nitric acid, HNO_3, was made using the Birkeland–Eyde process. This imitated the effect of lightning (photo A). A high-voltage electric arc was created between two electrodes. Nitrogen and oxygen in the air reacted to form nitrogen monoxide, NO. This further reacted with oxygen to form nitrogen dioxide, NO_2, which was then dissolved in water to form nitric acid. The process used huge amounts of electricity and the **yield** of nitrogen monoxide was only around 4%. Today, nitric acid is made from ammonia using the Ostwald process (diagram C).

Stage 1
ammonia + oxygen ⇌ nitrogen monoxide + water
$4NH_3(g) + 5O_2(g) \rightleftharpoons 4NO(g) + 6H_2O(g)$
(forward reaction is exothermic)

↓

Stage 2
nitrogen monoxide + oxygen ⇌ nitrogen dioxide
$2NO(g) + O_2(g) \rightleftharpoons 2NO_2(g)$
(forward reaction is exothermic)

↓

Stage 3
nitrogen dioxide + oxygen + water → nitric acid
$4NO_2(g) + O_2(g) + 2H_2O(l) \rightarrow 4HNO_3(aq)$

C Flow chart for the industrial production of nitric acid using the Ostwald process. Stage 1 is carried out at around 220 °C and 4 atmospheres of pressure with hot platinum as the catalyst. Under these conditions, the yield of nitrogen monoxide is around 95%. The reactions are so exothermic that the gases must be cooled.

4 Compare stages 2 and 3 of the Ostwald process with the Birkeland–Eyde process for making nitric acid.

5 Compare and contrast stage 1 of the Ostwald process with the Birkeland–Eyde process.

6 Explain the reaction conditions chosen for stage 1 of the Ostwald process.

Exam-style question

Stage 2 of the Ostwald process happens at about 50 °C (see diagram C). State and explain what this shows about the rate of the reaction at stage 2. *(2 marks)*

Checkpoint

How confidently can you answer the Progression questions?

Strengthen

S1 How does the time taken for a reversible reaction to reach equilibrium depend upon the reaction conditions?

S2 How are the reaction conditions chosen for industrial processes?

Extend

E1 Evaluate the use of high temperatures and pressures for industrial reactions.

SC16a Chemical cells and fuel cells

Specification reference: C5.25C; C5.26C; C5.27C

Progression questions

- Why do batteries go 'flat'?
- What happens in a hydrogen–oxygen fuel cell?
- What are the strengths and weaknesses of fuel cells?

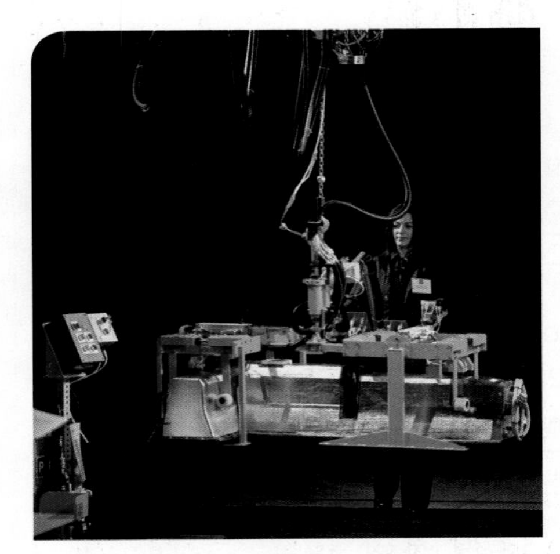

A This lithium ion battery pack is being moved into position, ready to fit into an electric car.

The everyday batteries used in mobile phones and torches are **chemical cells**. A simple chemical cell has these components:

- two different metals, each dipped into a solution of one of their salts
- a 'salt bridge' to allow dissolved ions to pass from one solution to the other.

A voltage (potential difference) is produced between the two metals. In general, the further apart in the reactivity series the two metals are, the greater the voltage. A current flows if the cell is connected to an external circuit. Photo B shows a simple chemical cell, invented in 1836 by John Daniell (1790–1845). The salt bridge is filter paper soaked with concentrated potassium nitrate solution.

B This Daniell cell is connected to a voltmeter, which measures its voltage.

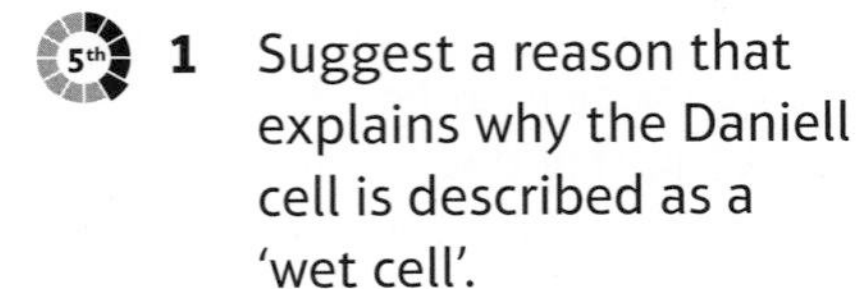

1 Suggest a reason that explains why the Daniell cell is described as a 'wet cell'.

The overall reaction that happens in a Daniell cell is:

zinc + copper sulfate → zinc sulfate + copper

$Zn(s) + CuSO_4(aq) \rightarrow ZnSO_4(aq) + Cu(s)$

This is an exothermic reaction, but the energy is transferred mainly by electricity rather than by heating. When one of the reactants is used up, the reaction stops and a voltage is no longer produced. This is why household batteries go 'flat', and why electric cars need recharging after a journey.

2 Explain what happens to the mass of each metal when a Daniell cell is in use.

Most modern batteries are 'dry cells' containing various reactants. Their solutions are mixed with a powder to make a paste.

Fuel cells

Chemical cells store all their reactants, but **fuel cells** are supplied with fuel and oxygen from outside. No burning takes place inside fuel cells, just like in chemical cells. Fuel cells do not go 'flat' – they produce a voltage for as long as reactants are supplied. Hydrogen–oxygen fuel cells use hydrogen and oxygen, and water is the only product. Diagram C shows what happens.

3 Write a balanced equation for the overall reaction in a hydrogen–oxygen fuel cell.

At the left-hand electrode, hydrogen atoms lose electrons and form hydrogen ions:

$$2H_2(g) \rightarrow 4H^+(aq) + 4e^-$$

Electrons flow through the external circuit to the positive electrode. Hydrogen ions pass through a membrane to the right-hand electrode, where they gain electrons and react with oxygen:

$$4H^+(aq) + 4e^- + O_2(g) \rightarrow 2H_2O(g)$$

4 Explain whether hydrogen is oxidised or reduced at the left-hand electrode.

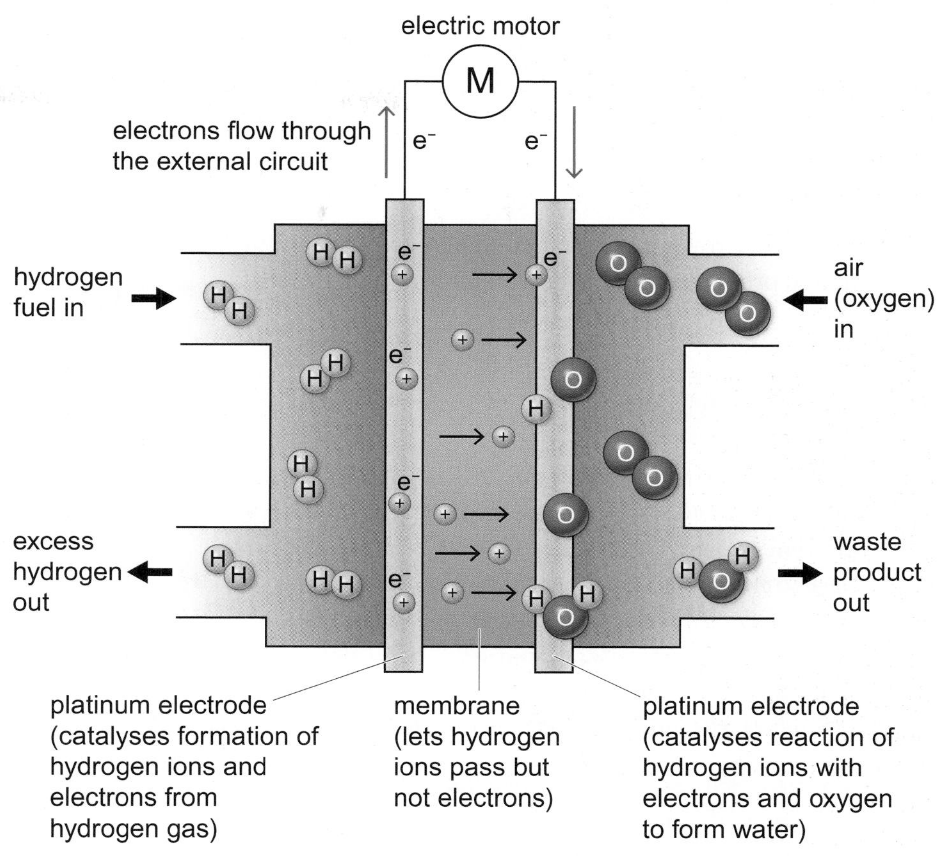

C a hydrogen–oxygen fuel cell with an electric motor in the external circuit

A hydrogen–oxygen fuel cell and electric motor are much quieter and need less maintenance than a petrol or diesel engine, but the hydrogen still needs to be stored in a tank.

Hydrogen–oxygen fuel cells do not produce carbon dioxide (a **greenhouse gas**). However, most hydrogen is manufactured by the reaction of steam with coal or natural gas. These processes do release carbon dioxide as a **by-product**.

5 Explain why a hydrogen–oxygen fuel cell car may cause the release of greenhouse gases.

6 In 2015, there were several thousand filling stations in the UK supplying petrol and diesel, but only four supplying hydrogen to the public. Explain why this limits the appeal of hydrogen–oxygen fuel cell cars, even though their range is similar to that of conventional cars.

Exam-style question

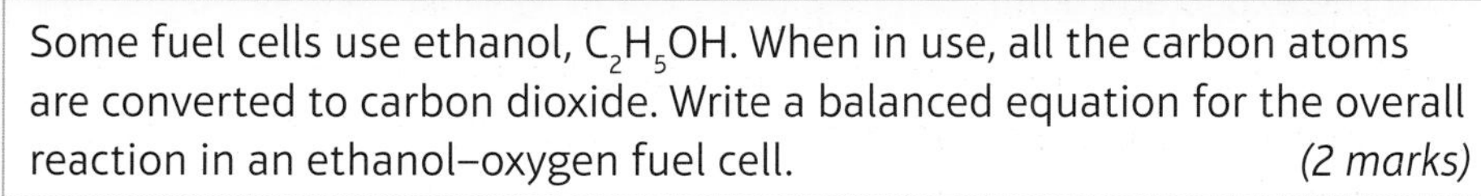

Some fuel cells use ethanol, C_2H_5OH. When in use, all the carbon atoms are converted to carbon dioxide. Write a balanced equation for the overall reaction in an ethanol–oxygen fuel cell. *(2 marks)*

Checkpoint

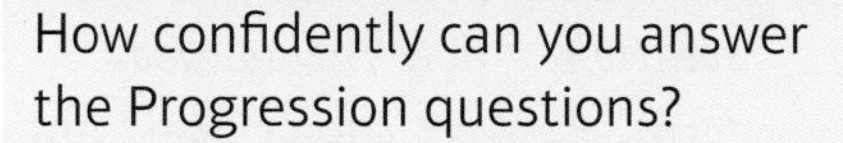

How confidently can you answer the Progression questions?

Strengthen

S1 How are chemical reactions used to produce electricity?

S2 What are the strengths and weaknesses of using a hydrogen–oxygen fuel cell to power a car's electric motor?

Extend

E1 Suggest reasons that explain why hydrogen–oxygen fuel cells *and* solar cells are used to produce electricity for the International Space Station.

Making a fertiliser

Ammonium sulfate is useful as a fertiliser. Ammonium sulfate solution can be prepared in the laboratory using dilute ammonia solution and dilute sulfuric acid.

Describe a titration experiment to prepare ammonium sulfate solution using 25.0 cm^3 of dilute ammonia solution, then to produce pure, dry crystals from this solution. **(6 marks)**

Student answer

Clamp a burette vertically and fill it with dilute sulfuric acid. Run out enough acid to remove any air from the tip. Record the burette reading from the bottom of the meniscus. Use a pipette with a pipette filler to transfer 25.0 cm^3 of the ammonia solution to a conical flask, and add a few drops of phenolphthalein indicator [1]. *Place the conical flask on a white tile underneath the burette.*

Add acid from the burette, swirling the flask gently. Add the acid drop by drop near the end-point until the indicator just changes from pink to colourless [2]. *Record the burette reading and calculate the titre (end reading minus start reading). Add the titre volume of acid to 25.0 cm^3 of ammonia solution, but this time without the indicator* [3].

Pour the mixture into an evaporating basin and heat over a boiling water bath to produce a concentrated solution. Allow the solution to cool and crystals to form. Remove the crystals and dry them in a warm oven [4].

[1] This is a good answer as it names a specific indicator (though methyl orange indicator would be a much better choice because it is more suited to titrations with strong acids and weak alkalis like ammonia solution).

[2] This is an important step to obtain an accurate titre and so it is important to include it in the answer. The answer could also describe washing the insides of the flask with distilled water near to the end-point.

[3] It would be better to carry out the experiment more than once to obtain concordant results (identical or very similar titres).

[4] The answer includes how to produce pure, dry crystals from the ammonium sulfate solution – a part of the answer that would be easy to forget to write.

Verdict

This is a strong answer. It shows good knowledge and understanding of how to carry out a titration and how to use crystallisation to produce pure, dry crystals. The answer describes the steps needed in a logical order. It gives practical details including the expected colour change at the end-point of the titration, and apparatus needed for safe working such as a pipette filler.

Exam tip

The specification contains a list of practicals that you should have covered in lessons. Make sure you have revised the practicals and can name the pieces of apparatus involved.

Paper 2

SC17 Groups in the Periodic Table / SC18 Rates of Reaction / SC19 Heat Energy Changes in Chemical Reactions

This light show, on the beaches of the Maldives, is generated by bioluminescent chemical reactions in tiny microorganisms called phytoplankton. Almost all of the energy transferred by the reaction is transferred by light, making it very efficient and of interest to scientists developing lighting systems that waste less energy. Understanding how chemical reactions occur and the energy transfers involved is fundamental to understanding our material world and the processes of life. This unit looks at some typical reactions of certain elements and general ideas about how chemical reactions can be controlled and used.

The learning journey

Previously you will have learnt at KS3:

- about elements, compounds and the periodic table
- what happens during chemical reactions.

You will also have learnt in *SC3 Atomic Structure, SC5 Ionic Bonding* and *SC8 Acids and Alkalis:*

- about the nature of atoms and ions
- how to write balanced chemical equations, including the state symbols.

In this unit you will learn:

- about the properties and reactions of the elements in groups 1, 7 and 0.
- how changes in conditions can affect the rates of reactions
- about the energy transfers that can occur during chemical reactions.

SC17a Group 1

Specification reference: C6.1; C6.2; C6.3; C6.4; C6.5

Progression questions

- What are the main properties of alkali metals?
- How do alkali metals react with water?
- Why do alkali metals have different reactivities?

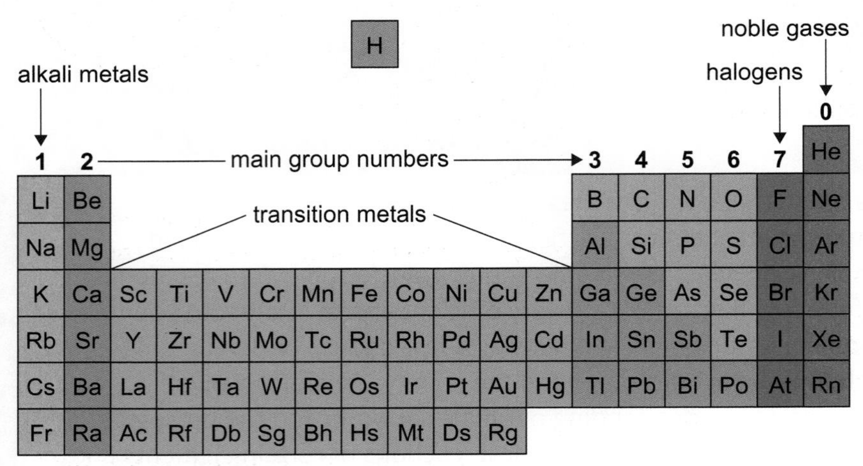

A Groups 1, 7 and 0 in the periodic table have special names.

The **periodic table** is arranged so that elements in the same vertical column or **group** have similar chemical and physical properties, and show trends in those properties.

The **alkali metals**, in group 1, have similar physical properties to other metals – they are all malleable and conduct electricity. However, they also have properties that are specific to this group. All alkali metals have relatively low melting points, are soft and easily cut. Alkali metals are also very reactive and readily form compounds with non-metals.

All alkali metals are easily oxidised and burn brightly in air. For example, the reaction of potassium with oxygen can be shown as:

$$4K(s) + O_2(g) \rightarrow 2K_2O(s)$$

potassium + oxygen → potassium oxide

The reactions of three alkali metals with water are described in table B. In each reaction, a metal hydroxide (an alkali) and hydrogen gas are the products. The **reactivity** of the alkali metals increases down the group.

$$2Li(s) + 2H_2O(l) \rightarrow 2LiOH(aq) + H_2(g)$$

lithium + water → lithium hydroxide + hydrogen

reactivity (increases down the table)

lithium + water	bubbles fiercely on the surface
sodium + water	melts into a ball and fizzes about the surface
potassium + water	bursts into flames and flies about the surface

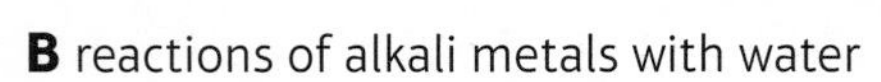

B reactions of alkali metals with water

1 Why are potassium and sodium placed in the same group of the periodic table?

2 Describe two physical properties of alkali metals that make them different from other metals.

3 Write word equations for the reactions of sodium with:

a oxygen

b water.

4 Caesium (Cs) is below potassium in the periodic table. Suggest how caesium might react with water.

Did you know?

Francium, discovered in 1939, was the last element to be discovered in nature. It is radioactive and extremely rare. Scientists think that only 20–30 g of francium exists on Earth at any one time.

To explain the trend in reactivity we need to look at the electronic configurations of alkali metal atoms. These atoms have one electron in their outer shells. When they react with non-metal atoms, the outer electrons are transferred from the metal to the non-metal. Diagram D shows an example. Each sodium atom loses its outer electron to form a positive (1+) ion, and each oxygen atom gains two electrons to form a negative (2–) ion.

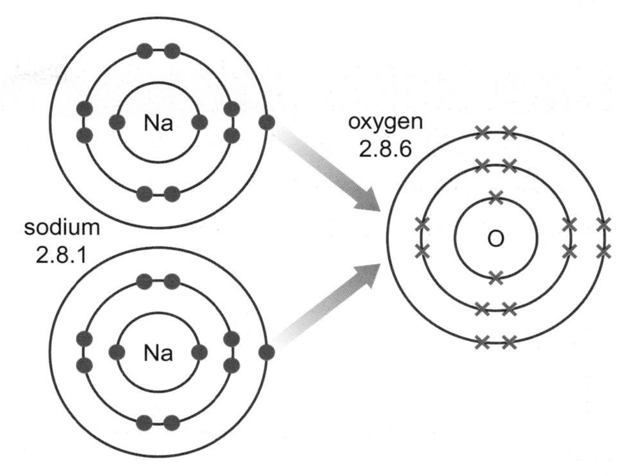

C dot and cross diagrams to show sodium reacting with oxygen to form sodium oxide (Na_2O, which contains Na^+ and O^{2-} ions)

 **5** Draw diagrams, like the ones in diagram C, to show the electronic configurations of the sodium and oxide ions.

As we go down group 1, the atoms get larger because an extra electron shell is added in each period. The force of attraction between the positive nucleus and the negative outer electron decreases as they become further apart. This explains the trend in reactivity of alkali metals. Sodium is more reactive than lithium because it is easier to remove the outer electron from a sodium atom.

 **6** Why do alkali metals form an ion with a 1+ charge?

 **7** **a** Why are alkali metals stored under oil?

 **b** How will the reactivity of rubidium (Rb) compare to potassium and caesium?

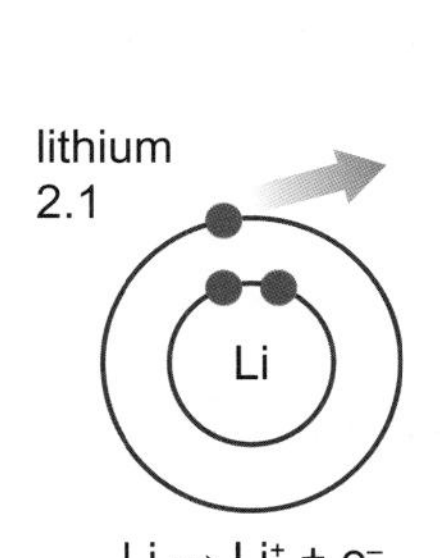

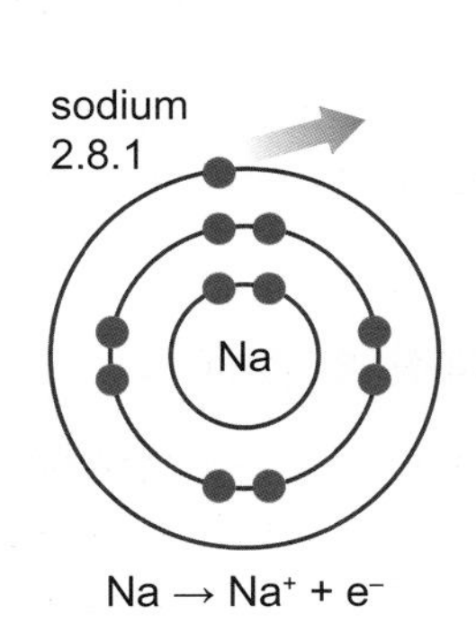

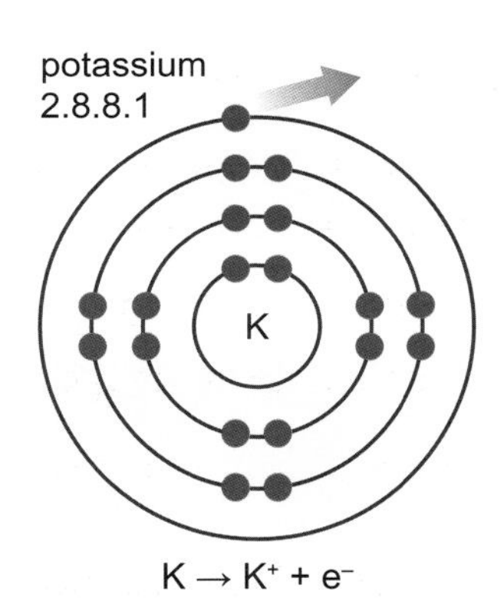

$Li \rightarrow Li^+ + e^-$ $Na \rightarrow Na^+ + e^-$ $K \rightarrow K^+ + e^-$

D As the distance between the outer electron and the nucleus increases, the alkali metals get more reactive.

 **8** By referring to atomic structures, explain why potassium is more reactive than sodium.

 **9** **H** Write an ionic equation for the reaction of potassium with water (hydroxide ion = OH^-).

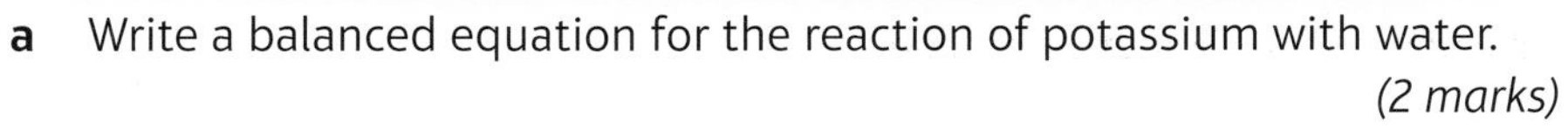

Exam-style question

a Write a balanced equation for the reaction of potassium with water. *(2 marks)*

b Explain why the reaction of caesium with water is not demonstrated in school laboratories. *(1 mark)*

Checkpoint

How confidently can you answer the Progression questions?

Strengthen

S1 Name three alkali metals and describe their main physical and chemical properties.

Extend

E1 **a** Explain the difference in reactivity between rubidium and caesium.

b **H** Write ionic equations for the reactions of rubidium and caesium with water.

SC17b Group 7

Specification reference: C6.6; C6.7; C6.8; C6.9; C6.10

Progression questions

- How do the physical properties of the halogens change, going down group 7?
- How can we test for chlorine gas?
- How do halogens react with metals and hydrogen?

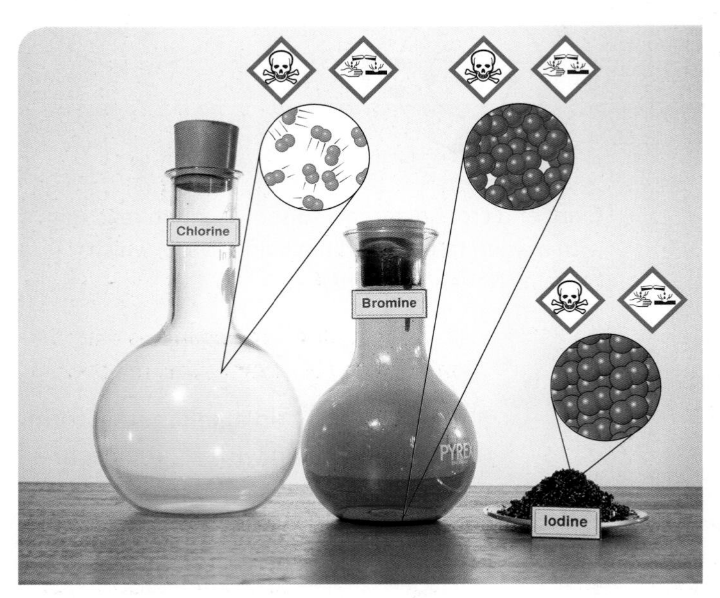

A the three most common halogens

Elements in group 7 of the periodic table are called the **halogens**. They all share similar properties and show a pattern in the way their properties change through the group.

All halogens exist as **diatomic** molecules, with two atoms held together by a single covalent bond. They are all non-metallic elements, which are poor conductors of heat and electricity. Care has to be taken when handling halogens, as they are all toxic and corrosive.

1 What pattern is there in the depth of colour of the halogens?

The physical properties of the three most common halogens are described in table B. As you go down the group the melting points, boiling points and densities increase.

Did you know?

The name halogen comes from the Greek words *hals*, meaning 'salt', and *gen*, meaning 'to make'. So halogens make salts – not just table salt (sodium chloride) but a range of metal halides that have a variety of uses.

Halogen	Melting point (°C)	Boiling point (°C)	Density (g/cm^3)	Appearance
chlorine	−101	−34	0.0032	green gas
bromine	−7	59	3.12	brown liquid
iodine	114	184	4.95	purple/black solid

B halogen properties

Most halogens react with metals and non-metals in a similar way. Halogens react with metals forming ionic compounds called **salts**, which contain **halide** ions (X^-). For example:

$$Cl_2(g) + Mg(s) \rightarrow MgCl_2(s)$$
chlorine + magnesium → magnesium chloride

$$F_2(g) + 2Na(s) \rightarrow 2NaF(s)$$
fluorine + sodium → sodium fluoride

Halide salts have many uses. For example, common sodium halide salts include sodium chloride (table salt), sodium fluoride (found in many toothpastes), sodium bromide (used in a disinfectant for swimming pools) and sodium iodide (added to table salt to prevent iodine deficiency).

2 Describe two ways that halogens are similar.

3 Look at photo A and table B.

a What do you think fluorine, at the top of group 7, will look like?

b Estimate the melting point, boiling point and density of fluorine.

 **4** What ions are formed when sodium reacts with fluorine?

 **5** **a** Name the product formed when calcium metal burns in fluorine.

 **b** Write a balanced equation for the reaction (calcium ion = Ca^{2+}).

All halogens can be used as **disinfectants** and **bleaches**, as they can kill microorganisms and remove the colour from materials. Chlorine is commonly used in swimming pools and many types of bleach. The test for chlorine, shown in photo C, depends on this bleaching action.

Halogens react with hydrogen to form hydrogen halides, which dissolve in water to form acidic solutions. For example, hydrogen and chlorine explode to form hydrogen chloride, which dissolves in water to make hydrochloric acid.

$$H_2(g) + Cl_2(g) \rightarrow 2HCl(g)$$

hydrogen + chlorine → hydrogen chloride

Hydrogen and chlorine molecules collide and the covalent bonds holding the atoms together break.

Covalent bonds form between hydrogen and chlorine atoms, making a new compound, hydrogen chloride.

When hydrogen chloride dissolves in water the molecules break up into two ions, H^+ and Cl^-.

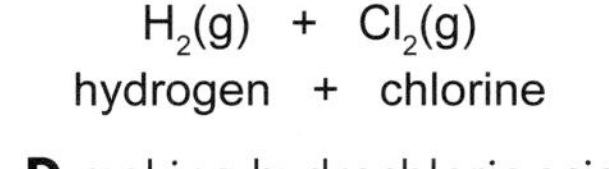

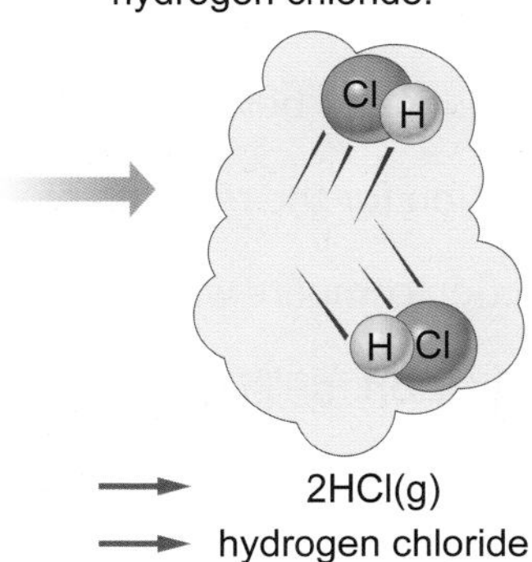

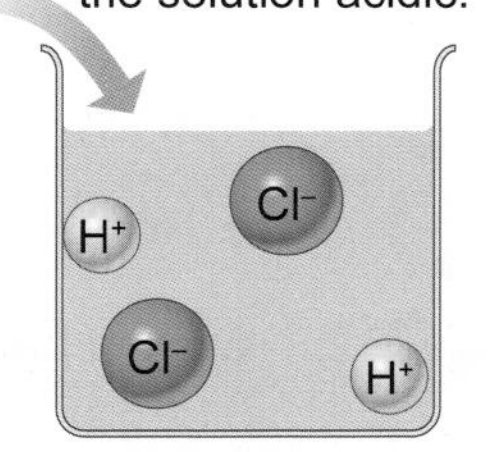

$H_2(g) + Cl_2(g)$ ⟶ $2HCl(g)$ dissolves in water to

hydrogen + chlorine ⟶ hydrogen chloride form hydrochloric acid

D making hydrochloric acid

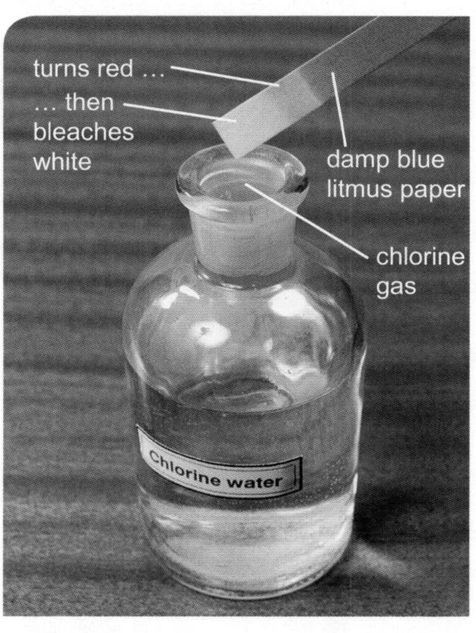

C If damp blue litmus paper is placed in chlorine gas, it first turns red then bleaches white.

6 Describe for chlorine:

 **a** two uses

 **b** a safety precaution for its use

 **c** a test for the gas.

7 In what state would each of the halogens in table B be at:

 **a** −50 °C **b** 150 °C?

8 Write word equations for the reactions between:

 **a** lithium and chlorine **b** hydrogen and fluorine.

 **9** Explain how hydrogen fluoride can form an acidic aqueous solution and name the acid.

10 Write balanced equations for the reactions between:

 **a** sodium and iodine **b** hydrogen and bromine.

Exam-style question

a	Predict the state and appearance of astatine (At).	*(1 mark)*
b	Explain your answer.	*(1 mark)*

Checkpoint

How confidently can you answer the Progression questions?

Strengthen

S1 Describe how the halogens chlorine, bromine and iodine are similar, and how they show trends in properties down their group.

Extend

E1 Describe, using balanced equations where appropriate, how bromine can be converted into:

a sodium bromide

b hydrobromic acid.

SC17c Halogen reactivity

Specification reference: H C0.4; C6.11; H C6.12; C6.13

Progression questions

- How can displacement reactions be used to work out the reactivity of halogens?
- How can we explain the reactivity of halogens?
- H What happens to halogen atoms and halide ions during displacement?

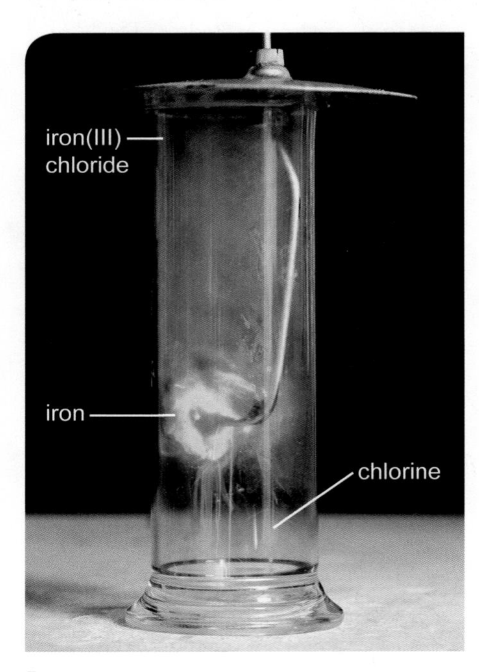

B $2Fe + 3Cl_2 \rightarrow 2FeCl_3$
iron + chlorine → iron(III) chloride

Table A shows the order of reactivity of different halogens when heated with iron wool. In general the halogens become less reactive as you go down the group.

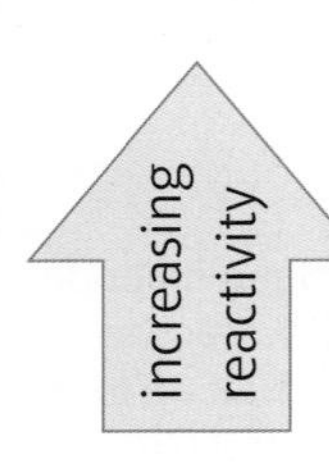

Halogen	Effect on iron wool
fluorine	bursts into flames
chlorine	glows brightly
bromine	glows dull red
iodine	changes colour

A halogens and heated iron wool

1 Astatine, symbol At, is found below iodine in the halogen group.

a Write a word equation for the reaction of astatine with iron wool.

b How will this reaction compare with chlorine? Explain your answer.

2 Write a balanced equation for the formation of magnesium iodide (MgI_2) from its elements.

The order of reactivity of halogens can also be worked out using **displacement reactions**. In a displacement reaction, a more reactive element takes the place of a less reactive element in an ionic compound. So, a more reactive halogen displaces a less reactive halogen from a halide compound. For example, chlorine displaces bromine from sodium bromide in solution, but bromine cannot displace chlorine from sodium chloride.

$Cl_2(aq) + 2NaBr(aq) \rightarrow Br_2(aq) + 2NaCl(aq)$
chlorine + sodium bromide → bromine + sodium chloride

3 Which of the following pairs of substances do not react? Explain your choice.

a $Br_2 + LiCl$ **b** $Cl_2 + NaI$

4 Write a balanced equation, with state symbols, for the reaction that occurs in photo C.

5 What would be observed if bromine gas were bubbled through potassium iodide solution?

C Chlorine displaces iodine from potassium iodide solution.

To explain the trend in reactivity we need to look at the electronic configuration of the halogen atoms.

Group 7 atoms gain one electron when they react. Down the group, the distance between the outermost shell containing electrons and the nucleus increases. This means that the force of attraction between the positive nucleus and an incoming negative electron decreases, and so the ions do not form so easily and the reactivity decreases.

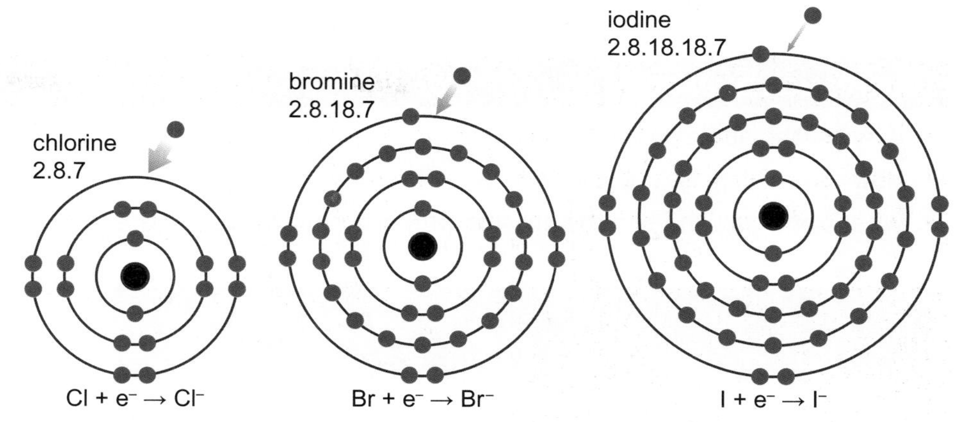

D Going down group 7, the outermost electron shell gets further from the nucleus and the ions are less readily formed.

 **6** Explain why fluorine is the most reactive halogen and astatine is the least reactive halogen.

H Redox

When a metal reacts with oxygen it loses electrons and so we can define **oxidation** as a 'loss of electrons'. **Reduction** is the opposite and is a 'gain of electrons'. Use the mnemonic 'OILRIG' to remember that 'Oxidation Is Loss, Reduction Is Gain'. These two processes occur at the same time in displacement reactions, which makes them examples of reduction–oxidation or **redox** reactions.

Diagram E shows the reaction between fluorine atoms and chloride ions. As the fluorine atoms are **reduced**, by gaining electrons, the chloride ions are **oxidised**, by losing electrons.

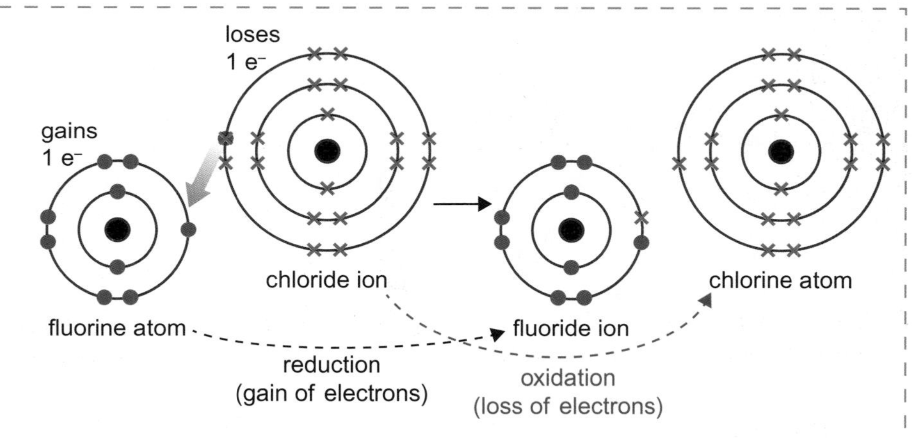

E Fluorine gains electrons more readily than chlorine. It displaces chlorine from chloride ions: $F_2(g) + 2Cl^-(aq) \rightarrow 2F^-(aq) + Cl_2(g)$

 **7** **a** What happens in all redox reactions?

b Identify the substances that are oxidised and reduced in the reaction below. Explain your choice.

$$2Na(s) + Br_2(g) \rightarrow 2NaBr(s)$$

 **8** Write an ionic equation with state symbols for the reaction that occurs in question 5.

Exam-style question

Compare the trends in melting point and reactivity of group 1 and group 7 elements. *(3 marks)*

Checkpoint

How confidently can you answer the Progression questions?

Strengthen

S1 Design a summary table or diagram to describe and explain the trend in reactivity of the halogens.

Extend

E1 H Use a displacement reaction to explain what is meant by 'redox reactions'.

SC17d Group 0

Specification reference: C6.14; C6.15; C6.16

Progression questions

- Why are the noble gases unreactive?
- How can noble gases be used?
- What trends are there in the physical properties of the noble gases?

Noble gas	Melting point (°C)	Boiling point (°C)	Density (g/cm³)
helium	−272	−269	0.00018
neon	−249	−246	0.0009
argon	−189	−186	0.0018
krypton	−157	−153	0.0038

A physical properties of noble gases

The **noble gases** are in group 0. They:

- are colourless
- have very low melting and boiling points
- are poor conductors of heat and electricity.

The data in table A clearly shows that there are trends in the physical properties of group 0 elements.

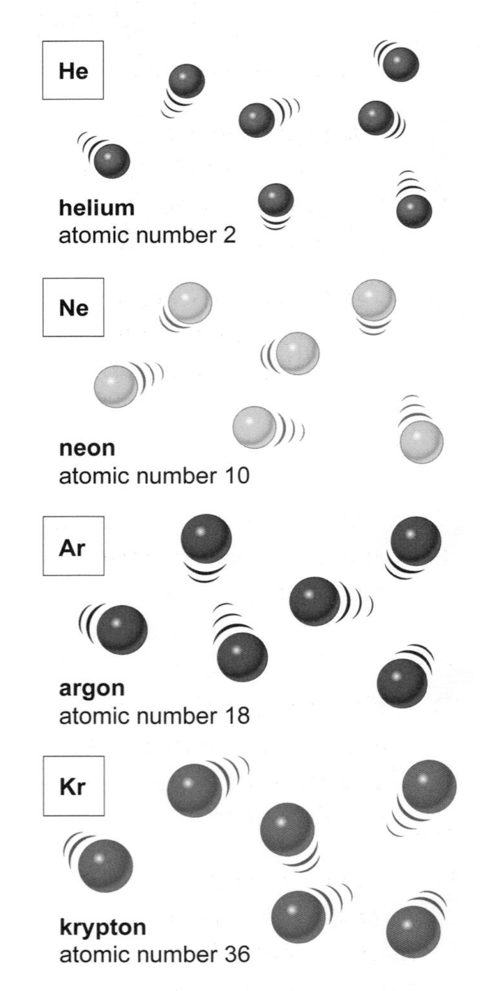

B Noble gases exist as single atoms with no strong bonds between the atoms.

The unique property of the noble gas elements is that they are **inert**, which means they do not react easily with anything. Noble gases all exist as single atoms, because they do not form bonds easily with other atoms.

1 **a** Describe the trend in density in group 0.

b Predict the melting and boiling points of the fifth noble gas, xenon.

c Explain how you made your prediction.

2 Nitrogen gas, formula N_2, is an inert gas. In what way is nitrogen:

a similar to neon **b** different from neon?

3 Explain which noble gas-filled balloons will float upwards in air. The density of air is about 0.0012 g/cm³.

The noble gas group was not known until the end of the 19th century. These elements were difficult to detect because they did not react with anything. There are only very small amounts of each noble gas in our atmosphere.

Noble gas	% in the atmosphere
helium	0.00052
neon	0.0018
argon	0.934
krypton	0.00011
xenon	0.000009

C noble gases in the atmosphere

4 Suggest why the noble gases did not appear in Mendeleev's first periodic table.

5 Look at table C.

a Place the noble gases in order of increasing abundance in the atmosphere.

b Explain why it was easier to discover oxygen gas than argon.

The noble gases have a variety of uses because of their unique properties.

Krypton is used in photography lighting. It produces a brilliant white light when electricity is passed through it.

Argon is denser than air. It is added to the space above the wine in wine barrels to stop oxygen in the air reacting with the wine.

Helium has a very low density and is non-flammable, so it is used in weather balloons and airships.

Neon produces a distinctive red-orange light when electricity is passed through it. This property makes it useful for making long-lasting illuminated signs.

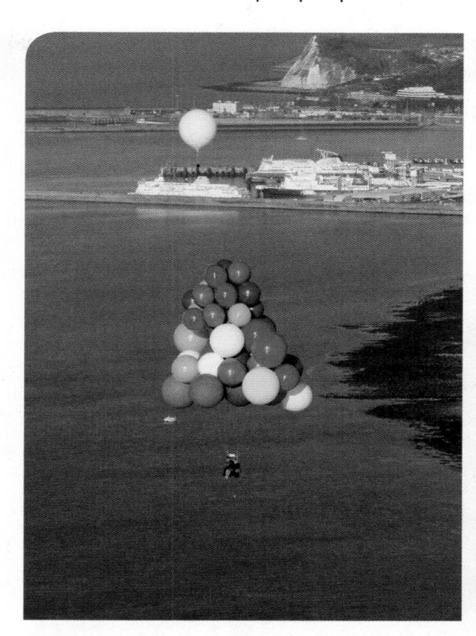

D helium-filled balloons

To explain why noble gases are unreactive, we need to look at their electronic configurations. Diagram F shows that all noble gases have a complete outer shell of electrons. It has been shown that, when atoms form bonds, they can become more stable. They do this by gaining, losing or sharing electrons to get an electronic configuration like a noble gas. So noble gases are unreactive because their atoms already have a stable electronic configuration with a complete outer shell.

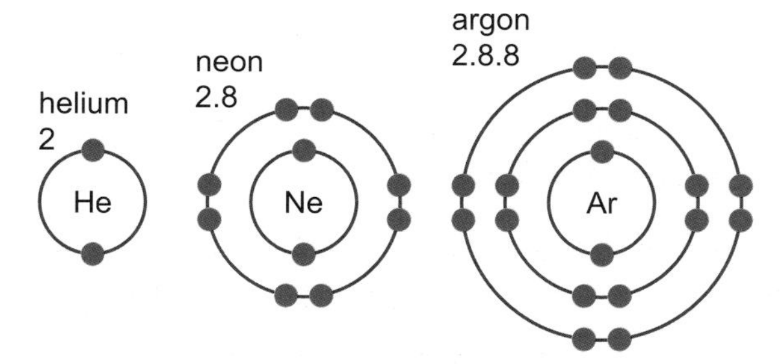

F Noble gases do not react as they already have a complete outer shell of electrons.

7 Explain why argon is very unreactive while potassium, with one more electron, is very reactive.

Exam-style question

Neon is a colourless inert gas.

a Describe what the term inert tells you about neon. *(1 mark)*

b Explain why neon exists as single atoms. *(2 marks)*

Did you know?

Helium atoms are continually being produced by radioactive decay in certain rocks. However, the atoms are so light that most of them escape into space as the Earth's gravity cannot hold them.

E a neon-filled advertising sign

6 **a** Explain how the properties of helium gas make it useful for weather balloons.

b Explain why argon can be used in fire extinguishers.

Checkpoint

How confidently can you answer the Progression questions?

Strengthen

S1 Explain how the electronic configuration of noble gases affects their properties.

Extend

E1 The noble gas radon is radioactive. Use the information on these two pages to predict other properties of radon.

SC18a Rates of reaction

Specification reference: C7.2; C7.5

Progression questions

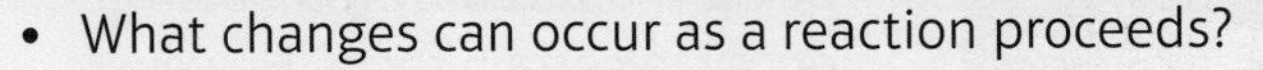

- What changes can occur as a reaction proceeds?
- How can we investigate rates of reaction?
- How are graphs used to show rates of reaction?

A The combustion of the wood is a faster reaction than the baking of the pizzas.

New substances are always formed in chemical reactions. The **rate** of a reaction is the speed at which **reactants** are turned into **products**. Rates vary greatly, from very slow (e.g. the rusting of iron) to almost instantaneous (e.g. explosions, precipitation reactions). However, we can control rates of reaction by altering **variables**, such as the concentration of solutions and the size of pieces of solid reactant.

1 Describe one example of a very fast and a very slow chemical reaction.

To investigate reaction rates, we need to be able to measure how the amount of reactants or products changes with time. Graph B shows how the concentrations change during a reaction. The gradient (slope) of the graph indicates the rate: the steeper the graph, the faster the reaction. Reaction rates are usually fastest at the start because that is when the concentration of the reactants is greatest.

Did you know?

Japanese scientists have developed a camera to observe extremely fast reactions. The camera records 4.4 trillion frames per second. A good smartphone would need over 1000 years to record as many frames as this camera records in the blink of an eye.

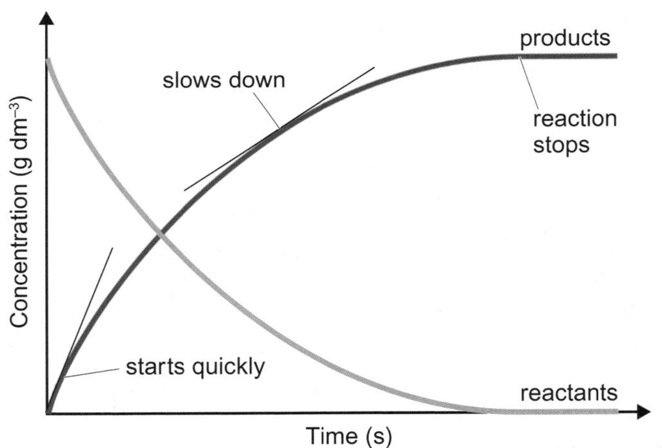

B Reactions are usually fastest at the start.

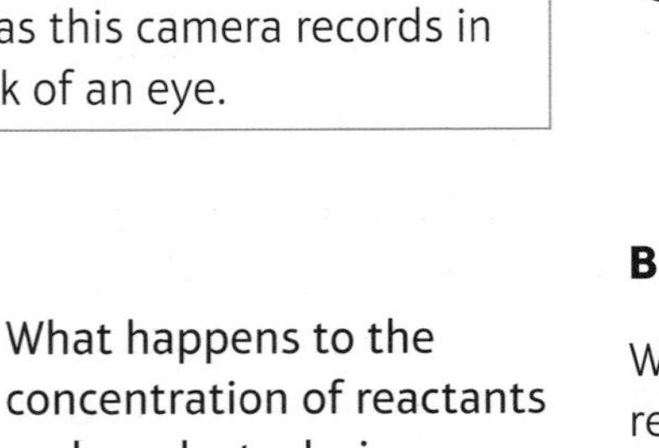

2 What happens to the concentration of reactants and products during a reaction?

3 Why do most reactions slow down in time?

We can also monitor rates by measuring changes in the mass or volume of reactants or products.

In the reaction between magnesium and sulfuric acid, shown in diagram C, we can follow the reaction by measuring the volume of hydrogen gas produced.

$$Mg(s) + H_2SO_4(aq) \rightarrow MgSO_4(aq) + H_2(g)$$

The results show the difference between using magnesium ribbon and magnesium granules. The graph for the granules is steeper and levels off more quickly. This shows that the granules, which are smaller pieces of solid than the ribbon, react more quickly.

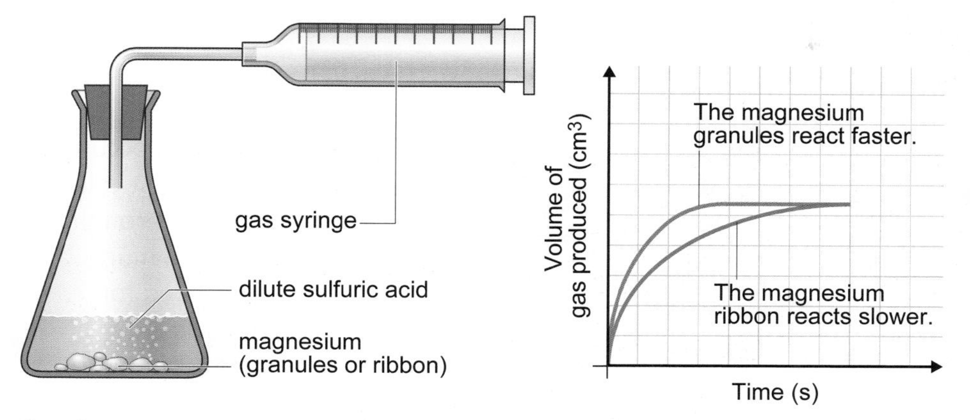

C In this experiment only the size of the pieces of magnesium is changed. All other variables are kept constant.

4 **a** What piece of apparatus can be used to measure gas volumes accurately?

b Explain why measuring gas volume can be used to monitor the rates of some reactions.

5 How does the graph in diagram C show that magnesium granules react faster than ribbon?

In the reaction between marble (calcium carbonate) and hydrochloric acid, shown in diagram D, we can follow the rate by measuring the change in mass. The mass decreases as carbon dioxide gas escapes from the flask.

$CaCO_3(s) + 2HCl(aq) \rightarrow CaCl_2(aq) + H_2O(l) + CO_2(g)$

6 Calcium carbonate is left at the end of the reaction shown in diagram D.

a Which reactant has been used up?

b How do you know when the reaction is complete?

c Sketch a graph to show how the mass of the flask will change as the reaction proceeds.

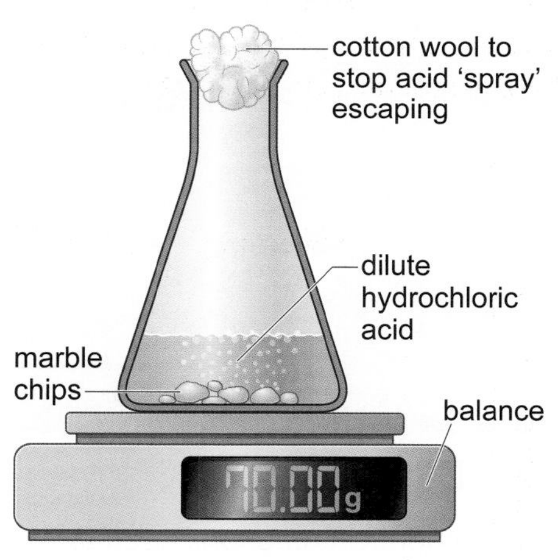

D As the reaction proceeds, the mass of the flask and contents will decrease.

7 Why would it be difficult to measure the reaction rate for the rusting of iron?

Exam-style question

When copper carbonate reacts with sulfuric acid, carbon dioxide gas is formed. Explain how an electronic balance could be used to investigate the rate of this reaction. *(2 marks)*

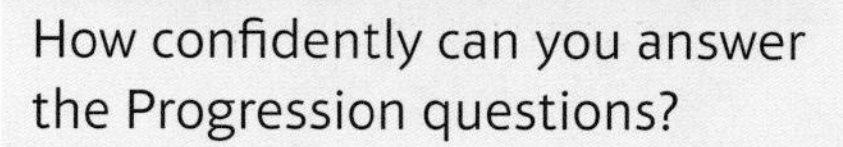

Checkpoint

How confidently can you answer the Progression questions?

Strengthen

S1 Look at the reaction in diagram D.

a What is being measured in this experiment?

b What happens to the concentration of the acid as the reaction proceeds?

c What other change could be measured to follow this reaction?

Extend

E1 Describe, including diagrams, how you could use a gas syringe to investigate the correlation between temperature and the rate of the reaction between magnesium and hydrochloric acid.

SC18b Factors affecting reaction rates

Specification reference: C7.3; C7.4

Progression questions

- What has to happen for two particles to react?
- How does the speed of particles affect the rate of reaction?
- Why do changes in temperature, concentration, surface area and pressure affect rates of reaction?

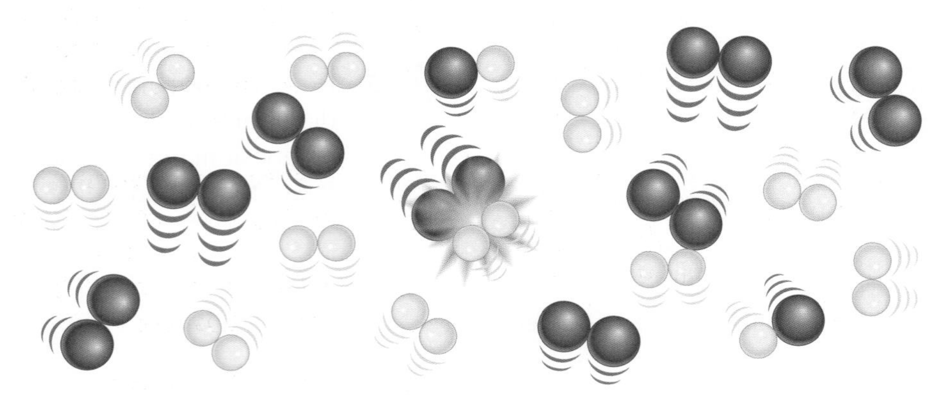

A The faster-moving hydrogen and chlorine molecules have more energy, and are more likely to react.

For chemical reactions to occur the reactant particles must collide or 'bump' together with enough energy to react. The minimum amount of energy needed for a reaction to occur is called its **activation energy**. During successful collisions, this energy helps to break bonds, so that the atoms can be rearranged to make new substances (the products of the reaction).

1 What two things must happen before hydrogen and chlorine can react?

When methane and air are mixed the molecules collide, but no reaction occurs until a spark or flame provides the activation energy needed. The reaction then keeps going because the reaction releases energy, which then provides the activation energy needed. Reactions which release energy are described as **exothermic** changes.

B The natural methane leaking out of these rocks has been burning for decades, having been set alight by lightning.

A few chemical reactions need to take in energy to occur. These reactions, called **endothermic** changes, will not keep going unless energy is continually supplied. For example, the electrolysis of copper chloride needs a continuous supply of electrical energy.

In general, reaction rates are increased when the energy of the collisions is increased, and when the frequency is increased (the number of collisions in a certain amount of time). More collisions occur if the particles are closer together or moving faster. The particles in any substance have a range of energies, but only those with enough energy can react. More collisions will be successful if more of the particles have the activation energy required.

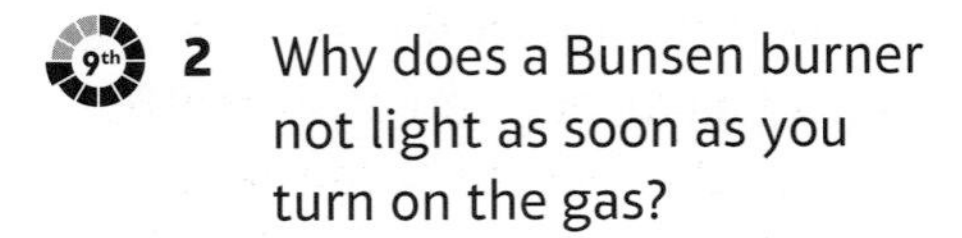

2 Why does a Bunsen burner not light as soon as you turn on the gas?

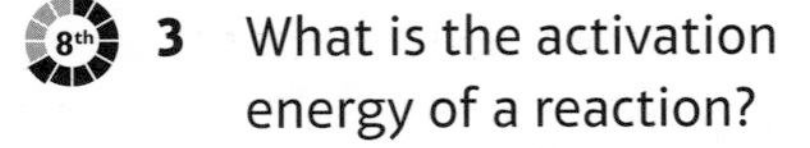

3 What is the activation energy of a reaction?

4 State two changes that would make the reaction in diagram A slower.

Concentration and reaction rate

Change: Increasing the concentration of solutions increases the rate of reaction.

Explanation: There are more reacting particles in the same volume so collisions occur more often.

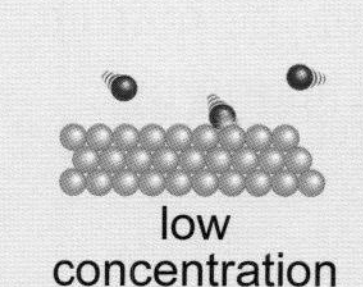

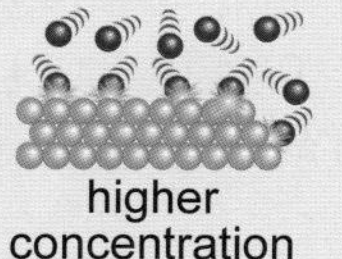

C

Surface area and reaction rate

Change: Increasing the surface area to volume ratio, by decreasing the size of solid pieces while keeping the total volume of solid the same, increases the rate of the reaction.

Explanation: There is more surface for collisions to occur on, so collisions occur more often.

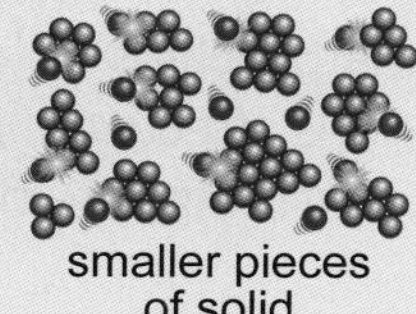

D

Pressure of gases and reaction rate

Change: Increasing the pressure of gases increases the rate of reaction.

Explanation: The reactant particles are squeezed closer together so collisions occur more often.

lower pressure   higher pressure

E

Temperature and reaction rate

Change: Increasing the temperature increases the rate of reaction.

Explanation: The reactant particles speed up and have more energy. They therefore collide more often and more particles have enough energy to react when they collide.

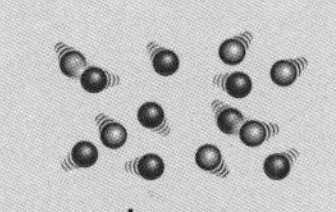

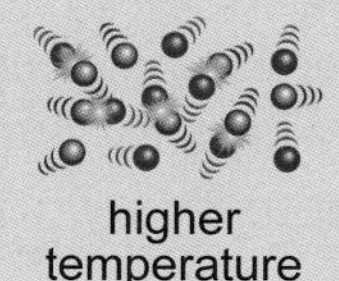

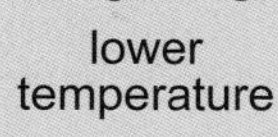

F

7th **5** **a** Which of the following burns most quickly in air: wood chips, wood dust or wood shavings?

8th **b** Explain your answer to part **a**.

8th **c** Explain how using pure oxygen instead of air would affect the rate of burning.

6 The reaction between hydrogen (H_2) and chlorine (Cl_2) gases produces hydrogen chloride (HCl) gas. For this reaction:

9th **a** write a balanced chemical equation, with state symbols

7th **b** explain how and why decreasing the gas pressures affects the rate

10th **c** explain how and why increasing the temperature affects the rate.

6th **7** Suggest a reason why reactions between gases are often slower than reactions between liquids at the same temperature.

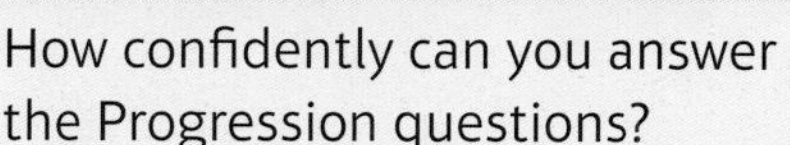

Checkpoint

How confidently can you answer the Progression questions?

Strengthen

S1 Use ideas about collisions and energy to explain how the rate of a reaction can be increased by changes in concentration, temperature and the size of pieces of a solid reactant.

Extend

E1 Explain four ways in which the rate of reaction between iron lumps and oxygen from the air can be increased.

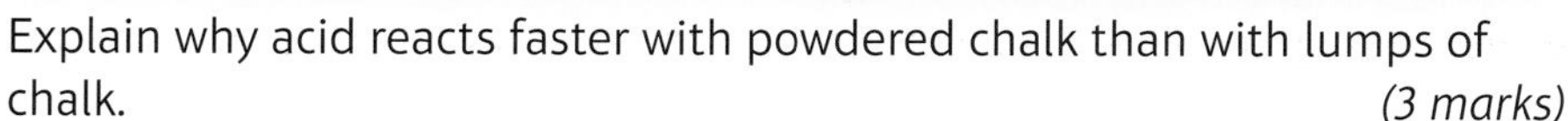

Exam-style question

Explain why acid reacts faster with powdered chalk than with lumps of chalk. *(3 marks)*

SC18b Core practical – Investigating reaction rates

Specification reference: C7.1

Aim

Investigate the effects of changing the conditions of a reaction on the rates of chemical reactions.

The progress of a chemical reaction can be measured by how the amounts of reactant or product change with time, or by the time taken for the reaction to reach a certain point.

Your task 1 – measuring volumes of gases

You are going to investigate the reaction between hydrochloric acid and marble chips (calcium carbonate) and how the surface area of the marble chips affects the rate. You will monitor the progress of the reaction by measuring the volume of carbon dioxide produced.

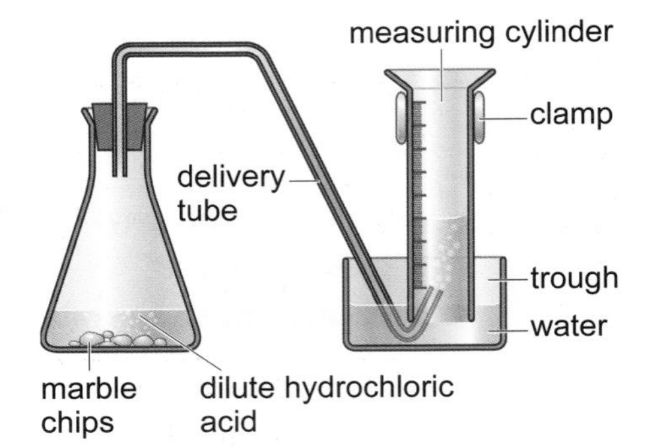

A investigating volumes of gas produced

Method 1

Wear eye protection.

A Set up the apparatus as shown in diagram A.

B Measure 40 cm^3 of dilute hydrochloric acid into a conical flask.

C Add 5 g of small marble chips to the flask.

D Immediately stopper the flask and start the stop clock.

E Note the total volume of gas produced after every 30 seconds until the reaction has finished.

F Repeat the experiment using 5 g of larger marble chips.

Your task 2 – observing a colour change

You are going to investigate the effect of temperature on the rate of reaction between sodium thiosulfate and hydrochloric acid. You will monitor the progress of the reaction by observing a colour change (as shown in photo B).

B We can follow the rate of the reaction between sodium thiosulfate and hydrochloric acid by measuring the time taken for a 'cross' drawn beneath the reaction beaker to disappear.

Method 2

Wear eye protection.

G Place 50 cm^3 of sodium thiosulfate solution into a 300 cm^3 conical flask.

H Measure out 5 cm^3 of dilute hydrochloric acid in a test tube.

I Clamp the conical flask in place in a water bath at a certain temperature. Place the test tube in a rack in the same water bath. Record this temperature.

J After 5 minutes, remove the flask and place it on a piece of white paper marked with a cross.

K Add the acid to the thiosulfate and start the stop clock.

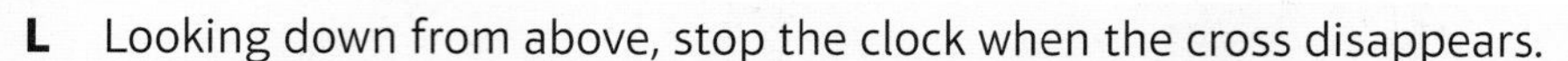

L Looking down from above, stop the clock when the cross disappears.

M Note this time and take the final temperature of the mixture.

N Repeat at three or four other temperatures, between 20 and 50 °C.

Exam-style questions

Look at Method 1.

1 Write a word equation and a balanced symbol equation for this reaction. *(4 marks)*

2 **a** State the dependent and independent variables in this investigation. *(2 marks)*

b State two control variables. *(2 marks)*

3 **a** State why you must immediately stopper the flask in step D. *(1 mark)*

b State the apparatus you would use to measure the mass of the marble chips. *(1 mark)*

4 Look at graph C.

a State when the reaction is complete. Explain your answer. *(2 marks)*

b Sketch graph C and add a curve that would be produced by smaller marble chips. *(2 marks)*

c Use graph C to calculate the average reaction rate in cm^3/min between 45 and 105 seconds. Show your working. *(2 marks)*

d Describe how you would use a tangent line to estimate the reaction rate in cm^3/min at 100 seconds. *(3 marks)*

5 Describe how you would modify Method 1 to investigate the effect of temperature on the rate of this reaction.

6 State one further variable that would effect the rate of this reaction. *(1 mark)*

Look at Method 2.

7 State why the investigation would be improved by measuring the initial temperature of the reaction mixture (just after the acid is added) and then measuring the final temperature (when the reaction is finished). *(2 marks)*

8 Some results from the experiment in method 2 are shown in table D.

a State why the cross disappears. *(1 mark)*

b Sketch a graph of the results (no graph paper required) with temperature on the horizontal axis. *(3 marks)*

c Explain what these results tell us about the effect of temperature on the rate of this reaction. *(2 marks)*

d Describe one way of improving the results obtained from this investigation. *(1 mark)*

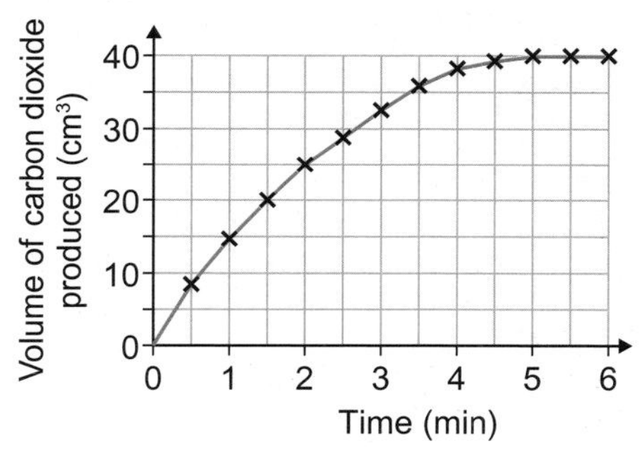

C volume of gas collected in the reaction between hydrochloric acid and marble chips

Average temperature (°C)	Time for cross to disappear (s)
20	165
30	81
40	42
50	21

D

SC18c Catalysts and activation energy

Specification reference: C7.6; C7.7; C7.8

Progression questions

- What is a catalyst?
- How do catalysts work?
- What are enzymes used for?

A The catalyst is not used up. So, if 1 g of manganese dioxide is added at the start, then 1 g will be recovered at the end.

Catalysts are substances that speed up chemical reactions without being permanently changed themselves and without altering the products of the reaction. Photo A shows the effect of a catalyst (manganese dioxide) on the decomposition of hydrogen peroxide.

Catalysts are often used in industry. For example, platinum is used as a catalyst in the manufacture of nitric acid from ammonia. These catalysts make industrial processes more profitable, by making products more quickly, and by allowing reactions to occur at lower temperatures, which saves costs. Catalysts also do not usually need to be replaced because they are not used up.

We can think about catalysts by using an analogy. In diagram B, the starting point and the finishing point are the same for all cars. However, those following the scenic route need more energy at the start to get over the hill. So, in terms of energy, most cars will use the road through the tunnel, which is the easier route.

B Not all cars have enough energy to go over the hill.

Like the tunnel, a catalyst provides an alternative reaction route, which requires less activation energy. **Reaction profiles** like graph C can be used to show the energy changes for a catalysed and an uncatalysed exothermic reaction. The catalyst does not alter the overall energy change. However, since less energy is needed to start the reaction, more reactant molecules have enough energy and so more collisions are successful. This means that the reaction is faster.

7th **1** Explain how catalysts reduce the costs in industrial processes.

7th **2** Platinum is a very expensive catalyst. Why might this not matter?

6th **3** How could you show that the manganese dioxide in photo A was not used up?

Did you know?

Many washing powders contain biological catalysts called enzymes to help break down different types of stains: proteases break down proteins like blood and egg, amylases break down starches and lipases break down fats and grease.

 **4** Explain whether a reaction with a high or low activation energy would be faster.

 **5** In terms of energy changes, what is the same for catalysed and uncatalysed reactions?

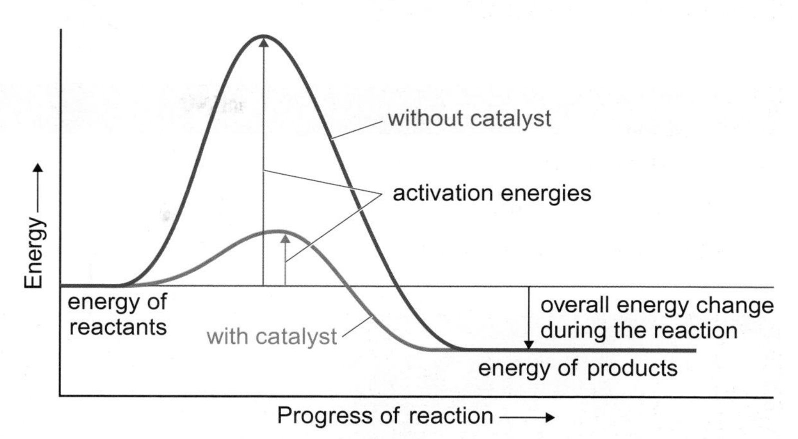

C This reaction profile shows that a catalyst lowers the activation energy.

In catalytic converters in car exhausts (shown in diagram D) the catalysts are platinum and palladium. Their presence lowers the activation energy needed to convert harmful gases into harmless gases. The metals used are expensive but don't need to be replaced as they are not used up.

6 Explain why the iron catalyst used in the manufacture of ammonia:

 **a** is in the form of small lumps

 **b** does not need to be replaced often.

Enzymes are large complex **protein** molecules that act as catalysts in biological reactions. Each enzyme molecule has a part with a specific shape called the **active site**. The reactant molecules (**substrates**) fit the shape of the active site, a bit like a 'lock and key'. So each enzyme only fits one substrate and only catalyses one specific reaction. Enzymes are sensitive to changes in temperature and pH as these can **denature** their molecules (make them change shape) so they will not work.

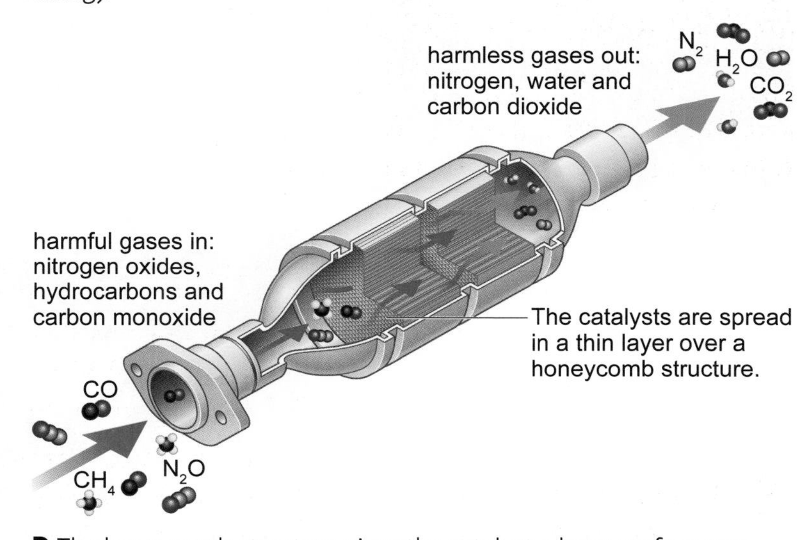

D The honeycomb structure gives the catalyst a large surface area.

Enzymes are essential in living things and many industries. For example, alcoholic drinks are produced using an enzyme in yeast. This enzyme catalyses the reaction in which glucose is converted into ethanol (alcohol) and carbon dioxide.

 **7** **a** Give an example of an enzyme and the reaction it catalyses.

 **b** Why will the enzyme not catalyse other reactions?

 **8** Explain why heating a reaction involving a catalyst will usually make it faster but heating an enzyme-catalysed reaction can make it slower.

Exam-style question

Explain how the following speed up chemical reactions by increasing the frequency of successful collisions.

a using a catalyst *(2 marks)*

b increasing the temperature *(2 marks)*

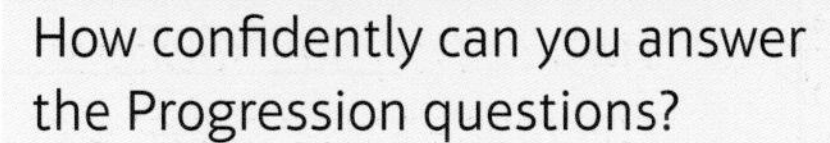

Checkpoint

How confidently can you answer the Progression questions?

Strengthen

S1 Explain, in terms of activation energy, how catalysts and enzymes work and why they are useful in industrial chemical reactions.

Extend

E1 Compare and contrast chemical catalysts and biological catalysts.

SC19a Exothermic and endothermic reactions

Specification reference: C7.9; C7.10; C7.11

Progression questions

- What are exothermic and endothermic reactions?
- What are some examples of exothermic and endothermic reactions?
- How can heat changes in solution be investigated?

A This self-heating can uses an exothermic reaction between sodium hydroxide pellets and water.

1 Explain why combustion reactions are described as being exothermic.

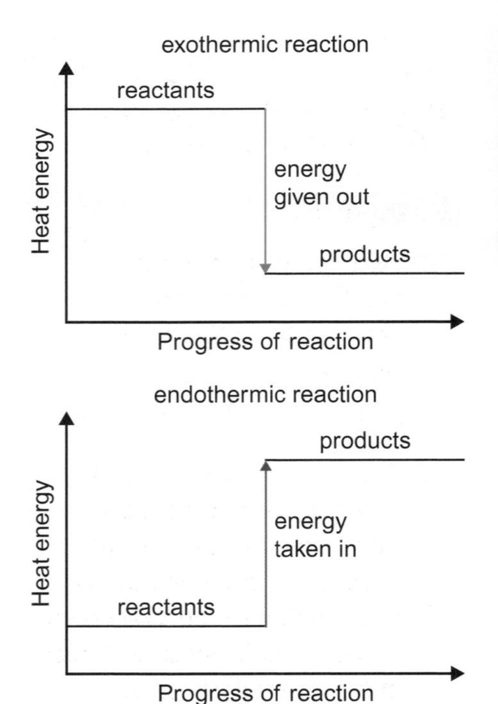

C simple reaction profiles

Energy is transferred between the surroundings and the reactants during chemical reactions. Energy is most often transferred by heating. Chemical reactions can be described as:

- **exothermic** – energy is transferred from stores of energy in chemical bonds to the surroundings.
- **endothermic** – energy is transferred from the surroundings to stores of energy in chemical bonds.

B Combustion reactions are exothermic.

You can use a **reaction profile** to model the energy change during a chemical reaction. In these diagrams, energy stored in bonds is represented as a horizontal line. The greater the energy stored, the higher the line.

2 Explain how you can tell from its reaction profile whether a reaction is exothermic or endothermic.

3 Sherbet sweets contain citric acid and sodium hydrogen carbonate. These react together to produce sodium citrate, water and carbon dioxide. The reaction makes your mouth feel cold. Draw a reaction profile for this reaction, labelling each horizontal line with the names of the substances involved.

Temperature changes during reactions

During a chemical reaction, energy is transferred between the reacting substances and their surroundings. This is usually by heating, particularly if a reaction takes place in solution. The stored thermal (heat) energy in the solution increases during an exothermic reaction, and it decreases during an endothermic reaction. This means you can determine whether a reaction in solution is exothermic or endothermic:

- the temperature increases in an exothermic reaction
- the temperature decreases in an endothermic reaction.

Diagram D shows a simple apparatus for these investigations.

 **4** **Explain why a lid and a *polystyrene* cup are used when investigating temperature changes in solution.**

In **precipitation** reactions, an insoluble product forms from two solutions. For example:

$AgNO_3(aq) + NaCl(aq) \rightarrow NaNO_3(aq) + AgCl(s)$

Precipitation reactions can be exothermic or endothermic, depending on the substances involved. However, two types of reactions are always exothermic:

- **neutralisation**, the reaction between an acid and a base
- **displacement**, the reaction between a metal and a compound of a less reactive metal, or between a halogen and a compound of a less reactive halogen.

When a salt dissolves in water, the change is exothermic or endothermic, depending on the salt. The temperature increases as calcium chloride dissolves, but it decreases when ammonium chloride dissolves.

 **5** **Explain the temperature change you would expect when sodium hydroxide dissolves in water.**

Exam-style question

Sodium carbonate solution reacts with calcium chloride solution. A precipitate of calcium carbonate forms. A student carries out an experiment to measure the temperature change in this reaction. These are her results:

temperature of reactants = 21 °C

final temperature of mixture = 12 °C

Explain what this shows about the type of energy change that happens.

(2 marks)

Did you know?

Photosynthesis is an endothermic reaction.

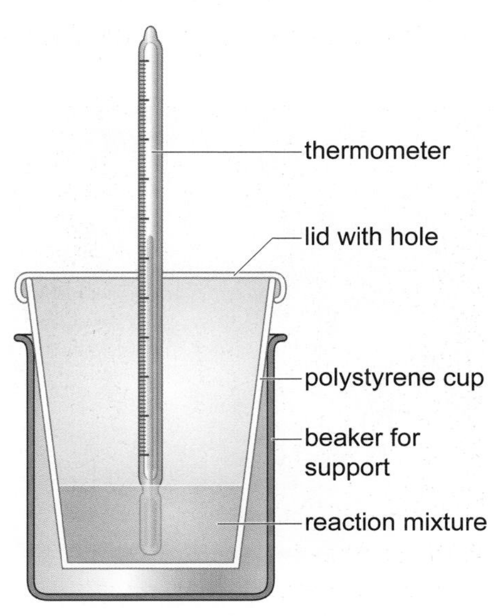

D The air trapped between the beaker and the cup reduces energy transfers by heating, to and from the surroundings.

Checkpoint

How confidently can you answer the Progression questions?

Strengthen

S1 How can you work out whether a reaction in solution is exothermic or endothermic?

Extend

E1 The temperature changes in displacement reactions between metals and solutions of metal compounds can be used to determine a reactivity series. Explain which variables should be controlled to obtain valid results.

SC19b Energy changes in reactions

Specification reference: C7.12; C7.13; H C7.14; C7.15; C7.16

Progression questions

- How can exothermic and endothermic reactions be explained in terms of bonds?
- How are exothermic and endothermic reactions modelled?
- H How are energy changes in reactions calculated?

A These bikes are fuelled with pure methanol.

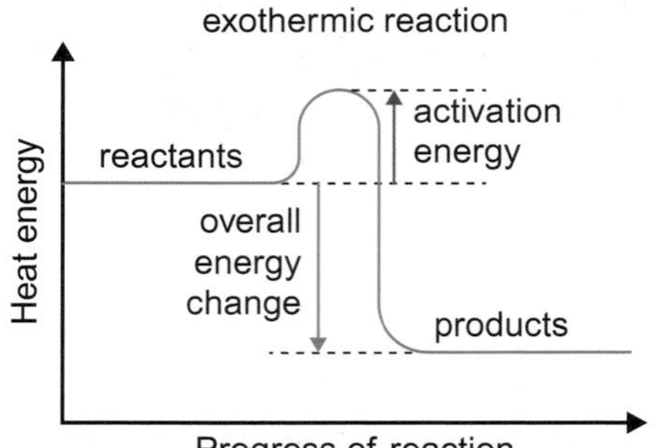

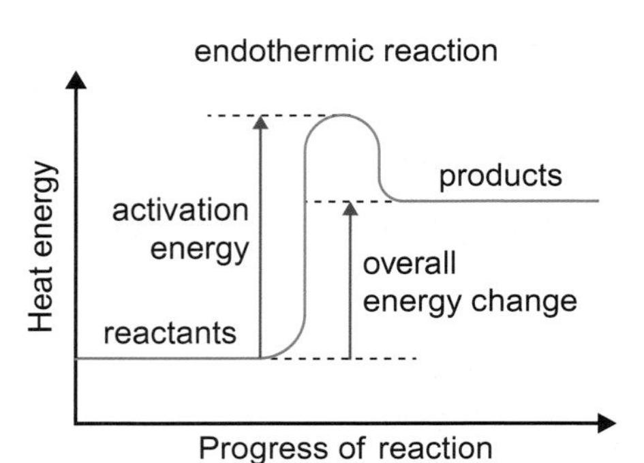

B The activation energy is the difference in energy between the reactants and the top of the 'hump'.

Reactions happen when reactant particles collide with each other with sufficient energy. The **activation energy** is the minimum amount of energy needed by colliding particles for a reaction to happen. Precipitation and neutralisation reactions have low activation energies, and start as soon as the reactants are mixed. Combustion reactions have higher activation energies.

 **1** Explain why methanol needs a flame to start it burning.

You can model activation energy in a **reaction profile** by drawing a 'hump' between the reactants and products lines. Some reactions, such as combustion, have high activation energies and need energy from a spark or flame to start.

2 Describe how the activation energy of a reaction is modelled on a reaction profile.

 **3** Explain, in terms of bond breaking and bond making, why the combustion of methanol is an exothermic reaction.

Breaking and making bonds

During a chemical reaction, bonds in the reactants break and new bonds are made to form the products:

- energy is transferred to the reactants to break their bonds, so breaking bonds is endothermic
- energy is transferred to the surroundings as bonds form, so making bonds is exothermic.

A reaction is exothermic if more energy is given out making bonds than is needed to break bonds. A reaction is endothermic if less energy is given out making bonds than is needed to break bonds.

H Bond energy calculations

A **mole** of something is 6.02×10^{23} of them (see *SC9c Moles*).The energy needed to break one mole of a particular **covalent bond** is its **bond energy**, measured in kilojoules per mole (kJ/mol or kJ mol^{-1}). For example, the bond energy of a C–O bond is 358 kJ mol^{-1}. This means that 358 kJ must be taken in to break one mole of C–O bonds, and 358 kJ is given out when one mole of C–O bonds is made. Table C shows some bond energies.

You can use bond energies to calculate the energy change in a reaction, as shown in the worked example below.

Covalent bond	Bond energy (kJ mol^{-1})
C–O	358
C–H	413
H–H	436
O–H	464
O=O	498
C=O	805

C a selection of bond energies

Worked example

Methane burns completely in oxygen to form carbon dioxide and water:

$$CH_4 + 2(O{=}O) \rightarrow O{=}C{=}O + 2(H{-}O{-}H)$$

D

Calculate the energy change during this reaction.

Step 1 Calculate energy in (bonds broken)

4 × (C–H)	= 4 × 413	= 1652 kJ mol^{-1}
2 × (O=O)	= 2 × 498	= 996 kJ mol^{-1}
Total in	= 1652 + 996	= 2648 kJ mol^{-1}

Step 2 Calculate energy out (bonds made)

2 × (C=O)	= 2 × 805	= 1610 kJ mol^{-1}
4 × (O–H)	= 4 × 464	= 1856 kJ mol^{-1}
Total out	= 1610 + 1856	= 3466 kJ mol^{-1}

Step 3 Energy change = energy in – energy out

= 2648 – 3466 = –818 kJ mol^{-1}

The negative sign shows that the reaction is exothermic (endothermic reactions have a positive sign).

4 Calculate the energy change when hydrogen reacts with oxygen:
2(H–H) + O=O → 2(H–O–H)

Did you know?

The strength of a given covalent bond differs between substances, and even between different places in the same molecule, so tables usually show mean bond energies.

Exam-style question

Explain, in terms of the energy involved in the breaking and making of bonds, why some reactions are endothermic. *(2 marks)*

Checkpoint

How confidently can you answer the Progression questions?

Strengthen

S1 What happens in exothermic and endothermic reactions when bonds are broken and made?

S2 What information do reaction profiles give us?

Extend

E1 Calculate the energy change when methanol undergoes complete combustion:
$CH_3OH + 1\frac{1}{2}O_2 \rightarrow CO_2 + 2H_2O$

Rates of reaction

Dilute hydrochloric acid reacts with solid calcium carbonate. A student carries out two experiments involving this reaction. She uses the same concentration of hydrochloric acid and the same mass of calcium carbonate each time. The table shows her results.

	Experiment 1	Experiment 2
calcium carbonate	lumps	powder
temperature of acid (°C)	22	45
reaction time (s)	225	25

Evaluate the student's results, explaining any difference in the rate of reaction between the two experiments in terms of particles. **(6 marks)**

Student answer

I think the data shows that the reaction in experiment 2 is nine times faster than the same reaction in experiment 1 [1]. *The greater rate of reaction in experiment 2 is for two reasons. Firstly, the particles in the powder have a greater surface area* [2] *than the particles in the lumps used in experiment 1. This means that more particles are exposed to the acid and there are more frequent collisions between reactant particles* [3], *so the rate of reaction is greater.*

The increased rate of reaction is also due to the increased temperature of the acid. The reactant particles in experiment 2 have more energy than those in experiment 1. So, a greater proportion of them have the activation energy or more. This means that the frequency of successful collisions is greater, causing a greater rate of reaction.

It would have been better to vary the size of the particles and the temperature separately, but the data clearly shows that the rate of reaction in experiment 1 is greater than in experiment 2 [4].

[1] The reaction times given in the table are used to make a conclusion about the rates of reaction.

[2] An accurate answer should refer to the *surface area to volume ratio* of the particles, not just to their surface area.

[3] The answer should refer to *successful* collisions (as it does later), not just to collisions.

[4] The answer finishes by looking at the data and the experiment, and evaluating how strong the conclusion is.

Verdict

This is a strong answer. It comes to a clear conclusion about the data. The answer uses scientific knowledge to link the greater rate of reaction in experiment 2 to the energy and frequency of particle collisions.

Exam tip

When you are asked to evaluate data, you must use it to form a conclusion. This may include interpreting and explaining the information, or considering its strengths and weaknesses.

Paper 2

SC20 Fuels / SC21 Earth and Atmospheric Science

Crude oil and natural gas are mostly used to provide fuels. However, burning oil and natural gas produces carbon dioxide, which is thought to be changing our atmosphere and climate. The photo shows a jet fighter, in which the fuel is kerosene (one of the 'fractions' that crude oil can be split into). The long flame is caused by its afterburner. Extra fuel is injected into the hot exhaust gases, producing additional thrust.

Crude oil also gives us the raw materials needed to make a huge range of products, including polymers such as polythene. Crude oil is, though, a finite resource and the substances we make from it are non-renewable. They will run out one day if we continue to use them.

The learning journey

Previously you will have learnt at KS3:

- that mixtures may be separated using fractional distillation
- about fuels and energy resources
- about the acidity of non-metal oxides
- about the production of carbon dioxide by human activity and the impact on climate.

In this unit you will learn:

- about the hydrocarbons found in crude oil and natural gas
- how crude oil is separated into useful fractions
- about the alkanes as an homologous series
- about the problems caused by some atmospheric pollutants
- how and why cracking of oil fractions is carried out
- about the advantages and disadvantages of different fuels for cars
- about how the Earth's atmosphere has changed in the past and how it is changing now
- more about the causes and effects of climate change.

SC20a Hydrocarbons in crude oil and natural gas

Specification reference: C8.1; C8.2; C8.15

Progression questions

- What are hydrocarbons?
- Why is crude oil so useful?
- Why is crude oil a non-renewable, finite resource?

A Hydraulic fracturing or 'fracking' is one way to obtain fossil fuels. A mixture of water, sand and other substances is injected into underground rock at high pressure. Natural gas or crude oil flows from cracks in the rocks to the well head at the surface.

Natural gas and **crude oil** are natural resources formed from the ancient remains of microscopic animals and plants that once lived in the sea. These remains became covered by layers of sediment. Over millions of years, the remains gradually turned into natural gas and crude oil. The sediments turned into rock, trapping the gas and oil. These resources are **finite resources** because they are not made any more (or are being made extremely slowly), which limits the amounts available to us.

Crude oil

Crude oil is a complex mixture of **hydrocarbons**. A hydrocarbon is a compound that contains hydrogen and carbon atoms only. Carbon atoms can each form four covalent bonds, so the carbon atoms in hydrocarbon molecules are able to join together in different ways, forming chains and rings. The number of carbon atoms in a hydrocarbon molecule can vary from just one carbon atom to many hundreds of them.

1 Explain why natural gas and crude oil are finite resources.

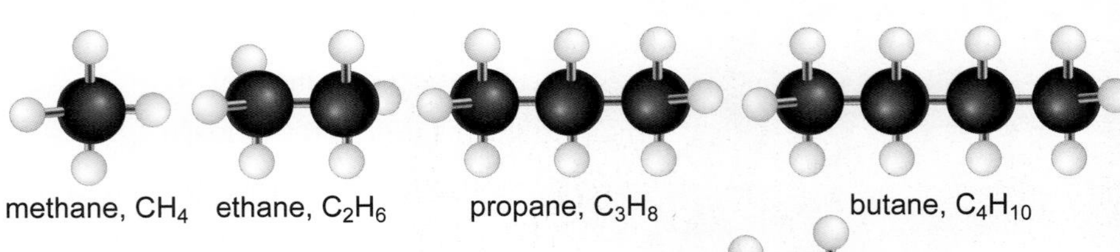

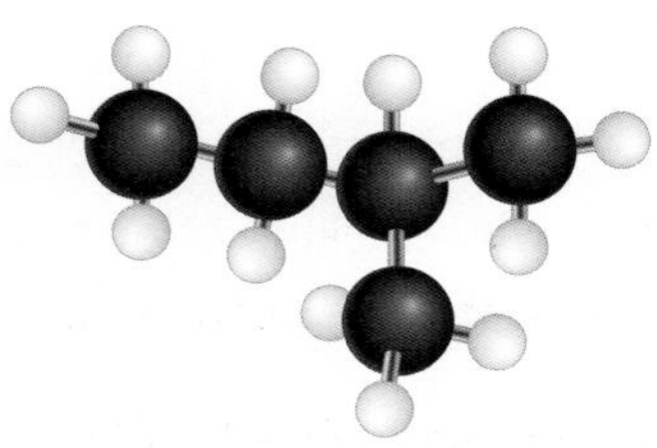

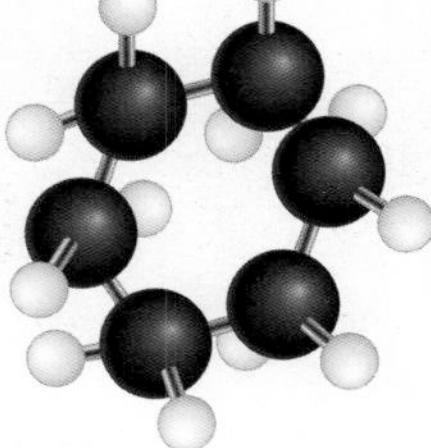

B These ball and stick models show some hydrocarbon molecules. The black spheres represent carbon atoms.

2 Explain what is meant by the term hydrocarbon.

3 Explain why carbon atoms can be arranged in chains or rings.

Hydrocarbons exist in different physical states, depending on the size and complexity of their molecules. Crude oil itself is liquid at room temperature, with hydrocarbons in the solid and gas states mixed with hydrocarbons in the liquid state.

Crude oil is an important source of useful substances, including:

- fuels for vehicles, aircraft, ships, heating and power stations
- **feedstock** or raw materials for the petrochemical industry.

Petrochemicals are substances made from crude oil, such as poly(ethene) and other polymers.

4 Describe two reasons why crude oil is useful to us.

Fuels

Natural gas is a mixture of hydrocarbons in the gas state. Methane, the main hydrocarbon in natural gas, is useful for cooking.

Several different liquid fuels can be obtained from crude oil, including petrol and diesel oil for vehicles, and kerosene for aircraft. These **fossil fuels** are **non-renewable** – they are being used up faster than they are being formed. If we carry on using these fuels, they will run out one day.

D Natural gas is used for domestic heating. This is a boiler with the cover taken off.

5 Explain why diesel and methane are *non-renewable* fossil fuels.

Exam-style question

Octane, C_8H_{18}, is one of the substances found in petrol.

a Explain why octane is a hydrocarbon. *(2 marks)*

b State why petrol is non-renewable. *(1 mark)*

C This oil industry engineer is pouring some crude oil into a container, ready for a test.

Did you know?

The barrel is the unit of volume used by the oil industry. One barrel of oil is 159 litres. The world uses about 96 million barrels of oil each day – about 180 000 litres per second.

Checkpoint

How confidently can you answer the Progression questions?

Strengthen

S1 What are the main features of crude oil and the substances it contains?

S2 Why are crude oil and natural gas useful?

Extend

E1 Why is crude oil an important finite source of non-renewable substances?

SC20b Fractional distillation of crude oil

Specification reference: C8.3; C8.4; C8.5

Progression questions

- How is crude oil separated into useful fractions?
- What are the names and uses of the main fractions from crude oil?
- What are the differences in the molecules found in different fractions from crude oil?

A Bitumen, a fraction obtained from crude oil, is mixed with small stones to make road surfaces.

Crude oil is usually not runny enough or ignited easily enough for it to be useful as a fuel. The different hydrocarbons it contains must be separated into simpler, more useful mixtures. This can be achieved using **fractional distillation** because the different hydrocarbons have different boiling points.

1 State why crude oil can be separated using fractional distillation.

In the fractionating column

The industrial fractional distillation of crude oil happens in a tall metal **fractionating column**. Crude oil is heated strongly to **evaporate** it, and the hot vapours are piped into the bottom of the column, where:

- the column is hottest at the bottom and coldest at the top
- the vapours rise through the column and cool down
- the vapours **condense** when they reach a part of the column that is cool enough (below their boiling points)
- the liquid falls into a tray and is piped away
- the vapours with the lowest boiling points do not condense at all and leave at the top as a mixture of gases
- bitumen has the highest boiling point and leaves at the bottom as a hot liquid.

The separated liquids and gases are called oil **fractions** because they are only parts of the original crude oil.

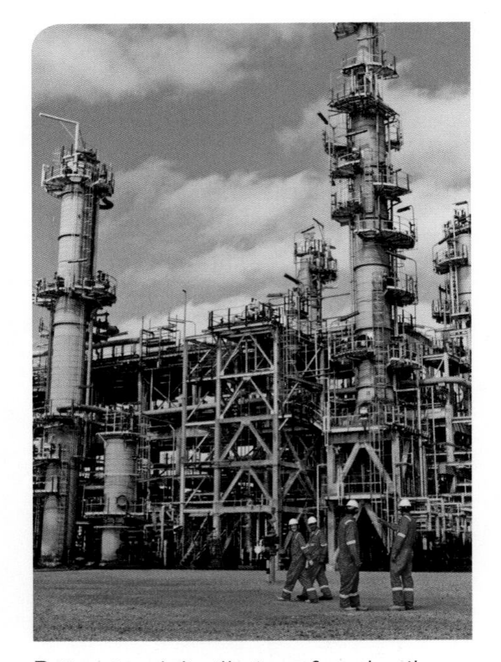

B Fractional distillation of crude oil happens at oil refineries.

2 Make a table to summarise the names and uses of the six main oil fractions.

3 Explain where changes of state happen during fractional distillation of crude oil.

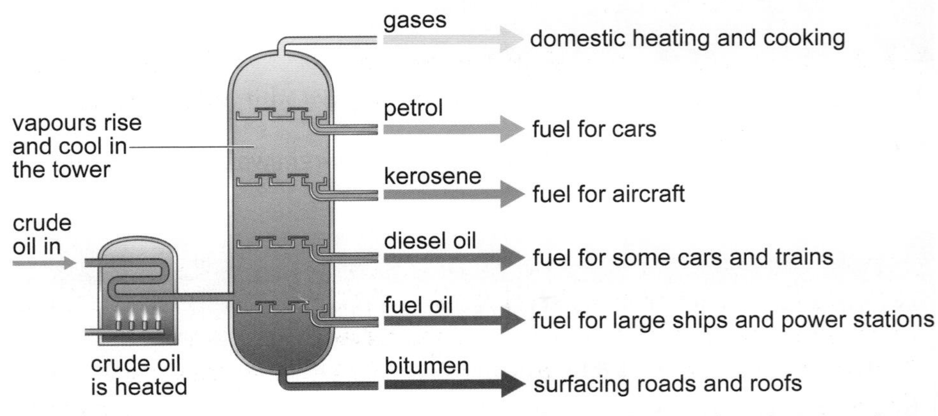

C These are the names and uses of the main fractions leaving an oil fractionating column.

Properties of fractions

Each fraction is a mixture of hydrocarbons, rather than a pure hydrocarbon. However, the hydrocarbons in a given fraction have similar numbers of carbon and hydrogen atoms in their molecules, and similar boiling points.

Different fractions have different uses because they have different properties. For example:

- the hydrocarbons in the gases fraction have the lowest **viscosity** (they flow easily) and are easiest to **ignite** (they are easily set alight), making them suitable for use as fuels
- bitumen is solid at room temperature, and waterproof, making it suitable for surfacing roads and roofs.

The other fractions are liquids at room temperature.

Fraction	Number of atoms in molecules	Boiling point	Ease of ignition	Viscosity
gases	smallest (1–4 carbon atoms)	lowest (<0 °C)	easy to ignite	lowest (flows most easily)
petrol				
kerosene				
diesel oil				
fuel oil				
bitumen	greatest (>35 carbon atoms)	highest (>350 °C)	difficult to ignite	highest (flows with difficulty)

D trends in the properties of the fractions leaving an oil fractionating column

4 Describe the properties of kerosene that make it suitable for use as an aircraft fuel.

5 Describe the relationships between the number of carbon atoms in a hydrocarbon molecule and the physical properties of the hydrocarbon.

Exam-style question

Petrol and fuel oil are different fractions separated from crude oil. Describe the difference in *one* physical property between these two fractions. *(2 marks)*

Did you know?

Over 100 million tonnes of bitumen is used globally each year. Around 85% is used for road building, and nearly all of it can be recycled when a road wears out and needs repairing.

Checkpoint

How confidently can you answer the Progression questions?

Strengthen

S1 How does fractional distillation of crude oil work?

S2 What do the substances in a crude oil fraction have in common?

Extend

E1 How is crude oil made into useful mixtures?

E2 Describe how the hydrocarbons in different fractions differ from each other.

SC20c The alkane homologous series

Specification reference: C8.5; C8.6

Progression questions

- What is the main type of hydrocarbon found in crude oil?
- What are the features of an homologous series of compounds?
- Why do alkanes form an homologous series?

A Methane, CH_4, is the simplest alkane. It is transported in large amounts as liquefied natural gas (LNG). It is distributed as a gas to homes and businesses through a network of pipelines.

The compounds in crude oil fractions are mostly **alkanes**. Alkanes are hydrocarbons that only have single covalent bonds between the atoms in their molecules. The alkanes form a 'family' or **homologous series** of compounds. There are several different homologous series but the members of a series have these features in common:

- the molecular formulae of neighbouring compounds differ by CH_2
- they have the same general formula (see the next page)
- they show a gradual variation in physical properties, such as their boiling points
- they have similar chemical properties.

1 Name the homologous series of compounds that make up most of crude oil.

Molecular formulae

The table shows information about the first three alkanes.

Name	Molecular formula	Structural formula
methane	CH_4	H–C(H)(H)–H
ethane	C_2H_6	H–C(H)(H)–C(H)(H)–H
propane	C_3H_8	H–C(H)(H)–C(H)(H)–C(H)(H)–H

B names and formulae of the first three alkanes

Going from ethane to propane, the number of carbon atoms increases by 1 and the number of hydrogen atoms increases by 2. You can see this in their **molecular formulae**, which show the actual numbers of atoms of each element in the molecules of these compounds. The molecular formula changes by CH_2 going from C_2H_6 to C_3H_8. You might find this easier to see in the **structural formulae** of ethane and propane. It looks as if an extra CH_2 group of atoms is fitted in between the two CH_3 groups of atoms.

2 Describe the difference between the molecular formulae of methane and ethane.

General formulae

A **general formula** represents the formula for a whole homologous series. The general formula for the alkanes is: C_nH_{2n+2}. This means that the number of hydrogen atoms is twice the number of carbon atoms, plus two. For example, propane molecules have three carbon atoms, so:

- $n = 3$, and $2n+2 = (2 \times 3) + 2 = 8$
- the molecular formula is C_3H_8.

3 Give the molecular formulae for:

a butane (an alkane with four carbon atoms)

b hexadecane (an alkane with 16 carbon atoms).

Trends in physical properties

The graph shows how the boiling points of alkanes change as the number of carbon atoms in the molecules increases. Notice that there is a gradual variation in this physical property. The difference in boiling points of the alkanes is the reason why alkanes in crude oil can be separated by fractional distillation.

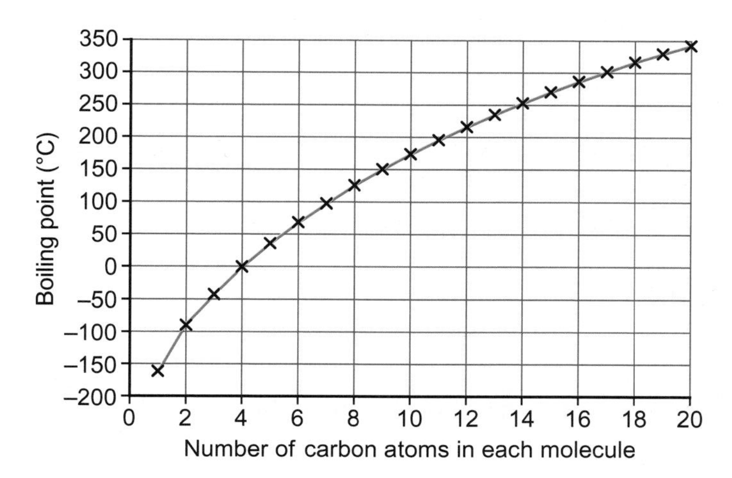

C The boiling point of a straight-chain alkane depends upon the size of its molecules.

Did you know?

The carbon atoms in alkanes can be arranged so there are branches as well as straight chains. There are only two ways to arrange the carbon atoms with butane but over 10 000 ways to do this with hexadecane.

4 Describe how the boiling points of alkanes change as the number of carbon atoms in the molecules changes.

Similar chemical properties

The alkanes have similar chemical properties. For example, they react with excess oxygen to produce carbon dioxide and water. These are the equations for propane, found in camping gas:

propane + oxygen → carbon dioxide + water

$C_3H_8 + 5O_2 \rightarrow 3CO_2 + 4H_2O$

5 Methane reacts with excess oxygen. For this reaction, write:

a the word equation

b the balanced equation.

Exam-style question

Ethene, C_2H_4, is a member of the alkene homologous series. The next two alkenes are propene, C_3H_6, and butene, C_4H_8. Explain why these three hydrocarbons are members of the same homologous series. *(2 marks)*

Checkpoint

How confidently can you answer the Progression questions?

Strengthen

S1 What are the features of an homologous series?

Extend

E1 Explain why the main components of crude oil form an homologous series.

SC20d Complete and incomplete combustion

Specification reference: C8.7; C8.8; C8.9; C8.10

Progression questions

- What happens during the complete combustion of a hydrocarbon?
- What happens during the incomplete combustion of a hydrocarbon?
- What problems does incomplete combustion cause?

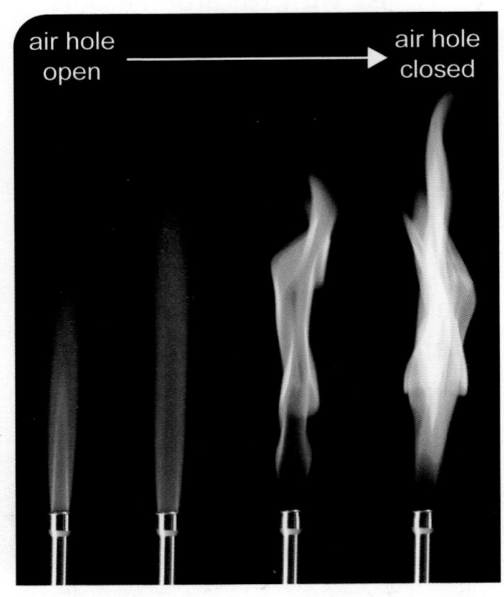

A Adjusting the air hole on a Bunsen burner alters the amount of air reaching the fuel, and changes the flame.

Hydrocarbon fuels react with oxygen in the air when they burn. This is an example of an **oxidation** reaction and is called **combustion**.

Complete combustion

Complete combustion of a hydrocarbon is a reaction in which:

- only carbon dioxide and water are produced
- energy is given out.

Complete combustion happens when there is a plentiful supply of air or oxygen, for example when the air hole on a Bunsen burner is fully open. Methane is the main hydrocarbon found in natural gas:

methane + oxygen → carbon dioxide + water

$$CH_4 + 2O_2 \rightarrow CO_2 + 2H_2O$$

1 Write the balanced equation for the complete combustion of pentane, C_5H_{12}.

2 Describe laboratory tests for water and for carbon dioxide.

The apparatus in photo B is used to investigate combustion. A pump draws combustion products from the Bunsen burner through the apparatus. Iced water cools and condenses water vapour passing through the U-shaped tube. White anhydrous copper sulfate in the U-shaped tube turns into blue hydrated copper sulfate, showing the presence of water. Limewater in the boiling tube turns milky, showing the presence of carbon dioxide.

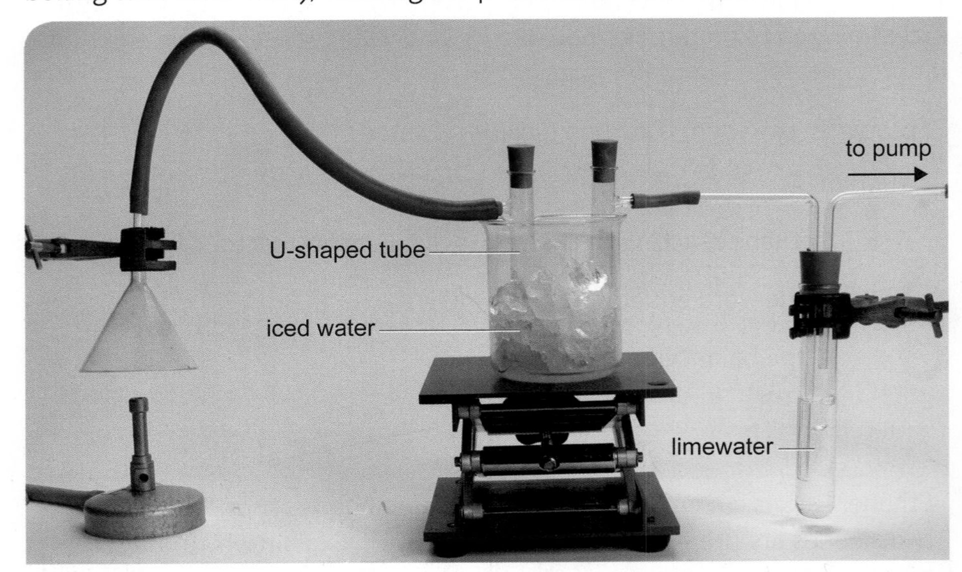

B This apparatus is used to investigate combustion products.

Incomplete combustion

Incomplete combustion happens when there is a limited supply of air or oxygen, such as when the air hole on a Bunsen burner is closed. During the incomplete combustion of a hydrocarbon:

- water is produced
- energy is given out (but less than with complete combustion)
- **carbon monoxide**, CO, and carbon are produced.

Some carbon atoms in the hydrocarbon may still be fully oxidised to carbon dioxide, but some are only partially oxidised to carbon monoxide. Some carbon atoms are released as smoke and **soot**.

Incomplete combustion problems

Incomplete combustion can cause problems in appliances that use hydrocarbon fuels, such as boilers and heaters, if they are poorly maintained or unventilated. Carbon monoxide is a **toxic** gas. It combines with **haemoglobin** in **red blood cells**, preventing oxygen combining. This reduces the amount of oxygen carried in the bloodstream, causing affected people to feel sleepy or to become unconscious. Severe carbon monoxide poisoning can even cause death.

Soot can block the pipes carrying away waste gases from an appliance. It blackens buildings, and it can cause breathing problems if it collects in the lungs.

D This wall has been blackened by soot from the exhaust pipe of an old boiler.

 **5** Describe *one* problem caused by soot.

Exam-style question

Describe a problem caused by *one* product of the incomplete combustion of natural gas. *(2 marks)*

 **3** Explain why incomplete combustion of hydrocarbons can produce carbon monoxide and carbon.

C Carbon monoxide is colourless and odourless, so electronic carbon monoxide detectors are used in homes using natural gas for heating or cooking.

 **4** Explain why carbon monoxide is a *toxic* gas.

Did you know?

After hydrogen, carbon monoxide is the second most common molecule in interstellar space.

Checkpoint

How confidently can you answer the Progression questions?

Strengthen

S1 Why can burning fuels in a lack of oxygen cause problems?

Extend

E1 Explain why adequate ventilation is important when using appliances fuelled by hydrocarbons.

SC20e Combustible fuels and pollution

Specification reference: C8.11; C8.12; C8.13

Progression questions

- Why do some hydrocarbon fuels release sulfur dioxide when they are used?
- Why are oxides of nitrogen produced by engines?
- What problems are caused by acid rain?

A The trees in this forest have died because of the effects of acid rain.

Carbon dioxide, like other soluble non-metal oxides, forms an acidic solution with water. Rain water is naturally acidic because it contains carbon dioxide from the air. **Acid rain** has a pH lower than 5.2, making it more acidic than natural rain water. Sulfur dioxide is a major cause of this extra acidity.

1 Name a substance that causes acid rain.

B New stonework and similar stonework (on the right) damaged by years of acid rain.

Sulfur dioxide

Hydrocarbon fuels (such as petrol and diesel oil) may contain sulfur compounds. These occur naturally as **impurities** and are not deliberately added. On the contrary, most of these impurities are removed at oil refineries in an attempt to reduce the environmental problems they cause. When the hydrocarbon fuel is burnt, the sulfur reacts with oxygen to form sulfur dioxide gas, SO_2.

Sulfur dioxide dissolves in the water in clouds to form a mixture of acids, including sulfurous acid:

$$H_2O(l) + SO_2(g) \rightarrow H_2SO_3(aq)$$

Sulfurous acid is oxidised by oxygen in the air to form sulfuric acid:

$$2H_2SO_3(aq) + O_2(g) \rightarrow 2H_2SO_4(aq)$$

This mixture of sulfurous acid and sulfuric acid causes problems when it falls as acid rain. Crops do not grow well when the soil is too acidic. Excess acidity in rivers and lakes prevents fish eggs hatching, and it can kill fish and insects.

Acid rain increases the rate of **weathering** of buildings made of limestone or marble, and breaks down their structures. These rocks are almost pure calcium carbonate, which reacts with sulfuric acid:

calcium carbonate + sulfuric acid → calcium sulfate + water + carbon dioxide

Acid rain also increases the rate of corrosion of metals, such as the iron in steel, weakening them:

iron + sulfuric acid → iron(II) sulfate + hydrogen

2 Write a balanced equation for the reaction between sulfur and oxygen.

3 Describe two environmental problems caused by sulfur dioxide dissolving in rain water.

4 Write the balanced equation for the reaction between calcium carbonate, $CaCO_3$, and sulfuric acid.

Oxides of nitrogen

Car engines are 'internal combustion' engines – fuel is mixed with air and ignited *inside* the engine. This causes temperatures high enough for nitrogen and oxygen in the air inside the engine to react together. The reactions produce various **oxides of nitrogen**, or NO_x, which are atmospheric **pollutants**.

C Spreading powdered limestone on a field reduces the acidity of the soil.

NO_x are a cause of acid rain. Nitrogen dioxide, NO_2, forms dilute nitric acid when it dissolves in the water in clouds. Nitrogen dioxide is a toxic red-brown gas, and it can cause respiratory diseases such as bronchitis. Catalytic converters in cars convert most of the NO_x in exhaust gases to harmless nitrogen.

D In sunlight, oxides of nitrogen react with other pollutants to form a harmful 'photochemical smog'.

6 Catalytic converters can reduce nitrogen dioxide, forming nitrogen and oxygen. Write a balanced equation for this reaction.

Exam-style question

Large ships use fuel oil, which contains sulfur as an impurity. Explain why this can cause environmental problems when ships travel the oceans. *(3 marks)*

Did you know?

Sulfur dioxide causes atmospheric cooling when it is released in volcanic eruptions. Scientists have suggested deliberately injecting sulfur dioxide high into the atmosphere as a way to reduce global warming.

5 Explain why:

a the use of some hydrocarbon fuels causes the production of sulfur dioxide

b oxides of nitrogen may be produced when hydrocarbon fuels are used.

Checkpoint

How confidently can you answer the Progression questions?

Strengthen

S1 Why are some non-metal oxides produced when hydrocarbon fuels are used in cars?

S2 What problems are caused by acid rain?

Extend

E1 How does the use of hydrocarbon fuels produce pollutants?

E2 Why might the problems caused by acid rain vary over time?

SC20f Breaking down hydrocarbons

Specification reference: C8.14; C8.16; C8.17

Progression questions

- Why is cracking needed?
- What happens during the cracking of crude oil fractions?
- What are the advantages and disadvantages of hydrogen and petrol as vehicle fuels?

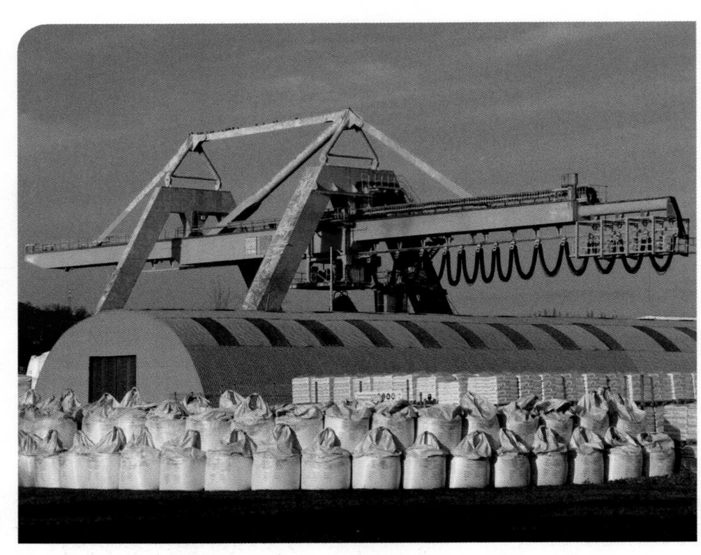

A This storage building has stockpiles outside because the supply of the products is greater than the customers' demand for them.

When crude oil is separated by fractional distillation, the volume of each fraction usually does not match the volume that can be sold. The supply of some fractions is greater than customer demand, while the demand for other fractions is greater than the supply. Oil refineries use **cracking** to match supply with demand. Cracking also produces hydrocarbons with C=C bonds. These hydrocarbons are used to make polymers.

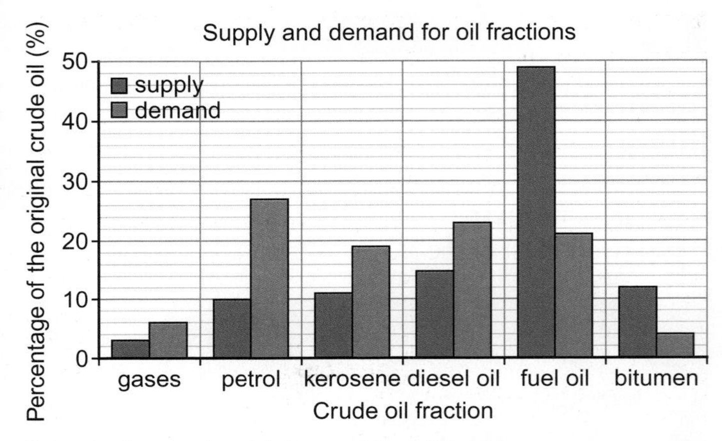

B example supply and demand for oil fractions

1 Use bar chart B to identify:

a the fractions in higher supply than demand

b the fractions in higher demand than supply.

Cracking

Cracking involves breaking covalent bonds in hydrocarbon molecules. Crude oil fractions are heated to evaporate them. The vapours are passed over a **catalyst** containing aluminium oxide and heated to about 650 °C. This speeds up reactions that break down larger hydrocarbon molecules. Smaller, more useful, hydrocarbon molecules form and these can be used as fuels or for making polymers. For example:

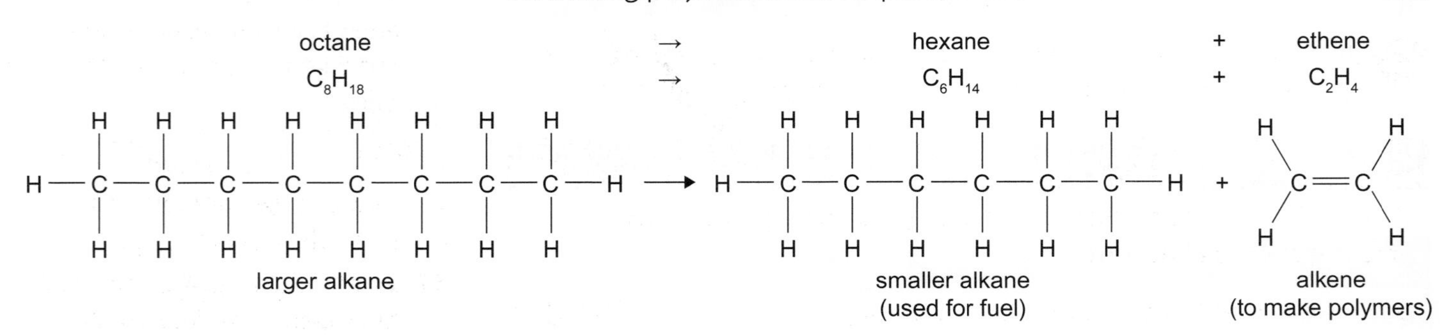

C a cracking reaction (modelled using structural formulae)

Notice that one of the products, ethene C_2H_4, is an **alkene**. Alkenes form a different homologous series to alkanes. Alkanes and alkenes are hydrocarbons, but:

- alkanes are **saturated** (their carbon atoms are joined by single bonds, C–C)
- alkenes are **unsaturated** (they contain a carbon–carbon double bond, C=C).

Fuels for cars

Petrol is in high demand for use as a fuel for cars. It is liquid at room temperature, so large amounts can be stored in the car's fuel tank and then pumped to the engine. Petrol is easily ignited, and its combustion releases large amounts of energy.

Hydrogen can also be used to fuel cars. It is a by-product of cracking and can also be produced by reacting methane (from natural gas) with steam. Unlike petrol and other hydrocarbon fuels, the combustion of hydrogen produces water vapour but no carbon dioxide. Hydrogen fuel has environmental benefits because carbon dioxide is a **greenhouse gas**, linked to global warming and climate change.

Like petrol, hydrogen is easily ignited and its combustion releases large amounts of energy. Unlike petrol, hydrogen is a gas at room temperature. This makes hydrogen difficult to store in large amounts unless it is compressed under high pressure or liquefied by cooling.

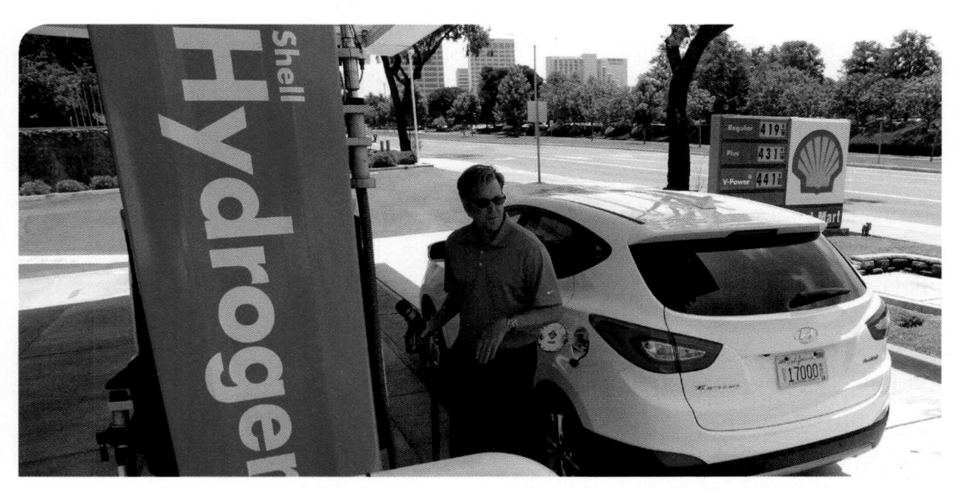

D In this car, electricity for an electric motor is generated by a fuel cell that uses hydrogen.

 **5** Explain, in terms of hydrogen molecules, an advantage of storing hydrogen in the liquid state rather than in the gas state.

Exam-style question

Ethene, C_2H_4, is used to make poly(ethene). Ethene is produced by cracking crude oil fractions.

a Explain what is meant by the term cracking. *(2 marks)*

b Complete this equation: $C_8H_{18} \rightarrow 3C_2H_4 +$ .... *(1 mark)*

 **2** Copy and complete this equation, which models a cracking reaction.

$C_{16}H_{34} \rightarrow$ .... $+ C_2H_4$

 **3** Describe the difference between saturated and unsaturated hydrocarbons.

 **4** Write a balanced equation, with state symbols, for the reaction between hydrogen and oxygen.

Did you know?

Scientists have discovered that graphene can store hydrogen. Roasted coconut or roasted chicken feathers work too.

Checkpoint

How confidently can you answer the Progression questions?

Strengthen

S1 How are crude oil fractions made more useful?

S2 What are the advantages and disadvantages of using hydrogen in cars, rather than petrol?

Extend

E1 How and why are relatively large alkanes broken down?

E2 What influences the choice of hydrogen or petrol as a fuel for cars?

SC21a The early atmosphere

Specification reference: C8.18; C8.19; C8.20

Progression questions

- What are the names of some common gases produced by volcanic activity?
- What evidence is there for the composition of the Earth's early atmosphere?
- How do scientists explain the formation of the oceans?

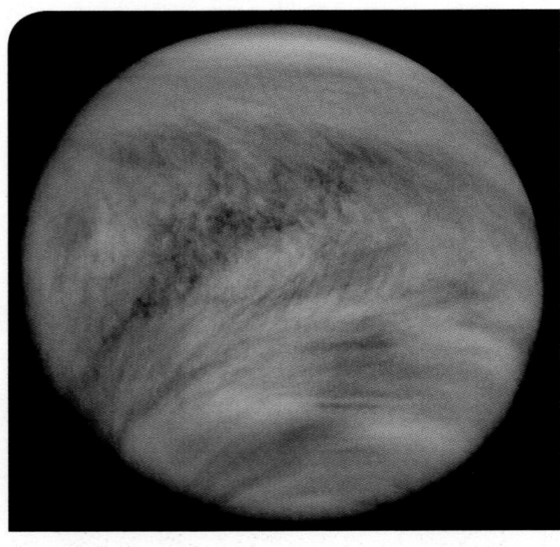

A Venus' atmosphere is 96.5% carbon dioxide and 3.5% nitrogen.

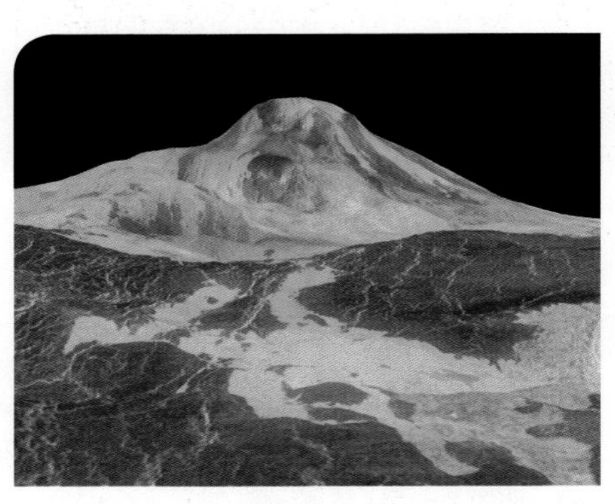

B Maat Mons (an 8 km high volcano on Venus) photographed by the NASA *Magellan* space probe

Did you know?

The largest volcano in the Solar System is on Mars. Called *Olympus Mons*, it is 27 km high (three times the height of Mount Everest).

Evidence indicates that significant changes have occurred to the **composition** of the Earth's **atmosphere** in its 4.5 billion year history. More recent changes are due to living organisms.

To investigate the atmosphere before life evolved, scientists look at evidence on Earth and study the atmospheres of other planets and moons. These bodies are unlikely to contain life, so their atmospheres may be similar to the Earth's early atmosphere.

1 Explain why scientists study the atmospheres of other bodies in our Solar System.

Earth's early atmosphere

The Earth's early atmosphere is thought to have been mainly carbon dioxide, with smaller amounts of water vapour and other gases, and little or no oxygen.

Volcanoes affect the atmosphere by releasing large amounts of some gases, such as carbon dioxide and water vapour, and small amounts of other gases (including nitrogen). There was a lot of **volcanic activity** on the early Earth, so volcanoes probably helped form its atmosphere.

Earth, Venus and Mars are rocky planets with volcanoes. The atmospheres of Venus and Mars are mainly made of carbon dioxide, thought to have been released by volcanoes. This supports the idea that Earth's early atmosphere also contained lots of carbon dioxide.

Some scientists think that the Earth's early atmosphere was mainly nitrogen. Evidence for this comes from Titan, a moon of Saturn. Titan's atmosphere is 98.4% nitrogen, probably also released by volcanoes. However, space probes have shown that Titan has an icy interior, unlike Earth, Venus or Mars. So, Earth's early atmosphere is less likely to have been like Titan's.

2 State how volcanoes affect the atmospheres of planets.

3 **a** Give the name of the gas most likely to have formed most of the Earth's early atmosphere.

b Explain why the discovery of Titan's icy interior does not support the idea that the Earth's early atmosphere was mainly nitrogen.

4 Explain why scientists think that the early Earth had an atmosphere similar to Venus.

The oceans

About 4 billion years ago, the Earth cooled down. This caused water vapour in the atmosphere to condense to liquid water, which formed the oceans.

5 Describe how the Earth's oceans may have formed.

C Many scientists think that the gases in Earth's early atmosphere came from volcanoes.

Oxygen

While the exact composition of the Earth's early atmosphere is uncertain, there is much more direct evidence to support the idea that it contained little or no oxygen.

D bands of iron oxide in an ancient rock

Oxygen is not produced by volcanoes. Further evidence comes from iron pyrite, a compound that is broken down by oxygen and so only forms if there is no oxygen. It is often found in very ancient rock.

About 2.4 billion years ago, rocks containing bands of iron oxide started to form. This oxidation of iron suggests that oxygen levels increased at this time. There is fossil evidence of microorganisms that may have produced this oxygen. So, scientists think that oxygen from these microorganisms reacted with iron in the early oceans, to produce insoluble iron oxides that formed layers on the seabed.

Some geologists suggest that it was only after microorganisms had produced enough oxygen to oxidise the iron in the ocean that atmospheric oxygen levels could rise.

6 Explain the evidence that supports the idea that oxygen was not present in the early Earth's atmosphere.

7 Why are scientists more certain about the oxygen content of the early atmosphere compared to other gases?

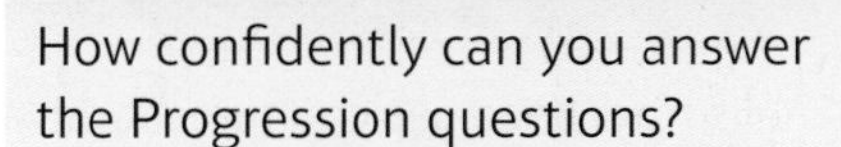

Checkpoint

How confidently can you answer the Progression questions?

Strengthen

S1 Describe two pieces of evidence that suggest that the composition of the Earth's early atmosphere was mainly carbon dioxide, with little or no oxygen.

Extend

E1 Explain why many scientists think that the Earth's early atmosphere was similar to that of Mars today (which is 95.3% carbon dioxide, 2.7% nitrogen, 1.6% argon and 0.13% oxygen).

Exam-style question

Describe how the Earth's cooling 4 billion years ago caused a change in the composition of the atmosphere. *(2 marks)*

SC21b The changing atmosphere

Specification reference: C8.21; C8.22; C8.23

Progression questions

- Why did the amount of carbon dioxide in the atmosphere change?
- How did primitive organisms change carbon dioxide and oxygen levels?
- What is the test for oxygen?

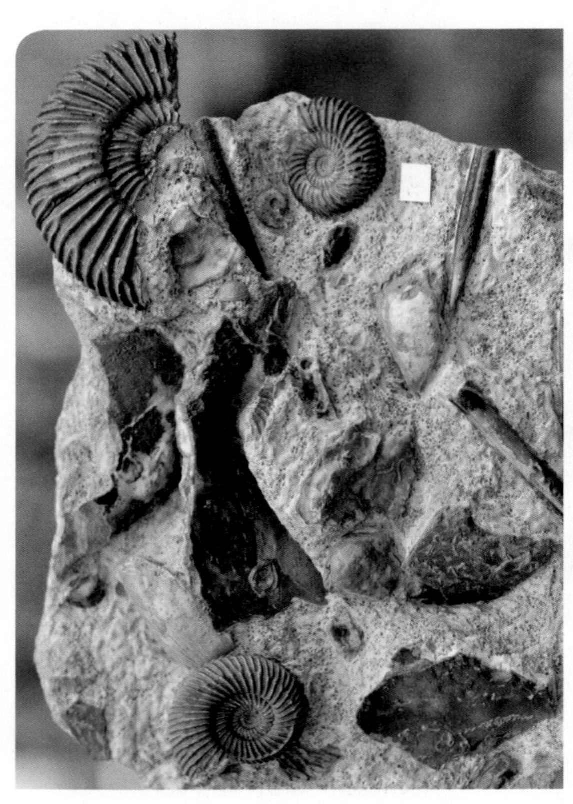

A Shells from dead sea creatures form layers of sediment that turn into sedimentary rocks (e.g. limestone) over millions of years. Shells can often be seen in limestone.

B Stromatolites are caused by oxygen-releasing microorganisms called cyanobacteria.

As the young Earth changed, so did the atmosphere. Over hundreds of millions of years the amount of oxygen increased and carbon dioxide levels decreased. Scientists have put forward many **hypotheses** to explain this. There is strong evidence to support some of these.

Oceans

As the young Earth cooled, water vapour in the atmosphere condensed and formed oceans. Many scientists think that carbon dioxide then dissolved in the oceans, reducing the amount of carbon dioxide in the atmosphere. Sea creatures used the dissolved carbon dioxide to form shells made of calcium carbonate, $CaCO_3$. This then allowed more carbon dioxide to dissolve in the oceans.

1 **State what happened to the water vapour in the Earth's atmosphere when temperatures cooled.**

Oxygen

Some organisms use energy from the Sun to make food by **photosynthesis**. These organisms change the atmosphere because photosynthesis uses up carbon dioxide and releases oxygen.

Some of the earliest photosynthetic organisms were cyanobacteria, which live in shallow waters. These bacteria grow in huge colonies and produce sticky mucus. The mucus traps a layer of sand grains and other sediments. The organisms need to move above the sediment layer in order to get sunlight. Over time, the sediment layers build up to form rocky shapes, called stromatolites.

2 **Explain why cyanobacteria need to move above the sediment as it collects in layers on a stromatolite.**

Some stromatolites are over 3 billion years old. They provide evidence that photosynthetic organisms were living at this time. It is thought that microorganisms like these caused a rise in oxygen levels in the oceans and then the atmosphere.

Cyanobacteria evolved into other forms of life, including plants. When land plants evolved, about 500 million years ago, there was another jump in atmospheric oxygen levels.

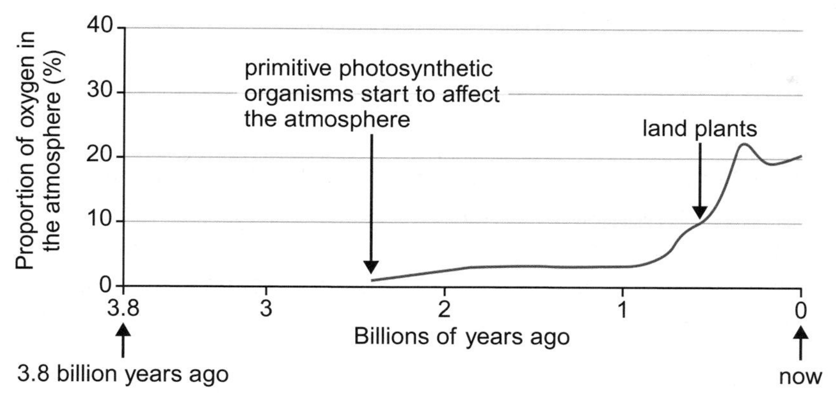

C Diagram showing how some scientists think that oxygen levels in the Earth's atmosphere may have changed over 3.8 billion years.

Today, oxygen makes up about 21% of the Earth's atmosphere. It is important for aerobic respiration in organisms. It also allows combustion (burning) to happen, and this property is used to test for the gas in the laboratory; pure oxygen will relight a glowing splint.

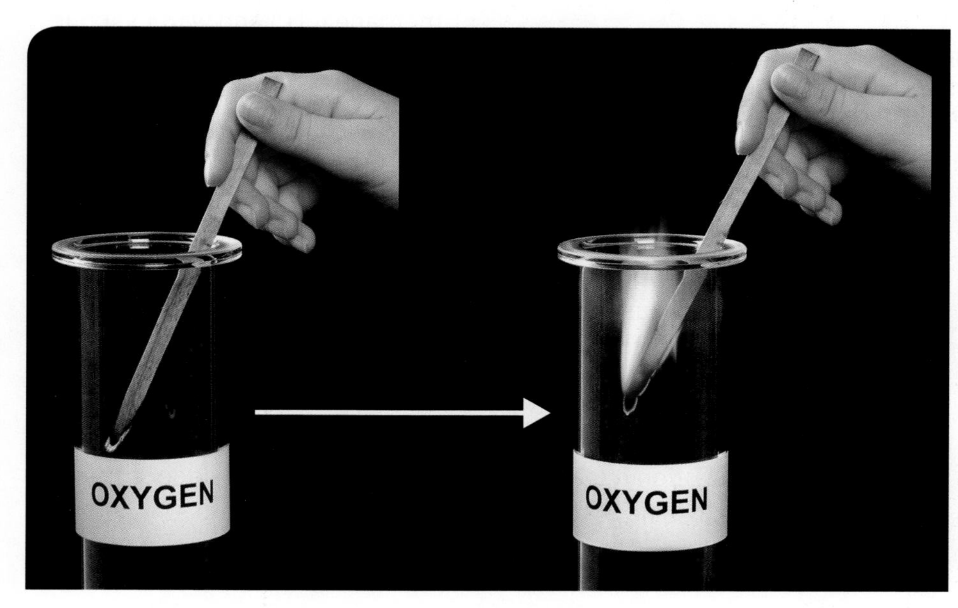

D the test for oxygen

 **5** **a** State the laboratory test for oxygen.

 **b** Why does oxygen relight a glowing splint?

Exam-style question

Explain why the formation of oceans on Earth may have caused a decrease in atmospheric carbon dioxide levels. *(3 marks)*

 **3** Explain why the presence of ancient stromatolites supports the idea of photosynthesis starting to occur over 3 billion years ago.

 **4** Describe how the evolution of land plants changed the composition of the atmosphere.

Did you know?

Oxygen is very reactive and would soon disappear from the atmosphere without photosynthetic organisms. Space scientists are very interested in trying to find other planets that contain oxygen in their atmospheres.

Checkpoint

How confidently can you answer the Progression questions?

Strengthen

S1 Explain how carbon dioxide levels in the Earth's atmosphere decreased.

S2 Explain how oxygen levels in the Earth's atmosphere increased.

Extend

E1 Explain how the development of life on Earth influenced levels of carbon dioxide and oxygen in the atmosphere.

SC21c The atmosphere today

Specification reference: C8.24; C8.25

Progression questions

- What are the names of some greenhouse gases?
- How is the greenhouse effect caused?
- What is the link between fossil fuel combustion and climate change?

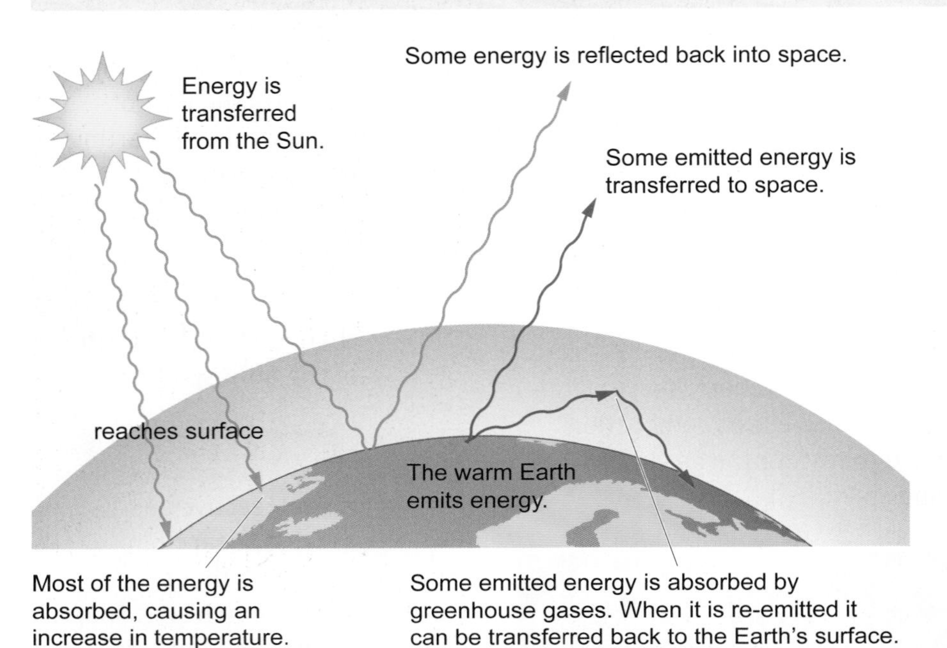

A The greenhouse effect keeps the Earth warm.

Energy from the Sun is transferred to the Earth by waves, such as light and **infrared**. Some energy is absorbed by the Earth's surface, warming it up. The warm Earth **emits** (gives out) infrared waves. Some gases in the air **absorb** energy transferred by these infrared waves. When the gases re-emit the energy, some of it goes back to the Earth's surface and warms it. This is the **greenhouse effect**.

The gases in the atmosphere that absorb energy are called **greenhouse gases**, and include carbon dioxide (CO_2), methane (CH_4) and water vapour (H_2O). Without them, the mean surface temperature of the Earth would be about −18 °C (compared to about 14 °C, which it is today).

1 List three greenhouse gases.

2 State the influence of the greenhouse effect on the Earth.

Correlation and climate change

There is evidence to support the idea that human activity is increasing the greenhouse effect and causing **global warming**. This is thought to be causing **climate change** (changes to average weather conditions around the world).

Since about 1850, there has been a steady increase in the burning of fossil fuels for industry. During this period, carbon dioxide levels have increased. We know that combustion releases CO_2, and so this is good evidence that increased fossil fuel use has caused increased CO_2 levels.

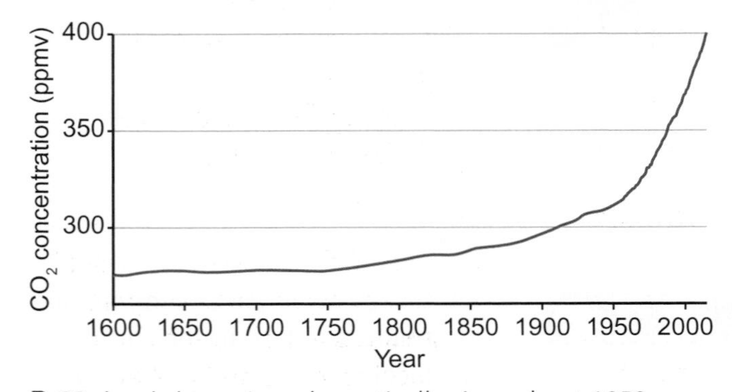

B CO_2 levels have risen dramatically since about 1850.

As CO_2 levels have risen, so has the average temperature of the Earth's surface. There is a strong **correlation** between CO_2 levels and surface temperature.

However, a correlation does not mean that there is a **causal link** (one thing causes the other). To show a causal link, scientists must collect evidence and explain *how* and *why* the correlation occurs. In this case, scientists want to know whether increasing CO_2 levels could actually cause global temperatures to rise, whether the reverse happens, or whether there is no causal link.

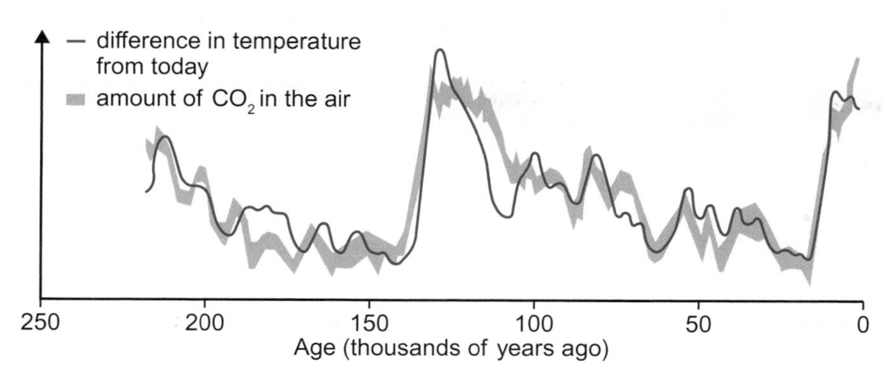

C Average global temperatures and atmospheric carbon dioxide levels are correlated.

Scientists can show in the lab that CO_2 absorbs infrared. Satellite data confirm that as CO_2 levels have increased, there has been a reduction in infrared waves from the Earth leaving the atmosphere. This supports the idea that CO_2 *causes* temperature rises because it shows how it could occur.

 **3** Why might industrialisation have led to an increase in greenhouse gases?

4 **a** Describe what global warming is.

b Compare global warming with climate change.

 **5** **a** What is a 'causal link'?

 **b** Explain why many scientists believe that there *is* a causal link between recent CO_2 level increases and a rise in temperature.

Evaluating the evidence

The amount of carbon dioxide in the air today is measured at monitoring stations around the world. Evidence for historical carbon dioxide levels comes from measuring concentrations of the gas trapped in ice cores. The oldest cores come from Antarctica and give data going back 800 000 years.

The oldest continuous temperature records are for central England and go back to 1659. However, these records cannot be used to assess global temperature changes because they are from only one place. Continuous temperature measurements from around the world exist from about 1880.

Earlier measurements were not very accurate. Modern thermometers are less prone to error and have a greater **resolution**. Today, we can also analyse huge amounts of data from around the world, including temperature measurements from many different sources (such as sensors and satellites).

 **6** How do scientists measure carbon dioxide levels from the past?

Exam-style question 

Describe why the greenhouse effect leads to increased average global temperatures. *(3 marks)*

D Gases are trapped in ice cores.

Checkpoint 

How confidently can you answer the Progression questions?

Strengthen

S1 Describe the evidence to support the idea that increasing levels of greenhouse gases have caused increased average global temperatures.

Extend

E1 Describe how scientists would collect evidence to support a causal link between carbon dioxide levels and global temperatures.

SC21d Climate change

Specification reference: C8.26

Progression questions

- What human activities influence the climate?
- What problems might climate change cause?
- How might we limit the impact of predicted climate change?

A Methane being released and burnt off on an oil rig.

The increased burning of fossil fuels has released more and more carbon dioxide (CO_2) into the atmosphere, which is thought to be causing global warming. However, CO_2 is not the only greenhouse gas produced by human activity.

Methane (CH_4) is a more powerful greenhouse gas than CO_2 because it is much better at absorbing infrared radiation from the Earth. Methane is the main component of natural gas, and is released into the atmosphere when oil and natural gas are extracted from the ground and processed.

Livestock farming (especially cattle) also produces a lot of methane. Cattle have bacteria in their stomachs to digest tough grass. Some of the bacteria produce methane. Soil bacteria in landfill sites and in rice 'paddy' fields also produce a lot of methane.

1 State three human activities that cause climate change.

2 How does livestock farming increase levels of greenhouse gases in the atmosphere?

3 Describe why an increasing world population might lead to more greenhouse gases being released into the atmosphere.

B Rice paddy fields produce significant amounts of methane.

Effects of climate change

Rising average global temperatures will cause ice at the South Pole and glaciers to melt. The extra water will raise sea levels, which will lead to increased flooding in some areas. Higher average temperatures will also result in a loss of 'sea ice' at the poles.

Some animals may move away from their natural habitats to find cooler areas. Some animals and plants may become extinct if they cannot survive at warmer temperatures or find new places to live.

As weather patterns change, some areas will become drier and others will become wetter. Scientists predict that there will be more extreme weather events (such as heavy rainfall, powerful storms and heat waves). These changes will affect wildlife and the growth of crops that people depend upon.

Did you know?

Sea levels have been rising at a rate of over 3 mm per year since 1993.

As more CO_2 is released, more of this acidic gas will dissolve in seawater, lowering its pH. This can harm organisms living in the seas and oceans. Additionally, as ocean temperatures rise, it causes coral to push out the photosynthetic algae that live in their tissues. These algae provide the colour of coral and so coral 'bleaching' may occur.

 **4** List four negative effects of climate change.

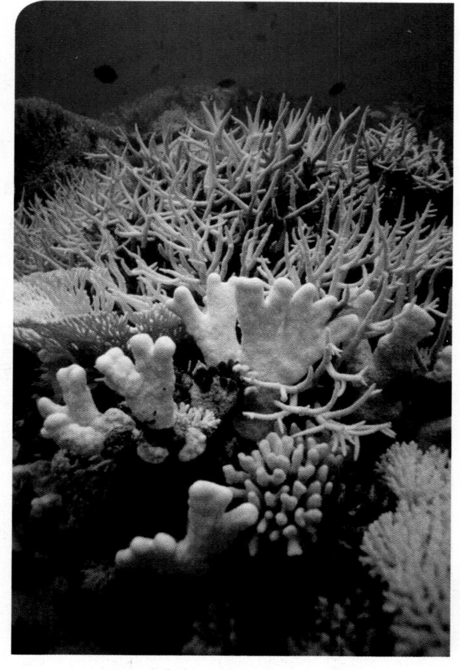

C If coral remain 'bleached' for too long they can die.

Limiting the impact

Using renewable energy resources can reduce greenhouse gas emissions, but there is a risk that this may not be enough to mitigate (lessen) the effects of climate change that we are already seeing.

Some people have suggested global engineering solutions, to reflect sunlight back into space or to capture CO_2 from the air and bury it underground. However, all countries will need to work together to reduce emissions and help pay for large-scale engineering. There is a risk that some countries will not help and that delicate ecosystems may be disrupted.

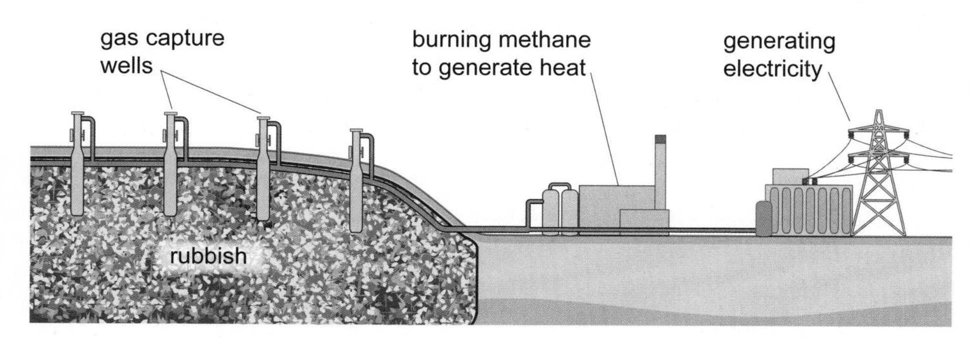

D Methane released from landfill sites can be captured and burnt to generate electricity.

Other ways of limiting the impact of climate change involve helping local people to adapt to new conditions. These include building flood defences, dams and irrigation systems. However, these ideas may destroy important habitats and there is a risk that they will not work.

 **5** Explain why an increased use of renewable energy might help to limit the impact of climate change.

 **6** Explain why international cooperation is important in dealing with climate change.

 **7** **a** Identify a way of limiting the impact of climate change.

 **b** State one risk associated with your suggestion.

Exam-style question

a State a problem caused by climate change. *(1 mark)*

b Describe what can be done to limit any harmful impact. *(1 mark)*

Checkpoint

How confidently can you answer the Progression questions?

Strengthen

S1 State an effect on the climate of increased carbon dioxide and methane levels, and identify whether the effect is global or local.

S2 Identify one way of reducing the harmful effect of your example above.

S3 State a risk associated with your suggested mitigation method.

Extend

E1 State the three most important policies you think the government should have for tackling climate change. Justify your choices.

Fuels

Useful substances are separated from crude oil by fractional distillation. The diagram shows the column used and the fractions it produces. The bitumen fraction leaves from the bottom of this column.

Look at the heights at which the kerosene and fuel oil fractions are collected. Explain the properties and uses for kerosene and fuel oil using the information.

(6 marks)

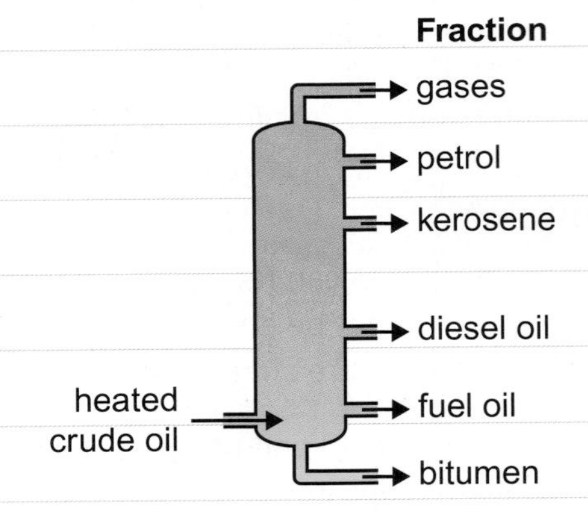

Student answer

The top of the fractionating column is cooler than the bottom. Kerosene vapours condense higher up the column than fuel oil. Kerosene has a lower boiling point than fuel oil. This is because the hydrocarbon molecules in kerosene have fewer carbon atoms and hydrogen atoms than the hydrocarbon molecules in fuel oil [1]*. Kerosene is more easily ignited than fuel oil* [2]*. It also has a lower viscosity than fuel oil, so kerosene flows more easily* [3]*. The differences in these properties make kerosene useful as a fuel for aircraft,* [4] *while fuel oil is used as a fuel for large ships and some power stations* [5]*.*

[1] The answer uses information given in the diagram, and the student's own knowledge and understanding, to link the size of the molecules in each fraction to its boiling point and position.

[2] This describes an important difference in the properties of the two fractions.

[3] It makes clear what low viscosity means – a less viscous substance flows more easily than a more viscous substance.

[4] It is important not to just describe kerosene as *used* in aircraft, but as a *fuel* for aircraft.

[5] More than one use of fuel oil is given, and both are correct.

Verdict

This is a strong answer. It shows good knowledge and understanding of the fractions obtained from crude oil, and uses correct scientific language. The answer uses scientific knowledge to link the size of the hydrocarbon molecules to their boiling points, and therefore the heights at which they are collected in the fractionating column. The answer is organised logically, explaining the differences in properties and then the difference in uses.

Exam tip

If you are given information in a question, make sure you use and refer to it in your answer. In this case, the question stated that you should use the information from the diagram.

Paper 2

SC22 Hydrocarbons / SC23 Alcohols and Carboxylic Acids / SC24 Polymers

Your body contains natural polymers including proteins, starch and DNA. Chemists discovered how to make poly(ethene), an artificial polymer, by accident over a hundred years ago. Nowadays, chemists know a lot more about polymers and how to make them using hydrocarbons, alcohols and carboxylic acids. They are able to develop polymers with astonishing properties, including light-emitting polymers that form flexible screens and polymers that mimic the appearance and flexibility of human skin. This robot head is covered with a spongy polymer, which helps the robot produce different life-like expressions.

The learning journey

Previously you will have learnt at KS3:

- about combustion of fuels
- about the properties of polymers.

In this unit you will learn:

- about the structures and properties of alkanes and alkenes
- how a concentrated solution of ethanol is produced from carbohydrates
- about the structures of alcohols and carboxylic acids
- about the chemical properties and uses of alcohols and carboxylic acids
- about the composition of biological polymers
- how poly(ethene) and other polymers are made
- about the disposal and recycling of polymers.

SC22a Alkanes and alkenes

Specification reference: C9.10C; C9.11C; C9.12C; C9.13C

Progression questions

- What are the names, formulae and structures of the four smallest alkanes?
- What functional group is present in all alkenes?
- How is the position of this functional group shown in alkene names?

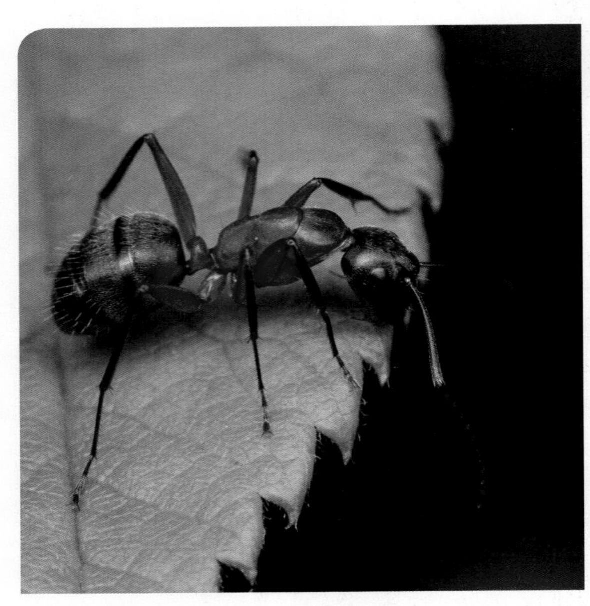

A Carpenter ants release the alkane undecane ($C_{11}H_{24}$) to signal danger, which other carpenter ants detect using their antennae.

Alkanes

Hydrocarbons are molecular compounds that contain only carbon and hydrogen. **Alkanes** are a group of hydrocarbon molecules based on a chain of carbon atoms. They all have the **general formula** C_nH_{2n+2} (where 'n' is a whole number). A series of molecules that have a general formula and vary in a single feature (such as carbon chain length) form an **homologous series**.

1 State why alkanes are hydrocarbons.

2 An alkane has six carbon atoms. Calculate the number of hydrogen atoms it has.

3 In what feature do members of the alkane homologous series vary?

The International Union of Pure and Applied Chemistry (IUPAC) developed the naming system for hydrocarbons. A prefix shows the length of the carbon chain and a suffix shows the homologous series. The suffix for alkanes is '-ane', as shown in table B.

Number of carbons in the chain	Prefix	Alkane	Molecular formula	Structural formula
1	meth-	methane	CH_4	H | H—C—H | H
2	eth-	ethane	C_2H_6	H H | | H—C—C—H | | H H
3	prop-	propane	C_3H_8	H H H | | | H—C—C—C—H | | | H H H
4	but-	butane	C_4H_{10}	H H H H | | | | H—C—C—C—C—H | | | | H H H H

B the first four members of the alkane homologous series

In table B the lines in the structural formulae represent covalent bonds between atoms. C–H shows a single covalent bond between carbon and hydrogen atoms. C–C shows a single covalent bond between carbon atoms. Molecules are **saturated** if all the carbon–carbon covalent bonds are single bonds. Alkanes are saturated hydrocarbons.

4 How many covalent bonds are there in one ethane molecule?

5 In an alkane, how many covalent bonds are found attached to every:

a carbon atom

b hydrogen atom?

Alkenes

Hydrocarbons with at least one double covalent bond between adjacent carbon atoms are **unsaturated**. Alkenes are an homologous series of unsaturated hydrocarbons with the general formula C_nH_{2n}. The first three alkenes in the series are shown in table C. The carbon–carbon double bond (C=C) is known as a **functional group**. A functional group is an atom or group of atoms that is mainly responsible for a molecule's chemical properties.

6 What feature is common to all alkenes but not alkanes?

7 How many pairs of electrons are there in a double covalent bond?

Name	Molecular formula	Structural formula
ethene	C_2H_4	$CH_2=CH_2$
propene	C_3H_6	$CH_3-CH=CH_2$
butene	C_4H_8	$CH_3-CH_2-CH=CH_2$

C the first three members of the alkene homologous series

> **Did you know?**
> Many plants produce ethene to help ripen their fruits.

Isomers

A functional group can be in different places in molecules with the same molecular formulae. Molecules with the same molecular formula but different arrangements of atoms are called **isomers**. Butene has two isomers. Numbers are added to the names to show where the C=C functional group is, as shown in diagram D.

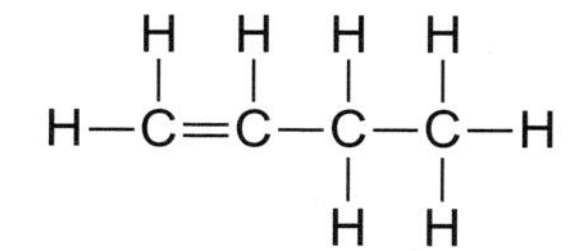
but-1-ene

$CH_3-CH=CH-CH_3$
but-2-ene

D The numbers in the butene isomer names show the position of the double bond. The 1 shows that the C=C bond starts at the end of the molecule on the first carbon, the 2 shows that it is in the middle. Carbon atoms are numbered starting from the end closest to the double bond.

8 In butene, how many of the following bonds are there?

a C–C

b C–H

c C=C

9 Which butene isomer is shown in table C?

10 Suggest why there is not a molecule called but-3-ene.

> **Exam-style question**
> Explain the difference between a saturated and an unsaturated hydrocarbon. *(2 marks)*

> **Checkpoint**
> How confidently can you answer the Progression questions?
>
> **Strengthen**
>
> **S1** Represent one saturated and one unsaturated hydrocarbon using their molecular and structural formulae, together with their names.
>
> **S2** Label your answer to **S1** with the similarities and differences between the two molecules.
>
> **Extend**
>
> **E1** Represent a five-carbon alkene using structural and molecular formulae.
>
> **E2** Suggest ways in which isomers of this hydrocarbon may be different.

SC22b Reactions of alkanes and alkenes

Specification reference: C9.14C; C9.15C; C9.16C

Progression questions

- What products are formed by the complete combustion of hydrocarbons?
- How can bromine water be used to distinguish between alkanes and alkenes?
- What are the structures of the reactants and products when bromine and ethene react?

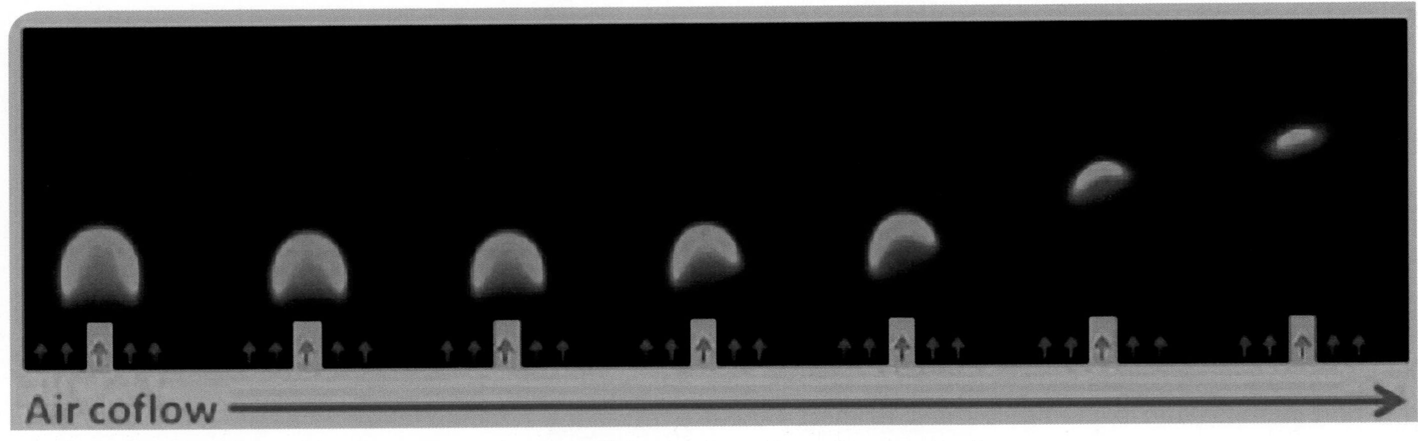

A This is ethene burning in space, where flames are a different shape from those on Earth.

Combustion

When hydrocarbons burn, carbon dioxide and water are formed when there is a plentiful supply of oxygen. During combustion, **oxidation** occurs. If all the atoms from the hydrocarbon are fully oxidised, the products are only water and carbon dioxide. This is called **complete combustion**.

Methane is the main alkane in natural gas. When it is burnt in a Bunsen burner with the air hole open, the following reaction occurs:

$$CH_4(g) + 2O_2(g) \rightarrow CO_2(g) + 2H_2O(g)$$

Ethene is the shortest alkene. The complete combustion of ethene is shown in the equation below:

$$C_2H_4(g) + 3O_2(g) \rightarrow 2CO_2(g) + 2H_2O(g)$$

If there is an insufficient amount of oxygen, full oxidation does not occur and carbon (soot) and carbon monoxide can be formed as well. In photo B, the orange flame is due to the presence of soot formed by **incomplete combustion**.

B Fire breathers use a fuel made of alkanes. The orange flame is caused by glowing particles of unburnt soot.

6th **1** What are the products of the complete combustion of propene in oxygen?

7th **2** What is the functional group found in alkenes?

7th **3** Explain why oxidation occurs in these combustion reactions.

6th **4** Why do the products of complete combustion not allow a scientist to distinguish easily between alkenes and alkanes?

The bromine water test

Bromine water is a dilute solution of bromine in water, Br_2(aq). It has an orange–brown colour. When it is mixed with alkenes a chemical reaction occurs, leading to colourless products. Alkanes do not cause decolourisation and so bromine water is used to test between alkenes and alkanes.

The test works because the C=C double bond reacts with the bromine to form a colourless product. The bromine is therefore removed from the solution, which loses its colour.

 **5** **a** Describe the effects of bromine water on alkanes and alkenes.

 **b** Explain the effects you have described.

 **6** Ripening bananas produce a gas. Describe how you would find out if this gas is an alkene or an alkane.

C The effects of bromine water on unsaturated hydrocarbons (containing C=C) and saturated hydrocarbons (containing C–C only) are different.

Addition reactions

Bromine gas is an orange–brown colour and reacts with alkenes. For example, it reacts with ethene to produce a colourless liquid called 1,2-dibromoethane. The 'di' in the name of the product means 'two' and the numbers show that the two bromine atoms are attached to different carbon atoms. If they were attached to the same carbon atom it would be called 1,1-dibromoethane.

ethene + bromine ⟶ 1,2-dibromoethane

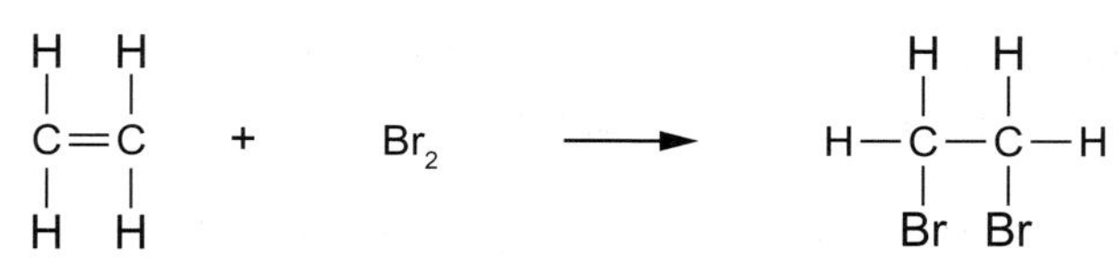

D Ethene reacts with bromine to form 1,2-dibromoethane.

Diagram D shows that in this reaction two reactant molecules add to one another to form just one product molecule. A reaction in which reactants combine to form one larger product molecule and no other products is called an **addition reaction**.

 **7** Explain what you would see happening during the reaction between ethene and bromine gas.

8 Propene reacts with bromine to form 1,2-dibromopropane.

 **a** Explain why this is an addition reaction.

 **b** Draw the structure of a molecule of 1,2-dibromopropane, showing all the covalent bonds.

Exam-style question

Bottles of two liquids, hexane and hexene, have been muddled. Explain how bromine water might be used to distinguish between them. *(2 marks)*

Did you know?

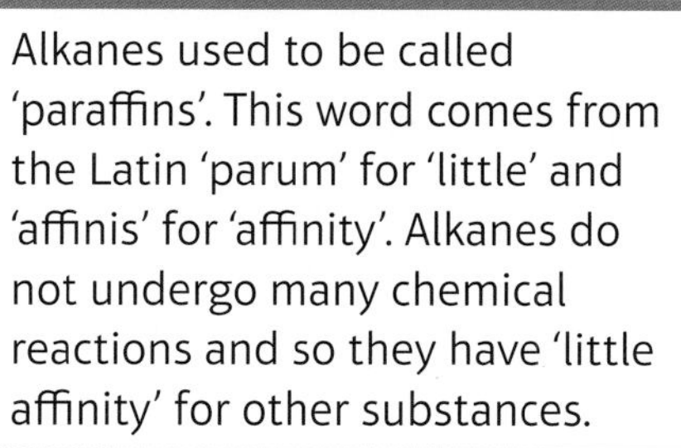

Alkanes used to be called 'paraffins'. This word comes from the Latin 'parum' for 'little' and 'affinis' for 'affinity'. Alkanes do not undergo many chemical reactions and so they have 'little affinity' for other substances.

Checkpoint

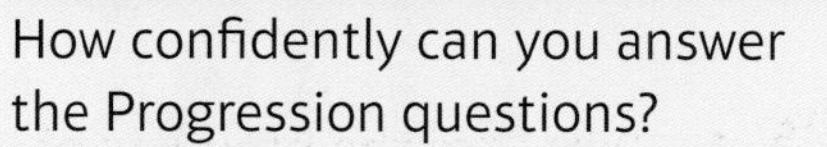

How confidently can you answer the Progression questions?

Strengthen

S1 Using the example of ethene reacting with bromine, describe what an addition reaction is.

S2 Explain why ethane does not undergo this reaction.

Extend

E1 But-2-ene reacts with bromine. Draw out the equation for this reaction using structural formulae, and name the product.

SC23a Ethanol production

Specification reference: C9.33C; C9.34C

Progression questions

- How are alcoholic drinks produced?
- What chemical reaction occurs during fermentation?
- How can we make alcohol solutions more concentrated?

A Drinks that contain a high percentage of ethanol are called spirits.

Alcoholic drinks have been made for thousands of years. These drinks contain a chemical substance called ethanol (although people often call it 'alcohol'). Its formula is C_2H_5OH. Ethanol can also be used as a fuel for vehicles and as a raw material for the chemical industry.

1 What is the proper chemical name and molecular formula for alcohol?

2 Alcoholic drinks can be described as spirits or non-spirits.

a What is the difference between them?

b Name an example of each type.

Did you know?

The ethanol content of spirits used to be measured in 'degrees proof', where 100° equalled 50% alcohol.

The ethanol in alcoholic drinks is made from **sugars**. Sugars are small, soluble substances that belong to a group called **carbohydrates** (compounds made of carbon, hydrogen and oxygen). Many fruits (such as grapes) contain a lot of sugars.

Seeds contain a carbohydrate called **starch**, which is a long polymer. Starch must be broken down into sugars in order to make alcoholic drinks. Seeds are germinated before using them to make ethanol because, during this process, **enzymes** in the seeds naturally turn the starch into sugars.

Drink	beer	wine	whisky	vodka
Commonly used plant	barley seeds	grapes	barley seeds	wheat seeds

B plant sources of alcoholic drinks

C During fermentation by yeast, sugars (such as glucose) are broken down.

Plant material containing sugars is mixed with water and yeast. Enzymes in the yeast turn the sugars into ethanol and carbon dioxide, in a process called **fermentation**:

glucose → ethanol + carbon dioxide

3 **a** Where are carbohydrates formed and what elements do they contain?

b Give the name of the group of soluble carbohydrates needed for fermentation.

During fermentation, the temperature and pH must be carefully controlled to help the enzymes work at their best. Photo C shows a fermentation flask. The air lock in the neck of the jar allows carbon dioxide to escape while keeping air out. This is necessary because yeast fermentation is a type of **anaerobic respiration** and only occurs in the absence of oxygen.

The fermentation process only produces alcohol concentrations up to 15%, as higher concentrations kill the yeast cells. More concentrated solutions of ethanol are formed by **fractional distillation**, as shown in photo D. This works because the boiling point of ethanol (78 °C) is lower than the boiling point of water (100 °C). The heated liquids evaporate and their vapours cool as they rise up the fractionating column. As the ethanol has a lower boiling point, it remains as a gas for longer, and separates from the water. As a result, the first **fraction**, or **distillate**, that is collected contains a higher percentage of ethanol.

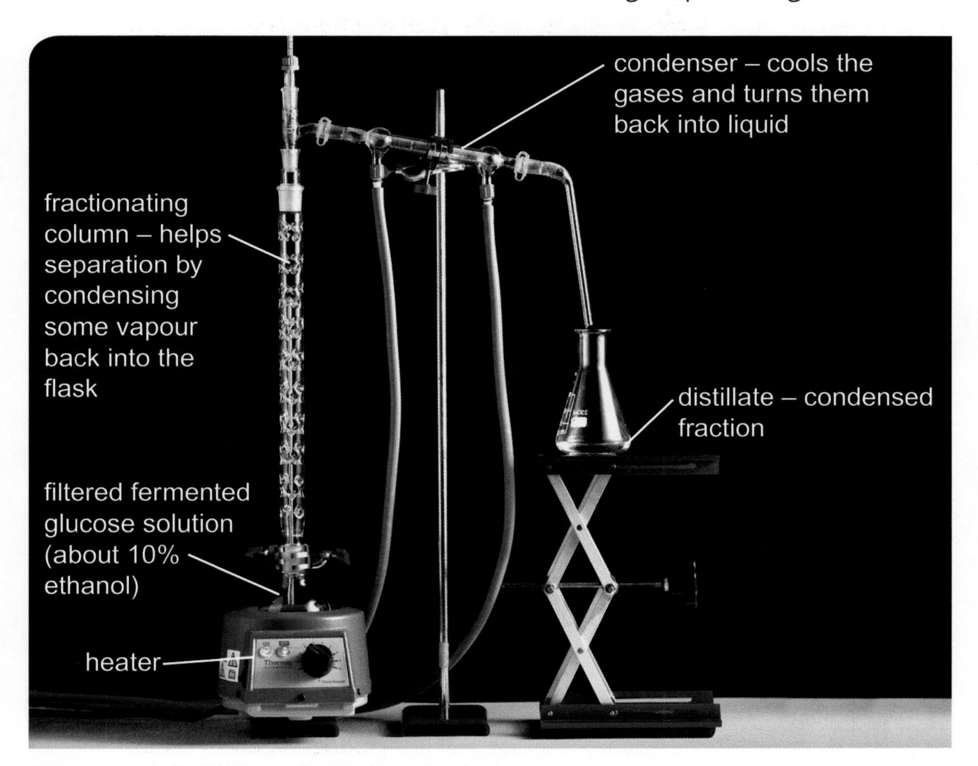

D fractional distillation of an ethanol solution

 **7** Explain how fractional distillation can be used to increase the concentration of an alcohol solution. Include the following words in your explanation:

boiling point; concentrated; condense; dilute; ethanol; evaporate; heated; water

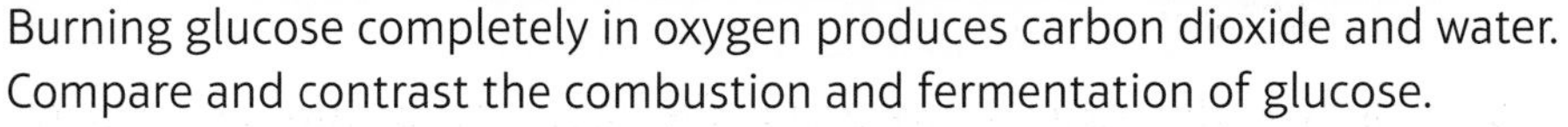

Exam-style question

Burning glucose completely in oxygen produces carbon dioxide and water. Compare and contrast the combustion and fermentation of glucose.

(2 marks)

 **4** Describe what is meant by 'anaerobic conditions'.

 **5** Explain why a grape and water mixture must be kept at a certain temperature when making wine.

 **6** Explain why beers rarely have an alcohol concentration greater than 10%.

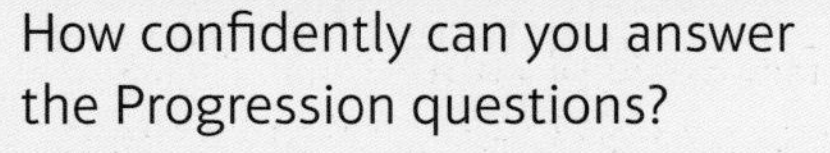

Checkpoint

How confidently can you answer the Progression questions?

Strengthen

S1 Draw a flow chart to show the stages involved in the production of a highly concentrated alcohol solution from a source of plant carbohydrates.

Extend

E1 In industry, ethanol can be produced by fermentation using a continuous process, in which the reaction is constantly kept going. Write a balanced equation for the fermentation of glucose ($C_6H_{12}O_6$), and explain what would need to be done to keep this reaction going at a constant rate in a continuous fermentation system.

SC23b Alcohols

Specification reference: C9.26C; C9.27C; C9.32C

Progression questions

- What are the names, formulae and structures of the four smallest alcohols?
- What functional group is present in all alcohols?
- What are some chemical properties of alcohols?

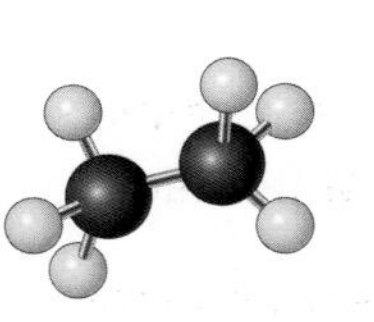

A Ethane and ethanol are both organic compounds but are in different homologous series.

1 Explain what is meant by an homologous series.

2 Describe one difference and one similarity in the structures of ethane and ethanol.

Did you know?

Ethanol, propanol and butanol are used in perfumes for two main reasons. They are all good solvents and readily dissolve the ingredients. They also evaporate easily, which helps to spread the perfume's aroma.

3 Describe the difference in molecular structure between propanol and butanol.

4 Hexanol has six carbon atoms. How many hydrogen atoms does hexanol have?

Organic compounds have a central framework of carbon atoms, onto which hydrogen and other atoms are attached. Ethanol, for example, is organic and has a central framework of two carbon atoms joined by a covalent bond.

Ethanol differs from a similar organic compound called ethane by having an additional oxygen atom. Ethanol and ethane have very different properties and are each in a different family or **homologous series** of compounds. Ethane belongs to the **alkane** series and ethanol belongs to the **alcohol** series.

Compounds in the same homologous series have the same general formula, have similar chemical reactions and display a trend in properties. Their names are also similar. All alcohol names end in '-anol' and have the general formula $C_nH_{2n+1}OH$ (where *n* stands for a number).

Name	Molecular formula	Structural formula
methanol	CH_3OH	H H–C–O–H H
ethanol	C_2H_5OH	H H H–C–C–O–H H H
propanol	C_3H_7OH	H H H H–C–C–C–O–H H H H
butanol	C_4H_9OH	H H H H H–C–C–C–C–O–H H H H H

B The naming of compounds uses a set of rules produced by the International Union of Pure and Applied Chemistry (IUPAC).

All alcohols have similar chemical properties. They all:

- produce carbon dioxide and water on complete combustion, for example:

  $C_2H_5OH + 3O_2 \rightarrow 2CO_2 + 3H_2O$

  ethanol + oxygen → carbon dioxide + water
- can be oxidised to form compounds called carboxylic acids (see *SC23c*)
- react with reactive metals, such as sodium, forming hydrogen gas as one of the products.

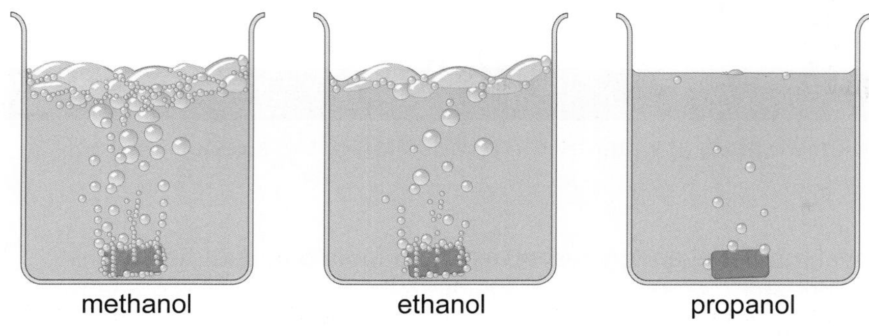

C Alcohols react with sodium metal but their reactivity depends on carbon chain length.

The atom or group of atoms in a molecule that is responsible for its main chemical reactions is called a **functional group**. Alcohols have similar chemical properties because they all contain one –OH functional group.

Alcohols have some important uses. Many alcohols are used as solvents for cosmetics, medical drugs and varnishes. Methanol and ethanol are widely used as fuels and can be made from **renewable sources**. Scientists are now working on developing processes to make propanol and butanol fuels from renewable sources, such as by fermenting plant cellulose using certain bacteria.

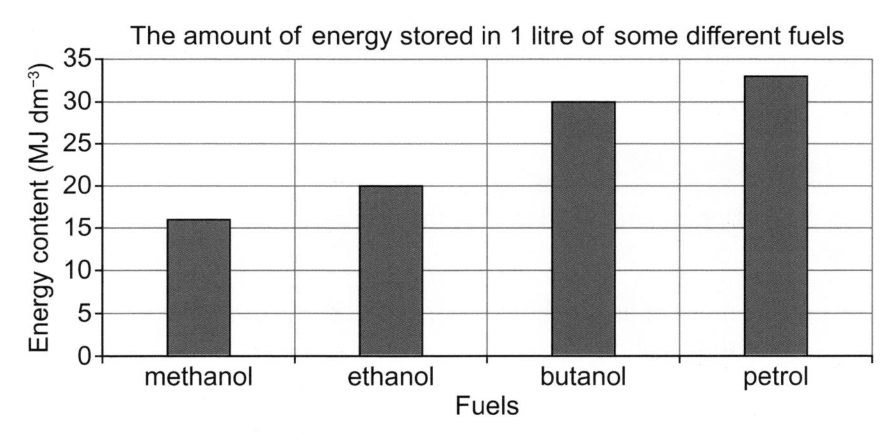

D Butanol has some advantages over some other alcohols used as fuels.

9 State three uses of alcohols.

10 a Explain why butanol produced by fermentation will be a renewable fuel.

b Use chart D to suggest why scientists are interested in using butanol as a fuel.

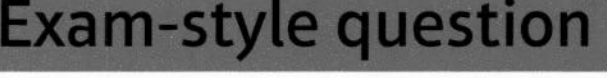

Exam-style question

The third member of the alcohol series has the molecular formula C_3H_7OH.

a Name this alcohol. *(1 mark)*

b Describe the functional group in this molecule. *(2 marks)*

5 Pentanol is an alcohol with five carbon atoms.

a State its molecular formula.

b Draw a structural formula for pentanol and circle the functional group.

6 Describe three chemical properties of pentanol.

7 a Write a word equation for the combustion of butanol.

b Write a balanced equation for the combustion of butanol.

8 What trend in reactivity is shown in diagram C?

Checkpoint

How confidently can you answer the Progression questions?

Strengthen

S1 Construct a table showing the names, formulae, structural formulae and functional groups of the four simplest alcohols.

Extend

E1 Explain, by referring to structures and properties, why the alcohols are an homologous series.

SC23b Core practical – The combustion of alcohols

Specification reference: C9.28C

Aim

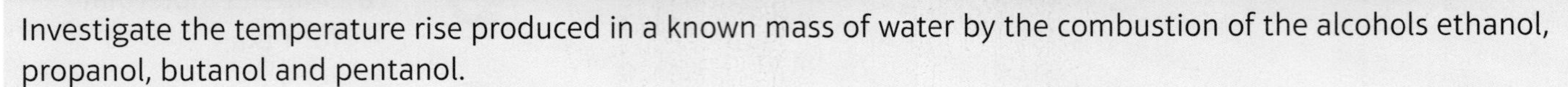

Investigate the temperature rise produced in a known mass of water by the combustion of the alcohols ethanol, propanol, butanol and pentanol.

A Most modern car engines can run on a fuel that is 90% petrol and 10% ethanol (often called E10). Some cars can run on fuels containing much higher proportions of ethanol, such as E85.

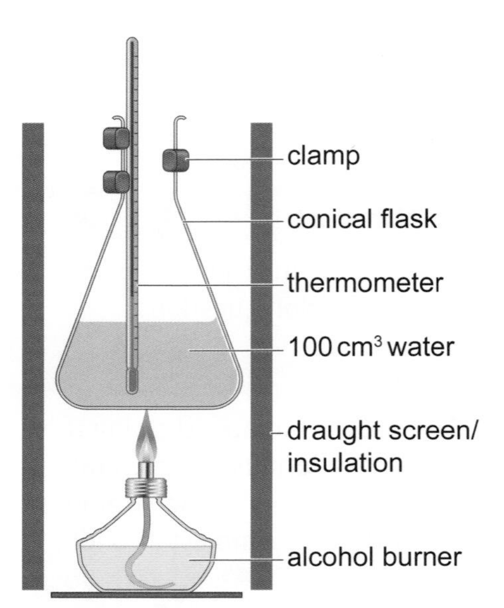

B investigating energy in fuels

Traditional fossil fuel energy resources are running out, and their use is also considered to be damaging our environment. We therefore need to find new sources of 'clean' energy. For example, ethanol, formed by the fermentation of sugars, is added to petrol to make it 'greener'. Scientists are now investigating ways of making engines that use other alcohols that are, at present, more difficult to obtain from renewable sources. There are a number of different characteristics that have to be considered when comparing fuels. These include availability, cost, toxicity, ease of combustion, environmental effects and the amount of energy released per unit mass.

Your task

You will investigate and compare the energy given out by the combustion of different alcohols. To do this, you will measure the temperature rise of a known mass of water caused by the combustion of ethanol, propanol, butanol and pentanol.

Method

Wear eye protection. Do not refill the alcohol burner if there are any naked flames nearby.

A Measure the mass of an alcohol burner and cap. Record the mass and the name of the alcohol.

B Place the alcohol burner in the centre of a heat-resistant mat.

C Use a measuring cylinder to add 100 cm^3 of cold water to a conical flask.

D Measure and record the initial temperature of the water and clamp the flask above the alcohol burner.

E Light the wick of the burner and allow the water to heat up by about 40 °C.

F Replace the cap on the burner and measure and record the final temperature of the water.

G Measure the mass of the alcohol burner and cap again and record the mass.

H Calculate the mass of the alcohol burned to produce a 1 °C rise in temperature.

I Repeat steps A to H using fresh, cold water and a different alcohol.

Exam-style questions

1 Look at the list of steps in the method described on the previous page.

a List *six* pieces of apparatus required for this investigation. *(3 marks)*

b State the dependent and independent variables. *(2 marks)*

c Explain why fresh water has to be used when repeating the experiment. *(2 marks)*

d State the measurements made during the investigation. *(4 marks)*

2 Look at the investigation apparatus set up in diagram B.

a Describe how the position of the flask and the alcohol burner will need to be controlled during each repeat. *(1 mark)*

b Explain the purpose of the draught screen/insulation. *(1 mark)*

c Describe another safety precaution that will need to be taken, in addition to wearing eye protection. *(1 mark)*

3 **a** State *four* possible sources of error in the investigation described on the previous page. *(4 marks)*

b State the main source of error in this investigation. *(1 mark)*

4 The results obtained by investigating two alcohols are shown in table C.

a Calculate the mass of alcohol burned and the temperature rise produced for each of the alcohols. *(4 marks)*

b By analysis of the results in table C, which of the two alcohols releases more energy for each gram burned? *(3 marks)*

Alcohol	ethanol	propanol
Initial mass of burner + cap (g)	291.60	284.25
Final mass of burner + cap (g)	290.50	285.25
Initial temperature of 100 cm^3 water (°C)	20	20
Final temperature of 100 cm^3 water (°C)	59	62

C

5 In another experiment, 1.5 g of butanol produces a temperature rise of 50 °C in 100 cm^3 of water. Calculate the mass of butanol that needs to be burned to cause a 1 °C rise in the same volume of water. *(1 mark)*

SC23c Carboxylic acids

Specification reference: C9.29C; C9.30C; C9.31C; C9.32C

Progression questions

- How are carboxylic acids produced?
- What are the names, formulae and structures of the first four carboxylic acids?
- How does the functional group in all carboxylic acids influence their chemical properties?

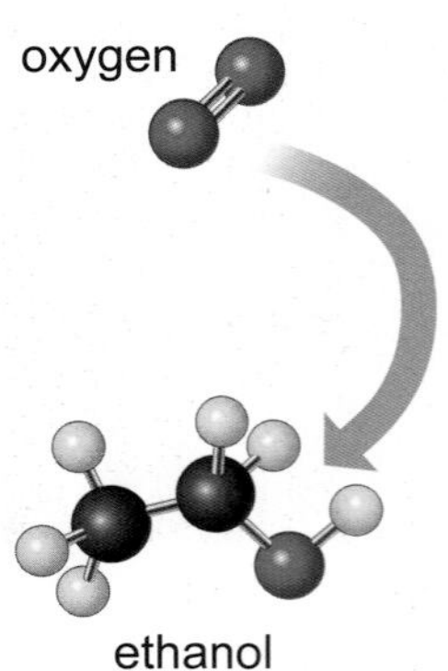

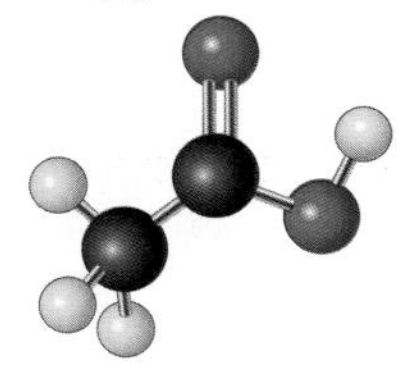

A oxidising ethanol

If wine is left open to the air, it turns into vinegar due to a reaction between ethanol and oxygen. The product is **ethanoic acid**, which is responsible for the distinctive sharp taste of vinegar. This **oxidation** reaction, shown in diagram A, occurs naturally due to the presence of certain bacteria. Vinegar can be made from any dilute ethanol solution like wine, cider or beer.

1 What substance produces the sharp taste of vinegar?

2 Describe the loss and gain of atoms when an ethanol molecule is oxidised.

Ethanoic acid is a member of an homologous series called the **carboxylic acids**. The first four members of the series are shown in table C.

Did you know?

Many chip shops do not use vinegar produced from fermented alcohol. Instead they use diluted ethanoic acid made from crude oil. It has exactly the same taste as the more expensive natural vinegar, but must be labelled as 'non-brewed condiment'.

B

Name	Molecular formula	Structural formula
methanoic acid	HCOOH	H–C(=O)–O–H
ethanoic acid	CH_3COOH	H–C(H)(H)–C(=O)–O–H
propanoic acid	C_2H_5COOH	H–C(H)(H)–C(H)(H)–C(=O)–O–H
butanoic acid	C_3H_7COOH	H–C(H)(H)–C(H)(H)–C(H)(H)–C(=O)–O–H

C the first four carboxylic acids

All carboxylic acids have the general formula $C_nH_{2n+1}COOH$ and contain the –COOH functional group. They are often formed by the gentle oxidation of alcohols using **oxidising agents** such as hot copper oxide. For example:

$$C_3H_7OH + CuO \rightarrow C_2H_5COOH + H_2O + Cu$$

propanol + copper(II) oxide → propanoic acid + water + copper

3 The fifth carboxylic acid is called pentanoic acid. Draw its structural formula and circle the functional group.

 **4** What carboxylic acid is formed by the oxidation of methanol?

5 Write word equations for the following oxidation reactions.

 **a** methanol + copper(II) oxide

 **b** ethanol + copper(II) oxide

The carboxylic acids have similar chemical properties. They all:

- form solutions with a pH less than 7 (if soluble)
- react with metals to form a salt and hydrogen
- react with bases to form a salt and water
- react with carbonates to form a salt, water and carbon dioxide.

The acidic properties are due to the presence of the –COOH group. In solution this group forms a hydrogen ion, while the rest of the molecule forms the negative ion that makes the salt. For example, propanoic acid forms propanoate ions, which make propanoate salts.

The equation for the reaction between magnesium and propanoic acid is:

$$2C_2H_5COOH + Mg \rightarrow Mg(C_2H_5COO)_2 + H_2$$

propanoic acid + magnesium → magnesium propanoate + hydrogen

Vinegar can be used to test for carbonate rocks like chalk and limestone (calcium carbonate). The ethanoic acid 'fizzes', producing carbon dioxide gas.

ethanoic acid + calcium carbonate → calcium ethanoate + water + carbon dioxide

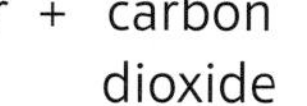

7 Write word equations for the following reactions.

 **a** methanoic acid + lead(II) oxide

 **b** butanoic acid + zinc carbonate

8 When ethanoic acid is added to sodium hydroxide solution the temperature increases.

 **a** Name the products of this reaction.

 **b** Suggest two possible names for this type of reaction.

Exam-style question

a Suggest names for the compounds with the formulae C_3H_7OH and C_2H_5COOH. *(2 marks)*

b Name the type of reaction that changes C_3H_7OH into C_2H_5COOH. *(1 mark)*

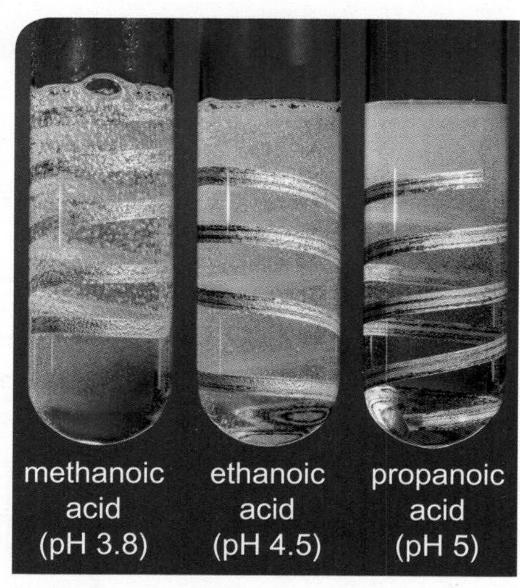

D the first three carboxylic acids reacting with magnesium

6 Look at photo D.

 **a** Write word equations for the three reactions.

 **b** Suggest what the reaction between butanoic acid and magnesium would look like.

Checkpoint

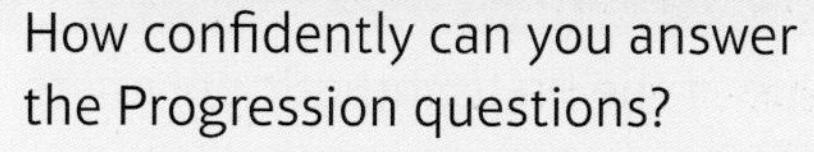

How confidently can you answer the Progression questions?

Strengthen

S1 Construct a table showing the names, molecular formulae, functional groups and salts formed for the four simplest carboxylic acids.

Extend

E1 Compare and contrast alcohols with carboxylic acids.

SC24a Addition polymerisation

Specification reference: C9.17C; C9.18C; C9.25C

Progression questions

- What is a polymer?
- What monomers join together to form DNA, starch and proteins?
- How do ethene molecules join together to form poly(ethene)?

A Polytunnels, used for growing crops, are made from poly(ethene).

Plastics are made from **polymers**. A polymer is a large molecule made from lots of small molecules, called **monomers**, joined together. The process in which monomers join together is called **polymerisation**.

A polymer has a high average relative molecular mass, anything from tens of thousands to millions. The polymer molecules can be different lengths, so they cannot be given a specific relative molecular mass.

Poly(ethene), more commonly known as polythene, is a polymer formed when a large number of ethene monomers join together. Ethene molecules have a double covalent bond between the carbon atoms. One of the bonds in the double bond breaks open and another ethene molecule adds on. This process happens again and again, forming a long chain. The process in which monomers add together in this way is called **addition polymerisation**.

6th **1** Describe what is meant by a polymer.

6th **2** State the type of bonds between the carbon atoms in ethene.

$H_2C{=}CH_2 \quad H_2C{=}CH_2 \quad H_2C{=}CH_2 \quad H_2C{=}CH_2 \quad H_2C{=}CH_2$ ethene molecules (monomers)

↓ addition polymerisation

$-CH_2-CH_2-CH_2-CH_2-CH_2-CH_2-CH_2-CH_2-CH_2-CH_2-$ part of a poly(ethene) molecule (polymer)

B the formation of poly(ethene), shown using structural formulae

This can be written as an equation:

$$n\ H_2C{=}CH_2 \longrightarrow \left[-CH_2-CH_2- \right]_n$$

repeating unit

D In the equation for the formation of poly(ethene), n is a very large number. The repeating unit is shown in brackets with the subscript n.

Did you know?

One of the first synthetic polymers was polyoxybenzylmethylenglycolanhydride. It was invented in 1907 by Leo Baekeland (1863–1944), and called Bakelite. Early telephones were made from it.

C

Equations for polymerisation show the structural formulae of the monomer and the **repeating unit**. The repeating unit shows how the monomer has changed and how it repeats throughout the polymer chain. The repeating unit does not have a double bond but has bond lines passing through the brackets to show that there is another repeating unit joined on each side.

Poly(ethene) is a **synthetic polymer** as it is manufactured in a laboratory or factory.

7th **3** Describe how ethene molecules join together to form poly(ethene).

6th **4** State the type of polymerisation that takes place when ethene forms poly(ethene).

7th **5** Draw a part of a poly(ethene) molecule, showing two repeating units.

7th **6** Describe how the repeating unit in poly(ethene) differs from the monomer.

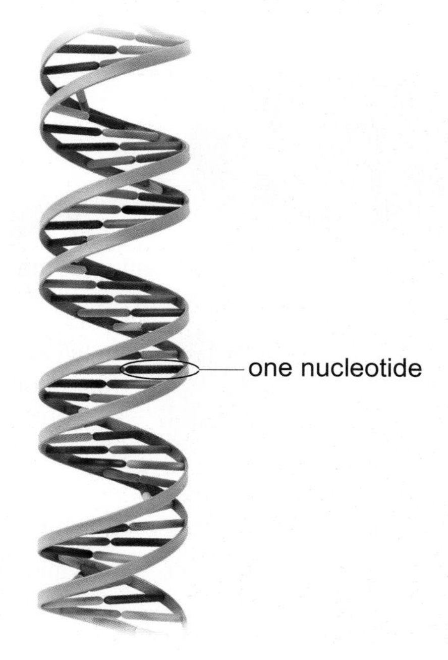

E part of a DNA molecule

Naturally occurring polymers

Some substances, such as DNA, starch and proteins, are **naturally occurring polymers**.

DNA is made from four different monomers called **nucleotides**. **Starch** is a polymer made from a **sugar** called glucose. **Proteins** are polymers made from **amino acids**.

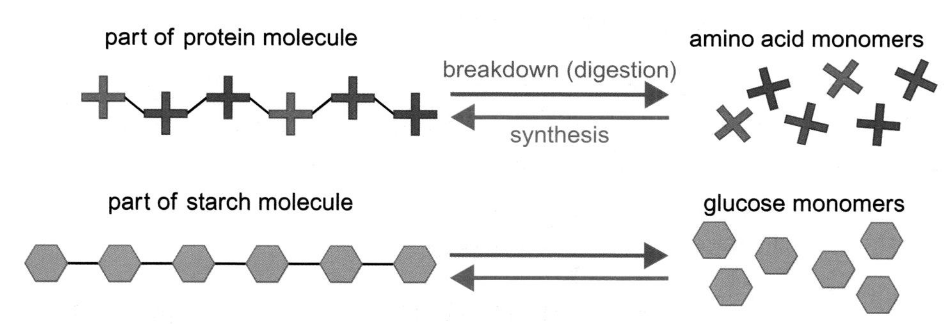

F Starch and proteins are polymers.

7th **7** Describe the difference between a synthetic polymer and a naturally occurring polymer, and give an example of each.

6th **8** State the name of the types of monomers that make up DNA.

6th **9** State the name of the naturally occurring polymer made from amino acids.

Exam-style question

Write an equation to show the formation of poly(ethene) from ethene, showing the structures of the monomer and the polymer. *(2 marks)*

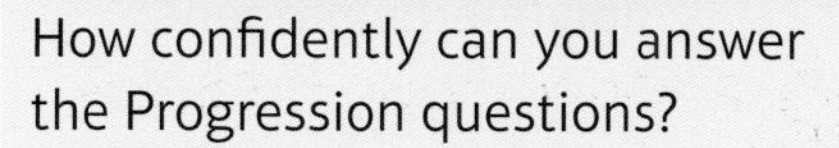

Checkpoint

How confidently can you answer the Progression questions?

Strengthen

S1 State the meanings of these terms: monomer, polymer, addition polymerisation.

S2 State the names of the types of monomers that make up these polymers:

a DNA **b** starch **c** protein.

Extend

E1 Explain, with the aid of diagrams, how two ethene molecules join together to form part of a poly(ethene) molecule.

SC24b Polymer properties and uses

Specification reference: C9.19C; C9.20C; C9.21C

Progression questions

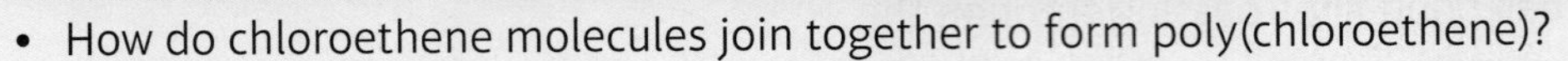

- How do chloroethene molecules join together to form poly(chloroethene)?
- How do you deduce the structure of a monomer from the structure of a polymer and vice versa?
- How are the uses of a polymer related to its properties?

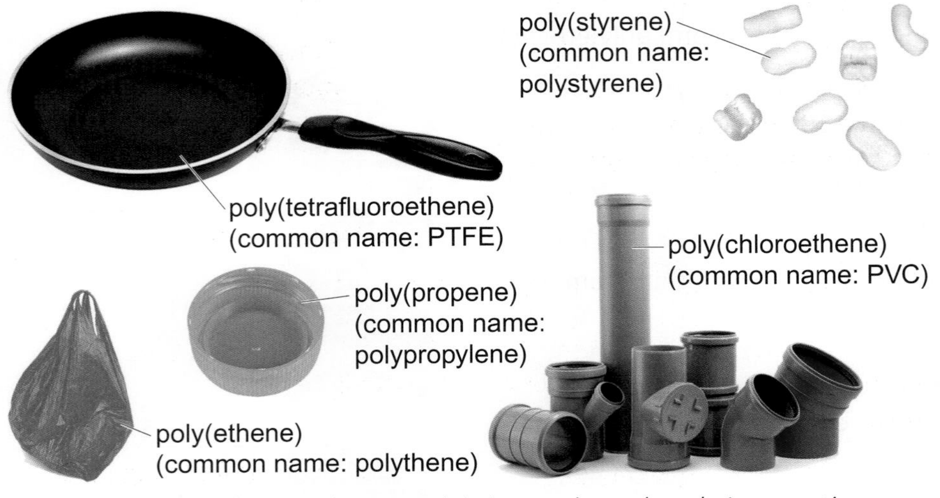

A There are many different polymers and their uses depend on their properties.

The name of a polymer is in the form of 'poly' followed by the name of the monomer in brackets, where 'poly' means 'many'. Some polymers have common names as well, such as polythene for poly(ethene).

Poly(ethene) is formed when thousands of ethene molecules undergo addition polymerisation. Many other polymers can be made from alkene monomers because they all contain a C=C double bond. The general equation for any addition polymerisation is:

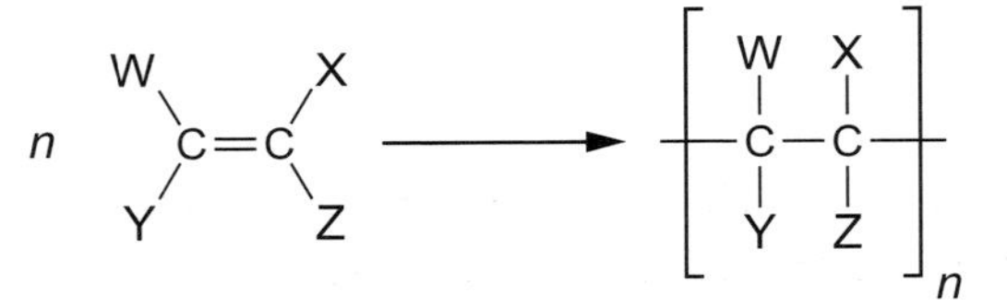

B In the general equation for addition polymerisation, W, X, Y and Z represent the atoms or groups of atoms attached to the C=C double bond in the monomer. Notice that these remain the same in the polymer.

1 Give the name of the polymer formed from butene.

2 Give the name of the monomer used to form poly(methylpropene).

Diagram C shows the equation for making poly(propene) from propene. There are only two carbon atoms in the carbon chain in the repeating unit. All the other atoms or groups of atoms that were attached to the carbons joined by the double bond remain in the same places.

$$n\ \mathrm{CH_2{=}CH(CH_3)} \longrightarrow \left[\!-\mathrm{CH_2}-\mathrm{CH(CH_3)}-\!\right]_n$$

C equation for the formation of poly(propene)

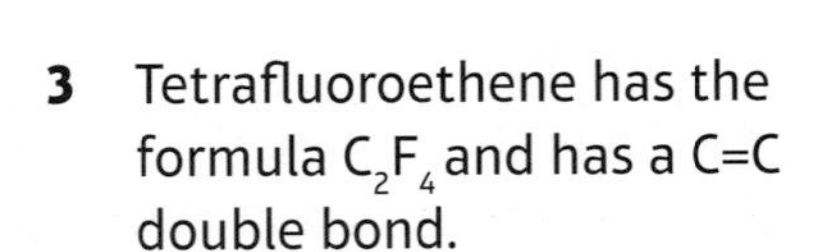

3 Tetrafluoroethene has the formula C_2F_4 and has a C=C double bond.

a Draw the structure of tetrafluoroethene, showing all the covalent bonds.

b Draw the repeating unit of poly(tetrafluoroethene).

You can work out the structure of the monomer from the formula for the polymer. Remove the brackets and the extension bond lines that go through them, and then draw a double bond between the two carbon atoms. Keep all the other atoms or groups of atoms the same.

For example, for poly(chloroethene):

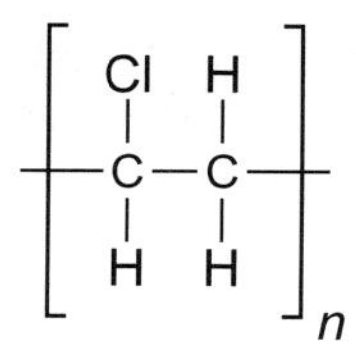

Cl H
C=C
H H

repeating unit monomer

D the structural formulae for the repeating unit and monomer of poly(chloroethene)

4 A polymer, X, has the repeating unit:

H CN
C C
H H
n

E polymer X

Draw the structure of the monomer that formed polymer X.

Polymers have different uses depending on their properties. Table F shows some common examples. New polymers are being developed all the time. For example, hydrogels are polymers that can absorb 500 times their own mass in water, making them useful for soft contact lenses and nappy linings.

Polymer	poly(ethene)	poly(propene)	poly(chloroethene)	poly(tetrafluoroethene)
Common name	polythene	polypropylene	polyvinyl chloride, PVC	PTFE, Teflon™
Properties	flexible, cheap, good insulator	flexible, does not shatter	tough, good insulator, can be made hard or flexible	tough, slippery
Uses	plastic bags, plastic bottles, cling film, polytunnels	buckets and bowls, crates, ropes, carpets	window frames, gutters, pipes, insulation for electrical wires	non-stick coatings for frying pans and kitchen utensils, burette taps, stain-proofing clothing and carpets

F some polymers and their uses

5 Select a polymer from table F that could be used to make each of the following items, and give a reason for your choice.

a a coating for a table that stops dust sticking to it

b a bucket and spade to use at the seaside

Did you know?

Old-fashioned waterproof coatings for clothing fabrics could keep water out but would not allow water vapour released as sweat to escape. This meant that the fabric still got wet on the inside. Modern polymer coatings for fabrics have now been developed that keep water out but also allow water vapour from sweat to escape so the wearer stays dry.

Exam-style question

Draw a diagram to show part of a poly(propene) molecule formed from two propene molecules. The structure of the monomer is shown in diagram C. *(2 marks)*

Checkpoint

How confidently can you answer the Progression questions?

Strengthen

S1 Give reasons that explain why:

a PVC is used as a covering on electrical wires

b PTFE is used as a coating on frying pans.

Extend

E1 Draw the structure of the monomer used to form poly(ethenol). The repeating unit of the polymer is:

H OH
C C
H H
n

G poly(ethenol)

SC24c Condensation polymerisation

Specification reference: H C9.22C

Progression questions

- H What is meant by condensation polymerisation?
- H Which two functional groups react together to form a polyester?
- H How do you draw the structure of a polyester?

H

A Most plastic drinks bottles are made from PET.

Many plastic bottles are made from PET (poly(ethylene terephthalate)), which is a **polyester**. The bottles are strong, lightweight, shatter-resistant and can be recycled. They can be made into items such as plastic garden furniture or into fibres for use in items such as carpets and fleece jackets.

Polyesters are synthetic polymers made by **condensation polymerisation** in which the monomers join together and eliminate a small molecule, such as water.

6th **1** State two properties of PET bottles.

6th **2** State two items that can be made from recycled PET.

6th **3** State what is meant by condensation polymerisation.

Organic compounds contain a **functional group**. A functional group is an atom or group of atoms that is responsible for the properties and reactions of the compound. The functional group in alcohols is –OH and in carboxylic acids it is –COOH. Esters are organic compounds that contain the functional group –COO–, which is drawn as:

```
   O
   ‖
—C—O—
```

B the ester functional group

Esters are formed when a carboxylic acid reacts with an alcohol, in the presence of a catalyst. This is a condensation reaction because water is also produced.

carboxylic acid + alcohol → ester + water

For example, ethanoic acid reacts with ethanol to form an ester, called ethyl ethanoate, and water.

```
   H  O              H  H             H  O        H  H
   |  ‖              |  |             |  ‖        |  |
H—C—C—O—H  +  H—O—C—C—H  ——►  H—C—C—O—C—C—H  +  H2O
   |                 |  |             |           |  |
   H                 H  H             H           H  H
ethanoic acid       ethanol          ethyl ethanoate
```

C This equation shows the formation of an ester from ethanoic acid and ethanol. The atoms in the red oval join together to form water. The yellow circle shows the ester link.

A polyester is a long-chain molecule that contains many **ester links** (in yellow in diagram C). The monomers that form a polyester contain alcohol and carboxylic acid functional groups. To form a long chain, each monomer must have two functional groups, one at each end of the molecule.

4 Write the equation for the reaction between methanoic acid (HCOOH) and methanol (CH_3OH), showing the structures of the reactants and the product.

H

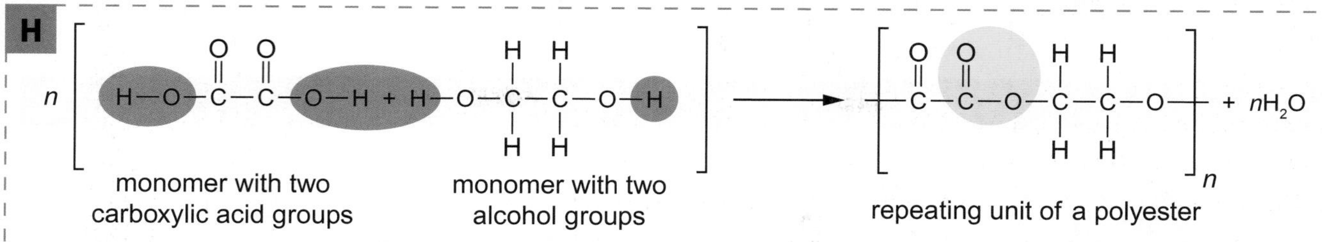

D This equation shows the formation of a polyester. The atoms shaded in red are eliminated from the monomers to form water. The group shaded in yellow is an ester link. Polyesters contain many ester links along the polymer chain.

Different polyesters can be formed by using monomers with different numbers of carbon atoms.

5 A polyester is formed from the following monomers:

```
       O   H   O                    H   H   H
       ‖   |   ‖                    |   |   |
H—O—C—C—C—O—H    and    H—O—C—C—C—O—H
           |                        |   |   |
           H                        H   H   H
```

E polyester monomers

a Write the equation for the formation of this polyester.

b Highlight the ester link in the polyester.

6 Explain how a molecule of water is formed each time an ester link is formed.

Polyesters are also used in the manufacture of synthetic fibres for weaving into fabrics for clothes and sheets.

Polyamides are another type of condensation polymer.

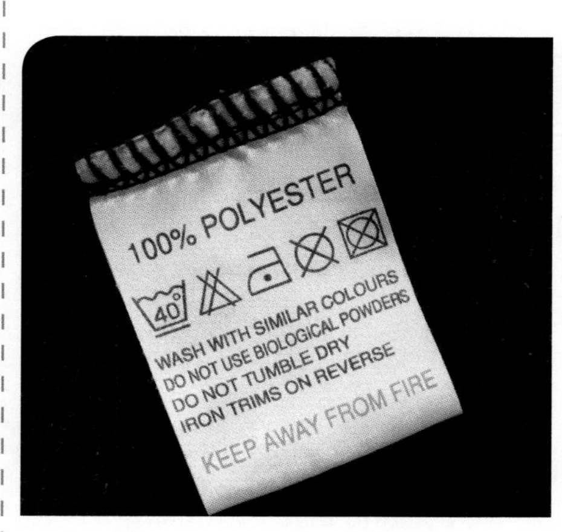

F Many items of clothing are made from polyesters or a mixture of polyesters and natural fibres such as cotton.

Did you know?

Nylon is a common synthetic polyamide formed by condensation polymerisation. Wallace Carothers (1896–1937) first produced it in 1935. Nylon was intended as a replacement for silk and was used to make parachutes and stockings during World War II. It is still used for parachutes but now has many other uses including cookware and car components.

Exam-style question

State the functional groups that react together to form an ester link.

(1 mark)

Checkpoint

How confidently can you answer the Progression questions?

Strengthen

S1 Explain what is meant by condensation polymerisation.

S2 Write the equation for the formation of a polyester from these monomers:

```
       O   H   O
       ‖   |   ‖
H—O—C—C—C—O—H
           |
           H

        and

       H   H   H
       |   |   |
H—O—C—C—C—O—H
       |   |   |
       H   H   H
```

Extend

E1 Write the equation for the formation of the polyester formed from $HOOC(CH_2)_2COOH$ and $HO(CH_2)_2OH$, showing all the bonds in the reactants and products.

SC24d Problems with polymers

Specification reference: C9.23C; C9.24C

Progression questions

- What problems are associated with making polymers?
- What problems are associated with the disposal of polymers?
- What are some advantages and disadvantages of recycling polymers?

A The extraction and transport of crude oil can have disastrous consequences for wildlife.

Crude oil is separated into fractions by **fractional distillation**. The fractions are further purified, **cracked** and refined to produce useful chemicals. Most of the monomers needed to make synthetic polymers are obtained from crude oil. Crude oil is a **finite resource** and is **non-renewable**, so chemists will need to find new sources of monomers in the future.

Materials such as wood and paper are **biodegradable**. This means that they rot because microbes can feed on them and break them down. Most synthetic polymers are useful for many purposes because they are not biodegradable and so they last for a long time. However, this also means that they do not rot when they are thrown away.

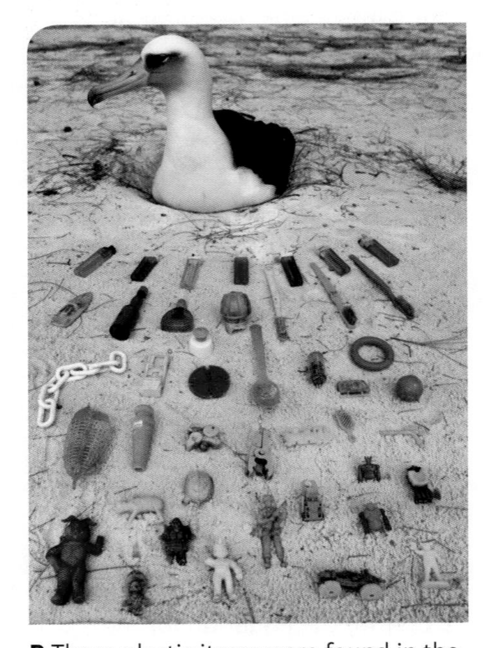

B These plastic items were found in the stomachs of dead albatrosses in Hawaii. The plastics are non-biodegradable and so they will not rot if they get into the sea. The albatrosses, such as the one in the photo, mistake the items for food.

1 State the meaning of the term 'biodegradable'.

2 Most synthetic polymers are non-biodegradable. State why this is:

a an advantage **b** a disadvantage.

Over half of the rubbish in the UK goes to landfill sites. The non-biodegradable plastic materials in the rubbish will last for many years. Some waste is **incinerated** (burned) and the energy released can be used to generate electricity. However, all plastics produce carbon dioxide, a greenhouse gas, and some plastics produce toxic substances when they burn. Most of these toxic substances can be removed from the waste gases, but this forms toxic ash, which must be disposed of safely.

We can reduce the amount of waste that goes into incinerators or landfill sites by reducing the amounts of materials we use and also by reusing materials. For example, we can reuse plastic bags rather than just throwing them away after a single use. If an item cannot be reused any more, it may be possible to recycle it by processing it to make a new item. This will also help to conserve the supplies of crude oil.

3 State three ways of disposing of plastics.

4 Describe why incinerating synthetic polymers can cause problems.

5 Explain the difference between reusing and recycling.

It is difficult to recycle polymers because many steps are needed to obtain a new item. The main steps are outlined below.

i Collect the waste – this may involve kerbside collection or people taking it to a collection point.

ii Sort the waste into different types of polymer – this is often done by hand, which is time-consuming and expensive.

iii Dispose of waste that cannot be recycled in a landfill site.

iv Clean the polymers and grind them into chippings.

v Purify the chippings.

vi Melt the chippings then process them into a new product.

To make the sorting of polymers easier, codes and symbols are used on plastic items to show what they are made of. These are shown in table C. The majority of recycled items are those with recycling symbols 1 or 2.

symbol	polymer	uses
1 PET	poly(ethylene terephthalate)	some bottles, food trays, duvet fillings
2 HDPE	high-density poly(ethene)	some bottles, buckets
3 PVC	poly(chlorothene)	soft toys, window frames
4 LDPE	low-density poly(ethene)	cling film, bags
5 PP	poly(propene)	crisp packets, carpet, rope
6 PS	poly(styrene)	egg boxes, foam packaging
7 OTHER	other polymers	

C polymer recycling symbols

Did you know?

Chemists are developing new polymers that are biodegradable. For example, poly(lactic acid) is made from cornstarch.

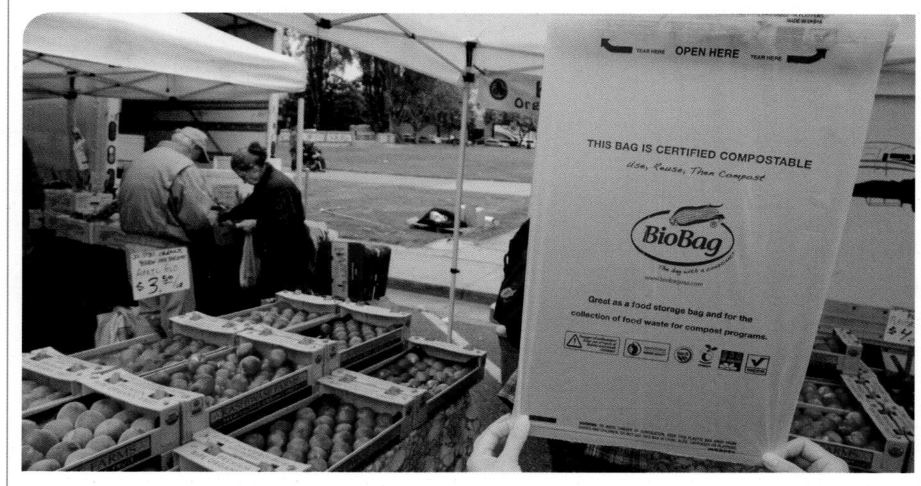

D a biodegradable bag will rot

6 Identify the steps in recycling polymers that require energy. State what the energy is used for.

Exam-style question

Polymers persist for a long time in landfill sites. State *one* way in which this problem can be overcome. *(1 mark)*

Checkpoint

How confidently can you answer the Progression questions?

Strengthen

S1 Describe some problems associated with:

a the starting materials for polymers

b the disposal of polymers.

S2 Describe the advantages and disadvantages of disposing of plastics by:

a putting them in landfill sites

b burning them.

Extend

E1 Evaluate the advantages and disadvantages of recycling polymers.

Alcohols and carboxylic acids

When heated together, acidified potassium dichromate solution oxidises propanol to form propanoic acid. The reaction can be modelled using this balanced equation (where 2[O] represents two oxygen atoms added in the reaction):

$$CH_3CH_2CH_2OH + 2[O] \rightarrow CH_3CH_2COOH + H_2O$$

Propanol and ethanol are members of the alcohol homologous series. Propanoic acid and ethanoic acid are members of the carboxylic acid homologous series.

Describe how ethanoic acid can be produced from sugar. The first step is to obtain a concentrated solution of ethanol. You may use equations if you wish. **(6 marks)**

Student answer

Dissolve the sugar in warm water, then add yeast. Yeast enzymes catalyse fermentation. The reaction mixture must be kept at 25–35 °C so that the enzymes work at their best. An air lock is needed so that carbon dioxide can escape, but air cannot get in [1].

Fermentation takes several days. When it is complete, remove the yeast by filtration [2]. *Separate ethanol from the filtrate using fractional distillation. This works because ethanol has a lower boiling point than water, so it is collected first* [3].

Use the concentrated ethanol solution to make ethanoic acid. Heat the ethanol with acidified potassium dichromate solution:

$$CH_3CH_2OH + 2[O] \rightarrow CH_3COOH + H_2O$$

This works because ethanol and propanol are both alcohols. They have the same functional group and similar chemical properties [4].

[1] The answer explains the temperature needed. It could also mention that fermentation is an anaerobic process, which is why air must be kept out.

[2] The reason for filtering the reaction mixture is given.

[3] The answer explains why a concentrated solution of ethanol can be produced by fractional distillation.

[4] The balanced equation given in the question is applied to predict the reaction of ethanol.

Verdict

This is a strong answer. It shows good knowledge and understanding of the production of ethanol by fermentation, how to produce a concentrated solution of ethanol and the similarity in chemical properties between members of an homologous series. The answer is presented in a logical order with good use of appropriate terminology.

Exam tip

Make sure you are prepared to *apply* information and so can, for example, predict the reactions of other members of a given homologous series.

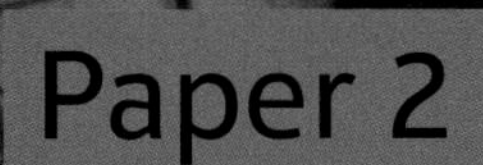

Paper 2

SC25 Qualitative Analysis: Tests for Ions / SC26 Bulk and Surface Properties of Matter Including Nanoparticles

A modern aircraft is made from many different materials, each with certain properties making it suitable for particular parts. Chemists and engineers test these materials to identify the substances they contain, and to ensure they meet the required specifications. Titanium alloys form strong, heat-resistant engine parts, while low-density aluminium alloys are used for the frame and leading wing edges. Carbon fibre and other composite materials are used for panels and floors, ceramics are used in braking systems, and the windows are made from polymers. Nanoparticle coatings are being investigated in efforts to reduce drag.

The learning journey

Previously you will have learnt at KS3:

- some properties of ceramics, polymers, metals and composite materials.

In this unit you will learn:

- how to identify metal ions
- the chemical tests for various non-metal ions and for ammonia gas
- about instrumental methods of analysis and their advantages
- how to compare the physical properties of different materials
- what composite materials are
- how and why materials are chosen for particular uses
- about nanoparticles and their properties, uses and possible risks.

SC25a Flame tests and photometry

Specification reference: C9.2C; C9.7C; C9.8C; C9.9C

Progression questions

- How are metal ions identified using flame tests?
- Why might chemists analyse substances using machines instead of chemical tests?
- How is the information from flame photometers used?

A The yellow light from these street lamps is emitted when an electric current passes through a vapour of sodium ions.

Flame tests are used to identify metal ions in substances. To carry out a flame test:

i Light a Bunsen burner and open the air hole to give a hot blue flame.

ii Pick up a small sample of the test substance using a wire loop.

iii Hold the sample in the edge of the flame and observe the flame colour.

The wire loop is cleaned in hydrochloric acid before testing each sample. Platinum wire has a high melting point and it is unreactive. It also gives no colour to the flame. However, nichrome alloy is often used instead. Although it produces its own faint orange colour, it is much cheaper.

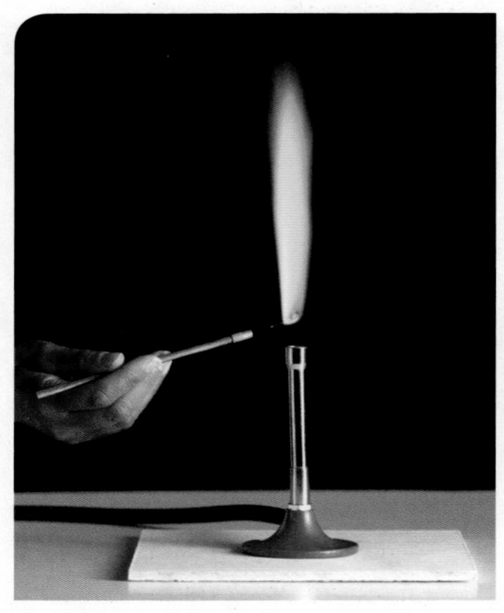

B Sodium ions produce a yellow flame test colour.

1 Wooden splints may be used instead of a wire loop. Suggest two reasons that explain why the splints are soaked in distilled water before use.

Different metal **cations** produce different flame test colours (as shown in table C). Flame tests work with solid samples and with solutions, but flame colours from solids are easier to see.

Metal ion	Symbol	Flame test colour
lithium	Li^+	red
sodium	Na^+	yellow
potassium	K^+	lilac
calcium	Ca^{2+}	orange-red
copper	Cu^{2+}	blue-green

C some flame test colours

2 Explain why potassium chloride and potassium iodide both produce lilac flame test colours.

3 Predict the flame test colours produced by the following compounds.

a $CaCl_2$ **b** Na_2SO_4 **c** $LiNO_3$ **d** $Cu_3(PO_4)_2$

Flame photometry

Machines can also be used to analyse substances. Compared to simple laboratory tests such as flame tests, using scientific instruments may improve:

- sensitivity (they can detect much smaller amounts)
- accuracy (they give values closer to the true values)
- speed.

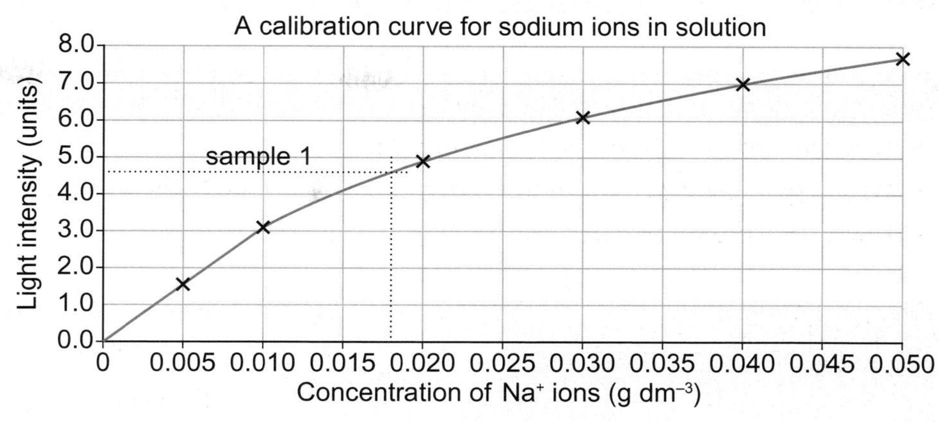

D a calibration curve from a flame photometer

The **flame photometer** measures the light intensity of the flame colours produced by metal ions. Its data is used to determine the concentration of a metal ion in a dilute solution. Graph D shows a **calibration curve** produced using different **standard solutions**, each containing known concentrations of the metal ion dissolved in distilled water.

4 Describe the relationship between light intensity and concentration shown in graph D.

5 In graph D, sample 1 gives a light intensity reading of 4.6 units, so its sodium ion concentration is 0.018 g dm^{-3}. A second sample gives a light intensity reading of 6.1 units. Determine its sodium ion concentration.

The colour of light that we see in a flame test is usually a mixture of different colours. A flame photometer can separate out these colours to produce a **spectrum** of the light emitted by each metal ion. Different metal ions produce different **emission spectra** (shown in diagram E). A metal ion in an unknown solution can be identified by matching its spectrum to the spectrum from a known metal ion.

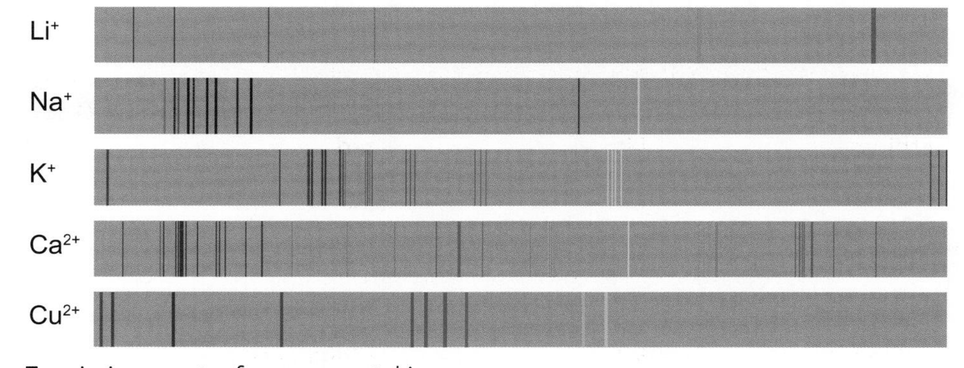

E emission spectra for some metal ions

6 Compare and contrast the emission spectra shown in diagram E.

Exam-style question

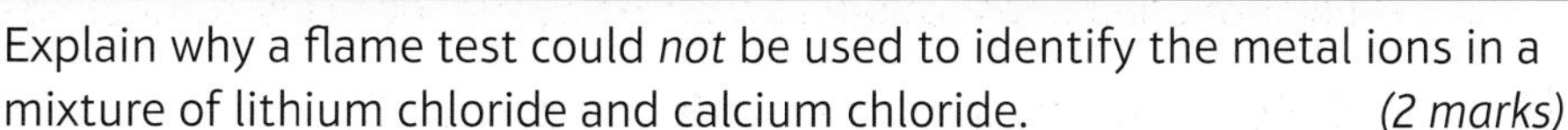

Explain why a flame test could *not* be used to identify the metal ions in a mixture of lithium chloride and calcium chloride. *(2 marks)*

Did you know?

Robert Bunsen and Gustav Kirchhoff analysed the spectrum of light given off by heated mineral salts. Using this method, they discovered caesium in 1860 and rubidium in 1861.

Checkpoint

How confidently can you answer the Progression questions?

Strengthen

S1 How are metal ions in solids identified using flame tests?

S2 How are the data from instrumental methods of analysis used?

Extend

E1 Evaluate the use of flame tests compared to the use of a flame photometer.

SC25b Tests for positive ions

Specification reference: C9.1C; C9.3C; C9.4C; C9.7C

Progression questions

- Why must the test for an ion only detect that ion?
- How are metal ions identified using sodium hydroxide solution?
- How are ammonium ions and ammonia detected?

A This stream is discoloured by metal ions in waste water draining from a mine.

Metal compounds dissolve in groundwater as it flows through mines. When it drains from the mines, the water contaminates rivers. One way to treat the water involves sodium hydroxide solution. This reacts with metal ions to produce **precipitates**, which settle out and can be removed.

Testing for metal ions

Precipitation reactions involving sodium hydroxide solution form the basis of a test to identify dissolved metal ions. A few drops at a time of dilute sodium hydroxide solution are added to the test solution. Different metal ions produce different coloured hydroxide precipitates, as shown in table B.

Metal ion	Symbol	Precipitate colour
iron(II)	Fe^{2+}	green
iron(III)	Fe^{3+}	brown
copper	Cu^{2+}	blue
calcium	Ca^{2+}	white
aluminium	Al^{3+}	white

B metal hydroxide precipitate colours for different metal ions

C A blue precipitate of copper hydroxide forms when sodium hydroxide solution reacts with copper sulfate solution.

For example, sodium hydroxide solution reacts with copper sulfate solution to form a blue precipitate:

sodium hydroxide + copper sulfate → sodium sulfate + copper hydroxide

$$2NaOH(aq) + CuSO_4(aq) \rightarrow Na_2SO_4(aq) + Cu(OH)_2(s)$$

1 A few drops of sodium hydroxide solution are added to a colourless solution. A faint green precipitate forms. Identify the metal ions present in the colourless solution.

2 For the reaction between sodium hydroxide solution and iron(II) chloride solution:

a write the word equation

b write the balanced equation, including state symbols.

These precipitation reactions can also be modelled using balanced ionic equations. For example, aqueous iron(III) ions react with aqueous hydroxide ions to form solid iron(III) hydroxide:

$$Fe^{3+}(aq) + 3OH^{-}(aq) \rightarrow Fe(OH)_3(s)$$

3 Write the balanced ionic equation, including state symbols, for the formation of calcium hydroxide, $Ca(OH)_2$.

It is important that the test for an ion should only detect that ion. For example, calcium ions and aluminium ions both produce white hydroxide precipitates. You cannot distinguish between these without a further test. Aluminium hydroxide disappears to form a colourless solution when excess sodium hydroxide solution is added, but calcium hydroxide does not.

4 Explain how you could use dilute sodium hydroxide solution to distinguish between calcium sulfate solution and aluminium sulfate solution.

Testing for ammonium ions

Dilute sodium hydroxide solution is also used to detect ammonium ions, NH_4^+, in a substance. Ammonia gas, NH_3, is produced when the mixture containing ammonium ions is warmed. Ammonia has a characteristic sharp smell, but a **confirmatory test** is used to identify it. Ammonia changes the colour of damp red litmus paper to blue.

5 Explain the meaning of the colour change seen when damp red litmus paper is used to test for ammonia.

6 H Write a balanced ionic equation to show the reaction between aqueous ammonium ions and aqueous hydroxide ions, producing ammonia gas and one other product. Include state symbols.

Did you know?

Aluminium sulfate is used to treat fresh water to make it potable (safe for drinking). Aluminium ions react with other ions in the water to produce an aluminium hydroxide precipitate. This catches tiny particles, such as rotted plant material and clay, forming a solid that sinks to the bottom of the treatment tank.

D In another test for ammonia, a glass rod dipped in concentrated hydrochloric acid is held near the mouth of the test tube. A white smoke of ammonium chloride forms.

Exam-style question

Ammonium iron(III) sulfate is a soluble solid used in waste water treatment. Describe how you could show that it contains ammonium ions and iron(III) ions. *(4 marks)*

Checkpoint

How confidently can you answer the Progression questions?

Strengthen

S1 How is sodium hydroxide solution used to identify positively charged ions?

Extend

E1 To what extent can sodium hydroxide solution be used to identify all positively charged ions?

SC25c Tests for negative ions

Specification reference: C9.5C; C9.7C

Progression questions

- How are carbonate ions and carbon dioxide detected?
- How are sulfate ions detected?
- How are halide ions identified?

A This geologist is testing tufa, a type of limestone rock, with dilute acid.

Geologists carry out simple 'acid tests' on rocks. If a rock contains carbonate minerals, it produces bubbles when dilute hydrochloric acid is added to it.

Testing for carbonate ions

Just as there are simple chemical tests to detect and identify positively charged ions (cations), there are tests for negatively charged ions (**anions**). Carbonate ions, CO_3^{2-}, are easily detected in solids and in solutions. Add dilute hydrochloric acid to the test substance and look for bubbling caused by the production of carbon dioxide. Since the bubbles could be due to a different gas, such as hydrogen, you should carry out a confirmatory test. If the bubbles do contain carbon dioxide, they turn limewater milky.

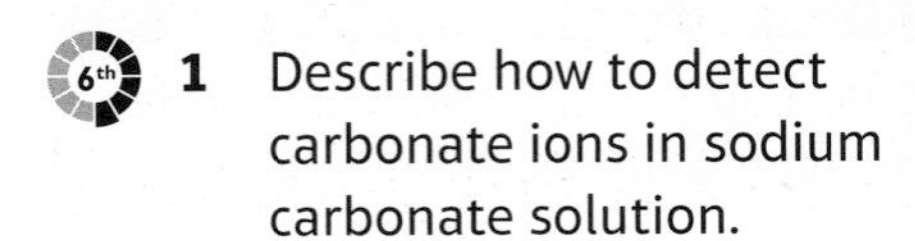

1 Describe how to detect carbonate ions in sodium carbonate solution.

2 H Write a balanced ionic equation to show the reaction between aqueous hydrogen ions (produced by acids in solution) and aqueous carbonate ions to form carbon dioxide gas and water. Include state symbols.

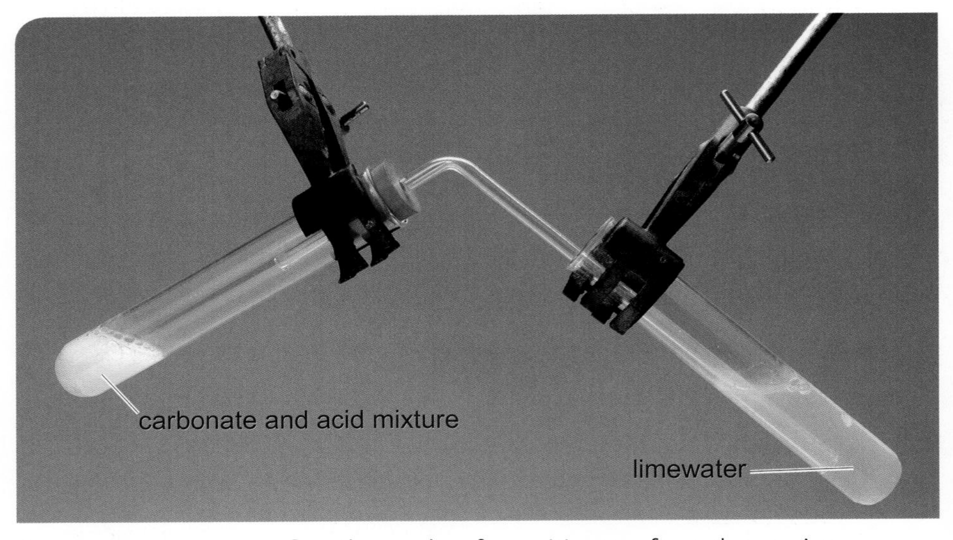

B using limewater to confirm the results of a positive test for carbonate ions

Testing for sulfate ions

To detect sulfate ions in a solution, add a few drops of dilute hydrochloric acid. This acidifies the solution and removes carbonate ions that might also give a precipitate in the test. Then add a few drops of barium chloride solution. A white precipitate of barium sulfate forms if the sample contains sulfate ions, SO_4^{2-}.

For example:

magnesium sulfate + barium chloride → magnesium chloride + barium sulfate

$MgSO_4(aq) + BaCl_2(aq) \rightarrow MgCl_2(aq) + BaSO_4(s)$

3 Suggest a reason that explains why dilute sulfuric acid, H_2SO_4, is *not* used to acidify the sample when testing for sulfate ions.

4 **H** Write an ionic equation, including state symbols, for the reaction between barium ions and sulfate ions.

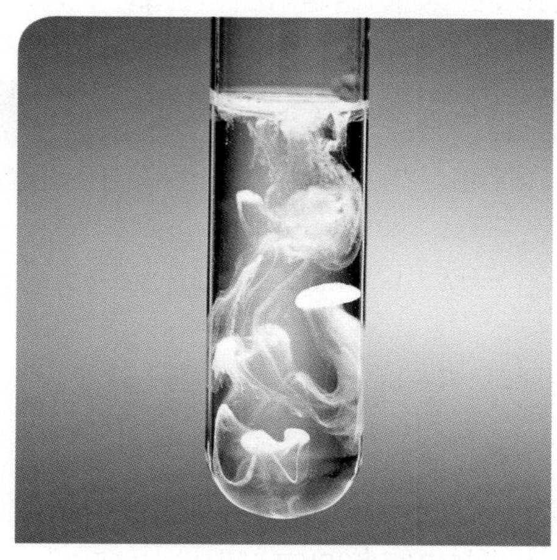

C A white precipitate of barium sulfate forms in a positive test for sulfate ions.

Testing for halide ions

The halogens are the non-metal elements in group 7 of the periodic table. They form compounds that contain **halide ions**, such as F^-, Cl^-, Br^- and I^-. Silver fluoride is soluble in water but the other silver **halides** are insoluble. This is the basis of the laboratory test for chloride, bromide and iodide ions. To detect these ions in a solution, add a few drops of dilute nitric acid. This acidifies the solution and removes carbonate ions that might also give a precipitate in the test. Then add a few drops of silver nitrate solution. Different coloured silver halide precipitates form, depending on the halide ion present (see table D and photo E). For example:

potassium bromide + silver nitrate → potassium nitrate + silver bromide

$KBr(aq) + AgNO_3(aq) \rightarrow KNO_3(aq) + AgBr(s)$

Halide ion	Symbol	Precipitate colour
chloride	Cl^-	white
bromide	Br^-	cream
iodide	I^-	yellow

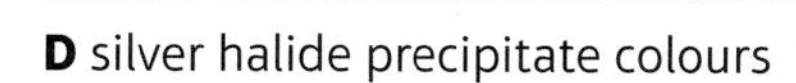

D silver halide precipitate colours

E silver halide precipitates

5 Explain why fluoride ions cannot be detected in the same way as chloride, bromide and iodide ions.

6 Substance X gives an orange-red flame test result and produces a yellow precipitate when silver nitrate solution is added. Name substance X.

7 **H** Write an ionic equation for the reaction between silver ions and bromide ions. Include state symbols.

Exam-style question

Silver carbonate is an insoluble yellow solid. Suggest an explanation for why dilute acid must first be added when testing solutions for halide ions using silver nitrate solution. *(3 marks)*

Checkpoint

How confidently can you answer the Progression questions?

Strengthen

S1 How are negatively charged ions identified in chemical tests?

Extend

E1 Explain why different dilute acids are used in the tests for negatively charged ions.

SC25c Core practical – Identifying ions

Specification reference: C9.6C

Aim

Identify the ions in some unknown salts, using the tests for the specified cations and anions.

Your task

You will use laboratory tests to identify the cations and anions in some unknown salts. You can then work out the name of each salt.

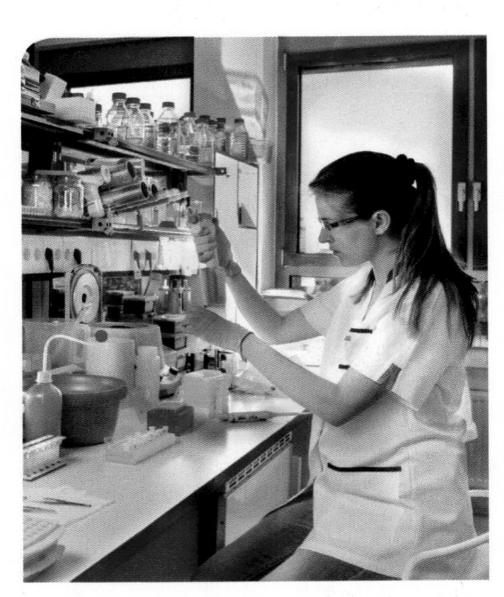

A Analytical chemists work in many areas, including chemical and forensic analysis, quality control, medical drug development and toxicology.

Analytical chemists use different techniques to determine which substances are present or absent.

Methods

For all tests, wear eye protection and avoid skin contact with all the chemical substances.

Flame tests for metal cations

A Light a Bunsen burner and open the air hole to give a hot blue flame.

B Pick up a small sample of a solid salt using a clean wire loop or a damp wooden splint.

C Hold the sample in the edge of the flame.

D Observe and record the flame colour.

Hydroxide precipitate tests for metal cations

E Dissolve a little solid salt in a test tube using distilled water.

F Add a few drops of dilute sodium hydroxide solution, one drop at a time.

G Record the colour of any precipitate formed.

H If a white precipitate forms, add excess dilute sodium hydroxide solution to see if it will disappear to leave a clear solution.

Testing for ammonium ions

I Dissolve a little solid salt in a test tube using distilled water.

J Add dilute sodium hydroxide solution and then warm gently.

K Remove from the flame. Hold a piece of damp red litmus paper near the mouth of the test tube. Record what happens to its colour.

Testing for carbonate ions

L Put a little solid salt in a test tube and add a few drops of dilute acid.

M Record whether any effervescence (bubbling) occurs.

N Use limewater to check that any bubbles contain carbon dioxide.

Testing for sulfate ions

O Dissolve a little solid salt in a test tube using distilled water.

P Add a few drops of dilute hydrochloric acid, then a few drops of barium chloride solution. Record whether a white precipitate forms.

Testing for halide ions

Q Dissolve a little solid salt in a test tube using distilled water.

R Add a few drops of dilute nitric acid, then a few drops of silver nitrate solution. Record the colour of any precipitate formed.

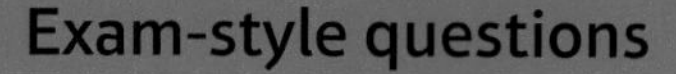

Exam-style questions

1 Copy diagram B. On your diagram, draw one straight line from each metal cation to its flame test colour. *(5 marks)*

2 Some metal cations react with sodium hydroxide solution to form metal hydroxide precipitates.

a Copy and complete table C. *(3 marks)*

b Describe a test to distinguish between aluminium hydroxide and calcium hydroxide. *(2 marks)*

3 Halide ions can be identified using silver nitrate solution. Copy table D. Place a tick (✓) in one box of each row to show the colour of the silver halide precipitate formed. *(3 marks)*

4 A teacher demonstrates how to carry out flame tests using a platinum wire loop.

a Give *two* reasons that explain why platinum is a suitable metal to use. *(2 marks)*

b Give a reason that explains why a luminous Bunsen burner flame is *not* suitable for flame tests. *(1 mark)*

c The teacher uses hydrochloric acid to clean the wire loop between each test. Explain why the teacher cleans the wire loop. *(2 marks)*

5 Describe the laboratory test for carbon dioxide. *(2 marks)*

6 A student tests a solution of an unknown salt. He adds a few drops of dilute nitric acid followed by a few drops of silver nitrate solution.

a Give a reason that explains why he adds dilute nitric acid. *(1 mark)*

b Explain why he should *not* use dilute hydrochloric acid instead of dilute nitric acid. *(2 marks)*

7 Barium chloride is toxic.

a Suggest a reason that explains why *dilute* barium chloride solution, rather than concentrated barium chloride solution, is used in tests to identify sulfate ions. *(1 mark)*

b State and explain a suitable precaution to reduce the risk of harm when carrying out tests for sulfate ions. *(2 marks)*

8 A solution of substance X gives a yellow flame test result. It produces a white precipitate when a few drops of dilute nitric acid are added followed by silver nitrate solution. Name substance X. *(2 marks)*

9 A solution of substance Y produces a green precipitate when sodium hydroxide solution is added. It produces a white precipitate when dilute hydrochloric acid is added followed by barium chloride solution.

a Name substance Y. *(2 marks)*

b On standing, the green precipitate gradually turns brown. Suggest a reason that explains this observation. *(1 mark)*

Cation			Colour
Li^{+}	•	•	orange-red
Na^{+}	•	•	red
K^{+}	•	•	blue-green
Ca^{2+}	•	•	yellow
Cu^{2+}	•	•	lilac

B

Metal cation	Colour of metal hydroxide
aluminium, Al^{3+}	white
calcium, Ca^{2+}	white
copper, Cu^{2+}	
iron(II), Fe^{2+}	
iron(III), Fe^{3+}	

C

Halide ion	Colour of silver halide		
	white	yellow	cream
chloride, Cl^{-}			
bromide, Br^{-}			
iodide, I^{-}			

D

SC26a Choosing materials

Specification reference: C9.38C; C9.39C

Progression questions

- What are ceramics?
- What are ceramics, polymers and metals like?
- How are materials chosen for a given use?

A Bathrooms contain many different materials, including glass and clay ceramics, polymers and metals.

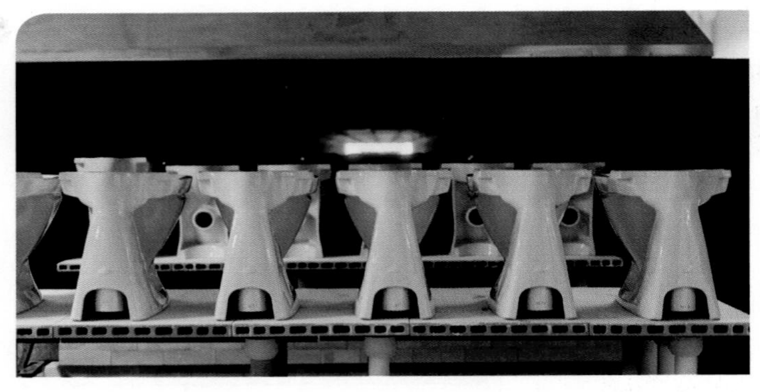

B These new ceramic toilet fittings have just come out of a kiln, a type of oven.

C a modern window glass factory

Glass and clay ceramics

Ceramics are a range of durable compounds that change very little when heated. They are chemically unreactive, hard and stiff but brittle. They are also poor electrical and thermal conductors, and have high melting points. Ceramic materials consist of giant structures with many strong bonds (covalent or ionic), giving them their typical properties.

1 State the typical physical properties of ceramic materials.

Brick, porcelain and china are **clay ceramics**. They are made from clay moulded into the desired shape. When the clay is heated to a very high temperature, tiny crystals form and join together. Bricks are usually decorated by adding a coloured substance to the clay before heating. A pattern may also be moulded into surfaces that will be visible in a finished wall. Porcelain and china are dipped in a 'glaze' and heated strongly again. The glaze forms the hard, waterproof, smooth surface you see on tiles, washbasins and toilet bowls.

2 Describe two properties of glazed clay ceramics that make them suitable for toilet bowls.

Glass is made by melting sand, then allowing it to cool and solidify. Glass and clay ceramics have similar properties because they both have giant structures. However, the atoms in glass are not arranged in a regular way to form crystals, so glass is **transparent** rather than **opaque**.

Modern window glass is made by the float process. Molten glass is poured onto a bath of molten tin, where it spreads out on the surface. The flat layer of glass is drawn away and cooled in a continuous process.

3 Describe two properties of glass that make it suitable for shower screens.

Did you know?

Medieval glass windowpanes are often thicker at the bottom, but not because glass flows very slowly. Instead, it is a result of the way the glass was made. A disc of molten glass was spun to make it spread out thinly, then cut into shape. It was installed thicker end down to make it more stable in the window frame.

Polymers

Polymers are substances with high average relative formula masses. They are made from **monomers** – smaller molecules that join together to form repeating units. For example, poly(ethene) is made from ethene, and poly(chloroethene), or PVC, is made from chloroethene (see *SC24 Polymers*).

Polymers can be moulded into complex shapes. The properties of a polymer depend on its structure and chemical composition, but polymers are usually strong and chemically unreactive. They are also poor electrical and thermal conductors. Rigid PVC is useful for underground pipes and window frames. PVC can be made softer by including substances called **plasticisers** in its manufacture. Flexible PVC is useful for indoor water pipes and waterproof flooring.

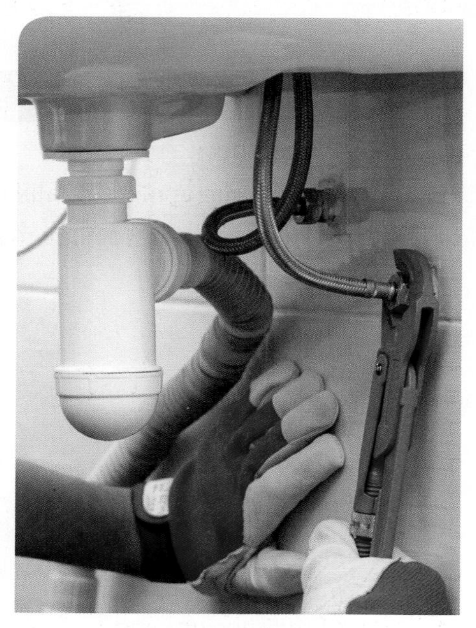

D PVC and metal plumbing fittings

 **4** Describe two properties of PVC that make it suitable for making toilet seats.

Metals

Most metals are strong, hard, shiny solids with high melting points (see *SC7 Types of Substance*). They are good electrical and thermal conductors. They are also **malleable**. Different metal elements can be mixed together to form **alloys**. The alloys are often stronger than the individual metals (see *SC13 Transition Metals, Alloys and Corrosion*). Metals can also be electroplated with an unreactive metal to improve their appearance or their resistance to corrosion.

 **5** Explain why bathroom taps are usually made from a metal electroplated with chromium.

 **6** Explain why bathroom mirrors are made from a sheet of glass coated on the back with a layer of aluminium.

Exam-style question

The table shows some information about copper and PVC, a flexible polymer.

Material	Relative electrical conductivity	Tensile strength (MPa) (resistance to stretching)
copper	1 000 000	220
PVC	1	22

Explain, using information from the table, why electrical cables are made from copper surrounded by a layer of PVC. *(3 marks)*

Checkpoint

How confidently can you answer the Progression questions?

Strengthen

S1 How are materials chosen for use in a bathroom?

Extend

E1 Evaluate the use of different materials for a bench at a bus stop.

SC26b Composite materials

Specification reference: C9.38C; C9.39C

Progression questions

- What are composite materials?
- What are composite materials like?
- How are materials, including composite materials, chosen for a given use?

A **composite material** is a mixture of two or more materials, combined to produce a material with improved properties. The individual materials often have contrasting properties. The individual materials are also usually visible in the composite material, and can often be separated out by physical separation methods. Pykrete consists of ice and about 14% wood pulp. Tiny pieces of wood can be seen in pykrete, and they separate out when the ice melts.

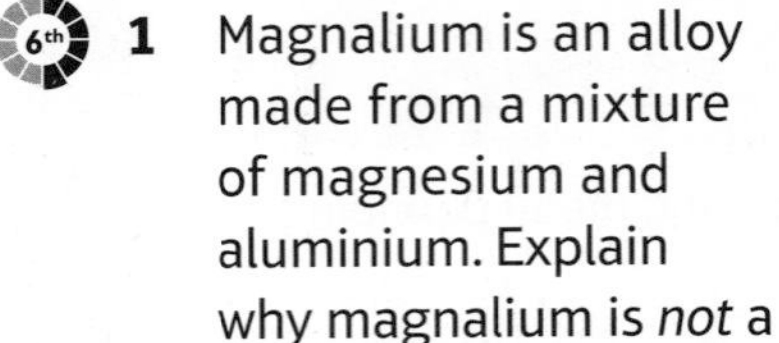

1 Magnalium is an alloy made from a mixture of magnesium and aluminium. Explain why magnalium is *not* a composite material.

2 Proposals for a pykrete aircraft carrier were put forward in the 1940s. Suggest an explanation for why this was impractical.

A The base of this ice dome is made from pykrete. Pykrete is almost half as strong as concrete but much more lightweight.

Reinforcement and matrix

Concrete is made by mixing cement, sand, aggregate (small stones and gravel) and water together. As the concrete sets hard, chemical reactions happen that bond the solid components together. The sand and aggregate form the **reinforcement** of the concrete. The reinforcement is bonded together by cement, which forms the **matrix**.

Many composite materials are like this. For example, in fibreglass, thin glass fibres form the reinforcement and a polymer resin forms the matrix. Glass fibres are brittle but have a low density and a high **tensile strength** (they resist being stretched). The polymer resin is hardwearing but not strong. The combination of these properties produces a lightweight, strong and tough composite material.

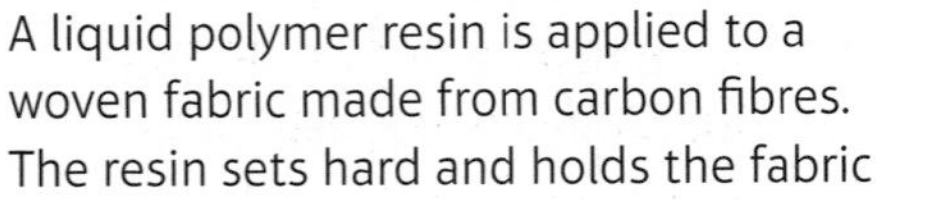

B These bicycle forks are made from a carbon-fibre-reinforced polymer. A liquid polymer resin is applied to a woven fabric made from carbon fibres. The resin sets hard and holds the fabric in shape.

3 Name the reinforcement and matrix in a carbon-fibre-reinforced polymer.

Concrete can be reinforced with steel. Table C shows some typical properties of concrete and steel. **Compressive strength** is a measure of how well a material resists being squashed.

Material	Tensile strength (MPa)	Compressive strength (MPa)	Density (kg/m^3)
concrete	4	40	2300
steel	500	300	7700

C some properties of concrete and steel

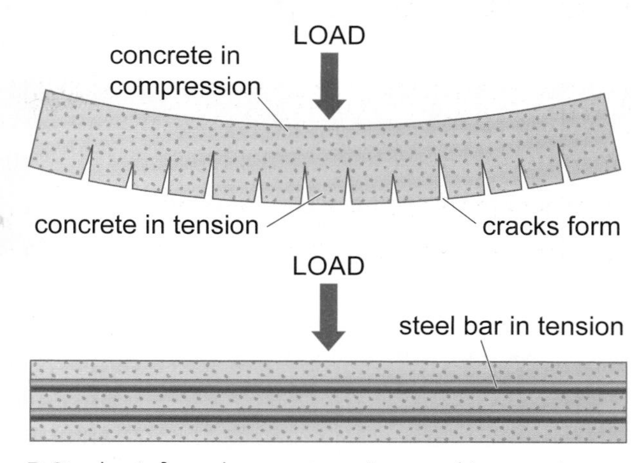

D Steel-reinforced concrete resists cracking much better than concrete alone.

Concrete is strong in compression but weak in tension. It is suitable for road surfaces and for foundations, where it will mainly be squashed. However, concrete beams tend to crack along their lower surface, which is stretched when a beam carries a load (see diagram D). Steel is denser than concrete but has a much higher tensile strength. Steel-reinforced concrete consists of a framework of steel bars with concrete poured in and around it. The composite material formed is strong in tension *and* in compression, and is less dense and cheaper than steel alone.

Laminates

Wood is a natural composite material consisting of cellulose fibres in a matrix of a polymer called lignin. It is stronger along its grain than it is across its grain. Plywood typically consists of odd numbers of thin sheets of wood, each glued at right angles to the sheet below (see diagram E).

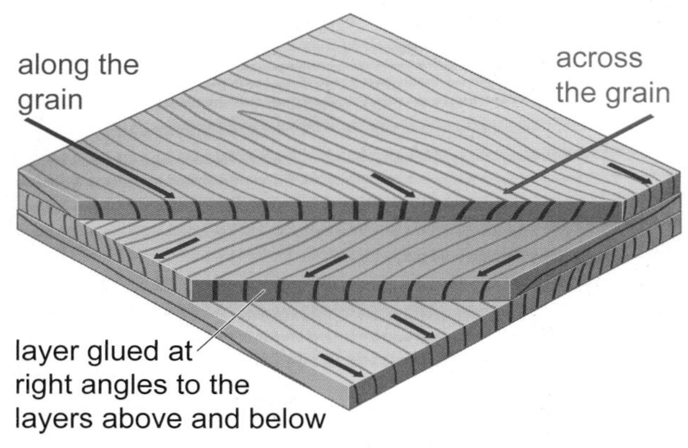

E In plywood, the glue that sticks the layers together forms part of the composite material.

Material	Tensile strength (MPa)
wood (along the grain)	80
wood (across the grain)	4
plywood (various directions)	25–40

F example wood and plywood strengths

4 Explain, using information from table C, which material is stronger when stretched than when it is squashed.

5 Suggest reasons that explain why steel should not be exposed at the surface of steel-reinforced concrete.

6 Compare and contrast plywood with wood. Use information from table F in your answer.

Exam-style question

Explain the meaning of the term 'composite material'. *(2 marks)*

Checkpoint

How confidently can you answer the Progression questions?

Strengthen

S1 What are the advantages of building a road bridge from steel-reinforced concrete, rather than from steel or concrete alone?

Extend

E1 Evaluate the use of papier mâché, expanded polystyrene or clear polymer made from recycled drinks bottles, to make egg boxes.

SC26c Nanoparticles

Specification reference: C9.35C; C9.36C; C9.37C

Progression questions

- Why do nanoparticulate materials have different properties from bulk materials?
- What are some of the uses of nanoparticles?
- What are some of the possible risks from nanoparticles?

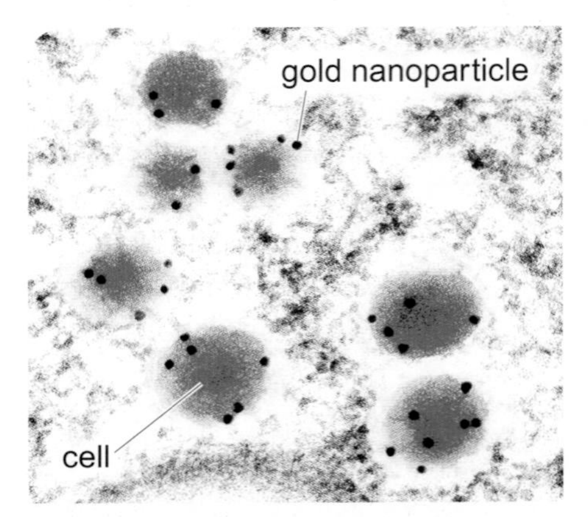

A 'Immunogold labelling' allows biologists to investigate the different types of cells in a tissue. Gold nanoparticles are joined to antibody molecules, which then attach to the surfaces of certain cells.

Lumps and powders are examples of **bulk** materials, and consist of huge numbers of atoms. **Nanoparticles** typically consist of just a few hundred atoms, and are 1–100 nm in size. Nanoparticles are larger than atoms (e.g. an oxygen atom is 0.1 nm in diameter) and simple molecules. Nanoparticles are smaller than cells (e.g. a typical bacterium is 1000 nm long).

Worked example W1

A gold nanoparticle is 32 nm in diameter.

a Calculate its diameter in metres, m.

$1\text{ nm} = 1 \times 10^{-9}\text{ m}$

$32\text{ nm} = 32 \times 10^{-9}\text{ m} = 3.2 \times 10^{-8}\text{ m}$

b The diameter of a gold atom is 0.28 nm. Estimate how many times larger the gold nanoparticle is compared to a gold atom.

Rounding each number to 1 significant figure gives 30 nm and 0.3 nm.

Number of times larger $\approx \frac{30}{0.3} = 100$

1 **a** A gold nanoparticle is 83 nm in diameter. Calculate its diameter in metres, m.

b The diameter of a methane molecule is 0.41 nm. Estimate how many times larger the gold nanoparticle is compared to a methane molecule.

B Michael Faraday (1791–1867) prepared the first pure sample of nanoparticulate gold in 1857. The pink colour in Faraday's nanoparticulate gold is caused by the way nanoparticles scatter light.

Nanoparticulate materials

Nanoparticles occur naturally. However, modern applications involve manufactured nanoparticles. Substances that consist of nanoparticles are described as being **nanoparticulate**. The uses of these materials depend on the small size of the nanoparticles, and their large **surface area to volume ratios**.

Did you know?

Smaller gold nanoparticles suspended in water give a red colour, while larger ones give a purple colour.

Worked example W2

A cube-shaped nanoparticle has sides of 20 nm.

a Calculate its total surface area.

surface area = $6 \times 20 \times 20 = 2400\ \text{nm}^2$

b Calculate its volume.

volume = $20 \times 20 \times 20 = 8000\ \text{nm}^3$

c Calculate its surface area to volume ratio.

surface area to volume ratio = $\frac{2400}{8000} = 0.3$

2 A cube-shaped nanoparticle has sides of 2 nm. Calculate its:

a total surface area

b volume

c surface area to volume ratio.

d Compare your answer to part **c** with answer **c** in Worked example W2. What happens to the surface area to volume ratio as nanoparticles become smaller?

Uses of nanoparticulate materials

Titanium dioxide in bulk is a white solid. It absorbs harmful ultraviolet radiation present in sunlight, which may cause skin cancer. Nanoparticulate titanium dioxide is transparent because its particles are very small, but it still absorbs ultraviolet radiation. This makes it useful for almost-invisible sunscreens.

3 Suggest an explanation for why nanoparticles are used in sunscreens.

The very large surface area to volume ratios of nanoparticles makes them useful as catalysts. Stain-resistant clothes treated with nanoparticulate materials stay clean because the nanoparticles catalyse the breakdown of dirt.

4 Suggest two reasons that explain why titanium dioxide nanoparticles are used to provide a self-cleaning coating for windows.

C The cotton fibres in this electron microscope image are coated with titanium dioxide nanoparticles, which make them self-cleaning.

Risks of nanoparticles

Some scientists are worried that nanoparticulate materials may pose hazards to human health and to the environment. The small size of nanoparticles allows them to be breathed in, or to pass through cell-surface membranes. Their large surface area to volume ratios may allow them to catalyse harmful reactions, or to carry toxic substances bound to their surfaces. The risks are difficult to determine because modern nanoparticulate materials have not been in use for long.

5 Some socks are treated with antibacterial silver nanoparticles, stopping the socks from becoming smelly. Describe a possible environmental hazard caused by these nanoparticles.

Exam-style question

Give *two* reasons that explain why some scientists are worried about the possible effects of nanoparticulate materials on humans. *(2 marks)*

Checkpoint

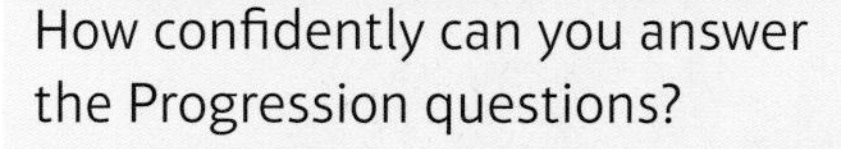

How confidently can you answer the Progression questions?

Strengthen

S1 What are nanoparticulate materials?

S2 State some uses and possible hazards of nanoparticles.

Extend

E1 Evaluate the use of nanoparticles in sunscreens.

Qualitative analysis

A school technician finds some white crystals in an unlabelled beaker in the laboratory.

The substance in the beaker could be sodium bromide, sodium sulfate, potassium bromide or potassium sulfate.

Explain how the technician could use chemical tests to determine which of the four compounds was left in the beaker. You may include equations in your answer. **(6 marks)**

Student answer

The technician can use flame tests to find out whether the substance contains sodium ions or potassium ions [1]. *A small sample of the substance is held at the edge of a hot Bunsen burner flame using a clean flame test loop. Sodium ions will produce a yellow flame colour and potassium ions will produce a lilac flame colour* [2]. *The technician will then need to find out whether the substance contains bromide ions or sulfate ions. A small sample of the substance is dissolved in distilled water and divided in two* [3]. *A few drops of dilute hydrochloric acid are added (to remove carbonate ions that would give a precipitate), followed by dilute barium chloride solution. A white precipitate of barium sulfate forms if the substance contains sulfate ions:*

$$Ba^{2+}(aq) + SO_4^{2-}(aq) \rightarrow BaSO_4(s)$$ [4]

A few drops of dilute nitric acid are added, followed by dilute silver nitrate solution. A cream precipitate of silver bromide forms if the substance contains bromide ions.

[1] Flame tests must be used because Na^+ ions and K^+ ions do not form precipitates with dilute sodium hydroxide solution (unlike Ca^{2+}, Al^{3+}, Cu^{2+}, Fe^{2+} and Fe^{3+} ions).

[2] The correct flame colours for the two metal ions are given.

[3] The answer might equally well have started with the tests to identify sulfate ions and bromide ions, rather than with the flame tests.

[4] The answer includes a balanced ionic equation with appropriate state symbols, but the written explanation is already very clear.

Verdict

This is a strong answer. It shows good knowledge and understanding of how to carry out tests to identify ions in compounds, and the results expected. The answer explains the steps needed in a logical order and includes practical details such as the need to use distilled water in a chemical analysis.

Exam tip

Make sure you know how to carry out tests for ions and the observations expected.

Glossary

absorb	To soak up or take in.
acid	A solution that reacts with alkalis, turns litmus red and has a pH of less than 7.
acid rain	Rainwater that is more acidic than usual due to air pollution, usually caused by sulfur dioxide and nitrogen oxides.
acidic	Containing or having the properties of an acid.
acidity	The amount of acid in a solution.
activation energy	The minimum amount of energy needed to start a reaction.
active site	The space in an enzyme where the substrate fits during an enzyme-catalysed reaction.
actual yield	The actual amount of product obtained from a chemical reaction.
addition polymerisation	A type of polymerisation in which the monomers add on to each other and no small molecules are eliminated.
addition reaction	A reaction in which reactants combine to form one larger product molecule and no other products.
alcohol	An homologous series of compounds that contain the –OH functional group.
alkali	A solution which contains excess OH^- ions, turns litmus blue and has a pH greater than 7.
alkali metals	A group of very reactive metals found in group 1 of the periodic table.
alkaline	Containing or having the properties of an alkaline.
alkalinity	The amount of alkali in a solution.
alkane	A hydrocarbon in which all the bonds between the carbon atoms are single bonds.
alkene	A hydrocarbon in which there are one or more double bonds between carbon atoms.
allotrope	A different structural form of an element, e.g. graphite and diamond are allotropes of carbon.
alloy	A metal with one or more other elements (usually metals) added to improve its properties.
alloy steel	Iron with other elements deliberately added to it to make an alloy.
amino acid	A group of compounds that are the monomers used to form proteins.
anaerobic respiration	A type of respiration that does not need oxygen.
anion	A negatively-charged ion formed by gaining electrons (usually a non-metal ion).
anode	Positive electrode.
aqueous solution	A mixture that is formed when a substance is dissolved in water.
aquifer	An underground layer of rock containing groundwater which can be extracted using a well or pump.
atmosphere	Layer of gases that surrounds the Earth.
atom	The smallest neutral part of an element that can take part in chemical reactions.
atom economy	The percentage, by mass, of reactants that are converted into useful products.
atomic number	The number of protons in the nucleus of an atom (symbol Z). It is also known as the proton number.
attractive forces	The weak forces of attraction between molecules.
Avogadro constant	This is the number of particles in one mole of a substance (6.02×10^{23} mol^{-1}).
Avogadro's law	If the temperature and pressure are the same, equal volumes of different gases contain an equal number of molecules.

balanced equation	Description of a reaction using the symbols and formulae of the reactants and products, so that the number of 'units' of each element to the left of the arrow is the same as those to the right of the arrow.
base	A substance that will react with an acid to form only salt and water.
batch process	A method in which substances are made in discrete stages rather than constantly.
biodegradable	A substance that can be broken down by microorganisms.
bioleaching	Using bacteria to extract metals from their ores.
bleach	To bleach means to take the colour out of something.
boiling point	The temperature at which a substance changes from a liquid to a gas.
bond	The force of attraction between atoms or ions holding them together.
bond energy	The energy needed to break one mole of a specified covalent bond. It is measured in kJ mol^{-1}.
bulk	A substance in the form of lumps or powders is described as being in bulk.
burette	A piece of apparatus used to accurately measure the volume of solution that has been added during a titration.
by-product	Substance produced in a chemical reaction in addition to the desired product.

calibrated	Marked with a scale for accurate readings.
calibration curve	A graph used to determine the concentration of a substance in a sample.
carbohydrate	A group of compounds made of carbon, hydrogen and oxygen. Sugars and starch are examples of carbohydrates.
carbon monoxide	A poisonous gas produced from carbon burning without enough oxygen.
carboxylic acid	An homologous series of compounds that contain the –COOH functional group.
catalyst	A substance that speeds up the rate of a reaction without itself being used up.
cathode	Negative electrode.
cation	A positively-charged ion formed by losing electrons.
causal link	When one thing can be shown to be causing another thing.
ceramic	A hard, durable, non-metallic material which is generally unaffected by heat, e.g. china and glass.
chemical analysis	Using chemical reactions or sensitive machines to identify and measure substances in a sample.
chemical cell	A device that produces a voltage due to reactions between reactants stored inside it, until one of the reactants is used up.
chemical property	How a substance reacts with other substances.
chlorination	The process of adding chlorine to a substance, often to water.
chromatogram	The piece of paper showing the results of chromatography.
chromatography	A technique for separating the components of a mixture, e.g. different food colouring agents.
clay ceramic	A hard, durable material including brick, porcelain and china.
climate change	Changes that happen to the global weather patterns as a result of global warming.
closed system	When substances cannot enter or leave an observed environment, e.g. a stoppered test tube.
combustion	A chemical reaction in which a compound reacts with oxygen.
complete combustion	Combustion of hydrocarbons with enough oxygen present to convert all the fuel into carbon dioxide and water.
composite material	A mixture of two or more materials with contrasting properties, combined to produce a material with properties of both.
composition	The substances and their proportions that make something up. For example, the composition of today's atmosphere is 78% nitrogen, 21% oxygen, 1% argon and other gases.
compound	A substance that can be split into simpler substances because it contains the atoms of two or more elements joined together.
compressive strength	A measure of how well a substance resists squashing.
concentrated	Containing a large amount of solute dissolved in a small volume of solvent.

concentration The amount of a solute dissolved in a certain volume of solvent.

condensation polymerisation When monomers join together and eliminate a small molecule, such as water.

condense When a gas turns in to a liquid.

confirmatory test A chemical test carried out to check the conclusion from the results of another test.

continuous process A method of manufacture in which substances are made constantly.

correlation A relationship between two variables, so that if one variable changes so does the other. This can be positive or negative.

corrosion The gradual deterioration of a substance when it reacts with substances in the environment, for example when a metal oxidises in air.

covalent bond The bond formed when a pair of electrons is shared between two atoms.

covalent, giant molecular structure Three-dimensional lattice of carbon atoms linked by covalent bonds.

covalent, simple molecular structure Two or more atoms covalently bonded together to form a distinct unit.

cracking A chemical reaction in which large alkane molecules are split into two or more smaller alkanes and alkenes.

crude oil A mixture of hydrocarbons formed from dead microscopic organisms by heat and pressure over millions of years.

crystallisation Separating the solute from a solution by evaporating the solvent.

crystals Solids that are made up of a regular, repeated pattern of atoms, molecules or ions which form fixed shapes with flat surfaces and sharp edges.

---

delocalised electron An electron that is free to move and can carry an electrical current.

denature A denatured enzyme is one where the shape of the active site has changed so much that its substrate no longer fits and the reaction can no longer happen.

desalination A process that produces fresh drinking water by separating the water from the salts in salty water.

desiccant A substance that absorbs water or vapour.

diatomic Two atoms chemically bonded together.

dilute A low concentration of a solute in a solution.

discharged In electrolysis, an ion is discharged when it gains or loses electrons to form an element.

disinfectant Something that destroys or neutralises disease-carrying microorganisms.

displacement reaction When a more reactive element displaces a less reactive element from one of its compounds.

dissociate Breaking up of a compound in to simpler components.

distillate The liquid produced by condensing gases during distillation.

distillation The process of separating a liquid from a mixture by evaporating the liquid and then condensing it (so that it can be collected).

dot and cross diagram A diagram to explain what happens when a bond is formed. It uses dots and crosses to represent the electrons of different atoms.

double bond The covalent bond formed when two pairs of electrons are shared between the same two atoms.

ductile A substance that can be stretched out to make a thin wire.

dynamic equilibrium When the forwards and backwards reactions in a reversible chemical reaction are occurring at the same rate.

---

effervescence The formation of gas bubbles in a liquid due to a chemical reaction occurring.

electrical conductivity Allowing electricity to pass through.

electrode A rod made of a metal or graphite that carries the current into or out of the electrolyte.

electrolysis The process in which energy transferred by a direct electrical current decomposes electrolytes.

electrolyte An ionic compound that is molten or dissolved in water.

electron A tiny particle with a negative charge and very little mass.

electron shell Areas around a nucleus that can be occupied by electrons and are usually drawn as circles. Also called an electron energy level or an 'orbit'.

electronic configuration The arrangement of electrons in shells around the nucleus of an atom.

electroplating Using electricity to coat one metal with a thin layer of another metal.

electrostatic force The force of attraction between oppositely-charged particles, and force of repulsion between particles with the same charge.

element A simple substance made up of only one type of atom.

emission spectra A set of wavelengths of light or electromagnetic radiation showing which wavelengths have been given out (emitted) by a substance.

emit To give out.

empirical formula The formula showing the simplest whole number ratio of atoms of each element in a compound.

endothermic A type of reaction in which energy from the surroundings is transferred to the products, e.g. photosynthesis.

end-point When just enough solution has been added from the burette to react with all the solution in the flask in a titration experiment.

enzyme A protein produced by living organisms that acts as a catalyst to speed up the rate of a reaction.

ester link This link is present in all polyester molecules. It consists of –COO–.

ethanoic acid The carboxylic acid which contains two carbon atoms and is the main acid in vinegar.

evaporate When a liquid turns in to a gas.

exothermic A type of reaction in which energy is transferred to the surroundings from the reactants, e.g. combustion.

extraction A process in which a metal is obtained from its ore.

---

feedstock Raw material. A substance used to make other substances.

fermentation Anaerobic respiration occurring in microorganisms.

fertiliser Soluble compounds added to soil to replace the minerals used up by plants.

filtrate A solution that has passed through a filter.

filtration Using a filter to separate insoluble substances from a liquid.

finite resource Something useful that is no longer made or which is being made very slowly.

flame photometer A machine used to identify metal ions in solution and to determine their concentration.

fossil fuel A fuel formed from the dead remains of organisms over millions of years, i.e. coal, oil and natural gas.

fraction A component of a mixture that has been separated by fractional distillation.

fractional distillation A method of separating a mixture of liquids with different boiling points into individual components (fractions).

fractionating column A long column used for fractional distillation. It is warmer at the bottom than at the top.

fuel cell A device that produces a voltage due to reactions involving a fuel and oxygen, for as long these reactants are supplied.

fullerene A molecule in which each carbon atom is covalently bonded to three other carbon atoms, forming spheres or tube shapes.

functional group An atom or group of atoms in a molecule that is mainly responsible for the molecule's chemical reactions and properties.

galvanising	Coating iron or steel with a thin layer of zinc to improve its resistance to rusting.
general formula	The formula showing the proportions of different atoms in molecules of an homologous series. For example, alkenes have the general formula C_nH_{2n}.
glass	A solid produced by cooling molten substances. The atoms are joined to form a giant structure without crystals.
global warming	The increase in the Earth's average temperature likely to be caused by increased amounts of carbon dioxide in the atmosphere.
graphene	An allotrope of carbon consisting of a sheet that is one atom thick, with atoms arranged in a honeycomb shape.
greenhouse effect	When gases in the atmosphere absorb energy transferred by infrared waves from the Earth, which causes the atmosphere to be warmer than it otherwise would be.
greenhouse gas	A gas that helps to trap 'heat' in the atmosphere. Carbon dioxide, methane and water vapour are greenhouse gases.
group	A vertical column of elements in the periodic table. Elements in the same group generally have similar properties.
haemoglobin	The red, iron-containing pigment found in red blood cells.
half equation	A chemical equation written to describe an oxidation or reduction half-reaction.
halide	A compound formed between a halogen and another element such as a metal or hydrogen.
halide ion	A negatively-charged ion formed from one of the group 7 elements.
halogen	An element in group 7 of the periodic table.
hazard	Something that could cause harm.
homologous series	A family of compounds that have the same general formula and similar properties, but have different numbers of carbon atoms.
hydrocarbon	A compound containing only hydrogen and carbon atoms.
ignite	To start burning.
impurity	Unwanted substance found mixed into a useful substance.
incinerated	This occurs when a substance is burned.
incomplete combustion	When a substance reacts only partially with oxygen, such as when carbon burns in air producing carbon dioxide, carbon monoxide and soot (unburnt carbon).
indicator	A substance which can change colour depending on the pH of a solution.
inert	Does not react.
infrared	Electromagnetic radiation that we can feel as heat.
insoluble	A substance that cannot be dissolved in a certain liquid.
intermolecular force	A weak force of attraction between molecules.
ion	An atom or group of atoms with an electrical charge due to the gain or loss of electrons.
ionic bond	A strong electrostatic force of attraction between oppositely-charged ions.
ionic compound	A substance made up of ions of different elements.
ionic equation	A balanced equation that only shows the ions that react together. The spectator ions are not included in the equation.
isomer	Molecules with the same molecular formula but different arrangements of atoms are called isomers.
isotope	Atoms of an element with the same number of protons (atomic number) but different mass numbers due to different numbers of neutrons.
lattice structure	An arrangement of many particles that are bonded together in a fixed, regular, grid-like pattern.
law of conservation of mass	The idea that mass is never lost or gained during a chemical reaction or physical change.
leachate	A solution produced when water or another solvent passes through a mixture of substances and dissolves some of them.
limiting reactant	The reactant that determines the amount of product formed in a chemical reaction. Any other reactants will be present in excess.
lubricant	A substance placed between two moving surfaces to reduce the friction between them.
malleable	A substance that can be hammered or rolled into shape without shattering.
mass number	The total number of protons and neutrons in the nucleus of an atom (symbol A). It is also known as the nucleon number.
matrix	In a composite material, it is the substance that binds the reinforcement material together.
mean	An average calculated by adding up the values of a set of measurements and dividing by the number of measurements in the set.
melting point	The temperature at which a substance changes from the solid state to the liquid stated when heated, or from the liquid state to the solid state when cooled.
metal	Any element that is shiny when polished, conducts heat and electricity well, is malleable and flexible and often has a high melting point.
metallic bonding	The type of bonding found in metals. You can think of it as positively-charged ions in a 'sea' of negatively-charged electrons.
mixture	A substance containing two or more different substances that are not joined together.
mobile phase	In paper chromatography, this is when the solvent moves along the paper carrying the dissolved samples with it.
molar gas volume	The volume occupied by one mole of molecule of any gas. It is 24 dm^3 or 24 000 cm^3 at room temperature and pressure.
mole	A mole of something is 6×10^{23} of it. The mass of a mole of a substance is the relative formula mass expressed in grams.
mole ratio	The ratio between the amounts, in moles, of substances in a balanced equation.
molecular formula	The formula showing the actual number of atoms of each element in a molecule of a compound.
molecular	Refers to substances that are made up of molecules.
molecule	A particle consisting of two or more atoms joined together by covalent bonding.
monomer	A small molecule that can join with other molecules like itself to form a polymer.
nanoparticle	Piece of a material consisting of a few hundred atoms, and between 1 nm and 100 nm in size.
nanoparticulate	A material consisting of nanoparticles is described as being nanoparticulate.
native state	The native state of an element is when it is not combined with other elements in compounds.
natural gas	A fossil fuel formed from the remains of microscopic dead plants and animals that lived in the sea.
naturally occurring polymer	A substance that exists naturally as a polymer in plants, animals etc., such as DNA, starch and proteins.
neutral	A liquid that is neither acidic nor alkaline and has a pH of 7.
neutralisation	A reaction in which an acid reacts with a base to produce a salt and water only.
neutralise	To make a solution neither acidic nor alkaline. During neutralisation, a base reacts with an acid, forming a salt and water.
neutron	A particle found in the nucleus of an atom having zero charge and mass of 1 (relative to a proton).
nitrogenous	Containing or supplying nitrogen, for example in a fertiliser.
noble gas	An unreactive gas in group 0 of the periodic table.
non-enclosed system	Another term for an open system.
non-metal	An element that is not shiny and does not conduct heat or electricity well.

non-renewable Any energy resource that will run out because you cannot renew your supply of it, e.g. oil.

nuclear fission When the nucleus of a large atom such as uranium, splits into two smaller nuclei.

nucleotide The monomers that make up nucleic acids such as DNA.

nucleus The central part of an atom or ion.

---

opaque Material that does not let light through. It is not possible to see through an opaque substance.

open system A system into or from which substances can enter or leave, such as a reaction inside an open test tube.

organic compound A compound that has a central framework of carbon atoms onto which hydrogen and other atoms are attached. Methane (CH_4) is organic but carbon dioxide is not (because it contains no hydrogen atoms).

outer electron shell The electron shell (or energy level) that is furthest away from a nucleus but which still contains one or more electrons.

oxidation A reaction in which oxygen is added to a chemical; loss of electrons by an atom or negative ion.

oxide of nitrogen Any one of a variety of gaseous compounds consisting of only nitrogen and oxygen atoms. Together they are often represented as NO_x.

oxidising agent A substance that causes another substance to be oxidised in an oxidation reaction.

---

paper chromatography Chromatography carried out by spotting drops of the same samples onto paper and then allowing a solvent to move up the paper. Different components in the samples travel up the paper in the solvent at different rates.

particle A tiny piece of matter that everything is made out of.

particle model Another term for kinetic theory.

percentage yield The actual yield divided by the theoretical yield, as a percentage.

period A horizontal row in the periodic table.

periodic table The chart in which the elements are arranged in order of increasing atomic number.

petrochemical A substance made from crude oil.

pH scale A scale going up to 14 showing acidity or alkalinity. Numbers below 7 are acids; numbers above 7 are alkalis; pH 7 is neutral.

photosynthesis A series of enzyme-catalysed reactions carried out in the green parts of plants. Carbon dioxide and water combine to form glucose. This process requires light energy from sunlight.

physical change A change in which no new substances are formed, such as changes of state.

physical property A description of how a material behaves and responds to forces and energy. For example, hardness is a physical property.

phytoextraction Using plants to extract metals from their ores.

pipette A piece of apparatus which can be used in a titration to accurately measure a set volume of a solution.

plasticiser A substance added to a polymer during its manufacture to make the polymer softer and more flexible.

pollutant A substance that harms living organisms when released into the environment.

polyatomic ions A group of atoms that have a positive or negative charge due to the loss or gain of electrons, e.g. nitrate NO_3^-.

polyester This is a polymer that contains large numbers of ester links.

poly(ethene) A common polymer made of ethene monomers.

polymer A long-chain molecule made by joining many smaller molecules (monomers) together.

polymerisation A reaction in which a large number of small molecules (monomers) join together to form a long chain molecule (polymer).

precipitate An insoluble substance that is formed when two soluble substances react together in solution.

precipitation A reaction in which a precipitate is formed.

precipitation reaction A reaction in which an insoluble product is formed from two soluble reactants.

prediction What you think will happen in an experiment (usually given with a reason of why you think this).

product A substance formed in a reaction.

protein A polymer made up of amino acids.

proton A particle found in the nucleus of an atom, having a positive charge and the same mass as a neutron.

pure A single substance with a fixed composition that does not have anything else mixed with it.

---

rate How quickly something happens.

reactant A substance used up in a chemical reaction.

reaction pathway A series of reactions needed to make a particular product.

reaction profile A diagram to show how the energy stored in a substance changed during the course of a chemical reaction.

reactivity series A list of metals in order of reactivity with the most reactive at the top.

recycling Converting waste materials into new products.

red blood cell A biconcave disc containing haemoglobin that gives blood its red colour and carries oxygen around the body to the tissues. Also known as an erythrocyte.

redox reaction A reaction in which both oxidation and reduction occur.

reduction A reaction in which a substance loses oxygen or gains electrons.

reinforcement In a composite material, the substance that is bound together by the matrix material.

relative atomic mass (RAM, A_r) The mean mass of an atom relative to the mass of an atom of carbon-12, which is assigned a mass of 12. The RAM of an element is the mean relative mass of the isotopes in the element.

relative charge The electrical charge on something compared with something else. The electrical charge used for the comparison is often given the value of 1.

relative formula mass (M_r) The sum of the relative atomic masses of all the atoms in a formula.

relative mass The mass of something compared to the mass of something else, which is often given the mass of 1.

renewable source Source of raw materials that will not run out.

repeating unit The part of a polymer that can be repeated many times to form the polymer chain.

residue Material remaining in the filter after a mixture has passed through it.

resolution The smallest change that can be measured by an instrument. For example, in a microscope it is the smallest distance between two points that can be seen as two points and not blurred into one point.

reversible reaction A chemical reaction that can work in both directions.

R_f value The ratio of the distance travelled by a solute on a chromatogram to the distance travelled by the solvent under the same conditions.

risk The chance of a hazard causing harm.

risk assessment Identification of the hazards of doing an experiment and ways of reducing the risk of harm from those hazards.

rusting The corrosion of iron or steel (water and oxygen must be present for rusting to occur).

---

sacrificial protection Using a more reactive metal to protect iron from rusting.

salt A compound formed by neutralisation of an acid by a base.

saturated A molecule that contains only single bonds between the carbon atoms in a chain.

saturated solution Contains the maximum amount of solute that can dissolve in that amount of solvent at that temperature.

sedimentation The process in which rock grains and insoluble substances sink to the bottom of a liquid.

side reaction A reaction which takes place at the same time as another main reaction.

simple distillation The process of separating a liquid from a mixture by evaporating the liquid and then condensing it so that it can be collected.

solute Describes a substance that dissolves in a liquid to make a solution.

solution Formed when a substance has dissolved in a liquid.

solvent Describes the liquid in which a substance dissolves to make a solution.

spectator ions These are ions that do not change during a reaction.

spectrum Individual components of light arranged in order of wavelength or frequency.

stainless steel Alloy steel containing elements such as chromium, to resist rusting.

standard solution A solution containing a known concentration of a substance.

starch A polymer carbohydrate that is made by the joining together of glucose molecules.

state of matter One of three different forms that a substance can have: solid, liquid or gas.

state symbol A letter or letters to show the state of a substance.

stationary phase The surface through which the solvent and dissolved substances move in chromatography.

still A piece of apparatus used to carry out distillation or fractional distillation.

stoichiometry The molar ratio of the reactants and products in a chemical reaction.

strong acid An acidic solute that dissociates completely into ions when it dissolves.

structural formula The formula showing the symbols for each atom in a compound with straight lines joining them to represent the covalent bonds.

subatomic particle A particle that is smaller than an atom, such as a proton, neutron or electron.

substrate A substance that is changed during a reaction.

sugar Soluble carbohydrate made up of small molecules, e.g. glucose formula $C_6H_{12}O_6$.

surface area : volume ratio (SA : V) The total amount of surface area of an object divided by its volume.

synthetic polymer A polymer that is manufactured in a laboratory or factory.

tarnish A thin layer that forms on a metal due to oxidation. A metal is also said to tarnish as this layer forms.

tensile strength A measure of how well a substance resists stretching.

theoretical yield The maximum calculated amount of a product that could be formed from a given amount of reactants.

titration A technique in volumetric analysis that is used to find the exact volumes of solutions which react with each other.

toxic Poisonous.

transition metal A metal element placed in the block between groups 2 and 3 in the periodic table.

transparent A coloured or colourless material that light can travel through without scattering.

universal indicator A mixture of different indicators giving a different colour at different points on the pH scale.

unsaturated A molecule that contains one or more double bonds between carbon atoms in a chain.

valency The number of covalent bonds formed by an atom, or the charge number of the ion formed by an atom.

variable A factor that can change.

viscosity How thick or runny a liquid is. Low viscosity is very runny; high viscosity is thick.

volcanic activity The release of gases and/or molten rock by volcanoes.

volumetric flask A flask which is accurately calibrated to hold a given volume of solution.

weak acid An acidic solute that does not dissociate completely into ions when it dissolves.

weathering When rocks are broken up by physical, chemical or biological processes.

X-ray Electromagnetic radiation that has a shorter wavelength than UV but longer than gamma rays.

yield The amount of useful product that you can get from something.

'ex

A

- A_r (relative atomic mass) 23
- absorption 166
- acid rain 158
- acidic solutions 52
- acidity 52
- acids 52–53, 54–55
  - reaction with metals 66
  - strong 55
  - weak 55
- activation energy 138, 146
  - catalysts 142–143
- active sites 143
- actual yield 108
- addition polymerisation 184–185
- addition reactions 175
- alcohols 178–179
  - ethanol 176–177
- alkali metals 128–129
- alkaline solutions 52
- alkalinity 52
- alkalis 52–53, 60–61, 64–65
- alkanes 154, 172, 178
  - homologous series 154–155
  - reactions 174–175
- alkenes 161, 173
  - reactions 174–175
- allotropes of carbon 44–45
- alloy steels 102
- alloys 102–103, 203
  - uses 104–105
- amino acids 185
- ammonium ions, tests for 197
- ammonium nitrate fertiliser 120
- ammonium sulfate 120–121
- anaerobic respiration 177
- anions 34, 80, 198
- anode 80, 100
- aqueous solutions
  - acids and alkalis 52
  - ionic compounds 39
- aquifers 15
- atmosphere
  - changing 164–165
  - composition 162
  - early 162–163
  - present-day 166–167
- atom economy 110–111
- atomic number 20
  - periodic table 28–29
- atomic structure 18–19
- atoms 2, 18
- attractive forces 3
- Avogadro constant 76
- Avogadro's law 118

B

- balanced equations 61
- bases 56
- batch processes 121
- biodegradable 190
- bioleaching 89
- bleaches 131
- boiling point 3
  - ionic compounds 38
  - molecular compounds 42
- bond energy 147
- bonding 42
  - covalent 40–41, 42, 48
  - giant covalent 48
  - ionic 34–35, 48
  - metallic 46, 48
  - models 48–49
- bonds
  - breaking and making 146
  - covalent 147
  - energy calculations 147
- bromine water test 175
- bulk materials 206
- by-products 110, 123, 125

C

- calibration 112
- calibration curves 195
- carbohydrates 176
- carbon allotropes 44–45
- carbon monoxide 157
- carbonates
  - reactions with acids 67
  - test for 198
- carboxylic acids 182–183
- catalysts 142–143
  - cracking 160
- cathode 80, 100
- cations 34, 80, 194
- causal links 166
- ceramics 202
- chemical cells 124
- chemical properties of substances 3
  - elements 26
- chlorination 15
- chromatogram 8
- chromatography 8
  - paper 8–9
- climate change 166–167, 168–169
  - effects 168–169
  - limiting the impact 169
- closed systems 74, 94, 122
- combustion 156–157, 174
- complete combustion 156, 174
- composite materials 204–205
- compounds 4
  - ionic 36–39
  - molecular 42–43
- compressive strength 205
- concentrated solutions 54
- concentration 53, 112–113
- condensation 10, 152
- condensation polymerisation 188–189
- conservation of mass, law of 74–75
- continuous processes 121
- correlations 166
- corrosion 91, 98–99
- covalent bonds 40–41, 42, 147
  - giant molecular structures 45
  - simple molecular structures 42
- cracking 160, 190
- crude oil 150
  - fractional distillation 152–153
- crystallisation 6, 57
  - laboratory practice 7
- crystals 36

D

- denaturing of enzymes 143
- desalination 14
- desiccants 99
- diatomic molecules 130
- dilute solutions 54
- discharged ions 84
- disinfectants 131
- displacement reactions 87, 132, 145
- dissociation 55
- distillate 177
- distillation
  - fractional 11, 152–153
  - simple 14
  - water 10–11, 14
- dot and cross diagrams 40
- double bonds 40
- drinking water 14–15
- ductile substances 96, 104
- dynamic equilibrium 94–95
  - factors affecting 122–123

E

- effervescence 66
- electrical conductivity
  - ionic compounds 38–39
  - metals 47
  - molecular compounds 43
- electrodes 80
  - reactions at 81
- electrolysis 80–81
  - products 84–85
  - salt solutions 84–85
- electrolytes 80, 100
- electron shells 18, 30
  - outer 40
- electronic configurations 30–31
  - noble gases 34
- electrons 18
- electroplating 100–101
- electrostatic forces 34
- elements 4, 18, 42
  - groups 29
  - periodic table 26–27
- emission 166
- emission spectra 195
- empirical formulae 73
- endothermic reactions 138, 144–145
  - equilibrium 95
- end-point of a titration 65
- energy changes during reactions 146–147
- enzymes 143, 176
  - denaturing 143
- equations
  - balanced 61
  - half equations 66, 81, 87
  - ionic 66
- equilibrium, dynamic 94–95
  - factors affecting 122–123
- ester links 188
- ethanoic acid 182
- ethanol 176–177
- evaporation 10, 152
- exam preparation examples
  - alcohols and carboxylic acid 192
  - atomic structure and periodic table 32
  - bonding 50
  - electrolysis 106–107
  - empirical formula 78
  - fuels 170
  - isotopes 24
  - magnesium sulfate 70
  - qualitative analysis 208
  - reaction rates 148
  - substance separation and purification 16
- exothermic reactions 138, 144–145
  - equilibrium 95
- extraction of metals 88

F

- feedstock 151
- fermentation 176–177
- fertilisers 120–121
- filtrate 7
- filtration 6, 57
  - laboratory practice 7
- finite resources 190
- flame photometry 195
- flame tests 194
- fossil fuels 151
- fractional distillation 11, 152–153, 177, 190
- fractionating columns 152
- fractions (of distillation) 177
- fuel cells 124–125
- fuels 151
  - for cars 161
  - pollution 158–159
- fullerenes 44
- functional groups 173, 179, 188

G

- galvanising 101
- gases, molar volumes of 118–119
- general formulae 155, 172
- giant structures of carbon 45
- glass 202
- global warming 166
- graphene 44
- greenhouse effect 166
- greenhouse gases 125, 161, 166
- groups (of the periodic table) 29
  - group 0 elements 134–135
  - group 1 elements 128–129
  - group 7 elements 130–131, 132–133
  - valency 41

H

- Haber process 120–121
- haemoglobin 157
- half equations 66, 81, 87
- halide ions 130
  - tests for 199
- halogens 130–131
  - reactivity 132–133
- hazards 7
- homologous series 154, 172, 178
- hydrocarbons 150–151, 172
  - breaking down 160–161

I

- ignition 153
- incomplete combustion 157
- incomplete combustion 174
- indicators (pH) 52
- inert electrodes 84
- inert substances 28
- infrared radiation 166
- insoluble substances 6, 69
- intermolecular forces 42
- ionic bonds 34–35
- ionic compounds 36
  - properties 38–39

ionic equations 66
ionic formulae 36
ionic lattices 36–37
ions 53
- neutralisation 64–65
- spectator ions 66
- tests for negative ions 198–199
- tests for positive ions 196–197

isomers 173
isotopes 22–23

L

laminates 205
lattices
- giant 46
- ionic 36–37

law of conservation of mass 74–75
leachate 89
life cycle assessment (LCA) 93
limiting reactant 76
lubricants 45

M

malleable substances 96, 104, 203
malleability of metals 47
mass conservation 74–75
mass number 21
masses 72
materials 202–203
- bulk 206
- composites 204–205

matrix 204
mean 23
melting point 3, 5
- ionic compounds 38
- molecular compounds 42

metals 46, 203
- biological extraction methods 89
- corrosion 91
- electrical conductivity 47
- extraction as reduction 90
- malleability 47
- ores 88–89
- properties 46–47
- reaction with acids 66
- reaction with carbonates 67
- reactivity series 66
- recycling 92
- structure and bonding 46
- uses 104–105

mixtures 4–5
- separation 10

mobile phase 8
molar volume of gases 118–119
mole ratio 114
molecular compounds 42–43
molecular formulae 40, 72, 154
- working out 41

molecular substances 40
molecules 2, 40
- diatomic 130

moles 76–77
monomers 43, 184, 203

N

nanoparticles 206–207
native state metals 88
natural gas 150, 151
naturally-occurring polymers 185
negative ions, tests for 198–199
neutral solutions 52
neutralisation reactions 56, 60, 64–65, 145
neutrons 18
nitrogen oxides 159
nitrogenous fertilisers 120
noble gases 134–135
non-enclosed systems 74
non-metals 46
non-renewable materials 151, 190
nuclear atom 20
nuclear fission 22
nucleotides 185
nucleus 18

O

oceans 163, 164
oil fractions 152
OILRIG mnemonic 66, 81, 133
opaque materials 202
open systems 94
ores 88–89
organic compounds 178
outer electron shells 40
oxidation 66, 81, 87, 90–91, 98, 174, 182
- OILRIG mnemonic 66, 81, 133

oxides of nitrogen 159
oxidising agents 182
oxygen in the atmosphere 163, 164–165

P

pair reversals 29
paper chromatography 8–9
particle model of matter 2
particles 2
percentage yield 108
periodic table 20
- atomic number 28–29
- electronic configurations 30–31
- elements 26–27
- group 0 elements 134–135
- group 1 elements 128–129
- group 7 elements 130–131, 132–133
- valency 41

periods (of the periodic table) 29
petrochemicals 151
pH meters 54
pH scale 52
photometry 195
photosynthesis 164
physical changes 3
physical properties of substances 5
- elements 26

phytoextraction 89
plasticisers 203
pollution 158–159
polyatomic ions 37
polyester 188
poly(ethylene) 43
polymerisation
- addition 184–185
- condensation 188–189

polymers 43, 184, 203
- naturally-occurring 185
- problems with 190–191
- properties and uses 186–187
- synthetic 185

positive ions, tests for 196–197
potable (drinkable) water 14–15
practicals
- acid–base titration 116–117
- alcohol combustion 180–181
- copper sulfate electrolysis 82–83
- copper sulfate preparation 58–59
- inks 12–13
- ion identification 200–201
- neutralisation 62–63
- reaction rates 140–141

precipitates 14, 68, 74, 196
precipitation 68, 145
precipitation reactions 196
predictions about elements 27
products 136
- masses of 75

proteins 185
protons 18
pure substances 4

R

R_f values 8–9
reactants 136
- limiting 76
- masses of 75

reaction pathways 111, 123
reaction profiles 142, 144, 146
reaction rates 136–137
- factors affecting 138–139

reactions 76–77
- displacement 87, 132, 145
- energy changes 146–147
- neutralisation 145
- redox 87, 133
- reversible 94
- temperature changes 145

reactivity 86–87
reactivity series 66, 86
recycling 92–93
red blood cells (erythrocytes) 157
redox reactions 87, 90, 133
reduction 66, 81, 87, 90–91
- metal extraction 90
- OILRIG mnemonic 66, 81, 133

reinforcement of materials 204
relative atomic masses (RAM) 23, 26, 29
relative charges 18
relative formula mass 72
relative masses 18
renewable sources 179
repeating units 185
residue 7
resolution 167
reversible reactions 94, 120
risk 7
risk assessment 7
rusting 91, 99

S

sacrificial protection 99
salts 56, 130
- insoluble 69
- soluble 57, 65

saturated compounds 161
saturated solutions 6
sea water purification 14
sedimentation 15
side reactions 109
simple distillation 14
solubility 68–69
solutes 6, 74
solutions 6, 74
- concentrated 54
- dilute 54
- saturated 6

solvents 6, 74
spectator ions 66, 87
spectrum of emitted light 195
stainless steels 102
standard solutions 195
starch 176, 185
state changes 3
state symbols 56
states of matter 2–3
stationary phase 8
still (distillation equipment) 10
stoichiometry 77
strong acids 55
structural formulae 154
subatomic particles 18
substances
- insoluble 6
- mixtures 4–5
- pure 4

substrates 143
sugars 176, 185
sulfates, test for 198–199
sulfur dioxide 158
surface area to volume ratios 206
synthetic polymers 185

T

tarnishing 91, 98
tensile strength 204
theoretical yield 108
tin plating 101
titrations 65
- calculations 114–115

transition metals 96–97
- chemical properties 97
- physical properties 96–97

transparent materials 202

U

universal indicator 52
unsaturated compounds 161, 173

V

valency 41
variables 136
viscosity 153
volumetric flasks 112

W

water
- distillation 10, 14
- for chemical analysis 14
- for drinking 14–15

weak acids 55

X

X-rays 28

Y

yields from reactions 108–109, 122

The Periodic Table of the Elements

Key

relative atomic mass
atomic symbol
name
atomic (proton) number

1	2											3	4	5	6	7	0
							1 **H** hydrogen 1										4 **He** helium 2
7 **Li** lithium 3	9 **Be** beryllium 4											11 **B** boron 5	12 **C** carbon 6	14 **N** nitrogen 7	16 **O** oxygen 8	19 **F** fluorine 9	20 **Ne** neon 10
23 **Na** sodium 11	24 **Mg** magnesium 12											27 **Al** aluminium 13	28 **Si** silicon 14	31 **P** phosphorus 15	32 **S** sulfur 16	35.5 **Cl** chlorine 17	40 **Ar** argon 18
39 **K** potassium 19	40 **Ca** calcium 20	45 **Sc** scandium 21	48 **Ti** titanium 22	51 **V** vanadium 23	52 **Cr** chromium 24	55 **Mn** manganese 25	56 **Fe** iron 26	59 **Co** cobalt 27	59 **Ni** nickel 28	63.5 **Cu** copper 29	65 **Zn** zinc 30	70 **Ga** gallium 31	73 **Ge** germanium 32	75 **As** arsenic 33	79 **Se** selenium 34	80 **Br** bromine 35	84 **Kr** krypton 36
85 **Rb** rubidium 37	88 **Sr** strontium 38	89 **Y** yttrium 39	91 **Zr** zirconium 40	93 **Nb** niobium 41	96 **Mo** molybdenum 42	[98] **TC** technetium 43	101 **Ru** ruthenium 44	103 **Rh** rhodium 45	106 **Pd** palladium 46	108 **Ag** silver 47	112 **Cd** cadmium 48	115 **In** indium 49	119 **Sn** tin 50	122 **Sb** antimony 51	128 **Te** tellurium 52	127 **I** iodine 53	131 **Xe** xenon 54
133 **Cs** caesium 55	137 **Ba** barium 56	139 **La*** lanthanum 57	178 **Hf** hafnium 72	181 **Ta** tantalum 73	184 **W** tungsten 74	186 **Re** rhenium 75	190 **Os** osmium 76	192 **Ir** iridium 77	195 **Pt** platinum 78	197 **Au** gold 79	201 **Hg** mercury 80	204 **Tl** thallium 81	207 **Pb** lead 82	209 **Bi** bismuth 83	[209] **Po** polonium 84	[210] **At** astatine 85	[222] **Rn** radon 86
[223] **Fr** francium 87	[226] **Ra** radium 88	[227] **Ac*** actinium 89	[261] **Rf** rutherfordium 104	[262] **Db** dubnium 105	[266] **Sg** seaborgium 106	[264] **Bh** bohrium 107	[277] **Hs** hassium 108	[268] **Mt** meitnerium 109	[271] **Ds** darmstadtium 110	[272] **Rg** roentgenium 111	Elements with atomic numbers 112-116 have been reported but not fully authenticated						

The lanthanoids (atomic numbers 58-71) and the actinoids (atomic numbers 90-103) have been omitted.

The relative atomic masses of copper and chlorine have not been rounded to the nearest whole number.

Published by Pearson Education Limited, 80 Strand, London, WC2R 0RL.

www.pearsonschoolsandfecolleges.co.uk

Copies of official specifications for all Edexcel qualifications may be found on the website: www.edexcel.com

Series editor: Mark Levesley
Designed by Poppy Marks, Pearson Education Limited
Typeset by Phoenix Photosetting, Chatham, Kent

Illustrated by KJA Artists Illustration Agency and Phoenix Photosetting, Chatham, Kent
Cover design by Poppy Marks and Colin Tilley Loughrey
Picture research by Rebecca Sodergren
Cover photo © **123RF.com**: Aafak Cakar, Maksim Kostenko; **SuperStock**: Corbis

First published 2016

19 18 17
10 9 8 7 6 5 4 3

British Library Cataloguing in Publication Data
A catalogue record for this book is available from the British Library

ISBN 9781292120218

Printed in Slovakia by Neografia.

A note from the publisher
In order to ensure that this resource offers high-quality support for the associated Pearson qualification, it has been through a review process by the awarding body. This process confirms that this resource fully covers the teaching and learning content of the specification or part of a specification at which it is aimed. It also confirms that it demonstrates an appropriate balance between the development of subject skills, knowledge and understanding, in addition to preparation for assessment.

Endorsement does not cover any guidance on assessment activities or processes (e.g. practice questions or advice on how to answer assessment questions), included in the resource nor does it prescribe any particular approach to the teaching or delivery of a related course.

While the publishers have made every attempt to ensure that advice on the qualification and its assessment is accurate, the official specification and associated assessment guidance materials are the only authoritative source of information and should always be referred to for definitive guidance.

Pearson examiners have not contributed to any sections in this resource relevant to examination papers for which they have responsibility. Examiners will not use endorsed resources as a source of material for any assessment set by Pearson.

Endorsement of a resource does not mean that the resource is required to achieve this Pearson qualification, nor does it mean that it is the only suitable material available to support the qualification, and any resource lists produced by the awarding body shall include this and other appropriate resources.

Acknowledgements
The following authors contributed text to previous Pearson publications and the publishers are grateful for their permission to include elements of their work: Richard Grime, Ray Oliver, Gemma Young, Penny Johnson and Peter Ellis. The publishers would like to thank Steve Gray and Penny Johnson for their original contributions.

The author and publisher would like to thank the following individuals and organisations for permission to reproduce photographs, figures and text:

Photographs
(Key: b-bottom; c-centre; l-left; r-right; t-top)

SC1-2 TheOceanCleanup.com; **SC1a Alamy Images**: Arctic Images (A); **SC2a Alamy Images**: studiomode (C). **Pearson Education Ltd**: (B). **Shutterstock.com**: sunny337 (A); **SC2b Alamy Images**: Vicki Beaver (A). **Science Photo Library Ltd**: Mark de Fraeye (C); Javier Trueba / MSF (B); **SC2c Corbis**: Anthony Rakusen / Cultura (B). **Getty Images**: Francois Guillot / AFP (A); **SC2d Fotolia.com**: nikkytok (A); **SC2d CP**

Shutterstock.com: Ralko (A); **SC2e Pearson Education Ltd**: (C). **Shutterstock.com**: Timothy Epp (A)

SC3 Reproduced with permission of D. Pearmain, S. J. Park, Z. W. Wang, A. Abdela, R. E. Palmer and Z. Y. Li; University of Birmingham; SC3a Getty Images: Tom Shaw (D). **Pearson Education Ltd**: Tsz-shan Kwok (A); **SC3b Shutterstock.com**: Paul Fleet (C); **SC3c Getty Images**: Corbis / Nagasaki Atomic Bomb Museum / epa (B)

SC4 Science Photo Library Ltd; SC4a NikNaks: (B). **Shutterstock.com**: Baloncici (A); **SC4b Alamy Images**: Jon Bower UK (A); **SC4c Shutterstock.com**: Domenic Gareri (A)

SC5-7 University of California, Berkeley: Felix R. Fischer Ph.D, Department of Chemistry; **SC5a Science Photo Library Ltd**: Andrew Lambert Photography (A); **SC5b Science Photo Library Ltd**: Gary Hincks (C); Dirk Wiersma (B); **SC5c Science Photo Library Ltd**: Tony Camacho (B); **SC7a Getty Images**: Photolibrary / Huw Jones (B). **Science Photo Library Ltd**: Alvis Upitis / AgstockUSA (C); **SC7b Shutterstock.com**: ribeiroantonio (D); **SC7c Fotolia.com**: Silvano Rebai (D). **Getty Images**: Image Ideas (A); **SC7d Science Photo Library Ltd**: Indigo Molecular Images (A)

SC8 Shutterstock.com: Science Photo Library; **SC8a Martyn F. Chillmaid**: (A, B); **SC8b Martyn F. Chillmaid**: (F). **Pearson Education Ltd**: Trevor Clifford (C). **Science Photo Library Ltd**: GIPhotoStock (A); **SC8c Shutterstock.com**: Industry and Travel (A); **SC8c CP Science Photo Library Ltd**: Andrew Lambert Photography (C); **SC8d Science Photo Library Ltd**: Mid Essex Hospital Services NHS Trust (A); Martyn F. Chillmaid (B); **SC8d CP Science Photo Library Ltd**: Trevor Clifford Photography (A); GIPhotoStock (B); **SC8e Martyn F. Chillmaid**: (C). **Science Photo Library Ltd**: Martyn F. Chillmaid (B). **Shutterstock.com**: Paul Prescott (A); **SC8f Getty Images**: Popperfoto (A). **Martyn F. Chillmaid**: (C). **Pearson Education Ltd**: Trevor Clifford (B); **SC8g Science Photo Library Ltd**: ER Degginger (A)

SC9 Getty Images: Corbis / Caroline; **SC9a Getty Images**: Auscape / UIG (C); **SC9b Fundamental Photographs**: Richard Megna (B). **Science Photo Library Ltd**: Martyn F. Chillmaid (A); **SC9c Science Photo Library Ltd**: Andrew Lambert Photography (A) **SC10-11 Alamy Images**: age footstock; **SC10a Alamy Images**: WENN UK (C); **SC11a Science Photo Library Ltd**: Charles D. Winters (B). **The Open University**: (A); **SC11b Dr. Antony van der Ent**: Sustainable Minerals Institute / The University of Queensland (C). **Shutterstock.com**: Steffen Foerster (A); **SC11c Courtesy of the Jersey Heritage Collection**: (C). **Shutterstock.com**: Ron Ellis (D); icarmen13 (A); **SC11d Alamy Images**: Stephen Saks Photography (B); AF archive (D). **Ocean Sole http://www.ocean-sole.com/**: (A); **SC12a Fundamental Photographs**: Chip Clark (D). **Pearson Education Ltd**: Trevor Clifford (A); **SC12b Alamy Images**: Corbin17 (A). **Science Photo Library Ltd**: Frans Lanting, Mint Images (B); **SC13a Alamy Images**: sciencephotos (D). **Shutterstock.com**: TinaImages (E); SasinT (A); **SC13b Fotolia.com**: pieropoma (D). **Pearson Education Ltd**: Gareth Boden (B). **Shutterstock.com**: S.Borisov (A); AHPix (C); **SC13c Fotolia.com**: Ilya Akinshin (A). **Shutterstock.com**: optimarc (D); Madlen (B); **SC13d Alamy Images**: David Hunter (A). **Fotolia.com**: zhu difeng (B). **Shutterstock.com**: Vereshchagin Dmitry (C); **SC13e Alamy Images**: TravelCollection (B); Heather Drake (C). **Fotolia.com**: kamilpetran (A); Andrey Armyagov (D)

SC14-16 Shutterstock.com: Jason.Lee; **SC14a Alamy Images**: robertharding (C); Branislav Bokun (B). **Getty Images**: Christian Science Monitor (A); **SC14b Alamy Images**: studiomode (B). Edinburgh Napier University: (C); **SC14c Science Photo Library Ltd**: Martyn F. Chillmaid (A, C); **SC14d CP Science Photo Library Ltd**: Martyn F. Chillmaid (A, B, C); **SC14e Getty Images**: Roger Viollet (A). **Pearson Education Ltd**: Trevor Clifford (C); **SC15a Science Photo Library Ltd**: US Department of Agriculture (A); **SC15b Science Photo Library Ltd**: Keith Kent (A); **SC16a Alamy Images**: Jim West (A). **Science Photo Library Ltd**: (B)

SC17-19 Shutterstock.com: PawelG Photo; **SC17a Pearson Education Ltd**: Trevor Clifford (B); **SC17b Science Photo Library Ltd**: Andrew Lambert Photography (A, C); **SC17c Science Photo Library Ltd**: Martyn F. Chillmaid (B); Andrew Lambert Photography (C); **SC17d Getty Images**: Nick Obank / Barcroft Media (D). **Shutterstock.com**: Karin Hildebrand Lau (E); **SC18a Alamy Images**: Bon Appetit (A); **SC18b Getty Images**: (B); **SC18b CP Science Photo Library Ltd**: Martyn F. Chillmaid (B); **SC18c Science Photo Library Ltd**: (A); **SC19a Science Photo Library Ltd**: (A). **Shutterstock.com**: M. Norris (B); **SC19b Shutterstock.com**: Stefan Holm (A)

SC20-21 Alamy Images: Plane Mad; **SC20a Alamy Images**: Daniel J. Cox (A). Getty Images: loonger (C). **Shutterstock.com**: Dmitry Naumov (D); **SC20b Science Photo Library Ltd**: Hybrid Images (B). **Shutterstock.com**: jocic (A); **SC20c Alamy Images**: Klaus Oskar Bromberg (A); **SC20d Alamy Images**: Alan Keith Beastall (D). **Pearson Education Ltd**: Trevor Clifford (B). **Science Photo Library Ltd**: (A). **Shutterstock.com**: Danny E Hooks (C); **SC20e Alamy Images**: Wayne Hutchinson (C). **Science Photo Library Ltd**: Simon Fraser (A); Monica Schroeder (B). **Shutterstock.com**: Hung Chung Chih (D); **SC20f Reuters**: Alex Gallardo (D). **Shutterstock.com**: NicVW (A); **SC21a Alamy Images**: World History Archive (A). **Science Photo Library Ltd**: Natural History Museum, London (D); NASA / JPL (B); **SC21b Science Photo Library Ltd**: Martyn F. Chillmaid (D); **SC21c Alamy Images**: Arctic Images (D); **SC21d 123RF.com**: warawoot nanta (A). **Science Photo Library Ltd**: Tony Camacho (B); Georgette Douwma (C)

SC22- 24 Alamy Images: epa european pressphoto agency b.v.; **SC22a Alamy Images**: Clarence Holmes Wildlife (A); **SC22b NASA**: (A). **Pearson Education Ltd**: Trevor Clifford

(C). **Shutterstock.com**: Vlad Ageshin (B); **SC23a Fotolia.com**: ra3rn (A/vodka); Givaga (A/whisky). **Science Photo Library Ltd**: Martyn F. Chillmaid (C); (D). **Shutterstock.com**: Nitr (A/beer); Dmitri Gristsenko (A/wine); **SC23b CP Alamy Images**: inga spence (A); **SC23c Alamy Images**: Mediablitzimages (B). **Martyn F. Chillmaid**: (D); **SC24a Artville**: Dennis Nolan (A). **PhotoDisc**: (D); **SC24b 123RF.com**: (A/bag, A/pan). **Shutterstock.com**: pryzmat (A/pipes); paijicha (A/bottle top); CrackerClips Stock Media (A/packing chips); **SC24c Alamy Images**: Alex Segre (B). **Science Photo Library Ltd**: Trevor Clifford (A); **SC24d Alamy Images**: Green Stock Media (D). **Getty Images**: Mint Images (B). **Science Photo Library Ltd**: Simon Fraser (A)

SC25-26 Science Photo Library Ltd: Patrick Landmann; **SC25a Alamy Images**: Roy Conchie (A). **Science Photo Library Ltd**: (B); **SC25b Pearson Education Ltd**: Trevor Clifford (C). **Science Photo Library Ltd**: Martyn F. Chillmaid (B, D). **Shutterstock.com**: K Steve Cope (A); **SC25c Alamy Images**: David Chapman (A). **Pearson Education Ltd**: Trevor Clifford (D). **Science Photo Library Ltd**: Trevor Clifford Photography (B); Charles D. Winters (C); **SC25c CP Shutterstock.com**: anyaivanova (A); **SC26a Alamy Images**: ITAR-TASS Photo Agency (C); Apelöga AB (B). **Fotolia.com**: slavun (A); ronstik (D); **SC26b Bart van Overbeeke Fotografie**: (A). **Getty Images**: matsou (B); **SC26c Science Photo Library Ltd**: Royal Institution Of Great Britain (B); Eye of Science (C); (A)

Cover images: Front: **123RF.com**: Aafak Cakar, Maksim Kostenko; **SuperStock**: Corbis

Text

SC3 Atomic Structure opener paragraph on page 17 adapted from Professor Richard Palmer, The Nanoscale Physics Research Laboratory, University of Birmingham. Reproduced with the permission of Professor Richard Palmer.

Websites

Pearson Education Limited is not responsible for the content of any external internet sites. It is essential for tutors to preview each website before using it in class so as to ensure that the URL is still accurate, relevant and appropriate. We suggest that tutors bookmark useful websites and consider enabling students to access them through the school/college intranet.